"IF I HAD MY WAY I WOULD REQUIRE STU-DENTS THROUGHOUT THE COUNTRY TO READ KENT STATE, particularly on 'The Threat to Education,' in which Michener spells out in stark detail the consequences to American education if events like those at Kent State occur on other campuses. The principal victims will be students, education, and the nation in that order. . . . Kent State is a lesson we neglect at our peril."
—Saturday Review Syndicate

"THERE WILL PROBABLY NEVER BE A MORE THOROUGH, MINUTE-BY-MINUTE ACCOUNT than Michener's of the three days of disorder that preceded the shooting. Valuably, the book shows how easily divisions within a community can escalate toward tragedy. Michener convinces the reader when he says: 'Kent could be your community.' "
—Time

"A SUPERBLY DOCUMENTED BOOK that deals with the basic estrangement of the young and older generation and the savage reaction of much of the public to what was happening on the campuses of the nation."
—Business Week

JAMES A. MICHENER

KENT STATE

What Happened and Why

FAWCETT CREST • NEW YORK

KENT STATE

Published by Fawcett Crest Books, a unit of CBS Publications, the Consumer Publishing Division of CBS Inc., by arrangement with Random House, Inc.

ISBN: 8-449-23869-5

Selection of the Book of the Month Club, February 1971
Playboy Magazine, March 1971
Selection of Psychology Today Book Club, March 1971

Printed in the United States of America.

17   16   15   14   13   12   11   10   9   8

CONTENTS

Photographs and a map follow page 256.

FOREWORD

I can recall no period of my life more fruitful and compelling than the time I spent at Kent doing research for this book, for I was thrust into the heart of great problems that will confront this nation for the next decade: What ought a university to be? What are the rights of students and what are their obligations? Is the clash in life styles a passing matter which will be forgotten as soon as hair is short and costumes change again, or is it a permanent modification of our national life? How pervasive is the malaise that has attacked university students? How strong are the semi-underground forces that are determined to destroy our universities and the society that supports them?

These are dreadful questions to occupy oneself with, but they are questions we had better face up to quickly and with all the intelligence we have.

In the days of May following the shootings at Kent State this nation stumbled to the edge of a precipice. Some 760 universities and colleges either closed down completely or came close to doing so, and students talked openly of revolution. Older citizens, outraged by what they were witnessing, began riding around at night with shotguns, threatening to shoot on sight any young people they spotted. Nomads, some of them on drugs and all of them looking like the murderous monsters from California, roamed the streets and gave substance to inchoate fears. Only those who were close to the scene, talked to all three groups, appreciated how dangerously close to catastrophe this country came in those critical days.

Fortunately, during the late summer and especially in the early days of October when students returned to college with a new seriousness, sage counsel prevailed and the incipient warfare between generations subsided. There was on all sides a de-escalation of emotion, a subsidence of threat. People of all ages began talking sense again and a most dreadful confrontation was avoided. It was a notable triumph of reason, one for which we can all be thankful.

This book deals with events leading up to the tension and explains why they involved so many young people. Also discussed are steps whereby our nation can perhaps avoid a repetition.

This could be your university. The students and National Guardsmen could be you, or young people of your neighborhood, or, if you are old enough, your sons and daughters. The city of Kent could be your community. That is why you need to know what happened to you, so that you can prevent it from happening again.

J.A.M.

I

VIEW OF KENT

In the spring of 1970 four large public universities in Ohio experienced destructive campus revolt. In descending order of violence, they were Ohio University at Athens in the southeastern part of the state, Ohio State University at Columbus in the center, Kent State University at the small city of Kent in the northeastern sector, Miami University at Oxford on the far western border. From this listing it can be seen that riots at Kent State were not the most destructive, but they became entangled in a bizarre combination of accidents that produced a tragedy which dismayed the nation and startled the world.

This book attempts to explain what happened at Kent State. It is a book about students, hundreds of them, and the first one we meet can stand as a representative of that enormous group of stable, solid young people who form the reliable central core of our great universities. He is a most attractive young man.

Bob Hillegas, whose father works for General Tire in nearby Akron, is six-feet-three, slight of build, with wavy blond hair and a long, intelligent-looking face. His hazel eyes are usually crinkled in laughter and he is a good student. He is also quietly patriotic and has volunteered to serve in the campus detachment of the ROTC. When he graduates in aero-space technology, for which his university is noted, he hopes to enter the air force, and after serving a normal stint there, to work his way into commercial aviation. Because of this he is careful of his appearance, wears his hair short and his trousers pressed. His three older brothers did well at their universities—Jon at Marquette, Dick at Cincinnati, and Jim at Ohio Wesleyan—so he lived within an academic tradition. Sometimes his brothers tease him with the popular clichés: 'If

9

you can't go to college, go to Kent' and 'Kent State, largest undiscovered university in the world.'

Bob considers it a pretty good operation. 'In 1944, 673 students. Today, 21,000. With that kind of growth, some things are bound to be rough, but we have some great professors, some brilliant kids, and one of the most beautiful campuses in America. I like the place.'

On Saturday evening, May 2, 1970, Bob Hillegas left his home in Akron, where he lives with his parents, and drove his 1967 Ford Fairlane some miles into the country to pick up his college date in the exclusive Twin Lakes residential district north of Kent. He had to be careful what route he took because the radio was saying there had been trouble on campus the night before and that a curfew had been imposed. He knew nothing about all this and cared less; anyway, by using back roads he could just as easily find his way to the university airport, for it lay west of town and outside the city limits.

When he got there he signed papers which would permit him, as a member of the Kent State Flying Club, to use one of the university Cessna 172's, a four-place job. He had gained his pilot's license in March, 1968, and had been flying for more than two years, but the interesting flight he planned for tonight contained features he had not attempted before. What he had in mind was a take-off in daylight, a short flight to the Cleveland airport, dinner there with his date and another couple who were waiting at the Kent airfield, and return about midnight in darkness. Since Kent lies at the western end of the time zone—it observes the same time as New York—twilight came late and there was still lots of light when he and his three companions strapped themselves into the Cessna. 'Should be a great flight,' he assured them, trimming the ailerons. The Cessna was in good shape and Hillegas taxied it to the end of the runway, which ran due north and south.

At Kent airfield, standard operation procedure required the pilot to take off from south to north, attain 450 feet altitude, then turn 45° left, attain proper altitude and clear the pattern. Hillegas decided to continue in a complete circle, counterclockwise, which would bring him back on a north heading, set for Cleveland. This plan had the added advantage of taking him directly over the city of Kent and the university, which he thought his companions would enjoy seeing from the air.

So when the Cessna attained the necessary 450 feet he turned slowly to the left, and in a wide, ascending circle, passed over the city of Kent, which is divided into four clearly defined quadrants. U.S. Route 59 runs due east and west, Route 43 due north and south, both intersecting at the dead center of the city.

The pattern Hillegas had chosen took him first over the northwest quadrant, with its wide streets and numerous trees. Kent is known as The Tree City; the famous Davey Tree Company started there and had sent its horticulturists throughout the nation. Martin L. Davey, son of the founder, had gone on to be governor of Ohio and had played a constructive role in helping the university to grow.

Crossing Route 59, as it headed west from the city, Hillegas entered the southwest quadrant and saw the many railroad lines that had once made Kent a railroad capital. He also saw the small manufacturing plants, the homes of the numerous Italian workmen who had built Kent into a good labor market, and more of the lovely trees and spacious homes. Hillegas had often viewed Kent from the air and considered it one of the most beautiful cities in Ohio. 'It has a certain sense of order,' he said as he headed for the southeast quadrant, which contained the campus.

Kent State University, as the young people saw it that evening in sunset glow, was a huge collection of academic buildings, most of them built of yellow brick and spaced generously on a broad green campus that rolled up and down slight hills. It was orderly yet varied, and it contained certain surprising aspects. For one thing, it had ample space. It was one of the few large universities in the world that had open land in three directions. Compared to the crowding at universities like Pennsylvania, Columbia and Texas, it was a marvel of broad perspectives and inviting vistas. This was no cramped, jammed-up collection of inadequate buildings. Its first impact was one of spaciousness. 'From the air it's magnificent,' Hillegas said, 'and from the ground it isn't too bad.'

He now pointed out something that always startled visitors to Kent: Tri-Towers—a huge, skyscraper nest of dormitories rising many stories in the air. The architecture was handsome and the buildings were set amid extensive landscaping, but what were skyscrapers doing in the heart of a modern university that had land to burn? They were an anomaly, the first sign that Kent was a university like all others, one with housing problems.

The next sight confirmed this, for at the dead heart of the campus, commanding the commons and disfiguring everything, clustered four long, low beige wooden buildings, holdovers from the end of World War II. Three of them had been prefabricated army barracks, never used for their original purpose but bought for disaster-prices when peace came unexpectedly. The fourth, which will figure largely in this story, was known as East Hall and had originally been intended as a field hospital; it had been bought by the university practically off the ship which was about to haul it to the Pacific war. Through the decades it had served the university well—as a dormitory, as a classroom, and now as the ROTC building. 'Look at ROTC,' Hillegas told his passengers; like everyone in Kent he pronounced the letters 'Rot-sie.' It was low and ugly and dirty and superannuated and it should have been torn down twenty years ago, but as a French philosopher once said, 'Nothing is so permanent as a temporary arrangement.' ROTC would probably stand crumbling at the heart of the Kent campus for another twenty-five years.

And there was one other thing Bob Hillegas saw that evening as he climbed to 3,000 feet. He remembers pointing it out. It was a remarkably lovely building, one of the most beautiful erected on any American campus in the last two decades. It stood on a hill across the commons from the old ROTC building, and commanded large perspectives in all directions. It was Taylor Hall, center of the School of Journalism, and Hillegas described it as 'a combination of the best classical and the best modern.' He was right. It was a very modern building, featuring dark glass and stone, set off by a Greek peristyle whose columns seemed exactly right for the purpose. It had balance and dignity, and the fact that it was so remarkably different from the yellow-brick buildings which surrounded it made it the cynosure of the campus. 'I always loved to see that building,' Hillegas says, 'even though I never took any classes in it.'

Dipping his wing over the campus, he completed his circle, passed over the luxurious homes that filled the northeast quadrant, found Route 43, running north, and followed it toward the shores of Lake Erie. There he turned left, tracked the shoreline west to Cleveland and received permission to make a straight-in landing at Burke Lakefront Airport, where they parked the Cessna and had dinner in one of the towers overlooking the lake.

When it came time to take off for the return trip, an

airfield attendant warned him of a procedure he had never before executed. 'Remember, SOP here is for a take-off to the west, then a quick bank right, which puts you over Lake Erie. You pass from the very bright lights of Cleveland into complete darkness. Watch out.' Bob's air instructor had warned him about this phenomenon, so he was prepared for it, but even so, when the long run down the strip ended and he was airborne, he was not prepared for that sudden turn into inky blackness. 'It was quite a thrill,' he says, but he made the big turn over the lake, then brought the Cessna back on a 180° heading, looked for Route 43 and, finding it, tied into the Akron ADF which would bring him south. Then he headed for Kent, but as he came within sight of the darkened city he saw to his astonishment that the university seemed to be all ablaze.

'God, what's that?' he called to his passengers, and they leaned in silence against the left-hand windows of the plane as he circled the campus, trying to avoid a huge pillar of black smoke and flame that reached high into the air. He did so because he feared that the heat might be producing convection currents that would toss his light plane about, but wherever he looked he saw the glare of fire.

'Nobody said anything,' Hillegas recalls. 'It was as if we were afraid to face what we knew was happening. But then I pushed the nose down and flew very low and after a couple of passes I said, "It's the ROTC building." I couldn't say anything more, because I sort of like the disreputable old shack. You see, I'm a member of ROTC. I'd had some good hours there, and I needed it to complete my training and get my commission. But most of all, I knew that if this symbol had been burned, trouble must follow. I think everyone in the plane knew this, for as we looked down at the charred timbers we realized that a great change had come to our university. None of us cared to speculate on what that change would involve, so we flew back to the airfield in silence.'

II

FRIDAY: TRASHING OF WATER STREET

The non-violent man

In order to evaluate what happened at Kent State in May, 1970, you must try to understand the new breed of student attending these large state institutions, and none could be more typical than a likable, somewhat confused, bearded young man with long hair and gentle face named Tim Butz, aged twenty-two and a native of Akron.

Like most of the students who take social change seriously, Tim had had part of his education in another institution, in this case Boise State, in Idaho. That he went to college so far from home was natural for a young man of this generation: he got caught in the draft, joined the air force, and after service overseas, attended Boise State because he wanted a college education and sought it even while in uniform.

He had served in Germany and with distinction in Vietnam. By the time he reached Kent State, he had become convinced on one point: 'I am non-violent.' When asked why, he says, 'My military experience convinced me.' Then he adds, 'Last spring I watched the air force ROTC fellows training, and I respected them for their willingness to serve in uniform, as I had. But when I heard them charging up Blanket Hill, making believe they had bayonets and shouting "Kill, kill," I knew the world was going crazy. What has killing to do with a university education? ROTC should never have been allowed on campus, and I wanted it off.' (ROTC officers deny that their troops ever shouted 'Kill, kill' on campus.)

Tim lived at 226 East Erie in what he remembers as 'excellent quarters, with a great landlord and a free garage for eighty bucks a month.' On Friday, May 1, he rose at

6:30 and took breakfast at home. 'I'm a fair cook, and this way I save money.' While eating he looked at the morning paper and said, 'Unh, unh! Trouble.'

What had caught his eye was news that President Nixon had ordered troops into Cambodia. 'I wasn't sure what would happen, but I was certain something would. Such an arrogant switch in national plans could not go unnoticed.' At 7:50 on his way to the campus, he saw that agitators had already painted the pavements with spray cans: *Free Bobby. Free Huey, U.S. Out of Cambodia.* Such signs, appearing all over town, had been painted between midnight and dawn.

'I went to my job in the library and at 10:00 some students came in with fliers announcing a noon rally on the commons to bury the Constitution. It seemed like a good idea, because, as one of them said, "If a nation can launch a war on Cambodia without declaring it, the Constitution as we knew it is really dead." '

At 11:45 the huge bell in the low brick housing in the middle of the campus started ringing. The bell, taken from an old Erie & Lackawanna train, stood only three feet off the ground, so that anyone could reach in and swing it back and forth. It had a penetrating sound, and throughout this long weekend would often be rung to summon students to gatherings of one sort or other. It was a provocative instrument, capable of creating its own sense of emergency, and to have kept it so easily available to anyone who wanted to convene a mob was a mistake.

Tim Butz responded to the bell the way a Pavlovian dog might have done. It had been the campus spokesman for the various causes he had espoused: it had called him to a rally at which he had signed up for one of the poverty programs in Mississippi; it had reminded him of the rally conducted by the professional radical, Jerry Rubin—that one had been a dreadful bust, with Rubin making a complete ass of himself and alienating everyone like Tim Butz who had gone to hear him; and it had sounded for the April moratorium, at which Tim had appeared as a Vietnam Veteran Against War. Now it was summoning students to the burial of the Constitution.

The crowd was disappointing. Only a few score appeared at first, but more straggled in, because any rally scheduled for twelve noon could count upon getting a lot of accidental participants who at that hour were passing from one class to another. Ultimately, there were about 300. 'What really impressed me,' Butz said later, 'was the brilliance of the speech made by Tom Dubis. He's a history teaching fellow and he knew what he was talking about. He was positively brilliant in explaining how President Nixon was really murdering the Constitution by his invasion of Cambodia and how we were excused from responsibility for any actions which we might mount in protest. Or something gripping like that.'

The highlight of the burial came, however, when a hero of the Vietnam war—Jim Geary, a graduate student in history, with the Bronze Star, the Combat Infantryman's Badge and Good Conduct Medal—got up and started speaking in a low voice. 'I could hardly hear him,' Tim Butz says. 'Geary is a stocky character with a crew cut—he looks like a football player—and he said, "I'm so disgusted with the behavior of my country in invading Cambodia, that I'm going to burn my discharge papers." It was electrifying! And as he was lighting his papers with a cigarette lighter that somebody loaned him, I remembered that I had mine in my pocket. I was engaged in a hassle with the Cleveland office of Veterans' Administration over some back pay they owed me, and on the spur of the moment I jumped up beside Geary and announced, "I'm going to burn my papers, too," and I did. If you want to check on Geary, he's one of the founders of WHORE, that's World Historians Opposed to Racism and Exploitation. They had organized the noon meeting.'

Since everything that happened during this violent weekend began with the burial of the Constitution, we had better take a closer look at this semi-serious prank. It was legal, and it was non-violent. Normally it would have passed without notice, the kind of thing that is apt to happen on any university campus. Its only unusual feature was that it was sponsored by an ad hoc committee, one convened on the spur of the moment, and that often meant trouble. In this instance WHORE had been the backroom brainchild of some wisecracking history assistants. The audience was normal, the behavior normal, and the general effect normal. 'Strictly blah,' one coed reported.

For the purposes of this book, however, it was of unusual interest, for it served to introduce two young graduate assistants. They had been roommates and were similar in certain ways, dissimilar in others. They got good grades in the classes they took and favorable attention in the ones they taught.

Robert Franklin, twenty-eight, is from Brooklyn and as a child had been recognized as a genius in chemistry. He had taught at Brooklyn College and Cornell and was now working on his Ph.D. at Kent. Short, alert, with narrow eyes and very white teeth, he gave the appearance, said one of his girl students, 'of being all hair.' He had a tremendous beard and a wild head of jet-black hair. When he added heavy tortoise-shell glasses, white sneakers and a small leather cap, he was an eye-catching figure.

'I am Robert Franklin, libertarian communist,' he would shout into almost any microphone he could get his hands on, a trick which gave him the reputation of mad genius. He had traveled widely to countries like Bulgaria, Yugoslavia, Turkey, Italy, France and Germany, acquiring accents and information from each. To the more serious radical student he was 'our coupon communist,' for it was rumored that he enjoyed a substantial income inherited from his parents. In the summer of 1968 he had lost some campus respect, he confesses: 'I shaved my beard and trimmed my hair in order to get a job. I sent inquiries to 250 different colleges and universities, but someone must have tipped them off as to my political activities, for I got a response from only one. When I pursued the matter, they said, "Sorry." That was all. Just "Sorry." So I let my beard grow again.'

It is difficult to know what Bob Franklin is trying to do. He says, 'Create a better society by destroying this one,' but when you ask him what character his new world will have, he is vague. He is not a revolutionary; meticulously he avoids any overt actions which would put him in trouble with the police. He is an unusual young man to be instructing the young—he no longer has a job at Kent State—but his type is familiar on all campuses: the talkative fellow who hangs around year after year, pursuing a few courses, working vaguely on a doctorate which may never be finished.

Franklin's roommate was a memorable young man in his early twenties. Tall, broad-shouldered, quick with a disarming laugh and able to tell a joke on himself, Steve Sharoff comes from Monticello, New York, where his father had been chief of police for thirty years. 'As a kid,' says Steve, wrapping his very long legs into knots, 'I wanted only one thing. To join the FBI.' But while working for his B.A. in history, at New York's State University at Plattsburg, he began to have doubts about America's social and political systems. Well able to handle himself and popular with girls, he had no trouble knocking around the United States after college: 'I had this Austin Healey 3000 sports car, a little money and friends across the country. A week in New Orleans, another in St. Louis, a month in Oklahoma City, seven months in Los Angeles. I worked as a vacuum-cleaner salesman. I did all right. Then ski instructor, and I did all right at that too. I figured I was set. But then I ran into a former history professor, who told me, "Steve, you're wasting a good mind." To my surprise, I wound up at Kent.'

When Steve talks he envelops the listener, studies him, tests him, tells him jokes to see what makes him laugh. His rapid-fire conversation is studded with references to bright people, the right books, the prevailing ideas. He says, 'Intellectually I was wakened by Noam Chomsky. I was much impressed by Che Guevara but couldn't accept his politics.' Later, going back to his awakening, he says, 'It was then I realized that Che Guevara was truly a great man.' He adds, 'I'm anti-war because I had a buddy killed in Vietnam. I have a strong yearning to accomplish something good for this nation.

'I became very anti-war. I decided that Vietnam was an abomination, and one evening made up my mind: "I will never go to war." From that decision I escalated to thinking about racism as it operated as a force throughout American history. And I got very uptight about the way the police were beginning to gun down Black Panthers. This was genocide at its worst. And the Jewish Defense League? What was it but Jewish fascism? Looking at the whole bundle, and listening to Agnew's assaults on reason, I developed the idea that the majority of Americans ought not be allowed to vote. They simply are not intelligent enough. And college students are not much better. All they really want is a piece of paper which says, "You're educated. You are now entitled to a good job." Real education? They couldn't care less.'

His arrival at Kent was a bombshell. A girl radical says, 'One week we had a normal campus. Next week Steve Sharoff had registered and you could hear reverberations starting. The week after that, he was leading the radical movement and everybody was asking, "Who in hell is Steve Sharoff?" We're still asking.'

It was typical that when the young historians of WHORE had their bright idea of burying the Constitution, Steve Sharoff should have appeared front and center to take charge of the affair. 'Steve is a take-charge guy,' everyone admits. We shall be seeing him often this weekend, and if we were at Ann Arbor, or Harvard, or Stanford we would see many like him. It is essential, therefore, that we get a reading on him.

Bob Franklin: 'We shared a room for eight months and I found that he had little visceral feeling for great movements or the genesis of big ideas. And I thought he was a poor leader. Too mercurial. Too much the prey of the moment's emotion. I always had trouble knowing where Steve stood. The administration accused him of being a crypto-member of SDS at the same time that the SDS accused him of being a secret member of the FBI. The boy has unquestioned energy, great charisma.'

Paul Probius, a committed radical: 'I wonder about Steve. At times he seems to be on an ego trip. Or maybe just career-hungry. At other times he looks a real solid sender. This cat knows.'

Debi Moreland, who would escape injury even though she was the person closest to the M-1 rifles when they fired: 'Steve is always big on forcing a confrontation and equally big on turning up missing when it occurs.'

Old-time radical: 'Where the hell did this Steve Sharoff suddenly come from? Last week I'd never heard of him. This week he's running the campus.'

Suspicious younger faculty member: 'Remember that his father is chief of police. I say the guy's a stool pigeon planted here to serve as an *agent provocateur.'*

Sorority girl: 'I know nothing about his politics, but he sends chills down my spine . . . nice ones.'

Law enforcement officer: 'We follow one simple rule. If we see Steve Sharoff on the scene, we know there's going to be trouble.'

History sophomore: 'Sharoff was the best teacher I ever had. Brilliant. And he didn't make you accept his interpretation of history, either. He made you think things out for yourself.'

It was not Steve's idea to bury the Constitution. He says, 'Chris Plant, one of the history buffs, and I heard that Nixon was going to speak on Cambodia. "What do you think he'll do?" Chris asked, and I said, "Only thing he would dare do is announce further withdrawal of troops from Vietnam and maybe some economic aid to Cambodia." But Chris was afraid Nixon might be thinking of invading Cambodia, and he said, "Why don't we bury the Constitution? To protest what he's up to?" And I told him, "Your timing is off. Let's wait till Memorial Day, when it'll mean something." Chris saw the logic of this and agreed, "We'll wait." But when we listened to the television we became so embittered that we swung into action right then. We worked all night. We printed leaflets. Sent kids out to paint signs on the sidewalks. Got Tom Dubis to give us some help, and shortly before noon some girl ripped a copy of the Constitution out of a textbook and we were in business.'

Stu Feldstein, a young newspaperman on whose recollections we will draw, had graduated from Kent State to a good job on a Cleveland newspaper. He says of the Constitution thing, 'Sharoff spoke well but said nothing exceptional. Then Bob Franklin took over, and he was a big hit. Former chemistry instructor, I think, with a real touch in handling an audience. They always accepted him as weird and lovable and anti-everything. On this day he showed up in green fatigues, wearing a green army cap over his great head of hair, and with a cigar butt jutting out from his huge beard. He said, "This is my Castro outfit," and he got a big cheer just for looking the way he did. People laughed hard as he paced up and down muttering revolutionary slogans and gesturing wildly.

'At the burial he took over as master of ceremonies and welcomed everyone to the event. I remember his pointing toward the Johnson Hall section of the crowd and saying, "I want you to welcome Officer Tom Kelley. He's the campus detective who comes to all our rallies. Now in case you don't know who Kelley is, he's standing over there." And he proceeded to describe Kelley in detail.

'Finally someone cried, "Shall we meet again to plan a real anti-war organization?" Most of the crowd shouted, "Yes!" and those in charge began shouting, "Monday. Monday at noon." The rally disbanded, but those who had been listening stood around, excited.'

Jeff Sallot, another Kent State graduate in journalism who had landed a good newspaper job, in his case with the Akron *Beacon Journal,* observed Franklin as the rally broke up: 'He moved along the edges of the crowd, passing the word, "There's going to be street action downtown tonight." '

Tim Butz has his own reaction to the two teachers: 'You have to admire Bob Franklin's gall; he was a chemistry professor but wild about politics. How do you square the two? Simple. He announced that he was teaching "liberation chemistry." Older professors took a dim view of this, and students asked, "When do we get to the chemistry?" and Franklin told them, "Liberation comes first." I always took him with a grain of salt. He preached, "We have got to smash industrial capitalism," but he kept his money invested in industrial stocks.'

Butz thought that Sharoff made a lot of sense. 'At the moment when the Constitution was officially buried, Steve said, "It is now our task to see that it is resurrected in its original form . . . in its true meaning." He could be a very moving guy.'

After the burial, Tim moved on to his 2:15-3:05 class, where he heard that the black students were going to have an important rally on the front campus at 3:00 that afternoon. 'There were rumors that something big was afoot, maybe taking over the Administration Building on Monday. afternoon, and I wanted to know what was cooking. I had great respect for the blacks on our campus because they handled themselves very well. No riots but constant pressure for the things they wanted. One of my professors was Marvin Holsey, a black sociologist and the finest man I've ever met. No ranting. No barn burning. Just pure, clean reasoning. So I wandered down to hear the news.'

BUS—Black United Students—was conducting the meeting and the big feature was the report of a delegation of blacks from Ohio State University in Columbus explaining how the riots which had closed down the campus were progressing. 'There was one OSU man in bib overalls, named Brown maybe, and he was listing the eighteen grievances that the blacks at OSU wanted corrected, and about fifteen of them had already been corrected at Kent State. We were way ahead of all the other universities in making sensible moves. I was proud of Kent State as I listened to that rally.'

There were about fifty blacks in attendance, perhaps three times that number of whites. When any speaker made a telling point about the need for vital change in either the university or the social system of the entire nation, blacks in the audience would call, 'Right on!' sometimes adding the approving appellation 'Brother.' 'I was surprised at how restrained the meeting was.' Butz says. 'But you could feel that it was only a surface calm. You knew that sooner or later these blacks were going to explode, and when they did, the university was going to explode from the repercussion.'

The rally had an almost schizoid quality because of the traditional observance of Derby Day on May 1. Each year on that day it was the custom at Kent for fraternity men to appear on campus wearing derbies, with the prettiest girls from the sororities obliged to chase them until they caught them, whereupon the girls gave the boys a kiss. The chase had always taken place on the precise part of the campus utilized by the blacks for their rally, so that, as Butz says, 'All during the time the blacks were discussing social revolution and the attainment of civil rights, around the edges of the meeting ran the fraternity men in their derbies, being chased by extremely pretty girls in miniskirts. One minute I'd be looking at Erwind Blount, the new president of BUS, a big, very black man with a personality like a charge of dynamite, and the next I'd be looking at some sorority girl as she tackled a derby man and fell squealing with him to the grass.'

When the black rally ended, with no violence of any kind, Tim sought out three of his instructors, young people little older than himself with a deep sense of social conviction—the Agtes, a married couple who taught English, and Ralph Bevilaqua, from the same department. 'We rapped for a long time about Cambodia and my having burned my discharge papers, and as I was leaving I remembered something Tom Dubis had said at the end of the ceremony when we buried the Constitution: "Don't forget the street action tonight at nine." Apparently something had been planned that I didn't know about. I meant to ask the Agtes but forgot.'

A banker takes a chance

The tragedy at Kent State was played against a community background in which the citizens of Kent were as important as the students at the university.

Bill Nash, a typical citizen, is a wiry, lean redhead, forty years old and vice-president of the Portage National Bank. Like many townspeople, he has the welfare of the university at heart, for he graduated from there as an expert in personnel management. 'That school gave me a great education,' he says 'and I needed it, because I was one of nine children and knew from the start I'd have to work hard.'

Conservative, good friends with the Republican county chairman, Bill lives in an exclusive development north of town at Dollar Lake. He rises every morning at 7:15, skips breakfast, jumps into his car and sets out for his office, where he is in charge of personal loans for the biggest bank in the county. He does not come straight south on Route 43, which would be his shortest way into town. He loves nature and so cuts across Diagonal Road on a rural route to State Road 14, which brings him into Kent past the reservoirs and their great natural beauty. Also, he has thirty acres of choice woodland in that direction on which he grows Christmas trees, and passing it not only starts the day right but allows him to check on an A-frame in which he has launched an experiment in human relations. More of this later.

After his country drive, Nash pulls into his bank parking lot, located in the dead center of town. It is a custom for community big shots to take their breakfast at Hahn's, across the corner from the bank, but some time ago Bill formed the habit of taking his at a less important restaurant, Mancino's. 'I could give you four good reasons why I do this,' he says, 'but the important one is that at Hahn's the coffee is twenty-five cents a cup, at Mancino's only fifteen.'

Bill would certainly be entitled to breakfast with the town's big shots, for he is one of them. As a driving force in Rotary he is well regarded by fellow businessmen, and as a member of the school board he helps determine civic policy. But just when you feel you understand this trim, hard-driving young business leader, he gives you a jolt. For example, he doesn't eat lunch. At 12:00 he jumps in his car and drives out East Main to the university gymnasium, where he dons a track suit, slips into his imported Onitsuka running shoes, and sets off cross country for a five-and-a-half-mile run.

He starts his daily trip by running up a hill which will be mentioned frequently in this book, Blanket Hill, which dominates the university campus and where on spring nights college couples have traditionally spread their blanket and watched the stars.

From there he runs east along Route 59 toward Ravenna, then loops back toward the lakes, and finishes the circuit in just under thirty-five minutes. 'I had been smoking two packs a day and the doctor said, "Give it up and do some exercise." So I do five and a half miles a day and I feel great.'

It would be incorrect to say that Bill Nash jogs. He runs at a pace that few in the community could keep up with. At the age of thirty-seven he ran the twenty-six miles of the Boston Marathon, gaining notice as one who finished the route in less than four hours. In other words, he is a considerable athlete, and says with pride, 'Kent State runs in a very fast league. The man who wins the Big Ten championship would finish fourth in our Middle America Conference.'

Like many Kent businessmen, Nash has great respect for

the university. 'It serves a marvelous purpose in this part of Ohio, and we need it economically,' he says, but he is perplexed by changes that have occurred in recent years. 'I can't understand what's been happening to our students. They seem to lack direction and discipline.' Events of the past week give him good cause to wonder.

Last Saturday when he came to work he found that college drunks had vomited all over the entrance to the bank. On Sunday, as he and his pretty wife, Betty, drove home from the Methodist church, he saw splashed across the front of the bank, in huge black letters, *End Imperelism.* After he deposited Betty at Dollar Lake he came back into town, and with soap and water, tried to scrub the words away.

On Monday the students who lived in the apartment over the bank got their toilet jammed, so that its contents seeped down on Bill's desk. When he went upstairs to see what could be done, 'I slipped on the steps because they had moved a motorcycle up to the top floor, but had parked it on an angle so that oil was dripping down the stairs. The rooms . . . well, I wouldn't try to describe them to you unless you had a strong stomach. I really cannot understand how people can live in such filth.' After he got the toilet straightened out he returned to his soggy desk and got what he terms 'one of the shocks of my life. Up the stairs went a tall student with a live goat draped around his neck. I was about to raise hell when I thought, "If there is any living thing calculated to feel at home in those rooms, it would be a goat." '

On Wednesday he had another example of a recurring problem. A huge, unkempt, shaggy-haired student dressed like Daniel Boone stalked into the bank and demanded that it cash a check without identification of any kind. When Nash politely and properly said, 'I'm afraid we can't cash checks from people we don't know and who have no identification,' the big fellow cursed everyone on the floor, bellowing as he left, 'No wonder we burn down banks. You be careful yours isn't next.'

On Thursday night Bill and Betty stayed home and listened as President Nixon, whom they like very much, announced that he was sending troops into Cambodia. 'I knew right then there was bound to be trouble,' Nash says. 'I grew terribly apprehensive about the coming weekend, because I'd been listening to what students said in the gym.'

On Friday the Nashes entertained friends from Athens, Ohio, and after talking with them Bill felt somewhat relieved.

'The wife told us that down there in Athens the townspeople were having real trouble with the students at Ohio University. "You're so fortunate in Kent," she assured us. "The petty things you're disturbed about are nothing. At Athens we have real anxiety. Drugs, agitation, threats against the downtown stores, violence. We're bound to have serious trouble. It's got to come. The townspeople won't stand this sort of thing much longer." They told us how much they envied us, living in a quiet area like Kent.'

On Friday afternoon, just as the black students at the university were breaking up the BUS meeting and planning what to do that night, Bill Nash drove back out State Road 14, and what he did at his tree farm explains why he was considered by the people of Kent one of the most unusual young leaders. He pulled onto his land, got out and walked over to the substantial A-frame building he had erected for housing his tools; during the Christmas season it came in handy when he sold spruce trees to families from Cleveland who liked to drive out into the country and chop down a tree they had personally selected.

'When I watched the growing estrangement between townspeople and students,' Nash says, 'I knew that something had to be done to bridge the gap. So I looked around for the most frightening young fellow I could find . . . someone living off the land . . . and I told him that he could move into the A-frame at no cost. I'd even help him fix it up.' He found a cadaverous young man, at odds with his family. 'He wouldn't take any money from his father. Said he insisted upon being independent. But he would accept airline tickets from his mother, so when he got tired of one spot he'd fly to another. A bum in the grand style, grace of TWA.'

Once or twice a week Nash stopped by the tree farm to talk with the young man. 'He has modified my thinking,' Nash told a business friend that night. 'He has many good ideas and I suspect that he may represent a lot of young people his age. At least we listen to one another.'

As Bill Nash spoke these hopeful words, in the quietness of his lovely home at Dollar Lake, where deer come down to drink and migratory ducks visit, students of Kent University were getting ready to smash all the windows in his bank and to heave an enormous manure spreader through the plate-glass front door.

The field marshal and his troops

The white students and the administration would have been justified had they expressed apprehension over the BUS rally. Anything might happen, because it had been following such a rally on November 13, 1968, that the Placement Office had been taken over, launching the series of confrontations which had not yet ended. Indeed, the campus was already shot with rumors that 'on Monday noon the blacks are going to close down the university.'

The blacks at Kent State now had an able cadre of leaders, some of them hardened in the ghettos of Cleveland, others the brilliant sons and daughters of middle-class families in which the fathers and mothers had long fought for civil rights. They were well disciplined, knew what they wanted, and were not afraid to press their demands with a most violent rhetoric.

Their campus newspaper, *Black Watch,* symbolized the radicalization which had occurred. In the issue of March 30, 1970, bearing the dateline Kenya (Kent State) there were furious articles depicting the black man's struggle for equality in AmeriKKKa, as it was invariably spelled. The basic message appeared in a front-page bold-face editorial:

In dealing with our present situation, the rhetoric of Revolution has been mouthed by many people. Black people must realize in speaking of Revolution that they speak of death. The lives of those who begin and carry out the violent end of this Revolution are forfeited.

We say we must achieve the liberation of our people on this campus and all over the world through any means necessary. We know what we are saying and we mean it even unto death!

One of the major articles exhorted the Kent blacks to 'end all forms of mental murder of black minds. This automatically calls for the firing or, if need be, killing of all racist deans, teachers, professors, coaches or university presidents.' Other publications distributed by the blacks called for the killing of policemen, and these appeared constantly.

Some of the writing in the Kent newspaper was moving, as when a male student begged black coeds to dress like true Africans and eschew the styles made popular by white girls: 'I don't want my Queen looking like a white woman, or reflecting the belief in the beauty standards of that white witch.' A coed wrote of the deep pride she had felt when the black poetess, Miss Gwendolyn Brooks, had read her poems at a Kent State convocation.

But the main cry of the *Black Watch* was for revolution, radical social change which would set the black man free. This call was constantly reiterated, as in the announcement to would-be writers explaining the kind of articles needed for future issues:

> We need articles by journalists that will inflame the people, that will spur on the revolutionary temptation to kidnap American Ambassadors, hyjack American airplanes, blow up American pipelines and buildings, and to shoot anyone who uses guns or weapons in the bloodstained service of imperialism against the people.
>
> —Eldridge Cleaver

The rally started at 3:00 in flawless weather. The sky was bright and the sun warm. Some of the coatless students took off their shoes and stretched out on the grass. Blacks tended to cluster together, and were surrounded by many whites who had come to listen to the recitation of black grievances. One participant judged, 'I'd say that about half the whites there did not agree with what the blacks were saying, but they did listen respectfully.'

To the disappointment of those who had come to witness fireworks, the rally began on a quiet note, for it dealt not with Kent State but with Ohio State University, where for the past week serious riots had disrupted the campus. Three visitors listed the eighteen black demands, and one, who gave his name only as Brown, explained that white students joined the demonstration with a nineteenth, 'ROTC must go.'

Then the black leaders from Kent State moved to the fore, and they were a toughly disciplined, impressive lot. President Blount, nineteen years old, was from the battlegrounds of Cleveland. He had a powerful face which resembled that of Joe Louis, and wore a huge Afro hairdo. 'I live in Glenville, man, and I've seen the riots. Those cats move in with rifles, man, they blow your head right off. I've talked to the Guardsmen who fought in the streets at Hough and Glenville, and they were scared stiff. A Guard sees me coming at him with my hairdo, he clutches up. Then he says, "Keep movin', boy," and I keep movin'.'

Blount's predecessor had been Larry Simpson, tall and patrician, with a beard like Bill Russell's. He was known as a brain: 'Every day of my life I feel completely blocked. I wouldn't object to being blocked by my own deficiencies, but when it's something over which I can exert no control, my color, I feel truly frustrated.'

Larry Hines, a lieutenant, was a languid fellow with an ingratiating smile who had placed his hopes in the Muslim movement: 'Blacks and whites are at total cross-purposes regarding Vietnam. We hope the war goes on. Because it teaches you whites that you can no longer sustain the master-slave relationship in any part of the world, and certainly not here. We are not going to demand any further. We are going to take.'

The logician of the group was a brilliant but sometimes erratic young man in pre-law. Bob Pickett had for the past year been writing a column for the campus newspaper, and he knew how to clobber white people who were hesitant about granting blacks equality, and the more exalted his target, the sharper his pen: 'Men like Nixon and Agnew seem laughable at first only because the dominance of the crypto-fascist right is new to this generation. There should be no mistake about the above: the right is definitely in power. And its strategy, plainly asserted, is to bludgeon and then silence the left and ultimately all the forms of change in America.'

Relying upon intelligent leadership, clever maneuvering and a laudable avoidance of revolutionary tactics which had alienated observers at Cornell and Columbia, the Kent blacks had maintained a steady pressure and had forced the university to make changes that were long overdue.

In fact, the condition at Kent was more satisfactory than at most universities in Ohio. There was an Institute for African-American Affairs headed by a black professor, and a Human Relations Center directed by a black dean. The faculty contained fourteen black members, plus five others whose jobs entailed faculty status. There were five specialists in an off-campus program at Akron, four teaching fellows, and seventeen staff members holding jobs like counselors, residence-hall directors and coordinators.

A most significant statistic, however, was that in a nation which contained 13 percent black population, only 2.9 percent of the Kent student body was black. White administrators said, 'Enormous efforts have been made to enroll black students, but they aren't prepared for college.' Black leaders responded, 'We've had a little tokenism but no real drive to correct the situation,' and they cited discouraging figures like these:

Category	Black	White
Graduate school	49	3,058
Doctoral candidates	4	532
Seniors	66	3,629

Blacks contended that these discrepancies must be corrected now, regardless of the dislocations involved, and BUS was prepared to enforce such a program by making three demands which the administration had to meet. Erwind Blount told the crowd which gathered beside Highway 59, 'We have tried to talk with this administration and they won't listen. This is the last time. We aren't taking any more. This is it.'

His assistant, Charles Eberhardt, took the microphone and said, 'The same thing that's happening at Ohio State is going to happen here at Kent if they don't do something.' Then he added a prophetic comment, 'The National Guard is on its way to this campus, if it isn't here already.' There were other fiery speeches, and one listener concluded, 'This is the roughest series of threats I've heard for a long time. If they keep talking this way, something is bound to break.' It was generally believed that the blacks would soon launch a demonstration that could close the university down unless their demands were met.

What did they want? Blount said, 'BUS is demanding three things, and we are demanding them now:

An enrollment beginning fall quarter this year of 5,000 students with no complaint that black high school students aren't prepared for college work.

A new black cultural center, big enough and good enough to take care of the students who will be coming here.

An all-black faculty to run the African-American institute.

The university can meet these demands and must do so.'

As he spoke, three black members of the audience were conspicuous. The first was a slightly built professor of German, thirty-eight years old, with flecks of gray in his beard and a perpetually sardonic smile on his lips. He was Edward Warren Crosby, director of the African-American institute and perhaps the most powerful black on the faculty. He was a Kent man, having enrolled from a Cleveland high school, but he had his Ph.D. from Kansas with a thesis on Medieval German History.

How a young man from the disadvantaged section of Cleveland had become a German expert tells much about Crosby. 'On my first day at East High, I knew I'd never like the place, so I played hookey. When the officer caught up with me he said, "Son, why did you run away from school?" and for no reason at all this crazy idea popped into my head and I said, "Because that one doesn't teach German." And damned if he didn't find me a school that did, so I had to take it. I had a great teacher and she encouraged me; and when I saw how easy it would be for me to lick this subject, first thing I knew I was writing a master's thesis on Richard Wagner and Wolfram von Eschenbach!'

His greatest contribution to education, however, was not in German, which he taught for many years, but as director of the Experiment in Higher Education conducted by Southern Illinois University in East St. Louis. 'We took the most disadvantaged people, black and white,' he says, 'and we took them as they were. If they needed third-grade spelling, that's what they got. But when we were through with them we sent them into the junior year of college. When we started, our students had a prognosis of 90 percent failure. When we got through with them, 76 percent were able to graduate from college. That's what you can do if you take people where they are and loosen up the structure so they can find a place to fit in.'

This is what Crosby is trying to do at Kent, but his success so far has been minimal, because the university has been afraid to open up. 'It'll take time,' Crosby says. In the meantime, he works with blacks and tries to keep them alert to educational opportunities. 'So as I listened to BUS that day I was reminded of the French proverb: *Plus ça change, plus c'est la même chose.* The demands Blount was making were the ones blacks had been making for years. The rhetoric was the same, and the indifference of the authorities was the same. I was afraid there would be trouble as a result of the BUS meeting, but I hoped that it could be avoided.' Later that night, when he heard of the rioting downtown, he would say, 'I hope our blacks weren't involved.'

One of the most persuasive speeches was delivered by a tall, gangling day student from Akron, conspicuous on campus for wearing a gray knitted tarboosh—a Muslim skullcap—which fitted neatly over his Afro hairdo. Known simply as Brother Fargo, he had an astonishing vocabulary, a gift for sly satire, and the ability to make jokes at his own expense. His real name, known only to his fellow blacks, was Dwayne White, son of a high-school teacher in · Louisville, Kentucky. He had come to Kent State on an athletic scholarship—football and track—but had also scored near the top in his academic tests. Lithe, golden tan in color, rapid of speech, he could be the archetype of a black leader, and it had been he who had engineered this rally in support of the blacks at Ohio State.

'As Ron Karenga has so well said of a death in Mississippi, "The only reason why he was killed instead of you was location. He was there. You were here. Next time, here may be there." But now we are beginning to see that there is no here or there. We are all living in Mississippi. We are all listening to the bell of which Hemingway wrote. If we believe for one instant that events occurring at Ohio State will not overtake us in Kent State, we are confused.'

If someone asks Fargo, 'Where did you pick up such a vocabulary?' he says, 'In all-black schools. Man, in those schools you meet women who pour their soul out in their teaching. I had one who said every day, "Words are power," and she gave us long lists to memorize, and I liked her so much I'd go home and read the dictionary, the way ordinary kids read comics.'

Fargo's week ended with the BUS rally. 'Me go for that kid exhibitionism! Are you crazy? We blacks were not remotely concerned with minor troubles on this campus when we had major troubles off. I did wander down Saturday afternoon to see the damage. You call that a riot? Hell, not a piece of jewelry was taken. They smashed the window of a hardware store and liberated nothing. Big deal!'

As he spoke at the Friday rally, bent over because of his height, neither he nor his listeners could have guessed that by this time next week he would appear on the cover of *Life* magazine, with millions of readers asking, "How do you suppose that good-looking Negro got there?"

Off to one side at the rally stood a small, handsome black named Rudy Perry. He did not thrust himself forward as a leader; indeed, except for a multicolored dashiki, he might not have been noticed, for he remained impassive as others spoke. Beardless and with a dark face of velvety smoothness, he looked like a tense young fellow getting ready to defend his welterweight title. He was the field marshal of the Black Protection Patrol, and like a small Napoleon he surveyed his forces. As he recalls the weekend he speaks softly but sometimes with a burst of excitement, conveying the fact that he is ready to die for what he believes 'Don't call me boy! Don't call me Negro! I'm a black. And our job from Friday on was to protect blacks. On Thursday night, when Nixon came on TV to announce the war in Cambodia, we took bets as to which unit of the National Guard would be on campus first—Akron barracks or Ravenna. And we decided right then, "No blacks visible if trouble starts. No sisters to appear anywhere on campus. Patrols of one or two trusted men to enforce the rules. For four nights I got no sleep, because as field marshal, I was responsible for maintaining order.

'Understand this. During everything that happened at Kent in those four days, you will find no blacks involved. Search the pictures of the rioters. Not very many blacks. And none throwing stones. Off to one side you may see a black standing with his arms folded. That's Bob Pickett, our chief patrol officer.

'I stayed in my room and took the messages. "Two black chicks seen crossing the campus near Tri-Towers." I call Pickett and tell him, "This is the field marshal. Get those chicks outa sight, right now!" Look at the pictures. Not one black girl visible.'

Even the briefest conversation with Perry produces insights into how blacks on a huge campus think: 'In Cleveland I attended four schools. Wonderful names. Best names in American history. Robert Fulton, Andrew Jackson, Alexander Hamilton and John F. Kennedy. And you know what? One hundred percent black students. I didn't get good grades in school because there was no challenge. I haven't found it in college, either.

'When you put it all together, every white man is my enemy. I have to look at all whites as potential enemies because, put them in the right position, they automatically become my enemy. There will never be a time when whites can live peacefully with blacks. The race war will come when the blacks can't hold it in any longer and start letting loose. The intensity of the war will depend on how far the whites let it get organized.

'What do the white people demand of me? Work in their factories. Fight their wars. Accept whatever pay they offer me. Do whatever they say to do. So I reject them. I'm not for blacks dating whites. That's an insult to my father and mother. If I went out with a white girl, it would be saying that black girls aren't good enough . . . that my mother wasn't good enough for my father . . . and I know she was beautiful.'

Perry has firm convictions about current history: 'A bunch of white cats in a truck offed President Kennedy. Then Oswald was offed by Ruby because he was too much on Cuba's side.. The CIA offed Bobby Kennedy and Martin Luther King. It's well know that both Sirhan Sirhan and James Earl Ray were hired by the CIA. They also offed Nasser. What's all this jazz about a heart attack? It's known he was a diabetic, but the autopsy showed sugar in his blood. He'd never have taken that sugar himself. The CIA slipped it to him because they had orders to off him.'

With these views, Perry wanted to participate in any protests agitating the Kent campus: 'Sure we wanted to be out there pressing our demands. Sure we wanted a piece of the action. But not with those guns on campus. Because we're black, and we know that when a white man has a gun and he sees a black he gets uptight. He has a compulsion to shoot. And the black man gets shot, no matter what he's done. Portage County is filled with immigrants from the south. To us, Portage County is Mississippi, and in Mississippi it's easy for a black to stay indoors when whites are running around with rifles.'

So during the entire weekend of violence, few blacks will be seen on campus. Bob Pickett will be spotted now and then, a magisterial figure standing aloof, surveying the action to see that no blacks are involved, and we shall see Field Marshal Perry slipping quietly onto the campus late at night to satisfy himself as to what is happening. On Monday, Brother Fargo, ignoring the order 'Blacks off campus,' will experience a sickening moment when he finds himself face to face with an armed Guardsman terrified by the sudden appearance of a black, but in the great Kent riots of 1970, blacks will not participate. Many people expected them to. Fantastic rumors flashed across campus that they were moving in. And after it was all over, some critics would try to pin the blame on the blacks, recalling the dreadful rhetoric that had flooded the campus, but they would be wrong.

Blacks were not involved, and they will be discussed no further in this book, except as we catch fleeting and unimportant glimpses of them. Field Marshal Perry kept his troops under control.

Five students

A university with a student body of 21,186 contains people of so many diversified interests, it is impossible to select even a hundred of them and say, 'These are typical.' During this weekend we shall follow with special attention the activities of five students. We shall see them drifting about the campus on their way to classes, engaged in missions of no particular importance, or in pursuit of their low-keyed love affairs. If their behavior appears banal, or even boring, this is good; and if we can accept them as typical, we will gain a deeper insight into what Kent State and the nation were like that weekend.

We meet the first, a girl, hurrying across Summit Street, off campus, early Friday morning, trying to keep up with a tall, statuesque Scandinavian beauty queen from Ashtabula. The smaller girl cried out, 'Wait a minute! I didn't want to go in the first place.' She was Sandy Scheuer, twenty years old, from Youngstown, a junior in the Speech and Hearing Clinic, where her professors considered her an ideal student. She contributed her spare time to caring for impoverished people with speech defects and charged them nothing for her help. Right now she was in an unhappy mood, because she was facing something not much to her liking. Sharon Swanson explains: 'I had walked over from Beall Hall, where I live, to Sandy's house on Summit Street for an appointment which had each of us scared. We were headed for the Ferrara Center, a low one-story building across the street from Sandy's house, and were nervous about entering. We were going to sell our blood. We were hurrying to get there, because if you give your blood before noon they pay you an extra dollar instead of the ten-dollar standard rate. I was really nervous because I'd never sold blood before, and even Sandy, who had done so several times, was kind of scared too. When we reached the door of the laboratory, Sandy drew back and cried, "I'm no good. I can't do this," and I had to reassure her, saying, "Sure you can. We both can." But when we got inside, what happened? They told me I was anemic. Iron count too low. So I left, and next time I saw Sandy was at our 1:10 organic speech disorders class. Sliding into the chair next to me, she whispered, "Wow, do I feel faint." Dr. Weidner told us, "Keep quiet over there or leave the class," but Sandy was a great favorite of his and knew he was teasing.'

Later that day Sandy felt sufficiently recovered to keep a date she had made with Bruce Pipman, a boy from Alpha Epsilon Pi, the Jewish fraternity, for a game of softball. She had associated with many of the boys from this fraternity— and they had shown their affection by naming her a fraternity 'little sister'—because of her parents, who had begged her to 'date only Jewish boys because dates with gentiles rarely lead to anything.'

'After the game,' says Ken Greene, one of the men who lived in the fraternity house, 'we all came back to the house and cooked up some barbecue. Sandy helped as usual, when she wasn't horsing around with the boys. She was everybody's pal. You just couldn't resist her.

'After we'd got a little beer in us, we started to slide down a mud bank behind our house. Since it was raining a little, you could get a really good slide going from top to bottom. Some of the girls didn't want to do it—they'd get their clothes dirty and that sort of thing—but not Sandy. She was right in there with the best of them.'

After everyone had washed up, the group adjourned to the Moonglow Roller Rink a few miles outside of Kent for a skating party which lasted well past midnight. At such affairs Sandy proved one of the most popular girls; boys enjoyed her and she was always invited to their busts, but she rarely had her own date, and when she next saw Sharon, she wailed, 'I'm getting worried. I'm going to be an old maid. I want someone special that I can care for and love the rest of my life, and what do I have but millions of good friends?' Her parents added to this feeling of insecurity by sending her newspaper clippings reporting the marriages of girls Sandy's age in Youngstown.

While the Constitution was being buried, Doug Wrentmore, a tall, thin sophomore from Northfield, Ohio, sat in his 1:10– 2:00 class in Satterfield Hall taking notes on American litera-ture of the nineteenth century. He was the kind of student a good university hopes to enroll, well behaved, intelligent, a boy with bright promise and one who prospered in academic surroundings in that he grew wiser with each class he took. When class ended he stood by the door and began distributing fliers for a meeting on ecology to be held next week to the other students as they filed out. 'I learned to love nature when I was a boy,' he explains. 'The earth is something we must look after if we expect to have a good life.' He believed in saving the environment, but he wasn't a freak about it.

When he finished distributing the notices, he chanced to hear that a BUS rally was to be held in a few minutes, so he stopped by to see what the blacks were disturbed about. 'It didn't look like a big deal to me,' he says. 'I've seen lots angrier crowds than that.'

Indeed he had. Two weeks before he had hitchhiked from Kent to Cleveland on an unusual mission. 'My brother and I were going as stockholders to the annual meeting of the A.T.&T. We wanted to see how a corporation ran its affairs. I certainly wanted no trouble, but because my brother had long hair, they gave us a bad time. It was my first experience with being discriminated against merely because I was a student. Things might have gotten pretty rough, because everywhere you looked you saw mounted policemen. Two of them arrested Bob Franklin, our communist professor of chemistry who had come to the meeting in his Castro outfit.

'A friend of my father's . . . he was wearing a business suit and looked respectable . . . he saw me and persuaded the police to let me in as a stockholder. They couldn't believe a guy like me would own stock. As I went through the doors I looked back and saw how angry the other students were. I'd never seen them so wrought up. No wonder arrests were made.'

From the BUS rally Doug went along to his karate class, where a long-time friend, Dennis Meredith, said, 'I watched that crowd bury the Constitution and I think there's going to be trouble.' Doug laughed and said, 'Relax. The BUS rally was really quiet. Nobody started anything. I'm sure things are going to be all right.'

Allison Krause, a stunning leggy brunette from Pittsburgh, had a passion for investigating everything that was going on, so naturally she had attended the burial of the Constitution, accompanied by her steady companion, Barry Levine. Together they made one of the most striking couples on campus. She was slightly taller than he, more aggressive, quicker intellectually, more contemporary. A beautiful girl whom many fellows tried to date, she had early and firmly settled upon Barry as the boy she loved and never deviated from this decision. Barry was a frail, sensitive young man with a seventeenth-century pointed beard and matching mustaches.

A friend said of him, 'If you put a plumed hat on him, he'd look just like Aramis in *The Three Musketeers*. The poetic one, remember?' Others said of the pair, 'They found the secret early and didn't have to keep looking.' Of all the young men interviewed at Kent by the researchers, Barry Levine was the most extraordinary, a cavalier in the wrong century, a cameo by Meissonier. By some great good luck he had stumbled upon the one girl, in the ten thousand at Kent, who suited him totally. It is amusing that everyone referred to them as Allison and Barry, never the other way around.

How were they as students? Above average. Nothing spectacular, but above average. Barry says, 'The most powerful influence on Allison was Tom Dubis, a history instructor with a really keen mind. We went to the burial of the Constitution only because we heard that Dubis was going to speak. Allison told me, "He's sure great!" but when we heard him at the Victory Bell we were disappointed. He wasn't on target. What did grab us was the moving manner in which Barbara Agte, our English teacher, spoke. Mrs. Agte was into Women's Lib real deep and Allison identified with her.'

Early that evening Allison and Barry left the campus intending to hitchhike to nearby Stow to visit friends, but as they passed through downtown Kent rain began to fall and Allison said, 'Let's forget it.'

'We went to some of the bars on Water Street and just messed around for a while,' recalls Barry. 'But then we saw the kids starting to gather in the streets, and it looked like there was going to be trouble.'

Since neither of them had ever been in trouble and wanted to stay clear, they left the area and returned to campus, but after they had been in Barry's room for a while a roommate appeared, flushed with excitement and shouting, 'Hey, man! They've liberated Water Street. The revolution has begun. The revolution is here!' Barry told him, 'Don't be absurd. You don't even know what a revolution is.'

At the far edge of the BUS rally were two white students, one a small fellow in well-worn Levis and shirt, the other a big husky young man with wavy reddish-brown hair and a well-trimmed red beard. The first was Jeff Miller; the second was Mark Cramer, high school football star and drummer in a rock group. Their conversation was well remembered by students who overheard them:

CRAMER: This whole affair is a bust. Nothing's going to happen at Kent.

MILLER: Man, you said it.

CRAMER: This dump is too apathetic. The blacks'll keep talking, but the whole thing will die down.

MILLER: It's better that way. Who wants trouble?

Jeff Miller was an undersized, extroverted junior from Plainview, New York, who had spent his first two and a half years at Michigan State and had appeared on the Kent campus only in January. He was a gregarious young man who would do anything for his friends—'Jeff Miller was ready to help you any time you needed him'—but who had a hard time trying to decide what to do for himself. He was most insecure around girls and often wondered if he was ever going to find anyone he could love. He told one girl, 'I know a dozen girls I'd like to ask for a date, but I'm sure they'd all turn me down.'

Early Friday evening friends from Columbus came in with the exciting news that Ohio State University was going through hell. 'Rioting for three days, confrontations with the police, the whole place in an uproar,' the visitor reported. Much discussion followed, and Jeff's friends contemplated the possibility of similar disturbances overtaking Kent. The consensus was that it wouldn't happen here, but about 12:30 a student who lived in the house next door rushed in with the news. 'They're smashing windows on Water Street!'

'We started out the door to see what was up, but only got two blocks down the street, when we saw a cop car. With that, we came back home. We didn't want any of that trouble, that's for sure,' says John Moir, one of Jeff's six roommates, and an ardent fan of the poetry of William Carlos Williams.

The most distinctive of the five students was a handsome six-foot basketball star from Lorain, Ohio, whom at least a score of his friends characterized as 'Bill Schroeder, all-American boy.' He had even features, blue eyes, an easy smile. People automatically liked him, for he combined the assurance of a top athlete with the congeniality of an average kid who enjoyed good company.

One of his close friends says of him, 'The perfect Nordic. Not a hair on his body.' He was a good student and, as another testifies, 'He could have succeeded in anything he tried. He'd have made a great doctor with that calm smile, or a good lawyer with his manner of asking "Now, what's wrong?" '

On Friday night Schroeder and his friend Al Springer were drinking beer at the Main Street bar frequented by fraternity men, when Bill said, 'Let's split. I want some of that apple wine at Orville's.' So they sauntered out of the bar, crossed Main Street and headed down toward Water Street, only to be confronted by a mass of students milling around.

'What's up?' Schroeder asked, but as he spoke he saw several friends who had just been evicted from Orville's. 'Police closed the joint down,' these men reported. 'Too much trouble on the street.'

Al Springer explains what happened next: 'We were just standing around, waiting to see what might break, when Bill noticed these two chicks off by themselves, away from the crowd and sort of lost. He moved right in to see if they were in trouble. Found out they had come over from Akron and were getting scared because of the rowdiness. So Bill right away offered to drive them home, and they gratefully accepted. That was the thing about Bill. He could usually get any girl he wanted.'

As the crowd piled into Bill's car for the trip to Akron, Al said, 'God, am I relieved to get out of Kent. There's going to be trouble and I want no part of it.' But before they could leave town, Schroeder saw one of his roommates headed unknowingly toward the heart of the action. Bill got out of the car and halted the fellow. 'I wouldn't go in there, pal,' he advised. 'They're going to start arresting people before long. I think we all ought to clear out.' And they did.

There they are, five students on a Friday in May. None is involved in any disturbance; all are well behaved. None is a radical; all are concerned. None is a freak; all are of the type sought by educational institutions. And each one, when disturbance does develop, shies away from it. Each is respected by his classmates, and each retains close ties with home.

The bars on Water Street

If a city in the year 1970 allows a railroad to run its tracks down the middle of its main street, piling up traffic as long lines of boxcars rumble past, that city has become confused on its priorities.

In Kent the main tracks of the Erie & Lackawanna run right smack through the middle of town. And these are not abandoned tracks on which a stray freight wanders through now and then. Not at all. Dozens of trains go by on some days, and each one ties up traffic on every east-west city street. When the trains are long, as they usually are, automobiles can pile up for tremendous distances and drivers sit in growing fury as the boxcars clang past, their names providing a review of American history: Norfolk & Western, Santa Fe, Union Pacific, Chicago & Northwestern, Monon, Louisville & Nashville, Toledo, Peoria & Western.

What makes Kent's position irritating is that when one of the extra-long freight trains forms up in the local marshaling yards, the engine begins to pull the endless boxcars at an agonizingly slow pace, often slower than a walk, and instead of picking up speed, the train actually slows down, for a reason that is unbelievable. Union rules forbid the use of an automatic switch in such instances, so the train has to stop when it is halfway through town, a brakeman has to climb down from the caboose, run over to the switch, throw it, run back to the caboose, climb aboard, then signal the engineer that he can proceed, picking up speed at a snail's pace.

This can tie up traffic for about twenty minutes, and Kent citizens learn to plan their movements east or west by train schedules. But on Monday morning, when thousands of Kent students are returning to campus in their cars, and on Friday evening, when they are leaving, the traffic jams are incredible. On Route 43, which brings students down from Cleveland, the cars can be lined up for as much as two miles out into the country, well past the Rusty Nail, Kent's posh restaurant for rural dining.

Then the townspeople curse the students and students curse the townspeople. All university settings throughout the world have a town-gown problem, but none more aggravated than Kent's, where one Erie & Lackawanna freight train, coming along at the inopportune moment, can infuriate thousands. Townsmen argue, 'If there weren't so damned many students, there wouldn't be so many cars,' and students argue back with equal logic, 'If the damned town would build a bridge over the railroad tracks, these massive traffic jams wouldn't happen.' The town does plan to build such a bridge. It has been an urgent item on the civic agenda since 1924.

Meanwhile the boxcars creep through the heart of the city, severing every east-west artery. Daring drivers have invented a hideous game to circumvent the train. If they see it about to close down one street, they dart ahead of it down narrow streets along the riverbank and dash across some street which the train hasn't quite yet reached. It is not unusual to see a staid banker from the town or a coed from the campus scream across the tracks two or three feet ahead of the train. Like dinosaurs from some ancient time, the boxcars continue: Pittsburgh & Lake Erie, Southern Pacific, Penn Central, Southern, Central of Georgia, Boston & Maine, New York, New Haven & Hartford, Denver & Rio Grande Western, Akron, Canton & Youngstown.

That the city indeed has its priorities confused is confirmed when one sees at the eastern end of town a massive concrete stadium belonging to the university and twice as large as the excellence of its football teams would have required. This overbuilding has happened at many universities, but what makes Kent outstanding is that at the western end of town there is an almost equally massive high school stadium, built of reinforced concrete and worthy of any university. Why a town of 28,000 requires two such elephantine structures is perplexing, especially since each is really used only six or seven times a year. One might have thought that with one good stadium the high school could have played its games on Friday night and the university on Saturday, but as one Kent businessman explained, 'For a high school to have its own stadium is absolutely essential.'

The city of Kent is even prettier in many of its aspects than Bob Hillegas saw on his airplane flight. The residential areas are excellent, and the constant avenues of trees keep the urban areas tied in with the lovely surrounding countryside. The sense of easy relaxation and space make it one of the most attractive college towns, and if one looks into its quiet corners, one can find an air of repose reminiscent of the late 1890's.

The two main streets are something else. Route 59, which runs east and west, is a tacky, grubby thoroughfare onto which all the ugliest enterprises of Kent have been piled. Near the university it contains one of the most pitiful fraternity rows in America, the gingerbread Gothic falling into disrepair and every house needing a coat of paint. Route 43, running north and south, is not much better, and if a visitor were to inspect only these two thoroughfares, he would be likely to dismiss Kent as one of the ugliest cities in the Midwest.

But the apex of this ugliness comes on North Water Street in the center of town, for here are collected all the sleazy bars frequented by the university students. Jammed one against the other, six of them compete with music, noise and a mild kind of underworld life. They form a remarkable appendage to university life, a grubby kind of Great White Way, and a good deal of the ferment that animates the university starts here.

The bars have become notorious across the state, so that on Friday or Saturday it is not unusual to find students from colleges as far away as Ohio University, Miami and Case. Motorcycle gangs also congregate here, the local Chosen Few often being joined by the Cobras, from Youngstown. Girls fourteen and fifteen who run away from home in cities like Pittsburgh and Cincinnati wind up here, as do older men trying to sell drugs to the university crowd. 'Kent is where the action is,' has become a popular saying throughout the area, and in Kent the action centers on the bars on Water Street, and Water Street revolves around a notable hangout whose history is interwoven with that of Kent.

'You can miss the library,' one habitué explains, 'and you can skip the gymnasium. You don't have to go to classes or even graduation, but if you miss Orville's, you miss everything important at Kent.' In old days, this was the saloon for men who worked for the Davey Tree Company, and it became famous across northern Ohio for its bean soup. The Davey dormitory lay just north of the saloon, and lumberjacks bunked there when they came to Kent for instruction in the Davey system of tree care. In those days only the toughest students dared appear in the saloon, but when the dormitory was sold to the university's art department for studios, painters and sculptors began to populate Water Street and quickly discovered the bean soup. Today this famous old saloon tells its story simply: On its bar stands a bowl of pickled eggs. Perched on the stools you find college instructors arguing with their students, pretty girls looking for dates, a score of young men with very long hair, and a host of kids not connected with the college who have dropped by to see what's happening.

Jammed up against Orville's are the five other bars: Big Daddy's with its pizzas; the Ron-de-vou for the rah-rah crowd; J.B.'s for the freaks who need music; the Kove for the Greeks;

the Pirate's Alley for the crowd with money. On any night of the week, North Water Street is a scene of rich nostalgia; on Fridays and Saturdays it's a jamboree always on the verge of explosion. One coed said with obvious affection, 'I went to college at Kent State, but I got my education on Water Street.' Students from all over Ohio felt the same way.

Artist with a spray gun

Researchers working on this book were able to interview every major figure with whom they needed to talk, except one, and this failure was galling, for this bizarre character was very much part of the background to this story.

For some years the university had been plagued by a mysterious word-artist whose palette consisted of only two colors, an iridescent red and a brilliant green, and whose brush was a spray can which imbedded the paint so deeply into stone that it could not be easily removed.

The unknown artist had a monotonous repertory: *Free Bobby. Free Huey. ROTC Off Campus. Off the Pigs.* These were often scrawled indelibly on white façades, and Lieutenant Crawford, of the campus police, says, 'We spent a lot of money undoing the work of this person. You could wash the letters with any kind of soap you wanted, and nothing happened. Sooner or later you had to sand-blast, and that costs real dough.'

The political sloganeering might have been tolerated, but the artist also had an ugly penchant for obscenity, and it was not uncommon for students and faculty to waken in the morning to find across their building such cheering reminders as *Fuck the Pigs* and *We don't want your fucking war.*

'We really had to find this spray-can expert,' Crawford says, 'but we were powerless. We had our eye on a couple of fellows who could have been doing it, but whenever the signs appeared, they had alibis. Then, late one night, as one of our professors was crossing the campus on his way home, he saw this figure with a spray can painting a slogan on the library. At last we had our man.

'He ran over, shouting, "You can't do that!" To his astonishment a young girl turned to face him, spray can in hand, and said quietly, "Mind your own fucking business." Well, we tracked down who she was, and it turned out to be Ruth Gibson, a girl with an I.Q. of at least 165. She was the daughter of a brilliant engineer who lived not far from Kent and she had a good academic record. She was known as an extreme liberal but not a revolutionary.

'Well, we arrested her, but the administration decided not to press formal charges against her. So every once in a while we'd see evidence of her spray can. She went everywhere with her signs, a one-woman propaganda machine, and wherever she went you'd find *Fuck the Pigs,* and other little gems.'

Ruth became president of the Young Socialist Alliance, a position she used to enhance her position as a critical force on campus, but her principal operation continued to be painting in as obscene a manner as possible. At the beginning of each quarter she would, says Crawford, 'slam open the door of the police department, stand in the middle of the room and cry, "Well, I'm back on campus, you motherfucking pigs. Keep your eye on me." '

Her younger brother, Noel Gibson, known to the campus as Richard, is a frail nineteen-year-old semi-genius with an I.Q. at least as high as his sister's: 'Our father is a great engineer, one of the best in Ohio. He worked on the *Nautilus* and for fun taught Ruth and me how to build an atomic bomb. He used to give me a dictionary and make me memorize words . . . just plain words.'

It is not easy to get young Gibson into focus. 'I was strongly in favor of the Vietnam war. Matter of fact, I enlisted and intended making the army my career. Very patriotic. You see, my father was in the navy, also an uncle, with a cousin in the army. My mother's family was frightfully gung-ho, but one day in the barracks I saw this television show of Vietnam, and in a flash of seeing the destruction, I realized that I didn't want to kill those little people who hadn't done anything to me. I tried every trick in the book to get out of uniform, and after five months and two days they were mighty glad to be rid of me.'

Noel says of his sister, 'Far above average as a person. Huge circle of friends who trust her. I think of her as a high achiever. Could do anything she wanted to in college, but I doubt that she'd be welcome back at KSU right now.' He says Ruth is now in hiding somewhere, maybe California, maybe Chicago, but he thinks she will complete her education. She has no desire to be a secretary or a clerk in some store, because she says the whole country wants to escape just that sort of drudgery. 'She and I are both convinced that society is going to come around to our way of life.' He says that he would always like to see his sister. 'She's a terribly vital sort of person.'

On Thursday night, following President Nixon's address on Cambodia, Ruth and three of her cohorts appeared on North Water Street. Joe Shannon, president of the Kent Tavern Owners Association, tells what happened: 'Somewhere around 9:00 this girl started using her spray can, painting the wall of J.B.'s. Joe Bujack, the owner of the bar, rushed over and grabbed her by the wrist—she had painted *"U.S. Get Out Of . . ."* When Joe grabbed her, she started yelling, "Let go of me, you're hurting me." Joe said, "Okay, I'm going to call the cops." He left his bouncer, Ron Mihalik, with instructions to hang onto the kids, but when he came back from the phone he found they had broken loose and run off. Ron told him they'd gone up Columbus Street, and when the police cruiser came by he got in it and drove with the two policemen all around the area. They never saw the kids again.'

Until Friday. That night, about the same time, Ruth Gibson and the same boys, plus three or four more, showed up wearing red armbands. Ruth did not have her paint can, but Joe spotted her in the crowd—slight, short, her stringy hair in ponytails. He said to her, 'I know you're Ruth Gibson.' (One of Joe's bartenders had supplied her name.) She turned on him and called him a 'capitalist pig.' The boys with her surrounded him. He broke out of their circle, went to the phone and called the police again. He mentioned the red armbands.

Says Bujack: 'Those kids were there all night long, standing in shadows, going out into the street, coming back into the shadows—agitating, egging the other kids on. Bob Franklin was there, too. The boys with the red armbands started the fire in the street. Then the cruiser came by and somebody slung a bottle and the riot was on.'

What happened on Friday

For each of the four critical events of this tragic weekend, an opening statement, factual in nature, will be made. It will endeavor to describe what actually happened, with no attempt to explain why it happened, who motivated it, or what it signified. After this unpejorative description, various viewpoints and interpretations will be given, which means that the same event may be seen from as many as eight or nine perspectives, some of them conflicting. It will be up to the reader to evaluate them. Here is the first of these accounts, a narrative of the events that took place on North Water Street on the night of Friday, May 1, 1970.

At dusk the usual crowd began to gather: hippies from California in buckskin suits and beads; a lot of young girls whose parents had not seen them for weeks, who hoped to find some university men with whom to stay for a while; members of two different motorcycle gangs; young instructors from the university who wanted to make the scene and talk with their students over a mug of beer; a horde of boys and girls from the campus, some moderately well dressed, the majority in the kind of weird historical costumes that pleased the young and confused the old. Many of the assembly wore beads, or Indian headbands, or military uniforms from past centuries. There were no less than eight Daniel Boones, six Davy Crocketts, and four young men in velvet jackets of the Edwardian period. Clean-shaven faces were rare, but there were some, and hair was worn conspicuously longer than it had been even a year before.

The coeds on Water Street that night were somewhat unusual. This was the first warm evening of the spring and the girls were dressed accordingly. Not too many of them were wearing blue jeans. Most were in miniskirts, their slim legs pale from the winter. Their hair was long, but for the most part, neatly combed. They moved easily from one bar to another where 3.2 beer was dispensed and eighteen-year-olds admitted, talking with boys they had known in class or with the young instructors to whom they had taken a liking. They drank little, behaved themselves well, and were extraordinarily beautiful in their unspoiled and youthful freshness. Some talked politics, but most did not.

Among these coeds was a tall, heavy girl who seemed to be about twenty years old, and mature even for that. She wore sneakers, ribbed brown pants, a red sweatshirt and a scarf, but what was memorable about this girl, so that many who saw her that night would easily recall her, was her large mobile face. It was that of a tragic madonna. It resembled certain Italian faces painted by Raphael, but it was also exactly the kind of female face one sees in the greatest paintings of Delacroix, say 'The Massacre of Scio' or 'Liberty Leading the People.' And before this week was over, it would become one of the best-known faces in America. Now, as the girl moved quietly from bar to bar, cadging drinks and making trivial conversation, everyone assumed that she was from the university. 'I think she's a senior in home ec,' said one of the men who bought her a drink.

At the beginning, the evening was about the same as on any Friday, except for the size of the crowd. A good many students had come in from other universities, and as the night wore on, there was a degree more noise than was customary. The bartenders attributed this to the sudden warmth after a long, cold winter. Whether there was also an influx of strange faces, determined men a little older than usual and from out of town, would be debated in the months ahead.

At 10:00 the excitement increased, because in several of the bars television sets were beginning to bring in pictures of the fourth game of the world championship basketball play-offs between the Los Angeles Lakers and the New York Knicks. The competition stood at two games to one in favor of New York, and in accordance with the rule that students in Ohio cheer for any team opposing New York, there was strong support for Los Angeles; Jerry West, who had played against Ohio teams while in college, was a particular hero, and the fans believed that he was going to lead the Lakers to victory.

At 10:15 an unprecedented occurrence for a spring night took place. Someone, somewhere, started throwing strings of firecrackers in the air, and they went off like a fusillade of distant shots. 'I thought it was gunfire,' one student said, 'but over in the next block.' The firecrackers excited the crowd, and someone tossed a beer bottle at a passing car, breaking one of the back windows. Arrests should have started now, but none would occur until 12:17, a delay of two hours.

At 10:30 Joseph Bujack, tough fifty-year-old refugee from Poland, grew worried. He says, 'On Thursday night I caught this band of people . . . girls and boys . . . painting signs with spray cans . . . on the pavements . . . on our bar. I tried to drive them off, but they simply ran away, then ran back. They wore red armbands and red Indian headdress. I know most of the students who come to Water Street . . . that's my business. But I'd never seen them before. They were real troublemakers.' Now, on Friday night, he saw them again, close to the dark building walls. One had a Vietcong flag. Seeing this, Bujack looked around for Patrolman Robert L. DeFluiter of the Kent police. A sensible arrangement had been made whereby DeFluiter was allowed to moonlight, wearing his uniform, after his regular hours with the police department, as a kind of watchman and bouncer for the Water Street bars, whose owners paid him a small salary in addition to the regular one he received from the city. Bujack told him, 'We'd better do something about this gang of people with the red armbands.' DeFluiter replied, 'I don't like the looks of that bunch. They keep themselves in the shadows and run out when I'm not looking. They know the tricks. Probably the best thing is for you to telephone the station and ask them to send a cruiser down here to pick them up.'

At 10:42 Bujack made the call, and shortly thereafter a patrol car did drive from south to north along the street, only to be hit by a beer bottle. The officers could not find the gang in the red armbands.

At 10:55 an elderly man and his wife came along Water Street in an old sedan. The troublemakers stopped them, pointed to the shouting crowd, and warned the man to back off. He refused to do so and edged his car forward, bumping ever so slightly one of the boys. 'What in hell are you trying to do, Chester?' someone called. Soon the car was being rocked back and forth and its windows were smashed, but the old man bulled ahead and drove it through the mob. A rain of beer bottles rattled off the roof, but the incident was forgotten as the damaged car disappeared. Still no police. The scene in the street grew rougher, with girls screaming at anyone who tried to negotiate Water Street, 'Pigs off the street! We won't go to Cambodia.'*

By 11:00 the crowd was getting increasingly unruly, and DeFluiter called the station himself and said, 'Send some men down here right away to break up the group.'

At 11:15 the crowd realized that they could continue to raise hell on Water Street with impunity, so when they saw

* Chronologies for the four major events were constructed with continuing review and care. They were based primarily on written entries in official logs, augmented by numerous interviews regarding each incident. Thus, for each event we started with a central core of highly accurate data into which we fitted related events, using the best available information. How accurate are the times we cite? This varies. Most are minutely so; others have had to be educated extrapolations, but even these, by force of circumstance, must be accurate to within a few minutes. There are discrepancies. For example, two top-flight witnesses differ by almost an hour in their estimates as to when this car tried to force its passage through North Water Street. We have accepted the earlier time, but with reservations. Five printed sources proved helpful: *Tragedy in Our Midst*, a commendable eight-page special summary in the May 24, 1970, Akron *Beacon Journal*; the Justice Department summary of the FBI report; the Kent State section of *The President's Commission on Campus Unrest*; the *obiter dicta* of the Portage County Special Grand Jury report; and the excellent full-length book *13 Seconds: Confrontation at Kent State* by Joe Eszterhas and Michael D. Roberts, Dodd, Mead and Company, 1970. Our timetables conform totally to none of those given in the four sources, for the good reason that they are sometimes contradictory among themselves.

a large tractor hauling a semi north, they formed a human-chain barricade and stopped it. A cheer went up at this second traffic victory. The driver good-naturedly tried to edge his huge vehicle through the mob, shrugged his shoulders, and backed it all the way to the traffic light. Now a huge cheer went up. This was a substantial triumph, and three more cars were forced to back up.

At 11:20 Ronald Pisanello, proprietor of Big Daddy's, made an experienced survey of the street and went right back inside to call the police. 'We need some patrolmen down here right now.' At this moment another cruise car, K-1, ventured down the street, from north to south this time, and it, too, was greeted with a beer bottle.

At 11:21 Patrolman Tony Filomena was awakened by a phone call. Along with numerous other off-duty Kent policemen, he was told, 'Report immediately. Full uniform. Riot in progress.' But it would be almost an hour before he and his colleagues would be ready to march forth to clear the streets.

At 11:27 a third cruiser came down the street, and it was struck with a real barrage of beer pitchers, bottles and glasses. Now DeFluiter called headquarters in some anger and shouted, 'If you're not going to send men to make arrests, don't send any more cars through here. This crowd is getting real bad.' The cars stopped coming, but no policemen appeared.

At 11:30 the serious trouble began. Trash cans were emptied in the middle of the street and their contents set afire. A small toolshed on a hillside across the street was set ablaze, producing its own considerable fire.

At 11:41 Sergeant Joe Myers of the Kent police, recognizing that he might soon have a full-scale riot on his hands, if indeed he did not already have one, broadcast, on his own recognizance, Signal 25. This meant that every available policeman was to report and that assistance from the police forces from neighboring communities was formally requested.

At 11:45 another cruiser driven by Patrolman Ronald Craige appeared on Water Street, moving cautiously and blinking its lights. This was a signal for DeFluiter to shift from his moonlighting job to normal status; he quit his post guarding the bars, climbed into his car, and reported to City Hall.

At 11:47, or perhaps a little later, an exhibition of motorcycle artistry was provided by the Chosen Few, a gang who would later be blamed for having incited the riot, even though they did not arrive until it was well started and then added little to the provocation. Some of the members, on gleaming machines with high 'nosepicker' handlebars, congregated at the far north end of the street and rode with considerable skill right at the bonfire, turning aside in screaming circles at the last moment and retreating to their starting position in wide swinging arcs, sometimes coming perilously close to their fellow cyclists headed in the opposite direction. A girl who witnessed the exhibition said, 'It was like a mechanical ballet. Those kids really knew how to handle their machines.'

At about 11:50, although some witnesses place the event earlier, part of the crowd, for no apparent reason, started moving rapidly away from the bars and south on Water Street toward the center of town. There someone threw a beer bottle through a store window, and the shattering glass echoed so musically that others began throwing whatever they could find at the big plate-glass windows. In the short distance from the bars to the traffic light where Routes 59 and 43 cross, forty-seven windows were smashed, including five large ones in Bill Nash's bank and thirteen small. It was the most destructive act of malicious mischief in Kent's history.

At 11:55 Mayor LeRoy Satrom roared into town from the north—for a reason which will be explained later—to find that because of the mob at the bonfire he was unable to negotiate North Water Street. Using side roads, he reached City Hall, where a contingent of nearly a dozen Kent police, who had been issued face shields, riot sticks and crash helmets, were awaiting instructions from him. Every member of this unit has testified that it would have been imprudent if not impossible to have dispatched solitary policemen or small groups to the riot area. 'We had to wait till a unit could be assembled,' they insist.

At 12:10 as the Kent policemen mustered at City Hall, preparing to wade into the trouble on Water Street, they could hear yelling and screaming and glass breaking. They had no doubts about the seriousness of the trouble.

At 12:15 the squad of fifteen riot police made their first contact with students at the big intersection of Main and Water. The young people who had broken the windows scattered immediately, vanishing up alleys and running east toward the campus.

At 12:17 the police reached the bar area and made a regrettable mistake: they ordered the bars closed. This arbitrary action threw a new mass of young people into the streets and infuriated many who up to now had done nothing wrong. A moderate student explains, 'Some of us had just paid for drinks which we were not allowed to finish, and money doesn't come easily. Those of us in the music bars had laid out a buck each to get inside, and so far we hadn't heard any music. But what made some of the athletic types really sore, the cops drove us away from the television sets, so that we couldn't see the finish of the Lakers–Knicks game. And the hell of this was that it looked as if the Lakers were going to win.' Says another student, 'If you want to specify one reason for the new rioting that followed, blame it on the police breaking up our basketball game.'

At 12:30 Mayor Satrom, in City Hall, reviewed reports coming to him of the scene that gripped the heart of his city: fire, rampaging students, broken glass, hundreds of new rioters erupting from the bars. 'You better give me a copy of the ordinance.' he told his assistant, and what happened next changed the complexion of that night's fun. Satrom declared a state of emergency.

At 12:35 the Kent city fire company received word of 'the large fire in the middle of Water Street' and dispatched a truck to handle the bonfire in North Water Street. The driver of the truck took one look down the street, saw the mob there, and prudently decided to approach the scene by a back street, keeping his truck hidden behind a building.

At 12:47 Mayor Satrom called Governor Rhodes in Columbus to alert him to the situation. He got John McElroy, the governor's assistant, on the phone and advised him that at this time he was not requesting assistance from the Guard, but that at some future time he might do so.

At 12:55 the riot squad had completed its drive to the north end of Water Street, sweeping it practically clear. It then turned back, and by the time it reached the bar area, saw with relief that a contingent of sheriff's deputies was moving north to join forces. Together the two units returned to Main and Water, then turned east and started sweeping all the rioters back toward the campus.

At 12:56, almost as they did so, a solitary rioter left Water Street, ran up an alley to the east, and set fire to a small wooden building on a hill overlooking the main fire below.

At 12:57 Mayor Satrom left City Hall, climbed into a cruiser driven by Patrolman DeFluiter and drove toward the center of town. He is certain of the time because as he approached Main and Water, the burglar alarm at Hickman's jewelry store was activated by rioters who had broken the window, and this fact was entered in the police log. DeFluiter pulled the cruiser to the side of the road and handed Satrom a microphone. The mayor announced the state of emergency and 'read the riot act.'

Practically no one who uses this critical phrase, which sets in motion severe legal sanctions, knows what the words mean. The Riot Act, *per se,* is never read. To do so would be ridiculous. The heart of the Ohio act is as follows:

2923.51 Dispersing of riotous group. When five or more persons are engaged in violent or tumultuous conduct which creates a clear and present danger to the safety of persons or property, a law enforcement officer, or commissioned officer of the organized militia or armed forces of the United States called to duty to protect against domestic violence, shall, forthwith upon view or as soon as may be on information, and unless prevented by such persons, order such persons to desist and disperse to their several homes or lawful employment. Such order shall be given by such means and as often as necessary to reasonably insure that it is heard, unless the giving or hearing of such order is prevented by such persons. Whoever refuses or knowingly fails to obey such order shall be fined not more than fifty dollars.

When an officer 'reads the riot act' he says something like 'This is an unlawful assembly. You must disperse.' Strict interpretation of the act would require him to 'order such persons to desist and disperse to their several homes or lawful employments.' The riot act would be read many times in the next three days, but never in that stilted phraseology. The essence of the act requires that the assembly be declared illegal and its members ordered to disperse. The word *immediately* is usually added, but it would be sufficient if the officer merely said, 'You are breaking the law. Get out of here at once.'

Once the riot act has been read, three grave charges can be made against those who fail to respond: riot in the first degree (one to three years in jail, fine of $1,000); riot in the second degree (one year, $1,000); or inciting to riot (one to three years, $1,000). First-degree riot exists when it leads to a subsequent felony; second-degree, when it leads to a misdemeanor. With the reading of the act, arrests began.

At 1:04, as Mayor Satrom concluded the last of several readings, he could see that some of his forward policemen were under a heavy barrage of rocks. At this point DeFluiter did an arbitrary thing. Indicating that Satrom must drive the car himself, he got out and said, 'I want to be with the other police who are taking the beating.' For the next hour or so Satrom would be his own chauffeur.

By 1:05 the police had compressed the students into a mass at Main and Lincoln, and now an impasse developed between the Kent police and the campus force. By tradition the city police were not allowed on campus, so it was expected that at this point the campus police would take over. None appeared. As one Kent policeman said, 'They let us down.' Others spoke more vehemently, and for the next four days this lack of cooperation would exacerbate feelings between the two police departments. What the city police did not know was that at this time the campus police were required elsewhere on campus to protect buildings being threatened with fire and bomb scares. Says Captain Donald L. Schwartzmiller, of the campus police, 'We needed every man we had. If we'd sent them to Main and Lincoln, anything could have happened.'

At 1:06 the firemen called in to headquarters, 'All fires extinguished. All clear on Water Street.' And they returned to the fire station.

At 1:10 the city police were well into the job of arresting students, some of whom were then piled into Mayor Satrom's car and driven by him to the police station, where they were placed in temporary custody in a small jail section, which at one point held fourteen students.

At 1:30 Marty Howard, popular radio figure in Kent, was awakened by the jangling of his phone. 'All deputy sheriffs to report to duty. Big rioting in Kent.' Since he lived close to the university and the downtown area, it was inconceivable that rioting could be under way without his knowing about it. 'But when I reached the courthouse in Ravenna and someone jammed a batch of riot gear in my hands, I knew there was trouble. Turning on my red light and siren, I zoomed into Kent, but as soon as I got there, two sheriffs flagged me down and started piling kids they had arrested into the back of my car. "To the jail!" they ordered, and for some time I ran a shuttle service.'

At 1:42 gas was used for the first time and was directed at the crowd gathered at Main and Lincoln, for when the mob from downtown was herded up to the campus area, they were joined by large numbers of students who had stayed on campus but who now clustered to watch. They were driven back with a stiff application of tear gas. The situation grew tense, for this was the first experience the students had had with this substance that choked them, irritated their nose and throat passages, and caused them to weep copiously. Angry words were spoken, but at 2:20 a curious traffic accident, which will be described later, so diverted the crowd that they turned their full attention to it. Within moments they were cheering the police who were speeding to the rescue.

At 2:10 one of those gratuitous and senseless things happened which give authenticity to a riot. Michael Weekley, crossing the darkened campus peacefully on his way to his dormitory, suddenly felt an urge to heave a brick through a ROTC window. He was nabbed by a watching policeman and became one of the students hauled off to jail in Marty Howard's red-lit car; he drew a sentence of thirty days. This was the first overt act against the ROTC building. But even as such arrests were being made, Sergeant John H. Williams of the campus police reflected upon the truism: 'When you arrest students, it's only the followers you get. You hardly ever grab the hard core. We see them stirring things up. We know they're there. But when the trouble starts we see them filtering out around the edges, and it's the innocent ones, the followers, who are getting picked up.'

At 2:27 a policeman was able to call back to headquarters: 'Students have returned to campus.' A bystander would have been justified in thinking at that moment that another spring outburst by college students had been safely negotiated and that when the cost of replacing the windows had been taken care of, everything would be all right. Such a supposition would have been dramatically wrong.

Proof of this came at 3:00 when through the quiet darkness that now enveloped the city, two speeding cars approached the outskirts of Kent. From the east came two uniformed officers of the Ohio State Highway Patrol, stopping by on the prudent guess that there would be more action in the city. And from the west, driving at breakneck speed from Columbus, came a young officer of the Ohio National Guard; he too was reporting on the good chance that there would be further action which might require intervention from the Guard. The two cars passed at Main and Lincoln, but the occupants did not recognize one another in the dark.

Why it happened

'It wasn't alcohol,' the bartender at Big Daddy's said, 'that's for sure. A couple of years ago the students used to drink a lot more than they do now. If the riot had occurred in 1968, I'd have said it was booze. This time impossible. You want my opinion? Spring. Something like this happens every spring, but this one was bigger.'

'It wasn't Cambodia,' says Paul Bossman, a senior in advertising. 'Every nut and weirdo in the vicinity was in town to celebrate spring. Most of the people on Water Street were high-schoolers or members of street gangs. They were much more interested in vandalism than Cambodia. Lots of KSU freshmen with time on their hands. I didn't see many upperclassmen, but I did spot a group of five or six older ones who triggered the action and who moved along the crowd, working up chants and generating excitement.'

'It was Cambodia,' says Jerry Persky, a secondary ed major from South Euclid and a strong liberal who should know what campus leaders were talking about that Friday. 'Nixon's Thursday night speech was the direct spark for the riot. What other reason could there be?'

At various points in this narrative, testimony by Charles Madonio will be cited, not only because he was double-bass for a combo which played at Big Daddy's, where he could watch the action and alert himself when new faces moved into town, and not because he was a Ravenna boy who had attended Kent State, but because he sat down when the events were over and typed out his recollection of what had happened. He was thus a first-class eyewitness whose impressions were spontaneous and not reconstructed long after the affair. 'It wasn't Cambodia,' he insists. 'At least not with the kids I saw. During an intermission Joe Bujack asked me, "How's business at Big Daddy's?" and I said, "Lousy," and he said, "So's mine." More people on the sidewalk than in the bars. I saw no evidence of malice over Nixon's Cambodian announcement.'

Hal Walker, editor of the summer-session newspaper, disagrees: 'The trouble must be blamed on President Nixon's decision to send American troops into Cambodia, thus, in the eyes of the students, widening the Vietnam war when he had promised to end it. This decision was the subject of much bitter comment in classes that Friday. When the students smashed store windows they also shouted anti-Nixon slogans.'

'It wasn't police brutality,' one student explains, 'because no police were in sight when it started. As a matter of fact, the police behaved pretty well, considering.'

'It wasn't the motorcycle gangs,' another student insists. 'The Chosen Few were in evidence, but only late, and the Cobras never did show.'

'It wasn't fighting over girls,' a coed reports, 'because there were so many girls around, anyone could have a date if he wanted one.'

'It was the weather,' opines one young man. 'First nice Friday night of the year. You know, the panty-raid spirit.'

'It wasn't a panty-raid thing at all,' declares his date. 'It was all planned and arranged by outsiders.'

Eddie Kaufman, a pre-law senior who is financing his way through college in part by bartending and working as doorman at J.B.'s, agrees with the girl. Eddie is twenty-three, slight of build, was a lightweight wrestler until he injured his back two years ago, and he speaks with the conviction of a trained observer. 'When you tend bar for a while you get a feel for what's going on,' he says. 'You can feel it when the crowd is ugly. You know there's going to be a fight before it starts. That Friday there was an ugly feel to the crowd. I knew there was going to be trouble.'

Steve Sharoff, who has a keen feeling for these matters, says, 'Who's looking around deep for reasons? I was sitting in Orville's having a beer. Everything normal. I hear a crash out in the street and somebody runs in shouting, "Guys are throwing bottles out there." All I could think of to say was, "Wow, man! That's pretty far out." That's how the trouble started.'

There is yet another factor that some responsible observers think touched off the explosion—the presence on North Water Street of at least one of the four SDS leaders who had been released from Portage County jail two days before. When questioned later, he admitted being in a bar on the strip that evening, but said, 'When I heard there were cops hassling kids outside in the street, I got out of town.'

Fortunately, three young men with first-class credentials were present during the riot, and their evidence is substantial. Rich Meilander, Alan Frank and Ken Tennant had known one another most of their lives and had remarkably similar tastes and habits. They had grown up in Kent and had attended the elementary and high school run by Kent State for practice teaching. Each had enrolled in the university later. They were good students, never in trouble with the police, and they lived at home. Rich was twenty, considered himself a liberal, and majored in psychology. 'I trust our government, but I don't believe in sitting on the sidelines keeping my mouth shut till I'm forty-eight. If I see something wrong, I'm going to say so.'

Alan is the nineteen-year-old son of one of the university's finest professors, Glenn Frank in geology, whose name will become familiar as this account progresses. Young Frank describes himself as 'a middle-of-the-road type who takes the swimming team very seriously. I am intuitively anti-radical and this must be considered in whatever I say.'

Ken Tennant is an eighteen-year-old jut-jawed ringer for the old-time movie actor William Bendix. Someone in the group described him as 'a conservative who drinks beer but hates the taste of it.' Ken protested vigorously, not about the description but the fact that if the beer bit got into print his mother would raise the devil. 'You can say I'm a conservative who digs the downtown scene, but I also take my courses seriously. By that I mean I manage to squeeze in about ten hours of study a quarter. I can't stand being alone. I need people.'

These three companions, representing three clearly defined points of view, saw the Friday rioting in this way. Alan Frank says, 'I know nearly everybody on campus, because I've lived here all my life and my father is such a hard-working guy. We have students around the house all the time. Now, there are two types of leaders at Kent State. The Student Union group and the downtown group, and they almost never meet. Certainly the Union gang, the ones who really run the protests on the campus, are never seen in the bars. But on Friday night there were fifty or seventy-five of them down there, talking things up. They mentioned Cambodia a good deal and I got the impression they were determined to start something.'

At the height of the fire, Ken Tennant did a courageous thing. He got Alan Frank, moved into the middle of the street and started to put the fire out. When rowdies tried to impede him, he fought them off. Of this incident he says, 'This was my town they were trying to burn. I was sore. Alan and I extinguished the fire . . . put it out completely . . . and when the mob tried to start it again, Alan asked, "Why are you doing this?" and they replied, "Kicks," but one girl said,

"There's a revolution about to start in this country and, man, you just got to be in on it." I started to tell her she was nuts, but some others crowded around me, shoving and pushing, and shouting, "Cambodia is a disgrace. Burn the whole damned town down." I could see myself in the middle of a fistfight, but just as it was about to start, the mob moved away from where the fire had been and I heard the smashing of windows. The real riot had begun.'

Rich Meilander had an equally sobering experience: 'I've often been at J.B.'s as a customer and I know the crowd. Boy, was it different this night! I didn't want to be with them, too violent in what they were saying. So I went out into the street and a stranger came up to me and said, "Hey! Stand right where you are." He moved close to me so that I would hide him, and when I looked down I saw he had a Molotov cocktail which he was going to throw over my shoulder. I told him, "No, thank you," and moved about a hundred yards away. A different stranger came up to me and asked, "What time is it?" and I asked, "What in hell is this all about?" and he said, "It's a planned movement to strain the National Guard. They're tied up at Columbus and on the truck strike in Akron and Cleveland, and we don't think they have enough men to cover this too." '

Meilander started to question the man, but he disappeared. At this point a tall, bearded, unkempt hippie came running right through the middle of a crowd of five policemen, slugging at them till one of them grabbed him to ask questions. 'Let go of me, you lousy pigs,' he shouted, whereupon one of the policemen belted him with a night stick. 'What goes on here?' the hippie yelled, cursing at them. A violent blow to the head dropped him and he looked unconscious, but the police hauled him to his feet and shouted, 'Now you better run!' He took off blindly, and when he reached the train tracks a freight was moving through and he crashed right into one of the boxcars. Meilander says, 'We could hear the thud. The police moved in and roughed him up. When they tossed him into a police car, I thought, "Boy, this isn't a game." '

When Meilander got back to the bars he found that a friend of his, a huge muscular merchant seaman called Tommy Rich, had climbed on top of a car and was trying to halt the riot and the destruction. 'You're going to get into trouble,' Rich warned, but nobody would listen, and when they had swarmed past him to kick in the windows of the bank, he sat on top of the car and cried to Meilander, 'This is going to get real tough.' He had seen riots before.

Tommy Rich had the word, right enough, but the question recurs: Why? What were the causes or factors or motives that turned a more or less typical Friday night on the strip into a full-scale riot?

Riots tend to follow certain patterns and they all adhere to the principle of accumulation, little things that somehow or other catch the crowd's fancy and increase the residue of excitement. Probably no less than thirty eyewitnesses, for instance, mentioned the Montoni pizza truck that tried to press through the crowd in the middle of the street. The kids flipped up the hood and either pulled the distributor wire and pushed it back down the street or the driver got it into reverse and backed away (you hear both versions). Then there was the car with the elderly couple that took such a beating—the man tried to drive through the crowd and nudged somebody. "What in hell are you trying to do, Chester?" somebody yelled. The car finally got through and roared on up the street. Both of these incidents were cheered loudly as demonstrable victories. Both raised the crowd's temperature.

Howard White, a student, inclines to rest the responsibility on people rather than events. 'I spotted the usual campus leaders,' he says. 'You know, Mike Alewitz watching everything with a cynical eye, the leather-jacket boys, Robert Franklin moving slowly up and down. Rick Erickson just out of jail. But none of them took action of any kind. They just watched. Then after a while someone yelled, "Let's go down and get the banks," and some kid from the middle of the crowd lobbed a brick through a store window. A big girl I hadn't ever seen before picked up a board and started bashing windows in the bank . . .'

Another student is adamant in his insistence that he saw an assistant professor of liberal political persuasions piling inflammable trash on the bonfire in the middle of the street. Allan Orashan, the Sigma Alpha Epsilon leader who spells Eddie Kaufman at J.B.'s door, says, 'I know the Water Street regulars. Friday night I saw half a dozen strangers who were giving the crowd direction. When the rock-throwing and window-smashing began, it was as much non-student as student.'

Another question: When did it all begin? Says Ken Tennant, 'With me it goes back to the music festival they held at Fred Fuller Park in September, 1969. Four Weathermen came down from Chicago, with insignia on their bib overalls. They were selling their organization newspaper, and I said, "I'll buy a copy if you'll tell me what your outfit stands for." They said, "We're going to destroy this corrupt American society and build a better." I asked how, and they explained, "We've decided to close down schools all over the nation. We're going to start in Chicago. But we have our eye on Kent State, too. It could be ripe." '

So, ripe or not, it is pretty clear that Kent State was the target of considerable outside interest and that this interest was expressed through violence the night of May 1. But Alan Frank's most lasting memory of that night is not of sinister Weathermen or red armbands or fires in the street: it is of the tall, mysterious girl with the Delacroix face. 'Which bar were we in? It must have been J.B.'s because she put the arm on Eddie Kaufman and me at the same time. She came up to us wearing that red shirt and no bra. She looked very mature, and with her big mouth drawn down in a kind of pout, she asked, "You fellows got any spare change?" In a place like J.B.'s you get hit all the time, so we said no, and without showing any disappointment she moved on, like a big, dark ghost.'

Then there is all the testimony concerning another Water Street irregular—Robert Franklin, the Castro look-alike who taught liberation chemistry. Like the big girl in the red shirt, Franklin has a striking appearance and chances for mistaken identity in his case are practically nil. 'He looks,' says one of his students, 'like a hairbrush coming at you.' Franklin had been mixed up in various campus movements, more like a student than a teacher, and was considered by many to be an extreme radical. Others thought of him merely as an activist who attracted a lot of students. Says Alan Frank, 'I can't ever remember seeing Bob Franklin on the strip before, but this night I spotted him moving along the edges of the crowd.' (Franklin, it will be recalled, was observed at the noon rally of WHORE moving on the outskirts of the crowd, announcing 'Street action downtown tonight.')

Robert Winkler, a campus detective, confirms Frank's report. Winkler was parked in a lot that commanded a view of most of the strip. 'We heard there was going to be trouble in town that night, and one of the first things we saw was Franklin walking up and down talking to kids one at a time. He has a way of doing this—he folds his arms across his chest and talks very confidentially, out of the side of his mouth. We'd seen him do it on campus many times.'

Then, with the first breaking of glass down the street, Winkler witnessed a phenomenon that is widely thought to typify the *modus operandi* of radical leadership—and which in this area makes law enforcement so difficult, the constant complaint being: 'We never get the real leaders. They're always there at the beginning. But as soon as the action starts and the police are on the way, the real leaders are long gone.' During the weekend no one saw Franklin perform any act of violence.

Winkler continues his account: 'When we heard the first windows go, we decided to get back to campus in case there was trouble there, too. As we were driving east on Main Street, we saw Franklin again. He was walking very fast, going in the same direction we were—away from the action.'

Field Marshal Perry had no trouble keeping his blacks away from Water Street that night. 'Man, that downtown bit may be hip for whites, but not for us blacks. We don't like beer. We don't like their music. We don't like to get blamed for things that happen by accident. So we never make that scene. But even if we'd been there, we wouldn't have thrown rocks through windows, because it didn't relate to us.' There is no report of blacks in the bars that night.

Perhaps the most accurate analysis was made by Stu Feldstein in a poetic paragraph he wrote when recollecting the night:

'My roommate told me in the afternoon, "Stu, you ought to watch downtown tonight. There's bound to be some street action." And when I got there I found a very light but tense feeling in the air. I said to myself, "This is like a mild static holding together a microcosm of the new youth culture." Predominantly, it was a freak crowd, where hair was long and straight, or thick and wavy, or curly and kinky in black or brown globes. The talk was among small circles of friends within a larger group of friends, so that while there was dialogue in a physical setup resembling the groupings at a cocktail party, there was in addition the freak spirit: talk of politics and drugs, school and revolt, creativity and philosophy and religion, all in an atmosphere whose soul would say, "We are together. We face many common problems and harassments. We have decided on new moral values and we live by them. We have discovered and use new ways to have fun. We have a language." ' It was to prove a language of violence.

A question of life style

The tragedy at Kent was partially the result of the current clash between two different life styles, which are contending for the spirit of America. Since the phrase *life style* will appear frequently, it must be defined.

In simple terms, a man's life style is composed of what he believes and what he does about it, in his choice of occupation, in his scale of values. It is even expressed in how he dresses, especially today.

The historic style is founded upon the accumulated experience of mankind, and in the United States is influenced by our Puritan heritage. It has many characteristics, and those which are most cherished are the ones against which the young rebel with most vigor. For example, the traditional style is based on a belief in God as manifested through organized churches. It respects authority. It is patriotic and sponsors a deep regard for the military, in which a large proportion of our population has served at one time or another. It believes that men lead happier lives if they practice thrift, charity and personal responsibility. It believes that honest work is good for a man and preaches allegiance to the firm for which one works. It believes in the sanctity of the home (except where divorce is necessary) and respect for elders (unless they become a burden). One of its basic tenets has always been a naïve and beautiful faith in universal education, not merely as a tool for getting ahead but as a way to attain a good life. Finally, it has adhered to conservative modes of dress, speech, music and ornamentation.

At least ninety percent of the American population subscribes to this traditional life style and considers it flexible enough to accommodate anyone willing to give it a fair test. It can be summed up in a series of aphorisms: 'A man's word is as good as his bond. If a man works he'll get ahead. America has usually tried to do the right thing. Get an education and you can accomplish anything. God is watching.'

The new style rejects almost every precept given above and is thus an assault on cherished tradition. To be even-handed in this analysis, first let us see how the new-style people describe themselves; then how the old-style people interpret these descriptions.

The new-style people say of themselves: 'We start with a positive interpretation of life, indeed an optimistic one. We preach love, freedom, interdependence, personal responsibility and a radically new theory of society. The beliefs which have traditionally kept society organized, we no longer accept, and the system of rewards which have encouraged the individual to operate within society, we reject.

'To be specific, our new life style ridicules the Puritan ethic as archaic and destructive. Saving money, hoarding against a rainy day, fear of what one's neighbor might think, and all the other bogeymen that have been used to make us behave are seen as ridiculous intrusions on the individual's freedom. God is sometimes respected more than He is in formalized religion, and religion acquires a deeper personal meaning. We are by no means atheists, but the religions we subscribe to are often the older religions of the East. Christianity is no longer acknowledged to be the primary belief, but many of us find ourselves at ease in Catholic, Protestant or Jewish churches, so long as the priest in charge does not try to force us to accept the ancient trappings of the religion. Pope John is one of our big heroes.

'The new life style can find no place for patriotism in the old sense, and respect for the military has been replaced by contempt. These are the direct consequences of the Vietnam war and the draft that was needed to support it. A generation of our young men have had to grapple with one of the most confusing draft systems ever devised by a democracy, and they have grown to hate it and everything associated with it. When an older man tries to tell us that he fought in Germany, or in the South Pacific, to preserve the American way of life, we tune him out as some kind of bore. Ancient symbols of patriotism, such as flags and martial music, we dismiss with impatience if we are philosophically minded, with contempt if we are activists, and with physical violence if we are revolutionaries. If America were to be threatened with invasion, enormous numbers of our group would volunteer to defend her, but the idea of going to Vietnam to fight in an undeclared war for uncertain principles is repugnant and must be opposed.

'We have a deep respect for work, but only if it is work we initiate and whose utility we understand. In many of our homes you find women baking bread in the old manner and men building the furniture they need. Farming is held in profound respect, and hand trades like carpentry, electric repair and automotive overhaul are dignified as arts. But the nine-to-five job, especially if it involves competition, is viewed with distaste. The more basic the job, the more acceptable. Many young men with long hair work incredibly hard as stevedores, truck drivers, day laborers and hospital attendants. What we all avoid is the respectable white-collar job which our fathers tried so hard to land. As for allegiance to a great corporation, this no longer exists among us and we believe it is diminishing among those who follow the older style.

'Problems of the family are discussed endlessly whenever we new-style people get together. Many of us, especially the girls, reject traditional marriage as a pattern of life, although we may accept it in our thirties after having lived with various partners during our twenties. Children are treated with special love, as are the inevitable pets one finds in our groups. Chastity is never mentioned and virginity is a temporary irritation. Love, the capacity to relate to other human beings, and the willingness to make concessions to them, is one of the noblest ideals of our group, and when marriages do result from long association in our free-and-easy world, they are apt to be good and well founded. Love, in the sense this word is used in the New Testament, is perhaps better understood by our group than it is by the old. Sex is unimportant in that it is no longer a hang-up and is therefore not the subject of endless discussion. If you are attracted to someone of the opposite sex, do something about it. Get it out of your system and then see what permanent values may result.

'Why do we dress the way we do? We interpret the sterile uniforms worn by old-style people as restrictive and stultifying. Why should a young man wear a gray-flannel suit merely to gratify the prejudices of his employer? We prefer the colorful costumes of American history. We want to look the way real heroes looked—Daniel Boone, Kit Carson, the women who crossed the prairies in Conestoga wagons. Girls reject the brassiere as a stigma of middle-class confinement and loss of freedom. Steel-rimmed granny glasses are preferred because they don't try to add fake prettiness to the human face. We go barefoot whenever possible because shoes are a drag. And although some of us incline toward shabby clothes as a mark of our disrespect, most of us are meticulous in personal cleanliness because we know it's good for our health.'

The confirmed adherent of the old style finds this line of

reasoning intolerable, and no tenet of the new philosophy is more infuriating than the one which claims a monopoly on love: 'They don't understand the meaning of the word. If you look at what the students did at Kent, you find far more hate than love. And as for being new, most of their ideas, when they can articulate them, are centuries old.

'Their rejection of religion is the normal twenty-year-old atheism that we've had for the last three hundred years. Their rejection of patriotism is plain old-fashioned cowardice based on a fear of facing enemy guns in Vietnam. Their retreat to living patterns of the nineteenth century is a matter of temporary style and won't last five years. You watch! Before long it will be Elizabethan or ancient Greece. You can expect to see togas on the street before long. Already we have the saffron robes of self-styled Buddhist monks.

'Their much vaunted "new analysis of society" is nothing but outmoded Marxism warmed over, and as for personal cleanliness, they never heard of it. Their new art is merely the *art nouveau* of the last century and their music is a retreat to African drums and ancient oriental chants.

'One fact is paramount. When the new-style people come downtown in a filthy group, wearing outlandish clothes and body paint, they terrify the citizens. They seem to us an incarnation of revolution. You can summarize it this way. Any life style which terrorizes a majority of the citizens and automatically raises antagonisms cannot be constructive, as they claim. It can only be destructive.' Such a clash in interpretations represents a real conflict, and it is this conflict that now concerns us.

In Kent, there is a house on Ash Street, not far from the university, which epitomizes this new life style. For legal reasons, the location of this house and the identification of its inhabitants have had to be masked. Old, clapboarded, with dormer windows, it was once inhabited by a hard-working middle-class family who rented two upstairs rooms to male students, in the days when Kent had an enrollment of 4,000. 'They were fine boys,' the owner remembers. 'They kept the place clean and were in bed by midnight.'

When enrollment jumped to more than 21,000, rooms near the campus were so badly needed that it became profitable to turn the entire house on Ash Street over to students, so the owners moved out and twelve young men moved in. 'It was the beginning of hell,' the owner sadly reflects. 'A whole new breed of student. A total lack of responsibility. Breakage, drinking, drugs.' If he was disturbed by those changes, he was jolted when the boys began moving their girl friends into the rooms with them. 'About three years ago I gave up. I no longer inspect. I no longer try to keep the place decent. I rent the house to one student, and what he does with it is his affair. My only concern is that the damned place doesn't burn down, and sometimes I think it might be better if it did.'

It is difficult to find a word that accurately describes this house and what transpires in it. One can use *commune,* but not in the California sense of that word. That is, the Ash Street house is not a closely organized unit with a common budget, common responsibilities and a generally understood political orientation—it is an experiment in group living.

When you enter the front door the first thing you see is an enormous American flag, big enough for a skyscraper or a battleship, suspended from the ceiling by grommets and hook-eyes. It serves as an effective room divider, and no matter where you move on the first floor, this clean and brilliant flag dominates.

Upstairs the rooms open onto one another in a free and easy manner, so that it would be difficult to say who sleeps where. The walls are decorated with posters, a few of them airline color photographs of places like Murchison Falls in Uganda or Hong Kong from the ferry. The more interesting ones are Che Guevara in brave uniform; two rhinoceroses copulating and accompanied by the legend *Make Love, Not War;* W. C. Fields playing a poker hand.

Who lives in the commune? Ten young men and seven girls, two of them married but not to people in the house. One of the young men is a college professor who has left his wife and is living with one of his more attractive girl students. One of the girls tried marriage two years ago and 'found out that it wasn't for me. My husband is in California . . . or somewhere.'

When you enter the house as a guest, the one who invited you says, 'I want you to meet Joe and Edith and Christine and Si and Carol.' Last names are never used when introducing someone to a stranger, and in some instances inhabitants do not know the last names of people with whom they have been living for weeks.

Who pays for what? Each member contributes as much money as his allowance from home will permit, and from this kitty the rent is paid. After that, budgets for food and household expense are established, and life proceeds as it might in an amiable but disorganized home. Cleanliness varies. If the commune contains a couple of girls who like to see things kept neat, the house may be spick and span. More likely it is a shambles. But the food is good, with emphasis on health items, whole-wheat banana bread of excellent quality, fine rice dishes made with Indian spices, and some of the best lasagna extant. Meal hours are something else again: breakfast at noon, dinner at midnight.

What is group living like? There is a sense of joyousness and hilarity. Discussion is lively. Adult comic books like *Mother's Oats* and *Zap Comics* are kept on low tables and everyone reads them; they provide clever comment on the current scene, with a heavy emphasis on psychedelic imagery. Each page is a unit by itself, crammed with in-jokes and observations on the new life style. The tabloid *Rolling Stone* is read avidly, issue by issue, and takes the place of the old-time *Playboy*.

Very popular, but rarely finished by students who start them, are two novels which exert a profound influence on young intellectuals: Hermann Hesse's *Siddhartha* and Robert Heinlein's *Stranger in a Strange Land*. Those who boast 'I'm not a brain' read *The Whole Earth Catalog*, which provides a guide through the zooming fads of the new culture: lists of the best books on Zen, how to avoid large bills while keeping a Volkswagen running, which science fiction has the wildest ideas, a list of practical tools for farming, how to build a sod house in your commune, where to exchange Janis Joplin records. But by all odds the most influential book to hit the house has been Noam Chomsky's *American Power and the New Mandarins*. One would not expect this collection of essays by a professor of linguistics at Massachusetts Institute of Technology to open young minds in Kent, Ohio, to what they call 'the reality of the world we live in,' but it does. Scores of thoughtful young radicals told us, at some time in their long interviews, 'I began to understand the structure of American society only when I read Chomsky.'

Music is important. It would be impossible to run a commune without a record player, and students will even study philosophy with a raga playing. Each house has an African-type drum, the best ones made from old soy-sauce barrels from Hong Kong over whose heads have been stretched wet cowhide; when it dries, it reverberates throughout the whole house.

Among many of the inhabitants of the house there exists a belief that 'James Dean still lives.' A girl says, 'One of the fellows felt this so deeply that he revved his motorcycle up and set out across country to pay homage at the spot where the squares said Dean had died. He wanted to pay homage and maybe get a psychic message as to where Dean was hiding out, but in western Nevada he went around a corner too fast and cracked up his machine. He never did make contact with Dean.'

The worst thing that one occupant of the house could say of another is, 'He gives me bad vibes.' When this verdict is delivered about another human being, conversation ended, for it bespeaks an evil so sinister that it could not be spelled out. To say of an acquaintance, 'He gives bad vibrations,' never specified, is to condemn him utterly. We heard numerous persons accused of emitting bad vibes, but never did we hear a cause. On the other hand, the best thing you could say of a friend is that he is 'into the peace thing real big,' or that he is 'into the protest thing real seriously.' To be into something, to be committed to action in defense of an idea, is the ultimate posture, but the noblest of man's aspirations is reduced to a 'thing.' Many residents of the house were described by their friends as 'being into the life-style thing real deep,' and a student contemplating the ministry was said to be 'all mixed up over the Jesus thing.'

At the house marijuana is as common as beer. LSD is no longer widely used and heroin is frowned upon as too dangerous. 'I used to be very deep into smack,' a gorgeous blonde confesses, 'but it scared hell out of me and I backed away.'

No question at Kent was more confusing than what to do about marijuana. Eighty percent of the student body would appear, from their own testimony, to have smoked the weed at least once.* This means that approximately 16,800 students were subject to the full penalties of the Ohio law, which is one of the strictest in the nation: 'For simple possession, first offense, two to fifteen years in jail and up to $10,000 fine.' (For selling or providing, twenty to forty years.) Thus, if only the eligible students at Kent were arrested, and if

---

*This statistic was researched with scrupulous care, not because we asked probing questions but because students wished to speak on the matter. Estimates were tabulated. Conservative newspaper people guessed 65 to 80 percent. Fraternities and sororities thought 80 to 90 percent. Many students said, 'A flat hundred percent,' but we met several who said, 'I've never touched it.'

each was given the maximum penalty, Ohio would have to provide jails for a total of 252,000 man-years, and parents of the students would have to cough up fines totaling $168,000,000. And this would take care of only one university. If similar proportions prevailed at Ohio State, Ohio University, Oberlin, Antioch and Ohio Wesleyan, to name only a few of the sixty-four Ohio schools, the situation could become, to say the least, awkward.

Ohio law contains another stipulation which was often discussed in the dormitories: 'Anyone having carnal knowledge of another person under the influence of marijuana is subject to two to fifteen years in jail and $10,000 fine.'

As a result, law enforcement agencies had to make arrests on a selective basis; students who smoked pot and lived together while doing so were not molested if they behaved themselves. A judge's son dating the daughter of a minister had little to fear, but any student who gave promise of causing trouble had to beware. Reefers circulated openly on the campus and in the town, with few arrests being made, but when one young man was suspected of being involved in radical causes, he was picked up for having given marijuana cigarettes to his friends and received three non-concurrent sentences of twenty to forty years each. When time came to make arrests for the May riots, much publicity would be given to the fact that certain of the indicted were already under arrest for marijuana cases; most of the choral society, a large percentage of the fraternity men, and many football players could have been similarly arrested had the state discovered a collateral reason for doing so. Only one of the residents of the house on Ash Street had been picked up on marijuana charges, but the others never knew when the lightning might strike, because most of the inhabitants were technically guilty and could be sent away for up to forty years at any time the state wished to press charges.

In a commune, who sleeps with whom? This always seems to be of greater interest to older people than it is to the young, who are the ones involved. The most explicit unraveling of this matter came from two high school sweethearts from New York who came west to college. He chose Kent State, while she preferred Ohio University, 165 miles to the south. Her father allows her to use his car, and each weekend she drives north to be with her lover. She says, 'A large percentage of college girls live with boys these days. Some of them do it because they love the boys, but a lot do it for convenience and the fun of having fellows around the house. It's not a big thing any more, and if you can get a good crowd together in your house, it can be a creative experience.' He adds, 'When parents first hear about it, they go right up the wall. The boy's parents often make more trouble than the girl's. But what can they do about it?' She says, 'It's natural for young people to live together. It does no harm. It helps them to study. And look at us. We intend to marry in July and our parents will be so relieved.'

This couple does not happen to live in the house on Ash Street; their commune is on the western edge of town and is smaller. In Kent there are about a dozen houses such as the one described and more than a hundred smaller units which two or three couples share, but rarely do the inhabitants come out even. There is usually an extra girl or two, and it is these spare ones who add color to the establishment, for occasionally they will come home with someone they have met in class. The newcomer will hang around for a few days, then drift back to his dormitory.

A pretty little Irish girl from New York has the simplest explanation of how group living comes about: 'I grew up with four brothers and I learned that boys are the nicest thing a girl can have. So when I came to Kent and found they were going to put me in Tri-Towers and I saw all those girls, I rebelled. I was sitting in the Student Union feeling sorry for myself and not knowing what to do next and this nice boy came up and asked, "What's the matter?" and I said I didn't want to live with a lot of girls, and he said, "Why don't you move in with us?" And I asked who us was, and he said, "A couple of guys who have a swell place," so I accepted the invitation and everything has worked out just great.'

Sometimes there are complications. An official confides, 'Last year we had sixty-three freshmen and sophomore girls who came to us pregnant. Real tragedies can result from group living.' But most who try it prefer it to older forms.

In group living, there is not much promiscuity. It wouldn't fit in nor would it be necessary. A girl tends to stay with one man for an extended period and would feel embarrassed if her friends watched her shift quickly to someone else. Besides, for this new breed, sex is not so important that it should be allowed to disrupt things. Boys and girls use the showers indiscriminately and undress with such extreme carelessness that one becomes accustomed to the opposite sex and is neither startled nor interested in chance nudity. In fact, sex is handled rather more intelligently in group living than it is otherwise.

How has such a radically new approach to college life developed? The key word is *parietal,* which means *having authority over residence within the walls.* In recent years students have insisted, and society has agreed, that university deans should stop exercising parietal functions. 'It is no longer our responsibility to check on where a girl sleeps nor with whom' is frequently cited as the new rule. 'The university does not stand *in loco parentis* and will not conduct bed checks to see that everyone is in his proper room at 11:00 P.M.' This is an outgrowth of the permissive society and permits men students to entertain girls in their rooms at hours that would have staggered their elders. As we shall see later, it also permits girls to smuggle boys into their rooms in even the strictest dormitories. By and large, the new rules are better than the old and they are not excessively abused. It is doubtful if any large university could easily reverse them, for they have become part of the new style of life.

Obviously, this style is difficult for outsiders to understand. It engenders deep animosities and of itself would alienate the average citizen who watches from a distance. What adds to the gap between the house and the city is the fact that the former is often radicalized and engaged in an open warfare against the social and economic system of the community.

The house on Ash Street is an example. Of its seventeen inhabitants, only twelve are enrolled in the university, two are under court orders to keep off campus because of previous misbehavior, one is on probation for a narcotics charge, one is wanted by the police in Cleveland on a riot charge, and one is fresh out of jail and lying low for a while. The other twelve are typical 1970 students: most of them want to alter society sharply; some of them want to destroy the university and build something they think is better; all are bitterly opposed to the war in Vietnam; most are in some kind of warfare with their parents.

From this house have come some of the plans for the various disruptions that have upset the university in recent years. None of the students is a revolutionary, in the sense that he would bomb or set fire to buildings; all are radicals, in that they would gladly see present forms of government and society collapse and be supplanted by something they like better. Since descriptive words such as these will have to be used throughout this book, their meanings must be understood. They arrange themselves in this way:

Anarchist Revolutionary Radical Liberal Conservative Reactionary Vigilante Anarchist

At the extremes, the leftist anarchist and the rightist are practically indistinguishable; each is prepared to blow up the nation, but from his own philosophical position. It is important to remember how Kent's 21,000 students divided. The university may have had an anarchist or two in the spring of 1970. The revolutionary is one who is prepared to take overt action against society; treason, arson, murder, bombing, sabotage are his weapons. Kent had perhaps a score of revolutionaries. The radical is opposed to the present system and will work by non-violent means to tear it down; his weapons are the demonstrations, the confrontations, strikes, campus disturbances, challenges to authority, disruptions of all kinds. Kent had about 500 radicals, of which some sixty or seventy were hard-core operators, but few of them committed illegal acts which would have sent them to jail. The liberal is well known in American history, and at least 15,000 of the Kent student body would have described themselves with this term, but that does not mean that they would have voted Democratic; more likely the vote would have been evenly split with the Republicans. Conservatives are also a fundamental part of the American system, and somewhat less than 5,000 of the Kent students would have been so described. However, many of the students who were liberal in college would become conservative upon leaving it, so that the balance between liberal and conservative might better be expressed as about fifty-fifty. It must be remembered that Kent was known throughout the Midwest as a conservative university, its nickname being Apathy U. The reactionary is the rightist equivalent of the radical; he wants to eliminate protest and prevent change, but he refrains from overt acts of violence. Kent State had about 200 reactionaries, but they maintained a low visibility. The vigilante is prepared to shoot people, in large numbers, to protect things as they are; his weapon is the shotgun which he is often eager to use. The university had no vigilantes, but the surrounding community had many.

There are other groups of words which must be understood. An *activist* is not one who throws a bomb, nor is he necessarily leftist; he can be a good Republican or a Democrat; he believes in taking action against the things he opposes or in behalf of those he supports. A *protestor* is one who can be counted on to work on committees or march in parades. A *concerned* student may also be of any political color but stops short of organized activity.

Students divide themselves into three other categories, depending upon life style rather than politics: *jocks* are the athletes and those who support them; *straight* people are the huge middle group of students who respect the old style; *freaks* are the long-hairs, the bead boys, the no-bra girls, the way-outs.

Finally, there are several organized groups whose activities dominate this book. The Greeks are the fraternity men, and they usually ally themselves with the jocks. The YSA (Young Socialist Alliance) are hard-core, left-wing radical socialists. The SDS (Students for a Democratic Society), now outlawed from Kent and many other campuses, started as moderates and quickly escalated into extreme radicals; indeed, when the movement broke into two sections, RYM-I and RYM-II (Revolutionary Youth Movement), the former segment became Weatherman, an avowed anarchistic group bent on bombing and total civil disruption. The Black Panthers are well known; the White Panthers are much more violent. And the YAF (Young Americans for Freedom) are the right-wing activists.

Political activity at the house on Ash Street is intense and interminable. Not only are there constant discussions of how best to assault society, but from time to time knowledgeable visitors from other campuses drop by to report on happenings at Berkeley or Michigan or Harvard.

The seventeen residents are unbelievably peripatetic. They leave Kent on a few minutes' notice to speak at Harvard, or

Wisconsin, or Michigan, or California. They attend conferences in Havana or Budapest. Some of them know Europe as well as they know Ohio, and maintain among themselves a list of addresses in all parts of the country to which they can flee in time of trouble. They are the traveling generation; their education comes not in books but in suitcases and airplane tickets. But always they return to the house on Ash Street.

An older person cannot be with the present crop of university students for long without realizing that he is dealing with a new type of individual, and after trying to isolate wherein the difference lies, he concludes that it derives from a cultural phenomenon whose influence he had previously underestimated. We are confronting America's first television generation, born and reared in the shadow of the tube, and the impact is tremendous.

These young people learn by means of a new synthesis of visual and oral sensation. They participate each night in the unfolding of history. To them the present is infinitely more significant than the past. Family patterns are eroded, both by program and commercial, in which fathers are shown as flabby moral incompetents and mothers as incredibly stupid, concerned only with the whiteness of their children's laundry. Passivity before the television set replaces the activity of the backyard. And non-sequitur transitions from subject to subject replace the orderly development of logic. Thought is fragmented into brief segments.

Two factors are paramount. In the average dramatic situation shown on television, a solution is found through immediate action, often through non-legal channels. That the action is almost always violent is not so important, apparently, as the fact that it by-passes the normal legal processes. If there has been an appalling reliance upon direct action—street action, non-negotiable demands, 'off the pigs,' 'we've talked long enough'—it must be because this generation has seen such action triumph in a thousand different television dramas. 'Taking things into our own hands' has become a way of life, and if it works so well on television, it'll work just as well at Kent State.

Perhaps even more important, however, is the visual impact of the young actors who appear on the screen. The most popular are loners, opposed to society, at odds with their fellows and prone to violent responses. They talk and dress in exaggerated style and allow no place for what used to be the responsible, well-behaved young man or woman who is concerned about ordinary problems which he grapples with in ordinary ways. It is futile for a family to argue with their son to keep his hair short when every peer-type he sees on television does just the opposite. The old adage that art imitates nature has been reversed; students now imitate art— in music, appearance, vocabulary, behavior and ideas. Thus the great popularity of Indian dress and western manners can be attributed only to television and motion pictures.

We are producing television children whom the university tries to educate as if they were the old-fashioned library students. It is not accidental that the young professors who are most popular with the students, and most influential in their growth, are closer to television than to the library, and we were constantly surprised in our conversation at the number of times someone said, 'Tim Butz made the six o'clock news' or 'Jerry Persky made Walter Cronkite' or 'Professor Lewis made the big television show out of Cleveland,' as if this were the greatest accomplishment a member of the university could aspire to. At the house on Ash Street, students watch television even when they are studying.

It is houses like this, existing around all campuses, which have made education such a difficult process in recent years. Why don't the universities rout them out and expel their inhabitants? The students have done nothing wrong. There is no longer any law against young people living together; you can't expel a girl because she has set up housekeeping with a boy she likes. And as long as young radicals merely preach the overthrow of the university while refraining from taking or precipitating overt action to speed their plans, they cannot be punished by either the civil authorities or the university.

The Haunted House

Kent contained one center of group living even more notorious than the house on Ash Street. This one would be difficult to describe—for its story is almost too bizarre to accept—except for one fact. The average reader has already seen the house and been terrified by it.

Some years ago a novelist lived in Kent, and when he

moved away, carried with him a haunting memory of a strange house. It stood on a high hill smack in the middle of Kent and was so surrounded by trees that it looked as if it existed in the middle of a Grimm Brothers' forest in medieval Germany. (A student who once lived in it said, 'It was less than a block from the Water Street bars, and if you climbed up to it half-loaded, you saw demons lurking behind the dormer windows.')

When the time came for the novelist to write a mystery, he naturally recalled Kent's Haunted House, and thus it became the setting for the story, and subsequently for one of the most shocking motion pictures of the last decade, Alfred Hitchcock's *Psycho*.

Hollywood dispatched a camera crew to Kent to photograph the weird old horror from various angles so that a replica could be built on the lot, and when Hitchcock saw the photographs he is reported to have said, 'Copy it just as it is. It looks evil.'

It had been built about 1810, a weather-beaten, ready-to-collapse gray-clapboard house which incorporated every Gothic extravagance. It could be approached only by perilous footpaths that climbed up from the city or by a twisting lane that only careful drivers would try to negotiate. It looked impossibly old, for its roof was about to blow off, its stairs were ready to collapse. The wooden clapboards which covered its walls were dangling and insecure, and the tall trees that overshadowed it kept it in constant gloom. To find such a house in the middle of a city and so close to a major university was miraculous.

A faithful replica was built in Hollywood—you can still buy color postcards of it—and it became the archetype of sinister houses. In a way, this was appropriate, for whereas the copy scared hell out of theater audiences across the United States, the original caused even greater consternation in Kent. Trouble started in 1968, when a charismatic couple moved into the six-room second-floor apartment and from this secluded foothold launched a series of extraordinary events that came close to destroying the university.

The husband was Rick Erickson, tall, long-haired, flowing-mustached, dynamic, and compelling to look at. Invariably he wore large black sunglasses, and numerous people who knew art commented on the fact that with his powerful, bending shoulders and his long face he was an exact duplicate of Paul Gauguin's famous self-portrait. He was the son of the former mayor of Akron and in high school had been a star athlete; one year he won the Kiwanis Service Award. He spoke rapidly, softly, and sometimes with terrifying force.

His wife, Candy Erickson, became almost as famous in Kent as he. She was from Tennessee, a petite, winsome girl whom everyone liked. A car accident had scarred her face, but in the opinion of many, this merely added to her charm. 'You'd have had to erase her face altogether to destroy its power,' a neighbor said of her at that time. An able girl, she got mostly A's and was invited by the university to teach English; her students thought she was super. She had known her husband only three and a half weeks before their marriage, and she was considered by her associates to be an almost perfect wife.

'Her father was very political,' a friend says, 'and that was the beginning of her powerful commitment to social justice. She was the political one of the two.' At first she had no success in her attempts to convince Rick of her beliefs, but in the spring of 1968 Rick and two male friends drove down to South Carolina to pick up some furniture one of Candy's relatives had given them as a wedding present.

The driver reports: 'We were in Harlan County, Kentucky, when we heard about the riots at Columbia, and they seemed to galvanize Rick. Everything fell into place. He began asking innumerable questions, and when we got back to Kent he dug in and read books like crazy for three and a half weeks. Marx, Marcuse, Fanon, anything radical he could lay his hands on. These were his "twenty-five days" and he came out of them a convinced radical.'

Now the big apartment on the second floor of the Haunted House became the liveliest intellectual center in Kent. One who lived there at the time says, 'You wouldn't believe it. Candy had fixed up her six rooms real swell. Straight middle-class culture-vulture. Prints, music, books. The bit. And just as she got everything in place, the locusts descended.'

They came in the form of the radical students who were then beginning to attack the university. 'Some days there would be twenty people staying with Rick and Candy, some days thirty. They slept on the floor, in the hallways; in good weather they spread their sleeping bags under the great trees. You'd wake up and there'd be maybe ten or a dozen sleeping bags. I remember one morning when the milkman puffed up the hill and asked, "Where did they come from?" All over America. This bag might contain a couple from Berkeley, stopping over for a few days on their way to Harvard. That one by the driveway would hold two fellows from Michigan. Terry Robbins stayed in the apartment for four months and talked incessantly of the coming revolution. Lisa Meisel slept there for a while and a lot of kids who are now on the wanted list of the FBI. On any given night half the kids might be from out of town.'

The most exciting times were when the gang gathered on a patch of grass under the big maple tree that dominated the back yard. One who attended the meetings says, 'It was like the old days. Socrates and his disciples. Or Jesus and His. We'd sit on boulders or in the lotus position, maybe thirty of us, and someone would stand on that rise over there and explain a concept or defend his view of the coming revolution. You'd sit there and hear really brilliant conversation, much better than we were getting at the university, and maybe this would go on for three or four hours, and when it was over, you had a better understanding of where you stood on the basic issues of the decade. Change was coming, we all knew that, and it was our job to see that it followed our direction.'

Among the speakers was one who would play a major role in the radicalization of Kent State. He was short where Rick was tall, cautious where Rick was impulsive, extremely well versed in radical thought where Rick was an improviser, and he came from a radical family, whereas Rick was from the middle class. He was Howie Emmer, a young man who in certain light looked as if he might have been a Manchurian or an Eskimo. His mouth was enormous and his eyes piercing. He wore his hair long but was without beard or mustache, and the dominant characteristic by which people remembered him was the acuity of his intellect. He was not well versed in a wide subject matter, for in many areas he was deficient, but in revolutionary tactics he was a master. He had one other attribute which made him invaluable to the movement. Dan Moore, of Grove City, Pennsylvania, admits that Howie had a strong influence on him. 'Simple explanation. He was fantastic at face-to-face persuasion. He listens to what you are trying to say, then picks up where you left off and shows you the consequences of your reasoning. Even people who disliked what he was trying to peddle liked the way he presented it.' In fact, the Ericksons were so impressed with Emmer that they invited him to move in with them, so that the Haunted House became known as the hangout of Rick and Howie, even though it was Candy who ran things intellectually.

Who owned the Haunted House when it was occupied by Emmer and the Ericksons? Technically their landlord was Monsignor Joseph Coke, spiritual leader of the Kent Catholic church, which had bought the house so as to use the flatland which came with it as a much-needed parking lot. When Monsignor Coke saw the shambles he had inherited on the hill he gave a peremptory order, 'Tear it down.' The students then inhabiting it pleaded, 'Don't do that. Raise the rents.' Someone had wired the whole upper area so that it could be controlled electronically: doors opened, windows closed, and water was turned on by clocks. It was this haunted place that became headquarters for Kent's radicals.

'Wait a minute!' Monsignor Coke says amiably when this ticklish subject is raised. 'I never saw the place when the Ericksons were running their famous meetings. The real estate committee of our church handles such matters, and to tell you the truth, when the Ericksons first moved in they were reported to me as "first-class tenants who pay their rent three months in advance." By the time people discovered what they were up to . . . did you know that both Rick and Candy went to jail? Well, the committee asked me if we should throw them out, but our lawyers warned that we might be legally liable if we broke a lease for such reasons. Actually, a little later Candy Erickson did sue somebody for something. I'm sure she would have sued us. After all, she was on the faculty.'

During the time it operated, the Haunted House dictated the ebb and flow of agitation on campus. Here policy meetings determined what tactic to use next, what handbill to distribute through the dorms. Demands were formulated here, and agonizing meetings were held to determine whether friends who had been arrested ought to plead guilty and go to jail, or plead not guilty and fight charges with a Cleveland civil-rights lawyer.

It was headquarters for SDS both at Kent State and for much of northern Ohio. (The biggest single SDS chapter in America was the one in Steubenville High School; at one time it enrolled 600 members.) National leaders and field organizers frequently passed through Kent, and usually they slept on the floor at Rick and Candy's. Someone who knew the movement well at this time says, 'The Kent SDS originally had about six members, no more. When they began to get publicity they boosted this to thirty. With their first big campus operation they raised it to fifty. After a group was formed to protest the way the administration handled the arrests at the Music and Speech Building, there were about five hundred who supported the movement. But when the administration got wise and used its head, the number dropped back to twenty, then to ten and finally to the original six.'

Who were the hard-core regulars? The undergraduates who edited *The Kent Daily Stater* were quick to grasp the significance of SDS and had the foresight to assign several of their best men to cover its development; two of the reporters were suspected of doubling as undercover policemen and thus lost their effectiveness; so the job had to be turned over to a pleasant, keen-witted little girl from Cuyahoga Falls named Debie Shryock. For two years she specialized in SDS activity and came to know more about it than the administration did. She made no secret of her newspaper affiliation and attended every meeting she could, but she assured the members that she was not working for the police, and while they never admitted her to their planning sessions, she attended most others.

'When I began to watch SDS, Rick Erickson was the dominant leader. He impressed me as being more intelligent and compassionate than the others. He had been really straight in high school and was very popular, but when he came to Kent a subtle change took place, maybe he was growing up. Of course, he and Howie Emmer were arrested in 1967 for having marijuana, and it was all over the papers. "Akron Mayor's Son Arrested for Drugs." It was a big commotion, but someone pulled some strings and got him off. On the whole, I suspect Rick was fairly disillusioned about his father's performance as mayor. I remember being amazed when I saw him at the Administration fracas. He was pounding on a policeman, and acted so mad, he seemed a completely different person. But from then on he became the real leader of the group. I remember at Music and Speech how he stood up when everyone was arrested and shouted, "Candy and I will operate a center for legal aid. We'll get you out of jail. If you get into serious trouble, see us at the Haunted House." He gave everybody his phone number, and after so many kids were suspended, they all moved into the Haunted House and that's when the great meetings were held in the back yard.'

For Candy Erickson, Debie had deep regard: 'It was obvious that Candy cared about politics, but she never seemed to be so personally involved as Rick. When they married she was fairly straight and I got the impression that what she wanted to do was settle down and have children. She was most attractive, very charming in manner, and it looked to me as if she had got swept up into what was eating Rick. She tried to be what he wanted her to be. Sometimes I felt sorry for her. She was playing a role for which she wasn't suited.'

Howie Emmer confused the young reporter: 'He scared me to death. I always felt he'd just as soon conk me over the head as talk to me. He was the one who unmasked the reporters who were working for the police and he suspected I might be their successor. But even apart from that, he didn't appeal to me personally, so I avoided him when I could. The only thing about Howie that you could be sure of was that day in, day out he'd be wearing the same plaid flannel shirt. I think it's the only shirt he had and I often wondered when he washed it. No matter what happened or when, there would be Howie in his plaid shirt. I think he'd have collapsed if anyone had taken it.'

Like the rest of the students at Kent State, young Debie Shryock admired Joyce Cecora, the free-swinging rabble-rouser of the movement: 'Joyce was so beautiful, with that long blond hair and appealing face! She became about the biggest draw at the rallies, but I got the idea the boys came more to look than to listen. After the arrests and suspensions, SDS was left without most of its male leaders, so Joyce had to take over. She'd been in SDS for about a year then, knew the ropes and had a pretty clear idea of what to do. She seemed to enjoy exercising the power suddenly thrust upon her. It was then that she began making her wildly inflammable speeches.'

There was one member of the leadership group Debie could not abide: 'Colin Neiburger could be really obnoxious. He was always ready with a nasty comeback if you ever offered a comment. He really delighted in taking people apart verbally. What gagged me, though, was when he tried to play the big revolutionary bit to impress the girls. You know, the tragic hero. I thought he was ridiculous. But on the other hand, I must admit that he did what he said he was going to do. He could be very brave when trouble broke out, and he wasn't afraid to take a stand in the front ranks. In fact, you couldn't keep him out of the front ranks.'

Like many women reporters before her, Debie Shryock

found herself getting personally involved with the group she had been assigned to cover. 'I used to go back to my room at night, sit down on the bed and tell myself, "Listen, you little fool! You're supposed to be checking on what they say. You don't have to believe it." Some of the SDS ideas were so convincing, like getting out of Vietnam and pushing ROTC off campus, that I felt attracted to them. Also, some of the leaders were unusually good at persuasion.' The most adept was a young man named Mark Real, who had studied in a seminary before entering Kent: 'Mark invariably wore a white shirt, a tie and either a sweater or a coat. He also kept his hair cut short and he shaved regularly. His looks were so extraordinary, with that shock of black hair falling neatly over his forehead, that he could have posed for advertisements. He looked so clean and normal that the administration felt secure in dealing with him, and he was the main reason why so many straight kids, especially girls, were ready to listen to the SDS line. But he was a lot more than just a pretty boy. He had come up through civil rights and the peace movement and was now a dedicated SDS man. He could be termed the brains of the movement, and just when it looked as if he was going to be the big man in the movement, maybe nationally, he contracted mononucleosis and, immediately after, infectious hepatitis. I went to visit him when he was recuperating. His family lived in a big house and must have been rather rich. When he returned to the campus he was too weak to exert leadership, but he still consulted with Rick and Howie on strategy. If the radicals produced one man who had the capacity for ultimate leadership, it was Mark Real. Where is he now? He's disappeared. In flight? Underground? Who knows? All I know is that if he came through here tonight, I'd do just about anything to help him.'

At the conclusion of her reflections, Debie offered a warning: 'You must not think of the gang in the Haunted House as just a merry band of men. They had a wild good life there, that's true, and they were generous to their friends. But they were also bent on destroying the university. They were determined to start revolution here. And sometimes this pressure made them ugly. They became quite paranoid about people they didn't know. They were most hostile to reporters and could be nasty when they wanted to be. As things grew more tense and members began getting arrested, the gay Robin Hood aspect vanished. Today many of the people I saw in those carefree days at the house are underground. Some are

Weathermen. And almost all are confirmed in their belief that society as we know it must be totally changed.'

Imagine a university trying to operate along historic principles with the house on Ash Street perched on one flank and the Haunted House on the other, each a haven for persons dedicated to its destruction. The history of Kent in 1968–69 is a record of the unswerving efforts of the university—sometimes brilliant in their insight and application—to contain the attacks emanating from these two houses. The history of May, 1970, is an account of how, at the very time when the original enemies were neutralized and disarmed, a series of chance accidents produced an even bigger confrontation than the clever young men in the Haunted House would have dared devise.

Regional travelers

It is obvious that the students living in these two houses comprised enough incipient power to bring the university down. But what made them additionally effective was that they were constantly being visited by older people who were in the process of becoming active revolutionaries. An investigation of who these visitors were provides an answer to the question: 'Was Kent State attacked by outside agitators?'

The national committee governing SDS had officers, loosely defined, whose job it was to supervise the progress of the movement on various campuses. It was natural for these people to visit Kent, and they did, laying over at one of the houses and encouraging the local SDS members in their work. The president, during one spell, was Carl Oglesby. He stayed at the house on Ash Street.

The interorganizational secretary was an amazing young woman who would become notorious in the months following her appearances at Kent. Bernardine Dohrn had been born in 1942 as Bernardine Rae Ohrnstein, but in 1958 her family shortened the last name, much to her disgust. In view of her later interest in Ohio colleges, it is interesting that she attended Miami (Ohio) for more than a year, but took her degrees, including a first-rate doctorate in law, at Chicago. In June of 1968 she created such a favorable stir at the SDS National Convention held at Michigan State that the delegates elected her interorganizational secretary of the national committee. When questioned regarding her qualifications for this crucial post, because upon her would depend the growth of the movement from one college to the next, she stated that she was a revolutionary communist. In September of that year she was in Budapest, meeting with leaders of Vietnam's National Liberation Front, but the best indication of her attitude toward universities came during a speech she delivered at the University of Washington in Seattle, where she advocated a program of closing down the schools. She maintained that students were being trained to serve not their own interests nor those of humanity in general but only the purposes of those who rule the world. She warned, 'A bunch of us who believe this, and a few well-placed bombs, could stop a lot of the institutions from functioning in this country.' Her most notable statement, however, came when she was discussing the Manson murders in California: 'Dig it, first they killed the pigs, then they ate dinner in the same room with them, then they even shoved a fork into a victim's stomach! Wild!'

Habitués of the Haunted House remember her as an extremely well-organized young woman with a keen sense of history and an assurance that what she was doing was right: 'Whenever she spoke, the general quality of the meeting improved.' A male admirer at Kent State put it more simply: 'Bernardine was a good-looking chick and I found her scintillating.'

Roman Tymchyshyn, recalling one of her visits to the campus, says, 'She was very strong-willed, very tough. A smart-looking girl of medium height and well dressed. She could foresee what was coming, for she told us, "They've shot blacks in Orangeburg, South Carolina, and they're certainly going to shoot whites here." She was conscripting members for Weatherman communes to be held that summer in Akron and Columbus, where students could learn total tactics. She persuaded some Kent students to try it, I think, but one of the couples was married and they couldn't buy that policy of "If you love someone, you can't sleep with him, but if you don't love him, you've got to lay him." I think all the Kent kids who tried Bernardine's communes busted out on that issue.'

In addition to the national officers of SDS, there was in Ohio a band of extremely able young people, often with college degrees, whose job it was to move about the area and keep things stirred up. They were known officially as regional travelers and the name describes their operations. Regional travelers out of Cleveland and Chicago were frequent visitors to the houses in Kent; in some instances they hung around for three or four months at a time, living off the local community as best they could. Whenever they arrived on the scene, exciting meetings took place, and after they had departed, the university faced new confrontations.

Most volatile of the group was Terry Robbins, known in Kent as V.I., in reference to V. I. Lenin; one student, who observed him in those days, says, 'Old V.I. knew more about the theory of revolution than any of the others. Of all the regional travelers who drifted through here, he was the most evil and started some of our chapter down the road to Weatherman.'

Robbins was a brilliant student from Long Island who had dropped out of Kenyon College at Gambier, Ohio, without graduating. In 1965 he had made an abortive attempt to organize a chapter of SDS at Kenyon, remaining active in the national organization until August, 1966, when he was made National Council Member at Large. Two years later he was appointed a regional traveler for Ohio and Michigan, and as such he once stayed at the Haunted House for a period of four months. He was so good at his job that in July, 1968, he was appointed national political organizer of SDS and played a major role in helping disrupt the Democratic National Convention in Chicago. In early 1969 he was arrested in Kent on a charge of first-degree riot, and in December of that year, started serving a forty-five-day jail sentence at Ravenna, having first participated in the Weatherman Days of Rage in Chicago that autumn.

The most notorious of the regional travelers was Mark Rudd, who had gained fame from his quarterbacking of the Columbia University shutdown. Alert, tricky, a fine debater, he was able to provide leadership in group discussions and encouragement to those in Kent who wanted to take direct action against the university. Kent SDS respected Rudd as an activist who gave specific ideas, as opposed to Terry Robbins, who stressed philosophical theories.

The other regional travelers responsible for Kent State were Lisa Meisel, a small, pretty girl who wrote well and contributed to SDS publications; Bill Ayers, who was known for his ability to organize groups for effective action; and Corky Benedict, who served as clean-up man, taking care of whatever needed to be done to coordinate actions across the state. In one official report we catch a glimpse of Benedict at work:

MR. WETTERMAN. The next speaker was Corky Benedict of the Ohio regional office of SDS, and he expounded, in one of the most vicious tirades, against every established institution of America that you could possibly think of. He used many obscenities. There wasn't a sentence that went by that didn't have such obscenities as we have heard prior in this testimony as being used.

He stated that when we, SDS, take over, the power structure will be eliminated.

Now, there were also expressions of killing for revenge in the course of his talk. He also listed teachers and social workers as being willing tools of the power structure and referred to them in many obscenities. He further stated that the ruling class possesses all the power and they will not relinquish it peacefully, and therefore it will have to be taken by force.

> —Investigation of Students
> for a Democratic Society.
> Committee Hearings,
> House of Representatives, 1969

In addition to the national officers and the regional travelers, there was a constant coming and going of young radicals who visited the university merely to see what was cooking. Jim Mellen, of the Radical Educational Project, was one such, and there were rumors that an intense girl named Diana Oughton drifted through at one time on her way to a blazing death, but the outstanding girl of this group was Kathie Boudin, Bryn Mawr 1965, magna cum laude. The daughter of a well-known civil-liberties lawyer, she had traveled widely, including summer study courses in France and England and a full-year course at Moscow University. She was an early member of SDS and gained notoriety during the Democratic Convention when she was caught planting a stink bomb in the Palmer House. She was arrested as a leading actor in the Weatherman Days of Rage, and in a statement joined in by Bernardine Dohrn and Terry Robbins, explained, 'Even though SDS has recognized the correctness of Chairman Mao's slogan "Political power grows out of the barrel of a gun," we have little experience with armed self-defense and little strategic understanding of how the Revolutionary Youth Movement is going to move to the level of armed self-defense.' She was also one of the authors of a handbook popular with young revolutionaries, *The Bust Book*, which explained how to behave when being arrested; she felt it was needed because 'more and more of us are getting busted more and more.' She slipped into Cuba, and after her return she was arrested for wielding something that looked like a club against two policemen, and two weeks later was nabbed again on charges of aggravated battery on another policeman. When Kathie visited she stayed at the Haunted House.

The significance of this constant movement in and out of Kent is appreciated only when the subsequent history of the travelers is known. Bernardine Dohrn became a Weatherman, served as one of their principal propagandists, went underground, helped devise and lead their program of massive dynamiting, appears to have made tapes threatening numerous installations, became recognized as one of America's leading anarchists, and finally escaped to Algeria, after standing high on the list of persons wanted by the FBI.

Terry Robbins became a Weatherman, participated in many acts of violence, went underground, and appears to have wound up in the famous Wilkerson house on West Eleventh Street in New York City on the day it disintegrated in one huge bomb blast. Fingerprints taken from a cadaver found in the basement led detectives to think that Robbins perished while making bombs to be used against Columbia University, but others have doubted that he really died. The FBI still carries him on its wanted list.

Kathie Boudin went underground on February 17, 1970, and has been a fugitive since. Great mystery surrounds her, because her purse was found beside the ruins of the Wilkerson house, and it is supposed that she was one of the two girls who appeared at the home of a neighbor shortly after the blast, their clothes blown off by the dynamite, and made their escape in borrowed outfits. She has not been seen since, but is wanted by the FBI and New York police. Diana Oughton, of course, perished in that blast.

Mark Rudd and Bill Ayres, after serving terms as regional travelers at Kent State, became Weathermen and went underground. In December, 1969, they attended a four-day secret war council in Flint, Michigan, where they are accused of having laid down plans for bombing forays in Detroit, Chicago, New York and Berkeley. Indictments charge the defendants with 'intending to use bombs, destructive devices and explosives to destroy police installations and other civic, business and educational buildings throughout the country and to kill and injure persons therein.' Bernardine Dohrn and Kathie Boudin were indicted on the same charge.

This doleful history of dynamiting and destruction raises several questions. Did the starry-eyed young people who entered places like the house on Ash Street and the Haunted House unknowingly take their first step toward an underground life when doing so? Is there an inescapable escalation toward violence when one begins to espouse radical protest? Judging from the regional travelers who serviced Kent State, the answer to each question must be yes; however, we know of many Kent students who occupied those houses at one time or another who avoided such escalation, withdrawing from the movement before it degenerated into violence.

One question which may become increasingly significant in American life cannot be answered conclusively by reference to the two houses: Does adherence to the new life style predispose a participant toward an eventual acceptance of a form of dictatorship? The answer would appear to be yes. The slogans, the uniform dress, the tendency to accept unproved ideas, and the ganglike yearning for simplistic solutions, all tend toward this, and it would not be surprising to see young people who once entered a commune with a dedication to freedom leave it with a commitment to dictatorship, whether of the right or left.

Operations of the regional travelers answer conclusively the question: Were there outside agitators? Of course there were, but they announced themselves and their intentions; indeed, their very title 'regional traveler' implies that they came to Kent to stir things up.

This in turn raises the tantalizing question of how their extensive travel was financed. Did they receive money from Cuba? For a long time there were only rumors to this effect, but certain university presidents whose institutions had been sabotaged by young revolutionaries were convinced that leadership was supported and encouraged by Cuba.

Recently Georgie Anne Geyer and Keyes Beech, two war correspondents of the *Chicago Daily News*, were brought home from Vietnam and asked to look into the assaults against American institutions as if they formed part of a foreign war. Their investigations led them directly to Cuba:

Fidel Castro's Cuba has become a revolutionary factory for the processing and refining of American radicals for export back to the United States.

No one believes that somebody is sitting in the Plaza de La Revolucion in Havana sending messages to American students to bomb the University of Wisconsin math center or kill policemen, but the roster of American radicals, white and black, who have responded to Castro's Utopian bugle call for world revolution, reads like a "Who's Who" of the American radical movement.

The pattern is clear: Mark Rudd, Bernardine Dohrn, Angela Davis, and Joudon M. Ford, who led the riots at San Francisco State University, all received instruction in Cuba. 'SDS was the group we concentrated on in those days,' says a Cuban who was in the government then. 'Oh, we didn't start it. But we radicalized it, we gave it form. Every leader came and left with new ideas.'

It is interesting that even in Kent, students trying to bring down the university signed their posters 'Venceremos!'—We Shall Conquer—the rallying cry of Che Guevara and the title of the Cuban revolutionary brigades.

It is believed that any funds which Cuba may have dispensed for such purposes came not from her economy but from either Russia or China, more likely the latter. We know that many of the young American revolutionaries who went to Havana met their representatives from North Vietnam with whom they discussed guerrilla warfare and the principles of street action, for to this they have testified. The proper conclusion would seem to be that Cuba is not actively planning the operational details for a revolution for the United States but is encouraging anyone, especially confused young idealists, black or white, who want to disrupt our society and maneuver its collapse.

However, those who study SDS financing caution against an easy assumption that major funds come only from abroad. Erwin Canham, member of the President's Commission on Campus Unrest, says:

It is reasonable to suppose that some Moscow money, some funds from Peking and even Havana, have gone to pay for radical activities in the United States. But it would be my guess that for every dollar that may come in foreign Communist money, there are $100 in native American wealth.

Here is one poignant example. An SDS leader in a major university area was the son of a millionaire in the Southwest. The father drank heavily, sometimes beat up his wife and son. When the young man reached twenty-one his father gave him $200,000 and said: 'I never want to see you again.' Every penny of the money went into the SDS coffers.

The most extensive analysis of where the money comes from was made by the Illinois Crime Investigating Commission charged with looking into the causes of the Weatherman Days of Rage which sacked areas of Chicago during October 8–11, 1969. Through the good luck of finding a detailed 1968 diary and address book left behind by Bernardine Dohrn when she fled her apartment at 4943 North Winthrop Street, Chicago, a detailed record of cash flow could be reconstructed. By tracking down all entries, investigators were able to show that a bank in Chicago handled $212,123.34 for SDS over a two-year period. One large tax-exempt foundation appears to have supplied cash directly to revolutionary activists.

Eugene Methvin, author of *The Riot Makers,* and perhaps the most informed investigator of this problem, provides these cautious conclusions:

I know that some cash comes in from Cuba, but I believe it is marginal. I find the persistent belief in Cuba financing distasteful because it reflects a basic lack of understanding of the nature of The Movement and how it works.

Phil Luce, who led the 1964 trip to Cuba and who became the only major hard-core leftist to defect, told me that when he was in Havana he and another Progressive Labor Maoist were given $15,000 in cash to finance a radical campus newspaper, so we know that money was coming in.

We also know that bundles of U.S. currency were skimmed from Las Vegas gambling tables, sold at a blackmarket discount in Mexico to intelligence agents for Communist governments, and sent back to the U.S. for subversive activity, because in Las Vegas the bills were secretly marked and noted later when they turned up in the hands of radical activists in the San Francisco Bay area. But the real money is found right here at home. Diana Oughton, who blew herself up in that Manhattan townhouse, had a credit card paid for by her wealthy father, and a dividend check from her share of an incorporated family-owned farm. Abbie Hoffman's royalties from his book *Free* and Jerry Rubin's from *Do It!* help. A crucially important role is played by underground newspapers, about 200 of them, who depend upon advertising from record companies. A business manager of Chicago's *The Seed* told a *New York Times* reporter that 80 per cent of the sheets would fold if the record companies stopped advertising. Fees paid to speakers who are members of the groups also help.

So it isn't a simple picture; and it isn't possible to embrace the assumption that if we can just cut off the flow of Cuban money the natives will no longer be restless. That the cash does flow from abroad is certain. But its significance is usually exaggerated.
—Letter to J.A.M.

There is a final comment on travel. Tim Butz reminds us: 'Today every student worth his salt travels all the time. This is the Age of the Knapsack. I feel no hesitation in starting out from Kent with fifty cents and a speaking engagement in Boston or Washington. I have addresses of places in almost every major American city where I can crash. And if I don't, I simply check in at the nearest university or center and report, "I need a place to stay" or "I have to get to Washington by Tuesday" and they arrange. We do the same for anyone coming to Kent. Perhaps we are too mobile. Perhaps we think of ourselves too much as citizens of the whole country and not enough as citizens of one place. But the peripatetic scholar is with us, and this isn't going to change, because to travel the way we do requires no money from Cuba, no money from our parents.' In the three months following the troubles, Tim Butz, at no expense to himself, traveled to Washington, New York, Virginia, four universities in Ohio, and Saigon, speaking in all these places on peace.

But to travel the way the professional revolutionaries do does require money, and where it comes from is a legitimate national concern. Captain Chester Hayth, of the Ohio State Highway Patrol, who has made a study of this problem, says, 'You'd be surprised at how much of the travel money comes from the sale of drugs.'

Assault on the university

The serious assault on the university began on October 24, 1968, when an exhibitionistic young man who had already brought Columbia University to its knees in the historic confrontation of the previous April visited the campus at the invitation of the Kent SDS. He spoke in the auditorium to a capacity crowd of 1,000 students, but was so chaotic in his philosophy and so turgid in his logic that he influenced few and repelled many.

'The schools are repressive, the media are closed; there is tremendous social control and fascism in the present system. The only way is outside the system,' he harangued the audience.

Arms upraised as if to embrace the audience, he continued his spiel: 'We in SDS do not propose a picture of what society should look like; we analyze this one. Our goal is to radicalize more people; it is not to seize power.'

That night, after the meeting was over and a collection had been taken, Mark Rudd left campus to hold court at the Haunted House, where a young student who was thinking about joining up with SDS went to tell him how deeply impressed he had been by Rudd's attack on the decrepit American society. 'But when I got to Erickson's apartment, there was no sign of Rudd, and I asked, "Where is he? I want to tell him what a great speech he gave." They pointed to a small room off the kitchen and said, "He's in there with a coed who met him this afternoon and fell in love with him." I waited around till he came out and he was pretty drunk. What appalled me, however, was that he immediately began heckling Rick Erickson for the money that had been collected ostensibly for the Columbia students' legal defense fund. They had a real big fight, with Rudd claiming that Rick was holding out and Rick arguing that he had a right to his share for local expenses and advertising. It was about $150 in all, I think, and Rudd said, "All that cash was intended for me as your regional traveler and I want it." In the end I think Rudd got it all, but I was disgusted with this view of what I thought was a burning revolutionary and I think my defection from revolutionary ranks started right there. I felt sorry for Candy Erickson, having to put up with such behavior and such brawling in her house.'

A more serious consequence of the Rudd invasion came next day, after Rudd had gone on to some other campus which he served as a regional traveler. It seems that two reporters from WKSU, the university radio station, had tried to conduct a tape interview with Rudd, but whenever they asked pertinent questions which showed up his inadequate logic, he replied with answers so full of obscenity that he knew the tape could not be used on the air. In the end, the SDS group demanded that they be given the tape, and an argument about its cost ensued. Howie Emmer and Rick Erickson volunteered to pay for the tape, and when they put up the money, got possession of it. However, a news story was published about the censorship exercised by SDS, and the phrase was used 'there is a cancer on the campus and the malignancy is SDS,' with the result that Howie and Rick, accompanied by three others, invaded the radio station and demanded equal time. This the station was willing to grant, on the customary seven-second delay which enables the station to eliminate obscenity or libel, but Howie and Rick insisted that what they had to say must go out live. A sharp argument ensued and the police were called, with the officers demanding that the SDS group leave quietly, which they did. This appears to have been the first official brush with the police, and the fact that Howie and Rick had faced up to them gave them cachet on the campus.

On November 13, 1968, officials of the Kent Law Enforcement Training Program had arranged a full schedule of interviews with visiting policemen from the Oakland, California, police department who sought to recruit a group of Kent's seniors for their force. This was offensive to black students, who believed that the Oakland police had mistreated blacks in California, and they intended to prevent the visitors from conducting their interviews or employing any Kent graduates. The SDS leadership grabbed at this as an opportunity to create widespread campus tension, and a classic confrontation of the 1960's was under way.

It started at 12:30 in the afternoon when the SDS leadership presented a list of three demands at Administration:

1. That Kent State University deny its facilities to the Oakland police department.
2. That the university sign a pledge of good faith agreeing not to infiltrate or otherwise intimidate recognized legitimate campus organizations. [SDS was not at this time officially recognized.]
3. That the Kent State police department disarm.

From there, a group of about 50 marched across campus to the Placement Office, which is in the Student Activities Center, and there they were joined by about 75 SDS adherents. Some 150 black students joined the group until there was a total of about 250 to 300, with blacks and whites maintaining separate groups. They proceeded to sit down in the Placement Office, so that the remaining interviews could not be held. It was about 2:00 P.M. and they stayed there for five hours. Since this was the university's first big sit-in, the administration moved cautiously but with studied determination. 'We wanted neither a riot nor a surrender,' one of the aides who played a conspicuous role says. Vice-President Robert A. Matson, head of student affairs, took charge. Adhering meticulously to university law, which was cumbersome, he tried his best to dislodge the students, but failed. (It is ironic that several days before, Matson, anticipating trouble of this kind, had met with Erickson and Emmer, trying to discover any legitimate grievances they might have whose correction would forestall trouble. 'At least tell us what the issues are,' he had pleaded. 'Hell no,' they had said. 'We tell you nothing.')

After two hours of futile negotiation, with Matson unable to commit the university to anything, he concluded that the sit-in was insoluble by ordinary means and telephoned the highway patrol, an excellently trained and disciplined police force whose responsibilities include the protection of state property such as universities. The nearest barracks was at Warren, Ohio, about thirty miles to the east. The commander there was one of the finest officers in the state, Captain Chester Hayth, a veteran of twenty-three years and a young-looking man in his early fifties.

Hayth had made Kent State a specialty. He loved the university and had often roared down Highway 59, past the huge ordnance dump that occupied much of Portage County, to help out at football games, or to make arrests for some minor infraction, or to lend general assistance. He had investigated thefts and traffic tie-ups and had reported to the campus so often that his wife said, 'If you go down there one more time, they've got to give you a diploma.'

With Matson's call for help, relayed through Captain Schwartzmiller, Hayth rushed over to the university. When he saw the situation, and the unprecedented number of students involved, he mobilized sixty officers of his patrol, but kept them out of sight in Ravenna. 'Wait there till I give you the signal to come over and make the arrests,' he instructed.

They waited an hour, then two hours, then three hours. But when no signal came after almost four hours of waiting— it was now 8:00 P.M.—Hayth got mad and sent his men home.

What had caused the mass arrest to be called off? The students had remained seated on the floor and had successfully prevented the Oakland recruiters from talking with any future policemen, so that the sit-in had to be termed a huge success. It seems that the college administration, faced with the enormity of almost 300 arrests, had decided to use the tactics made famous by Fabius Maximus three centuries before Christ: do nothing and hope the enemy will fade away. Matson and President Robert I. White went out to dinner, leaving Captain Hayth holding the bag without any instructions. When they returned from dinner the students had left the building.

In the days that followed, there was much talk of possible legal action against the leaders of the sit-in and the principal participants. When rumors thickened, the black students who might have been culpable startled everyone by announcing a walk-out, and under a severe discipline enforced by their own members, saw to it that all black students left the university. To the accompaniment of flashing cameras and television crews, 250 black students stalked majestically out of Kent, their bags packed and their fists in the air.

The SDS now mounted a vigorous campaign for amnesty for all blacks, but the university pointed out that the word was being misused, in that no penalties had yet been invoked, so that amnesty could not be granted. To this, the SDS replied that what they sought was amnesty in advance for any action which the university might be thinking of taking. To this sophistry President White retorted that KSU did not have sufficient evidence to substantiate charges of disorderly conduct against the students involved in the sit-in. Another university spokesman asked that in the future black students give advance notice of events which might carry possible racial overtones.

The outcome of this messy affair was that Fabian tactics had won an immediate victory by defusing a dangerous situation, but the police had been made fools of, and the SDS was left in a position to claim a stunning victory, on which they capitalized to the hilt. It must be remembered, however, that the potentially explosive racial situation had been handled with commendable calm, establishing a pattern which would prevail at Kent throughout this troubled period. And as we shall see, the cleverness with which the SDS had whip-sawed an accidental situation into a propaganda victory alerted the university to the seriousness of the problem which faced it. The next major encounter would not be so easily won by the SDS.

It came on April 8, 1969; the leaders put together a noon rally outside the Student Union to present their four famous demands:

1. Abolish ROTC.
2. Abolish the Liquid Crystals Institute.
3. Abolish the Northeast Ohio Crime Laboratory.
4. Abolish the Kent Law Enforcement Training Program.

It was decided to take these demands in person to the trustees' office in Administration, but before doing this, an impromptu parade was organized behind a Vietcong flag borne aloft by Colin Neiburger, one of the SDS leaders and a huge fellow of some 200 pounds. Elements of this parade stormed through Bowman and Satterfield Halls, disrupting classes with the contemptuous summary of what SDS thought the average university student was committed to: 'Work, study, get ahead, kill!' They shouted this slogan in various classrooms, then returned to the campus and headed for Administration.

Campus police had been alerted to their coming and tried to block the most likely entrance, but the students were upon them before they could secure the doors, and a hassle developed. To David Ambler, a tall, athletic, scholarly-looking associate dean of students from the University of Indiana, fell the unpleasant job of trying to bring some kind of order into the situation. With coolness and a degree of personal bravery, he squeezed open one of the doors, muscled his way through the crowd, and confronted the SDS leaders: 'If you behave in an orderly fashion, three of you may enter the building and present your petition to whatever authorities you wish.' To this, Rick Erickson shouted, 'We all come in or none of us do.' Ambler did his best to persuade the students to appoint a committee to handle their grievances, but Erickson insisted, 'We are a committee of the whole, and we act only as a body.' The doors were slammed shut.

The students then ran to another set of doors, and again the police anticipated them, but not quite quickly enough, because students had pushed their way into the building before the doors could be locked. More serious brawling ensued, with at least six SDS men physically assaulting the campus police. Lieutenant Jack Crawford, of the campus police, says, 'I was in the line of officers trying to protect the building and watched as the students began screaming and shouting obscenities. Then they began throwing punches and quite a few landed. Our officers were under strict instructions not to retaliate, because if we did, we knew the students would charge police brutality. So we stood there and took it for about fifteen minutes.'

Neiburger says of the affair, 'They charged me with slugging one of the officers for fifteen minutes. Did you see the size of the guy? I'd have broken him in half with one swing.'

Out of this melee came six arrests—Rick Erickson, Howie Emmer, Colin Neiburger, Alan DiMarco, Jeff Powell, George Gibeaut—of whom the last two were not students, nor then in any way connected with the university. The four who were students were immediately suspended. In addition, President White sought and obtained an injunction forbidding all but DiMarco from entering upon the campus at any point or for any purpose. (DiMarco was excused because he was judged to be of lesser importance in the SDS leadership.) Also, the university immediately rejected the appeal of SDS for a charter permitting them to operate on campus, which meant that the chapter had no legal standing at Kent State. When the six cases came to trial, all except DiMarco and Gibeaut got six months in jail.

It can be seen from this that the university acted with determination and dispatch. The administration did everything it conceivably could to discipline the individual SDS members who had resorted to violence and it took the further step of banishing the organization itself from campus. But the strategists from the Haunted House were far from defeated. They had, in fact, a provocative gesture planned for the next week.

On April 16 hearings were scheduled to be held regarding the suspensions of two of the students, DiMarco and Neiburger, as required by provisions governing the Student Judicial Board, which consisted of two students, two faculty members, plus one additional faculty member appointed by the dean of the college to which the student belonged. (Federal court decisions in recent years had insisted that strict procedures be followed in any attempt to suspend or dismiss students from a state university.) Normally such hearings are routine affairs, with the student usually getting the better of the bargain, since the operation of the system favored him, but today the SDS people had come up with a neat variation which would convert a routine hearing into a cause célèbre which would come close to shutting down the university.

DiMarco would ask that his hearing be conducted in secret, which was standard under rules designed to protect the innocent, but Neiburger would demand that his be held publicly on grounds that he was being persecuted, a fact which the general student body ought to be allowed to witness itself;

he also thought it would be a good idea if the hearings were collective. Both his requests were denied.

The hearings had been scheduled for a small room in Administration, where they were normally held, but because television cameras had caught some of the action of the previous week when Neiburger was fighting with the policeman, the authorities decided to shift the hearings to Music and Speech, where a closed-circuit television system would allow the film to be shown to the Judicial Board. However, those SDS students who had not been arrested or banished from the campus had gathered at Administration to protest the hearings, and now they felt betrayed because of the sudden change of venue. Accordingly, they organized a large and rowdy parade which stormed across campus to Music and Speech, but as they approached the sprawling building, they found that a large group of athletes and fraternity men had assembled to keep them away and to protect the building. 'We are not going to let you in!' they shouted. A mass fight occurred.

Now the second half of the SDS gambit was put into operation. Neiburger had made the logical request that the four banished SDS men be allowed on campus to testify on his behalf, and the judge to whom the petition was made immediately saw the reasonableness of the request and the injunction was modified so that Erickson and Emmer and their two associates were allowed permission to come on the campus.

What happened next became a source of great contention, leading to a bitter debate. First the official police explanation. Again Lieutenant Crawford is a good witness, for he participated in every step of the operation: 'As soon as we got word that the hearing was to be shifted to Music and Speech, we started securing the building. It's big, and it has many doors, and we did not want uncontrolled mobs rushing through it, trying to break up the hearing. I sent eight officers over there with locks and chains and they did a good job of securing every door so that students could have no possible way of entrance. In the few instances where the doors could not actually be padlocked, I stationed my best officers to guard them personally so that no one could gain entrance.

'So the building was locked up tight and we felt safe. However, when the SDS parade succeeded in breaking through the line of fraternity men, its members came up against the padlocked doors. Someone kicked in a glass panel in one of the doors, and before long more than 250 students were streaming into the building and roaring up the various stairs to the third floor, wrenching open a locked door there by using an improvised crowbar, filling the hallway outside the room where the hearings were to be held and making any further attempt at conducting the hearings futile. The mob was in control. Their battle cry had been "Open it up or shut it down," and they had succeeded in shutting the hearings down.'

Now the student explanation of how 250 SDS sympathizers reached the third floor of a building that was apparently totally locked and secured. The witness this time is the SDS leader Paul Probius, who says, 'It was a plot on the part of the administration. A classic example of entrapment. It's true that most of the ten doors to the building were locked, and it's also true that policemen were stationed at those where chains and padlocks weren't used, and it's finally true that someone kicked in the plate glass at the bottom of one of the doors. But the big question is: What happened next? We have sworn testimony that only a handful of students got in through the broken glass. To do so they had to get down on their hands and knees and carefully work their way past the jagged edges of glass plus the splinters on the floor inside. Even the administration admits not many could have got inside that way.

'I got inside and I'll tell you how I did. I went around to the door they call in evidence Door Number 2 and I simply walked in, and more than a hundred kids walked in with me. It was very simple, because the policeman standing there kept the door open for us, but when we were all inside, he carefully locked it, and that's when the administration claimed the "students had broken into Music and Speech."

'I climbed the two flights of stairs, and all the time I could hear Howie and Rick yelling, "You're our brothers and sisters. Come and get us!" It was a great encouragement. I was about twenty rows back when someone used a piece of steel from a coat rack to pry open the door leading to the third floor. When it was pushed aside, we all rushed into the hallway and found Howie and Rick raising a great commotion and keeping the hearings from being able to go ahead. It was a madhouse.

'Then, when our goal of shutting down the hearing had been accomplished, we all decided to leave the building, only to find that all doors were locked and the police were moving in to hold us in position until buses could be driven up to haul us off to jail. It was really terribly funny. There were several TV sets on the third floor and we sat around listening to the 6:30 news from Cleveland, and this dude came on real excited, to announce, "At Kent State, students from the SDS have occupied one of the major buildings and cannot be driven out." Everybody burst into cheers, because there we were, doing our best to get out of the building while they were claiming that we had taken over the darned thing.'

(Steve Paul, a fraternity man who tried to keep the SDS parade away from the building, says, 'As a member of student government I attended a meeting at which a university official said, two days before anything happened, "We're going to change the hearings to Music and Speech because it's easier to cordon off and control the door. We want to get all the SDS types inside and keep them there so that we can arrest them all at one time, without the chasing around that occurred last week." ')

At any rate, when the 250 students were penned up on the third floor they put on an exciting show. Howie Emmer and Rick Erickson took charge, got a bullhorn, and from an open window in the men's room, shouted wild encouragement to a mob of milling students outside, and food was sent up by means of cloth toweling that had been tied together to make improvised ropes. It was a festival.

The students had entered the building—broken into it, if you wish—at about 5:30 and were kept there till 10:00. At 5:45, when the situation had more or less stabilized, Captain Schwartzmiller telephoned Captain Hayth at the Warren barracks to inform him, 'You can come over now and make the arrests.' But Hayth, remembering his futile efforts at the Center sit-in and the wastage of sixty troopers, asked, 'Have you the authorization of President White for this phone call?' Schwartzmiller replied, 'I have cleared it with everybody. Come ahead.' So Hayth sped west on Highway 59, and after inspecting the broken doors, held a brief meeting with Schwartzmiller, asking him, 'Now you're sure that everybody up there is guilty? I don't want to be arresting innocent people.' Schwartzmiller assured him, 'I took up two faculty members who checked to find out if anyone was there legitimately for a class, and the innocent have been taken out. The rest are your people.'

So Hayth went to the third floor to confront the students. The first two he met were Howie Emmer and Rick Erickson. 'In as loud a voice as I could muster, because there was a lot of shouting and screaming, I said, "Everyone in this hall is under arrest for unlawful trespass. And if you try to resist, we're going to charge you with resisting arrest, which is a much more serious matter." This calmed things.'

Hayth returned to the first floor and spent the next hour calling for thirty officers from the Warren barracks, a set of buses to transport the students, photographic equipment to register them, and a table for processing arrest papers. During this time Lieutenant Crawford, who had been on the third floor all evening, was told by a group of students, 'When this is over we're going to kill you.'

At this point occurred a puzzling incident, whose significance is still being argued. Hayth says, 'When I inspected the third floor I was particularly concerned about the elevator, a big one which I saw might be used by students trying to escape. I asked the campus police, "What about that elevator?" and they told me, "Nothing to worry about there. It's kept on the ground floor and only a few people have keys to operate it."'

One of the men who had in his possession a key to this elevator was a man described in official reports only as 'red-headed with a beard.' Quietly moving onto the first floor of the building and working his way to the elevator doors, he opened them, started the elevator upward, halting it on the third floor. Opening the doors very quietly, he signaled to the first students he saw; the entrance to the elevator was so situated that no police on the third floor could see it. Deftly the students slipped in until the elevator could hold no more. The red-haired man then closed the doors and returned the elevator to the first floor, repeating this rescue operation ten or twelve times.

Hayth says, 'We have no idea how many of the arrested students escaped in this manner. We think we lost about as many as we kept. We didn't discover the operation until one of the building custodians on the first floor saw a mass of students running out of the elevator and escaping to the outside.'

(Late in the work on this book, one of the researchers met with Professor Carl Moore, whose office was in Music and Speech. Moore, with his handsome red beard, so fitted the description of the mystery man that the researcher tried probing Moore with some questions which he deemed both subtle and clever. After only a few, Moore broke in, 'Are you trying to discover whether I was the man who operated the elevator? Sure I was. I wish I had got the whole crowd out of there. I'd have done the university a profound service and we'd have avoided the bitter confrontation that resulted. There should have been no arrests or trials over that silly business.')

In view of later charges that the university had been supine in its handling of radical students, it is interesting to record what happened as a result of Music and Speech. Charges were filed against fifty-eight persons. Four of the SDS members—Erickson, Emmer, Neiburger and Powell—were charged with inciting to riot, and this indictment was added to charges carried over from the previous week; each would wind up in jail for more than half a year. SDS elder statesman Jim Powrie was charged with the more serious offense of having pried open the third-floor door, and he would spend one to seven years in jail. Twenty-six people were charged with trespass and received only minor penalties, and Candy Erickson was indicted for first-degree riot and drew down eighteen days in jail, but since she was a faculty member responsible for a course in English, the judge decided to allow her to spend her weekends in jail, over a period of six weeks, so that she could continue to meet with her students. This judgment drew down harsh criticism, all of it leveled against the university, the critics forgetting that it had been the decision of the court and not of the university. However, as the critics pointed out, it was the university that allowed her to continue teaching. Most important, SDS as an organization had been effectively expelled from the campus.

Music and Speech should have ended there, but it didn't. Students and faculty alike became incensed over the fact that the arrested students were summarily suspended without due process of university law. 'There should have been public hearings at which students could have proven their innocence' was the usual protest. Many students honestly believed that those arrested had been entrapped on the third floor by a university trick. Others argued that if Neiburger had wanted an open hearing, he was entitled to one, according to university law.

With the SDS banned, some organization was needed to carry on the protest, so an ad hoc Committee of Concerned Citizens of the Kent Community (CCC) was hastily formed, and after a confused and stormy first session, Steve Sharoff turned up as its leader; the campus was in turmoil. Knotty legalisms which grew out of the CCC protest will be discussed

later, but the end result must be observed now. The Kent
campus was radicalized. Students who had previously been
indifferent to SDS began to think, 'Maybe those radicals have
some good points,' so that SDS sympathizers jumped from
fifty to 500, and throughout the university there developed a
foreboding of greater confrontations to come.

The president

The administration which so doggedly defended the university
against the attacks of those who were determined to bring it
down was led by a taciturn, level-headed, retiring scholar
whose ambition was to make Kent into a first-rate center for
education. President Robert Isaac White had earned his three
degrees from the University of Chicago and had started his
professional life as an elementary-school teacher in Thornton,
Illinois. He had progressed rapidly through the various levels
of secondary education, had served as principal of a junior
college in Burlington, Iowa, and had been brought back
to Chicago as a professor in the graduate school. In 1946,
at the age of thirty-seven, he was offered the job of head of
Kent's College of Education. From this position, which he
filled with distinction, placing emphasis on scholarship and
character, he rose to vice-president for academic affairs. On
October 25, 1963, he became the sixth president of the university.

In some ways it was ironic that this quiet gentleman should
have been called to head a university that would soon have
21,000 students and where classes of 400 and 800 students
would be routine. Of his days at Chicago he says nostalgi-
cally, 'In my freshman and sophomore years at the University
of Chicago, I sat in classes taught by five Pulitzer Prize winners and three Nobel laureates. In our most ordinary classes
we had men like Thornton Wilder, Albert Michelson, who
did the great work on the speed of light, and J. Paul Goode,
the famous geographer. Learning was an adventure led by
outstanding minds and populated with the noblest ideas.'

Robert White had no illusions that his Kent students were
going to study with Nobel and Pulitzer winners. 'Kent was
destined to become a different kind of university . . . one to
which every high school graduate in Ohio had right of entrance. With the tremendous growth after World War II
and the results of this baby boom hitting us in the 1960's,

we had to find buildings to put the students in and professors to teach them. Our primary obligation was to keep the place running.'

He developed his own theory of administration. 'Bob is a strict constructionist,' says one of his admiring assistants. 'He has helped create what might be called a body of university law and he adheres to it as if it were sacred. He insists that everything go through channels and is meticulous about not hurting anyone's feelings through thoughtlessly bypassing him. If Kent has been a happy university, with a sense of cohesion among its faculty, it's primarily because Bob White has made it a place where faculty privileges are respected.'

Another highly placed member of the staff says, 'The one thing Bob hates is an ad hoc committee . . . one that a group of agitated professors or students dreams up on the spur of the moment, to deal with some burning issue. Properly and coldly he tells them, "Go back and submit your complaint through channels." He spent years building up those channels and he knows they're there to protect the freedom of everyone.'

From the beginning White has been a stubborn champion of academic freedom. He protected his faculty against attacks from outside, gave them his assurances on internal matters. He was adamant in his defense of students' rights, and even though he was one of the first big-university presidents to use the injunction against dissident students and police arrest of lawbreakers, he was stalwart in defense of legitimate protest. In speeches, in editorials in the college paper and in administrative procedures he consistently came out on the side of freedom, so long as it was self-disciplined and did not lead to violence. It could be said of him that he handled this delicate matter as well as any major university president and markedly better than most. Concerning his academic policies, one of his faculty has called him 'the last of the Jeffersonian liberals.' It is an apt description.

He has also managed to keep a testy Board of Trustees in Portage County happy and the state regents in Columbus from breathing down his neck too strongly. He has maintained excellent relations with the Ohio legislature, whose committees have found him always forthright yet restrained; from them he has obtained enormous grants of money for the yellow-brick buildings that have been growing like mushrooms across the campus during his presidency.

Growth has been inescapable. Whether White wanted Kent to become a multiversity or not, his hands were tied. The open-admissions policy forced on him by state law meant that any student, regardless of how illiterate he might be, who succeeded in grabbing off a high school diploma from any Ohio school, had an inalienable right to enter Kent State, and hordes came who were capable only of low-grade high school work. As a result, some university classes had to be conducted at a pathetic level of learning, but to protect themselves the faculty had devised a clever tactic: would-be entrants who were known to be miserably prepared were told, 'Of course you are entitled to enter Kent, but not until spring quarter. Registrations for fall and winter are all taken.' By the time spring rolled around, such young people had usually developed other interests, which spared Ohio the expense of offering them an education for which they had no capacity.

Bob White is a very good university president, marred by three weaknesses. In public speaking he belongs to the Dwight D. Eisenhower school of oratory: long sentences, hopelessly complicated, with subjects and predicates refusing to acknowledge each other. (Students and faculty delight in compiling lists of his outstanding efforts, and everyone has his favorite story of President White's losing battle with the English language.) 'I sit in faculty meetings,' says one dean, 'and keep asking myself, "How was that again?" ' This painful ineptness has keep White from communicating to others the sharp conclusions he has reached in the privacy of his study, and in a massive institution where verbal leadership was needed, he has been incapable of providing it.

He is also very shy. This prevents him from mingling with his students, who consider him so aloof that knowing him personally is impossible. They like him; they respect his fighting integrity; and they feel that if they could know him they would agree with many of his ideas. But he keeps aloof, finding himself incapable of providing the kind of charismatic leadership given by Kingman Brewster at Yale, Robert Goheen at Princeton, and Alexander Heard at Vanderbilt. At one point during the troubled weeks after May 4 he sought to gain temporary respite from pressure by taking his number-5 iron out on the back lawn and pitching a dozen or so balls over the hedge into the field beyond. It was late afternoon, and as he started to retrieve his pitch shots a couple of students passing by in the dusk called and waved to him. As he headed back for his yard another group waved and shouted, 'Hang in there, Dr. White!' When he recounts this incident, there is gratification in his voice. There is also a touch of astonishment, as though he is surprised that the kids should have recognized him.

His greatest handicap is that he followed in the presidency a remarkable man, George A. Bowman, who had served for nineteen years. Tall, magnetic, slim as a buggy whip, a brilliant speaker, Bowman ran Kent State as an emperor might rule his private domain. One who worked under him says, 'Bowman did not govern us from his vest pocket. He did it from a very small inside watch pocket.' A student from those days recalls, 'Eleven of us got very excited about the Congress of Racial Equality and decided that as practicing Christians we should do something to support the Negroes. So we painted two signs *Back CORE* and started a solemn march back and forth in front of Administration. President Bowman heard the commotion, came out, stood on the steps and stared silently at each of us as we walked sheepishly past. When he had seen us all, he rose to his greatest height, stretched his right arm out toward us and uttered one imperious word, "Disband!" Not to have obeyed him would have been unthinkable, so Kent's first demonstration ended.' To follow a man like Bowman was not easy, particularly when White's style was so conspicuously different. An aide who knew both men says, 'They were both needed, Bowman to give the place a touch of class, White to give it scholarship.'

Dr. White rises each morning at 5:00, works a couple of hours, walks down Main Street to some hash house for breakfast, spends a long morning at his desk in the KSU Administration Building and then drives out East Main to the Brown Derby, where he customarily occupies the corner table just inside the door. He likes to be waited on by a Chinese waitress named Flora who has the highest birdlike voice ever heard in a human being.

He sits hunched over, reading reports or just thinking, and although he is a gracious host if some member of his staff is sharing the table with him, he prefers lunching alone. He is of medium height, with a handsome, deeply lined face and graying hair. He wears solid-color ties, held in place by a Phi Beta Kappa clasp, and on most days of the year wears gray-flannel trousers topped by a sedate jacket which does not match.

He has a sense of humor and particularly appreciates jokes on himself. He enjoys Saturday afternoons when the Kent football team plays at home—it once set a record of going twenty-four games in a row without scoring—for then he can invite some thirty or forty of his friends to the spacious glassed-in room atop the new stadium, where in comfort they dine on beef Stroganoff, fruit salad, doughnuts and cider as they watch the home team try to squeeze out a victory.

His greatest pleasure, however, comes on the occasional evenings when he and Mrs. White invite a few distinguished guests from various parts of the nation to the Silver Lake Country Club west of Kent. There, in splendid surroundings overlooking rolling farmland, he speaks quietly of the problems of American education and listens as others tell of their experiences. The club is a lush affair, maintained by the wealthy rubber families of nearby Akron, and boasts the best menu in Ohio, a staggering choice of ten international dishes and thirty-five standard American items. It is a reassuring place to be after the storms of administering a modern university.

Robert White is a gentleman when the breed is going out of style; he is a scholarly administrator in an age when businessmen are taking over. In the rough days of May, 1970, Kent University needed his guidance as never before, and it was a tragedy that at every crucial moment this grave and tested administrator was missing from the campus. It was as if *Hamlet* were being performed while Hamlet was absent from Elsinore.

He missed the Friday troubles for good reason. In recent years a considerable honor had come to Kent State in that White had been chosen chairman of the Board of Trustees of the American College Testing Program, a powerful agency whose national headquarters were in Iowa City, and he had for some time planned to work there that weekend. But he was apprehensive about leaving the campus. From the room in which he had lunch that day he watched over the burial of the Constitution and was gratified to see that things had gone quite calmly. From his office he had watched the BUS rally and was relieved when nothing violent happened there. After a brief consultation with his aides, his student leaders and the police, it was unanimously agreed that White should proceed with his plans to attend the educational conference in Iowa City, so he caught a late afternoon plane to Mason

City, Iowa, where his sister-in-law lived and from which he would drive the 176 miles to Iowa City. He would rent a car and enjoy the leisurely drive across a state he had grown to like.

The trustees

The other important element of Kent's administration is the Board of Trustees. In recent decades it has become fashionable in American academic circles to downgrade such boards, as if they were intellectually embarrassing when compared to professors, or politically insignificant when compared to administrators. Indeed, Jacques Barzun, in his otherwise excellent analysis of the archetypal American university— *American University: How It Runs, Where It Is Going*— painstakingly investigates the most arcane faculty committee, but does not even mention the Board of Regents, which supposedly controls the university; yet when Columbia and sister universities were overrun, everyone called upon the boards to rescue them. Such boards are going to be much more important in the 1970's and 80's, because society will hold them responsible for a closer supervision than they have exercised in the past.

In Ohio, a Board of Regents, operating distantly and impartially out of Columbus, governs the entire system of state-supported advanced education. It sets policy; for example, it determines what the relative emphasis shall be in each of the universities, which ones shall give which advanced degrees, which ones shall have medical or law schools. Some years ago it made what many experts consider a barbarous decision: All Ohio universities must operate on the quarter plan (four short terms a year) and none on the semester (three long terms). This is a plan which has many drawbacks. Although it functions well when a year-long course is divided into three fragments (for then it enables the instructor to test his students three times instead of two), it tempts the university to offer a plethora of one-quarter hasty reviews of subjects rather than the intensive study that can be accomplished when adequate time is available. It is especially destructive of good language teaching, the development of ideas in philosophy. and history, and the deep pursuit of any science. Especially harmful is the fact that it encourages students to drift in and out of the university, quarter by quarter. The orderly sequence of both education and responsibility is thus disrupted. In general, however, the Board of Regents has worked hard to bring order into the Ohio system, and since it works under the sharp surveillance of the state legislature, provides liaison with the general public.

In addition to the regents, each university has its own Board of Trustees—largely local people—and they are responsible for the smooth operation of their institution. Kent State has been fortunate in having as the president of its trustees a short, choleric, Republican newspaper publisher with a deep interest in education and a face which turns angry-red when anyone attacks Kent. Robert Dix is like any of a hundred men across America; as the son of a prosperous publisher he inherited an empire of papers, radio stations and television companies. He started quietly, and colleagues said, 'He got the job because he was the boss's son.' But he matured steadily, exercising his power with discretion, until he found himself in his early fifties 'our local leader.'

He did one other thing which strengthened his position: he married a resolute young woman with a sharp voice and a penetrating mind. She has kept him from becoming parochial. At their home across from the campus, it is customary to find the speaker of an Asian parliament, or a novelist from Peru, or a delegation from Ghana. Helen Dix is apt to say, when endeavoring to recall a date, 'Wasn't that when we were trying to get down from Katmandu to Darjeeling?' They have been everywhere.

She has also been a modernizing influence. Recently her daughter Darcy telephoned from Madison, where she is attending the University of Wisconsin, to report, 'The university is allowing Abbie Hoffman to speak on campus. Lots of parents have forbidden their daughters permission to hear him. What should I do?' Mrs. Dix snorted, 'Do? Go hear him. You're a big girl now and it's time you learned the four-letter words.'

Dix had become a trustee while still a young man, had played a major role in having Kent promoted to university status, encouraged the hiring of sociologist Oscar W. Ritchie, first Negro faculty member at any Ohio state university, and had benevolently supervised the expenditure of hundreds of millions of dollars and the accumulation of 21,000 students.

He formed a good team with President White, whom he supported vehemently and whose style of administration matched his own. The Two Bobs, as they were called, had much in common. Both were retiring, both soft-spoken, both patient, both very stubborn, both dedicated to the building of a greater Kent. Neither was flamboyant, neither charismatic, neither bold in appearance, and neither eager to dictate to the university community. They were low-key, stubborn men who believed in the virtues of Middle America, and each had the capacity for courage when pushed against the wall.

They had worked together for almost a quarter of a century and had created a university which may not have been scintillating in its academic brilliance or athletic prowess but which was stubbornly determined to educate the maximum number of young people in the best possible manner within a climate of freedom. The Two Bobs had not created a hick university; it did not, of course, compare in endowment or faculty with private schools like Harvard and Stanford, and it had not yet attained the reputation of the top state universities like Minnesota, North Carolina and Michigan; but it compared favorably with schools like Nebraska, Missouri and Penn State and exceeded a good many other state universities whose names will come to the reader.

The mayor holds a big hand

This had been a long day for the city officials.

Throughout Ohio, May 1 was celebrated as Law Day, and major communities held public meetings extolling the virtues of law as opposed to mob action. Centuries ago May Day had been one of the liveliest holidays of the year, especially in Anglo-Saxon countries, for it not only signified the end of winter but was also the excuse for revels around the countryside. In the late nineteenth century it became a day on which workingmen in America demonstrated for labor reform. Soon after it was preempted by European socialists, but recently, conservative groups in America launched the idea of a completely new celebration stressing the virtues of law and the freedom we enjoy therefrom.

For example, Roy D. Thompson, Kent's chief of police, had addressed a meeting of the Kiwanis Club on Thursday evening, April 30, at which he said, 'Kent is exceedingly fortunate in that most of the 20,000 students at Kent State University are well balanced.' He went on to explain something that would become painfully apparent as this day wore on: 'Our city has only twenty-one police officers, but we should have fifty. That is, based on national standards for a city our size.' He assured his listeners that the twenty-one police in Kent worked overtime to give the city the best protection possible under the law, and concluded, 'We have been very fortunate in Kent.'

That evening LeRoy Satrom, a tall, very thin, soft-spoken Norwegian whose family had grown up in North Dakota and by diligent effort had seen him through a college degree in engineering, put on one of his good suits and headed twelve miles due north for the intersection town of Aurora, where the political leaders of Portage County were convening at the Treadway Inn to celebrate Law Day. Satrom was the mayor of Kent, a Democrat newly elected last November and in office only four months; prior to that he had been 'the best city engineer Kent ever had, because he knew every technical operation and kept a record of every piece of city property.' He was a member of Rotary and had always respected the university, from which two of his sons had graduated; his third son attended the excellent high school maintained by the education department of the university for use of its practice teachers. LeRoy Satrom was no educational yahoo.

Now, as he drove north to Aurora, he reflected on conversations he had had that day with his son, Thomas LeRoy Satrom, a third-year medical student at Ohio State University in Columbus. Tom had scurried out of Columbus because of the riots there. 'The students are raising hell,' he told his father. 'It was really getting dangerous.'

Tom, a member of Nu Sigma Nu, the medical fraternity, had witnessed heavy rioting on Wednesday and had been gassed while sitting on the second floor of his fraternity house. 'That was enough for me,' he told his father. 'Events had gotten completely out of hand. Students are fighting the police and the National Guard are filling the campus.'

Accompanied by such gloomy thoughts, Mayor Satrom proceeded to the Treadway Inn, in whose spacious Colonial-type quarters he found the political conviviality he liked. Those in the know suspected that Satrom owed his job— Kent had never previously had a full-time mayor—to Portage County's Democratic boss, Roger Di Paolo, a young-minded Italian politico, but others believed he had been hand-picked by Judge Albert Caris, eighty years of age, still active on the bench, and one of the finest men in the county. Judge Caris will be important in this story, and it is interesting to see him moving about the inn, greeting old friends and long-time enemies. He was a spry man with all of his hair and most of his teeth. He had a dry wit, could accept humor at his own expense, and was incredibly sharp for a man his age. He was glad to see Satrom, for if it was true that he had more or less nominated the tall Norwegian, he could be proud, for Satrom was making a good mayor.

One of the first men Satrom greeted was crusty Seabury Ford, chairman of the Republican party in Portage County and possessor of the most distinguished name in the district: his great-grandfather had been one of the most famous of the early residents, ending his career as governor of Ohio. Ford was approaching seventy, was known as the top lawyer in the area, and was being prominently mentioned for a judge-ship, now that Republicans controlled the state.

It was a good meeting, with the law properly extolled, but what followed was better: an old-time Ohio back-room poker game. It was a game Satrom would never forget, because the cards seemed to flow to him. The man across the table would have two pair, kings and queens, and he would have a pair of deuces and three treys. It went like this for more than a hour, with Satrom garnering most of the chips and the canny experts warning him, 'Wait till that streak cools off. We're going to clean you.'

When Satrom had most of the chips piled up before him, an embarrassing thing happened. He had an inexplicable urge to telephone the police in Kent to assure himself that every-thing was going well in the city, but when he went to make the call, he found he had no small change, so with all the money in the poker game before him, he had to ask Seabury Ford for a dime. Ford's reply was on the salty side, but Satrom got his dime; the Kent police reassured him: 'Every-thing just fine.' And the Portage County politicos settled down for a long, rough night of cutthroat poker.

Before long the phone rang. It was the police department in Kent. 'Street trouble. Yep, Water Street. Real bad.' Satrom asked if he was needed, and the voice said, 'You sure are.'

'I'll be there,' he said.

Now he had to explain to the poker players that even though he was the big winner—bigger, indeed, than ever before—he was going to have to quit early. This information drew a groan, but Satrom said he could do nothing about it. The politicians insisted that the phone call had been rigged, and Satrom said, 'I wish that were true.'

Recalling what happened next, Satrom says, 'Even though rain had begun to fall, I drove down Route 43 at about ninety-five miles an hour. Trouble with students! That's all I needed, especially after what I'd heard about Ohio State.'

Six miles south he roared under the broad lanes of the Ohio Turnpike. Two more miles and he was zooming across Route 14. He then had a clear run into the posh suburb of Twin Lakes, with its two country clubs, and before long he was screaming his way into Kent. But there he was stopped.

'I crossed Cuyahoga River at the Crain Street bridge and then over the railroad tracks and tried to turn right onto Water Street, but it was blocked. There seemed to be a bonfire in the middle of the street and the mob occupied everything.' Satrom backed away from the riot-torn street and used side roads to get to his office.

Unfortunately, City Hall at this time was undergoing extensive renovation, so that both the ground floor, which housed the police department, and the second floor, which held the mayor's offices, were chopped up. In fact, at that moment they looked as bad as Water Street, and it was through this unavoidable confusion that Satrom had to pick his way.

'My men had called the sheriff in Ravenna for help and we also decided to bring in policemen from neighboring communities.' Satrom is silent as to why his police force of twenty-one men and Chief Thompson had allowed the riot to rampage for two hours before action was taken; others would say, 'If Kent had sent its few policemen into that mob, they'd have been chewed up and spit out.'

As we have already seen, Satrom next asked his assistant for a copy of the ordinance empowering him to declare an emergency, and since he insists upon an inordinately neat office he got it promptly and made a formal announcement that Kent was in a state of emergency. This decision was broadcast.

For the next half hour Satrom stayed at his desk, listening to reports of the street action. 'They grew increasingly rough,' he says, 'and at 12:47 I had to make a decision. I called the governor's office in Columbus. I got hold of John McElroy, the administrative assistant, and told him, "I may have to make formal application for assistance from the National Guard." I'm sure no governor wants to hear such a message.' As soon as the conversation ended, McElroy telephoned Colonel John Simmons, the National Guard duty officer, who called the adjutant general, Major General Sylvester T. Del Corso, who would determine which units would report in the event that the Guard was officially summoned. This latter decision, of course, could be made only by the governor. Del Corso did one other thing which helped the situation noticeably. He dispatched immediately a bright young officer, Lieutenant Charles J. Barnette, to Kent to serve as liaison with the civil authorities while they tried to make up their minds as to whether they wanted the Guard to intervene or not. Nor did Del Corso wait till dawn to get Barnette on his way; the young man started driving east within a few minutes of Satrom's call. It was he who drove into Kent at 3:00 A.M. to serve as a stabilizing influence in the hours that followed.

After alerting Columbus, Satrom dug out his copy of the Riot Act, and with this in his hand he ran downstairs and jumped into a police car driven by Robert DeFluiter. 'Take me to North Water Street!' he commanded, and the car picked its way through scattered groups of students who had moved out from the bar area and who seemed intent upon smashing windows in other parts of town.

When Satrom saw the havoc that had been visited upon his city—people around him estimated that more than $100,000 worth of damage had been done, though in succeeding days this would be de-escalated to $50,000, then to $16,000, and finally to 'something around $10,000'—he felt sick. Directing DeFluiter to drive the automobile into Water Street, he placed himself right in the middle of the mob and proclaimed the state of emergency to the rioters, then read the riot act: 'This is an illegal assembly. You must disperse.' After repeating this many times, he then announced a new measure: 'This city is under curfew! As of right now!' For the ensuing days the city of Kent would operate under an 8:00 P.M. to 6:00 A.M. curfew, but by some incredible mixup, the university would be under a 1:00 A.M. to 6:00 A.M. curfew, which meant that a student on one side of the street at 10 P.M. would be subject to arrest, whereas if he crossed to the opposite side, he was home free. This, of course, was an invitation to chaos, which would be compounded when the hours for the university curfew were changed without making sure the students knew about it. In the next few days anyone could be arrested for practically anything and some kind of justification could be found for it. The remarkable thing is that under these circumstances, so few were arrested. In the widespread rioting of Friday night, with about a thousand people involved over a period of many hours and in full sight of the police, only fourteen were arrested.

In addition to the other measures he had initiated, Mayor Satrom also declared a ban on liquor sales, but Charles Madonio, who had been watching this aspect of the riot carefully, was of the opinion that Satrom might just as well have ordered a ban on sugar. 'My guess is that the demonstrators didn't have a case of beer among all of them in their systems. These people weren't drinkers. Most of them were long-hairs. The people in the street were the crowd that hangs out at J.B.'s, and that place sells about as much beer as a laundromat.'

So the city of Kent was closed down. Forty-seven windows in different establishments had been broken. A few people had been arrested, but none of the instigators nor real troublemakers. And on the outskirts of a small town to the west, three companies of National Guardsmen slept in tents, preoccupied with truckers and unaware that they would soon be moving upon Kent to face one of the most complicated situations ever to confront the Ohio Guard.

Guards in bivouac

We must now double back several days to observe a group of men who would soon be called upon to play a crucial role at Kent State.

At 11:00 on Wednesday morning, April 29, James Ronald Snyder, a captain in the Ohio National Guard and commanding officer of Charlie Company, 1st Battalion, 145th Infantry, had received an alert call from the High Street armory in Akron to the effect that he should be prepared to get his company together and ready to roll. It was another civil disturbance, specifically, an illegal work stoppage by a group of truck drivers. The drivers were interfering with truck movements out of the city on the way to the Ohio Turnpike; there had been some shooting of tires, a couple of people had been wounded. Charlie Company's mission would be to protect the working truckers and keep the traffic moving.

Snyder, who was at home on his day off as an investigator for the Summit County coroner, called his first sergeant and told him to prepare all the necessary papers. Next, he tried to reach Larry Van Horn, his communications non-com, but learned that Van Horn, an executive pilot for Goodyear Tire and Rubber, was on a flight to New York City. He had better luck with Sergeant Gordon Bedell. Gordon said he would get right down to the armory as soon as the executive order came through.

This came at 12:30. Snyder got into uniform, threw his gear into the car, and with his wife Donna at his side, made the twenty-minute drive from his home in Stow to downtown Akron. Ron Snyder, short, stocky, crisp in manner, describes Donna as a 'typical National Guard wife, always ready for anything. She gripes a lot, like all of them, but always does whatever there is to do.'

At 3:35 that afternoon, Charlie Company had three quarters of its manpower mustered and armed, and at 4:00 Snyder started trucking everyone out to the bivouac area in the Rubber Bowl, a U-shaped football stadium southeast of the city. Tents were pitched, sleeping bags rolled out, field kitchens set up. Van Horn had arrived by this time, and shortly after dark, the first sergeant could report a hundred-percent sign-in for Charlie Company—153 officers and men, all except those who were away at camp. Snyder says that each of his men had had the required six months of basic training, plus thirty-two hours of riot drill and instruction. Nor were real, live riots anything new to his men, he proudly points out. 'All but twenty of them had had riot experience before, what we call o.j.t. [on-the-job training],' he says. 'Many of us had participated in the Akron race riots of 1968, and after that, a few renegade truckers raising a little hell would be a piece of cake.'

It would be two days before the Guardsmen heard anything about Kent State. This night old Apathy U was sleeping away peacefully some fifteen miles to the east.

At first daylight on Thursday, Charlie Company was getting ready to move again, this time to the field behind the town hall at Ridgefield, scene of the most serious trucker harassment. Besides rifles, the strikers had citizen-band radios, so that their attacks on single trucks were well coordinated. Cars would dash out of side streets, weave in and out, shoot at the tires. The Guard plan was to move the trucks in convoy during hours of minimum traffic. Every fifth truck would be spaced out by a jeep full of soldiers. Guardsmen would be placed on overpasses from Ridgefield north on Route 21 to the turnpike.

As was his practice before committing his men to any kind

of action, Captain Snyder held his company formation and talked to them about the job ahead. He read to them from a pamphlet entitled *Disturbance Control: Guidelines for Small Unit Commanders and Troops.* Under the heading of *Legal Considerations* he read:

'Criminal sanctions may be imposed against any Guardsman who exceeds his authority in accomplishing his mission. The rule of "necessity" is the guide used to determine whether or not a Guardsman exceeded his authority. However, if acting in good faith and pursuant to lawful orders, the Guardsman's conduct is usually not criminal.'

Under *Troop Civilian Relations* he read:

'The restoration of law and order in an Ohio city is not exactly a combat situation, but rather it is a situation wherein our guideline is *minimum application of force consistent with our objective.*'

From the *Summary* he quoted:

'In a civil disorder the Ohio National Guardsman continues to serve his state and country by restoring law and order, and by providing an atmosphere where the rule of law will prevail. The successful accomplishment of this mission with a *minimum of force* must be recognized by the Guardsman as one of great honor and service to his state and country.
'And so the keynote of all operations aimed at the curtailment of civil disorder is *restraint.* The Guardsman acts confidently and with a firmness, but he must gauge his action to the seriousness of the disorder he seeks to deter or contain.'

He cited the three situations in which an individual Guardsman may fire his weapon: when he feels his life is endangered; when ordered to do so by his officer; to save someone else's life. He talked to them about tear gas. Ron Snyder is a great believer in the power of this gas to disperse threatening crowds of people and keep them from pressing ranks too closely. His copious use of it in the '68 Akron riots earned him the nickname of 'Cyanide.' His troopers have their own name for him. Not without affection, they refer to him privately as 'Captain Gas.'

Finally he ordered them to load and lock. Snyder is also firm on this subject. He says, 'The law states that it's the local unit commander's decision whether to load or not. I would never put my troops into a civil disturbance situation without loaded weapons. And,' he adds, 'I don't believe in firing warning shots, either. Firing into the air can be dangerous. It creates confusion. Sometimes shooting into the air invites a strong response from the very people you're trying to control.'

Charlie Company's show of force in the truck strike was completely successful: striking truckers gathered before the beer parlors on Route 21, did a lot of yelling and catcalling when the first convoys came through, but they did not try to interfere. In two days Snyder's men moved upwards of 300 trucks without incident. Those Guardsmen not actually riding convoy were deployed with fixed bayonets around the beer halls as further deterrent to any highjinks by the strikers. 'The spirit of the bayonet,' Ron says in reflection, describing this tactic. 'Bare steel can have a wonderful calming effect.'

By Friday night the situation had cooled to a point where Snyder was thinking of letting some of his men go home next day for a meal with their families and a change of uniform. Indeed, he actually put this plan into effect. But even as the idea occurred to him, trouble was brewing in the streets of Kent. Saturday would hold some wild and uncomfortable surprises for the men of Charlie Company.

Marooned on a traffic light

When the rioting students surged back on campus, sometime around 1:00 A.M., they were ready to continue their hell-raising, but a bizarre accident halted them. The principal witness to this strange development was a highly politicized girl from Sudbury, Massachusetts.

When Jamie Haines graduated from high school she enrolled at Miami University (Florida)—in Ohio there's only one Miami University, at Oxford, Ohio, and if you refer to the other you have to add (Florida)—but after a brief experience there she found the place much too apathetic: 'I was deep into the political thing and nobody down there wanted to talk politics, so I applied to seventeen different colleges, and my record must have looked pretty good, because all seventeen accepted me. I chose Kent. I figured that since it was so near to Cleveland and Akron, it would have some politically-minded students, and that's what I wanted.'

Jamie hungered for political action because she was a red-hot Republican determined to elect Richard Nixon President of the United States. 'My parents were dedicated Republicans, and they wanted Nixon too. They were delighted when I became secretary of the Young Republican Club at Kent and a pledge to the best sorority. We had a fantastic group of kids and we did everything we could to deliver Ohio to Nixon. We had a wild celebration when we won.'

It was not in her capacity as a Republican politician that Jamie participated in the closing event of Friday night. 'I was in charge of Inspiration Week for our sorority pledges and we'd convened at a house on Linden Street opposite the university. We'd had a fine, sentimental evening and I'd laid down the laws. But about 11:15 we got a phone call from the president of the sorority and she said, "Big trouble downtown. You get those girls back to their dorms immediately." I thought maybe she was choked up and that there wasn't any hurry, so we decided to stop by Burger Chef for a snack, but when we got there, we saw thirty motorcycles parked outside. The Cobras of Youngstown were on the scene and we sure didn't want to tangle with them, so we ducked back into the house. Again the phone rang. Again it was the president, real uptight: "All pledges are to sleep where they are. Don't allow any of them out of the house. Things are rather serious." I went down to Main Street to see what she meant and for the first time in my life I heard shots. It was tear gas exploding, and I thought, "She's right. This is serious." '

Jamie returned to her charges and told them, 'You stay here tonight. Sleep as you can.' The girls then clustered about windows, each of which provided a good view of the campus, and in the softly falling rain they watched as a repair truck from Tree City Electric Company driven by Glen Kruger pulled up at the intersection of Linden and Main and began cranking out a long ladder up which Blaine Baldasare climbed to repair a traffic light. It had ceased to function and could, in the rain, constitute a hazard.

'In a way it was providential that the truck arrived at this time,' Jamie says, 'because it provided a diversion. The kids who a moment ago were threatening the cops and looking around for things to throw now stopped and watched as Baldasare climbed the ladder, followed by Kruger. When they reached the light, students cheered and even policemen stopped to watch.

'Then a frightening thing happened. The repair truck was in the middle of Route 59 and it must have had half a dozen lights flashing off and on, so that no one could possibly fail to see it, but a car came swiftly down Main Street from the east, ran smack into the truck, knocked it forty feet onto the campus, tore away the ladder, leaving Baldasare clinging to the traffic light, knocked down Kruger, ran over him, and screeched to a halt. The driver, aware at last of what was going on, took one look at his havoc, opened the car door, and ran down an alley, and we saw him no more that night.'

There was a third member of the work crew, the nine-year-old Kruger boy in a toy hard-hat. He was the son of the man who had been run over, and now, seeing his father lying in the street, became hysterical. Jamie knew what to do. 'I ran out of our house, grabbed the child and took him away from the accident. He kept shouting, "That's my daddy!" and I told him, "He's going to be all right." This turned out not to be true, but at the time he looked dead. Finally Mrs. Kruger arrived, a large woman in a faded print dress, and she tried to take charge of her son but she became hysterical, too, so I did what I could to comfort her.'

All this time gales of laughter and cheering came from the students, for Baldasare, high in the air, clung to the traffic light, his feet dangling and his body swaying in the darkness as the light continued to blink from green to yellow to red. 'Hold on, buddy!' a voice shouted, and a score of students began giving advice and encouragement.

'Suddenly,' Jamie recalls, 'everybody forgot the misbehavior of the students. Cops and kids set up rescue teams together, their one design to save that fellow on the traffic light. One group huddled under the traffic light to catch him if he fell, and when somebody finally found a ladder, we heard more cheering than we do at a football game.' Tension was relieved; the crowd dispersed; and normally the Friday riot would have ended there. If it had, it would have merited in the news accounts of that day no more than an one-line postscript after accounts of the really serious troubles at Ohio State, Ohio U and Miami: 'There was also minor trouble at Kent State.' Historically, the whole affair was a rowbottom and no more.

This evocative word originated at the University of Pennsylvania in the latter years of the last century, when a woebegone student named Rowbottom enrolled as a freshman. At the end of two quarters he had made not one friend, but come spring he decided to do something about it, so each night toward 1:00 he would stand in the middle of the quadrangle and shout in a loud, mournful voice, 'Hey, Rowbottom! Come on out and have a beer.' He would call three or four times. 'Rowbottom, come on out and join us!' Then he would run to another part of the campus and yell back, 'Sorry, fellows. Can't make it tonight. Go along without me.'

By exam time everyone was inviting Rowbottom to their parties, and he passed into the legend of his university. Today, if anyone at Penn wants to start a riot, he runs to the middle of the dormitory area and shouts, 'Rowbottom!' and students storm forth to overturn trolleycars, bait policemen and make the city fathers furious.

At Kent the spring rowbottom had for many years taken the form of a mud fight, which one coed described as 'Glorious! All the girls piled out of their dorms on some rainy day, and we fought with the boys, rolling down Blanket Hill in the mud, and you'd get an arm broken or a jaw dislocated and it was just beautiful.' We have already seen Sandy Scheuer engaging in such a fight, but in 1970 spring was unusually late, there had been no warm rainy days and, consequently, little mud. Spirits were high and Water Street took the place of Blanket Hill.

But there was a darker aspect, too, for as Jamie Haines checked to be sure that her pledges were safe, she heard on the campus some student with a bullhorn shouting, 'The revolution has begun! Join us! We're going to burn ROTC!' That night the police forestalled him, but he would return at dusk on Saturday.

Conclusions

At the end of each day we shall offer our reasoned judgment as to what happened.

The events on Water Street constituted a riot involving about 1,000 persons, downtown and on campus, and Mayor Satrom was justified both in reading the riot act and in establishing a curfew. The damage to Kent was not nearly so great as excited witnesses made it out to be then and as those opposed to the students have repeated since; in fact, the

Friday riots were minor when compared to damage that had been done in other university communities.

In endeavoring to determine causation, two different types of participant must be considered. The great majority saw the disturbance as merely another spring frolic and were activated by nothing more serious than a desire for fun. There was, however, a hard core of radical activists—abetted by a few real revolutionaries, not necessarily from the university—who grasped at the disturbance as a means of advancing their own well-defined aims. President Nixon's Cambodian speech had minimal effect upon the first group but a profound one upon the radicals, who would have approved nothing he proposed. Alcohol and drugs played no significant role in this riot, nor in anything that was to happen during the next three days, and to claim otherwise is fallacious.

The police would have been justified in arresting about 100 young people for misdemeanors which would have warranted fines but no jail sentences, another twenty for arson and malicious breaking of windows, and perhaps as many as nine others for having incited to riot and given it impetus when it started. If arrests for misdemeanors had taken place early, the felonies that followed would have been obviated, and if the arrests for felonies had been made this night, the troubles that followed on the three succeeding days might have been avoided. That the police required two hours (from 10:15 to 12:17) to swing into effective action is astonishing, and that the campus police did not radically adjust their plans so as to provide aid when needed is regrettable. When the fourteen arrests were finally made, they included none of the leaders.

No fault accrues to the over-all administration of the university, for it responded at least as well as the average administration across the country. The fact that its president, Dr. White, was out of town had no bearing on the matter; he was absent on educational matters of the highest import and the entire Kent community should have been proud that his counsel had been sought elsewhere.

III

SATURDAY: BURNING OF ROTC

Day of a faculty marshal

For Professor Glenn Frank, of the geology department, the academic year of 1969–70 had been unusually pleasant. Not only were his classes more popular than ever, but he had an unexpected extra $1,000 to spend. Faculty and students alike had voted him the outstanding teacher on campus, principally because he made geology so exciting, with his precise lectures, fascinating illustrative material and great sense of humor, that students who had no conceivable interest in the subject fought to get into his crowded classrooms. If a coed was entertaining a date from another college she would often slip him into Professor Frank's class. 'It's better than a movie,' was the general opinion. The $1,000 in cash had been given him as a public testimony to the respect in which he was held.

He had no doctorate. After graduating from Kent State in 1951 he had driven a milk truck, served as local gravedigger, and had gone on to the University of Maine to pick up his master's. Of medium height, trim, with graying sandy hair, which he wore in a crew cut, Glenn Frank was the epitome of the professor interested in everything his students did. His squarish face, set off by two-tone horn-rimmed glasses, was customarily wrinkled in a smile, and his close-set hazel eyes looked on campus life with a mixture of deep seriousness and detached amusement.

On Friday night he had missed the action, for he had driven the thirty miles to Cleveland to attend a dinner party. As he was leaving, someone who had been listening to the radio told him, 'Students wrecked downtown Kent. Trouble with the blacks.' As we have seen, no black students were involved, and Frank suspected that that might be the case,

125

so he reserved judgment, hoping that the rest of the story was equally false. Since his new ranch-style home lay at Twin Lakes north of town, he would reach it on the way back from Cleveland before he got to Kent, so that night he did not see the damage.

Early Saturday morning his phone began ringing, for he was secretary of the Faculty Senate, and at 8:00 A.M. he went to the campus to make preparations for what he knew would be a long, hard day. 'I had this gut feeling that the rioting downtown had been merely the prelude to something important. I was apprehensive about the recent release of Erickson and Emmer and the others from the Haunted House. And I thought it ominous that townspeople were reporting hundreds of smashed windows instead of the relatively few that really were broken. For example, we were told that over $100,000 worth of damage had been done, and that's the figure that stuck in people's minds. In actuality, less than $10,000 would have restored everything. In other words, the whole atmosphere was supercharged. And when we began to get rumors that the ROTC building was going to be burned, it was only prudent that we take steps to cool things down.'

Frank attended a meeting at 8:00, another at 10:00, another at 1:00 and still another at 3:00. The faculty, at least, could not be charged with indifference to the disasters which threatened to overtake it, and at 4:00 that afternoon Frank made up his mind. Jumping in his car, he drove west on Main Street till he reached the intersection that marked the middle of town, then turned south on Route 43 till he came to the large shopping center where the huge Clarkins store dominated the area. There he purchased ten yards of a robin's-egg blue ribbon and the same amount of a pale white, using his own money to do so.

Returning to the campus, he cut the ribbons into foot-length pieces, which were later distributed: blue to a score of tough-minded faculty members, white to a selected group of graduate students whose job it would be to keep other students out of trouble. These would be the marshals for the rest of the weekend. In all, there were thirty-two of them to contain a crowd that would ultimately number more than 2,000.

'We then set up a command post . . . Can you imagine anything so preposterous on a college campus as a command post? We had it on the second floor of Administration and were supposed to call in and report any significant developments. As twilight approached we tied on our armbands and went forth to try to save the university.

'We did not visualize ourselves as extensions of the police. We were faculty members, and student leaders, and our job was to try to cool tempers, prevent extravagant acts, mediate between contending forces. I really couldn't summarize in words what we saw our job to be. I think you could say that we loved this institution and wanted desperately to see it survive what we knew was going to be a violent weekend.'

Among the people who got themselves blue armbands, signifying faculty status, was Steve Sharoff, whom we saw burying the United States Constitution and commanding his listeners that they must now work for its resurrection. His sudden appearance as a protector of law and order offended some, for they remembered that the vice-president for student affairs, Robert E. Matson, had brought a grave accusation against Sharoff: 'He was spotted by the highway patrol attending the secret meeting of the SDS control board in Akron.'

However, Louis Harris, vice-president for faculty affairs, had cleared Sharoff of this charge: 'On the evening when he was alleged to have attended the SDS meeting in Akron, he was in Kent working with me and Ombudsman Kitner.'

Kitner, gifted professor of art and the man charged with the ticklish job of handling complaints between faculty and administration, says flatly, 'I've had numerous contacts with Sharoff and have found him to be intelligent, responsible and dedicated to the best for this university. Ignore the gossip. He's a good man and you can rely on what he tells you.'

Frank says, 'Steve's driving compulsion was to be considered a member of the faculty. He fathomed himself a scholar and believed that if he was teaching students he ought to be in on decisions relating to them. I had heard about his sudden emergence as a student leader but had never met him until Saturday afternoon. When I saw him in the crowd of would-be marshals I thought of him as a student and was about to hand him a white band, but by some sudden movement he appropriated a blue one, and from that moment on he functioned as a full-fledged faculty member. He was invaluable. Everything he did was constructive, and when you get around to looking at what happened on Monday, you'll see that Steve Sharoff played a highly commendable role. He did the same on Saturday night.'

In this curious way, a man who had helped start the violent

weekend with his imaginative burial of the Constitution became an agency of its control. In this respect his actions were exactly contrary to those of the average student, who entered the weekend apathetic and emerged radicalized.

After Glenn Frank finished distributing the armbands, he went onto the campus and looked at the building he was supposed to defend. It was old and shabby and needed paint. It had been intended to serve as a temporary field hospital on some fever-stricken island in the South Pacific. Its location on the campus had been hastily determined, and at first no one bothered much about the totally inappropriate position it occupied because everyone knew it would be torn down as soon as something more substantial became available. When erected, it had had a probable life span of five years, for it was miserably constructed; the army had intended to use it briefly, then leave it behind as the war moved into new areas.

It should have been torn down twenty years ago, but had lingered on, and generations of students had cursed it as an eyesore on the campus and a pitiful place in which to study. Not long ago an instructor teaching an English class in the building had fallen through the floor. Fortunately, his legs straddled a beam and he was thus saved from what could have been a nasty accident.

What was the value of this antique? In subsequent weeks many citizens would recall the building as something rare and valuable, combining the best features of the Taj Mahal and the Parthenon. They would claim it was worth more than $100,000. It could have been worth as much as $5,000, but if money had been available, for a new and permanent building, the university would probably have had to pay twice that amount to get the old shack torn down.

As Professor Frank stood in its shadows, he found himself surrounded by people, many of them strangers, who were determined to save the university the trouble.

'Hooked into the revolution bit'

Paul Probius, one of the most powerful radicals enrolled at Kent State, asked that his right name not be used. 'I'm not ashamed of anything I've done, and I'm not afraid of going to jail. It's just that anything I say involves a lot of people and I don't want to muddy up whatever they're into.' With that apologia, he talked for seven hours in a bravura performance that left no doubt of his intellectual brilliance, his phenomenal memory and his complete dedication to the destruction of Kent State University. 'I work for the eventual overthrow of America's social and political systems as we know them,' he said forthrightly in his opening comment. In what follows, certain facts have had to be obscured to preserve his anonymity.

'I grew up in a mid-Ohio city where my father was a banker with a lot of collateral interests. He and my mother had met at Ohio State University, where they had been big in the fraternity thing . . . well, what you would have to call social leaders of the campus. I have an older brother and a sister who take after them.

'I went to good schools and did well. I've never had any of the big hatred-bit against my parents or my teachers and I still see both when I go home. But I don't go home much any more.'

He would be welcome at home, or almost anywhere else in America, for he is a congenial young man, not too tall, and very trim in appearance. He is clean and wears his hair short and his clothes pressed. The first suspicion you get that there is something quite different about him is the rapidity of his speech and the intense manner in which his eyes dart from one object to the next. It is easy to believe that he got good grades in school.

'How did I get hooked into the revolution bit? I simply looked around me in high school. I saw the whole stupid system for what it is . . . the phoniness, the lies, the corruption, the people working their lives away for nothing. And I decided right then that I was against it, that I hated it, and that I would do everything in my power to tear it down. And whenever I began to waver in my conviction, there was the Vietnam war to prove that my first interpretation had been right on.'

Did any of his high-school teachers encourage him in these revolutionary thoughts? 'Teachers? They were too stupid even to know what I was doing. They were pathetic. During my whole last year in school I kept my mouth shut and kept thinking, "Wait till I get to college." As soon as school was out I bummed around the country . . . met kids a little older who had it figured the way I did . . . talked, talked, talked . . . learned about social justice. And it was with those ideas that I came to Kent State.

'Now, in 1965 we had a guy on this campus who was frankly sensational. Howie Emmer. He was a short guy from Cleveland who wore a plaid shirt. But he had charisma he hadn't even used yet. This powerful kid could think . . . and speak . . . and argue with you. He understood society like none of the professors. A dozen times I've been sitting in the Student Union when things were sort of blah, and Howie would walk through the door and suddenly there was life . . . action. People would go up to him and ask what was cooking, and he would tell them. He always leveled with you. I'd say he was much more important on this campus than any of the professors. At any rate, he exercised more leadership.

'The only thing Howie had going for him in 1965 was a puny little committee with thirteen people. Kent Committee to End the War. Ruth Gibson, George Hoffman, a freshman named Bill Whittaker and a couple of us who had sort of agreed to listen to whatever Howie decided was important. He used to tell us that with the support of our committee he could change this whole university so nobody would recognize it.

'In 1967 Howie was real big in the New York peace march. It was held in April and I went along. I stood with Howie as we saw Martin Luther King and Harry Belafonte and Dr. Spock. You stood there with millions of people and realized that you were part of a movement, and it was going to change the face of America. Man, I came home ready to chew steel. Then there was the Washington march of November, 1967, which Howie and I attended, of course.'

Probius says that in 1968 Emmer hooked up with a sharp, lanky fellow named Rick Erickson, who was even more committed to total social change than Howie. 'From that moment on they were the team. The intellectual history of Kent State for the next two years was Howie and Rick. We've had some good professors and we've had some good movements, but the two people who counted were Howie and Rick. They were the university, because wherever they went, the university had to follow, trying to undo what they had done, reacting to their leadership.'

In May, 1968, Howie and Rick organized the big walk-out when Hubert Humphrey came to the campus. 'We decided to show Ohio what a mealy-mouthed fascist he was. We allowed him to say about two sentences, then we raised hell and left the hall. It was on television that night and helped start him on the downward path. We felt if we could elect

Nixon we'd get to the revolution that much sooner. The French student strike encouraged us enormously. We invited speakers to slip on campus quietly and tell us what the French bit meant, and we could see that it was close to us . . . very close to what we were attempting.'

At this time the Students for a Democratic Society started to become a big factor at Kent State. Organizers from the head offices in Chicago and Cleveland appeared on campus to talk over national programs and to tie the Kent operation into what the other chapters were doing elsewhere. Howie and Rick spent a good deal of their time putting together a hard-core cadre who could be trusted to work for revolutionary change in the social system and submit to intellectual discipline. Probius was one of the hard workers.

'We had five good planks going for us. At every public meeting we stressed them. We toured the dormitories night and day, arguing with students about them. Wherever we went we tried to find the liberal students and edge them over into the radical camp. And we tried to make the conservatives take wrong stands against us, so they'd look silly and alienate the middle students . . . drive the non-committed into our arms. What were our five planks?

'We were against the war in Vietnam. We were against ROTC. We were for whatever demands the black students might want to make, although we had no blacks in our leadership group. We insisted that the Northeast Ohio Crime Detection Center get off campus. And we kept protesting against Themis and its military experimentation at the Liquid Crystals Institute. I was in charge of keeping these ideas before the students, and at times I thought it was worthless, but Howie and Rick kept telling me that one of these days one of these planks would catch on and then even the squares would see we were right. When that happened, this campus would never be the same. Literature from headquarters started speaking of Kent as the battleground and it was widely understood that this school was going to go up first. We had a sensational girl named Joyce Cecora, who did a lot of our speaking for us, and she believed.'

During Christmas vacation of 1968 Paul Probius visited the University of Michigan at Ann Arbor and there met with SDS types from all parts of the country: 'There were Harvard men prepared to tear that university apart, and men from Stanford, and some fellows from Iowa who told us they had gained a foothold on that campus. It was even more exciting than the big peace march in New York, because Martin Luther King and Dr. Spock had been big men . . . older than us . . . they'd done their thing. But at Michigan it was young people of great dedication, determined to tear the universities down and build a better world. Howie Emmer knew what they were talking about and so did Rick Erickson.

But on the return to Kent State the movement split down the middle. 'Howie and Rick had become dedicated to direct action. I and some of the others believed in education, which was natural for me, seeing as how I had been in charge of the education wing. We spent the winter discussing the options before us in what we planned as our spring offensive. By some strong action we would radicalize the students and force the university to accede to our demands. Both factions agreed that SDS should do two things: mount a big education drive and take steps to isolate ROTC. But how to accomplish this? The direct-action crowd argued in behalf of a confrontation at Administration. My faction believed that we should wait for the Asian Affairs Conference and take it over with big publicity. We went through a real polarization, but by the beginning of April it was apparent that the direct-action people had won. I waited to see how their plan would work out.

'On April 8, 1969, Rick and Howie initiated the big effort. They got a large crowd together and tacked their petition on the door of the trustees' office. Before they knew it they were involved in an assault on the campus police, and this led to six arrests and the court injunction keeping them off campus. The university's determination to protect itself had proved much stronger than our leadership had anticipated. The big confrontation had not worked, and we were the big losers. I remember two aspects of this defeat most clearly. The big march around the campus did excite the non-committed students and did win some of them over to our side, but the invasion of classrooms by SDS leaders rushing in with pamphlets startled the professors and antagonized the students. It was a dreadful mistake, an action which lost us a lot of support. In the long run, I'd have to say that April 8 was a victory for the administration, a setback for SDS.'

When it looked as if the university had not only defended itself against SDS but had also destroyed it as a campus power, the vast confusion at Music and Speech erupted to revive the movement. Probius says, 'I almost missed the action. On April 16 Mark Real gave me a hurried telephone call, about thirty minutes before it began, and told me, "Get over there. They need you." We organized a great march from Administration to Music and Speech, where 200 jocks were waiting to beat us up. We made a tactical mistake by trying to force our way through them, because this backed them up against the wall and they had no escape but to fight back. Very stupid of us. Anyway, we broke into the building on one side, while the police were letting people in freely on the other. I didn't take part in prying open the third-floor door, but I approved of the kids who did the job. Ironically, it was my partner in non-violence, Jim Powrie, who was busted for hacking open the door. Got one to seven years in jail.

'It was weird. We gathered in this big hallway on the third floor and watched ourselves on television. A Cleveland station said that we had taken over the building, and there we were trying to get out. Two Cleveland reporters who were there broke into laughter. One of the strangest parts of the operation was Bob Pickett's role. The police sent him in to evacuate all the black students. "We want to keep race out of this," they explained, "because we have enough trouble as is," but when Pickett reached the third floor the blacks told him, "Get the hell out of here. We're in this to stay." Bob pleaded with them, almost with tears in his eyes, "Please get out of here. Blacks aren't prepared to fight this battle." In the end he persuaded them, and the blacks were quietly whisked away. I saw the police seek out two black girls, Tibi Heard and Pam Thomas, scared to death, and slip them out the door.'

SDS member Bill Whittaker went down on the last elevator that succeeded in getting people out. On its next trip it took Probius, Emmer and Erickson down, but before they could escape, the police moved in and made their arrests. Evidence against Probius was not conclusive and he did not go to jail; he did something more dramatic.

'Can you imagine?' he asks. 'On the weekend after Music and Speech, with all of our leaders either arrested or under indictment, we had the courage to hold a big regional meeting of the SDS leadership for Ohio and Michigan right here in Kent. We hid out at the Holiday Inn south of town and planned our next moves. Regional travelers from all over moved in to give us encouragement and ideas. We came out of it stronger than we had gone in. We were determined to close the university down, since it would not adjust to our demands for reconstruction.' At this clandestine meeting, plans were also drawn up for activities against other Ohio institutions, and Probius concluded that the dissident students at Ohio State and Ohio University would probably succeed in closing those universities down, too.

'How did I evaluate Music and Speech? We were all astounded that the university showed the ability to respond so rapidly and with such force. They did arrest us. They did drive us off campus. And yet at the moment of their apparent victory, SDS was about to have one of its greatest triumphs, because the student body was being radicalized, as we had planned. After Music and Speech, thousands of moderate students were willing to listen to us, and the big confrontation of May, 1970, was only a matter of time. We didn't know when the big blow-up would occur or why. But we were certain it was on the way.'

We can be fairly sure that Paul's analysis of the situation was accurate because an official SDS publication carried this summary:

The situation at this point in the struggle is very mixed. On the one hand, the repression has clearly hurt us: Over sixty of our people have been banned from the campus, at least eleven face heavy charges, with total bail exceeding $120,000, and the administration has succeeded to some extent in scaring a lot of people and obfuscating our original demands, allowing the civil-liberties whiz-kids to spring up.

On the other hand, SDS has made several key advances: We have fought hard, making it clear that we are serious and tough. We have constantly stressed the primacy of the four demands, maintaining that political repression is only an extension of the people's oppression, never getting hung up in civil-libertarian or pro-student privilege defenses of our actions. We have demonstrated tactical flexibility, using confrontations, rallies, dorm raps, wall posters. And we have clearly raised the political consciousness of almost the entire campus, winning over many new people, and making it possible to win over many more in the future.

And, of course, the struggle is not over. New leadership for the chapter is emerging with great rapidity. We're working on more elaborate explanations of the demands, getting back into the dorms, hitting back at the organizational suspension and raising money for the legal defenses.

—"War at Kent State,"
from *New Left Notes*, April 24, 1969

Music and Speech had one unexpected by-product. 'I found myself a traveling field agent for new communes which the Weatherman faction was setting up. Publicity over SDS at Kent State made anyone from our campus big news at other colleges, and Jeff Powell and I were invited to Mount Union College, very small, very strict, to address the student body. It was something. Police everywhere, deans watching us, a whole congregation of jocks eager to beat us up. I gave the best speech of my life, and in a beer-hall session afterwards signed up three perfectly straight students for the communes that summer. Bernardine Dohrn had explained them when she visited us and made them sound great.

'We established our communes in three Ohio cities, one in Columbus, two in Akron, two in Cleveland. The idea was to teach severe discipline. Every single decision—was a girl member entitled to buy an ice cream cone?—was decided by group discussion. The object was to produce revolutionaries programed to obey orders, even if they involved severe personal sacrifice or death. You surrendered all personal money, idiosyncrasies and will power, assured that you would come out of the experience with total dedication.'

The literature explaining the new communes was exciting. 'On university campuses, the battle that began in earnest at Columbia and in the streets of Chicago last summer is intensifying and deepening its roots in the American consciousness. The war is on. It will be a long war, a protracted war.' The report stigmatized SDS as 'isolated on elite university campuses' and challenged it to 'transform itself from a student movement into a working-class youth movement.' To achieve this end, each commune would stress three activities: work in the community—cabdrivers, waitresses, barmaids—at menial jobs if necessary, so as to get to know the working classes; study and research into revolutionary theory and the construction of a fall strategy, presumably for use when they returned to campus; organizing protests against pigs, or on behalf of black defendants, or for the enlistment of high school students 'who will be ready to move directly into SDS stuff on campus in the fall.'

Pamphlets gave ample warning that life in a commune might become difficult: 'Several significant tensions will probably develop during the course of the summer.' Areas suggested were: 'tension between collective life and political outreach into the community; tension between isolated elitism and group action; tension between three types of activity proposed.' (The greatest tension, the one that would wreck most of the communes, was not anticipated.) But if the members resisted the tensions and stuck to the program, the commune might become 'a major step forward in the development of a revolutionary youth movement in Ohio. All over the country young people are in motion. It remains for us to get into the struggles of the masses of people in America, and to learn from them the real meaning and possibility of revolution in America.'

Probius explains, 'Rick and Candy signed up, of course, so did Howie Emmer and a dear girl called Lorraine. I got several people interested and would have gone in myself except that my wife couldn't see herself in that situation. So the communes started. How did they end? We were at home one night in August—had just gone to bed—when a girl we had talked into joining the one in Columbus called us on the phone and said, "My God, drive over right away and get me out of here." It was from her that we first learned how horrible the experience had been. The thing she complained about most was the total lack of privacy. "I had to ask group permission even to go upstairs to read a book. I'm a private sort of person, but was never allowed to be alone. I broke under the pressure."'

Rick and Candy lasted a week longer, then they had to break out, too. 'They met their moment of truth in mid-August when the leadership of the movement handed down the famous dictum: "Smash monogamy." This meant that husbands and wives, or sweethearts who were getting too addicted to each other, had to split up. The idea was that if a man became too attached to a woman, it might impede his judgment if he were ordered to perform some dangerous task or involve him too deeply if he saw his girl being sent off on a mission from which she might not return. So the edict went out: "Smash monogamy." That's when the phrase became popular, "I'm prepared to make the ultimate sacrifice." This meant that as a husband, you were prepared to turn your wife over to the guy next door. Scores of couples found no difficulty in this, and there was a lot of on-the-minute change of partners. But Rick and Candy found themselves incapable of making the "ultimate sacrifice." So they just quit their commune. So did Howie and Lorraine. So did several other couples I'd helped enroll. "Smash monogamy" was the rock on which the communes split. The weak were weeded out, but those who could adjust to this new concept of group living came out of it much stronger revolutionaries than they were when they went in. Because now they had no sentimental attachments which might hold them back if they were directed to dynamite this building or blow up that police station.'

Probius says sadly that the Joan of Arc of the Kent movement was also lost. 'Joyce Cecora pretty much took over the leadership of SDS when the others went to jail, and she was planning an ambitious program of keeping pressure on the university, but it came to nothing, because one day near the end of the spring quarter her father drove down from Cleveland and made her come home.' Probius was now pretty much alone, and it would be appropriate to inspect him a little more closely.

What does he believe? That the present system of politics, economics and society in the United States is doomed and that men of intelligence are obligated to see that its demise comes as swiftly as possible. When asked for proof of our nation's incapacity to survive he points to 'Vietnam, and our treatment of minorities. Corruption, and our indifference to ecology.'

What are his values? 'I reject totally and without qualification everything my father stands for. I do not want to gear my life to the making of money. I do not want to get ahead. I do not want to occupy a prominent place in his society. I do not have his sense of patriotism toward a nation that cannot behave decently. I do not believe in the military, or the Republican party, or the First National Bank, or Rotary International, or football games at Ohio State. What values do I subscribe to? Brotherhood of peoples, brotherhood of nations. Working at a job which reaches you as a human being. I believe in love between people. And I believe that we can achieve a better society than the one we have now. Yes, and I also believe in education. I think a man ought to read and listen to music and philosophize. Above all, he ought to do his own thing, and if he wants to wear a beard, or dress like the early American heroes, he should be encouraged to do so.' It is the conviction that American society will not allow him to live by these values that has made him a radical.

Is he a revolutionary? This question must be answered in two ways. Thus far he has avoided any overt action which would lead to the overthrow of our government. He has never technically been a Weatherman, and his whole history at Kent—propaganda to win converts as opposed to terrorism which might alienate them—proves that he will probably never become one. But he is a revolutionary in the sense that he gives moral encouragement to those who feel that violence is the only solution. Also, he anticipates revolutionary action in the streets and counter-revolutionary action to suppress it. He feels no compunction about supporting blacks who preach 'Kill the pigs' because he feels that the police are subservient to the establishment and will sooner or later have to be removed. This question can therefore best be answered by asking two others. Has Paul Probius so far done anything criminal for which he could be arrested? No. Has he done anything for which he should be expelled from the university? Yes, he has tried to destroy it.

What is his attitude toward the university? He sees Kent State as a craven servant of the establishment, a factory committed to turning out replacements for big business, the military, corrupt political systems. He considers its professors paid lackeys without character or knowledge, in the Marxist sense. And he thinks that the many universities that carry on research work for the military could properly be bombed. He is totally committed to tearing down Kent State, for he can see it accomplishing no good end. In its place he would like to see some kind of people's college. In the meantime, he will avail himself of whatever it has to offer; indeed, he will probably continue at Kent till he gets his Ph.D., and might then consider a teaching job, to spur the revolution. During periods when his SDS obligations have been strenuous he has registered for one course a semester, in basket-weaving, which he attends one day a week; he does this in order to qualify for full student rights, and they allow him to move about the campus as he wishes.

What is his attitude on sexual morality? Surprisingly, he follows the behavior of his mother and father. When a senior, he married the daughter of a Cleveland doctor; his wife is more radical than he, and they serve more or less as the parents for a large group of other young people who plan never to marry. They were acquainted with communes, where sex was remarkably free, but preferred each other. They feel no concern over what other students do, nor how they care to live. It is doubtful that either Probius or his wife would cheat in an examination, but they would surely provide refuge and get-away money for anyone who decided to dynamite a building.

What is his attitude toward drugs? In long hours of conversation, drugs were never once mentioned, not because Probius and his wife frown upon them, but because drugs are no longer of sufficient importance to discuss. It was assumed that any Kent student who wanted marijuana or mescaline would get it as easily as he would get a quart of milk. For one two-year period, LSD was not much used, but now it is coming back. A few students have escalated to heroin, but most dropped it quickly. As another radical student said, 'The only problem with heroin is that the pushers are always trying to unload it on you: "Want a real sniff, kid? Take one on me." I get offered heroin every damned time I buy grass.'

What are his thoughts on international relations? Probius has acquired a series of clearly defined attitudes, picked up from left-wing journals and speeches. 'The most corrupting force in the world today is America, and if it cannot be halted in its foreign aggressions by reason, it must be immobilized by action in the streets. The Vietcong must be supported in every way until they win a total victory, drive us out of Asia and unite the whole country under their rule. Bigger than Vietnam, however, is the problem of Israel; the Arab guerrillas must be supported until they build up the power to liquidate Israel completely. South Africa must be exterminated. But fundamental to everything, in the power struggle under way in the world today, it is obligatory that Red China be protected against the pressures from the American–Russian coalition.' If you ask Probius which country in the world today commands the respect of most radical students, he says, 'Red China.'

How does he see the immediate future? 'Kent State is existing right now only because it's propped up, and we're going to keep the pressure on until it folds. Wisconsin can't last much longer. We think Harvard and Columbia have got to go down, and probably Michigan and Ohio State. The movement is spreading down into high schools, and every freshman class is going to bring us new recruits.' On the national scene he expects that by the summer of 1972 President Nixon will be in exactly the position that Johnson was in 1968. 'He won't be able to appear in public and won't dare to attend the convention of his own party.' After a debacle of some kind in 1972, with George Wallace getting a lot of votes, things will go on pretty much as before, 'but every day the present society operates, it brings itself nearer to collapse.'

How does he see his own future? 'Well, I'm married, so I expect to be around for some time. My father's stopped my allowance, but my wife works and gets some money from her folks, so we get by. I'm more convinced than ever that the whole structure has got to come down, and most of my friends with intelligence feel the same way. I doubt that I will ever do anything that will force me to go underground, but I do expect to spend the rest of my life fighting the system in every way possible. And, of course, I wouldn't rule out the possibility that society, by some self-defensive trick or other, will force fellows like me to take stands which will drive us underground. If things degenerate to that point, I couldn't care less about my personal position.'

Does he fear the hard-hat counter-revolution? 'Not a bit. It's bound to come and will probably cost a lot of lives, but it's needed to radicalize the rest of the nation. It may persist for a long time, but its conclusion can only be what I've been talking about. The old things are going to collapse. The universities, the armies, the churches, the patterns of marriage . . . everything is going down. You will never seduce this generation, or the ones to follow, back to the worn-out values. This year it was the dead at Kent State who radicalized the middle-of-the-roaders. Next year it'll be something else. I expect to be in this movement for as long as I live, and I expect to see it triumph.'

One of the happiest periods of his life, Probius says, 'was that autumn when I worked with Rick Erickson and Candy at the Haunted House. In the afternoons we had interminable discussions under the trees, outlining the various attacks we could make on university complacency. It was a time of high discussion and vast ideas. When night came we'd go inside, and my idea of home is the way Candy had that apartment arranged at the beginning. You know, she had original Chagalls on the walls, and some great color reproductions of Matisse and Picasso. I think she had gone to Vassar, but somewhere she'd picked up a beautiful idea of what a home ought to be. One room nothing but a huge, lovely carpet, some easy chairs and a great stereo set with the best music. The bathroom was an art gallery by itself. The food was good. The refrigerator always had cold beer. And the talk was even better than it had been outside.' Probius frowns. 'Of course, it all ended when the others began to move in. First came Howie Emmer. Then they kind of adopted a girl named Jill. Then a whole flood. Candy told me one day, "It's sort of sickening. You get up in the morning and find these bodies lying all over the place, and they never pick up anything or contribute anything to the refrigerator to replace what they've taken." The trouble was, as I saw it, poor Candy had to do all the work to keep the place functioning. Rick was big on ideas and politics, but Candy found herself a domestic slave. The rug went first, splashed to hell. Then the stereo was busted. The bathroom was a shambles, with twenty or thirty kids using it some nights. And the whole beautiful place fell apart. If you spoke to Rick about it, he said, "These kids are being persecuted by society. They have to crash somewhere." Trouble was, in crashing at Rick's, they destroyed the lovely thing Candy had created. In the end she didn't even bother to try to keep the place cleaned up. It became one huge filthy dormitory, with the powerful figures of youthful revolution using it as their way station when they passed from Chicago to Columbia or from Harvard to Michigan. Camelot was lost.'

Just how does a sophisticated radical like Probius view the Friday riots? 'Completely insignificant. Of no weight whatever. There was no plan, no slogans, nothing to capitalize upon. I'm told that Rick Erickson and George Gibeaut were seen on Water Street early in the evening, celebrating their release from jail, but you can be sure they got out fast, because there was nothing to be gained. I don't think Cambodia exerted a shred of influence on that riot. It was a bunch of drunks . . . the usual spring thing. But I do believe something was started there that we can build on—maybe something very powerful, because the police were called out and there was a confrontation.'

Like the blacks, who were not often seen during the four days of May, Paul Probius and his immediate cronies stayed away from the campus troubles. They sensed that something so big was afoot, it required neither impetus nor guidance from them. Rigorous search by various agencies has failed to uncover any evidence proving that Howie Emmer, Rick Erickson, Paul Probius or any of the other original SDS leaders engineered or participated in the riots; these men had been effectively neutralized by a determined administration. However, a younger group and less conspicuous had arisen on campus to take their place, and there is much evidence showing that these people, lifting their ideas from SDS, were operating this weekend with conscious plans to burn ROTC, confront the National Guard, and keep alive the demonstrations that would lead to the death of four students. That they were abetted by older revolutionaries, some not connected with the campus, will become apparent.

The young revolutionaries

We now have enough general information to grapple with four perplexing questions.

Was the SDS committed to closing down the university? Certainly the national organization was determined to confront all American universities. Proof of this came from an unexpected source. In the autumn 1969 issue of the *American Scholar,* a quarterly published by Phi Beta Kappa, Michael Kazin, who described himself as 'a senior at Harvard University and active in SDS,' reported as follows in a long, prideful article on the achievements of his organization:

> SDS chapters have been confronted with the responsibility of building white support actions for the black demands in question and of educating the campus about the connection between the particular demands and the radical movement's analysis of the larger society. At schools like Columbia and Kent State University in Ohio, SDS initiated action that has successfully curbed racist actions (at Kent State, SDS stopped recruiting by the Oakland, California, police department, and at Columbia, the infamous gymnasium was the issue). The virulent repression visited recently on the Black Panther Party and on other revolutionary forces in the black movement has brought in turn a new seriousness of purpose and determined maturity to the work of most SDS members.

> SDS had become an organization of self-consciously *revolutionary* students and ex-students. Debating policy resolutions and programmatic suggestions at the national convention that year were more than one thousand young Marxists of widely varying schools of thought, all attempting to apply the methodology of class analysis to the 'objective reality' of the world's most advanced capitalist society. Furthermore, there were few candidates for national office who did not define themselves as 'revolutionary communists' when queried about their politics.

> The general SDS strategy is geared toward the development of a revolutionary youth movement, since young people are judged to be more aware of the social contradictions of American capitalism at this period in history and are thus the group that is taking militant action in cities and schools across the country.

Kazin included comment on the 'sharp rise in the number of wildcat strikes, protests and disruptions at working-class high schools throughout the country' and announced that SDS organizers 'are working with radical students in high schools.'

The specific relationship of SDS to Kent State is spelled out in a series of remarkable documents written, published and circulated by the regional travelers whose territory included Kent. Non-students like Terry Robbins and Lisa Meisel made no secret of their determination to wage war against the university until it surrendered to their demands or shut up shop. One of the most instructive broadsides opened with a quote from an educational leader in whom the regional travelers placed much confidence:

> *Historically, all reactionary forces on the verge of extinction invariably conduct a last desperate struggle against the revolutionary forces, and some revolutionary forces are apt to be deluded for a time by this phenomenon of outward strength but inner weakness, failing to grasp the essential fact that the enemy is nearing extinction while they themselves are approaching victory.*
>
> —*Chairman Mao Tse-tung*

The war is on at Kent State University. Two weeks of intense struggle have seen the SDS lead several major actions, rallies marches, and raise the political consciousness of thousands on the campus, while the pig-thug adminstration has responded with swift and heavy repression.

Kent State is part of the spidery web of institutions which are currently developing sophisticated weaponry to be used against people's struggles for their freedom. Liquid crystals are extremely sensitive to heat, and are used in devices to detect campfires in jungle areas and in some cases to detect body heat at long range. (The 'sniffer' is currently used in Vietnam and a similar device was used in Bolivia to find and kill Che Guevara.) A struggle has begun and will continue on Kent's campus—the development of liquid crystals must be stopped.

Jim Mellen—an 'outside agitator' down for the week—addressed the crowd. 'We're no longer asking you to come and help us make a revolution. We're telling you that the revolution has begun, and the only choice you have to make is which side you're on. And we're also telling you that if you get in the way of the revolution, it's going to run right over you.'

Most important of all, through struggle, we have made it absolutely clear that the war being waged in Vietnam, in Guatemala, in the black colony in America, will be fought as well at Kent State University.

—"War at Kent State"

Joyce Cecora, the firebrand of the SDS movement, had not been hesitant about stating publicly, on February 27, 1969, 'that if the university does not stop politically repressing SDS they would burn and level the campus.' Later, on May 6, 1969, she appeared at another meeting.

Joyce Cecora, SDS member, speaking to the approximately 200 persons sitting under the searing post-noon sun called for the use of arms to end what she called the 'repressive actions of the administration.' 'Sitting on the grass in front of the Administration Building is not fighting!' she emphasized. 'They used guns at Cornell, and they got what they wanted,' she said. 'It will come to that here!'

—Committee Hearings, 1969

On April 28, 1969, she had delivered one of her fieriest speeches, appearing just before Bernardine Dohrn addressed the Kent student body.

The initial speaker at the meeting was Joyce Cecora. She spoke on repression and suppression of the American working class, which she described as being subjected to the imperialistic society. I might add that during the course of her address she was very adept at numerous obscenities, and some obscenities that are quite shocking to hear young ladies say.

—Neil Wetterman,
Investigator for Committee on Internal Security
United States House of Representatives

Rick Skirvin was the next speaker. He also came into the discussion of the revolutionary action and obtaining their aims by either peace or the violent aspect. He stated that at the time— well, first he stated that there could be no obtaining of their aims through peace. It had to be through force, and definitely there would be a revenge aspect involved. He said at the time he was confined in the Portage County jail he had one obsession, and that was 'to take a machine gun and kill every bastard there.' And that is his exact quote.

—Neil Wetterman

It was left to Skirvin to summarize in brief, powerful form

the thoughts that at this period interested the hard-core enemies of the university: 'We'll start blowing up buildings, we'll start buying guns, we'll do anything to bring this motherfucker down.' An unidentified speaker, but definitely not a student at Kent State, told the local SDS leaders, 'It is important out of this meeting comes a real sense of militancy and determination to act immediately, because like now the initiative is ours and I would like to see us go over and take this campus by storm.'

In our desire to represent Paul Probius fairly, we read our report of his interview to him, and he took vigorous exception to the sentence 'He wanted to close down the university,' insisting that we add the clarifying phrase 'as it then existed.' By this he meant that if Kent State accepted the reforms demanded by SDS, it would be allowed to function, but if it stubbornly continued to serve as a slave of the establishment, training its workmen, indoctrinating its teachers and doing the dirty work of the military, it would have to be shut down. Since there seemed small likelihood that Kent would conform to the SDS demands, its demise was imminent, but if this happened, the fault would lie with the university and not with SDS.

Why did these things happen at Kent rather than somewhere else? National leaders of the revolutionary movement had for some time appreciated the fact that if the educational system of a normal, unspectacular state like Ohio could be brought down, the propaganda value would be enormous and the reverberations nationwide. Radical triumphs in likely places such as California and New York had been depreciated, but to succeed in bucolic Ohio would constitute a significant victory. Starting as early as 1965 radical leaders gave Ohio special attention; there are numerous instances in which knowing visitors predicted that 'things might very well explode here first of all.' The choice of Ohio, with its sixty-four major universities and colleges, was no accident.

Within Ohio, the reasons for selecting Kent were the same as those for selecting the state in the first place. It was big; it was wonderfully average; if it could be brought down, people would realize that 'it could happen anywhere.' There is no evidence that Kent was accorded any special treatment; to the contrary, most believed that Ohio State would crumble first, or Ohio University. But pressure was maintained on Kent on the off chance that something might explode.

But in addition to large philosophical concepts, there was also the impact of personality. Bernardine Dohrn had been educated in Ohio, and she appreciated the peculiar structure of the state, with its outward propriety and inner revolt. She knew that the labor agitations dating back to 1880 and continuing through the depression had insured the propagation of revolutionary ideas. Grandchildren of the radical leadership of those times would provide a cadre to work with, and this made Ohio an attractive target for the SDS leadership.

The reason Kent was struck so hard stems from another of those irrational accidents that seemed to plague this university. Back in 1965, when Howie Emmer and Paul Probius were first establishing their contacts with the SDS, the national president of the organization happened to be Carl Oglesby, thirty years old, tall, with a beard, soft-spoken and unusually gifted with words. He'd had a play produced by the Margo Jones Theater in Dallas, another optioned for Broadway. He'd written a novel and had a mature insight into student problems. He wore thin-rimmed tortoise-shell glasses and had an attractive brush of hair which drooped over his right eye. He looked like any of a dozen young English novelists, but his specialty was student revolt against universities and the society which supported them.

SDS nationally was then a struggling movement, its philosophy well defined but its operating principles insecure. It had started in 1960 as the student branch of the old League for Industrial Democracy, which had been founded in 1905 by a group of thoughtful men like Upton Sinclair, Jack London and Clarence Darrow. In its first two years it got nowhere.

Then, in 1962, at an old-time CIO summer camp at Port Huron, Michigan, forty-three young intellectuals met to study a sixty-three-page provisional statement of principles drawn up by a self-contained, triangular-faced student from the University of Michigan. Tom Hayden's *Port Huron Statement* was adopted as the bible of a movement that was to sweep the nation and harass great universities like Columbia and Harvard.

The statement appealed to young activists because it presented a total view of their society: all the things they disliked were shown to be interacting—the war, the bomb, the military, ROTC on campus, the corruption of the universities, the unfair treatment of blacks, poverty, politics—so that the student was for the first time invited to tear this whole structure down and rebuild it on some better pattern. An attractive feature of the *Port Huron Satement* was its freedom from organization, cant, orthodoxy and severe systems of control. Unlike the Communist party, if you wanted to join, you simply joined. If you could pay the dues of $5 a year, you were encouraged to do so, but not many did. And instead of the long period of indoctrination required by communism, the SDS preached action now.

Also, at the same convention which adopted the *Port Huron Statement,* restrictions against communist membership were dropped, so that henceforth the SDS became the gathering place for leftists of all persuasions: anarchists, syndicalists, populists, Maoists, Trotskyites, plus well-intentioned old-fashioned liberals.

What has Oglesby to do with Kent State? Why should his advancement to the presidency of SDS have constituted a warning signal? For one thing, he was born in Akron, where his father worked in one of the rubber factories. He was thus a fellow townsman of Rick Erickson. More important, in 1953 he had enrolled at Kent State University, had disliked it because it was not then involved in the agitation that was enmeshing students in more lively universities, and had dropped out. Later he returned to Kent State, met a girl he liked, and got married. But again he dropped out. Obviously, he remembered Kent.

The powerful personality of Howie Emmer also encouraged a speed-up of campus friction, for at every moment when the movement seemed about to perish for lack of steam, he moved in to exert a dynamic leadership which kept it functioning. He remains an enigmatic young man. Observed one night at Orville's in the company of his jail associate, Colin Neiburger, he looked like a clean-cut, intense young man who had flunked his senior year because of lack of attention and was now back on campus to clean up a few missing credits. He was alert, very quick to catch on when someone spoke, and willing to laugh at jokes directed at himself. He had a conspicuously large mouth and penetrating eyes. He wore, of course, the plaid shirt which had become his trademark. He seemed definitely above average in intelligence, but looked as if he could be mean if anyone crossed him. He talked easily and always made sense. It was obvious that people around him considered him a leader.

Howie has an interesting background. At a Congressional hearing, the following colloquy took place.

MR. ASHBROOK. In trying to ascertain the degree of involvement of SDS throughout the country, there are some names that keep coming up. There were two names you mentioned that have been before us in another capacity. I have been sitting here trying to think. Lencl and Emmer ring a bell. Have they formerly been cited before this committee?

MR. WETTERMAN. Mr. Ashbrook, in 1961, I was assigned to investigate the activities of the Communist Party in the Cleveland, Ohio, area. In June of 1962 we had hearings before the predecessor committee on that subject matter, and as I recall you were on the dais at that time. Our witness was a Mrs. Julia Brown from Cleveland, Ohio. During the course of that hearing she identified a Ruth and Jack Emmer as being members of the Communist Party. As soon as I heard the name Howie Emmer, I further investigated and ascertained that he is the son of the Ruth and Jack Emmer. In addition, the name Mark Lencl, who was very familiar to me—the name Lencl is familiar—on further investigation I ascertained that he is the son of the Ruth Lencl, who also was identified as a member of the Communist Party in that same hearing.

Certainly the presence of one dedicated leader like Emmer could draw down the lightning of civil disturbance when otherwise it might have passed by.

Thus, without too many people being aware of it, Kent State had in its background Carl Oglesby and Bernardine Dohrn, two determined antagonists, who were aided on the scene by Howie Emmer and Rick Erickson. It was this combination of circumstances that made Kent State so attractive a target.

Are all American universities in danger? There is good evidence that the average university is becoming adept at handling crises that evolve naturally from the nature of academic life. If the general student body seeks curriculum changes or different dormitory hours, ways have been devised for tackling the problem. If blacks insist upon a segment of the university for their own, to experiment with as they wish, even this profound alteration can be dealt with. But there has developed recently a much different kind of confrontation, and its intrusion into university life threatens the entire academic structure, for universities are not equipped to handle this new type of disruption, nor should they be asked to do so.

Nothing better illustrates the cleverness with which SDS was able to attack a university on matters over which it exercised no control than two incidents which Paul Probius helped ignite and keep ablaze. We have seen how, on November 13, 1968, white students had grabbed hold of a black complaint—the visit of the Oakland police to the Kent Law Enforcement Training Program—and had come close to shutting down the university. How was this possible?

It so happened that the Black Panther Minister for Defense, Huey Newton, had been arrested in Oakland, California, charged with first-degree murder. The SDS had seen a chance to enroll black students in a protest not against the university but against the Oakland police department as 'pigs who had persecuted Huey.' Probius and his group plastered the city of Kent with *Free Huey* signs, and when it appeared that trouble might get out of hand, the Oakland police were asked to leave without completing their work. Thus the university found itself embroiled in a race agitation for which it was not responsible and which it could scarcely have anticipated or avoided.

In some ways the second assault was even more adroit, for now the reasoning behind it was more oblique and the university more in the dark and therefore less able to defend itself. For some time Kent State had sponsored a Liquid Crystals Institute under the direction of a world-famous authority on that subject, Dr. Glenn H. Brown, whose interest lay in the general development and utilization of liquid crystals, 'an intermediate state of matter between the liquid and the solid, with the flow properties of the former and the optical properties of the latter.' It was widely hoped the liquid crystals would prove effective in the detection of cancer. The Department of Defense, through its Themis Project, expressed an interest in the Kent institute and offered a small research grant; work done under this grant occupied only a small percentage of the institute's time or resources. Yet suddenly there was a great outcry against it, accompanied by threats that its building would be blown up. Why?

Someone at SDS headquarters in Chicago had read a story, largely fanciful, that liquid crystals were used in the manufacture of temperature detectors so sensitive that they could pick up body heat some distance away; such detectors were believed to have been used to track down Che Guevara, the revolutionary out of Castro's Cuba, who was endeavoring to overthrow the government of Bolivia. A beautiful female spy, so the story went, hid liquid-crystal detectors in Che's pocket, enabling federal troops to track him down in the jungle. Since Guevara had become a hero of the SDS, liquid crystals must go, and again the university was enmeshed in a near-riot which it could not in any way logically have anticipated.

The irony of the whole affair was well expressed by Professor Martin Nurmi, a quiet, conservative man from the English department: 'One of the saddest aspects of the student rebellion was the fracas over liquid crystals. Because some propagandist linked crystals with their big hero, Che Guevara, they felt they had to close down the institute. If the rumor had been correct, this would have been unfair to the university, but I looked into the matter and found the rumor to be preposterous. If they wanted to track down Che Guevara by detecting liquid crystals hidden in his clothes, you'd have to stand so near him that you could hit him with a baseball bat.'

In one crucial comment Probius said, 'We work and wait. On the Liquid Crystals Institute, we were able to enlist only the people who loved Che Guevara and wanted revenge for his death. Not many. On the Oakland police, we were able to get only the blacks. Not many. Vietnam is a dying issue. We simply couldn't pump more life into it because, frankly, the kids were bored. And the black civil-rights thing was not good because the riots in the big cities and the speeches of the Black Panthers had alienated too many. So all we had to work on was ROTC, and that turned out to be the big issue on which we got the support of nearly the entire student body. But even then we couldn't have got it off the ground if President Nixon hadn't moved into Cambodia. We had been dead, and suddenly we were alive. We were eight or ten people working in the dark, and suddenly we had eight or ten thousand with us.'

It seems probable that any university in the United States can be closed down if it harbors as few as eight committed students, assisted by younger faculty members of similar persuasion, who are determined to wreck the place. They cannot do this at the moment of their own choosing; they must wait for an accident which makes it possible for them to excite the sympathies of a large percentage of the student body, using such students as the spearhead for their assault. In most universities, such cadres already exist, waiting for the eruption of some popular cause to inflame the mass of the student body. When the upheaval comes, the small group will be prepared to initiate extreme measures to keep it boiling and to produce the sort of confrontation which will enrage the great middle group of students and radicalize them.

The American university is, therefore, in substantial peril, because it nurtures in its bosom persons dedicated to its destruction. It is doubtful if the university can speedily build up enough antibodies prepared to defend it against those who have announced their determination to destroy it. If even one of the hard core is willing to dynamite a building, explode a grenade in a crowded place or shoot from a rooftop, he alone can close down the whole university.

Do some members of the faculty participate in this attack on the university? One of the most difficult problems relating to advanced education today is the unraveling of charges of revolutionary activity made against the younger teaching staff. Depressing dossiers can be constructed on certain instructors who have jumped from California to Massachusetts to the Midwest, sowing discord wherever they landed, and one is not in Kent for long before he hears of the nefarious influence exerted on young minds by certain teachers of this type.

When we started our work we were not concerned with this matter, and never did we ask any student, 'What did you think of Professor Blank?'—for this was neither our duty nor our right. But inevitably students volunteered information that this instructor had been a positive influence for intellectual enlightenment and that one a mere propagandist. After scores of interviews, central tendencies began to appear with such clarity that no one familiar with university life could miss them.

Certain of the younger staff were so universally commended by students of all political persuasions for having 'broken open our minds and made us reconsider our preoccupations' that they emerged as precisely the kind of teachers a university ought to sponsor. True, there were occasional students who found the questions of these provocative young scholars disturbing, but one suspected that they might have been distressed by any incursion of ideas. Academic freedom means providing a home and security for young instructors who can produce as handsomely as these.

Like all universities, Kent State had another group of teachers—usually not regular members of the faculty—who seemed to be following personal prejudices rather than scholarly conclusions, and some of these appear to have had a devastating effect on their students, and an even greater one on the university within which they existed. There can be no doubt that some of them intended to close down the place, and that others were so totally alienated from contemporary American society, they were unable to criticize it constructively.

The former presidents of Brandeis, Duke, Columbia and Cornell, the former chancellor of California, and current administrators across the nation can testify to the power of the unaffiliated young instructor who owes allegiance to nothing but himself and who sets out to tear down the academic system he has inherited. In recent years these young revolutionaries have acquired too much leverage; they should either work within the system and accept responsibility for changing it according to the traditions of education, or they should resign to pursue their revolution by other means. Kent State had a much smaller percentage of such disaffected teachers than the five schools mentioned at the head of this paragraph, but it had its quota.

Jocks, Greeks and other squares

Anyone writing of an American university today finds himself in the predicament John Milton faced when writing *Paradise Lost:* against his will he is making the devil more attractive than the angels. Thus it may seem that this book is dominated by the radicals with their enticing theories and bravura style. Residents of the Haunted House get more attention than those plodding students who are concerned with a traditional education. But since it was the former who triggered the action at Kent State, it is inescapable that they appear front stage during most of the drama. Also, it is essential that we assess their motives and capabilities.

But the overwhelming majority of Kent students were straight; cynics, seeing no hope for moving this huge residue of suitcase scholars from dead center, called them squares and their university Apathy U. They were better than that; they were well-behaved young people, concerned but in no way radical.

Of the traditional-type student, the crowd at Delta Upsilon was representative. The D.U. house, like that of all the fraternities at Kent, was a ramshackle affair on East Main. It looked awful, with dirty peeling paint, unkempt lawn, Greek letters that needed painting, and dark inadequate rooms. One of the miracles of Kent was why anyone in his right mind would pay good money to live in one of the fraternity houses when he could, for less, live in one of the bright, clean new dormitories.

'There's a story about that,' Bob Perko, president of D.U., explains. 'We haven't put any money into keeping this old house in repair because we set aside our funds to build a new one. A local real estate wizard had a nice piece of land next to the university, and he proposed to build a dozen fraternity houses with dormitory facilities for about $300,000 each. Two sororities sold their old houses and a lot of the fraternities coughed up a down payment of $5,000 each for architect's fees. When plans were completed, they looked great. At last Kent would have a beautiful Greek Row. But when the time came to finance the operation, banks said, "Fraternities are on the downswing and this is a lousy risk," so the plan collapsed. There went the money. There went the houses. But a lot of fraternities have some great architectural drawings.'

The men of Delta Upsilon—sixty actives, fourteen residents—are a good bunch. They look much the way collegians of 1950 looked, except that their dress is markedly sloppier. Their hair is not overlong; their teeth are even and white; they like beer; they are big on dating; they go out for the athletic teams. In other words, like millions of college students before them, the D.U.'s of Kent State follow the old life style.

But there the resemblance ends. If any reader believes that the modern problems of the university can be solved merely by getting rid of the new-style people, he is badly advised. From a series of meetings with fraternities and sororities— Delta Upsilon, Sigma Alpha Epsilon, Gamma Beta Phi, Delta Zeta—we see that many of the straight students share the attitudes of the new-style people.

They oppose the war in Vietnam, and are as outspoken in their criticism of it as any radical. They see it as a fruitless adventure having little or nothing to do with American interests.

They oppose the draft, and it is not uncommon for a fraternity man to ask a stranger, 'Do you think there would be any chance of my escaping into Canada? Would I have to face a jail term if I ever came back?'

The girls are especially worried about the swift depletion of our natural resources and believe that the federal and state governments must do something about this right now. Many speak of looking for jobs in work that relates to ecological decisions.

The men are not eager to find positions in large corporations, and although some say that after law school or business training they would consider such jobs, most appear to be looking for work that would be personally more fulfilling and rewarding.

All of them like the new music, the new art, the new attitude toward women, and they are not going to revert to the tastes of their parents. In other words, they do not reject the new life style completely, nor do they feel themselves opposed to those who practice it. 'If it's their thing, let them have a go at it,' is the general attitude.

Some of them are just as much at odds with their parents as the new-style people are with theirs, and they appear to find it as difficult to conduct meaningful discussions with them. They reject quite strongly the life-goals and opinions of their parents, but they seem to retain a closer relationship —apart from the field of ideas—with their parents than do the more radical students.

They do not, as they talk, sound like Republicans, and whereas in later years they will probably vote Republican, it will be for a liberal Republicanism. At present they are bitterly opposed to many government policies and scorn the palpable weaknesses and contradictions of all political parties. No one could term them radical, but they are certainly not conservatives of the old stamp.

They can be very critical of the college administration, and it is not uncommon to hear them growl, 'This university really screwed things up.' They want more say in setting up curricula, more part in establishing the goals of education. They are more temperate in their demands than the blacks, for example, but not less insistent. One frequently hears a Greek concede, 'The blacks may have a point there.'

They cannot accept adult society's morbid fear of marijuana. LSD and heroin, yes. Those drugs are too serious to play around with, but marijuana is so commonly used on campus and with such little apparent effect that the fraternity men and sorority women cannot believe the stories about it, and when local judges hand down sentences of twenty to thirty years for drug cases, they are appalled.

They are for change in almost all fields of endeavor. They find no satisfaction in a mechanistic society and do not visualize their lives as a search for a safe haven in the machine age. They are not great brains, sitting around the fraternity house devising bold new patterns of life, but they are not afraid of the conclusions of men who do dream of better ways of doing things.

Finally, they are young people who will be deeply moved by the events of this weekend, for they will find themselves aligned with students and against the National Guard. They will not commit arson, nor throw rocks, nor encourage those who do. But they will stand aghast at what they see happening to their campus and they will retreat with disgust when the police fire tear gas, for no apparent reason, at the fraternity houses, 'just because they're filled with college kids.' And when the long weekend is over and the D.U.'s witness the indecent gesture that will be visited upon the Sigma Chi house a few doors away, they will be revolted.

Bob Perko, the D.U., twenty-one years old, is from Mentor, Ohio, standing six feet and weighing a well-proportioned 170 pounds. He gets good grades in his major, political science, and could well exemplify the fraternity man. The nature of his involvement in what had been happening at Kent State over the past two years indicates the way many of his friends were reacting, too.

'I heard there was going to be this big riot by the freaks at Music and Speech, so I went along to see what might happen. It was a nice day, sort of quiet in the afternoon, when here comes this huge crowd waving flags and shouting. It was obvious they were determined to break into the building, so a group of straight fellows formed a block to prevent them from getting to the doors. Not all Greeks, as the stories said. Just a good cross section of the average student body. And it was certainly not a riot.

'They came at us shouting, "Pigs off campus!" and we yelled back, "SDS go home." There was a scuffle for about fifteen minutes and not a tooth was lost. I've seen better fights in grade school. After it was all over I read in their radical papers how they had gallantly fought off 300 jocks. The real jocks were having football practice. If they'd been there, it would have been a massacre. Anyway, we were stopped by the faculty, and the freaks broke into the building, and you know what followed.

'I tell you how strongly I opposed them because it makes what happened next significant. From what I saw that day I became convinced that due process of law was ignored in the suspension of the troublemakers. I came to the conclusion they got a raw deal. I was one of many fraternity men who started out against the SDS—very strongly—only to find myself supporting them when I thought they'd been shafted.

'I attended their protest meetings. I listened to what the brighter young faculty members were saying. And I could easily have been caught up in the frenzy except for one thing. As I listened to the new leader, Steve Sharoff, I began to suspect, "That guy is doing this whole thing as an ego trip." And when I analyzed what he said and why he said it, I saw that the CCC was probably only a front for the same old agitation. I attended no more of the meetings, and shortly after I quit, everyone else caught on and the movement died.'

Bob Perko was not radicalized by Music and Speech, but many less analytical students were, so that the SDS operation at that time must be counted a conspicuous success, even though some of the members went to jail thereafter and the brotherhood itself collapsed.

On Thursday night Bob Perko and his friends listened to President Nixon speak on Cambodia. 'I didn't like what I heard! It took no genius to know that this meant more war, more draft. I think it was then that I began to grow a little scared about what might happen on campus.

'I was with the fraternity gang drinking beer at Towne House on Friday night when the trouble started. I went down to look in on the rioting on Water Street, and I'd have to say there was no visible leadership. It seemed to be sporadic and accidental, but when I looked along the edges of the crowd I saw a lot of figures that you didn't normally spot on Water Street, and they were giving everyone encouragement.

'And when I saw the amount of damage and the ugly spirit of the mob and the reaction of the police, I went back to the house and called my parents. "You can expect me home for the rest of the quarter." When they asked why, I said, "This university is going to be closed down." '

Fraternity men, that spring at Kent State, were caught up in the full passion of what was happening. They were moved to the left by the violence and by the presence of strange forces on their campus. They sensed that their country was undergoing great changes from which they could not hide. The spirit of Delta Upsilon was epitomized by the young man of nineteen who sat disconsolately on the front porch of the house and replied to a stranger who asked what he was majoring in: 'What does it matter when your number in the draft is 31?'

'Cow college in a cow town'

The official seal of Kent State University shows a brilliant sun coming over a mountain and illuminating a meadow on which stand a sheaf of arrows and a shock of wheat, with the misleading date 1910. That was the year in which the Ohio legislature authorized the establishment of a two-year normal school in some northeastern town; classes did not start till 1913, but when 1960 rolled around KSU celebrated its fiftieth anniversary.

As its first president, Kent had the good fortune to find a fighting bantam-cock of a man, an Illinois schoolteacher named John McGilvrey, who, from the first day he saw the empty rolling hills east of Kent, determined that here would stand a great university. Kent State is the product of the single-mindedness of this able and dedicated man.

The charter under which the normal school operated stated specifically that it was to be a two-year institution limited to the training of elementary-school teachers, and this directive was to be enforced not by the state itself but by Ohio State University in Columbus, which was then as now 'the darling of the state, the Chartres Cathedral of Ohio.' OSU then had a flamboyant president by the name of William Oxley Thompson, who had no intention of seeing the new normal school grow big enough to threaten his security or the legislative grants that belonged to the university.

For thirteen years the educational history of Ohio was the bare-knuckle brawling of John McGilvrey of the normal school versus William Oxley Thompson of the university. The two men despised one another, and each used every known device to strangle the other's aspirations. McGilvrey won.

In 1913, before even one class had been convened at the new normal school, McGilvrey was issuing bulletins announcing his intention of offering a full four-year course with a degree of Bachelor of Pedagogy. By the time classes began

in May, McGilvrey was already on his way to converting his
normal school into a university, and on June 5, 1915, over
the most bitter opposition from Ohio State, McGilvrey's
little school became Kent State Normal College, with a four-
year course and an enrollment of 625.

In 1929 it dropped the word *normal* and became a full-
fledged liberal arts college, with an enrollment of 832, and
in 1935 John McGilvrey, now a silver-thatched old man,
wearily, but triumphantly, left Columbus to return to Kent
bearing with him a copy of the bill creating Kent State University.*

In the years that followed, it seemed that Kent State faced
but two serious problems: how to field a winning football
team, and how to find parking space for all the automobiles
that wished to cram the campus. One of the reasons that Ohio
State University has always held such a lofty place in the
esteem of the state legislature, so that its coffers have continuously been filled while those of the lesser schools have
remained empty, is that it has consistently produced good
football teams. Kent has always hoped to do likewise, but
the results have been disastrous. In one inglorious stretch
Kent State lost thirty-nine games in a row, reaching its nadir
in 1932 when it not only lost every game, as had been its
custom, but failed to score a single point.

A major reason for Kent's failure in football has been the
nature of its student body: a huge proportion of the students
commute to classes or hasten out of town after their last
course on Friday, not reappearing till the last minute on
Monday morning. As we have seen, the traffic jams at those
two times can be tremendous. A collateral problem is where
to park. In fact, Kent's permanent crisis reminds one of Clark
Kerr's statement when he was serving as head of the University of California: 'The job of a college administrator in
America is threefold. To provide football for the graduates,
sex for the undergraduates, and parking space for the faculty.'
Since the huge campus has vast open spaces, one would suppose that Kent, alone of American universities, would have
enough parking space, but the contrary is true. Nearly every
one of the students seems to have a car, and it is almost
impossible to park that many anywhere.

The campus was well on its way to being strangled when
someone came up with the bright idea of initiating an endless chain bus service, linking all campus buildings to depots

*Phillip R. Shriver, *The Years of Youth*. Kent State University Press, 1960.

spread along the boundaries of the city. Now thirty-six blue and gray buses circulate every ten minutes, picking up students for $4 a quarter and dropping them where their next class is meeting. One of the most sought-after jobs on campus is that of bus driver, but even this service has not solved the problem. Kent still requires massive parking lots for the professors and special visitors, plus a large campus police force to hand out tickets for parking violations.

When the notoriety of May, 1970, overtook Kent State, the university was frequently referred to as 'a cow college in a cow town.' Neither of these descriptions was warranted. The city of Kent, as we have seen, was an attractive place except for the two main streets and that awful railroad track. The university was impressive, with a student body of 21,186* and a faculty of 970 (29,168 and 1,174 if you counted the nine flourishing branches in nearby communities). It had ninety-seven buildings valued at $108,000,000 and a yearly budget of $57,766,100. It contained fifty-five residence halls providing space for 4,913 women and 3,678 men, plus some of the most convenient quarters for married students seen on any campus.

Nor was the university in any way third-rate. An excellent way of judging the precise quality of any university is to read a year's issues of the campus newspaper, to see who was speaking at the assemblies, what plays were being given in the drama department, what music was being heard, what art being seen, what ideas exchanged. This enables the visitor to determine for himself, not what the university said it was achieving, but what it was actually doing. Kent State passes this inspection with rather high marks.

On January 6, 1970: *The Daily Kent Stater* intends to catalogue the events of life on campus in a world that can never be shut out. Everything is relevant, and everything has reverberations. After viewing the headlong rush of mankind to both heaven and hell at the same time during the past ten years, *The Stater* fervently prays that 1970 will be the true dawning of the Age of Aquarius.'

The newspaper also had the good policy of throwing its columns open to campus leaders for the expression of whatever ideas were eating them at the moment. Three of the leaders wrote repeatedly: Mike Alewitz the socialist, Bob Pickett the black, Robert Rust the conservative—and their

*This is the official figure for the 1969–70 academic year. However, in each spring quarter, enrollment drops about 2,000.

comment was somewhat more intelligent and well organized than that in comparable campus journals. In the first issue of 1970 Mike Alewitz anticipated a movement which was to sweep the country: 'Women form the oldest and largest oppressed section of mankind, their oppression dating back to the very beginnings of the rise of the class society.'

The university's annual invitational exhibition of painting provided the students with an opportunity to see works by such American artists as Jack Beal, Ben Cunningham, Edwin Dickinson, John Ferren, Edward Giobbi, Al Held, John Koch, Saul Steinberg and the Canadian Jean-Paul Riopelle, a group which would have graced any New York gallery. In addition, there were some new paintings by Richard Anuskiewicz, a leader of the new simplistic optical school and a graduate of Kent State. In this field, certainly, the university was not provincial. In music Andrés Segovia, the Spanish classical guitarist, was appearing, and in drama the university players were to give Brecht's *The Caucasian Chalk Circle*. And in athletics, a dinner was being held at which the football jersey Number 79 was being retired, it having been worn by Kent State's first all-American, the linebacker Jim Corrigal, who would surely be drafted by one of the professional teams for the 1970–71 season.

Robert Rust, the conservative columnist, said, 'Five words of Robert E. Lee on education "Teach him to deny himself" comprise the formula for the life-span of our democracy.'

On January 7 came the first faint rumbling of campus disturbance. Mike Herron, a conservative, said, 'Police teams patrol the corridors of many of our public schools, while at the same time the silent majorities in our great universities are muzzled by fear of knives and clubs.'

On January 27 the ominous note continued. In a heated discussion over the propriety of allowing campus police to carry guns, after the accidental shooting of a student at Wittenberg College some miles to the west by a campus policeman there, Lieutenant Crawford testified that to a policeman a gun is just a tool. Captain Schwartzmiller said, 'The disarming of a policeman would not solve anything except to make him a target, because the main purpose of the guns on campus is not to shoot but to deter the would-be criminal from committing a crime. Besides, the history of our country since its inception has been teethed upon the barrel of a gun. After all, even the Constitution recognizes guns as a social necessity.'

On January 30 Robert A. Van Bergen, a junior, wrote a sharp letter protesting the plan to name the new campus skyscraper The Kennedy–King Library. 'The new community center in Ravenna is going to be dedicated to Kennedy and King. I don't see any point in naming everything in the country after them.'

And on this day Bob Pickett launched his campaign against Frank Truitt, the basketball coach. He started with a complaint by a black athlete: 'One morning I walked into his office to see him and when he got off the phone—he slammed it down—he yelled, "You will play for me only if you cut your hair and *that*." I asked him what *that* was, it was my mustache that had to be cut. I think Truitt has a personality hang-up about mustaches. He thinks something is wrong if you have one. So after that I refused to submit, and so I'm not playing.' This confrontation continued over many issues of the newspaper, with Pickett charging Truitt with being anti-black and avowing that Kent State would never have a good basketball team until Truitt brought in more black players, 'since everyone knows they dominate this game.' One student was ungracious enough to go back in the files to find that the 1966–67 team had contained four black starters and had compiled a record of five wins and eighteen losses. Another discovered that when Coach Truitt did bring a top black high school basketball player to the campus, Pickett had advised the boy to go elsewhere. Things got so heated that at the Florida State game blacks cheered for the visitors and refused to stand when The Star-Spangled Banner was played.

On March 10 a different kind of agitation began, one that would have shaken any university campus a decade ago. A front-page article protested that the KSU health services would not dispense the pill to coeds or administer pregnancy tests to girls who requested them. Dr. R. J. Honzik, the director, said, 'Previously, the Student Health Center was never asked for this type of service. Pregnant students avoided the Health Center because they thought we would cross-communicate with the administration. Now we are dealing with a new attitude. Those that come to us don't really care who knows.'

Next day details were offered as to how pregnant coeds could obtain counseling, and in the rare case, contact with the Cleveland Clergy Consultation Service on Abortion, where ministers of various faiths took steps to locate sound medical service for girls who needed it. Dr. Lawrence Litwack, chairman of counselors for the university, said, 'I don't pass moral judgment. My concern is that if it must be done, it should be done by someone competent and not a butcher.'

Later a vigorous protest, signed by seven girls and five boys, pointed out that often a pregnancy test was the most important thing in a coed's education, and that refusal to administer it was unfair to students.

'Where does a coed go if she is under twenty-one years of age and is unable to have a parent accompany her? Where does she receive information concerning sex—on a campus which has no facilities or faculty specifically designated for sex counseling? Without a pregnancy test, she may have waited too late for any alternative other than having a baby. Had she been counseled about contraception, her pregnancy probably would have been prevented. If she has the baby, she either turns him over for adoption or keeps him. In either case, an unwanted child is brought into an already overpopulated world.' Two of the signers said that they had applied for such tests and had been refused.

Kent was not parochial. In the issue of March 13, it was announced that thirteen Kent students would be doing their spring-quarter student teaching in the American School in Vienna; ten others were attending a work-camp program in Europe, with $150 grants to help pay expenses. And still others were being given the opportunity of signing up for a year's study in Verona, with the tag line: 'If you liked *Romeo and Juliet,* you'll love Verona.'

To honor Beethoven's birthday, members of the music faculty were giving concerts of his complete works for piano and cello, in addition to which the Istomin–Stern–Rose trio would be giving a memorial concert. Dr. Carl Woodring of Columbia University was visiting to lecture on 'Wordsworth's Humanity in "Tintern Abbey." '

The outside world kept creeping in to disturb both the students and the campus. Mike Alewitz began stressing a theme which would perplex many students, that Israel was a menace to world peace and should be liquidated: 'Israel, like any other capitalist country, breeds barbaric wars and racism. The just cause of the Palestinian refugees and the Arab revolutionaries must be supported. Revolution until victory . . . defend the Arab revolution!'

More pertinent to the Kent situation was the premonitory news from Puerto Rico:

Helmeted riot police occupied the University of Puerto Rico campus Thursday and classes were suspended after student rioters set fire to the ROTC building and a nineteen-year-old girl was killed. Three other youths were treated for gunshot wounds, and fifty other persons, including several policemen, were reported injured in the day and night of violence that began with a demonstration by 300 coeds against the university's military training program. During five hours of violence, the ROTC building, a warehouse and a construction shack were put to the torch. Damage was estimated at $30,000. The rioters then surged into the streets, smashing windows and setting off Molotov cocktails. It took nearly seven hours to restore order.

As April ended, ominous news began filtering in from other Ohio campuses. There was an editorial defending the right of student newspapers at Ohio State to use obscene words if they wished:

A school paper is aimed at students. Most of the students who read the paper do not object to the use of so-called obscene words because they themselves use them. The readership should determine the limits of the paper and not some distant bureaucrat in Columbus who is out of touch with today's students. Any attempt to prevent college students from expressing themselves puts all of us in danger.

Student rioting at Miami University attracted special attention, and as one reads the editorials relating to it, one has the feeling that it was a trial run for the Kent State uprising:

Some men just don't seem to learn from the experience of others. Last week at Miami University an incident involving a student take-over of a classroom building illustrated ignorance and ugliness on the part of that school's administrators. Their response was rapid, costly in terms of academic prestige and tragic because of resulting violence.

The university might have called upon the courts, as so many other schools have successfully done, to issue injunctive orders breaking up the assemblage. Or it might have let the students have the hall until they were cold and hungry and went home in self-defeat.

Why did Miami have no plan to peacefully control disruptive efforts? Was police violence necessary? Have officials there studied similar disturbances on other campuses? Miami University has badly bungled its first serious student disruption. The philosophy behind its reaction demonstrated ignorance and jeopardized academic freedom. Such blunders need not be repeated anywhere.

Close attention was paid to the rioting at Ohio State University, but it was a stockholders' meeting at American Telephone and Telegraph in Cleveland that excited the campus: 'April 16. Police, marchers clash at AT&T about the stockholders' meeting in Cleveland. Six Kent State University students, including chemistry instructor Robert Franklin, were arrested in the melee on charges ranging from assaulting an officer to displaying an anarchist flag, according to Cleveland police.'

In the midst of this tension the campus had an unlikely visitor, Jerry Rubin, who attracted a crowd of about two thousand. *The Stater* reported:

What was impressive was the reaction of the crowd after the speech: there was little vulgarity or obscenity, no violence and hardly any shouting. 'I have no respect for the court systems of this country,' Rubin said. 'Being young in America is illegal. We are a generation of obscenities. The most oppressed people in this country are not the blacks, not the poor, but the white middle-class. They don't have anything to rise up and fight against. We will have to invent new laws to break.

The Stater did not report the most notorious passage from his speech: 'The first part of the Yippie program is to kill your parents. And I mean that quite literally, because until you're prepared to kill your parents, you're not ready to change this country. Our parents are our first oppressors.'

But the mood of the campus as April ended—the mood, that is, of those who felt that society stood at a great watershed— was expressed by Ralph Bevilaqua, a teaching fellow in English and a leader of the New University Conference, who wrote demanding that students bring pressure to end the war in Vietnam:

Certainly Nixon and his cronies would like to 'win' this war in Asia with as few of our boys as possible so as to keep dissent controlled at home; but the meaning of Vietnamization should be clear to us all. It is not a plan to end the war; it is a plan to continue fighting it with mercenary troops trained and supplied by the U.S. I think it should be clear to us all that the ruling class in America . . . turns a deaf ear away from any plea the content of which speaks for change that imperils its power and profit-making ability. Therefore, I urge everyone to think about the difference between begging on the one hand, and active dissent and resistance on the other. It seems to me that at this stage in our history the latter is the only visible course for us to take if we expect to win.

In other words, Kent State, at the end of April, was like many other American colleges and universities, and to believe that deaths occurred here because the school was in some way different is to miss the whole point. The shootings could have happened at almost any large university, given the series of unfortunate events that plagued Kent during the first days of May.

Throughout the various issues of *The Stater* in these first four months of 1970, there appear cryptic observations on the new hockey rink, which few of the students seemed to want. Its cost was cited variously as a million to two million dollars, and several times students pointed out that this was rather a high price to pay for a rink when Kent State had no hockey team and few students who wished to skate. Others, defending the expenditure, reminded the protesters that a plebiscite had been taken some years before with the then student body approving the erection of a rink, to which the critics replied that students in that day would have approved anything, especially if they were getting it for nothing.*

This argument did point up one of Kent's deficiencies, a lack of teaching space. Classes in the art department were unbelievably crowded, but plans were under way to correct that. It was the normal freshman and sophomore classes which raised problems, and some of these would have startled the average graduate from one of the typical small American colleges.

Scott Mueller, the trim, conservative, well-dressed senior who helped in gathering interviews for this book, in recalling his freshman year, says, 'You get a real shock when you enroll at a big university and find that for the first two years you are merely a Social Security number. You don't use your name on test papers, just your number. And when the grades

---

*This debate brought into focus a major complication facing universities today. If it is desirable to invite students to full participation in academic decisions, will such decisions have to be scrapped each four years when a new generation of students arrives with its recently acquired pressure positions? Who will provide the long-range judgment upon which any social institution must build? And who will defend that long-range judgment against the spontaneous reactions of the movement? When a given generation departs, it is no longer concerned whether the decisions it made were right or wrong.

are posted, you don't look for your name, because the IBM doesn't work by names. You run down the endless list of numbers, and zero in on your own. There's your grade. I remember how grateful I felt in my junior year when I finally had a professor who knew me by name.

'Size is another problem. My class in Philosophy 260 had 1,100 students, in Psychology 162 we had 1,000. It's not easy to teach philosophy to a class with over a thousand students. I sat so far back I couldn't even see the professor's face, and as to questions and answers, it took you a couple of minutes even for him to see your hand, and then he always said, "We'll get back to that tomorrow." I can't tell you how amazed I was in my junior year when for the first time I heard a professor who wasn't speaking through an electronic sound system with loudspeakers. It was amazing to discover that he had a human voice just like anyone else. Also, it was fun to be in a small class of 400.'

Harold Walker, the photographer from York, Pennsylvania, whose pictures appear in this book, says, 'This philosophy class I was telling you about had 700 students and was taught by six different professors who appeared for individual lectures in no way related one to the other. The only professor we saw more than once was a very brilliant Chinese who lectured on metaphysics in a weird language of his own that nobody understood. Finally, things got so hopeless that for comic relief we talked a coed into throwing a mock epileptic fit in the balcony, and on that day at least something happened that we could understand. At the end of the course they gave us a long true-false test, and when they fed the papers into the computer, the scores were so low that the machine gave everybody an F . . . 700 of us . . . and this created such a scandal that there were meetings to decide whether it was possible to fail everybody, and after a long discussion it was decided that the only fair thing to do was to admit that things had gotten a little bit out of hand and that all 700 should be given pass-in-course and let it go at that.'

Both Mueller and Walker are quick to add that most of the teaching at Kent State is of a high quality, and anyone who talks with students for any length of time finds most of them referring to one or two of their professors as 'real brains' or 'great men to know.' The average is rarely higher elsewhere.

In summary, Kent State was a good university beset by all the customary problems of the age. (Its catalogue carried far too many courses marked with a diagonal, 163/463, which meant that the same course was given for both undergraduate and graduate levels. Also, funds for the purchase of new books for the library were less than they should have been, especially since a huge new library building would soon be available.) In addition to the normal problems, Kent State had a special one: there was far too great a chasm between the three governing agencies of the university: the trustees, the administration and the faculty. The nine trustees appointed by the governor had considerable power but did not use it; the faculty wanted more power but was denied it. This meant that the control rested in the hands of the administration, which, more than in any college with which the researchers were acquainted, acted as a body separated from the generic functioning of the school. In other words, administration became an art in itself, and no one, looking at Kent's operation, would ever confuse an administrator with a faculty member. Further, there was a tendency to appoint to the lesser administrative posts athletic coaches who had grown too old to handle teams. An outstanding characteristic of the May crisis will be the failure of the administration and the faculty to work together as a unit, or to communicate sensibly with each other. Too often, as we shall see, administrative functions that were left unattended had to be assumed by the faculty.

This does not mean that the faculty was blameless. When a great university employs somewhere around 2,000 scholars to teach young people but admits only 970 of them to faculty status, denying the other 1,100 participation in the running of the institution, even though they are the ones who are most closely touching the younger students, something is wrong. That was the condition at Kent. In hundreds of interviews young students spoke of the teachers they admired, of the faculty members who seemed really to be trying to help them adjust to the contemporary world, and with appalling frequency the instructors referred to were not members of the faculty. They were either graduate assistants (young scholars with the A.B. degree and usually the M.A. who were working for the Ph.D.) or teaching fellows (almost anybody of any age and any academic condition who could be found to teach a part-time load, especially in late August, when it was discovered that registrations were unexpectedly high).

There is nothing wrong with the system of employing graduate assistants and teaching fellows; every great professor started his career that way, and on his first day in the classroom he was probably a better teacher than most of the older men then working. Certainly at Kent an unusually gifted and dedicated group of junior instructors had been assembled; the testimony of students who loved their teaching is too consistent to deny that. But sometimes it was their very dedication that caused the trouble. Without the responsibility of membership on the faculty, acknowledging no accountability for the progress of the university as a social organism, often not married and unburdened by the obligations of a home, these young instructors were free-wheeling spirits dedicated to a wild variety of causes. To have one or two of them in the course of one's freshman and sophomore years would be a tonic for the average high school graduate, testing his intellectual powers in the university, but to have a succession of them without the leavening of older professors who had been at the game a little longer could be unsettling. At Kent it was. And so it has been at hundreds of other universities.

The problem is threefold. Pedagogically it is a matter of providing adequate teaching. Economically it is a question of whether any university could survive if it were deprived of the moderately paid services of its beginning scholars. (Professors who have prospered in the system think back on it fondly as part of an honorable apprenticeship.) But there is also a moral problem. Are not the teaching fellows and the graduate assistants exploited? Are they not, as some have called them, wage slaves? It would appear so, and the outsider's whole inclination is to say, 'If these young scholars perform the duties of the faculty, they should exercise the rights of the faculty.' Put simply, if they teach, they vote.

But this simplistic solution would be abhorrent to faculty members trained in the rigorous German tradition of Harvard, Chicago and Johns Hopkins. They argue that the path of scholarship has always been difficult, with recognition coming late and full participation even later. They reason that a university is a precious instrument, hewn out of man's experience over the past seventeen hundred years, and that one of the gravest of all responsibilities is that of the full faculty member who is endeavoring to keep alive the university which he and his tested fellows inherited. Such men question the propriety of allowing young scholars to participate fully in faculty votes and decisions.

Two comments can be made. Later in this narrative we shall see that one of the crucial documents was a statement made by the faculty as it convened in haste and anguish in a rump session at a church in Akron, where a statement that did the university much damage was drawn up and circulated. One of the reasons why this understandable but unfortunate document was promulgated was that fellows and assistants had forced their way into the meeting and were exercising a privilege to which they were not entitled. On the other hand, we will later see several vital instances in which fellows and assistants were not even told of major decisions and were left in an ignorance which imperiled their lives.

There is one final observation necessary about the operation of Kent State, and it applies to all of America's institutions of advanced learning. The system of tenure, whereby faculty members of the upper grades are protected in their jobs and cannot be fired, shows so many creaking defects that it ought to be reconsidered. The justification for tenure has been that it protects faculty members against the willful and arbitrary persecutions of the community, and is essential for the conduct of free investigation.

The weaknesses of tenure have exposed themselves increasingly in recent years when professors with tenure have used it as an excuse for non-performance, non-involvement, and non-availability to their students. Its most grievous manifestation came not long ago at Kent, when a department head grew weary of receiving complaints from students in his field that Professor So-and-So was appearing for his fifty-minute lectures forty minutes late. (It is tradition that the students must wait twenty minutes for a full professor.) The head of the department visited the tardy professor in the latter's office and said, 'There have been complaints about your being so very late to your classes,' to which the professor cried, 'What are you doing, spying on me?' Next day he stormed into the office of the head of the department and shouted, 'You seem to forget, I have tenure and there's not a damned thing you can do about it.'

Calling the guard

When he reported to his office on Saturday morning, Mayor Satrom was angry and disturbed. He was angry about the destruction in downtown Kent. Robert G. Hickman, who ran a jewelry store whose front had been caved in by students, was trying to clean up the glass. He reported that about $100 worth of jewelry had been looted. A policeman reported, 'A squad of good college kids came down early this morning with buckets and brooms and swept up all the glass in the street. They said, "We're ashamed of what the other students did last night and want to prove that not all of us are bums." They did a fine job.' Satrom was impressed by the gesture, and calmed down somewhat, but when he saw the buckling which the fire had caused on Water Street, he grew angry again.

He was disturbed by reports which continued to filter in throughout the day. A trusted detective told him, 'We spotted two carloads of agitators coming into town from Chicago. Each car had six passengers. Loaded for bear. We saw them on Water Street and later one of our informants at the university caught them prowling the campus.'

Police Chief Roy Thompson, a solid man not easily given to exaggeration, reported, 'A man we have always been able to trust on the campus has warned us that students are going to burn the ROTC building tonight, and if they get away with that, they're going to try the army recruiting station downtown and the Kent City post office.'

False fire alarms, bomb threats and violent rumors kept the day ugly, and always at the mayor's elbow stood Lieutenant Barnette of the National Guard, warning him, 'If you're going to call the Guard, you have to do it before 5:00 this afternoon.'

Satrom, dressed in his customary flannel slacks and trimfitting sports jacket, moved methodically from one meeting to the next, trying to determine what he ought to do about the safety of his city. The scar on the left side of his chin deepened when he scowled as he listened to the confusion over who was responsible for what. He was caught up in a jigsaw puzzle whose pieces he was powerless to fit together.

'I had to deal with five separate police departments,' he explains. 'Kent had a total of twenty-one police, who obviously could not guard downtown Kent if trouble started. So we wanted to call in as many county sheriffs as we could. We could have used as many as seventy-five, but we never got them. The university, on the other hand, had only twenty-four campus police, and they preferred to call in the highway patrol. They considered Chester Hayth the best officer in the business, but the patrol showed no eagerness to come to Kent unless they were needed for special arrests. So we had four different agencies, all of them either inadequate in number or unwilling. What could I do? My only solution was to call the Guard.'

Satrom postponed his decision till the last possible minute. A man who was near him at the time says, 'Lieutenant Barnette kept giving him the eye. "It's almost 5:00." Roy tried every alternative he could, but when he could get neither deputies nor highway patrol, he picked up the phone and called Columbus.'

Satrom says, 'I delayed until 5:27. The lieutenant was afraid it might be too late, but I got John McElroy and he called General Del Corso, and about five minutes later Del Corso called back to assure me that troops would be available if they were needed.'

George Pierson, owner of a yarn store in the middle of town and a former ROTC instructor at the university, had served as president of the Kent City Council and in 1969 had opposed LeRoy Satrom in the race for mayor. He judged that Satrom did a good job during the crisis, except for one thing.

'Many people have asked me, "George, if you had been elected mayor instead of Satrom would you have called in the Guard?" I always answer as honestly as I can, "No, I don't think so." The situation on Friday night seemed to have been handled about as well as could be expected. Local police, sheriff's deputies and members of the highway patrol did a great job.

'As a former military man I would never want to call in the Guard. I am only too familiar with its training and preparation, and neither is adequate. I do not believe the Guardsmen were mentally or physically equipped to handle a troublesome situation like the one at Kent State. The city administration acted too hastily in calling for the Guard, and Governor Rhodes was too hasty in agreeing to send them.

'But I must admit, when the situation deteriorated and the students threatened to invade downtown again, I did appreciate the fact that the Guard was on hand.'

Mayor Satrom has an answer to such comments: 'If, tomorrow, conditions in Kent were the same as they were that Saturday morning, and if they developed as they did that Saturday afternoon, I'd still have to call the Guard. I'd have no alternative and I'd be very relieved when I saw them rolling into town.'

Volunteer fireman

Since the focal event on Saturday was a fire, it may be interesting to note the reactions of David Helmling, who has been a volunteer fireman for the past sixteen years, an enthusiastic kid following fire engines before that. He is about forty, born in the Kent area, married with six children, and his own boss. 'I dig holes. I have a back-hoe, a grader, some bulldozers, a couple of trucks. I probably know the Kent State campus better than anyone you could find, because I've dug miles of sewer lines up there, conduits, basements, excavations for new buildings. I know the university and I used to love it.'

Helmling's chief joy, however, is transplanting trees. 'I do a lot of digging for the Davey Tree people. One of their specialists and I have developed a system whereby I come in with my back-hoe and he sprays the leaves with a special preparation. We can dig, hoist and ball a large-sized tree in fifteen minutes. We've planted parks and playgrounds and beautiful areas from here to Cleveland, and I think I'm happiest when I'm out pulling a tree out of the ground and putting it down where it'll do some good.' On a recent weekend he had helped his son in a school project; within a few miles of his home he had found fifty-two different kinds of leaves for the school's nature notebook. 'This is truly a town of trees,' he says.

He knows every inch of Kent and says of it, 'What a beautiful town! As a boy living on a farm I always dreamed of living here, and as soon as I had saved a buck I started paying installments on a piece of ground. When I married, we moved into a house we had built. Kent was lovely in those days . . . trees . . . neighbors you could trust . . . a few well-dressed, well-behaved college students. You weren't crowded and your wife could walk downtown without fear of being insulted. I wish Kent had stayed that way. I wish the crowds hadn't moved in.' He pauses, seeming to reflect upon the quiet days, then says, 'You can't imagine how wonderful this town was for an ordinary workman like me. You'd get up early, work like hell, and at noon you'd go down to Seaver's bar and have a bowl of bean soup with men you knew. One guy would be cleaning sewers, another working in stone, another selling farm machinery. But we all met together like friends. What's Seaver's now? A saloon they call Orville's —and you can't get in the place for the college kids with their long hair. I often wish the university would just go away. I wish we could take the town back . . . as it used to be.'

He says a startling thing. 'A week before trouble started, Fire Chief Fred Miller called us together and said, "Fellows, we have pretty good intelligence that the university kids are going to burn down the ROTC building. We don't know when they're going to do it . . . could be any time. But we've got to lay plans for handling it when they make their move. If you leave town, you've got to give us a phone number where you can be reached, because we're not going to lose that building."

'So on two different nights that week we discussed what we would do when the fire started. Truck No. 3, which is our best unit, would rush onto the campus, hook onto the hydrant near the power station and attack the fire from the west. There was a brief discussion as to what we ought to do if students tried to interfere with us, but as I recall, we didn't take that possibility too seriously.

'When Thursday turned out to be a nice day, I sort of expected the building to burn, so when I took my wife out to my brother-in-law's place, the Rusty Nail, for a steak dinner, I called the firehouse and told them, "If the kids burn the building tonight, you can get me at the Rusty Nail." But nothing happened.

'On Friday I went to bed early, but at 12:01 the fire phone in my bedroom sounded. This is a system where we have two fire stations, and the one that gets the original call lets the other station take charge of summoning the firemen. They do this with a master phone that automatically rings all us firemen. I have five different phones at my place, because I want to hear the warning no matter where I am. This night I was in bed.'

In four minutes Helmling was at the station. 'I usually beat the fire truck to the fire,' he says. 'This night they gave me a sort of special duty. Students had set a fire in the middle of Water Street and were starting a riot around it. The truck had already got there, but I noticed that the driver had been real cute. Instead of driving into the middle of the street, where the students would probably have attacked us, he had kept the truck hidden in an alley. As I stood there in the darkness I saw a student with long hair sneak up an alley, take rags and matches out of his pocket, and set fire to a building some distance from the main fire. When it was blazing, he came running back to Water Street, shouting,

"There's a fire up there! My God, let's all help put it out!"
And damned if he didn't lead the firemen up to that fire.
But by then the building was gone.'

Helmling remembers one other thing about Friday night.
'A friend of mine who I can trust without question says that
the whole thing started with an incident at Orville's.' His
friend told him, 'I saw this little, skinny, puny bitch, a gal
with dirty hair, and she smashed her beer glass against the
table and shouted, "I want some action!" She stormed out
of the bar with a can of red spray paint and went to J.B.'s
and wrote on his wall *Fuck the pigs*. That got everybody
cheering and the riot was under way.'

Helmling says, 'I went back to bed on Friday night surprised that no one had tried to burn ROTC. But I was pretty
sure it would go sometime within the next two days. You
could sense it in the air.'

What happened on Saturday

About 7:00 P.M. Saturday evening, May 2, while there was
still ample light, a small crowd of young people gathered at
the Victory Bell. Most were casual sightseeing students, but
there were also a good many visitors who had stopped by to
see the action, the way they might have gone to a circus.
There was also a substantial cadre of hard-core radical leaders
and perhaps one or two revolutionaries who had their eyes
on much more than the rickety old ROTC building; among
them, too, were many who had no connection with the university. Throughout the evening this leadership group would
know precisely what it was supposed to accomplish and how
to go about it. They were going to burn down ROTC, symbolic in their minds both of American involvement in Asia
and the growing United States militarism, and when this was
achieved, they hoped to spread the resulting riot throughout
the campus and into the city. As larger crowds gathered, one
of this determined group circulated with handbills inveighing
against ROTC. It looked as if he were distributing programs
for what was about to happen.

At 7:10 Glenn Frank was on his way to an emergency
meeting of faculty marshals scheduled for Johnson Hall, and
with his improvised blue armband in place he happened to
pass by the ROTC building. He was stopped by a rather pretty
girl in dirty Levis, sweatshirt with sleeves to her fingertips,

and a ribbon in her long hair. Frank did not recognize her as a student, but she seemed to know him, and warned, 'You better tell those fucking photographers to stop taking our pictures or they're going to get hurt.' It was at this point that the twenty-four campus police should have gone into action to isolate the ringleaders; instead they remained in their headquarters. Had they acted, they could have forestalled what was about to happen.

At 7:30 a university official telephoned headquarters of the Ohio State Highway Patrol to report that the crowd on the commons had grown to more than 600, who now seemed bent on troublemaking. The patrol spokesman asked, 'Are you asking our help in making arrests?' and was told by university officials, 'The situation at present doesn't warrant arrests.' The patrolman pointed out that under existing law his men were allowed on campus only for the purpose of making arrests. 'When you make up your mind that you want some arrests, call us back.'

At 7:35 a long-haired young man climbed onto the brick structure housing the bell and began haranguing the crowd: 'We are going to need support tonight from the kids in the dorms. They're trying to keep them penned up. Let's go.'

At 7:36, while the orator was still shouting, three determined youths, never identified, circulated through the crowd to warn each newsman present not to take photographs. 'We don't want to go to jail again,' the spokesman said. Three *Record-Courier* reporters, at three different times, were warned by this young man that he would kill them if they used their cameras.

At 7:40 Professor Frank, returning from the meeting, admonished some young people who were participating in the threats against the photographers, 'There's no need to condone violence,' but one young man in very long hair and western outfit shouted, 'The point of discussion is past. The time for action is here.' To this Frank replied, 'Let me make one point,' but the young man cried, 'I don't want to hear anything a fucking pig like you has to say.' And with this he spat at Frank, aiming at his face, but Frank dodged.

At 7:45 everyone in the crowd moved purposefully across the commons, quitting the ROTC building, which had not yet been touched, and heading for Taylor Hall, behind which they disappeared. The commons was now empty, except for Professor Frank, who remained leaning against a white Ford, and as the darkness deepened he asked himself, 'Why are you hanging around?' Like everyone else, he expected more action and as a marshal he felt it his duty to prevent it from getting out of hand.

At 8:00 the sheriff's department of Portage County dispatched sixty men to help control the situation, but they would not arrive on campus in time to prevent major trouble.

At 8:03 the swirling mob of students reached Tri-Towers, from which they extracted a large contingent, picking up more and more supporters as they prepared for their dash back to the commons area and their announced target, the waiting ROTC building.

At 8:10 Professor Frank was still leaning against the white Ford. 'Then suddenly, from behind Taylor Hall, I heard a rising beat of voices: "Down with ROTC!" The crowd was still invisible on the other side of Blanket Hill, but the sound increased, and like a burst of wild energy a mob of about 2,000 students came roaring over the crest of the hill and down across the commons, zeroing in on the ROTC building. As soon as they came within range, they began hurling large rocks at it, and one of them struck me in the chest. When this happened I thought, "Glenn, you stupid idiot, get out of here!" and I moved to safer quarters.'

At 8:15 the barrage of rocks ended, only a few windows having been broken. At 8:19 a group of students improvised a battering ram from an empty gasoline drum and used it in an attempt to knock down the main door of the building, but they miscalculated their aim, missed the door, hit the side of the building and found themselves thrown backwards onto the grass.

At 8:20, as the crowd cheered this abortive effort, two railroad flares were hurled at the building, but fell harmlessly beside it and sputtered out.

A good many witnesses testified later that the appearance of ten or fifteen determined policemen could have prevented the fire, but none were in evidence. The Kent city force had not yet been summoned, and the campus police were being held in readiness in a building only 200 yards from the site. Not all the campus force was indoors; witnesses saw some of them standing in shadows during the next forty minutes, watching but attempting nothing.

At 8:24 another flare, thrown inside the building, set fire to a pair of curtains, which blazed vigorously, making it appear that at last the building was on fire. The crowd cheered enthusiastically, then groaned as the flames sputtered, died down and failed to revive. The first attempts at arson had failed miserably, and again strong police action could have saved the building, but none was forthcoming.

At 8:26 a young man who may have been a student, but whom none of the marshals were able to identify, whipped a fair-sized American flag from around his middle, where he had been carrying it, fastened it to a makeshift flagpole which he had secreted down an arm of his coat, and set it ablaze with a cigarette lighter. It burned slowly. Then, as the crowd cheered, it burst into vigorous flame and made a compelling picture against the evening sky.

When flames from the flag were at their height, an extremely big and heavy man, who looked as if he could have been a tackle for the Chicago Bears, tried to photograph the many faces illuminated by the blaze. As soon as they saw what he was doing, those nearest him began to yell, 'Kill the bastard!' and five or six husky men tackled him, knocking him to the ground, where about a dozen persons started kicking him in the head and stomach. Professor Frank leaped into the crowd, trying to rescue the beleaguered giant, but two men grabbed Frank from behind in a stranglehold and he had a bad time until Ruth Gibson shouted, 'Christ, it's Professor Frank! Let him go!' She led him to safety.

As Frank brushed himself off, he heard more cries of 'Let's kill that bastard!' and various people resumed kicking the fallen photographer, but an older man pushed them aside and said calmly, 'The smart thing is to destroy the film.' Someone knelt down, took the camera, a Brownie 126 Instamatic, and expertly slipped open the cartridge area, removed the film, exposed it, then almost apologetically returned the camera. The big man had now regained his feet, and Frank heard someone say to the man, in surprise, 'Hey, what are you doing here?' And another added, 'I bet you'll never take photos around here again!'

During this time the amateur incendiaries continued to have miserable results in their efforts to burn the building. Flares, Molotov cocktails, and even matches held against draperies failed to produce a blaze, and one group who did have the equipment to do the job wasted their efforts in trying to set afire the only wall of the building that was metal-sheathed. At any other spot on the perimeter their gasoline and rags would have kindled a sharp blaze, but against the metal the combination merely flared up, singed the paint, then died down again.

But at 8:28 two boys who may have been high school students, or even younger, smashed one of the windows, ran over to a waiting friend, took from him two railroad flares, set them ablaze and tossed them through the window. The operation took about a minute and was conducted in full view of hundreds, any one of whom could have terminated it. Nobody did.

At 8:30, a time confirmed by many witnesses, the ROTC building was truly ablaze, with students cheering 'Burn, baby. Burn!' Fire could be seen licking its way up curtains and across windows. A good deal of smoke accompanied it, and as it started to billow out through one of the smashed doors, the crowd cheered wildly. But witnesses also testify that one good fireman with a hand extinguisher could have stopped it at this time. None appeared, for the very good reason that no one had thought to turn in a fire alarm!

At 8:35 Mayor Satrom, informed of the new trouble on campus, called General Del Corso's office to make an urgent appeal for troops. Del Corso and another general left for Kent after Satrom's first request in the late afternoon, so Satrom phoned Colonel John Simmons, the duty officer at Guard headquarters at Fort Hayes in Columbus. Simmons called the battalion that had been policing the truck strike, which at that moment was in the Rubber Bowl, in Akron, and acting under instructions previously worked out with Del Corso, gave them the signal to move out. According to the plan, the troops, about 400 in number, were to proceed to Kent, but could not be committed to the Kent streets until they were notified that Del Corso and General Robert Canterbury had arrived in Kent.

At 8:40 a contingent of twenty highway patrolmen arrived on scene and took up a position which placed them between the home of President White and the distant rioters. As we shall see, this was a prudent move, because one irresponsible group of students would conceive the preposterous idea of burning this building, and had it been unprotected, might have done so.

At 8:49, when the fire at ROTC was well ablaze, a call from an unknown person finally reached the Kent fire department, which dispatched its Truck No. 3 with a normal complement of men, including volunteer Dave Helmling.

At 8:53 the fire truck arrived and the men in charge quickly saw two things. Putting out the relatively small fire would be easy, but getting to it through the mob was going to be difficult, especially since no police were visible to help protect the hoses and the men. Trouble started as soon as they hooked a hose to a distant fire hydrant and began playing it out, for students grabbed the nozzle and ran away with it, hauling it far beyond the firemen's reach. The latter attached a second hose to the hydrant and began dragging it to the fire, but the same ones who had commandeered the first now attacked this with knives and ice picks, which inflicted such damage on the hose that little water could be delivered to the fire. Worse, a large gang of students grabbed this punctured hose and wrapped it around a lilac bush, so that no water at all could get through. And finally a student with a machete hacked it into two pieces.

At 9:05 one of the most offensive incidents of the weekend occurred. Three young men, irritated by the slow burning of the building, decided upon bold action. They left the crowd, walked purposefully over to a pair of parked motorcycles, opened the gasoline tanks, dipped rags inside, walked back, lit the rags, and tossed them into the building. When a fireman tried to stop them, they beat him with a heavy wooden club, knocking him to the ground.

At 9:15 the firemen had had enough. Realizing that they were going to get no police protection while they fought both the fire and students, they announced their intention to withdraw, telling Professor Frank, who seemed to be representing the university, 'We're not going to put out that fire until there's police protection.' He pleaded with them to fight the blaze, but they snapped, 'With what? Your students ran away with our hoses.' And after reeling up their remaining hose, prepared to leave.

At 9:17, as if a comedian were writing the script for this chaotic night, the fire mysteriously subsided, then went out. The crowd groaned and milled about, not knowing what to do next.

At 9:20 ten men from the county sheriff's office arrived on scene, so that two police units were now available, sheriffs and highway patrol. At 9:22, when everything was apparently under control, the campus police arrived from their nearby headquarters, to be met with a barrage of catcalls and jeers. They were two hours and twelve minutes late (7:10 to 9:22).

At 9:27 the combined forces loosed their first attack of tear gas and drove the crowd back from the ROTC area, but this measure was no longer necessary; by now the building was merely smoldering.

At 9:28 the clerk at the city fire department entered the information that 'our truck left the campus.'

At 9:30 a contingent of city police arrived to protect the firemen, but found none on the scene, nor were they needed, for the fire was out. At this same time the two National Guard generals, Del Corso and Canterbury, arrived in Kent and went directly to City Hall, where they conferred with Mayor Satrom.

At 9:34 the determined students, now cordoned off from ROTC, moved a hundred yards away and set fire to a shed maintained on the commons by the athletic department for the storage of girls' archery materials. It started to burn rapidly, setting fire to the tree under which it stood. This enraged the ecology buffs in the mob, so within the space of a few minutes students who had been urging destruction of ROTC became firemen lugging buckets of water to save the tree. Frantic girls from nearby dormitories, who had applauded the ROTC fire, helped rescue the tree but were unable to save their archery shed or the equipment inside.

At 9:35 four campus police called in to report that they had been injured by rocks thrown by students at the two fires, but none was hurt sufficiently to warrant his removal to the hospital and all resumed duty after first-aid treatment.

At 9:40 the demonstration took an ugly turn, which some apologists for the students have preferred to overlook. A small determined group, irritated by the presence of police on their campus and the frustrations which this engendered, swept eastward in an attempt to burn another target. One student shouted to Professor Frank, 'They're going to burn the president's house.' While it seems possible that the group was led by older persons not registered at the university, students made up the bulk of the crowd, which contained many determined girls. They were easily deterred by the sight of the highway patrolmen.

At 9:45 a preposterous thing happened. The smoldering ROTC building burst into flame at many points. It is likely that in the confusion, some determined youths had succeeded in tossing at least two Molotov cocktails into the shattered windows, where they ignited inflammables that had not been reached before, but some believed that the fire had re-ignited itself spontaneously. At any rate, it was now truly ablaze, and as flames raced from one section to the next, new materials provided additional fuel, and a few rounds of ammunition which had been left in the building could be heard exploding in the fire. Soon the tarred roof was aflame, producing black smoke intermixed with flames which billowed seventy-five feet high in the air, visible in Ravenna to the east. When Captain Ron Snyder and his men of Charlie Company, who had been called in from Akron by Colonel Simmons, reached the edge of town they could see the towering flames; this unit of the Guard reported to the William A. Walls Elementary School gymnasium at the northeastern edge of town, some distance from the university. Two other units also arrived: Alpha Company, led by Captain John E. Martin, and G Troop, led by Captain Raymond J. Srp, whose last name would give reporters on the scene much trouble.

Meanwhile, at City Hall, Del Corso and Canterbury conferred with Mayor Satrom and decided on a twofold plan of action: one detachment of Guardsmen would be dispatched to prevent students from entering downtown Kent, another sent to protect firemen returning to the burning building. As Satrom had been warned earlier in the day, once the Guard was called to Kent, it would make no distinction between city and campus. Del Corso and Canterbury had assumed complete control of the entire area, and the former issued a terse command to his troops: 'Shoot any rioter who cuts a fire hose.'

While this conference was taking place, Vice-President Robert Matson, in charge of student affairs, was conferring with Vice-President Dunn, whose responsibilities included supervision of campus security. Safety Director Chester Williams and Captain Donald Schwartzmiller reported to Dunn that the Guard were needed: the highway patrol, the university's first choice when in need of outside help, had already dispatched twenty men to the campus, since there was a basis for arrests, but it was feared the main contingent could not reach Kent in time to be of service. Dunn so informed Matson, who prepared to summon the Guard, not aware that they were already on campus and taking charge. Thus, for all practical purposes, neither Del Corso nor Canterbury had requested permission of any university official before sending troops onto campus. Their rationale was that because the ROTC building was located on state property, the Guard needed no specific invitation to enter the campus.

On the streets, trouble was now in full swing. About 9:55, as the Guard unit answering Del Corso's call rode down East Main Street, it was stoned by persons who had left the commons and were hiding among the trees. Several Guardsmen later reported they were hit by pieces of flying glass and bricks, and one had to be taken to the hospital in Ravenna for treatment. One group of students tried to set fire to the library, but was diverted from this target to an information booth at the edge of the campus. As they tried to ignite it, Reverend William Jacobs of the United Christian Fellowship House ran up to them and yelled, 'Go home!' The group abandoned their attempt at arson. But while Reverend Jacobs was thus occupied, other activists wrecked a telephone booth that was not on campus, tried to uproot traffic signs, and hauled an air compressor into the middle of Main Street, using it as the base for the erection of a barricade. The students were on a rampage again, and the townspeople were apprehensive, if not downright terrified.

At 9:50 Del Corso made his decision known to state officials by telephoning John McElroy, the governor's aide, to report his troops' deployment in Kent.

At 9:55 a sickening bit of news flashed across the campus: 'The library's on fire.' Some idiot had tried to set it ablaze but had succeeded only in starting a substantial fire near one of the walls. This was quickly extinguished before it could cause any real damage.

At 10:10 the Kent city firemen ventured back on campus with a new hose and twelve policemen to protect it, but they were too late to do any good. Photographers caught several striking shots of them posed against the night sky, with flames darting upward from the doomed building, but just at this time a cache of about 1,000 rounds of .22 ammunition which had been kept in the north end of the building began exploding, and everyone retreated to a safe distance. As the police withdrew, a student heaved a sizable chunk of concrete, which struck a policeman on his helmet, denting the metal deeply and sending him to the infirmary with a cut head.

By 10:30 National Guardsmen were on hand in sufficient numbers to protect any firemen fighting the ROTC fire, but by this time the building was a total wreck. Only the curious frame box that served as a kind of entrance hall still stood. University officials would announce the financial loss as $86,000. While in the vicinity of the ROTC building, eight Guardsmen of Alpha Company and G Troop were injured by rocks and flying glass.

The appearance of National Guard at strategic points near the campus had prevented the students from entering the town, forcing their return to the campus and the ROTC area.

The Guard cleared this group from the campus with dispatch shortly after 10:30, using tear gas freely. As they approached the students, they announced over large bullhorns: 'Ladies and gentlemen, go back to your dormitories. If you remain outside, you will be arrested. We do not want to arrest you.'

At 11:55 General Canterbury was able to report by telephone to his staff headquarters at Fort Hayes: 'The situation at Kent is under control.' At about this time one of the university Cessnas arrived overhead, flying back and forth as witness to the macabre events. It was piloted by Bob Hillegas, returning from Cleveland.

Why it happened

Debi Moreland was one of the prettiest of the activists. She had hazel eyes, waist-length hair, a lovely face and a great figure. This weekend she was wearing multicolored bell-bottomed Levis, a floppy blue T-shirt and sneakers. Her home was in Cincinnati, but for some time she had been living in Akron, and it was there, on Saturday afternoon, that she heard the exciting news. 'Not about Friday on Water Street. I gave up the bars a long time ago. The grapevine said, "ROTC burns tonight." Later a lot of kids would claim, "We were there by accident." Not me—I was there because I wanted to see ROTC go.'

There was an aura of mystery about the actual burning of the building. Why were the arsonists granted an uninterrupted interval of seventy minutes (8:10 to 9:20) in which to try to set the building afire? And who were the leaders of this riot? An eerie comment on the second question comes from a tall, unbearded sophomore who asked that his name not be used: 'When the original crowd left the commons to swing past the dormitories, picking up members, I joined at Tri-Towers. We roared past the unfinished library building, singing and shouting that we were going to burn ROTC. But as we passed Manchester Hall, I overheard a strange conversation. Two young fellows just ahead of me . . . I think they couldn't have been students, at least not at Kent State. They were in serious discussion, and the first said, "How are we going to get off this campus when we're finished?" and the other replied, "The same way we got on." Impressed by the implication of these remarks, I continued to watch the two. They led the group. They were always a few feet ahead of the crowd, and where they led, the others followed.'

In this formation the mob stormed over the crest of Blanket Hill and rushed down at the ROTC building, screaming as they went. The young sophomore kept close to the leaders, and reports: 'A lot of people broke windows, but these two fellows were the ones who did their best to start the fire. They reached in and applied matches to the curtains, but they wouldn't burn. "Fiberglass," one of the men said. So they got some large flares and threw them in. When the firemen came, I watched these two fellows wrestling with the fire hose, and they kept it tied up till the building was pretty well ablaze.'

Several witnesses testify to a ghostly incident which occurred just before the fire began. From the mob, one young man, well dressed and so agitated that he could not control himself, ran wildly from group to group, crying, 'You have no right to do this! You must not burn this building! It belongs to your government. It belongs to you!' He made a deep impression on many who heard him, but he had no effect upon the mob's action, and in time one of the faculty marshals caught him and led him away.

Carl Moore, the red-bearded professor who had operated the elevator, says, 'As a faculty marshal I stood ten yards from ROTC as the junior arsonists tried for forty-five minutes to set fire to the metal sheathing on the building. The other three sides of the building are wood, and what do they do but go for the metal. I tried to drive them off and warned them about the live ammunition inside, but they kept plugging away. I saw many fraternity men in the crowd chanting, "Get it! Get it! Burn it! Burn it!" '

Howard Ruffner, photographer for the campus yearbook, had an exciting evening. 'My job was to take photos, so I reported on campus about 4:00 in the afternoon and picked up rumors that there would be an important rally at either 5:00 or 7:00. Nothing happened at 5:00, so I decided to hang around the union, and as I was about to enter, a man I had never seen before stopped me and said, "Where's the Student Union?" I remember a curious thing about him. He carried a paper bag in which he had two rolls of toilet paper.' Whether they were to be used as incendiary material or as improvised gas masks, Ruffner didn't know.

When the rally started at 7:00, a modest affair, Ruffner saw one student jump on the bell structure while others rang the bell: 'He began to shout, "Let's go over to Tri-Towers!" but I had never seen him before. In fact, I didn't recognize many of the initial crowd that gathered about ROTC. I thought this so strange that I started taking crowd photos, but eight or ten men came over and started to grab at me. I'd never seen any of them. They surrounded me, and one of them asked, "Did you take any of our pictures?" I told them no, and he said, "You damned well better not."

'I worked my way around so that I could take photos of the people working the bell, but by the time I got there, the man who had been on top telling everyone to get moving, climbed down. He himself stayed back, and joined the crowd that had threatened me. I noticed that he had an eight-inch bowie knife taped along his left leg.'

The essential spirit of Saturday night was best caught by Barbara Agte, a teaching fellow from Texas Western at El Paso, and one of the faculty with whom the radical students felt they could discuss politics without inducing shock. She says, 'As I was standing by ROTC trying to keep students out of trouble, I saw with horror that one of my brightest boys was coming across the commons with a large barrel which he was evidently going to crash through the windows. "Stop that!" I shouted at him, but he replied, "We've just got to do this. This building has got to go." I argued, "You must go away or you're going to get hurt," and he yelled back, "Six years of peaceful protest got us nowhere. They'll listen only when they see flames, and tonight they're going to see them." And there went the window.' There would be many students on campus this weekend who were convinced that a minority which had made repeated protests was entitled to take violent action if their demands had not been granted.

Mike Alewitz missed the fire. 'I had gone to Ohio State to attend a Young Socialist conference. Big ideas. When I returned to my room in Columbus, totally polluted, a friend said, "Mike, I have some bad news for you. They burned the ROTC building on your campus." I sobered up right away, because I knew this meant trouble. Nobody had told me there were any plans afoot to burn the building.'

Craig Morgan, a meteoric young man who was about to be elected president of the student body for the 1970–71 academic year, had a more ominous experience: 'I was trying to police the campus as a student marshal, but was getting nowhere. Boy, that mob wasn't about to listen! But I did see this one student with a hefty length of chain which he was swinging over his head in order to wrap it around a fireman's neck, and I grabbed his arm and said, "What are you trying to do? You could kill somebody with that." And a couple of us immobilized him.'

And Joe Pezzino, a sophomore from Clarence, New York, who had come to the rally with some friends, found himself in the thick of trouble: 'I was sitting up by Taylor Hall, watching the ROTC building go, because the gas down on the commons was too much for me. A large group, about 400 kids, started to form around me, and many "organizer types" appeared. I heard much talk: "That's right, kids, stay here, there's safety in numbers. Don't run if the pigs come toward us, just stay here." One guy not far from me had a whole bagful of Molotov cocktails, and he didn't bother to keep it a secret.'

Murvin Perry, head of the School of Journalism, heard a battle cry which reminded him not of jovial student disturbances but of hard-core street-fighting by professionals: 'As ROTC burned I stood on the walk north of the tennis courts, watching the National Guard clear the commons area. It was then I heard someone shout, "Here they come! Chicks up front!"' This was the traditional cry of street fighters who rely on the hope that neither the Guard nor the police will fire at girls.

One of the journalism students who helped on this book has a curious reason for remembering the ROTC fire, but it has nothing to do with arson. Larry Rose says, 'That night my wife and I were out of town. We'd gone to a small-town carnival in Barbeton, on the other side of Akron. I'd been assigned by my photography professor to take some blurred-action night shots, and when we got there we found the major attraction was Bob Hope. In the middle of his monologue, which was very funny, he got deadly serious and referred to the window-breaking in Kent the night before. He said something about still having faith in the youth of this nation, and at that very moment they were burning down the ROTC building, twenty miles away.'

Two conservative students saw the start of the fire. Lou Urbano was born in Naples, Italy. The parents of Nick Haskakis had been born in Greece, and the two boys had absorbed from their families the fundamental tenets of old-style patriotism: 'Our fathers worked. They saved pennies to send us to college. They taught us that this country was a blessing to the ordinary man. Again and again they explained that in the old country we would have been peasants, but that here we had a chance. And we took what they said seriously. To us the university was a privilege.'

Lou Urbano, medium height, very dark hair and eyes, good-looking, confesses, 'I'm an old-line conservative. I love this country. So I kept a close eye on SDS. And I went to the BUS rally on Friday and listened to their inflamed oratory. Burning a building was the logical next step, and I had a pretty fair suspicion that ROTC would go.'

Urbano shakes his head in bewilderment: 'Isn't it obvious that society has developed because we have evolved a set of tested rules? Why do mere kids want to destroy everything we've inherited? Today a university seems more like a high school, the students so immature . . . so unable to think things out for themselves.'

Urbano was close to ROTC when the arson began. To one young man about to toss a railroad flare into the building, he protested, 'Don't burn this place down. This is my university,' to which the man with the flare replied, 'It's sure as hell not my university.' Urbano stayed near the center of the rampaging group and overheard enough to get the clear impression that a hard-core cadre had determined to lure the National Guard on campus, hoping to radicalize everybody.

When the first flare was thrown, Urbano experienced a strange sensation. 'I wanted to rush over and cover it with my coat. Extinguish it, because it was burning my university. But I held back. Why? I suppose I was afraid. Maybe I'd get kicked. Maybe they'd laugh at me. I've been ashamed of myself ever since. Maybe if a half a dozen kids like me had taken a stand right then, it would have stopped.'

Nick Haskakis, a huge, muscular fellow with a powerful head which seems larger because of the heavy horn-rimmed glasses he wears, has also been ashamed of himself since that fiery night. He explains why: 'At about ten minutes after eight that night, I heard a mob making noise at Tri-Towers. Grabbing my camera, I went over to see what was happening. I got caught up in the first wave of students who were rushing down the hill to storm ROTC, and I stayed with them all the way. You couldn't say there were leaders who were directing, "Hey, you! Go over there and do that!" but there was strong leadership of the sort that says, "Let's do this next." And when they spoke, people acted.

'When we reached ROTC a pitiful thing happened. A little man who must have been a professor tried his best to halt the students, yelling at them, "Please don't burn this building." The mob shouted, "We've argued about this damned place long enough. Burn it." And the little man cried, almost in tears, "But if you burn it I'll have no place to teach." '

It was the incident that happened next which Haskakis remembers bitterly: 'A student whipped out a flag and set fire to it. I thought, "Man, what a shot!" And I took several great photographs on my Instamatic, but as soon as I had done so, a crowd of about a dozen men surrounded me and began cursing me and shouting, "Get that guy with the camera!" and they knocked me to the ground and began kicking at my stomach. I remember thinking, "Oh, God! I'm going to be killed." But I rolled over on my belly and hid the camera, and they really began working me over, and when they gave me one extra hard belt I had the crazy thought: "No, I won't die. Twenty years from now I'll remember this as an interesting experience."

'I was saved by a girl who threw herself on me and pleaded with the men to stop kicking me. I don't know who she was. She wore granny glasses, wire-rimmed, and had pigtails. She told me, "Be sensible, give them the camera," and all I could say was, "But it has pictures I took last week of my best friend's wedding." When she saw I wasn't thinking too clearly, she took the camera away from me and handed it to one of the men who had been kicking me.'

The cause of Haskakis' discomfiture was juvenile, but it lends authenticity to his account: 'What really irritated me, still makes me sore, is that when I was just a kid I was larger than the others, and also a Greek, so that boys from the upper grades found pleasure in knocking hell out of me. They came at me in gangs and I couldn't lick them, so I developed a tactic. When I saw them closing in, I focused on the smallest kid, grabbed him around the neck, and beat the living hell out of him. No matter what they did to me, I murdered that kid, and pretty soon they learned that eight of them could beat me up, but one of the eight was going to wind up in very sorry shape.

'You know? At the burning of the ROTC building I didn't land a single lick on any of them. A big guy like me, and I didn't even break a nose. Why not? I was terrified.'

When college authorities finally called for help from the Kent fire department, Chief Miller put into effect the plans he had devised the week before. Fireman Helmling says,

'When I reached the station, Chief Miller had everything ready. "Well," he told us, "they finally did it. Someone threw a flare into the building. Dave, I want you to go out on Truck 3." He assigned six of us to the lead truck—four volunteers, two regulars—and we roared off to the campus.

'We drove up Summit, turned left into Portage Drive. As soon as we found a hydrant, our youngest member jumped off, hooked the end of his feeder line onto the hydrant and turned on the water, which meant that by the time our truck had pulled ahead to a spot just west of ROTC, the water would be arriving there with us. The free end of the feeder line ends in a clamp. That's what we call the head, where the water is delivered and where we can attach two different hoses. But before we could even unwind our dry hose, the clamp was gone. Students had moved in, grabbed the charged line and run away with it. I could see them on their hands and knees . . . a mob of boys and girls with knives and ice picks . . . hacking it to pieces. This stuff isn't easy to cut, but they were using bolo knives. We recovered two of them and have them on display at the station.

'Two other firemen helped me pull a length of dry hose off the truck and we hooked it directly onto another hydrant closer to the fire, but when it was fully activated with water, the fire had died down and we had no use for it.

'But now the real trouble started. Three white males with Afro hairdos detached themselves from the mob and approached two motorcycles—one red, one black—took the lid off one of the gas tanks, dipped a rag into the gas tank, walked over to the window into which someone had thrown the earlier flare, laid the rag on the windowsill, lighted it with a match, then flipped it into the room with a stick. When it landed, the room was pretty well ignited.

'As the three students walked slowly back to the commons to rejoin the crowd, I took my hose up to the window to try to put the fire out, but as I did so I was attacked by the three men, who knocked me down with a heavy wooden club, struck me three times, then jumped on me and began beating me up. They grabbed my fire hose and took off with it.

'I was in real pain, because one of the shots had struck my left arm. I was also mad as hell over the loss of my hose, especially when I saw that fire inside. And then the damnedest thing happened. Six students with full beards saw my condition and ran at me. When they reached me, they ran right past, went into the crowd, grabbed the hose and brought it back to me. Without saying a word, they handed me the hose and returned to their positions at the far edge of the crowd.

'One look at that crowd convinced me that they weren't going to let me use that hose, so I abandoned the attempt. Instead I took two men with me and we chopped our way into the west end of the building to put the fire out before it could reach the ammunition at the other end. We chopped through a steel wall only to find ourselves facing a stud wall, and when we hacked our way through that we found ourselves inside a walled closet, and at this point we decided there was no reason to sacrifice a life for a building which the students were determined to burn down.

'So we left the building and went back to the truck in time to hear Chief Miller on the radio telling us to get out of there. We weren't being allowed to fight the fire and had no police protection against the kids who wanted to beat us up. So we climbed aboard Truck No. 3 and left the campus. When we got back to the main fire station Chief Miller and Mayor Satrom were waiting for us, and when they saw how badly beat up I was, they told me to find a bed and lie down. They wanted me to undress and quit for the night, but I said, "Nothing doing. I started this job and I'm going to finish it." You see, I'd been a marine in Korea and I'd feel ashamed to quit.

'Seventeen minutes after I lay down, we had the same six men on the same truck headed back for the same fire. The area around ROTC was now under some kind of police control, but the building itself was pretty far gone. Our job was to save the other wooden buildings around it, because the fire was so hot that the paint was blistering and the tar was beginning to ooze out. We kept our hoses on them, and after they were secured we recovered our other hoses and left the campus.'

Fireman Dave Helmling's testimony was so striking that we spent a good deal of time trying to find verification, and almost on the day we were leaving Kent we came upon another fireman who had ridden Truck 3 that night. Richard Workman, skilled firefighter for twenty years, says, 'I wasn't bugged by the appearance of the crowd. I have two boys of my own. One went real long-hair. It was red and he looked wild, but I didn't make a big thing about it. Now he's in Vietnam, short haircut, and doing a great job. I remember when the Air Force ROTC building was set on fire. That was some years back. The students gathered around us as we fought it and cheered like crazy whenever the flames burst forth, then booed us when we put them out. But that was sort of in fun. This time, no. Real savage professionals who brought specific weapons with them to chop the hoses in half. Two of the ugliest parts of the night were when the men beat up Dave Helmling and the coeds standing by yelled at us, "Leave that hose alone and come on up in the dorm. We'll make it worth your while." That's what they yelled at me as I received orders to lead the men back to the firehouse even though the building was still burning. First time I ever left a building that was still ablaze.'

Jamie Haines, the Young Republican, witnessed the burning of the archery shed: 'I was sitting in Tri-Towers lounge when the news broke about ROTC. A few minutes later a girl came running in sobbing and crying hysterically. She said someone had set fire to the shed with all her archery equipment in it. She cried, "They're burning everything and nothing can be salvaged." She didn't even mention the ROTC building. So we piled out to watch.'

When it was seen that the archery shed was flaming and that nothing more could be accomplished there, the young arsonists set off across campus to burn down the president's house, an old frame building. This would be much easier to ignite than ROTC had been, and some students in the group who did not want to see it lost ran to Professor Frank, shouting, 'They're going to burn the president's house!' He rounded up some policemen, yelling at them, 'We've got to get to the president's house,' but one of the officers took him aside and said, 'Glenn, we got word this afternoon they were going to try to burn it and we have it well protected.' When the arsonists reached the old building they were met by highway patrolmen who turned them back, and there was no more burning that night.

In a good number of discussions concerning the burning of the ROTC building, the researchers were amazed at the pleasure with which many students remembered the incident. That the burning of the building was destruction of public property was of no concern; what mattered was that it had effectively been removed from campus. 'I was really glad to see it go—it should have been done a long time ago' or 'I wouldn't have burned it myself, but I certainly wouldn't have stopped anyone doing the job' were standard refrains, even from many students who would have to be considered political moderates.

Writing to a friend shortly after May 4, Rita Rubin, a junior, expressed the sentiments of many students: 'We watched the building burn. I was glad it burned. I'm against the war in Vietnam. I'm against anyone getting military training on a college campus. We've been trying to end ROTC for a year, and burning down the building was a reasonable answer to an administration that doesn't listen to its students.'

A pathetic sidelight: Taylor Hall—a lovely building on the opposite side of the commons from ROTC—was protected by the respect in which the students held it . . . all but one. On his way across campus he ran along the pillars of the peristyle and heaved a large rock through one of the handsome plate-glass windows. Other students tried to catch him, shouting, 'You damned fool! Not this one.' He evaded their grasp and pitched his rocks through three more of the windows. Professor Harvey Saalberg, born in Germany and a survivor of Nazi concentration camps, was working in Taylor Hall when this happened. Tears came to his eyes as he saw his beautiful building being defaced. He was reminded of the glass that had shattered throughout Germany on that infamous Crystal Night when the Nazi hoodlums finally asserted their leadership.

The varied reactions of the army officials connected with ROTC are interesting. 'Everyone knew ROTC would go sometime or other,' says Captain Terry Klinger, a young assistant professor of military science, 'and for some reason I had a feeling it would be Saturday night. You could almost feel it in the air. So, late Saturday afternoon, after spending the day with the ROTC rifle team at a practice range outside of Kent, I came back to campus and took my camera and radio out of my office in ROTC headquarters. What a hunch! I was sort of ashamed when it paid off!'

Others were not so lucky. Colonel Arthur Dodson, in charge of the ROTC program, lost mementos he had collected over thirty years of military service: 'We have the most senseless act that I can possibly recall in a place which is supposedly very highly civilized and, I thought, a very nice academic environment. I haven't been to Vietnam. At the present time, I think that Vietnam would probably be a pleasure.'

It remains unclear as to why no arrests for serious offenses were made Saturday night. There had been open incendiarism, assaults on firemen and photographers, the smashing of windows, and an attempt to burn down the president's home, with ample chance to identify many of the perpetrators although perhaps not the instigators. Jeff Sallot says, 'The university had asked that afternoon for five hundred John Doe injunctions against any violent activity on the campus, and the administration had these in hand, but they were never used.' By the end of the evening the Kent city police had arrested only thirty-one persons . . . for violation of the 8:00 P.M. city curfew.

'That curfew business was wild,' says a student named Pete Holmberg. 'My girl and I decided we wanted to see the Film Festival in University Auditorium, but we weren't sure whether the town curfew applied to traffic as well as pedestrians, so I called the police department for information. When I asked the cop who answered what would happen if I drove to campus, I couldn't believe his reply: "If you're caught out after the curfew in a car, you'll either be arrested or shot."

'With that, a friend of mine who was with me, Stu Feldstein, called Mayor Satrom, because we couldn't believe that such a thing could be true. Feldstein told him about the cop's comment, and Satrom reacted without surprise. He merely said, "We intend to use all force necessary to maintain order." '

Chester Williams, on duty Saturday night, says, 'That mob which swept down over the hill to attack ROTC was the best organized I have ever seen on this campus. A handful of leaders knew exactly what they wanted to do and how to do it. I can state flatly that we had information in advance that the hard-core leaders were going to attempt serious trouble, and we took steps to neutralize them, but they were very clever in leading the students away from the commons, then coming back with their screaming supporters. They came at us so swiftly and with such discipline that we could never take the initiative away from them.'

Williams adds reflectively, 'I have reviewed the incidents of that day many times and do not see how my force could have acted other than it did.' He had been away from campus Friday night, attending the wedding of his nephew in Dayton. 'Some people have asked, "Why were you in Dayton?" Well, on Friday noon I'd checked on the burial of the Constitution. Nothing illegal about that. The speeches were not inflammatory and we felt rather lucky to have got off without trouble.

At 3:30 in the afternoon Lieutenant Crawford called me at the airport as I was about to fly to Dayton and reported, "The BUS rally was real quiet. Things look good." Then Paul Petrella, one of our finest detectives, called me and said, "There'll probably be some trouble downtown tonight, but nothing serious. Just first-of-spring stuff. We'll be able to keep it under control." So I went to the wedding.'

At 1:30 Saturday morning a phone call informed him of the rioting on Water Street, so he jumped into a Plymouth and drove all night, getting back on campus at dawn. 'At 8:30 we had a meeting with campus police and the officials downtown. We had five more sessions later on, three on campus, two downtown. We took into account everything that might possibly happen. Naturally there were rumors about ROTC, had been for five years. But we had plans for everything, and looking back on them, they were good plans. Then as dusk came, students in numbers greater than we could have anticipated came roaring down that hill, and when I took one look at them I realized that everything was lost. Specifically, to have sent a handful of campus policemen into that mob would have been insane. We had taken everything into account except the determination of the mob. My conclusion is that we lost the ROTC game by one point in overtime.'

Lieutenant Crawford agrees with Williams' assessment: 'If the National Guard had not arrived when they did, I'd have faced one terrible decision. Either run and let other buildings burn, or hold my ground and start firing. Don't you let anyone tell you we weren't stoned Saturday night. We were, heavily. One of my men was sent to the hospital and my knee is still bad because of a blow from a hunk of concrete.'

Few people lamented the loss of the building itself, and there were many rumors Saturday night that the administration had known it was doomed and was not unhappy when the campus police did not interfere, seeing this as a chance to get rid of an eyesore and a focus of student agitation. The police say, 'That charge is not true. We wanted to save the building but were powerless to do so.' People who knew the ramshackle affair did laugh, however, when claims were made that the ROTC building had burned at a loss of thousands of dollars. To repeat, the university would have had to pay out money to get it torn down. Also, everyone remembered when West Hall, a sister building and almost as ugly, had been set afire by student arsonists in 1968. It was then serving as a temporary classroom for art students and was so poorly equipped for that task that many students had threatened to burn it. When it was finally ablaze, great resentment was felt throughout the university that the firemen had been called.

Martin Nurmi, a responsible older member of the faculty who had investigated the business about liquid crystals and Che Guevara, recalls, 'An English teacher was using one end as an emergency class and it was she who reported the fire. The rest of the faculty humorously ostracized her, claiming that she had retarded progress.'

News of the arrival of the National Guard changed everything. Word that Charlie Company might be moving to some new assignment came Saturday afternoon at 1:00, a radio message for Captain Snyder from the Battalion command post in the Rubber Bowl. The voice of the operations officer, who liked to exercise a Biblical turn of phrase upon occasion, came drawling out of the receiver: 'Cyanide, be ye prepared! Be ye prepared to move to Kent no later than 1800 hours. I don't know what the hell's going on over there, but you're needed.'

Since the truck strike had obviously cooled, Snyder had let half his troopers go home for the day. Fortunately, this absent half of the roster had orders to be back by 1800. From past experience, however, Snyder knew that a number of his men, returning at the last minute from spending a pleasant afternoon with their families, would end the day by chasing Charlie Company's big two-and-a-half-tonners up the highway en route to Kent.

Sergeant Gordon Bedall was one of the stragglers. With his wife and daughter in the family car, he raced after the troop convoy, caught up with it at the Rubber Bowl, and jumped aboard a truck, confident that some buddy would have packed his duffel for him.

Bedall will never forget the sight that greeted the Guard as their trucks rolled up onto Route 80-S, the expressway that leads east of Akron. There was a low overcast that night and they could see the crimson glow of fire against the sky. The Kent State ROTC building was more than a dozen miles away, but the reflection of the flames consuming it could be seen even farther in all directions. Says Bedall, 'It looked like the whole university was going up.'

Two skilled photographers, Paul Tople and Don Roese, greeted the Kent city policemen when they came on campus, and Tople remembers how they looked: 'They came in riot dress, with clubs and visored helmets, and they looked real tough, but I saw they were shaking. I knew one of them, and said "How's it look?" and he said, "This is a really bad scene." He began to sweat—drops all over his face—and his hands were trembling. "I wish I were out of here," he said as he walked gingerly up to some students and said quietly, "You have to push back from here." '

As the police moved into action, Tople and Roese heard a loud squeaking noise. 'I knew right away it was a tank,' Tople says. 'I'd heard that sound on television, so we ran toward the street just in time to find ourselves in the middle of the barrage of rocks which greeted the arrival of the National Guard.' Roese started swearing at the students, but was hit hard in the left leg by a rock. 'The Guard fired gas at the mob,' Roese says, 'but the wind was in the wrong direction and blew the gas right back at them. Just then I was hit by a second rock—same leg, same spot.'

It was then that Tople saw something which foretold what was going to happen on Monday. 'One student in particular, wearing a light-colored outfit, kept running up to the Guard, jamming his face into theirs and cursing them most obscenely. When they made a move, he would retreat to the mass of students and lay low for a while. Then he'd feel brave and run out again. "Keep an eye on that loudmouth," called a Guard officer. "We'll take care of him." The Guardsmen got a good chance to identify their tormentor, because he kept running at them a number of times.'

As the Guard formed up to move onto the campus, Tople and Roese heard an officer warn: 'You guys got to listen to me. You spread yourselves out too far. Keep together. That's the important thing. You guys got to listen to me. Watch my hand signals. This is going to be tough.' As the Guardsmen marched past the two photographers, the latter saw some coeds crying and heard one of them say, 'I can't believe this is happening on our campus. I just can't believe it.'

One of the more level-headed views of Saturday comes from Lieutenant Barnette, the Guard liaison officer assigned to advise with Mayor Satrom. 'The whole thing was most familiar,' he explains. 'I had gone to Kent and knew most of the professors involved, and I had lived in the city, so I knew most of the politicians. Also, this was my sixth such civil action with the Guard and I knew pretty well what to expect.'

From the moment of his arrival, Barnette warned the city officials, 'You must understand that we can't move 600 Guardsmen around in a few minutes. If you want them here tonight, you've got to tell me so by 4:00 this afternoon. Later, under pressure, I changed that to 5:00.'

Barnette is firm on one point. 'Everybody I worked with was honestly trying to do the very best thing for the city and the university. Nobody tried to grab center stage. Nobody blamed the other guy. These were real professionals trying to do a job. Trouble was, the city tended to overreact, the university to underreact. You wouldn't believe the type of intelligence that kept pouring into City Hall. One man reported, "I saw an Illinois car loaded with six Weathermen armed with shotguns." Several townspeople warned us, "Students in the house next door are lugging in shotguns and rifles. Preparing for a big shoot-out." Talk about a town being uptight!

'The university, on the other hand, took things too coolly. At one session they threw four big problems at us. Should they allow beer to be served on campus that night? Should they call in some bands to play for dances? Should the film festival be canceled since it was well known that several of the proposed films were revolutionary? And should BUS be allowed to hold a dance at which all black students would gather? Big deals, and the town ready to explode.

'But the university people were consistent. No one up there wanted the Guard to be called in. Even Williams said no. Captain Schwartzmiller said no. When the combined group asked me what the situation would be if the Guard did come in, I explained that the Guard would not assume control of the city. That would remain in the hands of elected officials. To take one point, Guardsmen would have exactly the same right to make arrests that an ordinary citizen has, and no more. The Guard could detain troublemakers, but arrests would have to be made by local or state police. The university people wanted assurances that if the Guard did come, they would stay clear of the university, but I made it clear that the Guard, if summoned, could respect no such arbitrary boundaries. They would have to operate throughout the whole of Kent. I knew this from my five previous Guard actions.'

When the 5:00 deadline came and passed, without the Kent officials being able to make up their minds, Lieutenant Barnette extended the time till 5:30, and at 5:27 Mayor

Satrom finally gave the signal. 'Outriders began arriving in the city at around 7:00,' Barnette says, 'and you know the rest.'

President White missed the fire. Dawn had barely broken on Saturday morning in Mason City when he received a telephone call from his aide, Ron Beer, who reported the trashing of Water Street and the meticulous plans which were being worked out by the administration to keep the university on an even keel. Beer assured White that the situation was under control, but White suspected it might not remain so. He therefore took two precautionary steps. He canceled his plans to go to Iowa City for the education meeting, and he asked that the Kent State Piper Aztec be flown immediately to Mason City, because he feared he might have difficulty arranging a commercial flight if he needed to get back to Kent in a hurry.

He spent Saturday morning on a series of nine phone calls, checking on precisely what was happening at the university, and was assured by his associates that his presence on campus would not be required that night and that a return flight was not warranted as of that moment. He then instructed the pilot to hold the plane in Mason City on the chance that the situation might worsen at Kent, requiring his emergency departure.

As he was preparing for bed, he received a phone call from his maid, Cora, who cried, 'Dr. White! The campus is burning!' He got in touch with the pilot, but bad weather had set in, and they could not fly to Kent that night.

He got no sleep, but at 7:45 Sunday morning he was airborne on the way back to the university.

Five students

It is noteworthy that each of our five students witnessed the ROTC fire. Allison Krause had spent much of the day in Engleman Hall, her dormitory, discussing the previous night's riot with her best friends Liz Troshane and Bonnie Henry. 'I think it's crazy, what the kids did in smashing windows downtown,' said Allison. 'It's just not fair to make small businessmen suffer.' And the others agreed.

'We kept wondering what would happen next. Rumors flying all around the dorm,' says Bonnie. 'And that night we found out. Allison and Barry would always invite me to tag along on their dates, and about seven o'clock we set out for some art flicks in Bowman Hall. We'd heard that one of the features showed Christ coming back to earth as a student at Berkeley, and thought it might be really far out.'

As the three approached Bowman Hall they saw crowds gathering at the ROTC building, so they stopped at the top of Blanket Hill to watch. Prudent Barry, afraid of what might develop, warned the two girls, 'Somebody down there is going to say, "Let's do this or that," and everybody will yell, "Yeah, man!" and they'll roar off in a mob and do it, no matter what. We better get out of here, because this whole thing is going to end in a mess. It's completely unorganized.' But Allison and Bonnie prevailed upon him to stay with them, and they watched as the crowd at the building swept up the hill, rounded Taylor Hall, roared over to Tri-Towers, returned from their sweep of the dorms and cascaded down the hill to set fire to the building. Bonnie, however, said, 'I was always afraid that I might get caught up in a crowd and be trampled. So when the mob swept past, I hid behind Allison, and she said, "That's all right. I'll protect you." '

They watched as the fire was lit and the building burned. 'Neither Allison nor I had any idea of helping burn the building, but we certainly weren't going to stop anyone. We both wanted to see it burn and get ROTC off campus,' says Barry.

Bonnie concurs: 'At the end, even though we could feel the tear gas, it wasn't really a scary situation. Kids all around us were laughing and cheering and the whole thing was sort of like a party. When the police came and ordered everyone off the commons, we headed for Barry's room in Johnson Hall. It was closer than our dorm and we spent the night there.'

Bill Schroeder did not see much of Kent that day. After he and Al Springer had taken the two Akron girls home they went on to Al's house and spent the night there. Waking late on Saturday, they took a tour on Al's motorcycle, winding up in the early evening at the Drafthouse, one of Akron's popular beerhalls, where talk turned to what they might do during summer vacation. Schroeder said, 'I'm going to sell my car and move out West for the summer. I've got a lot of friends in Colorado.' He had spent his freshman year at the School of Mines at Golden. 'I'd like to see my buddies, and besides, I think I might be able to pick up a construction job. They pay good money out there. I could use some, the way I've been spending it.'

Just about then, someone who recognized Bill as a student from Kent rushed in, shouting, 'They burned the ROTC building over at your school!' Bill leaped to his feet, yelling to Al, 'This I got to see.' They jumped in Bill's car and sped back to the campus, arriving in time to see the final flames consume a building which had come to mean a great deal to Schroeder.

As one of Ohio's most promising high school students, Bill had won a valuable ROTC scholarship, which he could apply to any college in America which offered a ROTC program. He had used it at Golden, and when he wanted to return East it was necessary to find a school which also had ROTC, for he did not want to waste the scholarship money to which he was entitled. He was by no means a gung-ho militarist and once confessed that he 'stuck with ROTC because I need the $1,600 a year it provides.' But he told another friend, 'It would hurt my mother if I cut out of ROTC. She's pretty patriotic.' He did well in his military work at Kent and gave every sign of becoming a first-rate army officer when he graduated. His professors ranked him as one of the finest prospects they had. Now, looking at the blazing building in which this part of his education had taken place, he was deeply perplexed. He told Al, 'I'd heard rumors and I'd seen the demonstrations against ROTC, but I just couldn't believe they'd actually burn it. ROTC may not be the greatest thing, but you can't just go around burning up things you don't like.' He watched the fire with a morbid fascination, then turned abruptly and headed home in deep confusion.

Jeff Miller rose at his customary hour of noon to engage his philosophical roommate John Moir in protracted debate. Jeff made these points: 'The Weatherman Days of Rage in Chicago last fall were a stupid operation. They accomplished nothing. But from what I can tell, what happened in Kent last night may have been different. It was justifiable. Nixon's adventure into Cambodia proves that he will never listen to the people. Maybe now the students will make themselves heard, because people listen only to violence.'

'Sure, Jeff, all that's fine,' Moir replied, 'but I tell you this place is going to blow. There's something freaky about this weekend, and I'll bet you Kent State closes down by Monday.

I'm getting out and going home while I can.' With that, Moir packed his bag and left for the remainder of the weekend.

Almost as he said these words, the phone rang. It was Jeff's mother, calling to make sure that her son was all right. 'It's okay, Mom,' he reported. 'Nothing's going to happen out here.' However, after dinner, which he scrounged from a coed who liked to cook, he wandered onto the campus to see what was happening and mingled with the mob that seemed determined to burn ROTC. As he felt the spirit of the crowd and became aware of its potential, he became worried when a student with whom he was standing grabbed a rock, ran boldly across the grass and hurled it at the ROTC building.

'Stop that!' Jeff protested. 'Let's get out of here before the cops arrive and start busting people. I'm getting paranoid.' But the friend who had thrown the rock assured him, 'Quit worrying. As long as we stay together we'll be all right.' So Jeff stood there as the building burst into flames.

The coed from whom Jeff Miller scrounged his Saturday night dinner—as he was in the habit of doing—was Sandy Scheuer. She had known Jeff for only a month; friends had introduced them, and although Jeff had rarely asked her for a date, he had often accompanied her in group parties. He liked her so much that he formed that habit of dropping by casually almost every day. Together they had painted a small mural which hung on Sandy's wall, but their relationship was more that of brother and sister than dating partners. On this particular evening, Jeff sat in Sandy's living room drinking wine and reading the paper, while Sandy stayed in the kitchen cooking. After dinner, as we have seen, Jeff wandered off to the campus.

For Sandy, it had been just another day. It started with a call from Sharon Swanson, who had news of Friday's trashing of Water Street. 'Sandy was really surprised when I told her what had gone on,' says Sharon. 'The TV in her house was broken and someone had borrowed her radio, so she hadn't heard anything. She rarely went to the bars downtown and thought the violence was terrible when I told her about it.'

In the early afternoon Sandy's mother and grandmother had driven to Kent, bringing some summer clothes which she would need now that the weather was growing warm. They had accompanied her to downtown Kent and been appalled at the broken windows, but were relieved when they heard

Sandy say on the telephone to one of her roommates who was spending the weekend in New Jersey. 'The worst is over. Things are going to be quiet.' Cooking dinner for Jeff Miller had been fun, and afterwards her date Bruce Pipman arrived and the two also headed for the campus, where they stood on the porch of Taylor Hall and watched the ROTC building burn. They tarried overlong, because on their way back to the Summit Street house they ran into policemen who had arrived to disperse the crowds, and for the first time in her life Sandy Scheuer got a large helping of tear gas. She didn't like it.

For Doug Wrentmore, Saturday had been uneventful. On a trip downtown to investigate the damage, he told a friend, 'Big deal. Everybody's running around saying, "What do you think? What do you think?" Me, I've got no reaction. It's just as if somebody's garage had burned down.' At dusk he and three friends prepared for something which did excite him: an overnight camping trip to lake-front grounds near Sandusky, but before they drove north they decided to take a swing around campus in case something might be happening. When they got out of their car near the commons they found themselves in the tail end of the group headed for Tri-Towers to enlist students for the assault on ROTC.

'All of a sudden we heard "On to Tri-Towers," and we were off!' When the crowd, much augmented, returned to Blanket Hill, Doug and his friends remained near Taylor Hall to watch the arsonists.

'I was quite content to see the building begin to burn, for I have no love for ROTC,' says Doug. 'I don't think it has any business on campus. Kent's a university, and the military shouldn't have anything to do with it.'

However, the first good whiff of tear gas sent Doug and his friends scrambling, but before they left the campus Doug very daringly ran across the grass and as close to ROTC as he could, doubling back in a big circle to inform his friends, 'Fire's out. The building's not going to burn after all.' They were therefore much amazed a few minutes later, as they were on their way to the Sandusky camping grounds, to see the sky ablaze from the rekindling of the building. 'Let's get out of this town fast,' Doug said, and as they left Kent they found themselves face to face with the Ohio National Guard coming down Water Street. 'It looks like the Czechoslovakian invasion,' Doug said, and he was relieved to know that soon he would be on the sand dunes, away from such things.

A rumble of tanks

With a sense of defeat, Professor Frank left the ROTC fire at about 9:50. All he had tried to accomplish that day with his marshals had come to nought, and now, off to the west, a small gang of irresponsibles was trying to burn down the library. They were driven off, and Frank was once more alone.

But as he walked dejectedly toward Main Street, there surged up behind him a group of rampaging students who had been repulsed from their attempt to burn the president's house. The mob swept past Frank, turned west on Main Street and headed in the direction of Prentice Gate. Frank followed close behind to check on possible trouble, when suddenly, at the edge of the mob, he spied Steve Sharoff. 'Steve!' he shouted. 'Steve, for God's sake, you've got to stop them!'

Sharoff nodded, bewildered. 'I'll try, Dr. Frank,' he said, and dashed off.

Frank saw him remonstrating with several young men in the lead, but the howling gang ignored him and pressed on. Finally Sharoff came back, the agony of total failure in his face. 'Dr. Frank,' he gasped, 'this has gone way beyond anything I imagined.'

'You should have thought of this sooner, when you helped start it,' Frank snapped.

Sharoff went over to the curb and sat down, holding his head in his hands. Frank thought he was weeping. The mob roared on toward the center of town, where the police would be waiting.

As Frank walked away from Sharoff, he heard a rumble coming from the darkness to the east. It grew louder, and he stopped to consider what it might be. At the end of a day like this, it could be anything.

Then he saw, coming out of the darkness, a half-track. He thought it was a tank—big, lumbering, ominous. It was followed by two troop carriers which looked to him like little tanks. They were filled with silent troops in helmets and with rifles projecting upward from the floor of the carrier. Then came a line of jeeps, each marked with army designations and containing four determined soldiers. Finally there were some trucks—big, brutal things that moved awkwardly but with force. It was an impressive column, a raw and terrible thing to see coming onto the campus of a university.

But to Frank's surprise, the column moved silently on,

right past the university entrance, as if ignoring the troubles to the south and the column of smoke still rising from the burned-out building. Like a twisting dragon with a purpose of its own, the army vehicles continued west on Main Street, passed through the traffic light at Lincoln Street, and disappeared in darkness over the hill which led to the center of town.

Frank says, 'I sighed with relief to see them pass us by, but only a fool could think that they would not be back.'

It was Ruffner who first saw the Guards enter the campus. 'I was taking pictures of the ROTC fire as it died down, when someone shouted, "They got the library on fire!" I ran down that way to get some photos and saw coming through the trees two uniformed men with rifles pointed right at me. "Halt!" they cried, and a guy who had run up back of me gasped, "My God, they've got guns." '

Conclusions

The burning of the ROTC building and attendant events constituted a riot involving about 2,000 persons, and if Mayor Satrom had not summoned the National Guard late Saturday afternoon, he would have been justified in doing so Saturday night, for if the Guard had not been present, it seems clear that several more university buildings, and perhaps some downtown, would have been burned. That an 8:00 P.M. curfew should have been in force in town and a 1:00 A.M. one on campus seems an invitation to trouble. Students who would normally have frequented Water Street now turned to the campus for action.

The fact that so many persons were aware that ROTC was going to be burned that night raises the question as to why no serious attempt was made to save it, and it is not preposterous for students to claim that 'the administration decided to give us ROTC.' The financial loss involved in its burning was vastly exaggerated, to the detriment of sober discussion in the days that followed May 4, when millions of Americans inclined to justify the execution of four students on the grounds of the damage they had done to government property. On the other hand, the moral wrong of burning this building cannot be stressed too strongly. It was a most serious dereliction, and the fact that it was not promptly and severely punished contributed to the deterioration which followed.

The police would have been justified in arresting about eighty participants for offenses such as ignoring an injunction, obstructing public officials in conduct of their duty, or failing to disperse. As many as fifty others could have been arrested for riot in the first degree and thirty for inciting to riot. At least a dozen others could have been charged with arson, and half that many more, with physically assaulting firemen. These latter offenses are grievous, and it would be shocking that the conspicuous ringleaders were not arrested, except that during their offenses no police were in evidence. Armed with the John Doe injunctions secured that morning against just such a contingency, the university would have had no problem in apprehending and prosecuting wrongdoers. That law enforcement agencies allowed the building to be brazenly burned is almost unbelievable, and once again the tardy arrival of the police, both campus and city, and their lack of cooperation on the scene was unprofessional.

The administration appears to have been pusillanimous in its response to the arson, and lacking in foresight in that it made no effort beforehand to warn students that the Guard might be called to the campus. The fact that Dr. White was unable to return in time to assume command of a rapidly deteriorating situation on his campus was unfortunate.

There is substantial evidence that mature leaders, not necessarily enrolled at the university, engineered this riot and quarter-backed the burning of the building, but the actual arson was so amateurish that one must conclude that the professionals stayed well away from an act for which they could have been arrested. Most surprising is the fact that four major investigations, all with power of subpoena, have failed to turn up even one photograph of the major participants in an event which covered three hours and twenty minutes (7:10 to 10:30) and involved at least 178 active rioters. This would seem to prove that the leaders who terrorized the photographers did so with this outcome in mind.

IV

SUNDAY: CARNIVAL

Day of a Guardsman

Guardsman Carl Caldwell—that is not his real name, for he is one of those in the ranks of the Ohio National Guard who have requested anonymity—was awakened for his first duty at Kent before dawn Sunday morning. Carl had already torn the cloth name tag from his jacket. He had heard that some of the more imaginative dissident kids on campus looked up Guardsmen's names in the Akron or Ravenna phone books. If a woman answered the phone, they asked in a bedroom voice, 'Hey, you beautiful chick, who are you fucking now that your pig husband is here on the Kent campus?' Carl had been recently married.

Caldwell's outfit had been billeted Saturday night in the gymnasium of the William A. Walls Elementary School three blocks north of Main Street. During a breakfast of fruit juice, eggs, pancakes and coffee he wondered what kind of duty he would draw. The ROTC building was now a heap of ashes—nothing there to guard any more. When he learned that he would be assigned to a fixed post at the Kent city waterworks, he felt mildly relieved that he would not be going on campus. He himself had gone to Kent and was at present taking a psychology course there—he had, in fact, been preparing to go to class when the call came to report to his Guard unit. He would know a lot of the kids on campus. And they would know him.

The eastern sky was beginning to color as he and two other men were trucked out to the waterworks on Mogadore Road a couple of miles southeast of town. They were armed with two M-1's and an M-79 grenade launcher. The day promised to be warm and clear and there was already a handful of fishermen dangling their lines from the bank of the reservoir.

Carl checked them out. He found no bombs or suitcases full of strychnine. Over the radio he called his company command post and reported that there were no problems, nothing out of the ordinary. Every fifteen minutes a jeep came by to make sure all was in order with his unit. It looked like a long day ahead.

So let us for a moment take a good look at anonymous Carl Caldwell, a person who could be picked from the middle of the spectrum of Ohio Guard manhood present in the Kent environs that tragic weekend. He is in his early twenties; tall, lean, clear-eyed and eager for all that life ahead of him will bring. He and his wife are still childless. He is in his first career job and squeezing a little extra education in on the side. He speaks rapidly, softly, with just a touch of bitterness concerning his experiences of that day and the next. He is proud of his outfit, its training and its accomplishments. 'They call the Guard "Mickey Mouse," ' he says, 'but as soon as I enlisted I was whisked off to Fort Polk, Louisiana, for nine weeks of basic training under tough army officers. When that was finished, and I'd lost eight pounds, I stayed at Polk for ten more weeks of advanced infantry instruction. They assigned me to mortars and I became an expert. I could have moved right into the regular army. I knew mortars as well as they did.

'Instead, I came back to Kent State, where I'll be in the Guard for the next six years. Each month I have to attend at least four drills. Each summer we go to camp run by the federal government. This is important, because it throws you back into the national army. Your training is geared to the federal scheme of things, not the state. Every bit of training you get fits you for national duty. Very definitely, the state of Ohio comes second . . .'

Throughout its history the Ohio National Guard has been called to restore order to civil disturbances more times than any other Guard unit in the country. It has served with distinction in most of America's wars abroad. It was formed at Marietta, Ohio, on July 25, 1788, under laws intended to provide what was then known as the Northwest Territories with a militia. It even has its own ballad, 'Billy Buckeye,' an adaptation of a poem by Rudyard Kipling:

We aren't no cheap tin soldiers, nor we aren't no loafers, too,
But Buckeye boys from Buckeye schools, remarkable like you;
An' if we're sometimes careless-like an' just a bit too gay,
We steady down to business when the band begins to play.

(*Chorus*) Then it's Billy this, an' Billy that
      An' 'Billy, where's y'r gun?'
But it's 'Please to march to music!'
      When there's shootin' to be done.

The Buckeye Boys were first ordered out in the spring of 1812 to garrison the American fort at Detroit, which was soon taken under siege by a combined force of British troops and Indians from Canada. The fort fell and the militia retreated to the south. The next year, fighting under General William Henry Harrison, commander-in-chief of the Northwest Army, it defeated the British for good at the battle of Fallen Timbers.

In 1846 Ohio provided nearly one eighth of all the land forces employed in the war with Mexico, some 8,100 men. Ohio militiamen fought at Vera Cruz and Monterey. Concerning these actions, their commander wrote to the governor: 'I am sure you would have been proud of them. They walked into the most galling and murderous crossfire of the enemy with the coolness of regular soldiers, not a man or an officer flinching.'

After the war the Ohioans returned to a state engulfed in the industrial revolution. Railroads were expanding, cities ballooning with immigrants bound for the newly opened California gold fields. Law and order were on the verge of breaking down and beleaguered county sheriffs were forced to rely on the militia as a back-up force.

In 1861 President Lincoln asked Ohio for 13,000 troops to back the federal cause; 30,000 responded. Two future presidents of the United States—James A. Garfield and Rutherford B. Hayes—were among them. Major General George B. McClellan took command of Ohio forces, which included volunteers from such companies as the Cleveland Grays, the Columbus Videttes, the Cincinnati Rover Guards and the Dayton Light Guards. All in all, an astonishing total of 350,000 Ohio men fought in the Civil War, earning battle pennants at Shiloh, Murfreesboro, Chancellorsville, Gettysburg and the Wilderness, to name a few.

Once again the veterans returned to a state in the throes of unprecedented civil disorder—violent strikes, mob rioting and vigilante rule. Miners deep in the bowels of coal-rich Ohio brought their grievances home to employers with clubs and cap-and-ball muskets. The employers responded with goon squads, kangaroo courts and, finally, using influence with the legislators, the Guard. The Guard muster for 1877 reveals that all National Guard units were used, all 8,737 officers and enlisted men at a cost of $35,000 to the state's taxpayers. Less than a century later, in 1970, that figure would exceed $2,000,000—again, mostly for crowd control.

Also in 1877 there occurred a railroad strike serious enough to paralyze the state. Seven years later a Cincinnati lynch mob estimated at 10,000 killed several enlisted Guardsmen and one captain in three days of street rioting. Called back to Cincinnati the next year to quell a labor dispute, Guardsmen prominently displayed a murderous Gatling gun, the forerunner of the modern machine gun. The sight of it had a marked, calming effect upon the crowd. But in 1894 rioting again broke out. A sampling from one unit's records shows eleven major call-outs between January and October, each involving mob action and some entailing death. Violence, then, is nothing new to Ohio.

In 1916, the majority of Ohio's Guard units were ordered to active duty on the Mexican border with General John Pershing and the campaign against Pancho Villa. They were there as World War I broke out. Ohio, then the fourth largest state in the union, made the fourth largest contribution of fighting men. The first of the units to ship out was the 37th Buckeye Division; the second, the 166th Infantry Regiment. Both units fought with distinction at St. Mihiel and the Meuse –Argonne offensives. The German general staff rated the Buckeye 37th as one of the five best American divisions in the field.

Following the war, the Guard was again frequently called upon for disaster relief and riot control. In May of 1934, when labor violence broke out in Toledo, civil authorities could not subdue the crowds and requested the governor to send troops. Nearly a thousand Guardsmen responded and found themselves almost immediately involved in pitched battles with rioters. Tear gas was liberally used and gunfire broke out more than once. When the disturbance was controlled, the Guard found themselves being accused of having shot a striker without provocation. An inmate at the Mansfield Reformatory later confessed that he had done the shooting. The Ohio Guardsman *Bulletin* reported in its June 20, 1934, issue:

Scores of Guardsmen nursed bruises and contusions resulting from the barrage laid down by strikers (mostly bricks). However, the troops exhibited admirable self-restraint during these trying situations and major casualties were relatively few. The training received by Guardsmen for this kind of duty was in evidence throughout.

In 1940, quick upon the heels of Germany's invasion of Poland, the Ohio Guard was mobilized for federal service, and as the 37th Division, fought in the Pacific at places like New Georgia and Bougainville. It landed on the beaches of the Philippines and fought its way through Luzon. Of the seventeen Medals of Honor awarded to National Guardsmen during World War II, seven were won by members of the Buckeye Division. During the Korean War the Ohio unit was again federalized, but this time its duties kept it at Fort Polk, Louisiana, as a training division.

When it became apparent that the Vietnam war might escalate, a new plan for using the National Guard during wartime was promulgated. The normal six-month training period required before a Guard unit could be fitted into the national army would be eliminated by the device of selecting certain Guardsmen and keeping them at a high level of training, so that they could step immediately into the federal army. Selected Reserve Force this was called, and more than 6,500 of Ohio's 16,000 Guardsmen qualified for this ready force. A consequence of this move, however, was that Guardsmen began to think of themselves primarily as units prepared to serve abroad, whereas their principal duty would continue to be the handling of local civilian disturbances, as the following roster shows:

April, 1968	2,600 Guardsmen called to duty to cope with civilian riots in Cincinnati and Youngstown.
May, 1968	650 Guardsmen in Akron to put down race riots, followed by a full-scale mobilization of all Guard units to forestall possible race riots.
August, 1968	1,624 Guardsmen sent to quell prison riot at Ohio State Penitentiary.
July, 1969	1,300 Guardsmen required to halt race riots in Youngstown and Columbus.
December, 1969	634 Guardsmen required to put down disturbances at Akron University.
April, 1970	984 Guardsmen on riot duty in the Cleveland suburb of Collingwood. Battalion on

standby at Miami University. Another battalion at Sandusky to prevent race riots.
4,000 Guardsmen at work guarding trucks
at Teamsters' dispute. Strong units diverted
to Ohio State University to quell student
disorder.

In brief, the Guardsmen who patrolled Kent State University may have been trained for front-line duty overseas against
an enemy army, but they could not be said to be novices in
the handling of civilian disturbances. Whether they had been
provided with the right weapons for the latter job is another
question. One additional fact must be cited. Ohio, which stood
sixth among the states in population, stood fifth in the frequency with which it experienced civil disturbance, but first
by a long margin in its willingness to call out the National
Guard to deal with those disturbances. In other words, the
state was trigger-happy.

It was this dual tradition of war abroad and riot at home
that stood squarely behind Guardsman Carl Caldwell as he
walked his post at the Kent waterworks that sunny Sunday
morning.

Bad-mouthing the establishment

It is difficult for an older person who attended college even
a decade ago to believe the restrictions which have recently
been imposed on university administrators. Father Hesburgh,
of Notre Dame, has said, 'When I was appointed president of
Notre Dame in 1952, I could make any academic decision
on my own authority. This has been gradually chipped away
so that now I have roughly one tenth the power that I had
then.' In late 1969 Notre Dame was faced with the exciting
possibility of playing the University of Texas in the Cotton
Bowl for the national championship. 'Before I could decide
this simple question I had to get the approval of five different
groups, and even then other campus personages complained
that they should have been consulted. In 1952 I would have
made up my mind without checking with anybody. Now the
faculty makes decisions, and that's as it should be.'

But the task of holding a faculty in line requires tact and
expenditure of time. 'The way things are now, your powers
of persuasion are taxed too much. Unless things are simplified,

I would guess that before long no intelligent guy in his right mind would want to be a university administrator.'

Dr. Clark Kerr, former president of the University of California, who lost his job when the first of the Kent-type confrontations exploded on his campus, reflects, 'There is a lot of negative power on the campus. It is loaded with veto groups. Any really important measure at the University of California must pass at least twelve checkpoints.'

Graphic illustration of the new limitations on discipline was witnessed by one of the researchers when he visited the office of President White and heard the black student leader Erwind Blount, in the presence of four women secretaries, call the president 'a motherfucking, racist, cocksucking pig.' The visitor was stunned, and waited to see what action would be taken against Blount.

'None,' an administrator explained. 'There's not a thing we can do about foul language. The Flanagan case tied our hands on that.'

On Wednesday morning, February 26, 1969, Officer T. F. Kelley of the campus police found a poster on the bulletin board in the Student Union which in his innocence he deemed indecent. It announced a 'Film and Revolution' festival; the first three paragraphs explained what the seven movies were intended to accomplish:

The Revolution grows, forcing a reevaluation of roles within all segments of society. Not the least of these areas is the arts.

The struggle for a free and just world continues. Its growth can be seen in the films created by some of today's young artists. From the underground film tradition there has developed a new documentary style.

Out of the recognition that true freedom in art occurs when art becomes one with action or with life itself, these films not only reflect but encourage the Revolution.

The fourth film listed was entitled *Panther* and depicted 'the vanguard of the black liberation struggle, the Black Panthers confront the immediate agent of their repression, the pig.' It was the last paragraph that made Officer Kelley wince:

Garbage: The shit of consumption piles high on the streets of New York while the ruling class enjoys its fruits. The Up Against the Wall Motherfuckers dump on Lincoln Center.
—Venceremos!

By Thursday, five complaints had been filed with the police by students saying that they did not think such language appropriate for a university bulletin board. Kelley took the offending poster to the prosecutor of Portage County, Ron Kane, and asked his advice. 'It's immoral, indecent and obscene under Section 2509.34 of the Ohio Revised Code. Bust them,' Kane said, so Kelley went back to the campus to try to find out who was responsible for the poster. He had little difficulty, for as he entered the Student Union a tall, thin young man, clean-shaven but with a wild head of hair, was sitting with a group of friends at a table in the lounge. When Kelley approached, this tall fellow rose, walked over to a nearby table and started distributing handbills to students seated there. As Kelley neared him, Flanagan turned to his friends, and in the standard jargon, said, 'Here he comes— Pig Kelley! Our number-one pig on campus!'

The speaker was well known on campus as Rebel Flanagan, an activist, an SDS supporter and an able rabble-rouser. He was well liked by left-wing students and in the opinion of his associates was 'no dummy.' He was even clever enough to have received a $250 national defense loan and a $100 Equal Opportunities grant during the spring quarter. His real name was Matthew J. Flanagan, nineteen years old, from Bedford Heights, a suburb of Cleveland, but everyone called him Rebel because of his vigorous opposition to our present society.

His arrest and incarceration in the Kent jail created a storm in SDS circles, as this exchange from a subsequent investigation proves:

MR. ROMINES. Miss Murvay, I would direct your attention now to the date of February 27, 1969. Did you have occasion on that date to witness an incident involving SDS?

MISS MURVAY. Yes. That was the date that an SDS member [Rebel Flanagan] was arrested for passing out the literature. It was that leaflet that was just entered as an exhibit. The SDS members were very upset that he had been arrested for passing out the literature because they considered it political repression, because they felt that the university had him arrested because he was an SDS member. So they decided to go to one of the meetings held at one of the dormitories on the campus that night.

MR. ROMINES. Will you describe briefly what happened during that meeting?

MISS MURVAY. May I refer to my notes?

MR. ROMINES. What are your notes from, Miss Murvay?

MISS MURVAY. These notes were taken from the meeting that I attended on the 27th.

MR. ROMINES. Why were you taking notes of the meeting?

MISS MURVAY. I was taking notes because I was working with the Kent State police department at that time. At that meeting, one SDS member, Joyce Cecora, made the remark that if the university does not stop politically repressing SDS, they would burn and level the campus.

MR. ROMINES. That statement was made by whom?

MISS MURVAY. Joyce Cecora.

MR. ROMINES. What generally did the students discuss at that meeting on the 27th?

MISS MURVAY. They were very upset that their fellow SDS member had been arrested. One member, George Gibeaut, was beating on the garbage cans, jumping up and down, swearing. He had the idea that they should go down to the jail to get this SDS member, Matty Flanagan, out of jail, get him out one way or another. He tried to get people to give him a ride down, getting people to go. But nobody had a car available, and they were more interested in talking to the other people, convincing them that the university had done such a thing, so he did not get to go to the jail.

There was no need for Gibeaut's proposed liberation force to attack the city jail, for even as the SDS meeting was in progress on campus, a lawyer, Gustav Goldberger, was arranging for a Portage County bondsman, Mr. Percoco, to post the necessary $1,000 bail, and at 10:42 P.M., the bond having been posted, Rebel Flanagan was released. Early next morning his SDS defenders were distributing on campus a flier with this message:

YOU MAY BE NEXT, BUDDY!

Yesterday, Rebel Flanagan was busted by the campus cops for passing out 'obscene literature.' What Reb was trying to let people know about was a film festival called 'Film and Revolution' sponsored by Kent SDS tonight in the commuters' cafeteria of the Union.

What Rebel got for his troubles was a day in jail, $1,000 bail and a *felony* charge for which he faced a possible *1-7 years*.

Rebel's arrest was a POLITICAL ATTACK ON THE MOVEMENT AT KENT; an obvious attempt to scare the movement into silence. Our response can only be to break that silence and fight back against the political repression that the MAN is bringing down, and against the system that needs repression in the first place in order to keep itself alive.

—KENT STATE SDS

The flier repeated the description of the film, and therefore the indecent language. As Officer Kelley pointed out in his report: 'This arrest is predicated on the fact that the printed material in its terminology is immoral and indecent to the average person. This is further supported by the fact that the material could have been viewed or read by the numerous young persons coming to the university for the annual "Little Sister's Weekend." This event traditionally brings several hundred female teenagers, or younger, to campus.'

When Flanagan's case came before Judge Lester Campbell of the Portage County Municipal Court, he had to dismiss the case in accordance with recent Supreme Court rulings, because the campus police could not prove that the language which Flanagan was distributing 'appealed to the prurient interest.' After that decision, you could say anything you cared to on the Kent campus, and to anyone.

No incident in recent Kent State history better illustrates the legalistic strait jacket in which a university must operate than the CCC protest which came close to shutting down the campus in the wake of those confusing events which had occurred at Music and Speech on April 16, 1969. Then, as you will remember, the university discipline committee intended holding a closed hearing in the case of Colin Neiburger, and his SDS supporters decided to break in and make it an open hearing. In the course of the confrontation, fifty-eight students were arrested and summarily suspended, while retaining full rights to subsequent appeal and dismissal of their cases in the event that substantiating evidence was not forthcoming. (Cases were subsequently dismissed without prejudice to the students involved.)

Faculty and students alike rose in protest over the suspensions, claiming that they were made improperly, illegally and in contravention of university, Ohio and federal law. Campus lawyers initiated a meticulous review of each step of the procedure which had led to the arrest and suspension, and numerous fine-point discrepancies were uncovered. At the conclusion of the faculty investigation, these principles were elucidated:

1. Every student is entitled to know the reason for any administrative action that may harm him.

2. A discretionary decision should not be made, or advised, by anyone who is biased or likely to be biased concerning the issue being decided.

3. A discretionary decision impairing a student's rights should not be based on inaccurate or inadequate information if it is reasonably possible to ascertain the full truth.

4. A student should not suffer derogation from his existing rights or privileges without his case in defense of them being considered; and for it genuinely to be considered, he should know in good time what case he has to meet.

5. Any administrator making a discretionary decision, who recognizes that a student might be adversely affected by it, should, before making it, take appropriate steps to give the student an opportunity (a) to learn what case he has to meet if he chooses to act in defense of his rights; and (b) to put before the person making the decision such evidence and argument as he (the student) thinks material.

6. Reasons should be given to justify a discretionary decision, for to decide an issue without giving the reasons upon which the decision is based approaches autocracy and is incompatible with the educational objectives of the academic community.*

The outside observer is easily convinced that these principles ought to be applied to students within the historical development of advanced education—say, the student who breaks university property or who absents himself from class for a month—but one is perplexed as to how these same principles ought to be applied to those few students at Kent State who:

1. Advocated that President White be shot.
2. Openly announced that they intended to destroy the university.

*Kent Chapter of the American Association of University Professors: *Report of the Special Committee of Inquiry,* September 1969.

3. Habitually called campus police, to their face, 'mother-fucking pigs.'

4. Openly threatened to kill campus policemen.

5. Distributed leaflets calling for the assassination of all policemen at random.

6. Threatened to blow up buildings.

7. Warned that if disciplinary action were taken against them, 'the sky would be the limit.'

8. Preached that the United States government must be overthrown, now.

It was in their attempts to discipline such students that the Kent State administration so often found itself hog-tied by intricate rules and labyrinthine interpretations of them. A classic example of what this can mean was displayed when a faculty committee looked into the Music and Speech disturbance, in which the fifty-eight students were suspended. The faculty lawyers argued, citing relevant United States Supreme Court cases to back them up, that because a well-intentioned administration agent, anxious to avoid complicating the case with an irrelevant black-white confrontation and eager to preserve racial peace on campus, took it upon himself to arrange for the release of the two black girls whom everyone knew to be in the building by accident, the suspensions of the other fifty-eight were invalid.

> In direct violation of legal due process *(Barker v. Hardway)* and academic due process, Negro students were exempt from the application of the policy simply because they were Negro.

If blacks had been discriminated *against,* this reasoning would obviously apply; but when blacks were discriminated *for* in a situation where to do otherwise would have been an incitation to further rioting, one would think that common sense would be able to differentiate between conditions.

Ten other faults were found with the attempts of the administration to discipline students. Three will indicate their nature:

> The provision of Item A-3 of the Code of Student Conduct that requires advance written notification of formal disciplinary action was violated with respect to at least one applicant.

> Item B-1 of the Code of Student Conduct, concerning inquiry

into the appropriateness of medical or counseling referral, was violated with respect to at least one student.

At that same student's hearing, Mr. Oates failed to explain their duties to the members of the Judiciary Board that was hearing it.

One would surely agree that in each of these cases the one student involved in what might have been a miscarriage of justice ought to have legal redress and full protection under the law; the administration would be bound to provide satisfaction. But it is difficult to believe that these isolated and partial errors constituted a basis for challenging the entire disciplinary process necessary in a time of potential riot. This was in the spring of 1969; by 1970 the administration was so powerless that it could not take effective preventive action when trouble started, and from the ensuing culminating troubles, disaster resulted. (Imagine the outcry that would have resulted if on Saturday morning the university officials had summarily suspended twenty or thirty students who had wrecked North Water Street the night before; to have observed every item of what some described as 'due process' would have required as long as a week, each day filled with protests, challenges and threats of further riots.)

The acme of this nit-picking, however, was reached when the faculty committee tackled the question of whether President White, prior to the suspensions, had warned the students that such suspensions might be invoked if they rioted. Said the committee:

The March 28, 1969 *Stater* account of President White's statement concerning disruptions reports him as saying, 'We are establishing procedures for immediate suspension in time of mass eruptions.'

President White's statement does not say that procedures *have* been established, but that they *are being* established. Students reading this report would have inferred from the wording that guidelines were being offered to the university community for their consideration and comment rather than that the report constituted a binding public notice.

It must be remembered that the end product of such reasoning was a huge mass meeting and protest which helped radicalize many students. As Bob Perko, from Delta Upsilon,

says, 'When I was told that the administration had denied
due process to the fifty-eight students suspended because of
Music and Speech, and when professors who knew their way
around assured us that the process had been illegal, and when
we heard that both the student constitution and the federal
had been ignored and ridden over rough-shod, I became
angry. I joined the CCC protest. I marched along with four
or five thousand other students, and I was ready to strike
to close this university down. Then I heard that the CCC
movement was an SDS cover operation and I withdrew.'

After that brief flurry in 1969, Perko remained outside the
protest movement, but hundreds of others who participated
in the riots of 1970 have testified: 'I was fairly indifferent to
campus agitation until Music and Speech. Then I saw how
the administration ignored due process.' To support them in
their conversion they had the statement of the faculty committee:

> We conclude that the university failed on numerous counts to
> satisfy both legal and academic due process.

In almost every crisis operation of the university during the
years 1968–70, this tendency toward a legalistic approach
which inhibited and often prevented decision is apparent.
Neither student nor faculty member could be disciplined, and
if committees did not go so far as to call openly for the creation of a *campus sanctuary* from which no student can be
arrested and taken to the jurisdiction of ordinary courts, they
erected so many barriers to effective police action that an
ipso facto sanctuary came into being. Meanwhile, certain
students committed to revolution abused the sanctuary thus
provided, using it as a base to call for rioting, dynamiting,
revolution and murder.

The faculty committee was mindful of this difficulty and
addressed itself to the problem:

> The decision to call for 'outside police' was taken without con-
> sultation with representatives of the faculty. Yet such a decision
> is of the greatest import, insofar as it departs from the tradition
> whereby the campus is a kind of sanctuary. The tradition of
> sanctuary does not mean that acts that would be illegal if com-
> mitted off campus should enjoy legitimacy and legality on
> campus. Rather it refers to the essence of the academic com-
> munity as a place where reason, truth and dialogue enjoy free
> play. Where police are to be called onto the campus, it seems

to us there should be genuine consultation with representative elements of the *entire faculty*.

It is precisely this concept of an inviolate academic sanctuary, which developed rapidly in the 1960's, that encouraged student misbehavior, outraged civil observers, and threatened the university with drastic reprisal from state legislatures. In the latter pages of this book we will see where the doctrine of sanctuary led the universities of Venezuela and Japan; no man in his right mind could want such devastating results for the United States. This doctrine is pernicious and destructive, not of itself—for in the chaos of the Middle Ages the sanctuary of the church was needed—but because it cannot be operated within a complex industrial democracy without engendering animosities and hatreds which must in time destroy the institution which is claiming the right of sanctuary.

Some theories of language

Additional comment is necessary regarding present-day use of obscenity on campus. It has become so common that the most demure coeds, dressed in Villager blouses and Bobby Brooks skirts for which their parents pay tidy sums of money, habitually use language which would be resented in a corner saloon. If any man persisted in it, someone at the bar would probably knock his teeth in.

In the text, we have avoided reporting the constant flow of obscenity that marked many of our interviews; we have used an occasional noun or adjective to indicate the general coloring of the conversation, but even this has been embarrassing when reporting what girls said. Partly we refrained because we did not want parents to see such words attributed to their daughters.

Students are irritated when an older person objects to this language or points out that it accounts for much of the rejection that greets them. 'Who cares what I say?' was a constant question. The answer is, 'A great many people do, and if what you say embitters them and makes understanding impossible, why persist?' The young person's reply is, 'It's our language, and they better get used to it.'

It is more serious than a mere problem of taste. The perilous gap existing between townspeople and students often stems from the use of foul language, especially by girls. When the incident of the jeep occurs on Monday, the reader will see the obscenity problem through the eyes of a young man with a wife and daughter. Later, when the grand jury condemns a whole generation it will include this paragraph:

> It should be added, that although we fully understand and agree with the principle of law that words alone are never sufficient to justify the use of lethal force, the verbal abuse directed at the Guardsmen by the students during the period in question represented a level of obscenity and vulgarity which we have never before witnessed. The epithets directed at the Guardsmen and members of their families by male and female rioters alike would have been unbelievable had they not been confirmed by the testimony from every quarter and by audio tapes made available to the grand jury. It is hard to accept the fact that the language of the gutter has become the common vernacular of many persons posing as students in search of a higher education.

No explanation of this phenomenon, which is apparently nationwide in scope, was offered us until Robert Franklin dropped by one afternoon for an unscheduled conversation. He announced himself simply: 'Robert Franklin, libertarian communist,' and said, 'I've taught at Cornell University and Brooklyn College, but I like Kent best. It has a very American quality which I appreciate. My radicalization started here in 1967 when two Catholic priests from Guatemala were shot at with BB rifles by some right-wing students on the sundeck at Johnson Hall. I began to see that SDS had certain correct ideas. You see, I'd always been an intellectual socialist. I really believed that the new system for governing the United States would spring full-blown out of our heads, but now I began to see the need for a step-by-step destruction of the establishment and a reconstruction along saner lines.

'I shy away from revolution,' he said, 'but I have to recognize that the present establishment is so powerful that it will not relinquish control until it faces violence, so I suppose it will have to come. I developed these concepts while I was traveling in places like Yugoslavia and Bulgaria.'

Franklin then discussed the problem of scurrilous language. 'When the university arrested Rebel Flanagan for having posted a sign containing the word *motherfucker,* I immediately saw the trap they had dug for themselves. Flanagan was in my chemistry class and I knew him as a bright student . . .

with electric hair like mine, only his was red. I went promptly to White and Matson and told them, "It's insane. It's irrational to put this boy in jail at this time. The Supreme Court decisions on the matter of pornography are so clear that you won't be able to keep him in jail one day. He'll be released by the judge and you'll look stupid. Because the fact is that under present law, nothing can be judged pornography." I warned them that if they had any sense they'd release Rebel right away and save themselves embarrassment.'

Here Franklin smiled condescendingly, then added, 'Of course, the courts behaved as I predicted. What else could they do? You see, the word *motherfucker* is now part of normal, everyday speech and no court in the land would dare to outlaw it.'

He then proceeded to explain his philosophy, one which other students would allude to later: 'The new-style young people have adopted these ultimate words out of a sense of frustration. What frustration? Seeing our earlier vocabulary coopted by Madison Avenue. We used to say "Cool it, man," and now you'll see this in advertisements everywhere. We said "Get it together, man," and now you see the Dodge people using it as their slogan. We said things like "blow your mind," and *Harper's Bazaar* is advising women whose husbands earn $50,000 a year to blow their minds with pink blouses. *Psychedelic, trip, right on, letting it all hang out, it's what's happening, getting it all together, laying down a good rap* were stolen from us and put to the most banal uses. So in self-defense we have retreated to the no-retreat words, and we defy Madison Avenue to steal them from us.' He pauses, twists his leather cap to one side so that he looks exactly like a frenetic character out of Dostoevsky, then laughs and slaps his knee. 'Damn it all, I'll bet that within two years Buick will come out with full-page ads claiming that the 1972 Buick is a real motherfucker.'

He concluded with a case history: 'I was scheduled to give the final lecture in our big seminar course, Great Contemporary Issues, and it seemed to me that the biggest issue university students faced was the protection of their own identity, and one of the surest indices of identity was an in-language, used only by them and protected by them. So I made my lecture an unbroken string of the liveliest gutter language I could conceive. Just one block-busting word after another, bound together by the ideas I've just mentioned. At first a few girls got up and left, but pretty soon the huge audience caught on to what I was trying to say. They applauded, because they understood. I was legitimatizing their language. I was showing them that their language was just as effective as the language of any other culture. And this is what's happening across the country. Young people are devising a language which older people cannot steal from them. We seek to outrage those who have been outraging us.'

Franklin avoided another explanation for the public use of obscene language, one which perhaps comes closer to the truth. Numerous committed revolutionaries have . preached that the debasement of language is one of the most powerful agencies for the destruction of existing society. They argue, 'If you destroy the word, you can destroy the system,' and they have set out consciously to do both.

The Free Speech movement at Berkeley was a brilliant improvisation of this theory. By encouraging students to use language which orderly society had for many generations outlawed, the leaders of the movement sought to show that most of society's laws were equally absurd and could be broken with equal impunity. The assault on language became the spearhead of an assault on all authority, and students who felt free to shout hitherto forbidden words also felt free to attack other restrictions.

There was a further rationalization. If language could be shaken apart and restructured, new types of communication might become possible, and young revolutionaries might very well end up in control of them, using them to say new things in a drive for new purposes. And the simplest way to shake language apart would be to break former restraints. The shock value of having a pretty coed shout obscenities at middle-aged women who had been brought up in older patterns was quickly recognized.

We found much evidence in Kent that middle-class families felt that they had been elbowed out of the local movie houses by the permissive language and frank sex that was now allowed. Numerous residents volunteered their thoughts on this matter: 'They've taken the movies away from us. They're beginning to take books and magazines.' There was some evidence that this middle group would begin to fight if television were also stolen from them.

There is a wide literature on this subject, one of the most instructive books being an extraordinary account by an Australian writer of his adventures in places like Nepal, Ibiza and Afghanistan. Richard Neville's *Play Power* eulogizes the underground press for having broken the shackles of language: 'A new generation has emerged who find that such terms contain no suggestion of prurience. The unequivocal use of language is not confined to the underground literary scene; it is part of the everyday politics of the movement. Obscenity is traditionally among the armoury of weapons employed by the alienated and frustrated.'*

It would be ridiculous to claim that every coed who blasts away with a chain of four-letter words is doing so because she sees herself as an agent of revolution, and it would be false to deny that literature has profited from the increased freedom of recent decades, but the crude assault on language as practiced by Professor Franklin in the big seminar he speaks of can be understood only as an attack on authority, conducted in hope that by breaking down one bastion, the ultimate destruction of all organization will become easier.

The danger in this game is one that has helped cause the downfall of many democracies. If the middle class begin to feel that their everyday standards of decency have been outraged, they will willingly follow the first repressive leader who cries, 'Let's restore decency.' This happened in pre-Nazi Germany, in Singapore, in Argentina and, recently, in Greece, to name only four instances among many. It could very easily happen in the United States, and soon. The way to avoid it is to follow a prudent line between Puritanical restraint on the one hand and offensive license on the other, and the young people of America had better find that line.

There is the final irony that the white leaders who complain that their colorful language has been filched from them by Madison Avenue, forget to state that they stole it from the blacks.

The governor moves in

In the material cited so far, the administration of the university has been shown waging a resolute battle to preserve the freedom and the integrity of education. Instead of being indifferent to the confusions of the age, or supine in the face of their challenge, Kent State was in the forefront in developing procedures to cope with new confrontations, and in this respect, led the educational institutions of Ohio. One must remember that Kent had taken these bold steps:

*Richard Neville, *Play Power*, New York: Random House, 1970.

1. By applying resolute pressure and sober judgment, it had forced SDS off campus.

2. By a restrained use of court injunctions, it had protected itself against students who sought to destroy it.

3. By making sensible adjustments, it had tried to win the support of its black students, and although it had been unable to satisfy all their demands, it had paved the way for solid cooperation in the future. Specifically, by resolving as many black protests as possible, the administration had kept the large middle body of black students from throwing their destinies in with the SDS.

4. By inviting specially trained units of the Ohio State Highway Patrol onto the campus to make arrests when serious trouble threatened, it had avoided both scandal and rebellion.

5. And while it took these innovative steps, the university remained zealous in defending the right of free speech, assembly and intellectual investigation.

President White, in particular, was a champion of academic freedom: 'All matters pertaining to academic credit are initially vested in the faculty and that is where they belong. Carefully constructed procedures, developed over many years, for the recruitment, tenure and final evaluations of faculty cannot be violated. We must preserve the integrity of these faculty relationships. The right of peaceful, non-disruptive protest will always be protected on this campus.'

The administrators of Kent State acted prudently in these years to keep their university functioning; they displayed both intelligence and courage. It is extraordinary, therefore, to witness how ineffectual they were during the May crisis.

In the absence of President White the university was administered by four young, able vice-presidents. Ronald Roskens, tall, handsome, natty dresser and excellent speaker, was a former speech professor with a doctorate from Iowa; his specialty was administration. Robert Matson, a crisp-looking, no-nonsense man of medium height, Ph.D. from Ohio University, had always been an administrator; he had the thankless job of student affairs, and opinions on his performance were savagely divided: older faculty, the board of trustees and most businessmen downtown considered him one of the ablest men on campus, but students whom he had to discipline and some of the younger faculty felt he was unyielding. Louis Harris, round-faced, gentle, was an outstanding professor of political science with degrees from Ohio State and UCLA and an expert in Latin American politics; he was provost; that is, the organizer of and spokesman for the faculty. Richard E. Dunn, B.S. from Bowling Green, was in charge of the business and financial affairs of the university.

Who, among these four, was in charge? There was some ambiguity about this. If the university had been a manufacturing plant, obviously the vice-president in charge of administration would take over. But Kent was an educational institution, and therefore the provost should have exercised primary responsibility. This would mean that Louis Harris, one of the best-liked men on campus, would stand in for President White, with Roskens, Matson and Dunn trailing in that order.

There were, however, certain confusions. In the late autumn of 1969 President White had circulated a letter among his vice-presidents which in their opinion blurred the table of organization, so that when the May crisis struck, the four young men could not ascertain among themselves who precisely was in charge of what.

A close reading of the letter fails to show why uncertainty should have arisen. It consisted of four items and spelled out exactly who should assume responsibility in case of four specific crises: breakdown of physical plant, weather emergency, student demonstration, national disaster. The third instruction read as follows:

3. *Student demonstrations.* In student demonstrations, these are largely the concern of the Vice-President for Student Affairs [Matson], Assistant Vice-President for Student Affairs, Dean for Student Group Affairs, Dean for Human Relations. It should be noted further that whenever such demonstrations are forming, the assistance of the Security Office is indicated, and where necessary the security officer is charged with seeking help from City Police and Sheriff, and/or the State Highway Patrol.

This seems forthright and clear, but as we shall soon see, the problem that confronted the university on Sunday morning was not so much a student disturbance, for that was in the past, but a confrontation with civil authority which threatened the very existence of the university. At this crucial time, the reputation and defense of the university rested in the hands of the second in command, in this case, the provost.

Unfortunately, during this turbulent weekend, when Kent State needed administration as never before, Harris was unable to provide it; on a trip to Mexico for the purpose of increasing his knowledge of Latin America, he had contracted a bad case of dysentery and was confined to his bed. Primacy among Roskens, Matson and Dunn was uncertain, and the intricate organization staggered around without a head, since, as we have seen, Dr. White had been detained in Iowa.

This meant that he was absent on Sunday morning, when one of the strangest meetings in the history of American education occurred. Events which would involve 760 American universities and colleges, close many of them down and imperil the future of advanced learning in this country were set in train by a group of men meeting in a city firehouse without the participation of a single educator.

At the table, making these momentous decisions whose repercussions will be heard for years, were James H. Rhodes, lame-duck governor of Ohio, fighting desperately to defeat Robert Taft in the Republican primary for United States senator; Kent's Mayor LeRoy Satrom, new to his job and edgy about what was happening to his city; a federal district attorney from Cleveland; Major General Sylvester Del Corso of the Ohio National Guard; Colonel Robert Chiaramonte, head of the Ohio State Highway Patrol; and Ron Kane, fiery county prosecutor of the district in which the university stood, a man who knew how to pick up votes when he got his teeth into a good issue and who was widely supposed to be preening himself for either United States congressman or governor of Ohio. These men had convened to decide the fate of a great university and, by implication, all universities, but their group contained no one who had paid much attention to how a modern university functioned. How did this happen?

At 9:00 Sunday morning Governor Rhodes announced by phone that he was flying into Kent by helicopter to look over the situation and would hold a meeting at City Hall. Since that building was under heavy renovation, the meeting was shifted to Fire Station Number One, and there in a room with a long plywood table and comfortable chairs, the chief executive of the state met with the men designated above. Not at the table, and never a functioning part of the meeting, were the three hesitant vice-presidents of the university, Roskens, Matson and Dunn, accompanied by John Huffman, assistant to the first-named, and Gordon Bigelow, assistant vice-president for student affairs. They stayed in a group, off to one side, and watched as the fate of their institution was being discussed. One cannot imagine James Bryant Conant, Robert Hutchins, Milton Eisenhower or Kingman Brewster being shunted aside when decisions were made about their schools.

However, Bigelow has a convincing explanation of why the administrators allowed this to happen: 'Governor Rhodes can be an impressive man . . . almost domineering. And right before he began his talk about declaring a state of emergency, he pointed his finger at the five of us and growled, "You university people stay out of this. We're taking over now." So we had to conclude that matters relating to discipline were out of our hands.' This was not an unreasonable deduction, since the university was a function of the state, and Rhodes, the chief executive officer of the state.

The informal meeting opened with the governor saying, 'Let's everybody sit down here and talk this thing over quietly.' The discussion that followed was orderly and made a lot of sense. Rhodes was angry but not intemperate. Satrom was quietly persistent, and young Ron Kane alternately listened and made suggestions. Rhodes pressed his main point several times: 'We have got to keep this university open at all costs. To close it down would be to play into the hands of all the dissident elements that are trying to do just that.' The discussion proceeded amiably, with the educators trying to eavesdrop as best they could.

Then an unfortunate thing happened, but one that should have been anticipated. Someone knocked on the door and told the meeting, 'The press is outside. They insist on a news conference.' One who was there reports, 'At that moment Jim Rhodes changed completely. He became a candidate for United States Senate. He has always been very much a take-charge guy, and I think he wanted to show the voters of Ohio that he was not going to be pushed around by a lot of young punks.' The press was given permission to enter.

When the room was jammed and the photographers had shot their pictures with Rhodes and Satrom center table, the governor was inspired to launch into a fifteen-minute spate of oratory calculated not to quieten the local situation but to gain him favorable attention throughout the rest of the state. Back-lane gossip had it that he was trailing young Taft in the Senate race, and he needed some telling action to impress the voters when they went to the polls two days hence. This was his last chance to make points. He would show them.

'We've seen here in the city of Kent, especially, probably the most vicious form of campus-oriented violence yet perpetrated by dissident groups and their allies in the state of

Ohio,' he thundered, and this was a regrettable statement because disorders in his own city of Columbus had been much, much worse. So had they at Athens and at Oxford.

He was correct, however, when he said, 'Now it ceases to be a problem of the colleges in Ohio. This is now the problem of the state of Ohio. We're going to put a stop to this.' But he was wrong when he intimated that the four SDS members who had recently been released from jail had been responsible. He was entirely accurate, however, when he said, 'They have one thing in mind and that is to destroy higher education in Ohio.' He then said something which careless listeners would interpret as an official estimate of the loss at Kent State. 'You cannot continue to set fire to buildings that are worth five and ten million dollars, because you cannot get replacements from the Ohio General Assembly.'

The governor next delivered a series of sentences that would be quoted across the nation, inflaming emotions wherever they were heard. They were quoted out of context, even in the reports of official inquiries, and did him much damage. Speaking only of the few who were determined to destroy the university, he said, 'These people just move from one campus to the other and terrorize the community. They're worse than the Brown Shirts and communist element and also the night-riders and the vigilantes. They're the worst type that we harbor in America.' Later he added, 'These people who are causing the trouble are not all the students at Kent State University . . . I'll say 99-percent-plus of the students at Kent State want it open. They're here for an education.'

The damage was done. Word was flashed throughout Kent and across America that the governor of Ohio had castigated students as being worse than Brown Shirts; accused young people conducting legal protests against war of being night-riders and vigilantes. The effect on the campus was depressing. Governor Rhodes had never said that, but to this day people everywhere believe that one of the principal reasons for the deterioration of affairs at Kent and elsewhere was the Rhodes rhetoric.*

---

*President Nixon suffered from this same tendency of listeners to misapply his words. During an informal tour of the Pentagon he stopped near the office of Secretary Laird and was surrounded by a group of admirers, one of whom said, 'I approved your speech on Cambodia. It made me proud to be an American.' This inspired the President to say off the cuff, 'Oh, how nice of you. I wrote the speech. I finished it at five o'clock in the morning the night before. I had been writing for a little while. I had a lot of help from my staff, including people over here. Well, we could not do it without the backing of all of you, you know. When I got down to the conclusion, then you say, well, the usual thing. You ask for support for the President and all that guff. Then you finally think of those kids out there. I say kids. I've seen them. They're the greatest. You

Things were not helped when Colonel Chiaramonte said, with proper pride in his highway patrol, 'We have men that are well trained. But they're not trained to receive bricks. They won't take it.' That much was all right; it was the following part that did the damage: 'The next phase that we have encountered elsewhere is where they start sniping. They can expect us to return fire.' Throughout the next days there would be an obsession with sniping, never justified but always in men's minds because of what had been said at the press conference.

When the reporters had their story, and tape recorders were put away, Ron Kane caught the governor's elbow. 'I want a private audience with you,' Kane said, maneuvering him into the men's room. Vice-President Roskens, seeing this, warned his aide, John Huffman, 'You'd better get in there and see what they're doing.' Huffman tried to edge his way into the room, but Kane rebuffed him, saying, 'No, this is private.'

As soon as he had Rhodes alone, Kane said, 'Governor, I want to close this university down.'

'No! You mustn't do that,' Rhodes protested. 'You'd be playing right into the hands of the Weathermen and the SDS and other dissident groups.' Kane responded that keeping the place open was bound to lead to trouble, and Rhodes said, 'I'm determined to keep it open. We must not knuckle under.' When the two men, talking softly, left the men's room, the university contingent over in their corner could only guess what decisions had been reached.

To assess the impact of Governor Rhodes' statement at the press conference is not easy. Taken in context it appears to have been merely a flamboyant expression by a man addressing, as was his custom and right, the constituency of an entire state. That parts of his speech were taken out of context and formed into meanings he did not intend cannot be denied, but this error cannot be charged against him. One must, however, take into consideration the manner in which his words were delivered, for tapes of his comments were broadcast several times in the Kent area, with inflammatory results. They were uttered in the hortatory style of a politician seeking votes

---

know, you see these bums, you know, blowing up the campuses. Listen, the boys on the college campuses today are the luckiest people in the world, going to the greatest universities—and here they are burning up the books, storming around the issue. I mean—you name it. Get rid of the war and there'll be another one. And then out there, we got kids who are just doing their duty, and I've seen them. They stand tall, and they're proud.' Nixon did not say that all college students are bums; he did say that those who blow up buildings are.

rather that the persuasive style of a leader trying to defuse a perilous situation. Heard on the air, his words sounded strident and challenging.

Myron J. Lunine, dean of the Honors College and professor of political science, was one of the coolest heads on the faculty and one whose job brought him into constant contact with the best student minds. He was not given to extravagant statement, and throughout the weekend was a source of temperate judgment and restraining action. He says, 'In trying to assess student attitudes, you must remember that they had taken four heavy psychological blows in a row. I know because they told me so. Their President had termed them "bums." He had sent troops into Cambodia when the announced plan of our government was the withdrawal of troops from Vietnam. Armed troops were occupying the campus. And now the governor of the state was calling them worse than Brown Shirts. Do you honestly wonder that many of them felt a deep sense of revulsion?'

It was this spirit of rejection, engendered slowly but with increasing force as the weekend progressed, that caused despair among many of the most stable students at the university. This group did not riot, nor burn, nor throw rocks, nor vilify the Guards, but they did look on with disgust at what seemed to them a determined effort by society to crush student opinion. As one quiet-spoken girl said, 'If the President thinks I'm a bum and the governor thinks I'm a Nazi, what does it matter how I act?'

'Equally important,' continues Lunine, 'was the effect upon the Guardsmen. Naturally suspicious of college students, whom they consider to be favored both economically and in the draft, they heard their suspicions confirmed by their President and governor. In addition, the head of one of the state's police organizations had warned them to beware of snipers, who could be expected to go into action soon. What conclusions could the Guardsmen reach but that the students were an evil lot against whom they would have to defend themselves, perhaps with bullets? Words were very important that weekend, and always in a destructive direction.'

The flower in the gun

If some of Mike Lunine's honor students were apprehensive when they heard Governor Rhodes' press conference, the general student body was not, for the spring sun shone that Sunday afternoon and the scene on campus was relaxed, people moving about as though it were a holiday. More than a hundred witnesses have used the same description: 'It was a carnival.'

Many students, disturbed by the rioting of the two preceding nights, and gratified that the troubles had apparently ended, went to church, where ministers preached against violence and deplored its consequences. At the Newman Center, the Catholic church for students at the edge of campus, double-bass player Charles Madonio heard the priest say, 'Your obligation as young people forming part of a great university is to spread the word of peace and love among your fellows.' Another observer saw some students cover their foreheads with their hands, as if they were weeping.

By midmorning the circus at Kent was in full swing. The charred skeleton of ROTC had been roped off and placed under heavy guard, but visitors filed past it continuously. From time to time children from the city found expended ammunition shells, detonated by the fire, and squealed the news to their friends, while their parents rubbernecked at the charred embers of the main part of the old wooden building and at the front entrance, which somehow remained standing.

So many sightseers from all parts of Portage County and from as far away as Akron and Cleveland wanted to visit the ruins that traffic on the major highways was backed up for miles. Of course, a Sunday morning freight train chugged its way through town, adding to the confusion. All traffic signals had to be switched onto blinker so that cars could be controlled by hand signals from sheriff's deputies. Traffic trying to enter the campus was interdicted by 1:00 in the afternoon, and parking jams along side streets were mammoth as people left their cars and walked over to the campus.

What was happening there? Jeff Sallot says, 'Since my wife and I live only a few blocks from campus, and since she's working for a degree, too, we decided to go over and look around. What a lovely day it was, real springtime. All the coeds were out for the first time in their spring dresses and no coats, and they made a great hit with the Guardsmen. There was a lot of flirting and a little surreptitious handholding. No fear, no anxiety, no animosity. The bad language of the preceding night was forgotten and all we heard were idle rumors of the most gentle kind. "Guards going to leave campus this evening." I certainly expected them to be gone by morning.'

Charles Madonio, on his way home from church, cut across the campus, and recalls: 'Everyone was having fun. Know what? Quite a few of the incoming families had brought picnics, and while the women spread the food, their children played. Many of the Guard were in their early twenties or maybe not even that old. Any time a couple of cute coeds would stop to talk, eight or ten Guardsmen would gather. A Salvation Army canteen all the way from Akron drove onto the campus to see that the Guardsmen had something to eat, and after that it wasn't uncommon to see a group of Guards lying around munching hot dogs. You couldn't find the slightest hint of possible violence. It seemed as if nothing violent or illegal occurred last night or would occur tomorrow.'

Craig Morgan discovered why the atmosphere was so friendly: 'One of the Guardsmen was willing to talk with me for quite a while. He said, "The officers ordered us to fraternize with the students so as to relieve the tension." They did a great job that day. They turned the whole campus into one friendly circus. People wandered aimlessly about as if they were in an art gallery.'

Ellis Berns confirms this: 'At the Student Union the Guards were rapping with us and taking it real cool. They even went so far as to show us two kinds of cartridges, one live, one blank, and showed us how to tell the difference by weight, so that nobody could mistake one from the other. As they spoke, a fellow came by passing out leaflets announcing a rally on the commons at noon Monday, and I heard a student tell the Guardsmen, "We're all fed up with having military on our campus." And from the way one Guard laughed, I got the idea that maybe he was fed up being here.'

Phil Haas, a freshman from Stamford, Connecticut, hung around for some time with the Guards in front of Administration. 'I asked one of them all kinds of details. One of them told me, "Hang around, buddy. There's a rumor that the state is going to cut our pay from $25 a day to $12.80. If they try that, Governor Rhodes will be calling you characters out to subdue us." I felt so good about the things he was saying, I went down and bought some oranges and offered him some, but he said, "We're not allowed to take anything like that." I asked him why not, and he said, "Didn't you hear what the girls did to us at Berkeley? Injected the damned fruit with acid and you had guys all over the place going off on trips." About this time a real far-out kid came by in long curls and a velvet jacket, and the Guardsman said, "Son, you sure got some wild-looking people on this campus," and the guy in velvet said, "We feel the same about you." '

The holiday atmosphere was added to occasionally by the appearance of a tall, handsome Indian student from Indore. Ramesh Garg was six-feet-two, with jet-black hair and a fine mustache. He smiled at visitors who had never seen a man from India before and talked with children, charming them with his lively eyes, extremely mobile face and gentle accent. Unlike many of the students, he was dressed quite conservatively in slacks and white shirt. His dark skin and courtly manner made him popular wherever he went, and he spent some time talking with Guardsmen and telling them about India, but he is remembered primarily because at one point he took a photograph of an attractive girl student placing a flower in the muzzle of one of the Guardsmen's guns. As she deposited her yellow flower she said, 'Flowers are better than bullets.'

Roman Tymchyshyn, wandering through the crowd, flashed one of the Guardsmen the peace sign, and the Guardsman winked, opened his tunic and displayed a T-shirt bearing a peace symbol. Tymchyshyn had some of the members of his cinema group on campus taking photos of the action, and some weeks later, when the films were being shown, someone in the audience yelled, 'Hey, stop the projector! Look at that tall coed!' They rewound the film and found that the photographer had unwittingly caught about four minutes of the girl with the Delacroix face as she wandered delightedly about the campus, smiling at Guardsmen and enjoying the scene.

Carl Moore remembers: 'As I walked around our beautiful campus that splendid afternoon and saw our fine young people and the manly-looking Guards, the easy fraternization and the fun, I said to myself, "Moore, you get less radical every day your baby gets older." It was a day of love and contentment, and I felt both.'

Highlight of the day was a trip across campus to the university high school football field where the helicopters were stationed. By 2:00 P.M. all streets leading to the field were jammed and people had to stand in line to see the choppers. They visited with the pilots, who were the celebrities of the day, and children climbed onto whatever part of the plane they could to be photographed. Occasionally the good-natured pilots, enjoying their status as heroes, would hoist a child into the cockpit and pose as the parents took pictures. Many students paused by the choppers, admiring their sleekness and air of efficiency.

While students and Guardsmen were engaged in frolic, certain of the faculty were agitating for the university to take a stand against the presence of military units on campus. They phoned their colleagues, visited them in their homes, and did all they could to whip up a sense of indignation. They had no success. At an ad hoc meeting convened in Bowman Hall, only twenty-three members from a faculty of nearly a thousand appeared. Those who did were profoundly concerned about what was happening on their campus and drew up a document which occasioned almost no comment at the time, for hardly anyone was aware of it, but which did become the occasion, some five and a half months later, for a violent castigation of the university and the subject of national debate.

Even if the document had received widespread circulation Sunday evening, which it did not, few could have anticipated the trouble it was to cause, for it bore every evidence of being one more minority statement. It was signed '23 Concerned Faculty, KSU, Sunday Afternoon, May 3, 1970,' and it merely supported certain attitudes which were being promulgated by major newspapers across the country and defended in Congress by leaders of the nation. There is almost no recollection of the statement's having been read by anyone at time of release, and those who did bother to scan it seem to have responded, 'Ho hum.'

The appearance of armed troops on the campus of Kent State University is an appalling sight. Occupation of the town and campus by National Guardsmen is testimony to the domination of irrationality in the policies of our government.

The President of the United States commits an illegal act of war and refers to his opposition as 'bums.' That students and faculty and, indeed, all thinking people reject his position is not only rational but patriotic. True, burning a building at Kent State University is no joke; we reject such tactics. Yet the burning of an *ROTC* building is no accident. We deplore this violence but we feel it must be viewed in the larger context of the daily burning of buildings and people by our government in Vietnam, Laos, and now, Cambodia.

Leadership must set the example if it is to persuade. There is only one course to follow if the people of this country—young and old—are to be convinced of the good faith of their leaders: The war must stop. The vendetta against the Black Panthers must stop. The Constitutional rights of all must be defended against any challenge, even from the Department of Justice itself. If Mr. Nixon instead continues his bankrupt, illegal course, the Congress must be called upon to impeach him.

Here and now we repudiate the inflammatory inaccuracies expressed by Governor Rhodes in his press conference today. We urge him to remove the troops from our campus. No problem can be solved so long as the campus is under martial law.

We call upon our public authorities to use their high offices to bring about greater understanding of the issues involved in and contributing to the burning of the ROTC building at Kent State University on Saturday, rather than to exploit this incident in a manner that can only inflame the public and increase the confusion among the members of the university community.

As the 8:00 P.M. town curfew approached, the circus shut down and the patrons headed for home, but now a massive traffic jam developed, and curfew had been in operation for some time before the campus could be emptied. 'I want to get off the streets, Officer,' many drivers protested, 'but the traffic won't move.' By nine, however, most of the cars were gone and the eerie silence of Sunday night was beginning.

It hadn't been all circus that day. Phil Haas, a young man eager for rapid social change, says, 'I was disgusted with the carnival. Parents who had no idea what a university was. Students who were so damned apathetic they couldn't care less about a real education. I got some of my friends together and we stormed down to the helicopter field, where pretty girls were having their pictures taken with the pilots, and we stood back and gave the pilots the finger and yelled, "Off campus, you pigs." One of them smiled down at us and said, "You look like a really cute bunch of bastards."'

The apparent carnival masked some solid soul-searching that many students were undergoing. Among those who paused in the bright sunlight to inspect the burned-out shell of the ROTC building was Bob Hillegas, the tall pilot from Akron who had surveyed the fire from the air. He came with a friend, to whom he expressed his ambivalent feelings.

'I didn't want to see this building disappear,' Hillegas said.

'To me ROTC's important. It's an opening to a way of life I admire. A commission, wings in the United States air force, serving my country, and when that's over, finding a job in commercial aviation. I'm different from you and some of the rest of the kids. I have three older brothers and I've watched how hard they've had to work to get into the professions they wanted. One's a doctor, one's a magazine executive, and that's not easy. For me ROTC was part of the training, and I'm sore as hell to see it in ashes.'

But no sooner had he made this assessment than he made another, of a much different kind: 'But I suppose that deep in my mind I knew the building had to go. I'm surprised it wasn't burned earlier. The violent agitation against ROTC on campus had to bear fruit.'

'You forget,' his friend reminded him. 'Last fall the student body was given a choice: "Do you want ROTC on campus?" They voted overwhelmingly to keep it.'

'I know. But the minority who wanted it off were so dedicated, so virulent in their attacks, I knew that in the end they'd win. I'll confess something. I was in favor of getting it off campus, myself. Even though I was a member of the outfit, I suspected it ought not be linked with a university.'

Now Hillegas used a phrase he had picked up in a recent sociology class. 'I suppose my peer group in ROTC will think me a traitor.' He reflected on this for a moment, then said bitterly, 'You fellows who have never been in ROTC can't appreciate the problem. Do you think it's fun to be called a pig every time you put on your uniform? Don't you think a guy like me gets disgusted when coeds scream at him and curse him as an imperialist? I really despise the name "toy soldier." And I don't want to be labeled a sadist just because I think that a man owes a debt to his nation.'

Hillegas kicked at the ashes and said quietly, 'It so happens that I'm against the war in Vietnam as strongly as the girls who curse me. I believe it's a waste and a sad error. I'd get out tomorrow if I could, and I sure as hell don't want to be flying over there. But I also believe that a man like me can honorably serve his country in uniform.' Embarrassed by this outburst, Hillegas stood silent, staring at the end of the building which had contained the live ammo. 'It's a wonder a lot of the kids weren't killed,' he said.

Lending color to the day was one couple who evoked comment wherever they went, Charles Madonio and his wife riding tandem bicycle with the two Madonio children perched on the handlebars. Because so many of the Guardsmen were from Ravenna, the Madonios discovered friends wherever they pedaled. At the helicopters, David Shere was one of the pilots, and the children posed with him. At the main entrance to the university, two particular friends were standing guard duty, Specialist 4 Jim Pierce and Geoff Lant. The former was a handsome young blond who on Monday would play a major role that would link him indelibly to the Kent tragedy. His appearance was so striking that coeds stopped to admire him, and one acquaintance said, 'Only natural. He's always fancied himself a ladies' man.'

'That's unfair,' Madonio says. 'I've known Jim Pierce for many years, and he's a very solid guy. He grew up in Kent, went to Roosevelt High, was a big track star. He knew how to handle himself . . . smart . . . a nice, free type of guy . . . good to be with. He used to spend a lot of time in the Kove when I played there, and we talked endlessly.

'After he graduated he went to the University of Hawaii but stayed less than a year. He didn't like Hawaii. Told me he had gotten beat up several times. Seems the characters out there took a dim view of any white fellow from the mainland who tried to move in on their girls. But Pierce kept trying, and one night they gave him a savage beating.' Madonio remembers that Pierce brooded upon this beating, coming back to it many times. 'He frequently brought up Hawaii and the beating he had taken there. He became afraid that someone was going to start something. On more than one occasion we'd be sitting in the bar and if anyone looked at him for any length of time, he'd become uneasy and insist on leaving.

'He also dreaded duty in Vietnam and was mighty happy when he found refuge in the National Guard. But he hated his basic training at Fort Knox . . . passionately. He counted the days till he got out. Then he went to Connecticut and married a girl from Stamford, and his letters became fascinating. Everything sounded like it came from a storybook . . . poor small-town boy meets beautiful rich girl and they live in a gorgeous apartment that reeks with success. Next I knew, he was in California. Then I lost track of him.'

When Madonio met Pierce at the main gate, he found him uptight. 'Nervous as a hawk. He told me of the great fear he had experienced at the ROTC fire. "That was more dangerous than the week I'd spent in Hough." This statement puzzled me, because that ghetto battle in Cleveland involved real snipers who were out to gun down Guardsmen.

'I figured maybe he was exaggerating, but he was deadly serious. He told me, "I'm nervous and I'm tired. We've been getting three hours' sleep a night. I just live a couple of blocks over there in Silver Oaks and I haven't been able to see my wife and son all this time. These college kids are out to kill us."

'To ease the conversation, I asked Geoff Lant, "How are things with the bank in Ravenna?" and he growled, "How in hell would I know? I haven't been there in a week." One of the Guard asked, "You hear any rumors that the Black Panthers are going to move in?" I told them I hadn't heard about it, but they were apprehensive.

'I got back on my bicycle and started up one of the paths into the campus, but Jim stopped me. "Don't go in there," he warned, showing real fear. "We just got word there's snipers on lots of the rooftops." He forced me to turn back, and as I left I told him, "When this is over, you and Barbara must come over and have dinner with us," and he said, "I'd like that. But watch out for the snipers."'

Jeff Sallot confirms that the Guardsmen were worried. 'Even during the height of the carnival Sunday afternoon, you could hear lightning-like exchanges of a most bitter kind. One group of students sidled up to a Guard and muttered, "We get you tonight, you bastard." One group of Guardsmen told me, "We've been astonished at what's been happening to us in this town. We've been hit by bags of human manure that students throw at us from car windows. And the coeds! They perform strip teases in their dormitory windows, appearing in shifts and suddenly dropping them and yelling, "Wouldn't you rather be up here making love with us than down there making war?"'

Captain Chester Hayth's men reported, 'Ten blacks from Akron, who had nothing to do with the university but were there only to see the carnival, marched past one unit of Guardsmen, and without speaking, spit all over the Guards. When it looked as if trouble would start, the blacks cursed the Guard violently, then marched on and were seen no more.'

Madonio, who continued touring the campus on his bike, talked with other Guardsmen. 'One of the favorite questions taunters threw at them was, "Who's been sleeping with your wife since you've been away?"' Coeds were particularly brutal in using that tactic, and many Guardsmen who accepted the ugly accusation when it came from men were bitterly resentful when pretty girls used it.

There were more than words. Rumors circulated all day that new fires were planned. Specific campus buildings were identified as sure to go up in flames that night, the air force ROTC and the president's house being most frequently nominated. Buildings in the downtown business section were also designated. At first these rumors were dismissed as irresponsible, but around 7:45 a Guardsman found a rope and two bottles of gasoline in bushes near the university police headquarters. It appeared to be the makings of a fire bomb, and fifteen minutes later five gallons of gasoline were found on the roof of Administration. What scared the Guard even more was the report of a Guardsman stationed near the growing crowd: 'I just saw two students go by with gas masks. They were moving rapidly among the crowd, giving directions.' The carnival was over.

What happened on Sunday night

Of the four major segments of the rioting—one for each day —the least flamboyant was the confrontation on Sunday night, and yet in a somber and almost vicious way, it represented the watershed of the weekend, for after it happened, an angry bitterness existed that would not be dissipated. Given the face-to-face ugliness of Sunday night, some kind of Monday showdown was inevitable.

At 7:10 it started with the ringing of that abominable bell, signaling the end of the carnival. After the bell had clanged for some minutes, a young man with kinky blond hair exploding in all directions from his head climbed onto the brick frame, shouting to the crowd and provoking them to a unison response:

'One, two, three, four!
We don't want your fucking war.'

After some minutes of this, he shouted new directions, and the chant changed to:

'Two, four, six, eight!
We won't live in a fascist state.'

Again he called new instructions, and again the crowd, growing larger as the cries attracted more passers-by, shifted into a new shout:

'Fuck you,
Agnew.'

At 7:20, as the antiphonal chanting died down, the young man asked a rhetorical question: 'What do you want to do? We can quit here or march on.' A throaty cry gave answer, but it was interrupted by another voice, metallic and final. It came from a jeep which none of the students had seen approaching on the road leading to ROTC, and issued from a bullhorn held by an officer in the National Guard: 'You are breaking the law. You must disperse. If you continue to demonstrate you will be arrested.' From the crowd came back the challenge: 'Fuck you, pig.'

At 7:45 a member of the National Guard, about to report for liaison duty with the campus police, happened to spot the makings of two Molotov cocktails. His report spurred the police to check on other danger points.

At 8:00 the gasoline was found on the roof of Administration. Reports continued to filter through of suspicious or dangerous acts, and the authorities began to think that it might be wise to close down the campus as far as possible.

At 8:45 it was decided to move the campus curfew forward from 1:00 A.M. to 9:00 P.M., fifteen minutes away. Hasty announcements were made through all available channels, but it soon became apparent that to inform all who might be subject to the curfew would prove impossible, so the idea was dropped. However, some officials and many students had heard that the legal curfew was now 9:00.

At 8:58 Major Harry Jones, battalion staff officer of the 145th, who would play a major role on Monday, used his own authority to read the riot act for the second time, but with practically no effect. Students were milling about the campus and some were conducting an informal kind of march.

At 9:05 things took an ugly turn. One of the leaders of the students shouted, 'Let's march and show them how we feel about pigs on campus,' and the curly-headed young man who had earlier led the crowd from the Victory Bell housing talked with some comrades, and from this unit came the cry, 'Let's march to White's house.' The crowd roared back approvingly and swarmed off Blanket Hill. It surged past the dormitories, hundreds of voices shouting, 'Join us, join us!' A rock was tossed through one dormitory window; many students cheered, but others yelled, 'Cool it.' The noise and the invitations to march influenced the residents of the dormitories, who piled out into the spring night, glad for an excuse to quit their studies. The crowd now numbered more than three thousand, and seemed to be moving in a random direction, except that the blond young man and his gang kept it headed in the direction they wanted. 'To the president's house!' the group in front kept chanting.

At 9:15, as they approached the old structure, they were unexpectedly halted by a unit of the National Guard, who tear-gassed them. Reeling back, screaming, cursing, covering their faces with handkerchiefs, they stumbled off in the direction from which they had come. Some grabbed rocks to throw at the Guard, who were much too far away to be endangered by such futile action. 'Back to the commons,' shouted the leaders, and back they went.

At 9:29 about 200 students detached themselves from the main march and decided to invade the city. Cheering and singing, they erupted onto Main Street and began a riotous procession to the corner of Main and Lincoln, but they stopped abruptly, terrified by what loomed ahead of them.

At 9:33 an armored personnel carrier with occupants whose guns bristled in the twilight placed itself across Main Street and defied the students to pass. There ensued a tense and frightening confrontation.

At 9:35 it ended, for the driver of the tank suddenly revved up his motor, wheeled the big vehicle about in the middle of the street, and retreated into a side street, where it remained, hidden by trees. The students cheered, as if their bravery had forced the retreat, and about forty proceeded down Main Street toward the center of town, where they would be in obvious violation of the city's 8:00 P.M. curfew.

At 9:38 they reached the Kent Motor Inn, where other students (who had not heard about the proposed change) warned them, 'Down there the curfew's at 8:00. On campus it's 1:00.' This stopped the adventurous group, who hesitated, milled about in the street for a few minutes, then quietly turned and went back toward campus.

At 9:42 the trouble should have ended, and Sunday night should have been a somewhat insignificant finale to the riotous weekend. If the retreating students had returned to their campus, the National Guard would have had no reason for remaining in Kent and normal procedures would have been resumed. This was not to happen. When the forty straggling students got back to Main and Lincoln, they found a group of girls and men sitting defiantly in the middle of the street and impulsively joined them. Here they would remain for about eighty minutes, and it was from this illegal act of defying curfew that the ill will and tension of late Sunday night developed. How many students were · involved? Some 3,000 had been milling about the campus, but most of these had been mere spectators, and although some had later wandered down to Main and Lincoln, most stayed behind and took no part in what followed. Estimates vary as to the number actually involved, but 700 seems an accurate guess, with about fifty sitting in the . intersection.

At 9:45 all units of the National Guard had moved into the positions they would occupy until 11:00. The 107th took the most conspicuous role, for it lined up along Lincoln Street, hooking up on the left flank with the Kent police, who were concentrated at the intersection at Main. Charlie Company, under Captain Snyder, stationed itself along a line jutting out from the library, which had been threatened with fire-bombing. This formed a large pocket enclosing the student demonstrators on three sides; the students were free at any time to retreat to the campus, but could not move in other directions. As for the Guard, wherever they looked they saw students, who, as the night progressed, inched constantly closer.

At 9:50 the battle lines were set and the confrontation assumed a new seriousness. Guardsmen were greeted with obscene challenges on the one hand and enticing pleas on the other: 'You're just like us,' girls shouted. 'Come on over to our side.' A student went up to a Guard with whom he had become familiar during the afternoon carnival and started to resume conversation, but the Guardsman lowered his bayonet into the student's belly and growled, 'Buzz off, kid.' A girl asked a Guardsman, 'Are those guns loaded?' and he told her, 'You're damned right they are, and if this keeps up, somebody's going to get killed.' Overhead there were the helicopters. They seemed omnipresent, dipping and swooping, flashing their penetrating anti-riot lights onto rooftops to flush out any would-be snipers.

Kent that night epitomized the triumph of mechanical man: the Victory Bell rang in place of a reasoned call to reasoned action; men amplified their voices by means of bullhorns, so that when they spoke they seemed more powerful than ordinary humans; young farmboys and clerks masked their faces and held steel bayonets before them; officers did not walk, they darted about in jeeps; semi-tanks dominated city streets; and skies were controlled by the terrifying helicopters.

At 10:00 there began a steady, non-spectacular rise to a peak. The students who had originally occupied the intersection were joined by hundreds of casual spectators, so that the crowd looked constantly larger. Emboldened by the fact that no one seemed able to disperse them, the leaders became more arrogant, pushing and shoving their way closer and closer to the Guardsmen, who stood with bayonets projecting outward.

At 10:10 three students detached themselves from the crowd and walked deliberately but not provocatively toward the police lines, believing apparently that they might have better luck with the plan they had in mind if they could talk with police rather than with Guards. They came face to face with Sergeant Joseph Myers of the Kent city police, a burly man with a thin mustache. They told Myers, 'We have three demands. We want to talk with President White. We want to talk with Mayor Satrom. And we want you policemen to give us fair warning before you start making arrests.'

At 10:15, after listening to them courteously and discussing their proposals with them, Sergeant Myers told them, 'I'll relay your requests to the officials. But it's not up to me to tell you whether they'll agree or not. But I can promise that before the police start making arrests, we'll warn you so that you can move this mob out of here.' Seemingly satisfied with these answers, the three students returned to report to the crowd sitting in the street.

At 10:23 a group of students wearing white bands on their arms and large white crosses in the middle of their backs took strategic positions from which they taunted the Guard and organized the resistance. Some sat in the middle of the street; others moved about giving encouragement. One Guardsman, fed up with the manner in which one member of this cadre kept moving toward and away from him, growled, 'Son, that white cross in the middle of your back makes a damned fine target, and one move out of you, I'm going to use it.' The student withdrew and shortly thereafter reappeared, but without his cross.

At 10:32 the confusion that had marked this night increased when it was decided to move the campus curfew ahead to 11:00—that is, twenty-eight minutes away—while knowing there would be no adequate means of informing the students. Legally the change was made, so that any student who was on campus outside his dormitory after that hour was there in defiance of the law and subject to arrest. Feeble attempts were made to announce the change, but they reached few students.

At 10:40 the three young men who had conferred with the police earlier, seeking the meeting with White and Satrom, now returned to make a strange request: 'Will you lend us your bullhorn?' Sergeant Myers replied, 'Yes, if it will do any good,' and he found a bullhorn for the students to use. Then he added, 'But we can do better than that,' and he signaled for a police car with a built-in public address system. The mildest of the three students climbed into the car, took the microphone and began haranguing the students in a non-provocative way, but making promises that only a segment of the law-enforcing agencies had agreed to: 'We can stay here. President White and Mayor Satrom are coming here to listen to our demands. The police will not move in without giving us fair warning.' The crowd cheered.

During this time Vice-Presidents Matson and Roskens were conferring in Administration over the demand of the students that President White come to the corner to confer with them. They did not like the idea. Matson would later report that he discussed the proposal with White, who rejected the suggestion; White would not be able to recall that he had been consulted. At any rate, the two vice-presidents decided that White ought not meet with the mob, and this decision was reported to Matson's executive assistant, John Huffman, who was told to communicate it to the students sitting in the street.

At 10:45 the student using the police microphone, emboldened perhaps by his own words, began reading the list of demands his committee proposed to press upon White and Satrom when they appeared:

1. The ROTC program to be removed from campus.
2. Total amnesty to be granted to all persons charged with burning ROTC.
3. Total acceptance of all demands made by the Black United Students, whatever those demands might turn out to be.
4. All National Guard to be removed from campus by Monday night.

5. The curfew to be lifted immediately.
6. Tuition for all students to be lowered.

At 10:46 John Huffman reached the corner, went to the police car and informed those present that President White would not come there to meet with the students, and shortly thereafter it was learned that Mayor Satrom would not be coming either. It appears that the three students heard these decisions but did not relay them to those sitting in the street. Instead, they did a most culpable thing.

At 10:50 the tallest of the three, 'a fellow with flowing sideburns,' grabbed the police bullhorn and circulated through the crowd spreading the heartening news, 'President White and Mayor Satrom have promised to come here to discuss our demands with us. The police will not arrest us, because the president and the mayor are coming.'

Then came the crisis of the weekend. Up to now neither the students nor the Guard had adopted positions of serious hostility; there had been minor skirmishes involving some shoving, but nothing that a night's sleep would not have cured. But what was about to happen did involve overt action, did harden animosities, and did create across the campus an aura of bad faith and broken promises. To comprehend it, we must double back to 2:00 P.M. that afternoon when the carnival was in progress.

Carl Caldwell was finishing his vigil at the Kent waterworks when a jeep drove up to take him back to the gymnasium for some badly needed sleep. He took a shower, grabbed a hasty lunch and played a couple of games of Ping-Pong, then hit the sack, intending to sleep till 10:00 or 11:00 P.M., when he would presumably return to night duty. However, at 5:30 he was awakened. Everyone was being routed out, for the word was that trouble had erupted on campus again. 'They're going to burn the air force ROTC,' was the intelligence, 'and we've got to stop them.'

Caldwell and the other men of Charlie Company were finishing supper when Captain Ron Snyder came along the chow line, shouting, 'Saddle up! Get that gear on and let's move out.' They assembled in full company strength.

Here is the way Carl remembers what happened, and his testimony is not second-hand, for throughout the night he stood close to the heart of the action. 'We loaded our weapons before we left the gym, and when we got out of the trucks at the University School, up on Summit Street, we were told to fix bayonets. By this time it was growing dark. We marched in double column across Summit and down Portage Drive to the site of the burned ROTC building—you could still smell the smoke. It was a dark night and it was quiet. Man, it was quiet—too quiet. Then all of a sudden the chopper goes by overhead and hits the rim of the hill along Johnson and Taylor with its searchlight and there they were—*two thousand students* all standing silent around the rim of the hill! The order came down the line, "There they are, mask up!"

'When the kids got hit by the light they started to scream and yell. Someone began ringing the bell. Then they quieted down again and the chanting started: *"Here . . . we . . . come. Here . . . we . . . come!"* What an eerie feeling. A hundred of us, two thousand of them—I tell you, we didn't like the odds. And all the time they're coming down the hill someone's ringing that damn bell.'

The demonstrators stopped about a hundred yards from the line of Guardsmen and fell silent again. Then, as though on command, they did an abrupt right-face and marched off the commons between the tennis courts and the Student Union, headed for the front campus and, presumably, downtown Kent. To cut them off, Charlie Company double-timed up past Merrill Hall and down the dark, heavily treed slope to the front campus.

A number of protesters were already there, hiding in the shadows of the Rockwell Library, and some forty or fifty of these tried to turn the Guardsmen from their line of march. Carl and those near him moved into the mob, swinging rifle butts and billy clubs and jabbing with their bayonets. The students broke and ran. Some of them darted into the library, others dashed around the back of the building and came at the Guardsmen from the rear. Officers and non-coms quickly positioned the company on a single line that ran from the library door along the front walk, across Main Street to the corner of University Drive. With rioters screaming and hurling bricks and rocks and bottles both before and behind, the men alternately faced front and back, half looking east and half west.

'We were taking abuse like you never heard before,' Carl recalls. 'I had to rifle-butt some of the tough ones in front of me. Beer bottles came at us and the man on my right was conked on the head. The fellow on my left had his helmet dented by a chunk of concrete. The language was horrible, especially from the girls. Coeds would throw open their shirts or lift their dresses and they'd be wearing nothing underneath and they'd shout, "Wouldn't you rather be sleeping with me than doing what you're doing?"

'I was sure we'd be rushed. I was afraid of what might happen if we were. Actually, there were some uncoordinated attempts and we had to drive the most aggressive students back at bayonet point. I thought then and I've often thought since that if they had really come at us that Sunday night, they could have knocked us off the street.

'Who was leading the riot? There was a hard core of about twelve, with white armbands and crosses on their backs, cutting around in back of us, linking hands at the far edges of the mob and pushing forward, making people crush in on us. "Move on in!" this determined crowd kept repeating, but they didn't come in themselves. Whenever they got one part of the crowd moving, they'd leave it and run to another area.

'At 10:45 our position was getting dangerous, so we shot out some canisters of powder . . . not tear gas . . . a powder that makes you sneeze and feel lousy. And this separated the men from the boys, because when the powder hit, all the mere spectators withdrew, leaving behind the hard-core operators, some in front of us, some in back. We began to get hit by stuff front and back and there was a lot of action. Really, you had to ask yourself, "Are these kids on dope?" We gassed them, powdered them, struck at them with rifle butts and the police jabbed them with billy clubs, but they still came right at us. Finally we had to get maximum rough, and they drew back.

'Now came the negotiations. A student committee led by a tall fellow with some kind of mustache or beard demanded that either the mayor, or the chief of police, or President White come out to consult with them. At 10:50 the major commanding the Guard told this committee . . . now I know what I'm saying, because I was standing right beside the major as he talked. He said, "Young man, at 11:00 we are going to move forward, and we're going to clear this area fast. So you better be gone." I personally heard the major tell the student this, face to face.

'But when the student leader left us, he raised the bullhorn and shouted, "The Guard is leaving. The Guard is leaving. We've won! The Guard will be getting back into their trucks and they're going to leave the campus." The major gritted his teeth and looked at his watch.

'At 11:00 sharp we moved out. We cleaned up the street and chased the students out of our way, but as we went we could hear the tall fellow on the bullhorn shouting, "They've lied to us. We've been betrayed."

'Boy, did that bring down a barrage of rocks! I was hit twice. The man beside me dropped as if he had been pole-axed. Overhead the helicopter told them to disperse. Our loudspeakers told them. Our bullhorns told them. And our officers told them. They had all sorts of warning, but they refused to listen and we had to chase them up the streets and back onto the campus. It was disgraceful. And all the time the man with the bullhorn kept crying, "White lied to us. The Guard lied to us. We've been betrayed." '

There can be no question but that the mass of students, who could not have heard either the hopeful conversation with Sergeant Myers or the more realistic one with the major, honestly felt that they were betrayed. They had been told by their self-appointed leaders that a firm deal had been made and within a few minutes of that announcement they had seen it shattered in a forceful and even brutal way. 'Liars, liars!' screamed the students as they were forced off the street. 'Filthy lying bastards!' they shouted at the Guards, who were breaking no promises they had made. It was in these confusing moments that the students were polarized and radicalized.

At 11:10 as the Guards moved out they bayoneted at least two and probably seven students. A white boy and a black girl were taken to the hospital, and these were put on record, but there were other incidents. One Guard says, 'One unit had to bayonet five kids, none very seriously, and to do so we didn't move six inches from our tracks. You could honestly say that the damned fools were throwing themselves at us and all we had to do was stand with our bayonets out.' These five cases do not appear in the records.

At 11:40 General Canterbury, after surveying the various Guard positions and the general condition of the campus, was able to announce, 'Campus secured. All quiet.'

Bitterness, recrimination, hatred and accusations of betrayal filled the campus as Sunday ended, and there is considerable evidence—some of it fabricated after the event, much of it with a tinge of authenticity—to the effect that many students that night, as they went to bed, or stayed up in dormitories ten and twelve to a room, discussing events, suspected that on Monday there would have to be serious consequences.

One coed, as she turned out the light, said to her roommate, 'I'm afraid of what's going to happen on this campus tomorrow. Too many guns. Too many people mad at each other. I'm not going to classes tomorrow.' And she made plans to quit the campus and visit her orthodontist in Akron, for, like so many young coeds we saw, she was still wearing braces.

Why it happened

The incidental sidelights to the events of Sunday night have this in common: they are seen in an eerie glow, suffused with a sense of macabre unreality. Nobody has expressed them better than Janette Wise, an extremely good-looking girl specializing in elementary education, with mostly A's and B's. She lives in Ravenna and considers herself 'a quiet liberal.' Meticulous in dress, careful about her make-up, she could have fitted into a 1950 musical about college life but now 'you get so many cross-currents from the entire world cutting across your campus, who can be detached?'

Of Sunday night she says, 'It was a night that none of us will ever forget. We would be in our rooms, studying, and the helicopters would come swooping down, only a few feet from our windows. You could have looked out and waved at the pilots, except that if you tried, the man with the bullhorn sitting beside the pilot would shout at you, "Get back indoors. Turn out that light. This is an order." It was a voice from the sky.

'And when the helicopter was gone, a National Guard jeep would come slowly cruising down your street, flashing its spotlight up through the trees, and someone with a bullhorn would bellow, "Turn out those lights." And when you were sickened by this, they really got you. Tear gas. Yes, even though we were on the second floor of our rooming house, one of the canisters they threw contained so much gas it filled our room, and we had to leave. Then the helicopters zoomed down and the voice from the sky shouted, "Get back inside!"

'It gave you the feeling that you were living in a police state. It was 1984 and George Orwell was in the background, smiling.'

Ben Post, a reporter for the Kent newspaper, thought not ahead to 1984 but back to an equally ugly, in a different sense, scene: 'When the crowd was at its wildest I found myself standing beside a tiny girl dressed in faded army fatigues. "Isn't it beautiful?" she shouted. I looked down at her eyes brimming with excitement and realized that she was screaming words which she herself could not hear. I felt chilled. I kept remembering old movies of Hitler youth, their arms piercing the sky, their mouths moving but making no sound: *Sieg Heil! Sieg Heil!*

Jeff Sallot was busy that night, checking incidents so that he could report accurately to his Akron paper: 'An important thing about this first face-to-face confrontation was that some-one had a large number of cherry bombs which he kept exploding on the edges of the crowd. They made a noise like riflefire and got the students accustomed to the sound. Also, there were two instances in which long strings of fire-crackers went off like blanks being fired from a gun. After the noise had ended I went up to one of the Guards, an-nounced myself as a reporter and asked, "What do you think might happen tomorrow?" He said firmly, "There will not be any demonstrations on this campus. Those are our orders." '

John P. Hayes is gargantuan in size, baby-faced in appear-ance, skilled as an actor—he was a rowdy success as Pseudolus the conniving slave in *A Funny Thing Happened on the Way to the Forum*—and a professional stringer for both the *Record-Courier* and the *Cleveland Plain Dealer*. In spite of his bulk, he moves like a ballet dancer, and can be seen in many of the photographs, notebook in hand, at the center of the action. He recalls, 'There must have been 3,000 kids on campus, so I decided to stay at the front where you'd expect to find the leaders. One white student ran up to say, "The blacks are going to invade us from Ohio State." I told him, "Rubbish."

'I stayed with the mob till we reached the president's house. The Guardsmen sent an officer over to us newsmen, and he said, "You fellows better keep running, because we may have to throw gas." I felt that the Guards were playing it fair by warning us before choking us with tear gas. So then the students, about 800 of them at least, went out into the street singing "America" and bellowing obscenities. For about an hour they taunted the Guardsmen, and demanded that White come to listen to their demands.'

Hayes, towering over all the other students, grabbed one dissident and asked, 'You think White will show up?'

'He won't be here. He doesn't give a fuck about us.'

But another student said, 'He'll be here. He's got a cool head and a lot of headaches. He wants to get this over with.'

At the height of the confrontation, two ill-matched figures walked through the shadows toward Administration, trying to keep out of sight—Erwind Blount towering over his field marshal, Rudy Perry. At his command post, Perry had heard that two black girls were lost on campus and couldn't get through the military lines. The two men were headed toward Tri-Towers when a contingent of Guardsmen suddenly blocked their way.

'Where you going, boy?' one of them asked Blount.

'Two of the sisters are lost.'

'You get your ass out of here.' An M-1 was pointed at Blount's head, a .45 at Perry's.

'Look, we got two black girls lost in there.'

'You take care of yourselves. We'll take care of the girls.'

Blount and his field marshal retired, circled about the edge of the campus and found the girls. 'Stay the hell off this campus,' Perry growled as he led them to safety.

Shortly after 11:00 John P. Hayes once more found himself in the middle of the action. 'When the Guard moved out with their bayonets I kept a little in front of them, letting them see my notebook so they'd know I was a reporter. Ahead of me a dissident fell to the ground, and as he started to get up he was stabbed in the back with a bayonet. He screamed, got up, clutched his back and ran into a house across from the campus. I saw him collapse on the kitchen floor.'

Ben Post also witnessed this action: 'I saw the student with the bullhorn telling the others, "Everything's going to be all right. We're going to talk with White." But as he talked, a National Guard officer walked up, looked at him and said, "You're not talking to anyone. The riot act has been read and we're going to make arrests." So the Guard moved in and the students were shocked by what they considered a betrayal. Hysterical screams filled the air, "Liar! Liar!"

'One demonstrator was not quick enough and was knocked to the ground. As he rose, a Guard jabbed his bayonet into the youth's lower back. He stumbled to the middle of Lincoln Street, where he ran into a house and collapsed.'

At the hospital it was discovered that Joel Richardson, nineteen, of Sterling, New York, had a punctured shoulder and Helen Opasker, twenty-one, of Cleveland, a stab wound in the abdomen. Neither was injured seriously, and a spokesman for the Guard announced that they could not have been inflicted by bayonets. Later an official of the Guard told an investigating committee, 'During the three days only one student was injured by a bayonet. One girl was attempting to climb a fence, lost her grip and fell backwards onto a bayonet.'

When the meeting at Main and Lincoln was broken up, Field Marshal Rudy Perry moved quietly through the crowd to see if any blacks had been involved: 'I really had to laugh. I could of split a gut. This cat, this white dude, grabs a bullhorn and cries, "They lied to us. We trusted them and they betrayed us." I asked a student, "Who betrayed who?" and the cat says, "They promised they wouldn't arrest anybody without warning. They broke their word." I didn't say anything, but I wanted to ask him, "How old are you, son? Don't you know they always break their word?" '

Jamie Haines tells her story: 'I walked to Van Deusen Hall and asked a Guardsman if I could take his picture. He glared at me and said, "You think this is funny, don't you? You think it's a big joke?" So I walked over to another Guard and said, "Hi!" and flashed him the peace sign. He aimed his rifle at me and told me to keep moving. I had my camera around my neck, and another Guard stuck a bayonet at my throat and said, "Get rid of that camera . . . now!" I'd had enough, so I went back to my dorm, but on the way I passed two Guards who spoke to me as if I were their little sister, "You better get back inside, it's close to curfew." Then the other added, "Don't come out till we're gone. There's going to be trouble and shooting and someone is bound to be killed." So I went home and listened to the radio.'

If she tuned in the campus station, WKSU, she heard a program called Operation Quell, which had been improvised that afternoon to quash rumors. It had been scheduled from 9:00 to 11:00, but had proved so popular that it had been extended first to 1:00 and then to 2:00. Professor Carl Moore was in the studio, accompanied by a group of other professors and concerned students, and they talked a lot of sense, but from the casual comments of those who called in, students picked up much erroneous information.

1:10 Official announcement: 'Classes are scheduled tomorrow as normal. All students are required to attend classes tomorrow.'

1:19 A young woman who may or may not have been a student: 'I am the Voice of Conscience. I live in Hudson. There's no turning back the revolution. It's a beautiful thing and we're all in it.'

1:25 Faculty member to a caller: 'Do you think there is going to be violence?'
Student: 'I don't think so. I think Governor Rhodes and the National Guard and all police officials are going to be very careful tomorrow.'

1:43 Alan Preis, a freshman who had witnessed most of the action at Main and Lincoln, called in with an impassioned statement which many students would recall in the months to come. They would remember it as the last advice they heard before WKSU signed off, the prediction of what was destined to happen tomorrow: 'I'd like to see this thing come to a peaceful settlement . . . without riots tomorrow night. Tomorrow night, after what happened tonight, those kids are going to be out there . . . they're going to be out there to kill.' Then came a pause as if Preis had realized what he had said, and he corrected himself. 'Not to kill people but to burn this campus to the ground. And that's my own fear.'

It was the fear of many.

When it became apparent to those working on this book that the confrontation at Main and Lincoln was the watershed of the weekend, vigorous efforts were made to identify the student who had spoken through the bullhorn, for if he had callously lied about the probability of President White's and Mayor Satrom's coming to negotiate with the students—as appeared to be the case—it was important to know why he had done so; and if he had spoken under an honest belief that the two officials were coming, it was necessary that the degree of his honesty be tested. We were unable to discover who he was; official inquiries fared no better. There appear to be no photographs of him, and while it seems likely that among the many students who talked with us about this incident, there must have been some who knew him, they kept their secret. From much questioning, however, we concluded that he spoke with malicious intent and that much of the bitterness which followed can be charged to him.

Then, on almost the last day of our visit, while we were conversing with a tall, beardless, intense young man about some insignificant problem, he happened to drop a startling bit of information: 'I suppose you've guessed that I was the fellow who borrowed the bullhorn from the police.' There was a moment of silence, then he continued, asking that his name not be used: 'I was the principal negotiator with the National Guard and the police that night. Nobody elected me to the job. I simply saw that if the students remained in the street, breaking curfew, and if the Guard waited around long enough with their rifles at the ready, something had to happen. Neither side appeared willing to give an inch, so I said to myself, "Why not me? Somebody has to get things started." So I nominated myself to go up to the police, and over to the Guard officers, and we organized a little peace treaty on the spot. Two other students and me. I served as the spokesman. I said to the police, "Gentlemen, I don't want any trouble I just want to talk with you about negotiating a peace." To my surprise, both the police and the Guard were very understanding. I got the idea they were relieved to find someone to talk to.

'They spelled out what the students must do, then told me what they would do in return. They were completely reasonable. They were sure eager to avoid trouble. So I told them, "I want to talk with General Del Corso, Mayor Satrom and President White. I'm sure we can organize a peace." The Guard officer got on his walkie-talkie and spoke with one of the generals. Then he told me, "If all the students will go back onto the campus, a meeting will be arranged and we'll leave you alone." So I asked if the police would lend me their bullhorn, and an officer said, "We can do better. We'll let you have a bullhorn and a microphone to end this thing." He signaled for a car which had a built-in address system, and I sat in the car and explained to the students what the deal was.' (At this point, as we know from other evidence, Huffman appeared at the car and told the occupants that President White was not coming. This announcement was not relayed to the students.)

The young man, whose testimony on three other matters was found to be accurate, said, 'A tall kid with sideburns used the bullhorn to circulate the cry "President White and Mayor Satrom have agreed to meet with us soon," and this news spread throughout the crowd. Students cheered, but at this moment one of the generals came down Lincoln Street, saw the size of the mob and where they were sitting, and said, "I've read the riot act. To hell with you people. I'm going in and break it up." And he did.'

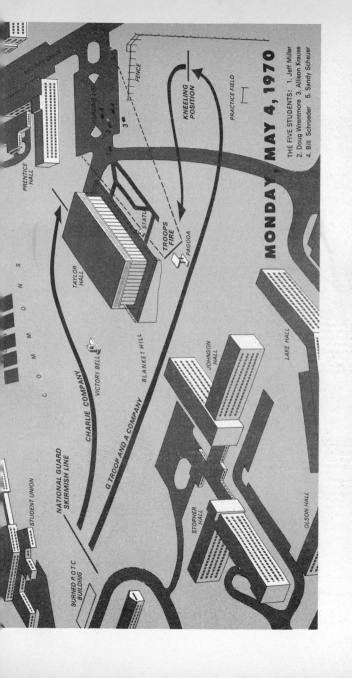

MONDAY, MAY 4, 1970

THE FIVE STUDENTS: 1. Jeff Miller
2. Doug Wrentmore 3. Allison Krause
4. Bill Schroeder 5. Sandy Scheuer

urday, May 2, 10:50 P.M. National Guard arrive to cordon
he burning ROTC building. DON ROESE

Sunday, May 3, midafternoon. Guardsman Myers, his rifle ◀ taining the flower given him by Allison Krause, flashes p◀ sign.

MARTIN LE◀

Sunday, May 3, late afternoon. The distance between the Gua *and the students increases.* RANDY L. WALLIC

*nday, May 3, early afternoon. Sandy Scheuer and the dog
eavy visit the carnival.*
MARTIN LEVICK

*Early October, 1969. Allison Krause collects funds for the S_
dent Mobilization Committee, which will sponsor a peace ra_
on October 15.* THOMAS L. DIFLOU_

Monday, May 4, 11:48 A.M. Students gather at Victory Bell. This photograph is a litmus test for the reader. Do you see the many peaceful students resting on the grass, or the avowed rabble-rousers on the bell housing, one of whom is already prepared for the action which he anticipates? JOHN FILO

...nday, May 4, 11:55 A.M. Jeff Miller, extreme left, greets the ...rd with two fingers. Behind him, in knitted tarboosh, ...ther Fargo.

JACK DAVIS

Monday, May 4, 12:04 P.M. Captain Srp's G Troop approa
the pagoda, to the right of which stands Allison Krause
identified by Barry Levine, who had moved farther down
other side of the hill). HOWARD E. RUFFN

...nday, May 4, 12:16 P.M. The recently uncovered photo-...ph which shows the seventeen Guardsmen assuming a firing ...ition to protect themselves from the encroaching students.

BEVERLY KNOWLES

Monday, May 4, 12:24:04 P.M. *The Guard have fired an op-
ing burst. General Canterbury is startled. Right foregrounc
left-handed Guardsman takes dead aim on the photograpʰ*
HOWARD E. RUFFⁿ

Monday, May 4, 12:28 P.M. *Captain Ron Snyder, left, w_i*
baton, and members of Charlie Company stand guard at t
body of Jeff Miller.   JOHN FI

onday, May 4, 12:50 P.M. The perilous aftermath. The ⎯ard are ready to resume firing. Students mass on the com- ⎯ns. Onlookers line the amphitheater. DON ROESE

Allison, Barry, Yossarian.

BARRY LEVIN

Monday, May 4, 12:27 P.M. *Anguish.*
1970 JOHN FILO. © 1970 TARENTUM, PA., VALLEY DAILY NEWS

The reason the young man wished his name suppressed bore no relation to his encounter with the police: 'So when the Guard came at us, I left the police car, ran across the street to the campus and started running toward the library, but I was halted by a Guard who suddenly appeared out of the bushes. He gave me the butt of his gun, and in self-defense I gave him a wild kick in the shin. He doubled up, forgot about me, and I got home free.' (A Guard was treated for a bruise acquired near the library.)

When asked if he knew who the tall man with the bullhorn was, he said, 'Never saw him before that night.' Did the man with the bullhorn know that White and Satrom were not coming? 'He heard everything I heard.' Finally, had he himself appreciated the gravity of misinforming the students? 'Why do you suppose I tried to calm things in the first place? Anyone could see that the way the situation was developing it had to end in tragedy. I went back to my dorm and wanted to cry. Instead I got mad and said, "What the hell? Tomorrow there'll be shooting." '

Five Students

What were the five students doing on this Sunday? A close look at them provides a fair cross section of the activities of the main university population.

Doug Wrentmore, like some 10,000 of the student body, had been off campus Saturday night. 'We had a bad time deciding whether or not even to come back to campus. It was so peaceful on the dunes at Sandusky, and we knew that three hours away was the big hassle at Kent. But we figured classes would be held on Monday, so we came back in.' They arrived in midafternoon and participated in the tail end of the carnival, tossing a frisbee on the commons. 'We were having a fun time until we accidentally threw it inside the line of Guards protecting the ruins of ROTC. There they were, standing with their guns protecting the ashes, and they wouldn't even allow us to get our frisbee back.'

After this, Doug returned to his quarters and spent the remainder of the afternoon and early evening with friends who had dropped by unannounced on a visit from Cleveland. 'That whole day was a series of physical shocks,' says Doug, 'so we didn't have such a good visit. In the afternoon the whole house shook from the impact of jeeps and tanks and troop carriers going up and down the street. Then, that night, the helicopters started buzzing us. Three of them, with giant searchlights. We couldn't figure out what was happening, so we headed for campus in a friend's car. You know, according to the curfew regulations, you could be out in a car after 8:00, but not on foot, so we didn't want to take any chances.' They arrived at the corner of Lincoln and East Main to find traffic blocked by students holding a sit-in, but the presence of the National Guard convinced Wrentmore that it would be prudent to turn around and go home, which they did.

While a great number of his schoolmates passed the afternoon on campus, Bill Schroeder sat in his room in a pair of cut-offs and studied for a test in ROTC war tactics to be held the next day. He paused briefly to talk to Lydia Casey, the fiancée of one of his roommates, who happened to pass by his open door.

'Bill, what do you think of all this?' she asked. 'Can you believe they burned ROTC?' The only reply he could think of was: 'Amazing, Lydia, just amazing.' He saw none of the action.

Sandy Scheuer did view the Sunday afternoon carnival briefly but did not participate in it. Getting onto her bike, one of her favorite possessions, she rode the short distance to campus to survey the ruins of the ROTC building.

'Things like the ROTC burning were always a big shock to Sandy,' says one bearded young man who was with her that afternoon. 'I was arrested at the A.T.&T. rally in Cleveland, and the next time Sandy saw me, she came running up. "I told you so," she cried like a mother. "I knew this would happen if you didn't watch out." She just couldn't take the demonstration bit. I tried to radicalize her, but it was hopeless.'

Later she returned home to do some last-minute studying, because she and her roommate, Jan Reinstein, planned to attend the rally called for that evening. These plans did not materialize, however, for Jan fell asleep in the late afternoon, and rather than waken her, or go by herself, Sandy decided to stay home and study. She too missed the action.

For Jeff Miller it had been a typical day: wandering about campus, noticing everything, participating in some of the action, then coming home for long discussions as to what it all signified. After scrounging dinner again, he became more angered about the state of affairs on campus than he had been at any other time during the weekend. He and several friends did go to the rally that evening and had been close enough to watch the group that defied the city curfew with their sit-in on Main Street. But when, at 11:00 P.M., the National Guard marched forth to drive the students back to campus, Jeff prudently withdrew, but did stay on the fringes to witness the confrontation and the Guard's use of tear gas on the students. He wanted no part of this and headed for home.

On his way, however, his natural gallantry led him into danger. 'We knew something was up,' says Rita Rubin, the junior from New York, 'so a couple of us girls left our house on the edge of campus and started walking slowly down to Main and Lincoln. It was real weird. We were carrying a transistor police radio and we heard the pigs talking about bombing some kids with tear gas and we listened as one of the Guards asked, "How do you operate this tear-gas stuff?" So another Guard told him how to use it, and as the explanation continued we suddenly realized that we were the people they were preparing to gas, so we started to run back to our house. Jeff saw us running and figured we were in trouble, and as he always did, he ran over to see if he could be of any help. He said, "If the cops come at you, I'll create a diversionary action." We told him to clear out, that we could take care of ourselves, and he said, "I don't want to see girls busted." And he led us through the police, staying with us until he was sure we were out of danger.'

Much angered by this series of events, Jeff returned home. 'They lied to us,' he blurted out to his roommates. 'They said we could talk to Satrom and White, and then what do they do but start gassing us two minutes later? Those fucking pigs lied to us.'

'Come on, Jeff, don't be so naïve,' said John Moir, back from his weekend at home. 'That's what cops are for. Besides, you've lost sight of what you're protesting—whether it's Cambodia or not—when all you do is get out in the street and break a curfew. All you're doing is forcing a showdown between the Guard and the students.'

'Maybe so, but we have a right to have rallies, and be on the street. It's our campus. And they'd better not try that stuff again tomorrow. Our rally is going to be peaceful because that's the way we want it.'

'Maybe that's the way you want it,' Moir said bluntly, 'but that's not the way it's going to be.'

The pretty girl whom Ramesh Garg had photographed on front campus jamming a flower into the muzzle of a loaded M-1 rifle while she told the Guardsman holding it, 'Flowers are better than bullets,' was Allison Krause. She had been seen at various sites that afternoon, walking casually about the campus. In the late afternoon she and Barry Levine saw their good friends Barbara and Lloyd Agte, who had just left the faculty meeting in Bowman Hall.

'Wow, Barbara, what are you doing with a dress on?' Allison asked.

'I figured the faculty would realize I thought all this was pretty important if I showed up in a dress, after wearing pants all the time,' Mrs. Agte said, 'but still we could get only twenty-three people to sign a petition asking that the Guard leave the campus.'

The Agtes then recounted what they had heard about Governor Rhodes' press conference, and Allison and Barry laughed as they talked, especially when they mentioned Rhodes' terming the students as being worse than the Brown Shirts.

'Oh, Barry, did you hear that?' Allison gasped.

As dusk fell, many of those with whom she had spoken during the afternoon participated in the Main and Lincoln sit-in, and the later confrontation with the Guard. But not Allison. With Barry she had remained on campus with a small group who were listening to reports coming in on a walkie-talkie. 'When we heard that the Guard was pushing the kids back from Main Street, and that we were all to go directly to the dorms, we set off for Tri-Towers with a couple of other kids, knowing there'd be people we could rap with about what had gone on,' says Barry. 'We cut back behind Taylor Hall and were walking across the football practice field when the shit hit the fan. Out of nowhere, about twenty to thirty Guardsmen appeared and started running with their bayonets lowered. They were going to cut us off at the only gate leading to the Towers from the football field. We panicked, and started running too, and luckily, got through the gate just before the Guard, who shot tear gas at us from over the fence. We were so relieved when we got to Tri-Towers. Allison and

I had both been scared out there. It felt like a war zone, with the Guard, and the helicopters flying overhead.'

But at the Towers, they faced a dead end, for the dorm directors had been instructed to forbid students not residing in the complex from entering the dorm. The students tried to push their way in. 'We thought for sure the Guard would come up from behind and try to surround us again,' Barry explains.

In the shoving and pushing that resulted, Allison became separated from Barry and found herself in the front line of students trying to force an entrance into the building; indeed, they had no other option, for return to their quarters was blocked. In the turmoil, she became quite hysterical. Losing all control, screaming and yelling, she fought with the directors, who with their arms locked were trying to prevent her entrance. For some reason that has never been explained, she began shouting, 'Hit me! Hit me!' A husky boy standing behind her thought that she was shouting, 'He hit me!' and was pleading for protection from one of the directors, Tom Rudell, at whom he then took a hefty swipe. Since Rudell's arms were locked with those of the other directors, he could not protect himself and was nearly floored. 'I have reason to remember this girl,' Rudell says. 'Her face was ashen-white and her hair was matted. She seemed completely out of control and rather pitiful, so I let her in.' After an interval of anguish, when she felt herself deserted, she found Barry and they tried to locate a place to stay. The open lounge was filled with other students who had no bed for the night—they would sit up till dawn talking about the weekend—so Barry asked around and found a friend who had a room in the dormitory. He took Allison there, but about midnight they happened to look out the window in time to see a curious incident involving the National Guard.

A stand-off

One of the dormitory directors who locked arms to keep the mass of invading students out of Tri-Towers was Jim Banks, a broad-shouldered, crop-haired young man who was working toward his doctorate in history. For Jim it had been a trying day, for it had brought hundreds of strange visitors to the dormitories. 'And the night was worse,' he recalled later. 'For one thing, there was the helicopter, chattering back and forth at tree-top level. You could hear it coming. You tried to evade its evil eye. You hated it. But there it was, still hovering above Tri-Towers when a mob of terrified students came bearing down upon us.'

Jim does not remember Allison Krause trying to push her way into Tri-Towers—he was defending another portion of the line—but when he and the other directors finally had to give way before the pressure of the kids, he fell back and watched them swarm into the pit area. No sooner had they found refuge there than a blond young man in a red sweat-shirt started shouting at them to leave with him and join in an attempt to burn another building. 'Listen,' the agitator cried, 'there's one more building out there that has to go.' He was referring to the air force ROTC, but before he had time to get the students sufficiently riled up, Banks ran up to him and yelled, 'What's your name?'

'Hey, man,' he shouted back. 'Don't bug me who I am. I'm with the people! What's a name, man? Don't give me any of that name shit!' But Banks kept after him, asking questions, keeping the pressure on him. He turned to the crowd and yelled, 'Satrom and White promised they'd meet with us! They bugged out on us!' But by this time the students were talking among themselves; they had a roof over their heads, their fear was subsiding. The man in the red sweatshirt had lost them. Within minutes he disappeared.

Jim Banks had taught in high school and college; he had supervised Wright Hall since the fall of 1968, and watched the Black United Student campus walk-out of that year. He was, in short, no newcomer to student turbulence. But reconstructing that Sunday night in Tri-Towers, he still shakes his head in disbelief. 'I never saw anything like it,' he says. 'Announcements kept coming at us constantly—"Go back to your dormitories, clear the building, you have fifteen minutes!" Curfew time had been moved up, but no one really knew when it was supposed to be. The kids were scared, they didn't want to go outside again—that damned helicopter, for one thing. My wife, Paula, was upstairs with the baby, watching television, and when I told her I'd be back in a few minutes she didn't know what I might be involved in. She was working on her doctorate, too, at the time, and when I say that, I get a sinking feeling, because she could have been walking across the campus the next day when the rifles fired . . ." '

Shortly before midnight, when the dormitories had begun to quieten down, some students at a window began shouting, 'The Guard is coming!' Banks first considered this just another rumor. Then he went to the window. Beneath a lamppost on the cement path south of Tri-Towers he saw a contingent of thirty or forty Guardsmen standing partially in shadows, their rifles slung over their shoulders, looking his way. He knew then that he had to act—fast! He had to go out and stop them before they could march on the dormitories. He had no idea how he was going to do it. He only knew he had to try.

The soldiers stood on a rise of ground, and as he approached their formation he discerned an older man in a raincoat and baseball-type cap talking with a highway patrol officer. By this time students in the dormitories had also discovered the Guardsmen, and some were leaning out windows, catcalling and jeering. Banks turned and called up to them to quiet down.

There was more catcalling in reply.

'Shut up!' Banks shouted. 'I'm going to talk to these people and find out what they want. You guys give me a chance now, okay?' The noise subsided and Jim Banks went up to the man in the raincoat—he noted a single silver star on his cap above the brim. He offered his hand and identified himself.

'We had a report there was trouble over here,' the man said.

'I'm afraid there could be if you stay here,' Banks replied. 'As you can see, there's no trouble here now.'

The man nodded toward the dormitories. 'I call that trouble.'

'Just a little noise,' Banks said.

'You put your boys to bed,' the man warned.

'I can't tell college students to go to bed,' Banks protested.

'If you don't put them to bed, we'll do it for you!' the man threatened.

For the first time that night Jim Banks got angry. 'Now wait a minute,' he said, 'you can't go into that building.' Then he added, 'I have a wife and baby in there and nobody's going in that building with guns.'

There was a stunned silence. In the brief instant that followed, both parties to the stand-off understood the options, the potential disasters that could be precipitated by a wrong decision, possibly even by a wrong word spoken aloud. It was a third man who broke the deadlock. The highway patrolman nodded to Banks and said, 'Do your job.' With that, the man in the raincoat turned and ordered his troops to march off.

Jim Banks did not know it then, but the man he had been talking with was General Robert Canterbury, tactical commander of all Guard troops in the Kent area.

Half an hour later the buildings had quieted for the night. Banks entered his apartment and found his wife in bed, trying unsuccessfully to sleep. Suddenly bone-weary from hours of keeping the lid on a series of combustible situations, he slumped to the side of the bed. For the moment at least the bomb had been defused. Catastrophe had been contained. 'Honey,' he said, 'I think tonight I did something good . . .'

The coach writes a letter

Late Sunday night, when the turmoil gripping the city of Kent finally subsided, with ashes from the ROTC building still emitting an ugly smell and windows of the downtown establishments boarded up as if in a deserted mining camp, citizens stayed home behind locked doors, obedient to the curfew. Out at Twin Lakes, however, the fashionable area north of town, lights in one house still burned. It was a low, rambling yellow clapboard New England house, tucked away among a nest of blue spruce. It did not stand beside either of the lakes but on a small hill called Knoll Road. It was occupied by the family of track coach Douglas L. Raymond, and its expensive appearance bespoke the secure position he enjoyed at the university.

Raymond was born in Beverly, Massachusetts, in 1915, and while he was an undergraduate at Boston University, he burned up the track, winning national championships in the 600- and 880-yard distances. He was rangy, crop-headed, and had wrinkles at the corners of his constantly smiling eyes. During World War II he was a Navy commander, and later the head coach for track at Boston University, from which he moved to Kent. He was a good coach, having turned out eleven all-Americans, and an even better father, with five children, three of whom were attending Kent State.

On this Sunday he was restless. All day his wife had tried to quieten him down, and during the evening, when neighbors dropped in, he found himself alone in his assessment of the gravity of the situation facing his university. 'I kept telling everybody that we were involved in a revolution . . . morals

. . . education . . . politics. But they kept teasing me, and one fellow said, "Hey, somebody better get Doug a tranquilizer or he's going to blow his gasket." '

Now his children were in bed and his wife had gone upstairs. But he stayed in his study, pacing the floor and trying to comprehend what had overtaken his way of life.

'It hasn't been easy for me to adjust to the new morality,' he says as he explains his feelings that night. 'I'm the twelfth lineal descendant of old Elder Brewster of the *Mayflower*. My folks on both sides settled in places like Plymouth and Duxbury and Beverly. As early as 1636. I was raised with certain standards that exist for all people in all times.

'You take what happened to me last year. I had brought these two great prospects to visit the campus. One boy from New York, another from New Jersey. Good clean-cut kids. It was normal recruiting. I put them up at McDowell Hall and treated them to movie tickets Saturday night. Great kids. They'd been to other universities, so they knew their way around. Anyway, Sunday morning I went to their dorm at 10:00. I always ask my boys if they'd like to go to church, but if they don't, it doesn't faze me.

'So I walk into McDowell Hall at 10:00 this Sunday morning, and what do I find? Two college couples on divans right in the middle of the lobby. The girls were practically naked to the waist. The boys were locked up with them and there was some pretty vigorous love-making of one kind or another going on. I was so outraged that I leaped at those divans, upset them and sent the two couples sprawling across the floor. They started to yell, and I said, "Get out of here! What do you think this is?" A girl behind the desk—you know the type . . . big glasses . . . long hair that hadn't been combed in a month . . . no bra. Well, she started yelling at me, "You can't come in here and do a thing like that!" And I yelled right back, "Young lady, you shut up! Or you're going to be down there on the floor with the rest of them." I took my track boys out of there. They see a thing like that —fellows who haven't gone with girls too much—they might decide to come to Kent, but for the wrong reasons.'

As he walked the floor, Coach Raymond had tried vainly to understand today's young people: 'The boys especially. Long hair and beads. If they want to be girls, why don't they register in the girls' dorm? If they want to be real men, let them work with me, or the football fellows.

'I simply cannot understand why a beautiful American girl who respects herself would waste her time on some cave-chested, long-haired boy with beads when she could be dating a real man on the football team.

'And I don't see why there has to be campus agitation about everything. Disadvantaged youth? You take Al Schoterman of Bayshore, Long Island, my boy in the hammer throw. A foundling. The Schoterman family lost a wonderful son at age eight, so they adopted Al to take his place. He turned out to be a perfect kid. They must be terribly proud of him.

'And Leonard Turner. He's a black student from Dayton. I beat my brains out trying to find good black students for scholarships, and when you turn up a boy like Leonard, it's worth all the trouble. Top violinist, split end of freshman football, and for me an outstanding sprinter and jumper. Why can't all students apply themselves like Schoterman and Turner?'

After contemplating this matter for some time and recalling an editorial attack on one of the few American leaders who seemed to understand how he felt about what was happening, he decided that he must speak out: changes had crept into so many aspects of American life, the whole fabric of our society was being threatened. In this mood, late at night, and on the eve of a tragedy much greater than he could have anticipated, he started to draft a letter for the local newspaper. In the months ahead it would be quoted often:

Dear Sir:

I must take issue against your editorial entitled 'Agnew's Tirades.' Vice-President Agnew has clearly and unequivocally warned us that a 'campus dissident' is no longer to be taken as a little boy, but rather as a full-fledged revolutionary, violently opposed to the government of The United States of America, law and order, the police, the Constitution, the courts, the administrators and the rights of others in the destruction of public and personal property indiscriminately on our streets. These same revolutionaries, basically, want to close down all our universities, libraries, courts, etc. This is what Vice-President Agnew is trying to tell us. He is calling an ace an ace and a spade a spade and it is about time that we had this type of leadership. He is showing up the shams in our society. It is disgusting to me to see what I saw last Saturday evening while standing on the sidewalks of E. Main St. and seeing rocks being thrown by students of Kent and others at the National Guard carriers and personnel as they passed down E. Main St. Also the breaking of windows in the library, the fire in the ROTC building, completely demolishing this facility, the destruction of downtown stores.

How useless and degrading it is to Kent State University to have this happen and I believe that the only course now open for us to follow is for the National Guardsmen and police to use real bullets.

Enough for now, but I am willing to wager that there are many more responsible citizens here in Kent who believe as I do and who feel that your editorial was untimely and ridiculous.

Douglas L. Raymond
Head Coach of Track and Field
Kent State University

Events would prove that far more than half the citizens of Kent were thinking similar thoughts and coming to similar conclusions that mournful Sunday night.

Conclusions

It is most difficult to classify student behavior on Sunday night as a riot, for it lacked both leadership and serious intent, but technically it must be so described, though of such limited dimension as not to warrant the emphasis some have given it. Those students who sat in the highway at the corner of Main and Lincoln were without question in defiance of a lawful order, for they had intruded six feet into the city of Kent, and those who pushed their way past the troop carriers were even more definitely in the wrong, for they had penetrated one block. As many as 100 students could justifiably have been arrested, but they should properly have been charged with violating curfew, and nothing more serious. About twenty others could have been arrested for inciting to riot.

The protest of students that 'we were betrayed' was believed by them, but there is no evidence that any of the authorities maliciously betrayed them; in the heat of confrontation, with several competing policing agencies in command, there was ample room for misunderstanding, but such as did occur was not a plot to entrap students. We know the young man who spoke from the police car and are convinced he did so in good faith; we were unable to discover who spoke with the bullhorn, probably because he knew that he had uttered information and promises which he knew to be false. He was guilty of a malicious act which had far-reaching consequences.

The confusing curfew on campus, twice changed arbitrarily

and without adequate notice to those most concerned, was clumsy and the cause of much subsequent trouble, for which students could not rightfully be blamed.

It is difficult to believe that the Guards were ever in serious danger; when they were pressed from time to time by rambunctious students, they showed admirable restraint. There were at least seven cases of bayoneting and possibly more, but no evidence exists that these were vicious or that students were pursued and run down in any sense of vengeance; when one studies the situation, he is impressed that so few bayonetings occurred, but to deny that any did is to deny facts.

The one event on Sunday that admits no explanation is the supine position of the university administration when its fate was being settled at the firehouse that morning; even the youngest assistant professor ought to have been in there fighting for the integrity of his institution and of American education in general. Failure on the part of all to do so constitutes a dereliction.

The speech of Governor Rhodes seems far less offensive when carefully studied than it must have seemed at the moment, for much of what he claimed was true; it is regrettable that he did not state his conclusions in language more calculated to subdue, rather than arouse emotions, but his words were in the flamboyant tradition of American political leadership and cannot be unduly faulted for that.

The statement of the twenty-three concerned professors at the meeting held on Sunday afternoon would later come in for vigorous abuse by those who felt that the sentiments expressed therein were provocative and conducive to riot. Far from it. They were sentiments which had been expressed at various times on the floor of the United States Senate, in the editorial columns of great newspapers across the country, and in university senates everywhere; they were in the great tradition of free education, and if no one at Kent State had voiced them, the university would have been further derelict. There is, however, a question of timing, and it is possible to make a case against the publishing of these impeccable opinions at this particular and heated moment, except that we could find no one who had bothered to read them that day.

Finally, throughout the day and evening the National Guard comported itself with good judgment and commendable restraint; its leaders gave the impression of knowing how to handle civilian mobs, an exercise in which they had had much practice.

V

MONDAY: BLANKET HILL

The black squirrels

Those students who had stayed at Kent State University over the weekend arose on Monday morning to greet another lovely day. Birds had returned to the campus and robins could be seen digging furiously for worms.

Shortly after 6:00 A.M. men in track suits appeared for their early morning jogs. Avoiding the campus, they ran out east on Main and back around the new stadium, from which the fleet of blue and gray buses set forth for their first circle runs of the day.

From Lake Erie to the north a brisk wind moved in, but by the time it had filtered through the trees it was reduced to a breeze. As the day progressed, this breeze would become important.

It wasn't long before all highways leading into Kent became jammed as usual with cars. As many as 6,000 students and 500 professors and teaching fellows returned to Kent, uncertain as to what had been happening on their campus and uninformed as to what strange laws were now in effect. Unbelievable as it seems, some had not even heard that the university had experienced rioting and that the National Guard had been brought onto the campus. The first they learned of this was when they parked their cars at the huge paved lot by the football field and boarded the bus for the trip to their classrooms.

'You hear about the burning?' some informed student would ask.

'What burning?'

Of course, when the buses halted at Administration and incoming students walked the brief distance to where ROTC had stood, they saw with shock the burned fragment, standing like the ruins of a broken tooth. Strands of white rope cordoned it off and kept it a thing hideously apart. Many students who in the past had said lightly, 'I'd like to see ROTC off campus,' were dismayed when they saw what had been done to accomplish this.

As the day warmed, couples began appearing on Blanket Hill, enjoying the warm earth and reviewing notes for their 9:55–10:45 classes. With each hour, more showed up, sprawling on the grass, so that by midmorning the area resembled a vast outdoor study hall.

Now, as masses of people began moving back and forth across the campus in their accustomed ways, many students observed with pleasure that the animals they loved most were out in lively force. These black squirrels were one of the happiest features of the university, a gang of unruly, beautiful, rambunctious little beasts whose antics were a source of joy. Every tree seemed to have its quota.

It was extraordinary that they prospered in Kent, for they were not indigenous to Ohio. In 1954 the university groundkeeper, Larry Wooddell, had visited Canada and seen in the northern woods 'a new breed of squirrel which might do well in Kent.' He had trapped a pair, brought them home in the trunk of his car, and set them loose on the campus. At the end of the next breeding season Kent had a nucleus from which sprang the huge population which now makes the university unique. Shimmering and sleek, the beautiful blacks drove off the browns, but accommodated to the grays. By 1965 they had spread to all parts of the city, and by 1970 had reached as far north as Twin Lakes, enjoyed as much in the residential areas as on the campus. By their frolics, they made themselves the mascots of Kent.

But on this day, returning students found that their pastoral campus had been invaded. One group of girls, turning a corner suddenly, came upon a massive armed personnel carrier stationed at Bowman Hall. 'A tank!' they screamed. As they continued along the footpath they came to the still-smoking ROTC building and saw along its perimeter a thin line of National Guardsmen. 'Soldiers,' they cried in disbelief.

'The Guard has taken over,' explained students who had spent the weekend on campus. 'It's a whole new ball game.'

Five students

It is now Monday, and there will be firing on the hill. Before it starts—a rain of fifty-five steel-jacketed bullets which could kill at a range of two miles—let us find out more about the background of the five students whom we have been following, for they are among the thirteen who will be hit.

In mid-October, 1967, freshman Sandy Scheuer sat in a bus heading down the highway from Kent to Akron, thinking of her first month at Kent State. Already she had made many friends in Fletcher Hall, her dorm, and felt at home as a student; she liked Kent but was happy at being able to get to Akron, to attend temple services for the Jewish high holidays. Religion was an important part of her life—her Hebrew name was Gittel, meaning goodness, kindness, all the joy one can think of in life—and she brought to it the same enthusiasm she did to all her activities. Beside her sat Steve Drucker, a freshman whom she had just begun to date, who was talking to a friend across the aisle, and with a smile she joined their conversation.

Two Octobers later, cute, pert Sandy Scheuer was still everybody's pal. 'If you were really down and out, the first person you'd want to see was Sandy,' says Steve, who had maintained his friendship with her over the years. 'Man, she had a laugh like you haven't heard. Made you feel good inside just to hear her. Within ten minutes, I guarantee, you'd be up on top again. There wasn't anything Sandy wouldn't do for you. She cared.'

Her warm personality and good sense of humor appealed to all who knew her; and the house on Summit Street which she shared with three other juniors was constantly filled with friends who dropped by. They recall, 'We could count on Sandy, or Barb Kass or Jan Reinstein, to find a bed, or a place for one more at table. There were always so many people at Sandy's you couldn't keep count.' Jan says, 'Sandy would be one of the first to try a new idea, and the one to enjoy it most. Once, after we got back from a trip to Florida, all we could boast about was how tan we were. So Sandy marshaled us into the front yard at 10:00 one night so we could keep it going with moon tan!'

'Sandy was one of the friendliest people I knew,' says Jerry Persky, the beaded Yippie. 'There was hardly a soul on campus she didn't know. She was pretty too . . . always smiling . . . really nice eyes. About five-feet-four. In a crowd you wouldn't pick her out as the best-looking chick—she dressed like everybody else, in jeans or a casual dress—but when you talked to her, you knew she was different. On a date you could take her to anything . . . parties, plays . . . she always enjoyed them all.' Jerry's face breaks into a sad smile whenever he speaks of her.

Although Sandy enjoyed all her studies, her main interest was in speech-and-hearing therapy, a course which she had decided upon early in her freshman year. 'I think the way to help people is to work individually, and gradually, rather than just sit around and talk about how unjust things are,' Sandy would say to friends. 'I just can't buy these people who beat their chest, and then do nothing. Why aren't they in the ghettos, or doing inner-city work? Maybe I'm not going to set the world on fire through speech therapy, but if I help a few people, that's good enough.'

Most of her courses were in speech, physiology and anatomy, and she was a diligent student, often spending long hours at her work and maintaining a 3.6 average out of a possible 4.0. She was elected to the speech-and-hearing honorary club, Alpha Eta.

'I never could figure out how somebody who acted as out of it as Sandy did at times could get such good grades,' says one friend, Rita Rubin. 'We used to tease her and call her "Space" because she sometimes seemed a couple of minutes behind in the conversation. If you've seen Judy Carne on *Laugh-In* you've seen Sandy.'

Much of her time was spent at the clinic, where she would administer hearing tests and do other volunteer work in line with her academic curriculum. As a speech-and-hearing major, Sandy had been assigned one student, who was in her special care and for whom she had to make up nightly care plans in speech therapy. 'Come on, help me think up a sentence that has five words starting with z,' she'd moan to Jan or Barb. 'I've already used every word I can think of.'

In addition to helping her therapy student, Sandy was greatly devoted to her friends, and beauty queen Sharon Swanson remembers her with special fondness. She had good reason to: 'In the fall of 1969 I broke my back in a car accident, and I couldn't have made it through finals without Sandy. Carrying my books for me, helping me to class, collecting class notes that I'd missed. You'd have thought she was my guardian angel, and I had no claim on her at all.'

Sandy was a girl very attentive to what others thought of her. 'I guess people don't take me seriously, because maybe I laugh too much. But I really do care what's happening. It's just that I don't show it.' During her sophomore year a number of her friends had become greatly interested in politics. At the time SDS was the hottest thing on campus, and word circulated, 'It's one of the few groups on campus that takes an interest in America.' So Sandy, who lived in Koonce Hall, where many of the hippies hung out, decided to investigate. 'So I walk up to SDS headquarters in the pit, and ask them to tell me what they want, what it is they stand for,' she reported. 'They wouldn't even talk to me, much less explain anything. Maybe they didn't think I'd be an asset to their movement!' Sandy told a friend. 'At any rate, for me that was the end.'

While living in Koonce, Sandy used to go over to Wright Hall to baby-sit for Jim Banks, the hero of the Sunday night confrontation, and his wife, who was studying, too, so they had frequent occasion to hire Sandy as their sitter. She fell quite in love with their one-year-old, David, and he with her, so much so that she often used to stop by their apartment just to play with David, who was always delighted when she appeared.

Banks says, 'My wife and I had ample opportunity to talk with Sandy about her plans, her ideas. We thought of her as apolitical.' She simply never discussed the topics which agitated the other students, and when one of the boys said one night, 'We must oppose the oppressive fascist elements in our society,' she said, "Like what?" and teased him when he tried to explain," Banks adds, 'Of course, that was 1968–69. This year she left Tri-Towers. For a while I wasn't sure where she was, but then she stopped by one day to see David, and she told us she had taken an apartment off campus and liked the freedom.'

But her feelings remained the same. 'You've got to understand the way it was with Sandy,' explains a friend. 'She was Jewish. So were her friends. And that almost automatically put her in with a lot of the long-hairs and the freaks and the big-thinkers. Like a lot of them, she had done the sorority bit and dropped out, but she wasn't really one of them. She was more the proverbial Jewish mother, worrying that the rest would get in trouble.'

A roommate, Barb Kass, who dresses very neatly and is the one who knew her best, concurs: 'Some of the guys who came over to the house were pretty much into politics and would rap for hours about the economics of the war, U.S. imperialism . . . the standard topics. But not Sandy. She'd just as soon be out in the kitchen fixing something for everyone to eat. Sure she was against the war, but who isn't? I guess the best way to explain it is this: she cared because people were dying, not because of the military-industrial complex.'

Sandy was one of two daughters, and the two girls retained a close relationship with their parents. 'Hi, how are you doing?' she'd say as she called her parents in nearby Youngstown. 'Just checking to make sure everything's okay.' She often referred to graduation, for her father had promised her a trip to Israel if she did well in her senior year. 'I don't know what I'll find when I get there, maybe I'll try life in a kibbutz,' she told her friends. 'But I sure want to see what it's like.' Around her neck she wore a Star of David.

She enjoyed all sports, especially tennis and swimming, and was an excellent roller-skater. In the spring of 1970 she had bought a second-hand bicycle and loved to ride over campus and around Kent. Once, with a friend, she attempted to cycle down to Mogadore Lake, but the five-mile distance was too great for them, and they turned back, confessing, 'We're worse than two old women.'

In one of her courses this spring Sandy had been required to write an essay, and had started with the phrase, 'Who is to say?' One of her friends, noticing this, had kidded Sandy about it, and the rest of their group used it as a constant gag, walking around the campus mournfully exclaiming, 'Who is to say?' On Sunday night, when asked her opinion about the weekend riots, Sandy replied, 'Who is to say?'

Jeff Miller, the constant free-loader at Sandy's, had been in Kent only four months, having transferred from Michigan State at the beginning of the winter quarter. He had adapted quickly and easily to life at Kent. 'A lot of people have tried to say that Kent radicalized Jeff . . . that he came in straight and went out a freak . . . but that's just not true,' says his confidant, John Moir, 'because he was never radicalized. Sure, he wore his hair long, with an Indian headband and the whole bit, but he was really just your standard easy-going kid. He wasn't a leader, and he pretty much did what his friends did.'

At Kent that consisted of a life of ease and fun, clouded

by the standard uncertainties of the draft, the war, the drug laws. Upon transferring to Kent, he moved into a house with several friends from his home in Plainview, New York. 'We were really a close house,' continues Moir. 'There were seven of us, and we'd always do things together. We didn't do the downtown bar scene, we preferred playing softball, or things like that. We got a really good team going, and were the terror of the neighborhood for a while there. Jeff used to tell the rest of us, "You ought to be glad I'm as small as I am [at five feet six inches he weighed 150 pounds] or I'd be up in the big leagues and leave all of you behind."'

Back at the house, everything happened on a rather haphazard basis; friends would drift in and spend several days in one bed or another. Class attendance was sketchy, and everyone was on the look-out for something new or exciting.

Things got a little tense in the spring. 'The whole place was a mess. No clean dishes, the sink was stopped up, no running water. And then the two best guys in the house, the ones who kept us at attention, moved out because they feared we were going to be busted. It was an unsatisfactory spring break, too. We only had a couple of days, so there was no time to unwind,' says John Moir.

Since none of the boys had much money, their diet was somewhat limited. 'Come on, Jeff, get on macrobiotics like me,' Steve Drucker would say. 'Good rich organic foods—lots of minerals and proteins.'

'No, man, I've got to stick to rice and vegetables. That's all I can afford.'

The one thing that enabled the boys to get by was the generosity of their girl friends, who could always be relied upon for a meal. 'Every time you'd turn around, there'd be Jeff at the door, with one of those silly Marx Brothers' grins on his face, waving his hands in the air,' recalls Barb Kass.

'Just truckin' on by, just truckin' on by,' he'd say.

'You just couldn't resist Jeff, because he was so good. He'd do anything for you. He spent practically his whole spring break helping me find a summer job near his home on Long Island, and he didn't even think twice about it. And he had such a hell of a good time doing everything. His house was near Sparkle Market, where we used to grocery-shop, and by spring quarter he and the rest of the guys in his house had liberated about ten shopping carts and brought them home. One day we were going together to do our laundry with the clothes in one of the baskets, and what does Jeff do but jump on top of the cart, yell, "I'm off," and go careening down the middle of Summit Street with his hair flying in the wind. I've never seen so many cars veer to the side of the road in my life!'

Although he got along very well with Sandy's roommates, he confided that he felt rather awkward around other girls. 'I don't know what it is with me. When I see a chick I like, either I get really quiet, or I get hyperactive and start jumping around like some kind of fool. I really feel inferior to women. When I was at Michigan, I hardly dated at all. I don't know when it's going to stop.'

It stopped about a month prior to his death, with a girl named Nancy. 'She was the stereotype hippie,' says one friend. 'Long frizzy hair, blue jeans, and kind of quiet. But Jeff really fell for her. They'd spend hours together, sitting on the roof of the house, talking or listening to music. But I've always suspected that the real reason he liked her was because she was one of the few people who didn't bitch when he practiced the drums.'

One of Jeff's main loves was music; he had always wanted to make the rock scene. For long hours he would sit with stereo earphones on and listen to popular music. At Michigan State he had been a disc jockey on the college radio station, but in April his big chance came along. A friend was forming a band and needed a drummer, and he told Jeff that if he could learn how to play well enough, he could be in the band. From that moment on, Jeff practiced incessantly, sitting hunched over borrowed drums, trying to play along with music from his record player, much to the dismay of his roommates.

'God, it'll be great,' he told his friends. 'We're going to call ourselves "The Acapulco Greasers" and wear overalls and slick back our hair. Then we'll come out with really hard rock and freak them out.'

In the opinion of Mark Cramer, who had earned his living with the drums and who was giving Jeff lessons on the side, 'He had a real knack. He learned faster than anyone I had taught before. He had a natural sense of rhythm . . . you know, the finger-snapping kind. What he wanted most of all—you might say his big dream—was to be third drummer with "The Grateful Dead." He'd play their records for hours and try to master the drum parts. I couldn't tell the difference between him and the drummer on the record.'

Although Jeff had declared himself a psychology major,

he told friends, 'I really don't know what I'll do when I graduate, or even if I will graduate. Sometimes I think I ought to split and find out what I want and then come back later. But who knows?' He frequently talked with friends about his time at Michigan State: 'When I got there, I played it straight. Joined my brother's fraternity, dressed right . . . button-down shirts, the whole bit. But pretty soon it just didn't seem to matter, and I let go. In the fraternity, they started calling me "the hippie" and "the radical." But here at Kent it's good. There's no hassle.'

For a time he did consider changing schools again. Barry Levine says, 'Allison had a class with Jeff and we grew to like him. In fact, he was thinking seriously about transferring to Buffalo with us. I respected him. I don't think you can go around all day talking with deep brains, and Jeff was a fun human being.'

Although he attended classes irregularly, he managed passable grades, and even maintained good relations with the faculty.

'I first met Jeff when he came to apologize for cutting so many classes in a course I was teaching,' says Dr. Wesley Zaynor, one of the leading lights of Kent's psychology department. 'I was impressed that he had bothered to drop by . . . most students don't . . . and we became fairly good friends. I found him to have very strong convictions on higher education, and to be very articulate in his beliefs.

' "Dr. Zaynor," he would say, "if college is supposed to be a period for individual growth, don't you think that this would be best in a community which encourages students to participate in community affairs? But we can't even vote. Unless the voting age is lowered to eighteen, the only outlet we have as students to get things done is to rally or demonstrate. Maybe that's not the best way, but now it's the only way. I'm not big on doing a lot of social work myself, but I could see being one of Nader's Raiders."

'I found Jeff very much concerned that the state legislature and other funding agencies weren't going to be able to keep up with the demands of the universities. He told me, "With so many kids enrolling now, how can they support the existing curricula, and keep adding the necessary new programs? The trouble with a lot of our courses now is that they aim at giving only superficial and transitory factual knowledge. We need the tools to apply and extend what we know to other fields. Take your statistics course, for example, that's good because you can use it in a lot of other fields, but a lot of the courses I take are just full of bull."

'One day he told me, "Sure, I'm against pollution, but I don't like the way Nixon and the administration are giving so much publicity to the problem. I think they may be trying to co-opt the whole country, getting us so uptight about the environment that we forget about Vietnam." '

Other than social concerns, Jeff was not very politically active. He was against the war in Vietnam, but did not harp on the subject. 'What can I tell you about Vietnam that you don't already know and feel?' he would say to friends.

He had written to his draft board for the necessary papers and was considering applying for status as a conscientious objector. 'We talked about his applying frequently,' says Dane Griffin, 'and he was certain he wanted to do it, but someone had told him, incorrectly, that if you did apply and were rejected, you'd be automatically drafted. That was enough to scare him off.' Other friends agree that if Jeff had been drafted, he would not have served. 'For me it's Canada or jail . . . nothing else.'

How can this drum-playing, irresponsible young man best be characterized? He had a continuing interest in social problems, but perhaps an even deeper addiction to apathy. He and most of his friends were more involved in play than in changing the world.

'I was amazed when Jeff got so upset that weekend,' says John Moir. 'All along, we'd been in our own detached little world, kind of thinking the whole thing was useless. He went to the Washington moratorium, and came away saying, "Liberals are strange, man, really strange," and that was about it. What kind of a radical is that?'

He was alienated from the standard patterns of American life, but as he expressed it, 'I'm more into the peace thing than into violence.' In the political spectrum he was on the left, but those who knew him best avow that he was far removed from radicalism.

There is no doubt, however, that he was more deeply concerned this weekend than ever before. Angered by the Cambodian adventure and frightened by the Saturday night fire, he reacted to the destruction of ROTC with confusion. He enjoyed seeing it go but was afraid of the consequences. Sunday night was crucial in his alienation because he felt the Guard actions to have been unjustified. 'They lied to us,' he repeated over and over to his friends. By Monday he was willing to listen to those who argued, 'Jeff, you've got to get into it now. You've got to be involved.' A friend stopped by to tell him, 'You've got to decide where you stand. When the fucking Guard comes on campus, what are you going to do about it?' In a fumbling, half-baked way he made his decision.

'Doug Wrentmore is the kind of fellow, like if you had a son and he turned out half as well, you'd be satisfied.' The speaker was a red-headed Kent coed who obviously liked the young man she was describing. 'What I mean, if you had been all-American tackle at Ohio State you might growl, "Why don't the boy eat and put some flesh on his bones? Why don't he fight?" What I mean, when you see him, he's six feet tall, very gentle. His hair isn't long but it isn't short, either, and what he really loves is nature. You might say that Doug was the very best kind of kid this university turns out.'

An anthropology buff since his early childhood, Doug elected to attend Kent because its anthropology department was reputed to be one of the best in northern Ohio. 'I've been an ecology and anthropology nut since age five, and I can't wait to get into those courses,' he told friends. 'I like to be out in the woods and do things with my hands, and get away from people every now and then. This ought to be just what I want.'

Upon entering Kent, however, Doug was somewhat disappointed. He found it too big for his liking: 'Too many students for a good faculty-student relationship. I like things a little more personal. I guess I'm just not cut out for a big school.' His interest in anthropology waned as the year progressed and Kent held little for him. Consequently, in the spring of his freshman year, he wrote to his parents that he wanted to transfer to St. John's College in Maryland: 'They offer a fabulous program in the great books. All you do is read and discuss them.' He was not accepted, however, because of inadequate grades, and had to reconcile himself to Kent.

During the summer between his freshman and sophomore years, Doug, who had been an outstanding scout for years, was selected to head the counselors' program at the main scout camp in Pennsylvania. It was about as high a position as a scout could aspire to, but Doug's general discontent invaded even this area. 'In a way, I feel badly about being the head counselor,' Doug confided to a friend. 'You know, I won the Eagle Scout and God-and-Country awards a couple of years ago, so I suppose I'm qualified. But now I'm not so sure I believe in God—in the sense of an organized religion—and I'm beginning to have doubts about the country.'

In his sophomore year Doug and his brother Hal, a freshman at Kent, and several of their friends rented a small house some blocks from campus. Doug had no steady girl, and he once commented wryly to a friend: 'Of over 200 graduating seniors in my high school class, when it came time for the senior superlatives, I was voted "Most quiet." How good can that make you feel?' Most of his activities revolved around his brother and a few friends.

In the middle of the fall quarter his dissatisfaction with Kent returned, and he dropped out, living with his parents in nearby Northfield. 'About the only thing that interested me at that time was working as a child-care helper in a local psychiatric hospital. I've always been interested in experimental education, and to be with children is a great joy. And then the November draft caught up with me.'

Although he had begun application for status as a conscientious objector—'I can't think of any war worth fighting for or dying for'—his number was so low that he realized he might be called for a physical at any time. To escape this, he got back into Kent for the winter quarter.

'I knew it was do or die this time at Kent, so I determined to get more involved in campus life,' he says. 'I still couldn't go the football-fraternity bit, but I sought out what organizations I did like.' In the spring quarter he joined the Kent sailing club, and grew to enjoy sailing on a reservoir near Ravenna. This, coupled with activities in the Kent Karate Klub and work in the school's ecological organization, led to a fairly busy and happy spring.

'I switched my major to psychology, and even decided I might shoot for a Ph.D. in it. I started talking to people more, and I seemed to be getting things together somewhat. My life had stopped being a series of ups and downs, and ins and outs.' Perfection was reached on April 30, when his mother called from Northfield with the news that the draft board had accepted his request for C.O. status.

That night he heard Nixon announce the entry of United States troops into Cambodia.

'If you were making one of the old-style rah-rah college movies, Bill Schroeder would have to be the star. You know the type: good build, easy smile, the campus hero,' says one of his friends. 'But there was a hell of a lot more to him than that. He wasn't your party boy, he was a real thinker.'

'Bill didn't have to search for an identity, like the rest of us,' adds another. 'He was so sound in the head. He knew himself and what he was capable of. He'd met success in a lot of areas already . . . sports, academics . . . and didn't have to hassle to prove himself.'

When Bill entered Kent as a nineteen-year-old sophomore in the fall of 1969, it was like old home week. He had been at Colorado the past year intending to major in geology, but had become dissatisfied with this program. 'After a while I realized that even though I loved geology, I didn't want to make it my career,' he told friends. 'I got more and more interested in psychology and people, so I came to Kent to get the courses I wanted. It's close to home, and I have high school friends here already, so it's a good deal.'

In the early fall Bill had moved into a house near campus with three of his hometown buddies from Lorain, and here he indulged his favorite habits. He confided that he wanted to be a writer and spent much of his time writing poetry, which he would then hide, saying he would let others read it 'when my time comes.' He was a voracious reader, especially enjoying *Psychology Today*, the manual of his chosen field, and current news magazines. He had part-time jobs on and off during the year, at a hamburger joint, in the school cafeteria, and in the assembly line of a local powder and metal company. 'I like to make my own way, and have cash when I need it,' he always said. One of his favorite possessions was a Fiat 850, which he had bought at the beginning of September. He loved music also, and had bought every album which the Rolling Stones, his favorite group, had released. He especially admired Mick Jagger, the Stones' leader: 'He lives as he wants to and doesn't take any shit from anybody.'

Frequently, when nothing else was going on, he'd make the three-block trip to Kent's strip of bars for a beer with some of his friends. He also spent some time at the Sigma Nu fraternity house, the club to which some of his roommates belonged. He was well liked by the members, and had been nominated for membership, but as he said to one of his friends: 'I like the free beer they give me, but I'm not interested in it as a full-time thing.' Although he tended toward the quiet side and was at times rather shy, he had no trouble getting dates when he wanted them. 'I enjoy playing the game and meeting different chicks. Hell, I'm too young to get serious,' he'd say. 'But sometimes I get discouraged. There just aren't that many girls around here that I can talk to on anything but a superficial level. They're all so damn flighty.'

'That was the main thing for Bill,' a friend recalls. 'A girl might be a good-looker, but she had to have a mind, too.'

'Although I lived with Bill for almost a year, and we had good times together, he was rather hard to get to know,' says Bruce Smith. 'Really self-contained. You kind of got the idea that he was always thinking great thoughts.'

'He was an extremely intelligent and perceptive guy,' says another. 'I'd say he had a photographic memory. Kent really wasn't a challenge to him. Oh, he'd bitch and say he wasn't doing too well, but he always pulled through. Never studied till the last minute, and still had a B-plus average. Once he walked into his physical science course in the middle of the quarter and was surprised to find that a test was being given that day. He went ahead and took it cold, and came out with an A.'

But all was not studies. A top athlete who had been named all-state in high school basketball, he was also a track star. Standing six feet one inch, he weighed 180 pounds and was devoted to all sports. 'Come on, let's go down to the courts,' he'd say to one of his roommates. 'Those little kids down at the Fulton School have probably been waiting for us all day. I promised them we'd teach them lay-up shots today.'

Much of his time was spent in ROTC activities. In return for the scholarship he had received from the military, he was committed to four years of active duty in the army after graduating from college. Because of his consistently high performance in class work and military drill, he was named first sergeant of his cadet company, and was running a close second to another cadet for the number-one position in the sophomore cadet corps. But the military was fast losing his allegiance.

'When I first got the scholarship,' he told friends, 'I thought it wouldn't be such a bad deal. I needed the money and figured I would travel a lot on my tour of duty. But now I just can't justify our being in Vietnam, and I don't think I could ever fight there.

'And the worst part of it is having killing drilled into you day after day. I can take the military history part. I even like that. But when they start telling us the best way to kill peasants, I hate it. And what can I say when people are constantly hammering at you for being in ROTC? Like the other day when I happened to be in uniform, one of my professors said to me, "What are you, some kind of fascist or something?" I know he was just kidding, but it really gets to you after a while.'

Bill told friends that he considered himself to be more in the middle ground on life style and politics than rigidly adhering to one set pattern. 'I'm not a freak, but I don't think I'm a square either. I can go either way, depending on the situation.' In line with this, he had few friends in the ROTC program, whose members he found too conservative.

'When the magazine reporters first started coming around right after the shooting,' confides one roommate, 'we pointedly stressed that Bill was "all-American" so that there would be no way anyone could link him up with the "liberal-commie-hippie" complex groups, because we knew that accusation would undoubtedly follow. Maybe we overdid it. Because we were denying what he had become. He was too complex and too much his own person to be described simply as the all-American boy he had been in high school. He understood a lot about America.'

One of Bill's close friends at Kent was Captain Donald Peters, assistant professor of military science. Captain Peters had answered Bill's initial request for information on transferring when Bill was still at Colorado, and the two met shortly after Bill entered Kent. Frequently Bill would drop by Peters' office in the ROTC building after class to talk.

'Over the course of the year,' says Peters, a twenty-eight-year-old Vietnam veteran, 'Bill and I discussed everything from Che Guevara to Kent to current best sellers. There wasn't anything he wasn't interested in. He wanted to analyze it all. And he worried a lot, too, about the kids his own age who were blowing their minds with drugs. He said he just couldn't see that. They were just wasting their lives.' Then Peters adds, 'Schroeder wasn't the average campus guy, out to sell himself. He wanted to buy. The whole time I knew him, he never lied or went back on his word.'

Although he had surrendered any interest in a geology degree, Bill still had a love of rocks and the outdoors and greatly admired Dr. Glenn Frank for his handling of the geology department. 'That man is really tops.'

'He used to take long walks around Kent,' recalls Robin Alexander, a petite blond coed, 'and describe to me in great depth what he'd seen. His favorite spot was the Akron reservoir. You could tell he really dug just being outdoors. He was really soft-spoken and gentle, and then he'd blush if he thought he'd been talking about himself too much.'

A couple of weeks before, he had gone on a camping trip with his father and several of his friends. 'Bill always stayed close to his parents, especially his mother,' recalls one friend. 'She knew him inside out and he really loved her. Used to tell her everything, and it mattered a good deal to him what she thought of what he was doing.'

It has been said, 'Bill Schroeder was apolitical.' That is not true. He was firmly convinced that history proved the efficiency and justice of the American system, but he was attentive to the criticism of that system by his peers. It was because of this openness that Schroeder found himself caught up in the maelstrom.

The most interesting, and certainly the most controversial, of the students was a tall, slender, attractive girl named Allison Beth Krause, who will be remembered for a flower, a kitten, and a wild concoction of accusation and rumor, some of it based on fact. She was a study in contradictions. Some found her to be quiet and aloof, while others thought her aggressive and forthright. Some saw her the symbol of the flower generation. Others branded her 'the pearl of the Weathermen.'

She came to Kent in the fall of 1969, dedicated to a career in special education so that she could help emotionally disturbed children work their way out of their psychological problems by means of art. She had such a good record and obvious ability that she was granted admission to the Honors College. She was definitely a girl with charisma, liked by both her teachers and her peers, and she did well at Kent. She was one of five freshmen out of 180 chosen by the staff of the Honors College to be on their policy council, and she told friends, 'I'm thrilled to have a vote equal to the deans. Students ought to have more say in making policy.' Professors found her suggestions valid and imaginative. In her dormitory she was elected by her fellow students to the judicial board, and here she served her classmates well.

'Allison was really big on individual rights, and as our representative to the dorm council, she personally saved a girl from disciplinary probation,' recalls a friend. 'This girl had been accused of having a boy in her room when she wasn't supposed to, but no one had actually seen the boy. So Allison challenged the rest of the judicial board: "This girl can't be convicted on mere hearsay," and the case was dropped.'

But there is one voice of dissent from the members of the dorm: 'Allison always took her own views to the dorm council, rather than representing ours. Since she was more liberal than the rest of us, it could be rather irritating at times.'

Early in the year Allison met the person who was to have more effect on her than any other. Barry Levine, from Valley Stream, New York, was also a freshman in the Honors College, and the two were drawn to each other immediately. A rather soft-spoken, unassuming person, Barry had a slight build and a full beard. He spoke with a quiet sureness and had great charm. He and Allison made a fine-looking couple. Carol Buchholz, one of three girls assigned to live with her at the beginning of the school year, says Allison was 'very natural. No make-up, high cheekbones, almond eyes, long curly hair. She had plenty of clothes, but always preferred to wear jeans and a top. But she was always clean, and never looked sloppy.'

From the time Allison and Barry met, they were inseparable. They had classes together, ate together in his dormitory —she would sneak in on borrowed meal tickets—and played pool in the lounges in the dorm complex. Barry was an excellent player and frequently financed their dates with his winnings. With him, she shared her joy in music; hard rock and the throaty sensuality of her favorite artist, Melanie.

'Barry's private entrance to our room in the dorm was the window facing the street, and through it he would come and go at all hours,' recalls Carol. 'Usually his being there didn't bother us, but when we had fire drills and things like that, when everyone had to evacuate the building, it was kind of a hassle figuring out where to hide him.'

Rather than frequent the bars on Water Street, Allison and Barry preferred to sit and talk with friends in the Student Union or in the pit of Tri-Towers. Their friends were the long-hairs of the campus, more interested in forming a student co-op than attending a football game. Allison was quiet around those whom she did not know well, but when she was with friends, she was vivacious, an extremely self-confident young woman.

'Allison was never really interested in going downtown and checking out the guys, or always going to parties and getting drunk, like a lot of freshman girls at Kent,' says Carol. 'She'd been on her own in D.C. the summer before she came to Kent, and I think she'd grown out of that sort of thing by the time she came to college. She was more interested in really talking to people, and finding out what they were like.'

'But that didn't mean she was all seriousness,' adds another friend. 'She and Barry were completely uninhibited: half the time they'd be out in the hall of our dorm wrestling, and early in the year Allison proved she wasn't the least bit bashful. We had two rock concerts open to the whole school, and at both affairs, Allison was the first person up on the floor to dance. I mean, nobody else was dancing, and there's Allison out in the middle of the floor, by herself, just grooving away. But Barry calmed her down somewhat, after they'd been dating for a while. He convinced her to stop smoking and drinking.'

In assessing these two young people, it is vital to know what happened to them politically, for Allison was the most politically aware of the five students. She had even begun in high school to be concerned about the war and national priorities, had determined to work for needed changes in the system while in college. In the early days on campus, she had gone to an SDS meeting—'If anybody is involved on campus, I guess it will be them'—but had come back thoroughly disgusted. 'They couldn't answer any of my questions, and they didn't know what they were talking about at all. I'm certainly not going to join up with that crowd!'

She participated in the October moratorium at Kent, as one roommate, Gail Travaglianti, recalls: 'She was one of the first of us to get into the moratorium thing. She did it because she really believed in it, while the rest of us just kind of tagged along because we thought it would be a cool thing to do.'

When the march began around campus, Allison was in the front lines, and as the group headed for downtown Kent, she was one of the people holding up the banner leading the rest.

'As we neared the main intersection,' Gail continues, 'there was a group of SDS types standing in the street holding a Vietcong flag, and they looked like they were going to start walking ahead of us, and ruin our march. So Allison yelled out "Don't let them get ahead of us!" and we swept around them, leaving them standing foolishly in the middle of the street.'

In November, Allison and Barry hitchhiked to the Washington moratorium. 'It was the first really big rally either of us had ever attended,' recalls Barry, 'and we expected a lot, but it wasn't much. Like everyone else, I guess, we wanted an immediate response from the government, and we didn't get it. What we did get was tear gas. First experience, and Allison was embittered by it. Said she'd never get involved in anything again where she'd get gassed.'

These two incidents were the height of Allison's political activity throughout the school year.

Although they proved themselves responsible students, faithful in attendance and good in exams, neither was satisfied with the academics at Kent. 'I just can't accept all these rules. "Take this English course. Take that history seminar,"' Allison told friends. 'I want to take what I want, when I want it. Besides, if I don't like a course or a prof, I'm not going to study the material anyway, so I'm just wasting my time. And the Honors College isn't much of a challenge anyway.'

Consequently, late in the fall Allison and Barry applied for transfers to the State University of New York at Buffalo, effective fall quarter 1970, and were accepted. 'Allison and I hitched up there once or twice to look over the school. I had friends from home there, and we were both quite impressed. We liked the emphasis on the humanities at Buffalo, and thought we had more in common with the students there. Most of them are from the East, while at Kent, you get mostly Ohio kids,' says Barry.

'Allison really had a hard time with her parents about the transfer,' Carol Buchholz recalls. 'They thought she should stay at Kent State because of the Honors College, but Allison and Barry had made up their minds to go, and that was it as far as Allison was concerned. She and her parents argued about the transfer many times over the phone—sometimes you could hear her yelling at them from one end of the dorm hall to the other—but in the end it was settled that Allison could go. She was to be entirely on her own, and pay for it herself.'

The remainder of the fall passed quietly. 'Kent is sort of a football players' school,' says Barry. 'No great mental output on the part of the students. If you stay there for any length of time, you fall into that, and we did.' Allison's younger sister, Laurie, age sixteen, came to school from the Krauses' home in Pittsburgh to visit Allison several times. The two were very close, and Allison always looked forward to her visits and included Laurie in her activities when she came. Over Christmas, Allison spent ten days with Barry and his parents in New York. It was the first time the Levines had met her, and they liked her. Friends report that her relationships with her own family, particularly her father, were not the best, and she was pleased with any opportunity not to go home, for Mr. Krause did not approve of her style of dress or her outlook on life, and the two clashed frequently. Allison had confided to friends that she had often locked herself in her room at home to escape her father's anger.

At the end of the winter quarter Allison moved out of the Honors dormitory into Engleman Hall, where she had a single room. She told friends, 'I'm glad to be in the center of campus now, rather than having to trudge back and forth to the edge of campus like I had to before. Besides, I like having a room to myself.'

Her former roommates viewed her departure with a certain amount of pleasure. 'We still got along fairly well,' says Gail Travaglianti, 'but Allison had taken to reprimanding us about everything we did. That we should study more, and drink and smoke less, and on and on. It wasn't that she was acting superior. It was more "I'm trying to help you, so listen to me." And that kind of thing gets old fast, especially coming from someone your own age.'

Carol Buchholz adds, 'Allison's natural tendency to tell anyone what she thought—in a very loud and forthright manner, without caring what they thought of her in return—began to alienate her from a lot of people. And yet, underneath it all, I thought some of her brashness reflected a lack of confidence in herself. Somehow, she seemed independent but insecure.'

Since her switch to Buffalo the next year was assured, Allison was no longer bound to Kent's required courses, so she enrolled in classes that interested her, such as art history, psychology and Afro-American studies. She and Barry were seen together so constantly that one of the graduate teaching fellows in the psychology department, Jim Brennan, referred to them as 'My bookends. You never see one without the other. They're good students, and I can always count on them to be prepared and to participate in class discussions. They always get my jokes, too!' Should an occasion arise when either she or Barry could not come to class, Allison would call the professor ahead of time to explain their absence.

One of Allison's special interests was art, and on a visit to Kent, her mother brought her a number of art books, which she read with pleasure. More and more, she began to think of a career in art, rather than in special education.

'Allison's one big desire was to own an art gallery,' says Barry. ' "It could be a little place out in the country," she used to tell me. "I wouldn't want to make a million dollars, just enough to live on." She started taking art courses and thought she might specialize in art at Buffalo. She was very good at college.'

As winter turned to spring, Allison and Barry began to live more outdoors; they would fly kites on the commons, or take long walks around Kent, or frequently just sit around on the grass and talk to friends or read.

'Hey, Bonnie, you ought to read *One Flew Over the Cuckoo's Nest*,' she'd say to her friend. 'It's really good. Next on my list is Ferlinghetti's *Coney Island of the Mind*.'

One of her favorite courses was an English class taught by Barbara Agte, the young woman who had spoken at the noon burial of the Constitution. 'I'm so glad we discuss what we read, Barbara,' she'd say. 'I get so tired of people telling me all the time what poets and novelists mean. If I can get a book of critical essays on a poet, I much prefer reading that and trying to understand on my own.'

At the start of the spring semester a girl in Allison's dorm was ordered by the authorities to get rid of a kitten she was keeping against regulations. It was a scrawny brown-and-gray-striped alley cat, and Allison took a liking to it. 'I'll take it,' she said. The girl explained that no kitten would be allowed in Engleman, but Allison said, 'You let me worry about that,' and she moved the kitten into her room without trouble. Yossarian, she named her pet, after the anti-hero of *Catch-22*, and it became a permanent member of her group.

Allison's mind was both inquisitive and objective. 'Frequently, when freshmen come to Kent,' says Barbara Agte, 'they are easily radicalized, just because they don't know anything. They have more people around to persuade them, more information at hand, so they just accept things as they come. But not Allison! She always wanted to know for herself what the whole story was.'

Randy Gardner, age twenty, of Columbus, Ohio, confirms Mrs. Agte's assessment: 'I was with Allison in her last class with Mrs. Agte. We both thought she was about the best teacher we'd ever known, and this day Allison asked, "All this talk about dirt in the air? How can we know the amount a human being can absorb? Is what we hear propaganda or is there a serious problem? It's hypocritical to have one day set aside as Earth Day, when everyone will so soon forget what needs to be done." '

So that she would not hear just one side of an issue, and accept that as truth, Allison would, with Barry's help, do research on her own. 'When Nixon's troop withdrawal was immediately criticized by our friends as being a sham, she went to the library and read through the back issues of the *New York Times* to see just how many men had been sent into Vietnam, and how many actually had been withdrawn,' says Barry. 'She was always reading: *Time, Newsweek, Ramparts, National Review* and underground papers, just to keep up.'

He then continues, 'Allison and I went to hear Jerry Rubin speak and he got us excited by the great force of his personality. But his ideas were too far beyond our frame of reference. However, when he limited his talk to facts about his trial in Chicago, he was very good and convinced us that it was an atrocity against reason. We found ourselves getting caught up in the excitement of the Black Panther cause. Their execution by the Chicago police horrified us. But when Rubin had left the campus, Allison and I sat down to rethink everything, and we were ashamed of our emotional reactions.'

One day Barry suggested, 'If things get bad enough in this country, maybe we ought to move to Canada.' To him this was a logical move to avoid the draft, which was beginning to breathe down his neck, and thousands of students across the United States were voicing similar thoughts; almost everyone in college knew of someone who had ducked out to Canada. On the other hand, Barry was skinny and friends were of the opinion that 'Man, you lose fifteen pounds, you're home safe. They'll never take you at that weight.' And there was serious discussion as to which was better, escaping to Canada or dieting to lose fifteen pounds. But other than that, they were two happy young people, with no plans for the future except to be together.

'I doubt that marriage would have been the right thing for us. We were afraid it was too demanding, and not in our style,' Barry would later confide to a friend.

What were Allison's basic attitudes as the spring quarter neared its conclusions? This is a vital question, for many of our reactions to this volatile woman-child depend upon what kind of person we see her to be. The best approach is to face some of the questions most often asked.

Was she a radical? No. Jim Brennan said, 'If she had gone to Boston University, she'd have been thought of by her fellow students as a conservative.'

Did she belong to any radical organizations? No. As a matter of fact, she belonged to no organizations, radical or otherwise. A fellow student, Meridy Therrill, said, 'I lived next door to her. I never heard her be abusive about Nixon or the war, but it was obvious from her hair and dress that she didn't see herself as one of Nixon's people.'

Did she participate in any campus protests? Yes, but only in legal and innocuous ones. Since like many other students she was opposed to the war, she was active in the October moratorium, and she did, as we have seen, attend the Washington protest against Vietnam.

Was she a responsible student insofar as academic work went? Unquestionably. The testimony of professors like Mike Lunine, Barbara Agte and Jim Brennan is conclusive. Lunine, in particular, says, 'She was an excellent student. Studied regularly, and attended all classes. No other student among the five, and few students in the total body, elicited the enthusiastic support from her teachers that Allison did.'

Had she done anything of a criminal nature? Like eighty percent of her fellow students, she had smoked marijuana; she used it frequently and kept a small supply in her room. The only charge that could possibly have been made against her was that she and Barry had hitchhiked to Buffalo University. She was no bomb-thrower.

Carol Buchholz sums up these questions with a definitive statement: 'Dope and politics are all people seem to care about when they think of Allison. Well, I'll tell you. She smoked pot, but no more than anyone else, and she was always lecturing people we knew who wanted to try heroin, about how bad it would be for them. And as for politics, she had always insisted on non-violence. She thought change was necessary, but she'd never be the kind to go out and burn down property. She knew that wasn't the way.'

What was her political posture? At the conclusion of at least a hundred interviews, a solid impression of this girl emerges: She was, like countless students on the Kent campus, against the war in Vietnam, worried about the environment, vaguely irritated by the deficiencies in American life, interested in new solutions to old problems. She was not a female Paul Probius, brooding about the coming revolution. She was not a Bernardine Dohrn, prepared to dynamite a building. She was not a Joyce Cecora, burning up the campus with violent predictions. She must be thought of as a girl with more than average ability, but a most average reaction to her society. If anything, she was more responsive and sensitive to the circumstances of her situation than many of her peers and was a girl who could become loud and demanding if her hopes were not met. But there is one thing more. In the spring of 1970 Allison Krause was only a freshman, just beginning to discover what she believed. It seems probable that had she progressed normally through her junior and senior years, the force of events would have more deeply cemented her alienation. This conclusion is ratified by observing what had happened to Barry Levine by the summer of 1970: 'When the ROTC building burned at Kent, I knew it was wrong and took no part, but I also knew that the kids had been forced into doing it by having been ignored for so long. I'm not yet ready to participate in burning or bombing, but I may get to it. I realize that students can't change the system, but you simply can't stand by and allow people to live as they do now. This country must change its priorities, we must wake up to the fact that it's wrong to kill. I wear my hair long so that I will be constantly reminded of what it feels like to be harassed. And I suppose that some day I'll be shot because of it. So I live for the moment. I don't really know what I'll be doing next.' That is the voice of Allison Krause as it might have been.

What mood was she in on May 4? Sleepless after the wild events of Sunday night, and still distraught over the Guardsmen on campus, she was at the raw edge of self-control. Twice we have seen her hysterical, but Barry says, 'She had things under control. She knew what she was doing.'

Legal confusions

Did a state of martial law exist on the campus that quiet and lovely Monday morning? No one really knew what the legal status of the university was.

Among others, Sue Greco, the Gamma Phi Beta from Canton, remembers the notice which appeared on the lavatory wall in her dorm.

WARNING!
You are under martial law.
—Governor James A. Rhodes

She says, 'Seven or eight rules were spelled out, telling us what we could and could not do. It was pretty clear to me that the Guard was in control.'

Sue was wrong. No martial law had been officially declared, in spite of thousands of handbills and announcements to that effect. For martial law to be proclaimed three conditions are essential: first, there must be a complete breakdown of civil authority; second, the National Guard must assume all civil powers and be able to enforce them; and third, a special proclamation must be signed by the governor. None of these things had been done. There was no martial law, nor was the National Guard in total control.

What was the legal situation? Mayor Satrom had declared an emergency, and troops had been sent in to assist a functioning civil authority. While in Kent, Governor Rhodes had said, 'We are going to ask for an injunction . . . equivalent to a state of emergency. We're trying to work on it right now.' No such injunction was ever sought or obtained, and the rules the governor intended to apply were never spelled out. In their absence, the emergency remained a local one, and the Guard's prerogatives would be whatever was worked out between Mayor Satrom and General Del Corso.

It was not difficult to decide what powers the Guard was entitled to exercise in the city of Kent; Del Corso and Satrom quickly handled that and made no errors. But when the time came to spell out the relationship of the Guard to the campus, much confusion arose. No one understood the law; no one was willing to speak clearly and directly to the point. Throughout Sunday a series of confused discussions were held, and with each the understandings became more murky. Finally Major Harry Jones, in some irritation, delivered an off-the-cuff opinion that the Guard was legally empowered to forbid public gatherings on campus, and although he had volunteered this judgment only because others were reluctant to decide anything, it was eagerly accepted as law.

Based on this discussion, the university prepared and distributed 12,000 leaflets which listed curfew hours; said the governor through the National Guard had assumed legal control of the campus; stated that all outdoor demonstrations and rallies, peaceful or otherwise, were prohibited by the state of emergency; and said the Guard was empowered to make arrests.
—President's Commission on Campus Unrest

Practically every statement in the leaflet was incorrect—

neither the governor nor the Guard had assumed control of the campus; outdoor rallies had not yet been prohibited; no state of emergency had been declared by the governor; and the Guardsmen were not empowered to make arrests.

Fortunately, the erroneous leaflet had little adverse effect on the students, because of two additional errors: it was signed by a university official and a student leader for whom the students had little respect, and it was distributed not generally but through mailboxes, which the majority of students would not open until after the shootings had occurred.

But the leaflet did have a deleterious effect on the Kent situation generally, because at a meeting held Monday morning at 10:00 in the firehouse, General Canterbury sought some statement of authority which would empower him to assume control of the campus, and this leaflet was adduced as legal documentary evidence, even though it had been founded on mere guesswork by one of his own assistants and lacked any legal foundation. Later he would cite it as his authorization. One cannot help but feel sympathy for Canterbury, working under this cloud of misapprehension and uncertainty; given the circumstances, he conducted himself rather sensibly.

It was ridiculous to think of the city of Kent and the university as two separate entities at such a time; they formed a unit, and the moment the Guard appeared the troops were entitled—indeed they were obligated—to occupy any area that might become a source of trouble.

It was preposterous to have different curfew hours for the two segments of a common problem; it was worse to permit the university to serve as a kind of sanctuary. And it was indefensible for five policing agencies to function within a small area without clarifying the responsibilities of each. Generals Del Corso and Canterbury cannot be faulted for arrogating to themselves too much power; one wishes they had exercised more and that they had done so early, clearly, firmly and with an effort to explain conditions to the students.

What happened on Monday

The crucial event at Kent State was, of course, the action of the National Guard on Monday, May 4. Here is what happened.

At 11:00 in the morning of a bright, sunny day, students

began collecting on the commons as their 9:55–10:45 classes ended. They came casually at first, then in larger numbers when some of their 11:00–11:50 classes dismissed early because the confusion on campus made it too difficult to teach. Many students wandered by, as they always did, to check on what might be happening. Another set of classes, 12:05–12:55, would soon convene, and it was traditional for students who were involved either in leaving one class or heading for another to use the commons as their walkway. Without question, they had a right to be on the commons. But were they entitled to be there this day? A state of emergency had been declared by Satrom, presumably outlawing any unusual gatherings. Classes would meet, and that was about all. Yet testimony from students is overwhelming that they believed their campus to be operating as usual. On Friday a rally had been openly announced for Monday noon, and invitations to attend it had been circulated on succeeding days; in fact, announcements for this rally had been scrawled on certain blackboards and were seen by students when they reported for classes on Monday. Furthermore, those students and faculty who had left the campus Friday afternoon could not have listened to local radio stations and would have had no personal knowledge of what the situation was. Later we shall watch several professors, absent over the weekend, as they specifically instruct their students, with the most laudable intentions, to leave class and observe the campus rally. The rally may have been forbidden, but there were too many who either were not aware of this fact or did not believe it.

At 11:15 leaders of the National Guard, in discussion with school officials, became aware of this confusion and asked that the university radio station WKSU and the school intercom announce: 'All outdoor demonstrations and gatherings are banned by order of the governor. The National Guard has the power of arrest.' This was repeated several times but reached only a small proportion of the students, because the intercom system operated in only certain classrooms and none of the dormitories. But the rally had been forbidden; everyone knew it except the students.

At 11:30 General Canterbury, fresh from the inconclusive and even contradictory meeting with university and town officials, arrived at the burned-out ROTC building, surveyed the commons which lay before him, and concluded that the crowd was orderly and did not constitute any kind of significant threat. He could not at that moment have known that the impending dismissal of the 11:00–11:50 class would promptly crowd the commons.

At 11:45 General Canterbury, unaware that the radio broadcast canceling the rally had been heard by so few people, and not knowing about the normal movements of students going from class to class, was astonished to see so many students proceeding as if the rally were still authorized. The crowd was growing larger every minute. He saw about 600 students massing not far from his troops and became justifiably concerned. Giving a clear order, he commanded that the students be dispersed. This order was given before any rocks had been thrown.

At 11:48 someone began ringing the Victory Bell. Two students climbed onto its brick housing to issue frenzied calls to action. The bell continued clanging intermittently during the next fifteen minutes, and this coincided with the end of another class period, so that a constant press of new arrivals kept pouring onto the commons, while a much larger group watched from various walkways, driveways and porches of classroom buildings.

At 11:49 Officer Harold E. Rice, of the campus police, stood by the ruins of the ROTC building and read the riot act over a bullhorn: 'Attention! This is an order. Disperse immediately. This is an order. Leave this área immediately. This is an order. Disperse.' Unfortunately, he was so far away from the students that they could not hear him, and his words had no effect.

At 11:50 a National Guard jeep was driven up, with a driver at the wheel and two armed Guardsmen perched high atop the rear seat. Officer Rice climbed into the right front seat and with his bullhorn proceeded to read the riot act repeatedly as the jeep moved slowly along the edges of the crowd: 'This assembly is unlawful. This crowd must disperse immediately. This is an order.' (Later, certain students would claim that Rice *asked* them to break up the crowd but did not *order* them to do so, and it is possible that in one or another of the repetitions he may have used those words, but the evidence is overwhelming that he recited the version, as given, at least eight times.) The jeep was greeted with catcalls, boos, cursing and a shower of rocks; few of the latter reached the jeep and none appear to have struck any of the four passengers.

At 11:52, as the jeep made its slow progress, with Rice still shouting over the bullhorn, he spotted in the crowd someone he recognized as a leader of riots on the two preceding nights, and he wanted to arrest him. So the driver edged the jeep right into the edge of the crowd, but the young radical saw what Rice was up to and slipped away. So that all students might be properly warned, the jeep made three complete circuits.

At 11:55 the order was passed to the Guardsmen: 'If you have not already done so, load and lock. Prepare for gas attack. Prepare to move out.'

At 11:58 it was obvious that Rice in the jeep was accomplishing nothing, so Major Harry Jones ran out, banged on the jeep with his baton, and ordered it to return to the ROTC building.

At 11:59 General Canterbury gave the order: 'Prepare to move out and disperse this mob.' There is considerable variance in published reports as to the number of troops he had at his disposal. Inaccessibility of accurate records makes any estimate arbitrary; some seem much too low. It would appear that the total contingent contained 113 Guardsmen, disposed as follows: three senior officers, Brigadier General Robert H. Canterbury, Lieutenant Colonel Charles Fassinger, Major Harry D. Jones in command of three units of troops arranged in this order. On the left flank, nearest to the tennis courts, Charlie Company, First Battalion, 145th Infantry, consisting of two officers (Captain Ron Snyder, Lieutenant Herthneck) and 34 enlisted men; in the center, headed for Taylor Hall, G Troop, Second Squadron, 107th Armored Cavalry Regiment, consisting of two officers (Captain Raymond J. Srp, Lieutenant Stevenson) and 16 enlisted men; on the right flank, headed toward Johnson Hall, Alpha Company of the 145th, consisting of three officers (Captain John E. Martin, Lieutenant Klein, Lieutenant Fallon) and 51 enlisted men, but to Alpha Company, two members of Charlie Company (Richard Love and Richard Lutey) had attached themselves because their own unit had moved out before they could catch up with it. The contingent therefore included 10 officers and 103 enlisted men.

According to the plan that General Canterbury had worked out with his commanders, the Guardsmen were to sweep the commons toward the southwest, driving all demonstrators across the crest of Blanket Hill, keeping Taylor Hall on their left, the pagoda on the right. The troops would then push the students down the far slope of the hill toward the practice football field, and the operation would be completed. Captain

Snyder had suggested an additional detail: his left-flank Charlie Company would sweep left of Taylor Hall and take a holding position between it and Prentice while the center and right flank completed the main sweep on the other side of Taylor. To this General Canterbury assented, adding, 'Before you step off, fire a barrage of tear gas.'

It is important to visualize the number of students confronting the Guard. At 11:45 Colonel Fassinger had estimated the number of students on the commons—that is, in position to constitute a threat of some kind to the Guard—as 'more than 500.' In the interval this number had grown to 600 and then to something over 800. Now it might number as high as 1,100; for students were piling in from all directions as their classes ended. But a much larger crowd had assembled on the terraces of halls like Johnson and Stopher to the west, Prentice and Engleman to the east. And the largest group of all filled the open spaces directly in back of ROTC toward Administration. All of these must be considered as spectators only, and they could have numbered as many as 2,500. Included among them were townspeople, high-school children, professors and, of course, university students. As they were situated that morning they formed a gigantic amphitheater focusing upon a small stage of green.[*]

At 12:00 sharp, before the order to march could be given, an unidentified spokesman for the students, perhaps a faculty member, ran up to Canterbury and said, 'General, you must not march against the students,' to which the general replied that the students congregated illegally. 'These students,' he told the intercessor, 'are going to have to find out what law and order is all about.' Then he nodded to his commanders; the first slim gray tear-gas canisters popped out in their long parabolas toward the demonstrators, and 103 Guardsmen plus 10 officers stepped off into the history of contemporary America. The three senior officers, apparently by accident, distributed themselves among the units: Major Jones stayed with Charlie Company on the left flank; Colonel Fassinger marched with G Troop in the center; General Canterbury went with Alpha Company on the right flank.

At 12:01 Captain Snyder positioned himself on the extreme

[*]Eszterhas and Roberts believe the crowd to have been much larger: 'By a few minutes before noon nearly fifteen hundred students had gathered around the bell. Another two thousand to three thousand students were assembled on the opposite side of the commons behind the National Guard lines. Another two thousand were on the northern edge of the commons near the tennis courts.' One member of the research team, working independently, came up with almost these same estimates, but other members, reviewing each available photograph, convinced him that his figures were too high.

right of his men, so that when the gas stopped and his troop broke off from the other units for the drive to the east end of Taylor Hall, he would be anchor man on the right flank. Following his custom, he kept up a barrage of tear gas. A tear-gas canister launched by an M-79 is a most effective crowd-control device; if fired on a level trajectory (none were), it has sufficient velocity to kill a man at twenty-five yards. A sudden cross wind blew up to spread it across the field and up the Taylor Hall slope—before long the smoke would be inhaled into the Taylor Hall air-conditioning system, filling that building and affecting all those inside. Now, as Snyder's men moved ever closer to the crowd, those among the more daring demonstrators came darting forward, seizing the hot canisters and flinging them back. Most of these fell short of the approaching Guardsmen. One says *most* because certain unusually aggressive—or brave, if you prefer—young men not only grabbed the canisters but also ran good distances with them back toward the troops, throwing them from such short range that canisters sometimes landed in the ranks.

At 12:02 Snyder's men reached the point at which they would detach themselves from the center unit for the swing left. As they reached the Victory Bell a 'bushy-haired young man' (Snyder's description) came darting down out of the trees on the slope and gave the bell a final swing. Then he wound up and hurled a fistful of small stones. Ron Snyder turned his back on the stones, spun around and brought his baton down across the boy's shoulders with such force as to snap off the tip of the baton. The young man then reached in his pocket and brought forth a piece of metal with four finger holes—a brass knuckle. Snyder hit him again. He dropped the piece of metal and dashed back up the hill.

At 12:03, as Charlie Company began to climb up through the trees, they could see a number of demonstrators along the brow of the hill. They fired more tear gas in that direction and kept climbing. At the top they beheld an even greater number of students gathered below them in the Prentice Hall parking lot, and here Snyder decided to form his line. He placed his men in a single row from the northeast corner of Taylor toward the nearest corner of Prentice, leaving twenty yards open at the Prentice Hall end as an escape route.

At 12:04 they were in the position they would hold for the next twenty minutes, and we shall leave them there as we follow the center unit, but before we do so, one incident should be noted. Clustered in front of Snyder's formation were a number of frantic coeds, and he began calling to them through the voice emitter in his M-17-type gas mask (all officers and non-coms were equipped with these special masks, through which voice instructions could be issued). He shouted to them, 'Come on, come on! It's safe.' Like a herd of frightened deer, the girls suddenly made their decision and bolted through the opening and around the side of the building. In the next few minutes Snyder estimates that he let upward of 100 students pass, all trying to escape the agony of drifting tear gas.

At 12:04, as Captain Snyder's troops were reaching their final position at the east end of Taylor, Captain Srp's center unit of eighteen soldiers was approaching the pagoda, undergoing as they marched a heavy barrage of curses and their own tear-gas canisters thrown back at them by determined students. The canisters were of little consequence to the Guardsmen, who, having anticipated this maneuver, were wearing gas masks, but this in itself posed a problem. As one Guardsman says, 'It was a hot day, and this was the hottest part of the day. The gas masks were heavy, and as soon as you put yours on, you were hemmed in and sweating. Your vision was restricted to a narrow field and sometimes you couldn't even see the man next to you. It was like being tucked away in a corner . . . sweating.' To the outsider, seeing a Guardsman in mask evoked a sense of the unreal, the mechanical, the monster from outer space, and this was an advantage, for it frightened the observer; but to the man inside the mask, there was a sense of remoteness, of detachment, of being alone in a crowd, and that was a disadvantage, for it cut a soldier off from his fellows and from reality.

At 12:05 the unit reached the pagoda, where it was met by a good deal more than returning gas canisters. Students began throwing rocks at them, and chunks of wood studded with nails, and jagged hunks of concrete. Where did they get such missiles? At least two witnesses swear they saw girls carrying heavy handbags from which they distributed rocks to men students, and some photographs would seem to substantiate this charge. At a nearby construction site some students had picked up fragments of concrete block. And some of the students had armed themselves with bricks. In addition, there were a few—not many—small stones and pebbles available on the campus itself, but these were inconsequential; on a normal day one could have searched this commons fairly carefully, without finding a rock large enough to throw at anyone.

Did any of the missiles hit the troops? Not many. The distances between the mass of the students and the Guards were later stepped off by expert judges, who concluded that students would have required good right arms like Mickey Mantle's to have reached the Guardsmen with even small stones. But as with the canisters, some students were bold enough to run back down the hill and throw from close range, and their stones did hit.

Worse, in a way, than the missiles were the epithets, especially when launched by coeds. A steady barrage of curses, obscenities and fatal challenges came down upon the Guard, whose gas masks did not prevent their hearing what they were being called. Girls were particularly abusive, using the foulest language and taunting the Guardsmen with being 'shit-heels, motherfuckers and half-ass pigs.' Others called them less explosive but equally hurtful names: 'toy soldiers, murderers, weekend warriors, fascists.' During the half hour that the Guardsmen were in action, this rain of abuse never let up.

In addition, a special few among the students—perhaps a dozen men and four girls—kept running at the Guardsmen, daring them to retaliate. One young man, with extremely long hair held in place by a beaded band, displayed a large black flag at the end of a pole, and with extreme bravado waved it at critical moments at the troops, almost in their faces, retreating to eight or ten yards at other times. Guardsmen behind their masks were unsure whether it was a Vietcong flag or not. Certainly it was not any with which they were familiar.

As this central detachment reached the top of Blanket Hill, they found that the mass of students had melted away before them. Never were the students very close, except for the daring ones, and people who have studied the facts and the photographs become irritated when someone asks, 'Why didn't the Guard surround the students and arrest them?' The Guards were never within a hundred yards of being able to surround this ebbing and flowing mass of people, and besides, there were not nearly enough men to have done so had they desired. It was like asking a group of six people why they didn't surround a flock of pigeons who kept flying in all directions.

At 12:06, with the central unit perched atop the hill, the officers faced an awkward decision. They now stood between

Taylor Hall on their left and the cement pagoda on their right, with almost the whole body of students, who a few minutes ago had been on the commons, facing them in the various open spaces that lay ahead. Also, many hundreds of additional students who could have known nothing of the preceding sweep, now arrived from their 11:00–11:50 classes, which had been held in buildings at distant parts of the campus, or were on their way to 12:05–12:55 classes in buildings nearby. For anyone to say of these students 'They had no right to be on the campus' is to misunderstand the nature of a university; they had every right to be precisely where they were, but they did add to the visual confusion. If at this crucial moment the Guard had returned to their ROTC station, they would have had an absolutely clear escape route, but in all likelihood the radical students would have followed behind them, so that the situation would have wound up exactly as it started, with the Guard at ROTC and the students occupying Blanket Hill.

So an understandable decision was reached that the Guard would push on and try to clear the large area that lay ahead, an open field used for practice football, with a soccer goal at the south end and a baseball diamond at the north. What none of the Guardsmen apparently realized was that along the eastern side of this field, ran a sturdy six-foot-high chain-link fence, topped by three strands of heavy barbed wire. What was worse, at the baseball end this fence took a right-angle turn to the west to form a catcher's backstop; it would be difficult to find on the campus a more perfect cul-de-sac. It was inconceivable that soldiers would march with their eyes open into such a trap, where they would be subjected to hostile students who would have large numbers of rocks at their disposal. But this is what happened.

At 12:07 the center unit, led by Colonel Fassinger and reinforced by large numbers from Captain Martin's Alpha Company on the right flank, marched down from the pagoda and smack against the steel chain-link fence. They had placed themselves in a position from which they could escape only by retreating, which, when it happened, would have to be interpreted by the watching students as a defeat for the Guard. How large was this combined unit? Photographs show at least 69 Guards against the fence, but one meticulous investigation augments that number. There were 75 Guards present, comprised as follows: two senior officers (Canterbury, Fassinger) with 53 men from Alpha Company, including three officers, plus the two casuals from Charlie Company, to which were added 18 men from G Troop, including two officers. However, Major Jones now ran across the grass to join the group. We have seen that he started with Charlie Company, which halted at the far end of Taylor Hall, so that during the first few minutes when the Guard stood penned against the fence, he had been with Captain Snyder. But quickly he discerned what was developing; elbowing his way through the crowd of students, he joined the larger contingent at the fence, where he would play a conspicuous role in what was to follow. The unit therefore consisted of 68 enlisted men led by 8 officers.

As soon as the students saw that the Guard was pinned against the fence, they began to close in from the parking lot to the north, cursing, throwing rocks, waving flags and tossing back gas canisters. The word *surrounded* has often been used to describe the Guard's condition at this moment. Nothing could be more inappropriate. To the east, across the fence, there was no one but Mike Alewitz, the socialist leader whose presence there will be explained later. To the south—that is, behind the Guardsmen on the practice field—there was no one for more than a hundred yards, as numerous photographs attest. And to the west, over the path to the pagoda which the Guard had just traversed, students had not yet re-formed. Far from being surrounded, the Guard had empty space on all sides.

At 12:10 the Guard underwent a heavy assault from the north, where students had grown bolder and were dashing in close to unload. What happened next remains obscure, but the sixteen enlisted men of G Troop, plus one other, believing their supply of tear gas to have been exhausted, knelt on one knee and assumed a firing position, aiming their rifles directly at the gadfly students who were pestering them. It appears that they must have been ordered by some officer to assume this frightening and provocative position, and if a further command had been given at this moment, students on the parking lot would have been mowed down, but no such command was uttered. (Actually, the beleaguered troops had more gas. Specialist Russell Repp of A Company still carried eight canisters, a fact known by his immediate superiors, Srp and Stevenson, but not by those in command.)

The brazen young man with the black flag ran close and waved it before the silent rifles, daring the Guardsmen to fire. When they refrained, he and others were convinced that they would never shoot, that even if they did, the bullets were blanks. That much of the situation is ascertainable; what is still unknown is what took place at the core of the unit, where General Canterbury discussed this dangerous and ridiculous situation with his officers.

At 12:18 Colonel Fassinger issued the order: 'Regroup back at ROTC.' And the contingent began to form up for retreat, assuming the pattern of a flying wedge, point foremost and flanks trailing, with officers inside the V. (It may seem strange that a colonel should have been issuing orders to the troops when a general was present, but this was not unusual. In the navy, for example, it is customary for a five-star admiral attended by three- and two-star admirals to choose some warship as headquarters afloat; when they do so, they are technically under the command of whatever captain is in charge of the ship they occupy, and all personnel attached to that ship take their orders from the captain and not from the admirals.)

At 12:19 Fassinger radioed: 'For the third time I am asking for more tear gas.'

At 12:22 Fassinger gave the order to march, and his unit left the fence, where they had suffered much humiliation, some of it at their own hands, crossed the service road, and at an increasing speed, hurried back up to the pagoda. They were hot, and angry, and disgusted at having been pinned down against the fence, infuriated by the students who had challenged them, and bitterly resentful of the girls who even now trailed them up the hill, cursing and reviling them. Their gas masks prevented them from seeing just what was happening, and they were only vaguely aware of students still massed on their right flank. They had a long hot hill to climb and they were sweating. Were they in danger? On their left flank there was nobody except a few Guardsmen stationed at Johnson Hall. In the rear there was a handful of gadflies, mostly girls, who posed no threat at all. Straight ahead the commons was almost empty. At Taylor Hall the porches were crowded with students, at least half of them girls, and some teachers who were observing the scene. On the right flank, however, at a distance of seventy yards, there was a large mass of students, including many of those who had been pestering the Guard at the practice field but also many who were merely passing by between classes. The closest student seems to have been at least twenty yards away; the bulk were more than a hundred yards distant. But there was movement, and in the confusion of the march, it could be interpreted as hostile.

At 12:24, with the escape route back to ROTC completely unimpeded and with alternate ones available either to the left flank or to the rear, some Guardsmen on the trailing right flank suddenly stopped, wheeled 135 degrees to the right—that is, they turned almost completely around—faced the students who had collected on the south side of Taylor Hall, and dropped their rifles to a ready position. It so happens that three tape recorders, operated by would-be reporters from the School of Journalism, were running at this moment, and their testimony as to what happened next is incontrovertible.

There was a single shot—some people heard it as two almost simultaneous shots—then a period of silence lasting about two seconds, then a prolonged but thin fusillade, now a single angry burst, lasting about eight seconds, then another silence, and two final shots. The shooting had covered thirteen seconds, which is a very long time under such circumstances, and fifty-five M-1 bullets seem to have been discharged, plus five pistol shots and the single blast from a shotgun. Twenty-eight different Guardsmen did the firing, but this fact should be remembered: If each of the men had fired his weapon directly at the massed students, the killing would have been terrible, for a steel-jacketed M-1 bullet can carry two miles and penetrate two or four or six bodies in doing so. Fortunately, many of the men found it impossible to fire into a crowd and pointed their rifles upward—avoiding what could have been a general slaughter.

But some Guardsmen, fed up with the riotous behavior of the students and in fear of their lives, did fire directly into the crowd, and when the volley ended, thirteen bodies were scattered over the grass and the distant parking area. Four were dead, and nine were wounded more or less severely.

On the afternoon of the shooting, a governmental agency took careful measurements (which have not previously been released); here are the dry statistics. Thirteen young people shot: eleven men, two girls. All were registered at the university and all were attending classes formally. If the wounded were arranged in order of their nearness to the Guard, the closest young man was 71 feet away from the rifles, the farthest 745 feet away, or nearly two and a half football fields. The seventh body—that is, the median one—happened to be Doug Wrentmore, who was 329 feet away. The distances of the four dead at the time they were hit are as follows:

Jeffrey Glenn Miller, fifth closest	265 feet
Allison B. Krause, eighth closest	343 feet
William K. Schroeder, tenth closest	382 feet
Sandra Lee Scheuer, eleventh closest	390 feet

Of the thirteen who were struck by bullets, two were shot in the front, seven from the side, and four from the rear. Ten of the wounded were struck directly, three by ricochets. We came upon fairly strong evidence that a fourteenth student was hit in the left arm, but not seriously; he fled the area with his wound concealed, apprehensive lest he become involved with police or FBI investigations. He was more than 600 feet away when hit, and obviously not involved in the immediate action, though what he might have been doing earlier, we have no way of knowing.

Ascertaining the correct time of the firing is difficult, for whereas most of the other events can be confirmed with minute accuracy, often by three or four people, it is impossible to state precisely when the shooting occurred, even though hundreds of eyewitnesses observed it. The time indicated here is by no means a consensus, but it does represent the best-educated guess. Estimates vary from 12:12, which hardly gives the Guard time to cover the distances involved, let alone take action at any of the resting points, to 12:45, which is the solid report of one of the most careful investigating committees but which seems ridiculously late to those who participated. A highly placed Guard officer who was in position to know what was happening, who looked at his wristwatch at the moment of firing, and who was responsible for calling the information in to the command post, affirms, 'The shooting took place at exactly 12:20, for I checked it as it occurred.' But the official log of the action recording his report times it at 12:26. The apparent impossibility of determining a precise time is not critical; if an early time is used, it means only that the Guardsmen had conducted all their operations on the practice field in less than three minutes, which seems impossible; if a late time is used it means that they dallied there for more than half an hour, which seems contrary to evidence and common sense. The time given here was noted by a journalism student at Taylor Hall, who made no great claim for its accuracy, but it does conform to the judgment of many.

At 12:25 (or 12:46, if the extreme time is accepted) the firing ceased, thanks to the energetic efforts of Major Jones, who can be seen in photographs beating his troops over their helmets with his swagger stick, pleading with them to stop. General Canterbury can also be seen, turning in surprise from the direction in which he had been heading—down the hill to safety—which lends credence to the theory that if an order of some kind had been given to fire, he at least had not been informed of it.

At 12:29, after a lapse of at least four minutes, during which frantic officers did their best to restore order, the unit re-formed, retreated in orderly fashion to their staging area at ROTC, and surrendered their guns for registry and inspection. Jack Deegan, a Marine Corps reservist majoring in history, who had followed the unit at extremely close range all the way from the link fence, reports, 'I saw one young Guard lying on the ground, tossing himself back and forth in hysteria and moaning something I couldn't hear.' He may have been William Herschler, whom the FBI reported as having cried, 'I just shot two teenagers.' At this point a veil of silence descended over the Guard.

A new danger was building and would be dissipated only by the cool action of the Guard's officers and an extraordinary performance by three professors. Before we deal with that, however, it is essential that many fragmented bits of evidence be brought together.

Why it happened

A unique aspect of the Kent tragedy was that its critical stage took place in the immediate vicinity of a school of journalism whose building, Taylor Hall, provided on four sides a spacious porch which not only permitted but encouraged observation by a score of professors and students trained in news reporting. Events were also photographed by a team of incredibly daring novices, of whom an older man said, 'They'll never be that brave when they have regular jobs.' Much of what is about to be said is based on testimony coming from trained journalists. Because Monday's events involved so many contentious situations and so much conflicting evidence, comment will be arranged by subject headings, not necessarily in chronological order.

Was the rally legal? It had been publicly announced, as we have seen, at the burial of the Constitution, at the BUS rally, and in many other legal situations during the succeeding three days. Professors announced it from their podiums and there were signs advising students where and when it would be held. There was certainly nothing surreptitious about it, nor was it planned as a protest against the Guard, for it had been announced eighteen hours before the Guard appeared.

But whether or not it was legal becomes a question of some consequence, because on this will depend the validity of subsequent indictments and punishment. Legality must be considered from three points of view: the university's, the Guard's and the law's.

As far as university regulations were concerned, the rally was unauthorized in that those sponsoring it had failed to move through official channels to obtain permission; they had not submitted a request to the Student Activities Board; they had not listed the time, place and purpose of the rally; nor had they named those responsible for its good conduct. Since official approval had not been obtained, the rally was a wildcat affair and, under university law, illegal.

The Guard was in an ambivalent position. It was basing its action upon an arbitrary guess by one of its officers (Major Jones) who had depended upon the assumption that Governor Rhodes had followed through on his promise to 'ask for an injunction, equivalent to a state of emergency,' whereas no such step had been taken. In the absence of any authorization in law, the Guard was acting solely on the verbal assurance of the governor, which would have to be interpreted as 'law by personal decree.' This is legal in no American state. One must therefore conclude that when the students assembled on Blanket Hill, their rally may have been illegal in university law, but it was certainly not illegal in civil law.

However, once Officer Rice began to read the riot act at 11:49—and especially when he got in a jeep and took the act into the heart of the crowd so that his words could not be misunderstood—the emergency thus proclaimed took supersedence over ordinary law. The assembly became illegal and those who failed to disperse were subject to arrest.

Also, it had been officially prohibited. Of this there can be no doubt. At 7:30 A.M. the campus radio announced: 'As a result of the governor's declaration of a state of emergency, orders have been issued to Guardsmen banning all outdoor rallies and demonstrations.' At 10:45 the same radio announced to all students: 'Under the governor's orders, Guardsmen will break up any outside rallies and demonstrations—peaceful or otherwise.' (Each of these announcements was inaccurate, as we have just seen.) This order was repeated over public-address systems and verbally to whoever would listen.

But it must be remembered that only a small portion of the student body and teaching staff heard it. Of the 21,000 persons involved—including nearly 1,000 professors—some would not have known what had been happening on campus over the weekend and what the situation was as classes reconvened. They were returning to a terra incognita where the rules had been changed without their knowing about it. Testimony on this is overwhelming.

Jeff Sallot, the journalism student, took the trouble to tour the campus at about 11:50, noting exactly what was happening, on the chance that his editor might want a report: 'Lots of traffic. Lots of sightseers, not necessarily from the university. Bell-ringing incessantly. Two fellows kicking a soccer ball. One boy on the hill flying a kite. Quite a few tennis games going on. Trees just coming into bud. Weather excellent.'

The experience of Jamie Haines, the Young Republican, was typical: 'I had an 11:00 English class in Satterfield with Professor Sanford Marovitz, who appeared before us wearing a black armband. Before he could start his lecture, someone asked, "Why the armband?" and he replied, "I'm showing my sadness at the death of democracy in America." He had just launched into his lecture when a National Guard officer in Memorial Stadium turned on his bullhorn to announce, "All right, you men. Get in line. Shape up." At this, Marovitz threw down a piece of chalk and said, "I cannot teach in such an atmosphere," and that was the end of the class.'

As Professor Crosby sat in his office in the African-American institute, waiting for his regular Monday morning interview with black students, one of Field Marshal Perry's lieutenants entered his room and said sharply, 'Professor Crosby, you've got to get off this campus, right now.'

'What are you talking about?'

'Off. Get off.'

'Why?'

'There are Guardsmen out there. They have loaded rifles.'

'What have they to do with me?'

'They like to shoot blacks.'

'What are you talking about?'

'Professor Crosby, you may be a very intelligent man. But there are some things you don't know. I'm from Newark, New Jersey. And I do know. You get the hell off this campus.'

And Crosby left.

Tom McGrew, who would take some of the good photographs of the action, had an 11:00–11:50 class in social problems with Tom Lough, whose courses were extremely popular because of the challenging manner in which he taught them. 'Normally the class would have had about 400 students, but on Monday there were only 225 of us. I took the course because Lough taught it, and he was one of the best, but before we could get going, a girl standing on a table in the rear interrupted to tell us, "I'm ready to tear this place apart." There was discussion of this, and Dr. Lough finally dismissed the class early. "I'll see you on the campus at noon," he told us.'

One of the young men Professor Lough dismissed early that day, Robert Stamps, says, 'I had a social-problems class with Tom Lough, and I knew it would be exciting because he was not only one of the best professors on campus, but we'd been discussing the primary election and now everything had come to a head. We met in Bowman Hall and dedicated the entire class to discussing things. It was the consensus that Governor Rhodes had sent the troops on campus in an attempt to win the primary on Tuesday. Everybody got real pissed off when his motives were explained. It was then I heard about the rally that would be held right after class. Everybody was encouraged to go to it.'

Tom Lough was the most controversial of the Kent professors. That he was also one of the ablest, no one could deny. Tim Butz, who studied with him, says, 'He originated this marvelous course on ghetto living in Akron, where the local blacks helped teach us what ghetto life was all about. But he damaged it by trying to align himself with us students against the other faculty members in the program. Some kind of inner power struggle, which didn't work. At a retreat held in February, 1970, for all members of the ghetto course, Lough asked us, "If you're so angry, why aren't you out there demonstrating?" But you can discount the Molotov-cocktail charge they bring against him sometimes. If a student wants to make a Molotov, he can find a dozen books in the library to tell him how, or he can ask any of the hundred ex-GI's around here. We all learned how in Vietnam.'

The Molotov-cocktail story recurs in every discussion of Kent. Craig Morgan, a leader of the student body, explains what happened: 'I was in the class, so I know. The front cover of *The New York Review of Books* consisted of a line drawing of how to make a Molotov. It had something to do with a story of revolutions around the world and had been used for shock effect. Lough was lecturing on how revolutionaries in different parts of the world had used the Molotov to fight off their adversaries. Like in Budapest, those who used Molotovs against the Russians were heroes. Well, to make his point he xeroxed off some copies of the magazine cover and passed them around the class—to show how simple revolution had become when gasoline was so easy to obtain and so simple to ignite. That's all there was to it. Preaching revolution? Never. Telling us to go out and make our own Molotov cocktails? Never.'

Many other professors dismissed their classes early that day. Many others referred to the rally. As we shall see later, one professor led her students unknowingly into the direct line of fire. She hadn't heard and hadn't been told that the rally had been forbidden.

The Victory Bell. There can be no doubt that the ringing of this bell played a major role in first assembling the students and then in keeping them agitated. Who rang the bell? Professor Saalberg, of the journalism department, had his office in a room which overlooked the bell, and while preparing notes for his next class, heard its incessant ringing. A student ran into Taylor Hall, shouting, 'Hey, we've got something going. Come on!' Saalberg went to the porch to look, and was greeted with tear gas blowing up from the commons.

Now another student ran into the building, his hair wild and his voice high. 'Wait till next time,' he yelled, but the first student challenged, 'If you've got so much courage, come on out and show it,' and the two departed, screaming 'Pigs off campus!' and 'Shut down the university.' Strings of obscenities trailed behind them.

The bell continued ringing, almost like a summons to violence, and Saalberg could stand it no longer. Striding down to the brick housing where students were operating the hand lever which rang the bell, he met Jim Bruss, director of the university news bureau and also a Kent City councilman. 'Can't we get that damned bell silenced?' Saalberg asked, but

Bruss said, 'I have no authority to do such a thing. I'll take it up later with Dr. Roskens.'

Saalberg, acting on his own, tried to stop the ringing, but he was ineffective, for young men in relays kept darting in, striking a few peals, and darting away again. 'They reminded me of members of an African tribe, seeking to prove their manhood by rushing in to touch the lion with their spears.'

He tried to inactivate the bell, shouting, 'Stop this noise!' but the young men replied, 'We'll go away when they go away. Troops have no right to be on our campus.' When he persisted, the students turned toward him, but were driven off by the arrival of four National Guardsmen who suggested that he leave the job to them, but as soon as they were called elsewhere, the bell resumed ringing and the venturesome young men kept it reverberating even when the soldiers surrounded it on their march up the hill.

Saalberg remembers that two students climbed to the top of the bell housing, waving therefrom a flag. 'It could have been a Vietcong flag. It is ironic that of the radicals' program for dividing and destroying our university, the only concept that caught on with the mass of students was Vietnam. All other slogans were rejected.'

Was the rally at the Victory Bell led principally by outsiders? Professor Murvin Perry says, 'We got together twenty-five of our most knowledgeable people in journalism—kids who know this campus inside out—and we inspected every photograph of the ones who led the rally at the bell, and no one could identify them as students who had ever been seen here before.'

Stu Feldstein thought he recognized one of the later speakers as a former theoretician for the SDS. 'He began telling us about Indochina, while he stood on top of the narrow ledge protecting the Victory Bell.'

The jeep. When Officer Rice warned the crowd that the gathering was illegal, and ordered them to disperse, Stu Feldstein said to the man standing next to him, 'Isn't that what the British said at Lexington or somewhere?'

On the next sweep, when Rice directed the driver to close in on the crowd, in hopes of arresting one of the ringleaders, there occurred a minor incident, of little consequence by itself but important when considering the provocations for the eventual shootings. Sergeant Gordon R. Bedall, riding rear-left shotgun, was thrust into the midst of the crowd, with students pressing in upon him from all sides. A tall young man who works as supervisor for a trucking company and who is married, he says, 'I sort of suspected there might be some rock-throwing, but what happened was much worse. The coeds in the crowd began yelling at us, and I wouldn't dare to repeat what they said. It was incredible. I'd never heard such filth from our truck drivers . . . at least not in the office where I worked. I looked at Dennis Lutey, who was riding right-hand shotgun, and he sat with his mouth open. We couldn't believe that such language was coming from young ladies. I was quelled. A very pretty girl stuck her hand right under my nose, gave me the finger, and uttered four words that I've never used myself. I've been on riot duty before, but I've never encountered such language, not even among the raunchiest whores on Wooster Avenue.'

It would be tedious to cite the numerous witnesses from among the Guardsmen and townspeople who have confirmed Sergeant Bedall's testimony, but scores of persons not connected with the university testified their shock at how the college girls talked, and if there was one element of the riots which alienated the ordinary citizens of Portage County, it was this. Guardsmen knew the words, but many of them had been reared in homes where it would have been unthinkable for even the toughest man to use them; to hear them in common usage by girls who could have been their sisters produced a psychic shock which ran deep. No one watching Bedall's face cloud up and his neck muscles protrude as he recalls this experience with the coeds could believe that he took it lightly. With the Guardsmen in general, the girls had removed themselves from any special category of 'women and children.' They were tough, foul-mouthed enemies. A fellow soldier says of Bedall's experience, 'He has a daughter and has always hoped to send her to college. He wasn't able to make it, himself. But when this pretty coed came up, gave him the finger and called him a motherfucking cocksucker, he began to think, "I'm not sure I want my daughter to go to college if that's how they teach her to talk." He hasn't got over it yet.' Scores of Guardsmen went through this experience; within half an hour they would be facing these same girls with loaded rifles.

The Guard moves out. Robert Stamps says, 'I was walking toward my 9:55–10:45 Spanish class in Satterfield Hall when I heard a voice calling, "Hey, Stamps!" I looked around and could see only Guardsmen, so I continued on my way to class, but two of the Guard came running over to shake hands with me. I recognized both of them. One was from my geology class from the year before, Robin Hefflefinger. We had a nice talk, and I said, "This is ridiculous, you standing there in your uniform and me standing here in mine." I had on my customary boots, blue jeans, fatigue jacket and shirt. He said "You know, it is sort of ridiculous for me to be on campus in this gear, and I sure want to leave." I told him, "And I want you to leave." So then I added, "Well, have a nice day," and all that rot, and we shook hands and I left.'

Steve Rowe, a studious sophomore in business administration, found himself on campus for a reason that would have seemed unbelievable to a college student even ten years ago but which today seemed quite normal. 'I reported to my 8:50 accounting class, but we were thrown out of the building because of another bomb scare. With nothing to do, I went to the Union and found that there was to be a rally at noon.' On this Monday morning the university was plagued with about fifteen different bomb threats, each of which had to be investigated. A brief section of the log shows:

    0752   Education Building
    0812   Roosevelt High School in Kent
    0851   University School
    0919   Bowman Hall
    0936   A threat from station 024
    0948   *Kent Stater* offices in Taylor Hall
    0955   Three calls from stations 041, 006, 026

Therefore, as the Guard moves out, the campus must be viewed not only as a casual gathering place for students but also as a scene of planned riot and open warfare.

As the time set for the rally approached, the mood grew ugly. Patrick Lamar, a conservative who held the rank of brigade commander in ROTC and who looked as if he had stepped out from an army recruiting poster, had been helping collect serial numbers of equipment burned in the fire. Pausing in this grimy work, he walked over to a Guardsman sitting in a jeep nearby. 'What are you going to do if something happens?' he asked.

'We're prepared.'

He walked to another Guardsman and asked, 'What do you think of being called up for duty like this?'

'We've been on the line for a week. We're tired of this. These kids just don't respect authority.'

When the time came for the Guard to move out, fifteen ROTC cadets joined up with Lamar, and one asked, 'Why doesn't the Guard move out and clean this up?'

'There they go!' one of the ROTC men cried.

'Give 'em hell, Guardsmen!' several of the ROTC cadets shouted.

Tom McGrew, who had been quietly photographing the Guardsmen, was standing close to Charlie Company when one of the soldiers walked over to him and said in a low voice, 'I'm sure we're going to start throwing gas pretty soon. If you'd like, you'd better move back and not get this stuff in your eyes. It can hurt.' And he left the line to show Mc-Grew where to stand.

Bob Hillegas was also standing with the National Guard when it moved out: 'Reporters from various newspapers flocked to the scene and two of them tried to bust through the line and stay with the Guards. One became most obnoxious and tried to elbow his way, but one of the men halted him. The reporter got tough and the Guard looked side to side, as if calling his mates. Four or five of them moved in real hard, backed the reporter up against a tree and slammed a gun butt into his groin. The reporter doubled over, and the first Guard said, "Now get out." From that point on, we knew things were going to be rough, so my group stayed clear.'

Hillegas was not impressed with the operation that developed: 'I thought it was pathetic when the Guardsmen engaged in a game of ball, throwing the gas canisters back and forth like high school kids. It was ridiculous and lost them a lot of respect. Boys began hooting and girls jeered, and I believe that's where the trouble started. You have enough girls throwing wisecracks at young soldiers, it does something to them.'

But he adds, 'I don't think any sensible observer can rule out the fact that we had among us that day a cadre of real, hard-core agitators. They moved about the campus with a sense of mystery. They had already been involved in the disturbances at Ohio University, at Ohio State, at Miami and now at Kent State. Understand, I differentiate between them and the life-style people with wild hair and amusing costumes. The latter were simply kids who didn't want to dress the way their old men did, and so far as I knew them, were in no way radical. The hell of it was, when the Guard moved on campus, these two groups came together and formed an accidental unit against which the Guard had to react.'

Professor Saalberg saw, at close range, 'a girl carrying a rather large bag of rocks, which she was distributing to boys in the crowd.' Another professor cautions, 'I was in position to see most of the crowd as it ran past ahead of the Guard, and I saw not one weapon that could have been considered lethal,' but the researchers saw two photographs of just that scene in which girls appeared to be lugging bags of rocks.

Coach Douglas Raymond, crossing the commons at this moment on his way to his office, recalled: 'When I looked at that mob of long-hairs, with their dirty clothes and no shoes, I felt certain that if I could have called in twenty good kids from my track squad I could have cleaned up the whole mess. I was so disgusted I went back later to pick up some of the junk that was being thrown and I still have it in my office . . . large chunks of cement block.'

As Paul Tople, a photography student who would take some stunning shots of the action, stepped out of the journalism office with a freshly loaded camera, he saw three or four male students vomiting in the grass: 'They were very hippie and one was trying to mumble obscenities and catch his breath at the same time. He had to give up both when he started vomiting again. Then I retreated to the safety of Taylor Hall. I couldn't believe it was happening.' One student, suffering from gas, cried, 'This burns like hell,' and another said, almost facetiously, 'It's different from what they used against us last time.' Tople left Taylor Hall again in time to see certain daring students darting out from the crowd to hurl still-fuming canisters back at the Guard. 'Very brave,' he said to himself. 'Very foolish.'

Patrick Lamar is the best witness to a critical scene which first demonstrated the ugly mood of the crowd and which might have brought on the shooting earlier than it did occur: 'As one unit of the Guard passed the Victory Bell, a student broke out of the crowd, ran directly at one of the Guardsmen, and grabbed his rifle. It looked like the beginning of a general assault on the Guard. The soldier appeared unsure of what he ought to do and just clutched his rifle tighter to him while the student struggled with him to tear it away. Another Guardsman ran up, struck the student with some kind of baton, and drove him off. Other Guardsmen, apparently afraid that they were going to be attacked, too, assumed a kneeling position and aimed their rifles during the incident, but when the man with the baton drove the student off, they got up and resumed their march. It was a miracle that nobody fired.'

Scott Mueller, one of the journalism students who helped collect such reports, was at the center of the action: 'I was shocked by the intensity of the hostility. Hundreds of students were shouting "Pigs off campus!" and raising clenched fists. I watched as the National Guard tried to chase the students off the hill, while the students were busy throwing canisters back at them. It was all sadly comical and I knew it would have to end badly.'

But Vaclav Koutnik, a visiting professor from Czechoslovakia, explained condescendingly to tall and pretty Christine Wilson, a mathematics instructor from North Carolina, 'This is children's games. When the Russians took over my country they moved in with tanks. Nothing will come of this. Just a pleasant exercise.'

The pagoda. In any discussion of what happened next, the pagoda plays a major role, for it served as the focal point for everything. As the photographic backdrop to events which swirled around it, this Japanese pagoda became the most familiar landmark in Kent.

'Don't call it a Japanese pagoda,' protests Robert Gressard, one of the five architecture students who built it as their contribution to beautifying the campus. 'It's really an *inverted hyperbolic parabaloid umbrella-like structure* and it ought to be called by its right name. Of course, you could call it H-P for short.'

It was born as a classroom project and was executed almost entirely by 'moonlight requisitioning,' that is, scavenging lumber and cement from more important university projects when the night watchmen were asleep. It was completed shortly before that weekend.

'We wanted the project to fit into the landscape,' Gressard says, 'as if it were part of the scene. So we planted grass seed, but before it could grow, there were the shootings and boots were trampling it.'

Gressard reflects for a moment, then adds, 'A lot of people tell me, "Your pagoda has become a kind of monument." I don't want it to be thought of as a peace symbol or anything political like that. But I suppose it will become whatever people care to make it. For us, it was a chance to learn about concrete.'

Confrontation on the practice field. Events here permit many different explanations. The non-involved observer closest to the action was Mike Alewitz, who got caught in the middle of the action quite by accident. 'When the Guard moved up the hill from ROTC, I was very brave. I defied them and took a snootful of gas. I ran into the washroom in Taylor Hall to wash my eyes, but gas had got into their ventilation system, so I decided to run across the top of the hill to Johnson Hall. What did I do? Found myself smack in front of the Guard, hoping they'd not hit me with more gas.

'Had no way of getting across to Johnson, so I retreated one step ahead of the Guard until I came up against the link fence. Now, sometime ago I had been looking at that fence. Don't ask me why. And I had spotted a small hole in it, so I dove for that hole and got on the other side. Next minute the Guard was up against the fence about three feet from me.' Unfortunately, Alewitz is of no help as to what happened next: 'I kept my head in the grass and didn't see a damned thing.'

Jim Banks had a view less intimate but more comprehensive. From the roof of his building he could see the entire panorama: 'When I looked at the campus and saw these strange, inhuman figures moving about in gas masks, confronting radical students who looked like Jim Bowie and Daniel Boone, with long-haired girls moving slowly about like figures in a dream, I thought, "My God, they've imported a bunch of Hollywood extras to shoot a movie!" '

As the Guardsmen took up their positions against the fence, there was a flurry of rocks from the students, and it was this action that led some witnesses to conclude that the Guard was 'in mortal danger.' Confirmation that the Guard considered the situation dangerous comes from Lieutenant Jack Crawford, who had seen more student disruption than anyone else on campus. He says, 'At the time the Guard was pinned down at the fence I was at their command post at the ROTC building. I was monitoring radio communications and heard an officer in charge of one section calling, "We're going to need more reinforcements down here. Send somebody down." Then he must have turned away, for I could hear the sound of rocks ricocheting off his helmet and him swearing.' There is much evidence of 'hordes of students' and 'mad, screaming masses of students encircling the Guard, and attacking them from all sides.' One investigator associated with this book felt strongly that 'the miracle is not that the Guard fired at the pagoda but that it did not fire when encircled at the practice field. If firing at the pagoda can be criticized, firing at the field could not have been. The crucial moment on Monday came when the seventeen Guardsmen knelt, aimed their rifles at the students encircling them, and then refrained from firing.' Newspaper stories and verbal accounts, especially the testimony of Guardsmen, seemed to substantiate the claim that the Guard were 'encircled and under great pressure from the students,' that they were 'in mortal danger' and subjected to a 'constant shower of rocks.'

When numerous photographs failed to show these hordes of encircling students, it was thought that perhaps the shots had been taken from 'blind' angles. With so much verbal evidence, we had to believe that the Guard had indeed been endangered. But the nagging doubt persisted: 'If there were hordes of menacing students, some one of those photographers must have seen them.'

Then, in the fourth month of our investigation, a remarkable photograph turned up. It had been taken by Beverly K. Knowles from an upper window of Prentice Hall and is a panoramic shot of the Guardsmen on the practice field. To the south, there are no students for at least two hundred yards; much of the field is visible and completely empty. To the east, not one student can be seen behind the fence. And where the mob was supposed to have been there was seen only empty space for nearly forty yards, then the high steel fence of the baseball diamond, then the famous parking lot. On or near it could be counted about a score of students, five of them, with books under their arms, walking away from the Guard. One researcher, an excellent baseball player, went down to the scene and placed a student where the Guard had been. Picking up what rocks he could find, he retreated behind the fence and tried to throw them at the supposed Guard. His conclusion: 'Joe Di Maggio couldn't have reached them.'

Confirmation came from Harold Walker, already a good writer and a skilled photographer. He looked like a hundred other young men who work on college newspapers: alert, well-spoken, reserved in manner, carefully dressed and sober in judgment. He had done so well in his college work that the university had offered him the job of running the summer-school newspaper. He was known on the campus as a comer.

When Walker saw the Guardsmen march toward the fence, he said to himself, 'They're boxing themselves in; good chance for some great shots.' He ran down beside them and, as his stunning series of pictures proves, was, during much of the time, the student nearest them. He says, 'It's true that a few kids, maybe ten, ran inside the baseball fence to throw rocks and junk at the Guardsmen, but very little of it reached them. Now and then a gas canister would roll among the Guards, but from where I stood I saw no damage being done.' On this he was emphatic.

But, he went on, 'I remember looking out of the corner of my eye and seeing off to the right, well removed from the rioting, a hard-core group of radicals wearing Che Guevara headbands and black suits and carrying Vietcong flags. The men wore green army jackets and kept themselves well protected from whatever might be about to happen. After the firing, I saw them move to the foreground and sort of take over.'

Another witness had good credentials insofar as guns were concerned. Richard Schreiber was an assistant professor of journalism who had lived an outdoor life in Minnesota. He startled students who met him for the first time because he had a huge red beard and piercing blue eyes, a Honda 305 and a red, white and blue motorcycle helmet. He was married to a girl from New Jersey whom he had met while they were both students at Heidelberg in Germany. He says, 'I was in the army three years and had served a lot of patrol duty, so I knew guns. I've gone hunting almost every year of my life and am a life member of the National Rifle Association. I keep in my office a pair of 7x35 Bushnell binoculars.

'On Monday morning at 0745 I had a class called the Principles of Advertising. Now, you must remember that at least 6,000 of our students had gone home over the weekend, and they didn't know what had been happening on campus. They were interested to find out, but I had a guest speaker from Ohio Bell who had come up to explain the advantages of advertising in their Yellow Pages. At 11:10 I had a different class in advertising but with the same guest speaker, but as soon as he ended his presentation, I said, "Let's wrap this one up," because the kids were restless and wanted to see what was happening out on the commons, where the Victory Bell was ringing.

'I saw the Guard come up from ROTC and disappear on the other side of Taylor. I thought that was that, but then I heard voices from the practice field, so I went out on the south porch of Taylor with my binoculars and saw something which has caused a lot of discussion. While the Guard was pinned against the fence, the students kept throwing rocks, but they were rather far away and most of the rocks were falling short. I happened to have this one Guard in my glasses and I saw him raise his revolver and bang away. I've fired many hundreds of rounds with a .45 and I know a shot when I see one. There can be no question but that he fired the first round of the day. But the damnedest thing happened. Even while he was firing, some student ran up with a gas grenade and threw it at him. Where could he have possibly got it? Didn't look like the ones the Guards had been using. One of the Guardsmen, foolishly I thought, picked up the grenade and threw it back. It seemed like horseplay, so I turned away.'

For a long time there was no confirming testimony to support Schreiber's contention; the Guard insisted that no shot could have been fired; Schreiber stuck to his story, but most observers felt that he was wrong. Then, slowly, more evidence began to filter out. Sergeant James W. Farriss of Alpha Company said, 'An officer I didn't recognize fired one shot from a .45-caliber pistol.' And Specialist 4 Gerald Lee Scaif found a spent .22-caliber shell casing near the edge of the field where the firing was supposed to have taken place, but the only officer with a .22 pistol that day was Major Jones, an impeccable witness, who swears he did not fire his Beretta either on the football field or anywhere else, and subsequent checking of weapons would tend to confirm this.

Brother Fargo and Jim Pierce. Among the crowd of students milling around the pagoda while the Guardsmen were pinned against the fence was a man who should not have been there. It was Brother Fargo, the tall black with the knitted tarboosh. 'I was there for four precise reasons,' he says. 'I was on patrol to see that no black sister got tangled in trouble. I sought to warn blacks in general that there might be Guardsmen who would fire at them for no reason. I am also a first-aid specialist and I suspected my skill might be needed before the day ended. And I was opposed to the war in Vietnam.'

Fargo can be spotted in a good many photographs, left hand to mouth, shouting to the Guard as they march past in their retreat. When the firing came, he was extremely close to the guns, and when it ceased he was among the first to run to the rescue of John Cleary, the wounded student who was the third closest to the Guard, and it was while in the process of administering first aid that he was photographed for the cover of *Life*. His dark face looks grave.

What Fargo could not have known at the time was the narrowness by which he had just escaped with his life. For in the group of Guardsmen clustered along the ragged and informal firing line was Specialist 4 James Pierce, the boy from Kent who had gone to the University of Hawaii. He had had a bad week, away from home, away from his son, standing guard against truckers in Akron and students in Kent. By his own admission his nerves were frayed and he was in no mood to take any further nonsense.

Among all the Guardsmen, he would give the most extraordinary testimony as to what part he had played in the shooting. Charles Madonio, the friend who had talked to him on Sunday afternoon at the gate, says, 'The next time I saw Jim Pierce was the day after he got off duty. He was nervous and scared, and refused to talk about it other than to admit to me that he was on the hill in the firing line. "They were going to kill us," was all he could say. He meant it. He also expressed fear for his family, said he planned to move out of Kent, not go back to school. I tried later to get a statement from him, but he refused to talk about it, saying he was sworn to secrecy. He, in my opinion, had no grudges against students, no ax to grind, as the others might have had. He was just plain scared. He claimed the crowd was within ten feet of them. He told the FBI that he had fired four times. One shot in the air. One at a male student ten feet from him who was about to throw a rock. Once into the crowd. And once point-blank at a Negro throwing a rock. It is sad. He's a good guy, and he was probably just scared.'

There are numerous photographs of the action. None shows Brother Fargo with a rock.

Was there an order to fire? As to the crucial question, 'When the Guard went into their huddle on the practice field, was an order given that they should fire when they reached the pagoda?' there is at present no evidence, and there may never be, for on this point no Guardsman will now allow himself to be interrogated. What follows is an educated guess based upon hours of investigation and speculation.

One photograph of the actual shooting shows General Canterbury, who had already passed the pagoda, turning around and storming back toward the troops who had done the firing, as if he were shouting, 'What in hell goes on here?'

Either Canterbury is a superb actor or he was truly astonished by the shooting. The same can be said for Colonel Fassinger, who would have had to give the order. And the well-known actions of Major Jones, who spent tremendous energy trying to halt the firing once it started, would seem to exonerate him. Among the three top officers, there was no order and no conspiracy to fire without one.

It seems likely, however, that on the football field, when the students were being obnoxious and stones were drifting in, that some of the troops agreed among themselves, 'We've taken about enough of this crap. If they don't stop pretty soon we're going to let them have it.' It was in this mood that they retreated up the hill—hot, dusty, sweating, and cut off from the rational world by their gas masks. Any sudden movement, any apparent attack would suffice to start the firing. A secret report contains this pregnant passage:

> As the troops marched back to Blanket Hill someone among the Guard said, 'If they charge us, shoot them.' Another spread the word, 'Armed dissidents in the area.' Another said, 'Snipers on the rooftops ready to shoot us.'

No order to fire was necessary and none was given. It must be remembered also that the men of G Troop had already knelt in the firing position and had awaited only the final order, 'Fire.' They must have been psychologically prepared and especially restive.

Jim Nichols, whose judgment is excellent, lends credence to the theory that some kind of understanding may have been reached before the Guard left the practice field: 'I was coming out of Taylor Hall just as the Guard reached the pagoda. They had not yet fired but they had stopped. I kept going toward them. Suddenly one of them saw me coming, turned around and pointed his rifle at me. He had a gas mask on like the rest of them, so I couldn't see his face and to this day I don't know his name. But I know he saved my life. I was going right out in front of them where the shooting would start in a few seconds. Oh, wow, a bad place to be! But *he* recognized *me* and sort of waved me back with his gun. He couldn't yell at me because he had a mask on. The only way he could stop me was with his gun.'

Jim halted, then watched in horror as the ragged volley of gunfire rolled down the slope of Blanket Hill. The shooting stopped. While the soldiers were still milling about beside the pagoda, Jim started back toward them, to see for himself what had happened on the other side of the hill, to conduct his own investigation, to 'get the evidence,' as he puts it.

'I wasn't sure of my safety at all. I remember thinking, "Screw you, buddy, if you kill me you'll have to answer to the Supreme Being—if there is one. If there isn't, you'll have to answer to my managing editor." '

Jim adds the clincher: 'A few weeks later I was picking up extra money pumping gas at the Sohio station on West Main Street when a fellow drives in and asks for a dollar's worth—I remember it was a Friday night in June. While I'm taking his dollar he asks me, "You still reporting for the *Record-Courier?*" "No," I told him, "that was last year." "Well," he says, "were you working for a newspaper on May 4?" I said, "Yeah, the Dayton *Daily News.*" Then he grinned and said, "Don't you recognize me?" I looked at him real hard and his face was kind of familiar, but I couldn't place him. He said, "I'm the guy that pointed his rifle at you." Then he drove off.

'A couple of days later I suddenly placed him. He was from Ravenna and I'd met him the year before when I was covering Ravenna high school basketball games for the *Courier.* But I still couldn't remember his name. And I had the feeling he wanted it that way.'

Then comes the big question: 'Jim, if a Guardsman stopped you from going onto that hill he must have known there was going to be a shooting? He must have known they had something planned?'

'I've wondered about that,' he says, 'but I don't think so. I don't think he actually knew there was going to be a shooting. All he knew was that the possibility of shooting existed. These Guardsmen were really strung out at the time and the students were all fired up and ready to go. I think he just didn't want to see me get myself in the middle.'

Finally, one must grapple with the perplexing story reported by the Canadian housewife. Mrs. Wilma D. Luckwitz lives just beyond the western boundary of Kent. She is an attractive, level-headed woman in her early thirties, a native of Canada, and since her accountant husband is a graduate of Kent State, she regards the university favorably. She says, 'About one hour after the shooting took place, our neighbor from two doors down the road came over to see us, badly shaken. Jack Albright—his real name is Harold—works as an electrician at the university and he had quite a story to tell. When I heard it I called for Dr. and Mrs. Robert Fernie, who live on the other side of us—he's a professor of psychology at the university—to come and verify it.' (The Fernies did come, do verify everything about to be related.)

This is what Jack Albright told them: 'A gang of us were wiring one of the floors in the new library, and since we were high up we could see most of what was happening on campus, but we were so far away we couldn't catch the details. So lunch-break came, me and three other electricians got on the elevator, went down to the ground floor, and crossed the construction site where the new Student Union is to be. We were there when the National Guard marched past the pagoda and we saw hundreds of college kids, some wearing white headbands and armbands and acting as leaders, run across the practice field and come to where they picked up rocks and bricks. I was all for the Guard. Those kids deserved whatever they got.

'So when the Guard retreated, I followed them and found a position near the pagoda. I was the closest person to the Guard and I heard an officer give the order, "Turn around and fire three rounds." He yelled so loud I could hear it very plainly.'

This statement was so startling that Mrs. Luckwitz, the Fernies and another neighbor, Mrs. John Smith, asked him to go over it again, and he repeated it four times, each time saying he heard 'an officer give the order, "Turn around and fire three rounds."'

Mrs. Luckwitz says, 'The reason we remember this so clearly is that whenever Jack said it, he explained, "I was for the Guards. They had to fire or they'd have had their rifles taken away from them by the students."'

Mrs. Luckwitz, standing with the Fernies, ends her narrative: 'All of us on Marsh Road who heard Jack recite his account insisted that he take it to the FBI. He did. We urged him to take it to the grand jury. He did. But the story has never appeared in any public record. Can it be that the investigators haven't wanted to believe that an order was given?'

A visit to Jack Albright's new home at 3304 Marsh Road does not clarify the matter. He appears at the door, a very tall man who looks exactly like a young Dick Foran. He smiles affably, is most courteous, leads the way into a tastefully furnished living room of which he and his petite blond wife are obviously proud. 'I've told this story a hundred times,' he begins, 'and no one believes it. I'm tired of telling it.' When asked for one more repetition, he says with keen interest, leaning forward as he speaks, 'You understand, I'm on the Guard's side completely and everything I say is intended to bolster up their case. The college kids were behaving insanely. They'd have overrun them at the pagoda and taken their guns away, that's for sure. The Guard were a hundred-percent right.'

'Did you hear the command given to fire?'

Jack Albright sits back. His enthusiasm vanishes, 'Well, there was a lot of noise, a lot of screaming. I was about 150 feet away, and what could I hear?'

'Did you hear an officer say, "Turn around and fire three rounds"?'

'Well, I heard . . . well, yes. I heard it.'

The retreat. It is important to visualize the condition of the Guard as they begin their retreat. They have been on duty for nearly a week, sleeping at odd times and in odd places. They have eaten irregularly and been subjected to taunts and ridicule. They are bewildered by the behavior of college students and outraged by the vocabulary of the coeds. It is hot. They have been stoned. They have chased a lot of oddly dressed kids back and forth and have accomplished nothing except the indignity of having their own tear gas thrown back at them.

And they experienced irritating physical limitations. Private Paul Zimmerman told a reporter from the Akron *Beacon Journal,* 'It was hard to see through that plastic. To look behind you, you'd have to turn your head all the way around. I was hot and sweaty.'

Sergeant Dale Antram, and any other Guardsman wearing glasses, had to take them off in order to get the gas mask on: 'We would be marching up the hill but we would be thinking behind us. We were always watching over our shoulders, and guys were saying, "Back there!" "Watch it!" "Here comes a rock!" '

Lieutenant Stevenson, platoon leader of G Troop, told one of the investigating groups, 'At the time of the firing, the crowd was acting like this whole thing was a circus. The crowd must have thought the National Guard was harmless. They were having fun with the Guard. The circus was in town.'

Jack Deegan added his bit of clowning: 'I was standing in

the roadway when the Guard started retreating up the hill, and they whizzed past me at a distance of a few feet. So I fell in behind them and called cadence for them. "Hep, two, three, four," stopping now and then to give them hell for being out of step. A lot of rocks were being thrown from the roadway, but most of them were falling short.

'I followed the Guards right to the position from which they shot, then looked aside to where my roommate Tom Masterson was being clubbed over the head with a revolver, but that's another story. As I ran past the Guards to help Tom, the detachment turned and fired. I saw no students encroaching on them and it seemed to me that an officer must have ordered them to do this turning and firing.'

Brian Fisher, a motorcycle fancier and tough-minded liberal who wanted to see ROTC and the Guard off campus, stood stolidly in their path as they charged back up the hill. A girl whom we will meet in a few moments was near him, and he says she was yelling at the soldiers. At any rate, one of them, a left-handed fellow without a gas mask, turned and shouted at the girl, "Come one step nearer, you bitch, and I'll blow your head off." '

Debi Moreland had risen early Monday in order to attend her field-study class in the Akron slums, but as she approached the bus which would have taken her there, she suddenly decided to go to the bank, so she cut class and headed downtown.

The bank she was going to was the one that Sandy Scheuer had patronized Friday morning, the blood bank in the Ferrara Building at 211 East Summit. Debi explains, 'You're allowed to sell once every two months. All my friends do. We need the bread. Some kids wangle double cards under fictitious names, so they can sell more often. But it's necessary to go there early in order to get the extra buck.' She produces the card she carries like a driver's license: *Debi Moreland, A RH positive. Before noon $11. Afternoon $10.*

After selling her blood, Debi wandered back to Johnson Hall, and as she was leaving, met Brian Fisher, a friend in liberal causes. She accompanied him right into the line of march of the National Guard. 'I wound up not more than two feet away from them as they came charging up the hill, and they were furious. I was in the middle of them fifty seconds before they fired. A short man on the end took out a revolver, waved it in my face, and dared any of us to do anything. It was my most vivid memory of the day.'

One of the more sober evaluations came from a young man well qualified to make it, by virtue of both his previous experience and his position on campus that morning. Peter Winnen, a rugged fellow from Cleveland, was married, and, like many students, dependent upon his wife's income as a nurse in Akron. He had had a typically broken career. After an initial trial at Ohio State he had decided that the American educational system held little for him, so he drifted out to San Francisco, where he hooked up with a crowd which had fallen under the spell of the then guru, Ken Kesey, whom Winnen found shallow. The draft caught up with him and he served in Vietnam as a forward artillery observer. 'My job was to see what guns did,' he says, but on one point he wants everyone to know where he stands. 'I'm a hard-hat. I'm the son of one, and I worked as one. I dig those workingmen and understand why they're sore at college kids. But I'm also an English major, which involves me in values and ideas.'

On Monday morning he had a class in history, but cannot now remember his professor's name. (It is extraordinary how many Kent State students cannot remember the names of professors who taught them only a quarter ago.) At noon he went onto the Taylor porch and watched proceedings on the football field, and as an ex-soldier, became increasingly disgusted by what he saw. General Canterbury was moving from group to group and seemed irritated by being trapped against the fence. 'But no one else appeared to be taking it seriously. Some tear-gas canisters were exchanged, and every time the Guardsmen fielded one, the girls cheered, so that it appeared like a game. Then you began to notice that the Guards were perplexed. They couldn't see too much in those gas masks.

'It's true that the Guards were surrounded, but only by the fence. I wouldn't say that the students in the parking lot presented much of a threat. A lot of missiles were in the air, but damned few of them reached the Guardsmen. Then I saw the Guards go into a huddle, and it was quite obvious that a decision of some kind had been reached.

'They came back up the hill a lot faster than they had gone down, and I judged they were withdrawing because they knew they had a clear run back to the ROTC building, with practically no students facing them. But suddenly they turned and fired. I heard no command, and I wasn't very far away. Yet they did turn, like a flock of birds. When they fired, it seemed to be sporadic and not on command. Certainly, if this had been at the front in Vietnam and an order to fire had been given, I'd have had to say that the execution was very poor. I have fired many rounds of M-14 and M-16 ammo, and I noticed three periods of fire. One blast . . . pause . . . then fifteen seconds of firing. And it was all over.'

Bill Montgomery, a Vietnam veteran from Sandusky, was another trained military observer: 'Most of the students were clean-cut fraternity types. Really, I saw very few people you would call radicals there. A lot of kids had just come back from the weekend and didn't even know what was coming off.

'What happened at the pagoda seemed to be planned. They sure didn't look like panicky men.' Nor could he believe that the firing had been triggered by a sniper. 'If there had been a sniper, you don't fire into a crowd. You try to spot him and maneuver in on him. They didn't react as if it were a sniper. It was nothing but murder.'

Were Guardsmen in danger? The testimony here is so divergent, it is as if witnesses were observing two different battle actions. One official who was responsible for studying all aspects of the situation says flatly, 'If they hadn't fired, they would have been killed.' General Canterbury testifies that they were in danger of their lives. The official statement of the Guardsmen issued after the firing agrees that the men were in mortal danger from which they could extricate themselves only with gunfire, and numerous witnesses, some of whom appear not to have been at the scene, testify to hordes of students about to overrun the Guardsmen. One says that Jeff Miller was dashing up the hill, shouting 'Kill, kill, kill!' and these words appear in one official report. (Miller was 265 feet from the Guardsmen when he supposedly threatened them.)

Available photographs do not support claims of extreme danger. In picture after picture, empty space surrounds the Guardsmen. They are under attack neither on the left nor right, neither from the front nor from the rear.

About a score of Guardsmen testified immediately after the firing that their lives were not in danger. One who gave an interview to James Herzog of the *Beacon Journal* said, 'The men were really on edge and disgusted, but I didn't feel my life was in danger.'

Larry Rose, Army Specialist 5 with experience against the Vietcong at Pleiku, watched the action from Taylor Hall, and says, 'Danger? What danger that would justify firing? In Vietnam, even when we were facing the enemy inside our barbed-wire enclosure, fire control was so rigid that we are not allowed to fire on our own . . . not even if we spotted Vietcong creeping under the wire. We waited till someone gave the command "Fire!" But on a college campus where there was no enemy, anyone could fire when he wanted to.'

And yet, there is substantial evidence that the Guard believed itself to be in mortal danger. It is based on a mysterious motion picture which purportedly shows that a large mass of students had suddenly surged forward at the Guard just before they fired, viciously enough to have warranted the shooting. We spent our first three months in Kent trying to see this film, but it had been impounded by the government. We did, however, get a description of it from an official whose duty had required him to review it several times:

Long after the pundits had guessed and miscalculated horribly in their attempts to explain what had happened at the pagoda, I had the good luck to see a film which showed it all. The film had an amazing history, apart from its content. Several weeks after the excitement had died down, a student reported to the authorities that he had been perched on a high tower to the southeast of the shooting, and with a cheap camera loaded with color film, had tried to take moving pictures of everything.

Since the film had not yet been developed, he didn't know what he had, and you can imagine the gingerly manner in which the police sent it off to a special lab. Believe it or not, the lab messed it up. Used the wrong chemicals or something. Anyway, the color was lost. But a grainy, jerky black-and-white came out, sometimes not too clear.

What did it show? It picks up the Guardsmen as they first leave the pagoda, a skirmish line of olive-drab, look-alike men from Mars in helmets and moving down the hill through their own tear gas. The kids, of course, are something else . . . dancing in retreat, waving obscene finger gestures, a few of them hurling rocks, railroad spikes, expended gas canisters. They appear in all varieties of garb, wild hair styles, flamboyant headbands, black flags. On comes the Guard. Away dance the students.

The original purpose of this march— 'to dispel the rioters'—has clearly become a joke, with no one in much danger. As you watch the fumbling movements of the Guardsmen, about sixty-five of them, you get the feeling that this is more a picnic than a battle scene, and when the Guard finds itself penned in by the link fence, it becomes downright ridiculous.

How close are the threatening students? Well, they move back and forth of course, some of them running forward to throw rocks or return gas canisters, but not even the most daring ones are very close. But as the Guard continues in its embarrassed position against the fence, the authority seems to shift from it to the mob. The Guard responds. One line of about fifteen soldiers drop to their knees, shoulder their rifles, and poke them out as if getting ready to fire. As a gesture it looks bewildering, unconvincing, something they had been taught to do but had not practiced sufficiently. The movement of the students increases, for they know very well that the Guard will not fire their guns, even if they are loaded, which seems unlikely.

The Guard now stands, forms a huddle, discusses things, forms into a big V and starts back up the hill toward the pagoda. The howling students pursue them, always at a considerable distance, picking up and hurling the same rocks and shards of concrete they had thrown on the way down. But you can see that most of the missiles are thrown from such a distance that they cannot possibly reach the Guard. There is not much smoke. Maybe the Guard have used up their tear gas.

Now comes the critical moment. As the point of the V reaches the pagoda, there is a definite surge of the students toward the right flank. You can see it on the film, a kind of pulsating movement. It never comes close to the Guard. I'd say fifty or sixty feet at the most. Is it a threatening movement? From the film you can't tell, but there it is.

So the Guard halts, wheels around, lets go, and bodies begin to fall. The film ends.

Confirmation comes from two trained observers. Writing on May 5, eyewitness Al Thompson, of the *Cleveland Press*, said, 'Now the Guardsmen begin to retreat. They had used up all their tear gas. They were heading back to their original stations. The students moved after them. Suddenly a small group of students raced forward to within close range of the Guard, some throwing rocks. In that instant there was a shot.'

Paul Tople was in an unequaled position to observe what was happening along the right flank; he was standing on the porch at Taylor Hall, with an unobstructed view all the way to the practice field. He saw the Guard start their retreat with only a few students between them and the pagoda. 'I don't actually remember any students in that area,' he says, 'nor any on the left flank, but as the Guard moved up the hill, somewhere around fifty to a hundred students followed them, and some of these were lobbing stones and rocks at the retreating figures. This group didn't appear to bother the Guards too much, but there was another group, moving up the path leading to Taylor Hall, that did. They were about fifty yards or so away from the Guard, and off to my left. How many students? Maybe forty. They seemed to be moving toward the Guard. At any rate, the Guard could have interpreted it as a surge. The lead student could have been as close as fifteen feet. It was after this that the Guard turned and fired, but by then the closest student was about twenty yards away.'

After much negotiation, we were finally able to see the secret film. To have claimed, as some did, that the group of students hurrying up from the right constituted 'a mortal danger' or 'a howling mob bent on killing the Guard' required either extrasensory perception or a new definition of words.

But that is not what is really relevant, for it answers only the question, 'What would a rational person viewing this film in a quiet library, long after the event, conclude?' The larger question must be, 'What would a hot, tired Guardsman think if he caught a glimpse of moving students coming at him on his blind right flank?' He could very reasonably think that he was about to be attacked by 'a howling, vicious mob prepared to tear him apart.'

Significantly, neither of the two unit commanders at the pagoda believed that their lives or the lives of their troops were in danger. Captain Srp, of G Troop, said, 'I was right in the middle of it and felt no danger.' Captain Martin of Alpha Company supported this opinion.

Certainly General Canterbury believed his men were in danger, even though, as is apparent from photographs, he could not have been watching them at the moment: 'Guardsmen on the right flank were in serious danger of bodily harm and death as the mob continued to charge. I felt that, in view of the extreme danger to the troops at this point, they were justified in firing.'

One must also take into account the strong feeling running through the Guard that 'we've taken enough.' During the truckers' strike tough union men had cursed them, thrown rocks at them, hit them with empty beer bottles and on several occasions actually brought them under sniper fire, and 'we weren't about to take a lot of guff from some snot-nosed college brats.' (However, in weeks that were to follow, hard-hats at the Portage County Ordnance Depot northeast of Kent would create much more violence than had occurred at the university, but in neither that strike nor the earlier truckers' was firing into a crowd deemed necessary.)

'The Guard is firing blanks.' Professional military men were infuriated when witnesses said, 'We assumed the rifles were not loaded' or 'We assumed they were firing blanks.' Sometimes the regular soldiers would curse and ask, 'Why would *anybody* assume that a gun wasn't loaded?' The testimony is overwhelming that a large percentage of the people on the campus that day did so assume.

They had reason to do so. After the Detroit riots in 1967, nationwide publicity was given to the fact that much of the killing was done by Guardsmen firing haphazardly at street lights, shadows and even at other Guardsmen. The commander of the regular army, upon moving in, had ordered the Guard disarmed, and in subsequent hearings it was widely reported that henceforth Guardsmen would go into such situations with rifles loaded only with blanks. Several commissions had so recommended, and it was reported that of the fifty State Guards, only a few permitted their men to carry loaded rifles. Apparently it was not widely known that Ohio was one of the few.

More specifically, at Kent the students had been assured that the Guard did not carry live ammunition.

Linda Peterson, one of the reportorial team, says, 'Over Station WKSU on Sunday night some professors held a rap session from 9:00 till 2:00 in the morning and everyone in the dorms was listening. The question came up, "Does the Guard carry loaded weapons?" And the wife of a Guard telephoned in to say, "I can tell you positively that the Guardsmen do not carry loaded weapons. They are unarmed." '

President White thought so. 'I did not know the Guardsmen were patrolling with loaded rifles,' he said to reporters.

Certain professors, who had had experience in those states where live ammunition was not permitted, told their students, 'Guardsmen do not carry ammunition in their rifles.'

Captain Martin of Alpha Company suspected the motives of anyone who spread such reports: 'Agitators had those kids believing we had blanks. Somebody told them that!'

Dan Fuller, assistant professor of English, wore the popular gold-rimmed granny glasses preferred by the in-group. He kept his reddish-brown hair moderately long in back and was always neat. He liked blue shirts, wide ties, blue jeans and wore one of those three-inch-wide leather wristwatch bands which were almost the badge of the younger intellectuals. Most conspicuously, he fancied yellow shoes made of an expensive soft leather. The thing he liked best was to quaff beer with the gang on Water Street. He was known as an excellent teacher, but must have been something of a problem to the elderly members of the Board of Trustees who conducted this interview with him one day before the troubles.

TRUSTEE: Why does an excellent English teacher like you feel you have to teach about politics?

FULLER: I don't teach politics. I teach American literature to college students who are more than twenty years old.

TRUSTEE: But why even mention politics? It isn't necessary.

FULLER: How can you not mention politics when you're teaching about James T. Farrell and Studs Lonigan?

TRUSTEE: Why do you have to teach such books? Why can't you teach the fine old books that didn't bother with such things?

FULLER: The authors who did the writing determined what I have to teach.

TRUSTEE: But can't you just teach the young people to write correctly, and how to read?

FULLER: I also have to teach them how to think.

He explains, 'I was able to view the Kent State thing without hysteria because I had seen agitations at Wisconsin, and believe me, they were much, much worse. In comparison, our kids at Kent were well behaved.'

Fuller started his day with an 8:50–9:40 class in the honors college on the meaning of fiction, and he spent that hour discussing with his students 'What shall we believe about the events of this past weekend?' The debate was lively. In the 9:55–10:45 period he met with his creative-writing students and told them that on this day their own campus provided them with one of the great subjects for writing: masses of people in conflict. He felt it only natural to dismiss this class early so that the students could see for themselves what mass action consisted of, and its dangers.

He started out with a sense of optimism, for when the warning jeep circulated through the commons, commanding the students to disperse, 'I was standing not far from it when the first barrage of stones came its way. "Whoops!" the man on the bullhorn cried, not a bit uptight, "here come the rocks," and the crowd cheered. I figured everyone was relaxed.'

He says, 'I wasn't aware of the greatest danger. Later on, some of my students saw me on the campus and asked, "Professor Fuller, the Guards are using blanks in their guns, aren't they?" and I assured them, "No danger. I saw the Guards in action at Wisconsin and they never had loaded weapons." Another batch of students, not from my class, asked, "They wouldn't have live ammo in those guns, would they?" and I told them, "Not a chance. They're not fools." '

Later, when the volley was heard, some students told Fuller, 'That must have been more firecrackers,' and he agreed.

Bob Dyal, assistant professor of philosophy, was a short, pipe-smoking New England gentleman who wore a Captain Ahab beard and trim blue trousers with a turtle-neck sweater. He was married, with two daughters. He spoke in a deep pleasant voice, and was memorable in that down the two sides of his beard ran white streaks about an inch wide. He still thinks of that Monday with a sense of shock: 'When the rifles went off I was a few yards behind the Guard, and I shouted, "They *are* using blanks, aren't they?" and Ken Calkins, professor of history, called back, "Of course they are. You can tell from the sound. They'd never use real bullets in a crowd." '

It may sound strange to read that such an exchange took place at the climax of a shooting, but it is not illogical when one remembers that a fusillade was in no sense a single burst of fire but a sporadic shooting which continued with pauses, for thirteen seconds. We have records of some extraordinary conversations that occurred during that confused interval, and many of them consist of the question, 'They are blanks, aren't they?' and the response, 'Of course.' The reader ought to time himself and see how many questions and answers he can exchange within a thirteen-second interval.

But now one of Dyal's girl students came running up, screaming, 'My God, those damned pigs have killed people!'

Professor Schreiber, on the south porch of Taylor Hall when the firing took place, said it had seemed to him that live ammunition was being fired, but one of his girl students who was standing closer to the rifles than he, shouted, 'They're firing blanks,' and he assumed she knew, but a man who was on the grass and saw some of the students fall, 'came up to us, absolutely white,' Schreiber says, 'and said bitterly, "Hell, I was in Vietnam for a full tour and never saw anyone shot down. Look at that campus. I had to come back to my own university to see kids killed." '

Mrs. Elizabeth Runyan might be considered the perfect prototype of the teaching fellow. She is married and lives with her lawyer husband in Hudson, about ten miles northwest of Kent. She has two sons attending Harvard, and when they left home she decided to acquire a Ph.D. Of Monday she says, 'Since I live off campus and do not regularly listen to the radio, I did not know that an injunction had been handed down forbidding outdoor assemblies at the university. However, when I got to my classroom, there was a copy of an injunction posted on the door, but it said nothing about forbidding rallies on the campus, of this I am certain.

'Only one third of my twelve o'clock class reported, so I told the others that as students of writing we all ought to go out on campus and test our powers of observation. I was therefore responsible for leading those six into the heart of the rally, none of us realizing that we were doing anything wrong.'

Unknowingly, Mrs. Runyan led her students to one of the most dangerous spots on the hill. 'We stood only a few yards in back of the Guardsmen, and if they had elected to turn left when they turned right, they would have killed us all. When the guns did go off, only a short distance from us, I assured my students, "Nothing to worry about. Those are surely blanks." ' In the confusion that followed, Mrs. Runyan and her student observers saw almost nothing. 'A girl did rush past, screaming, "A National Guard has been killed," but we were standing right beside the Guard and knew this wasn't true, so one of the boys grabbed the girl and said, "You're a rabble-rouser. No Guard was touched." '

One of Mrs. Runyan's students, who had cut her noon class, came running up: 'My God, they've killed people down there!' But the only part that Mrs. Runyan recalls clearly occurred at least ten minutes later. 'My students and I walked in a kind of daze to that big piece of steel sculpture in front of Taylor Hall and we saw where one of the bullets had cut its way right through the thick steel. Only then did we appreciate what had happened.'

The professors may have been confused, but there were some students who knew. From the very beginning, they knew. Cindy Sudberry must be one of the most beautiful girls at Kent State. She has a superb figure which she shows off in a white piqué open-midriff dress. She uses lipstick intelligently and adds a touch of rouge and eye make-up. Her hair falls in braids, held in place by two handsome gold clips, down the side of her face. She is a black—in her case, a golden tan. Of the shooting she says, 'It was pathetic for a black like me to watch the nice white boys and girls growing up so fast. "Are the guns loaded?" they asked. "Are they using real bullets?" What in hell did they think the Guard have in their guns? You didn't hear any blacks asking damn-fool questions like that. But the poor white kids never knew what hit them. So many came to me later and said, "We never knew it was like that." And I had to bite my tongue to keep from saying, "I knew when I was born. The guns are always loaded." '

Field Marshal Perry summed it up in his tense, crisp way: 'Amazing. You could get five thousand white cats on that hill with the National Guard running around. But you couldn't get five blacks. What was the difference? Education. We had learned.'

Jeff Miller's body. When the Guards left the area, the scene in front of Taylor Hall was a shambles. In the middle of the roadway lay the body of Jeff Miller, his head blown apart and an appalling amount of blood running out of it and into the gutter. No one, not even veterans from Vietnam, could believe that so much blood had come from one human being. We know a good deal about the death of Jeff Miller because three photography majors were there.

Harold Walker, photographing the scene, followed the Guardsmen in their retreat and found himself in their direct line of fire. The bullets that killed three of the students had to pass him, and it was a miracle that he was not killed. When he turned back after the firing and trained his camera upon the scene of devastation, he captured the greatest comprehensive shot of the day: it showed the entire panorama, with the exact location of the dead and wounded, the shattered automobiles, the students lying huddled on the ground. It is a terrifying photograph and halts in the heart any easy comment about students being where they were not supposed to be.

Another photo, however, was to bring him more notoriety. Earlier he had noticed the Che Guevara gang off to one side, but now they moved out in force to surround the dead body, while the student who had been taunting the Guard with his flag ran up to dip that flag in the blood, jumping up and down on it in a kind of war dance to insure that the blood was well smeared across the fabric. No sooner had Walker taken this photograph than he was grabbed by two of the Guevara gang, who shouted, 'You fucking cop! Taking our pictures for identification.' They slugged him in the stomach and tried to grab his camera, and he was about to collapse when the driver of one of the ambulances came to his rescue, driving them off.

The second photographer, Harold Ruffner, had been a sergeant in the air force before returning to Kent State to complete his education. He had served in the Philippines and was not afraid of guns, and this fearlessness enabled him to get one photograph which will undoubtedly haunt him the rest of his life. 'I had gone out early in response to the bell and had got a series of great shots of the jeep, the men ringing the bell, the Guard. You know, the whole bit. I went down to the practice field and watched the kids throwing rocks, but they weren't hitting anything. When the Guard retreated, I stayed on their right flank, shooting away. They stopped twice and turned, as if to defy the students. Once they even threw back some rocks.

'I wound up less than forty yards from them when they stopped. There was only one man in front of me and he got shot. I was aware of no barrage of rocks, no large crowd behind me, no one following up the hill from the football field, no one behind them at Johnson, and certainly no one ahead of them on the way back to ROTC. But nevertheless, they turned and fired.'

The photograph that Ruffner especially treasures was taken a second before the shots, and it shows one of the Guardsmen on the left flank aiming directly at Ruffner. As you look at the photograph, you can see straight into the barrel. Ruffner hit the dirt; the shot that would have struck him passed through the steel sculpture.

The third photographer is a tall young fellow named John

Filo, and he, like Ruffner, wound up in the direct line of fire, but someone from the porch at Taylor Hall reassured him, 'Don't run! They're firing blanks.' So unlike Ruffner, who hit the dirt, Filo remained standing near a large piece of steel sculpture, taking shots of the Guard in the act of firing. 'Then, to my amazement, a bullet came ripping through the sculpture and two more rattled through the tree with such force that they knocked my camera out of my hands. I hit the ground very fast. They were real bullets!'

When Filo got down to the roadway he took several shots of Jeff Miller, and in doing so, caught the Delacroix girl lamenting over the body. This picture was widely reproduced throughout the world, appeared on the cover of news magazines, and could win Filo a Pulitzer Prize, but one of his later shots had special interest. Critics would charge that Filo had staged his famous photograph, coaching the girl in how to hold her arms and contort her mouth. To appreciate this second photo, we must go back for a moment and find out what Captain Ron Snyder's Charlie Company had been doing.

While Alpha Company and G Troop were making their sweep up to the top of Blanket Hill and down to the practice field, Snyder and his men held their position between Taylor and Prentice. They had expended all their tear gas, and Snyder said, 'We're in trouble with no gas!' but the action had moved away from them and they were left to one side, surrounded by demonstrators who swarmed like maddened hornets, dodging in and out among the trees, running up to his men, throwing things, and retreating. Boys in-headbands and Daniel Boone shirts seemed determined to challenge the Guard, and Snyder says, 'Never in all my years as a Guardsman had I seen a more electrifying sight. I really could not guess what was going to happen next.'

When the troops on the field began their retreat, Snyder alerted his men to be ready to move also, if necessary. He did not see the shooting—too many students milling around, he says—but as soon as the bodies began falling a few yards ahead of him, he sprang into action. One glance at Jeff Miller's body and he knew that the boy was dead. He caught a glimpse of another body that had to be dead, too. But some idea of the strain he was under can be gleaned from the fact that as a coroner's investigator with more than 300 cases behind him, he thought the second dead student was a boy. It was Sandy

Scheuer, and days later, when confronted with evidence of her identity, he had trouble accepting it.

Snyder now posted about eight men around the hideous body of Jeff Miller, but as soon as he did so, his unit was surrounded by a swarm of bitter students who screamed, 'Pigs! Murderers! Motherfuckers!' Erroneously, they believed that it had been Snyder and his men who had done the killing, and the situation grew most perilous. It was this moment that Filo captured in his second photograph: in the midst of the Guards, screaming at them, stands the Delacroix girl, and her face is no less tremendous than in the shot where she is seen kneeling.

It was a moment of decision. Howard White, from Poland, Ohio, reports, 'I was standing near the body when one of Snyder's men, in full battle gear, gas mask, and rifle came and looked down at Jeff Miller, with the blood gushing out of his head. I shuddered when the Guardsman started to turn the dead body over with the toe of his boot. A girl screamed, "No!" and the Guardsman drew back. I do believe that if he had rolled Jeff over with his shoe, the crowd would have torn him to pieces.'

Prudently, Snyder ordered his men to move on. As they departed, one Guardsman, who had been subjected to extreme cursing by several girls, turned and lofted a hand grenade at the crowd. Filo says, 'He tossed it underhand from about forty feet away, and it exploded nine feet in the air. Someone said it was an M-80 practice grenade made of plastic rather than steel.' It cut one student's lip very badly, and it was lucky that no one was killed.'

Myron Kukla, a student with a brilliant high school record which he was continuing in college, saw this incident differently: 'I walked down to where Jeff Miller was lying in that ghastly pool of blood. I saw John Filo taking his picture of the girl with the expressive face. Then, suddenly, from out of left field, appeared this contingent of the Guard. They took a lot of abuse, their buddies having just killed a bunch of kids, and as they passed us, one of the Guardsmen turned and fired his M-1, but the bullet went into the ground near Steve Tarr. I saw the splatter and believe the whole thing was an accident.'

Steve Tarr, a short, rugged fellow with a huge head of hair, mutton-chop beard and the gold-rimmed granny glasses that complete such a costume, says, 'Boy, was I startled! Last year I was an all-star high school athlete in three sports . . . a real jock practicing legalized violence for good old Archbishop Hogan High. My only concerns were the three C's—clothes, car, chicks—and here I was, a year later, reading books and arguing philosophy and getting shot at by an M-1. When I saw the splatter mark of the bullet, nor far from my toes, I said to myself, "Tarr, you may not be college material." ' It seems likely that the supposed shot was actually a fragment from the grenade.

There now occurred the scene which horrified all who have seen photographs of it but which seemed an acceptable symbolic gesture to those who witnessed it. Paul Tople describes it best: 'As the Guards disappeared up the hill, a student ran up with a flag and ceremoniously dipped it in the blood, got it well saturated, then waved it aloft in vast swirls, shouting, "See what you've done! Are you happy? Are you happy?" He was addressing the Guard, who weren't even there.' We have talked with as many as six students who got blood across their faces and shirts from this madly waving flag and unanimously they agreed with Tople's final comment: 'The approximately twenty-five students standing around him were being splattered with blood spurting out from the whipping flag. They just watched, said nothing.'

Many students noticed that when the first ambulance screamed across the commons, up the hill past the pagoda and down to the roadway where Jeff Miller lay, the first man out to take charge was Professor Frank. 'You'd sort of expect it from a guy like him,' one of the students said.

Peter Winnen says, 'I left Taylor and went down to inspect the bodies. The first fellow I saw was wounded and was bleeding a lot, but I assured him: "From what I saw in Vietnam, buddy, you're going to be all right." But when I saw the second guy . . . wow . . . no top to his head . . . he was really dead. The ambulance rushed up and the first man out was Glenn Frank. I couldn't take my eyes off his face, because he seemed totally unprepared for the fact that the first two students he started working over were absolutely dead. A lot of girls came unglued when they saw Frank's grief, and fellows had to lead them away.'

Jeff Miller's pistol. When Captain Ron Snyder ran over to inspect the fallen bodies of Sandy Scheuer and Jeff Miller, he was either the first or among the very first to reach them. We have seen how he mistook Sandy for a boy, but this was understandable. What happened at the Miller boy's body will be long debated. Snyder says, matter-of-factly, 'While we were in readiness at the east end of Taylor Hall, I spotted this especially obstreperous demonstrator with long hair, headband and cowboy shirt. Jeff Miller, I was to learn later. He kept charging up the hill to torment the retreating Guards, and this was damaging enough, but he also kept shouting at the top of his voice, "Kill! Kill! Kill!" And then he whipped a pistol out of his blouse and started pointing it at the Guardsmen by the pagoda. I had just about decided to shoot him down with my revolver when the volley began at the top of the hill. Halfway through the thirteen-second fusillade Miller spun around and fell on his face in the middle of the road, mortally wounded.

'I was the first person to reach his body, and as I bent down to assure myself that he was dead, I saw protruding from under his chest the handle of the revolver. Quickly I snatched it up and stuck it inside my blouse.' Snyder did not disclose his knowledge of Miller's revolver for about two months; why, he does not say.

This story has never before been published, and when Jeff's close friends were told of it, they exploded. They simply would not listen and became profane if anyone tried sensibly to discuss the possibility that Jeff might have been carrying a gun that day, or threatening the Guard with it if he did have one.

'Absolutely preposterous!' his close friend Neil Phillips snaps. 'I knew Jeff intimately. He wouldn't have been able to shoot down a fly that was tormenting him. He loathed guns.'

John Moir, his roommate, says with great vehemence, 'That Jeff could have been carrying a gun that day is ridiculous. I saw him thirty minutes before he went to the rally, and I know he didn't have one then. I am positive that if he'd been planning anything so unusual as carrying a gun, he'd have told me. I just can't believe anything like that.'

Jerry Persky, who is seen in photographs standing beside the body, runs his fingers through his long black hair and snorts, 'That's crazy. Whoever's saying that about Jeff is just trying to discredit him. I was standing near him before he was shot, and I certainly didn't see him running around anywhere waving a gun. After I got to him lying in the road, I saw this girl kneeling over him crying, and grabbing at some beads she had around her neck. Anyway, nobody had touched Jeff, so I got another kid, Brian Fisher, and we turned him over. There sure as hell wasn't any gun on him then, or I'd have seen it. And I've never heard anybody say anything about him waving a gun that day. The whole story is bullshit.'

We have seen the gun attributed to Miller, an old-fashioned, rusty .32-caliber rimfire revolver. It was unloaded, unfired, and because it had no hammer mechanism, unfirable. It had a short barrel, wooden handgrips and a trigger that folded out of the way. No one could tell us whether .32-caliber rimfire cartridges were still being made.

Obscene gestures: In every report, including this one, the accusation is entered that students 'made obscene gestures against the National Guard.'

Many students made obscene gestures. Victim Jeff Miller was one of this group. *FBI summary.*

Jeffrey Glenn Miller, twenty, a junior, was present in the crowd on the commons when the dispersal order was given and made obscene gestures at Guardsmen. *Scranton Commission.*

It is now necessary to spell out what the phrase *obscene gesture* means.

Forty years ago it meant that the accused had thumbed his nose at someone. Depending upon the tension at the moment, or the amount of liquor that had been consumed, this could be considered cause for a fist fight on grounds that 'I don't take that from no man.' There were probably instances in the Far West when men were shot down for having made this gesture. More often it was intended and understood as a sign of contempt, to which the classic reply was, 'Same to you.'

In recent years, and especially with younger people, thumbing the nose has gone out of style, and no photograph of the Kent weekend shows anyone resorting to this outmoded gesture. Starting in World War II, comedians and others adopted from Europe a sign made by holding the palm of a hand face-in, clasping the thumb and three fingers while raising erect the middle finger and thrusting the whole forward and upward in a menacing manner at the object of one's contempt. This is known as 'giving him the finger' or 'throwing a bird,' or, simply, 'up yours,' and carries with it a mild sexual connotation.

Photographs taken on Sunday night and Monday noon show many students throwing a finger at the Guard, usually at distances beyond fifty yards, but occasionally at closer range. The grand jury appears to have been especially incensed at this, and indicted one young man, who had already been struck by a bullet, for a felony which carried punishment as high as three years in jail and $10,000 fine. One national magazine justified the fatal shooting of Jeffrey Miller on the grounds that he had made an indecent gesture against the Guard.

We doubt that the United States seriously intends to make thumbing one's nose at a policeman or throwing a bird at a National Guard a mortal offense justifying execution on sight.

Was there a sniper? A copious body of literature has grown up around this question, but it is so turgid, that to summarize it would be tedious; it resembles the literature relating to the Kennedy assassination in Dallas and will undoubtedly be augmented in the years ahead. We have studied all available documents and find no need to postulate the existence of a sniper and nothing to support the theory that one existed. The Guard, the highway patrol, the FBI, the Scranton Commission and the grand jury all investigated this theory exhaustively, tracking down at least a dozen alluring tales of snipers seen here and there, and no shred of evidence was found to support any of them.

However, three incidents merit brief comment. A score of reliable witnesses testified that they saw a sniper atop Johnson Hall, and in a sense they did, for up there, standing against the sky, pointing a black rifle-like object directly at the Guard, stood a mysterious figure, silhouetted ominously against clouds. A sharp-eyed photographer from the *Record-Courier* spotted him and took his photograph; it turned out he was Jerome P. Stoklas, an enterprising photographer from the college paper, who had climbed up there with a tripod and a long-distance lens that could easily have been mistaken for a rifle.

Scott Mackenzie, a student from Richboro, Pennsylvania, was more than 750 feet away from the Guard when the firing broke out, but a bullet reached him and shot away part of his jaw. An elderly doctor in Akron issued a statement to the effect that he could tell from looking at the wound that it had not been caused by a military bullet but by sniper fire coming from the opposite direction. This opinion was enthusiastically received by those who were committed to the theory that a sniper had started the shoot-out, but evidence from other experts established the fact that the injury had been caused by an M-1 bullet. Mackenzie himself pointed out that he had heard the first volley of shots, had run several steps, and had then been hit, so that even if the Akron doctor were correct and the wound had been caused by sniper fire, the sniper did not shoot until the fracas had been well launched by someone else.

The third incident was totally bizarre, but it received so much publicity that many people to this day offer it as proof that students fired the first shot and were thus to blame for all that followed. Some pages back we saw Jack Deegan trailing the Guard up the hill and calling cadence for them. It was said then that he was diverted from this perilous game when he saw his roommate, Tom Masterson, getting clobbered over the head by a revolver. It was held by a student with a camera, and when the police apprehended him, the story flashed across America: 'Kent Mystery: Armed Student.' It was generally assumed that a shot from his pistol had launched the riot.

Deegan says, 'When Masterson approached him, the boy assumed that he intended snatching his camera, it being a tactic of radical students to prevent photographs on campus to forestall identification in subsequent investigations. So the fellow jerked out this revolver and started pistol-whipping Masterson about the head. Tom yelled for help, and I rushed over, but when the photographer saw me bearing down on him, he started running like hell, all the way back to the ROTC building, where he ducked for safety inside the perimeter established by the Guard.'

Mark Malick, a boy from Weirton, also witnessed this scene: 'I was on the south porch when they started to fire, and a kid next to me said, "No sweat, they're firing blanks." I paid no attention because my eye was on a cameraman in civilian clothes. He was having an argument with someone. Looked as if he were afraid he might lose his camera. So he whips out a pistol in his right hand, and as I watched, he fired it. Then ran like hell down the hill toward ROTC.'

Who was the mysterious cameraman? When the story finally broke, there were some red faces. He was Terry Norman, a nineteen-year-old Kent State student who was rumored to have been hired by the FBI and the campus police to photograph disturbances. (Later the FBI denied that he had ever worked for them.) He appears to have been armed illegally, and to this day many students are convinced that he had been sent on campus to provoke a riot and that it was his flashy display of a revolver which triggered the shooting. However, this theory is damaged by the fact that testimony is contradictory as to whether he went into action before or after the shooting began. One meticulously researched report says, 'He was seen with a pistol after the Guard fired,' but we have already heard Jack Deegan say that he saw Norman with the revolver before the firing. The testimony of Mark Malick, cited above, would indicate that Norman did not swing into action until after the shooting, but Harriet Wolin, a nineteen-year-old sophomore from Long Island, was in position to see what happened, and she says, 'The photographer pulled a gun out of his jacket and struck a friend of mine on the side of the head. Shortly after that the Guardsmen opened fire.' Another witness, who asked that his name not be used, said, 'Norman ran away from the attacking students, gun aloft, right at the Guardsmen, who were only ten yards away. The soldiers, thinking themselves under attack, opened fire. He caused it all.' We are of the opinion that Norman's movement toward the Guard—if indeed it took place, which we doubt—occurred after the firing of the first round and could not have been a cause of that firing.

Norman's revolver was retrieved within minutes by the campus police, who examined it and reported, 'It was not fired.' To this, the sponsors of the *agent provocateur* theory respond, 'The police lied. Norman did fire the first shot, as he had been ordered to do. They're covering up for their boy.' We found no evidence of this and no substance to the theory.

First news. Jeff Sallot was completely immobilized by the confusion of wild movement, screaming girls and prostrate bodies. Three times he tried vainly to do something intelligent . . . anything . . . then got mad and mumbled to himself, 'Hell, Sallot, you're supposed to be a reporter. You ought to be noticing something. And what do you suppose I did? I started counting the fallen bodies and noting where they were. Thirteen. I walked slowly down to where Jeff Miller was lying and thought, "My God, that one's got to be dead." Then I walked back, trying to notice everything but seeing only that ghastly body. I called my paper in Akron and told them, "Look, the Guard did shoot. They did hit people.

Thirteen bodies are lying on the ground. One of them, I am morally sure, has got to be dead. But don't print it until you get confirmation from the hospital." '

More experienced newsmen were not so meticulous. During the move up the hill an unfortunate accident had occurred. Sergeant Dennis L. Breckenridge overexerted himself climbing Blanket Hill and breathed so heavily that he experienced hyperventilation, which carries the symptoms of a heart attack. He collapsed, had to be carried on a stretcher to an ambulance and whisked off the field. Almost everyone who watched him go was certain he had been struck by sniper fire from some student, and most believed that he was dead. This started the rumor that two Guardsmen had been shot, and the local newspaper printed a banner headline to that effect and six thousand copies were distributed before the error was detected. In a community where, as we shall see, natural sympathies lay with the Guards rather than with the students, this was a most unfortunate circumstance and did much to polarize the citizens. The big black headlines were remembered long after corrections were made, and there are still residents of the area who remain convinced that students slaughtered Guardsmen.

The true explanation for this gaffe was a long time in coming. Captain Ron Snyder, of Charlie Company, having seen the bodies of Jeff Miller and Sandy Scheuer, radioed back to Guard headquarters at the ROTC building, 'This is Snyder. We have two dead up here. I'll give you a further sit rep [situation report] in a few minutes.'

These words, received through a loudspeaker in the emergency operations center in Administration, were heard by two reporters who erroneously assumed that Snyder's *we* referred to two dead Guardsmen, and the damaging flash went out.

As the bodies were being removed from the campus, an ironic coincidence occurred. In New York the directors responsible for awarding Pulitzer Prizes in journalism were announcing that Thomas Fitzpatrick, a Kent State student in 1950, had won the prize for an article he had written in the Chicago *Sun-Times* about the Weatherman faction of SDS. He had called it *Days of Wrath,* but he would not be listed as a graduate of Kent because he had quit the school in 1950 after having been told by Professor Taylor, after whom the building was named, 'You have no aptitude for writing.'

Guard reactions. Stu Feldstein, continuing at the center of things, followed the Guard down Blanket Hill after the firing and heard one of the men say, 'Now they'll know we mean business.'

Richard Schreiber, still using his binoculars, studied the Guard as they lined up at the ROTC building. 'Those are the ones who did the shooting,' he told a companion. 'It looks like they're really catching hell from someone.'

Schreiber may have had Ron Snyder in his glasses, for Captain Cyanide had his Charlie Company lined up for an ammunition check. 'And right here was where I got a big surprise,' Snyder says. 'I discovered that two of my men had arrived late at the noon formation and had tagged along with Alpha Company on the initial sweep up to the pagoda. They had stayed with it on the trip down to the chain-link fence and back to the firing line. Each of them showed up with one round of M-1 ammunition expended. What did I do? I ordered them to fill their clips because the students massing on the commons behind us looked ominous. I wanted to be prepared for the worst.'

Peter Winnen, continuing his role of observer, walked slowly down to the ROTC building, where the Guard were standing, and sought out the unit that had been at the pagoda: 'You fellows know that you killed two people up there?'

The Guardsmen did not answer, so Winnen went on, 'You really went crazy, didn't you?' And they replied, 'Buddy, you're the ones who are crazy.'

Dan Fuller, who had assured his students that the rifles were not loaded, also moved along the silent Guards, and asked one young man, 'Was there really shooting?'

'There was.'

'Was anyone killed?'

'Yes, I'm sorry to say.'

Crystallizations. In the moments after the shooting, terrible crystallizations of sentiment occurred. Bob Hillegas was at the ROTC building as the Guardsmen returned: 'The Guards who had done the shooting marched back, stood at ease, and put their guns into a pile which was commandeered. The other Guards got real tight. One had a Thompson machine gun. Of this I am absolutely certain, because I was standing close to him and saw him brandish it right at me. Now the ambulances started arriving, and students came down the hill, running and screaming at the Guards. One girl kept shouting, "Those murderers, they killed four of our students." There was a rain of terrible obscenities, and in the midst of this screaming, and the wild movements of the bodies, and the confusion, I realized that my sympathy lay with the students and would forever remain with them.'

For Stu Feldstein the change was simpler and more abrupt: 'I was walking around dazed and finally found Mike Alewitz sitting on the hill. Mike always had a wisecrack for me, because he considered it his duty to educate me. Coldly, he said, "Now I could kill someone." '

Ron Snyder and his men looked at the matter professionally. He says, 'My men were not remorseful. I have men who are students and instructors at Kent State and not one has ever expressed to me any regrets for what happened.'

But Sergeant Dale Antram took off his gas mask, put his glasses back on, and said, 'I feel like crying. I'm getting out of this Guard. I'm a C.O., baby, and I don't care who knows it.' And he told several friends, 'I'm a conscientious objector to this sort of thing!'

Vaclav Koutnik, the visiting professor from Czechoslovakia who had been sure it was all a game, was dazed. He told a colleague, 'Russia took over my whole country without killing one student. Your soldiers couldn't take over a plot of grass.' What Koutnik left out was one fundamental difference between the two events: in Czechoslovakia, no one could have conceivably imagined that the Russian guns were not loaded or would not be fired.

Five students

That Monday Jeff Miller rose at what for him was an early hour, about 10:00, and dressed in his usual way: blue jeans, cowboy shirt, brown Indian headband. He knew that a rally had been called for noon and he proposed to attend it, but first he would stop by the Student Union to see what was up.

He left his house on Summit Street, being careful not to waken his sleeping roommates, crossed Lincoln Street, and ambled across campus. On his way, he passed Mary Hagan, from Boston, a girl with long hair and extraordinary eyes.

'Hey, Jeff, you gonna be out there today playing war games?'

'You bet I am.'

At the Union he saw one of his former roommates, and the

two speculated on what might happen at the rally. 'God, I hope everything's going to stay cool,' Jeff said, but as he left the cafeteria, someone was passing out small slips of paper on which were phone numbers of medical and legal aid groups. He took one—as a precaution. Later it would be found in his pocket.

It was now about 11:30 and Jeff decided to return to his house, to waken his roommates and see if they wanted to accompany him to the rally. He first tried John Moir, who had so steadfastly predicted trouble throughout the weekend. Moir said, 'No rally for me. All hell's going to break loose out there.' So Jeff propositioned another roommate, who said, 'I've got some work to do on my motorcycle and can't be bothered.'

Thus rejected, Jeff set off alone for the commons, but on his way back to campus, as he was crossing Lincoln Street, he ran into a friend, Dane Griffin, a recent graduate of Roosevelt High in Kent, who was carrying a camera.

'Hey, Jeff, I got some great shots of the action yesterday, and I'm going out for more now! Want to come along?'

'Sure.' When they reached the commons, about 600 people had already gathered near the Victory Bell, and the two joined some friends on the grass by Johnson Hall.

Most of the gang were discussing events of the previous nights, but stopped when the jeep came up, telling the group to disperse. 'As the jeep came up, some idiot threw a rock,' says Dane. 'How crazy can you get? We didn't want to hassle the Guard, but when they started shooting tear gas Jeff and I both got mad. We held our ground during two rounds of the gas, but it was getting pretty thick there for a while.'

'You motherfuckers,' Jeff yelled at the Guard. (He dominates one photograph, his two middle fingers high in the air as he yells, 'Pigs off campus, you motherfuckers!') He continued his shouts as the Guard marched past on their way to the fence. When the Guard began to retreat up the hill after the interval at the football practice field, Jeff assumed that the confrontation was over, at least for the time being, and he started jumping around in excitement and glee. 'We really showed them that time!'

As the Guard neared the top of the hill, Jeff and Dane were standing on the side of the road that separated Taylor Hall from the football field, expecting to see the Guard disappear beyond the pagoda. Jeff stood facing the rear Guardsmen, while Dane was on an angle, facing Jeff, with his back to Taylor Hall. When the first shots rang out, Dane looked away from Jeff to see what was happening on the hill. 'It must be blanks,' he said, but as he saw the guns pointed in his direction, he turned back to Jeff. 'I was going to say we'd better get out of there, no matter what was in the guns,' but by the time he started to speak, Jeff was already lying in a rapidly expanding pool of blood, for a bullet had caught him full in the face.

Walking to campus early Monday morning, Bill Schroeder remarked to one of his roommates, Bruce Smith, 'It feels like we're walking through a war zone, rather than going to class.' As they left Franklin Street, where they lived, and turned up Summit, the first thing they spied at the gas station on the corner of Summit and Water was an old Plymouth, its trunk open, while an attendant poured gas into large five-gallon containers. Schroeder commented, 'I thought gas sales of this sort were banned by the mayor,' but Smith shrugged it off as another of the many laws aimed at students which townspeople did not feel obliged to obey.

As they continued up Summit they found more symbols of violence. First came an empty tear-gas canister, which they spotted lying in the street. 'I'll get it,' Bill said as he picked it up and turned it over to a Guardsman who was sitting in a nearby truck. Next they came across a rather crudely made Molotov cocktail—a Coke bottle filled with gasoline, with a wick at the end which had not been used, so Bill picked it up, too, and poured out the gas. Finally, as they reached the campus, they were confronted by an armored personnel carrier waiting at the gate of the school. At this, the two boys just shrugged and parted ways. Bill headed for Kent Hall to do a little last-minute studying for the ROTC test scheduled for later that morning.

Although Bill was attending ROTC that day, he wasn't required to wear his uniform. Instead he was decked out in his favorite pants: some gold-orange bell-bottoms he called his 'Brian Jones pants,' after the late member of the Rolling Stones. He had on a striped T-shirt and a blue denim jacket that his grandfather had given him; from its zipper dangled two enamel flowers, one yellow, one purple. He frequently kidded friends: 'You know what this is, don't you? My Purple Heart.'

Promptly at 11:00 Bill entered 4 North Hall, and began to take his test in war tactics, in which he was called upon to write an order to accomplish a theoretical military mission. Completing the test shortly before noon, he left the building, which was located next to the remains of the burned-out ROTC building, and saw an old high school friend, Gene Pekarik. 'Going to the rally, Bill?' Gene asked.

'Yeah, I just want to see what happens. Come along.'

As they started off, they saw Bill's friend, Captain Peters, standing near the ROTC ruins. Bill said, 'I just can't understand why they burned this building,' and the captain agreed. Then Peters warned Bill, 'Stay out of the way today. Don't get mixed up in any crowd.' Bill answered, 'Yeah, sure,' and he and Gene continued toward Gene's dorm, Johnson Hall, from which they intended to watch the rally.

As they walked, Gene told Bill about the events of Sunday night, since Bill had been at home and didn't know too much about the confrontation. They were both of the opinion that there would be no violence at the noon rally, because people would have fairly well released their energies during the previous night. Gene said, 'I sure hope there are no trigger-happy reactionaries with their guns in the Guard,' and Bill reassured him, 'A lot of the Guards I've seen don't even have clips in their guns.'

As they neared the crowd on the commons they could hear the chant: 'Pigs off campus!' When the jeep came up to order the crowd to disperse, the two boys started up the hill toward Johnson Hall, while the main body of the crowd stood firm. When the Guard launched their first advance toward the students, behind the canisters of tear gas, Bill and Gene were separated as they retired toward Taylor Hall. While the Guard proceeded to the practice field, Bill went down to the parking lot, where a few minutes later he heard the opening round of gunfire. Instinctively, he hit the ground, face pointed away from the pagoda, and either as he was on the way down or as he lay prone, one of the steel-jacketed bullets entered his back at the seventh rib, continued up past the next two, shattered the fourth rib, deflected inward to penetrate his lung, then exploded outward through the left shoulder. He was thus shot from the rear, from the lower portion of his body toward the upper, and at a great distance from the Guard.

As he lay on the ground, those about him saw the look of agony on his face. When the firing stopped, he was surrounded by a group of students attempting awkwardly to help him. He asked weakly, 'Is an ambulance coming?' and remained conscious for the interminable ten minutes before its arrival. As the medics tried to hoist him on the stretcher, he moved his leg up to help them. At this moment Gene, who had heard that Bill had been shot, rushed up and looked on in anguish. There was nothing he could do, for the young ROTC man was dying.

On Monday morning a very tired and keyed-up Allison Krause returned to her dorm. She had spent the night in Tri-Towers and had been unable to sleep because students from all over the campus had flocked there after the confrontation with the Guard.

Allison and Barry had split up after leaving the Towers, deciding that they would eat in their respective dorms, not go to class, and meet for the rally at noon. When Allison reached Engleman, she went to see her close friend, Bonnie Henry, and recounted the previous night's adventure, concluding, 'The whole thing was very hectic.' Allison told Bonnie, 'I have to feed Yossarian, so I won't be coming to lunch,' but she arranged for Bonnie to join her and Barry for the rally. As they were parting, Bonnie told Allison, 'I'm afraid something might really happen at the rally.'

'Don't be afraid,' Allison said, but then she added, 'I'm a little scared too.'

Bonnie arrived at the rally too late to find Allison and Barry, for the two were deep in the crowd and were on the commons when the order came to disperse. Dressed in jeans, sneakers, a gray T-shirt with the name 'Kennedy' across the chest, and an old army jacket, Allison was a rather conspicuous figure as the Guard pushed the students over the hill by Taylor Hall. Hovering near Taylor, and one of the last students to move before the advance of the Guard, Allison had gotten over her fear, and was completely incensed by the actions of the Guard.

'You motherfuckers,' she yelled at the Guard, 'get off our campus.' Turning to the students running by her, she yelled several times, 'Do something! Do something!'

With Barry, Allison then ran toward the pagoda. As Barry yelled directions to her over the noise of the crowd, the two headed for the base of the hill, entered the parking lot, and watched as the Guard milled around on the practice field. Although there wasn't much chance to talk, they shared the same sentiments: this wasn't as frightening as Sunday night, when the Guard had been a bayonet-thrust away.

They became more cautious, however, when the Guard knelt and raised their guns at the students. For some curious reason Allison said, 'Since the Guard is actually pointing their guns at the students, they can't possibly shoot.' Barry agreed. 'If they had fired a warning shot, it'd be a different story, but this is nothing.' When the Guard rose from their kneeling position and began their ascent of the hill, Barry and Allison exchanged victorious glances, and Barry yelled to Allison, 'They ran out of gas. The whole thing's over.'

They remained in the parking lot as the Guard neared the pagoda. Suddenly they heard shots, and Barry called to Allison, 'Get down!' They both knelt behind a car. For at least ten seconds after the firing stopped, Barry congratulated himself that they were safe. Then he heard Allison whisper, 'Barry, I'm hit.'

He glanced at her, unbelieving. He saw no wound, no blood. 'No, no!' he reassured her.

'Barry,' she repeated, 'I'm hit,' and now he saw blood coming from under her arm.

'Ambulance, ambulance!' he began to scream, and after a long time one arrived.

On Monday Doug Wrentmore decided to allow himself the luxury of sleeping a little later than usual. 'For the first time this quarter, I decided to cut my 12:05 English class in order to go to the noon rally, and there was no thought of attending my 7:45 geography class, so I lay in bed until about 10:30.'

After dressing, he crossed the parking lot between his house and the town's only A&P, where he bought several small pies to take to school for lunch. He returned home, got one of his roommates out of bed, and walked up East College to campus, where the two of them waited at the Union for another roommate to join them.

By noon Doug became impatient and decided to set out on his own for the rally. Crossing behind Van Deusen, he arrived on the ridge by Johnson Hall just in time to see and hear the warning jeep. He witnessed the exchange of tear gas and watched as Guards drove the students past Taylor Hall. Still alone, he decided he wanted to see what would happen on the other side of Taylor, but rather than follow the crowd over the hill, for that might be dangerous, he made a wide and prudent swing to the tennis courts, around Taylor Hall and back to the pagoda. This put him in position to see most of the action, and as he stood between Taylor and Johnson he saw four or five students in the parking lot throwing rocks at the Guard, while the Guard knelt and aimed their guns directly at the students.

'With that, I decided that things were getting much too dangerous for me. I've never had a gun pointed at me before, so I started to leave, walking toward the parking lot at Prentice Hall.' As he left, he was careful to stay free from the main body of students, telling himself, 'I'll be a lot safer if I'm not in the middle of a crowd.' Consequently, most of the students were to his left, closer to Taylor. He also kept looking anxiously over his shoulder, charting the movement of the Guard, who were now retreating up the hill, away from him, and right toward the pagoda, where he had been standing.

As Doug reached the parking lot, the Guard reached the pagoda, and he was now more than 300 feet away from them. However, he continued to walk even farther away. Then he heard a noise which he took for firecrackers, and as he turned to investigate, he saw the distant Guardsmen kneeling down as they had done on the football field. (We know that they did not kneel; it only looked that way.) He took two steps back toward the Guard, in order to determine what was going on, but on the third step, his right leg gave way, pitching him onto the ground. Crouching beneath a car, he inspected his trousers and saw a little hole outlined by red. He realized that he'd been hit. 'Buckshot,' he said. Half standing, half sitting, he again tried to see what was happening. As he looked up the hill, he saw three or four students running, while others were prone on the ground. In bewilderment he heard a boy yell to him, 'Get down! That's live ammunition!' Obediently, he sank to the pavement.

After the shooting stopped, he dragged himself erect, calling out for help. No one came, and before he limped away, he paused to inspect the blue Chevrolet which had shielded him, and noted that it had been completely shot up. A fragment of one of the bullets which had wrecked the car had penetrated his leg. We know these small details because Doug was the only one of the five students we have been following who lived. (Of course, eight other wounded students also survived.)

Returning to her house on East Summit after Monday morning classes, Sandy Scheuer happened to meet a boy who lived just around the corner from her, Ellis Berns. During the year the two had become fairly good friends and they immediately started talking about topic number one: events of the weekend. Ellis came directly to the point: 'Too much gas had been thrown on this campus for this to continue as a game. It's got to come down to a life-death situation.' Sandy shook her head as if this were impossible. The two spoke for a few minutes, and as Ellis left to go to class, Sandy said to him, 'I'm not sure whether I'll go to the rally or not.'

When she reached home, however, about 11:15 or 11:30, she found one of her roommates, Jan Reinstein, sitting on the front porch, and the two girls decided to risk a look around campus. 'We weren't exactly sure whether the rally had been banned . . . off-campus students are usually the last ones to know anything. But we thought it was on, since we'd both been to class and nothing had been said. I'd even taken the precaution to ask one of the Guardsmen on Sunday if his gun was loaded, and he told me no,' says Jan.

She waited while Sandy left her purse and books in the house, taking only a pencil and a piece of paper with her; these she would use during her 1:10 class. Tucking them into the tan leather coat she was wearing over a red shirt and jeans, she was ready to go.

As they walked toward the campus, Nick Mamula came over to see if they were going to the rally. The three set off together, accompanied by Heavy, a dog that belonged to three girls living on the upper floor of Sandy's house. The group walked up Summit, crossed onto campus by McGilvrey Hall, and went straight to the Student Union. Outside the Union, Sandy met a boy whom she tutored in speech therapy, and these four continued on to the rally. Since they couldn't go directly from the Union to the commons, they detoured around Engleman Hall, and came onto the commons beside the tennis courts.

As soon as the Guard began shooting gas into the crowd, Nick and Jan decided they'd had enough, and ran to the safety of the tennis courts. Sandy meanwhile had found two other friends, Joel Schackne and Roy Zagon, and with them, ran into Johnson Hall and waited until the tear gas cleared. They left Johnson, then watched the antics on the practice field, where students and Guardsmen were heaving rocks back and forth.

Sandy, her eyes streaming from the effects of the tear gas, decided to quit the crowd, and headed toward Music and Speech, where her 1:10 class was to meet. As she crossed the roadway leading into the parking lot, she happened to see Ellis Berns again.

'I saw Sandy, and what do you suppose?' says Ellis. 'She's walking through a demonstration where there's bound to be a lot of tear gas, and what does she have? A little corner of Kleenex. So I tore my rag in half and gave it to her to wipe the gas off her face, because her eyes were still streaming. She had a class, I think. Anyway, I had my books and she had a coat. We sort of started walking away from the whole scene. I was headed to talk things over with my girl friend, and Sandy was walking along with me, just rapping about the morning.'

As they left the area, they heard a noise behind them, and half-turned to see what was happening. This meant that they were facing right into the volley of shots coming from the hill. Ellis grabbed Sandy, intending to run toward a car, but instead the two hit the ground, with Ellis' arm around her waist. They lay there for a moment until the firing ended. Then Ellis turned to Sandy and said, 'Let's go.' She made no movement, and he looked again and saw that she had been hit somewhere in the neck, and that the pavement was being stained with her blood.

The peacemakers

When the Guards completed their retreat after their fusillade at the pagoda, they reported to the ROTC site, where they entered a large defensive circle which Guardsmen from other units had formed, backs to the center, faces outward, guns at the ready as if they were members of a wagon train preparing to hold off Indians.

This may seem unnecessarily cautious, but it was a prudent move on the part of General Canterbury, for something was happening on the commons which only he, who was familiar with riots, could have foreseen. The students, who had witnessed the deaths of four of their members might have been expected to withdraw in terror from the Guard with their deadly M-1's, but they did just the opposite. Canterbury, from experience, had anticipated this. The students followed the Guard down the hill, took up menacing positions, and prepared for random battle. Far from being frightened by death, they were emboldened by it.

From the crowd rose many voices demanding that a frontal assault be made on the Guard. 'Let them splatter us if they want to,' was the defiant cry.

'Let's drive those fuckers right off our campus.'

'Let's finish it here and now.'

'If they want to use their goddamned guns, let them splatter us now.'

A girl kept crying, 'Let them shoot us too, if they want to.' She was ready to run down the hill and grab at the M-1 rifles.

There happen to be tapes of the tumult on the hill at this time; some were made by the journalism students who had earlier taped the firing on the hill but others were made by professional radiomen who had reported to the scene. On them one hears enough of the anguished cries of students to know that they indeed were prepared to rush the Guard, even though they knew the power of the M-1. The rhetoric was so inflamed, and the hideous phrase 'Let them splatter us' so nihilistic, that further bloodshed seemed unavoidable.

How was this human powder keg defused? By the insight and energy of three determined professors.

Seymour H. Baron, a psychologist from Tulane, bald and bearded, carried the main burden. Mike Lunine, the political scientist from Iowa and Istanbul, in those few minutes demonstrated his mastery of the politics of force. And as one might have suspected, Glenn Frank behaved like the good father he was. During this great crisis, no administrators were in evidence, no coaches, no counselors. But in a way, it was appropriate that guidance should have been given by faculty members, for historically that should be their purpose in a university.

The quality of this meeting—five hundred unarmed students massed on one part of the commons; a couple of hundred National Guardsmen, less than fifty yards away, expecting an assault; a tense audience of several thousand watching from the sidelines—can best be understood by listening to fragments of the tapes:

VOICE: . . . Are we going to have any kind of retaliation? Because people were killed.

BARON: All right. This guy's asking about retaliation. Now what does retaliation mean? Retaliation means escalation. Two students have been shot. I saw one with a hole in his arm.

VOICE: I just mean justice.

BARON: What justice? Leave them alone, will you?

VOICE: Let's go down there and get them.

BARON: They killed somebody, and I'm sure the guy who did it is going to sweat blood. I wouldn't want to have his conscience.

VOICE: We're going to try and get a loudspeaker. Okay?

While they searched for a bullhorn, Baron left the students and walked down to the Guard, where he asked, 'Who's in command here?' A captain pointed to General Canterbury and said, 'Talk with the man in the suit.' Baron went to him and said, 'Look, you've got to stop this. You've just shot four students and you can't shoot any more.' Canterbury, pressured on all sides by advice and requests, brushed Baron aside and growled, 'Take this man away.' The captain took Baron by the arm and started to haul him off, but Baron slapped his hand away and said crisply, 'Don't grab me. I'm going back there to see what I can do.' The captain dropped his hand and said, 'Good luck.'

The students found two bullhorns, and thereafter Baron spoke with both held to his mouth. At first he was able to accomplish little, for through the entire mass of students ran an insane desire to charge the Guards, to have the shooting over with once and for all. It was a suicide wish that is clearly audible on the tapes and attested to by many students who participated: 'If they want to kill us all, let them do it now.' Baron realized that some kind of break in the confrontation was necessary, so he ran down the hill again to consult with General Canterbury, pleading, 'You've got to give those kids some kind of sign.' Canterbury asked, 'Sign of what?' and Baron said, 'That you're not going to shoot. That we can quieten this thing down. Isn't there some kind of order, like "parade rest"?' Several Guardsmen, hearing these words, dropped their guns, whereupon Canterbury shouted, 'Shoulder those guns!' Baron's voice broke, and he begged, 'General, can't you make them stop pointing those guns as if they were going to fire?' General Canterbury reflected, looked at the massed students, and said, 'Parade rest.' Down went the guns.

BARON: Let me tell you, I spoke to the general down there, and believe me, we've got a real live general. He doesn't wear a soldier's suit but he's a general, and I said, 'Listen, you guys have caused enough trouble here today. Now for God's sake, will you put your guns away?' and he said, 'Soldiers have no right to put guns down. That's against their rules and regulations.' So I said, 'Well, what do you do when you hold your guns so the people know you're not going to shoot them?' They've got them now in what I think they call 'parade rest.' Now let me tell you this. I said to him, 'You have already committed a couple of crimes here today. You've already caused some very serious problems. You've killed at least one student that I know of and another was helped into the ambulance. Another one got a .30-caliber round through his shoulder.' Now they've got live ammo. I wouldn't have believed that. They've got live ammo in those guns. Now if you walk down toward them, I promise you they'll kill you. Now the reason they'll kill you is because they're scared to death. They're a bunch of summertime soldiers. They have no idea of what soldiering is about or what war is about. These guys aren't pros. They're scared stiff. There is only one way you're going to stay alive, and that is to stay here. I don't want you going down there. I don't want you going after them. Some of you guys feel that you have to be heroes. You can be heroes, but there are girls and people here who don't want to get shot and killed. That includes me. Now I don't know when they're going to go home. All I can say is don't go down. Don't go near them. They've got guns and live ammo.

VOICE: Who ordered them to shoot?

BARON: My answer is I don't know. I can tell you this. You put live ammunition in a gun with a scared kid behind it and you've had it. And we've had it. Please, don't let anybody start you again in going across this campus. We've had bloodshed. It's a terrible thing that's happened here today. This campus will never forget it. Don't start chasing across this field again. I want you to understand that the faculty is with you with regard to this Vietnam thing. We're with you. We're with you all the way. So for heaven's sake, cool it, calm it and enjoy the sun. Those guys will stay there for a while. Their feet will start to hurt and maybe they'll go home.

Mike Lunine now ran down to the Guard, located General Canterbury, and said, 'You've got to do everything you can to keep your troops under control. There must be no more shooting.' Canterbury merely stared at him, but two university functionaries standing with the Guard volunteered the comment, 'Those students shouldn't be on that hill. There has to be a line drawn somewhere. We've got to have law and order.' Lunine went back to tell the students what they faced.

VOICE: Let them splatter us.

VOICE: Let's face this thing right now.

BARON: Wait a minute. Wait a minute. Are any of you kids hungry? I'm damned hungry.

LUNINE: For God's sake, some of you fellows who want to move, go get us something to eat. We'll have a bite to eat, then we'll get the hell out of here.

He then returned to the Guard and again begged them not to shoot, and again one of the functionaries warned him, 'Professor Lunine, the National Guard does not negotiate under siege.' Lunine asked who was besieging the Guard, and the official pointed to the students. Lunine was trembling when he returned to the students, and told those standing near him an extraordinary thing, the precise sort of thing a professor would say at such a crisis, 'Students, the imminence of slaughter is great.'

BARON: I'm scared to death that somebody else is going to get shot and killed.

VOICE: Man, you take Martin Luther King. He wouldn't be scared.

BARON: Martin Luther King would not have stayed. Martin Luther King was a man who understood that to win you must live. If you die, you cannot win anything. You must live to win. I don't want you kids to die. That won't win you kids peanuts.

VOICE: Let them splatter us right now.

BARON: There are too many of you who are too damned good to die in this stinking field here.

At this critical moment of the impasse, a tall, ubiquitous figure with red hair and flowing sideburns left the mass of students, walked with dignity toward the National Guard, and announced, 'I am here to speak with General Canterbury.'

'Who in hell are you?' asked one of the men guarding the perimeter.

Pointing to his blue armband, the young man replied, 'I am a member of the faculty, here to do what I can to prevent a tragedy.' When asked his name, he said, 'Steve Sharoff.'

He spoke with such authority that the Guardsman not only allowed him to pass within the perimeter but also took him to Canterbury.

'General,' said Sharoff, 'I can't get those kids to move.'

'You get them out of there,' Canterbury snapped.

'You don't understand. Four of their friends have been killed.'

'I have my orders. They have got to go.' When Sharoff heard these harsh words he started to protest, but Canterbury repeated bluntly, 'Those students have got to go.'

Trembling, Sharoff left the Guard. He realized that the students were determined not to move and the Guard were equally determined to move them. He says, 'A further tragedy was about to happen, and during the few steps it took me to get back to the students, who might be shot at any moment, I broke down. I started to cry, but then I said to myself, "Christ, I'm well known on this campus. If I lose my head, it would look pathetic." So I pulled myself together.' Several students in the seated mob have testified that it was Sharoff's cool behavior that encouraged them to get themselves under control. 'He moved among us and talked sense,' they reported. A few hours later, when Steve reviewed his actions with Bob Franklin, the latter looked at him in amazement and said, 'Sharoff, sometimes you are out of sight . . . man, you are out of sight.'

Now the day's most dramatic interview with General Canterbury occurred. It involved, of course, Glenn Frank, who had left the students in order to make one last appeal. As he moved toward the Guards he was met by a contingent under the leadership of Major Harry Jones, who up to now had tried to calm the action. It looked as if Jones intended leading his men into the mob of students, and Frank pleaded with him, 'For God's sake, don't come any closer.' Jones replied, 'My orders are to move ahead,' and Frank said quietly, 'Over my dead body.' There was a moment of dreadful indecision, and the Guard refrained from trying to force the issue at that moment.

Frank then went over to where Canterbury was discussing strategy with Captain Ron Snyder. 'You have got to give us a little time,' Frank begged. Snyder remembers the general as replying, 'They're going to have to find out what law and order is all about.' Frank was close to hysteria as he pleaded, 'Give us time, General.' Canterbury told him, 'I'll give you five minutes,' but Major Manly, in command of 181 members of the highway patrol, told Frank reassuringly, 'Take all the time you need.'

Frank was already distraught when he left the general, but as he walked back uphill to the waiting students, he saw a sight which truly terrified him. Quietly, but giving forth a sense of deadly power, a line of Guardsmen had taken a position running from Taylor Hall past the pagoda to Johnson. The students could now be attacked from three sides. Scores of them have testified as to the terror of that moment, none more profoundly than the girl who said, 'My heart went out of me.' A tape from a radio station best tells what happened next.

(MUCH YELLING, THREATS, CURSES, GENERAL NOISE)

VOICE (over the mob): Here's Glenn Frank.

VOICES (over the mob): Hold on, hold on. Wait a minute. Hold it.

FRANK (with deep, choking emotion): I don't care whether you've never listened to anyone before in your lives. I am begging you right now. If you don't disperse right now, they're going to move in, and it can only be a slaughter. Would you please listen to me?

That was all he said, but the students did listen. They reacted to the anguish in his voice, and after a while they did move away in small groups. The slaughter was averted.

There was a minority report on the peacemakers. Stu Feldstein says, 'I stayed with the group on the hill and sat down with them while Dr. Baron and Dr. Frank pleaded and, I thought, worked themselves up to a point of hysteria much more extreme than the students felt. They seemed convinced the kids were about to charge the Guard in some kind of kamikaze operation, so, while everyone stayed on the hill, Frank and Baron were running around trying to prevent more slaughter by reasoning with both sides at a time when nothing was going by logic. I suppose they didn't do any harm, although I was tremendously annoyed by Baron's comment that the faculty was behind the students a hundred percent this time, because I knew that was an outlandish exaggeration. There would be plenty of profs, maybe most, who, while they wouldn't condone the murders . . . maybe some did . . .

would at least be saying, "If the protesters hadn't started up in the first place . . ." This past fall it was like pulling teeth to get profs to excuse students from classes for the October 15 moratorium, and last spring the faculty agreed unanimously not to change the status of ROTC the least bit. I knew some profs personally who were right-wingers, and more who were ten years behind the times, still wondering what all the fuss was about.

'I left campus, but not before hearing that vigilante groups were forming in the town to get any students who remained.'

Professor Perry, leaving the campus in the opposite direction, heard a hard-core group of radical students calling to friends, 'Now we've got the sons of bitches. This whole thing was President White's fault. Let's find some guns and drive that bastard off this campus.'

And Mike Lunine, after waiting to be sure that the students were safely dispersed, 'walked like a zombie back to my quarters, and as I was going I heard someone from the city shouting, "It's going to be very bad. Five hundred Black Panthers are on their way here from Cleveland with carloads of dynamite. They're going to level every building in the university." '

Conclusions

Strict interpretation of Ohio's riot act—'five or more persons engaged in violent or tumultuous conduct which creates a clear and present danger'—would legally justify terming the conduct of students on Monday as a riot, but all investigative agencies have refrained from doing so, primarily because the students assembled peacefully, conducted themselves at the beginning non-tumultuously, and never acted in concert. Experts have concluded that there was no riot, in the commonly accepted sense of that word, but there were individual acts of 'tumultuous conduct' which should have been halted and, if persisted in, punished. We agree.

The National Guard was in control at all times and present in such numbers as to protect its members from critical assault. Of the 3,600 people, more or less, who watched the proceedings, most of them at great distances from the action, only a small number were involved in overt actions against the Guard. Police would have been justified in arresting some 120 for individual 'tumultuous conduct,' but none of this group would have deserved serious sentences. About thirty others could have been charged with riot in the second degree, but again their provocation was of a minor nature and would not have warranted major jail sentences. Perhaps as many as ten could have been charged with the serious offense of inciting to riot and impeding agents of the law in the performance of their duty. (It is ironic that if all the arrests justified for Friday, Saturday, Sunday and Monday had been made, not one of the major radical figures mentioned in this book would have been taken into custody; the groundwork for the May disturbances had been laid far in the past, and those responsible were long absent from the scene; furthermore, the new cadre of secret leaders who did operate on campus were not visible during the trouble and thus were not subject to arrest; only the minor and obstreperous figures could have been caught.)

There was no sniper. There was no order from General Canterbury to fire. There is no acceptable proof of collusion on the part of officers or men to account for that sudden and dramatic turn of 135° before firing, but it seems likely that some kind of rough verbal agreement had been reached among the troops when they clustered on the practice field. The Guard was in no mortal danger at the time of firing, for the nearest students were at least twenty yards away and in no menacing number. That so many of the Guard elected to fire in the air was a miracle for which everyone can be grateful.

As to the testimony of the Canadian housewife, we remain confused. That she and her professor neighbor are reporting accurately what they heard, there can be no doubt, but how to interpret what they heard, we do not know. Regarding the charge that the Guardsmen assembled after the firing and fabricated a story that they had considered themselves to have been in mortal danger, we suspect that this happened but that its significance has been overstated and falsely interpreted. Certain of the Guardsmen did so believe and did act upon that belief; what they did later was to convince their friends of their own fear.

We have dissected all adverse evidence, explored each ugly rumor, but we cannot convince ourselves that murder was committed by the Guard. It was an accident, deplorable and tragic. If evidence should surface to prove there was collusion or that certain Guardsmen boasted on Sunday night that 'tomorrow I'm gonna shoot me some students,' this conclusion will look ridiculous, but such evidence was not available to us, even though we searched for it most diligently. There was death, but not murder.

There remains the question, 'Was it the presence of the Guard that triggered the Monday disturbance? Were they the true outside agitators?' We have been much impressed by the pastoral calm shown in photographs of the commons taken before noon that day and have had to conclude that the students did not gather to riot. It has been these impressive photographs that have restrained other committees from declaring Monday's action a riot, so it is logical to argue that had the Guard not been there, no disturbance would have developed. But this is irrelevant; the Guard was there and for understandable reason. Society had assembled combustible materials, and no one should be surprised that they ignited.

Of the final group of students standing on the porch at Taylor Hall or traversing the parking lot in the distance, a good 70 percent were entitled to be exactly where they were, and it is improper to argue, 'They shouldn't have been there in the first place.' Of the remainder, 25 percent had constituted the mobile cheering section for the harassment of the Guard and about 5 percent the hard-core rock-and-canister throwers.

Professor Murvin Perry made a conscious effort to identify the leaders and found no recognizable students among them. Photographer Harold Walker took special notice of a gang of Che Guevara types off to one side at the practice field, shouting encouragement, so it seems probable that there were some agitators from off-campus, but there is little evidence that anyone did much leading, which is another reason why investigative agencies have been reluctant to term this a riot. Campus figures who had arranged the noontime rally, beginning on Friday noon, did not have university permission, and when they circulated notices on Saturday, they were still acting outside university law, but had broken no civil law. As to the legal status on Sunday and especially Monday, there is such confusion that we have always suspected that major indictments issued for Monday would not stand up in court. That the outdoor rally had been prohibited, there can be no doubt, but that thousands of students and scores of professors did not know this is incontrovertible.

No student performed any act on May 4 for which he deserved to be shot. We do not believe that Jeff Miller carried a gun.

The National Guard of each state determines whether or not it will use live ammunition in curbing riots; Ohio is one of the few states that does. It is noteworthy that in a public-opinion poll held in Columbus, long after the troubles, 72.2 percent of Ohio residents believed that their Guardsmen should continue to load with live ammunition and use it whenever the officers deemed it necessary. There can be no doubt but that the actions of the Guard on May 4 were approved by the majority of Ohio citizens, but the question still remains whether the death of four students should in some way be punished. No matter what one's personal feelings in this matter may be, Ohio law is specific:

> 2923.55 *Liability of law enforcement officers for use of force during riot.* Members of the organized militias when engaged in suppressing a riot or in dispersing or apprehending rioters and after an order to desist and disperse has been issued, are guiltless for killing, maiming, or injuring a rioter as a consequence of the use of such force as is necessary and proper to suppress the riot or disperse or apprehend rioters.

It may be argued, as these conclusions do, that no riot existed on May 4, but a riotous condition did, and that would seem to justify application of the above law.

That no military court-martial was convened to look into the shootings and to explain them to the public was deplorable; if the Guard is exempt from civil law, as many believe it has to be, then there is treble responsibility for the military to clean up its own affairs, not to punish but to explain. One of the most dangerous conditions that could exist in America would be for the civilian population to turn its sympathies against the military, and the best way to prevent this is for the military always to present clean hands to civilian eyes.

The United States cannot allow young people to be shot down in its streets, for if this were to become common, a revulsion would result of such dimension as to sweep away our forms of government. Young people who brazenly defy soldiers, daring them to shoot, commit more than suicide; they commit a grave crime against organized society. And soldiers or policemen who fire without ultimate provocation run the grave risk of alienating the support which sustains them.

We were driven to one final and significant conclusion. The hard-core revolutionary leadership across the nation was so determined to force a confrontation—which would result in gunfire and the radicalization of the young—that some kind of major incident had become inevitable. It was bound to come within the twelve-month and it could have happened on any campus which experienced physical unrest. That it happened at Kent State was pure accident, but the confrontation itself was not.

VI

REACTION

Day of a photographer

John Filo was scared. A huge man six-feet-three and over 215 pounds, he would have looked like a football guard except for his full Abraham Lincoln beard. He probably could have handled anyone who wanted to give him trouble, but he was scared.

'I'd seen so many photographers attacked in the last few days . . . Well, all the radicals were uptight about getting their photos taken, because they might be used for identification later on. They'd already clubbed me when I was taking my photos of Jeff Miller, so I was real scared.'

It was about two hours after the shooting, and ugly rumors were scurrying through the campus. Vigilantes were going to shoot up the place. They were stopping all cars and searching them for guns or cameras. Who knew what to believe?

'What I did believe,' Filo says, 'was that on the six rolls of film I'd exposed—that's thirty-six to a roll, or over 200 shots—I simply had to have something important. What it might be I didn't know, because I'd been shooting in a daze, but I had tried to stand at the heart of the action. I'd been gassed and shot at and run over and knocked down and clubbed over the head, and I ought to have something on those films.'

He was gripped by an obsession: 'I've got to get these films out of Ohio.' So he hid them in various parts of his Volkswagen, made his Nikkormatic as inconspicuous as possible, and slipped down back roads till he made his way across the Pennsylvania line. Only then did he pause to telephone his hometown newspaper, the *Valley Daily News* of Tarentum, Pennsylvania. With restraint he told the editor, 'I think I might have something good,' and the editor said, 'Bring them in and let's see.' Filo explained, 'They aren't developed yet,' and the editor said, 'We'll take care of that.' So Filo continued east along the turnpike.

He had grown up near Tarentum, north of Pittsburgh, where his father worked as a foreman for Allegheny Ludlum Steel. The old man had always dreamed of having John go into dentistry, 'a clean, dignified profession,' but one wrestling match with chemistry and math satisfied the boy that this was not for him. 'Besides, I liked reading too much. So I switched to journalism and discovered that I had a feeling for photography, but I kept philosophy and sociology as my minors. So that I'd understand a good story if I came upon it.'

As he sped east, he thought it was pretty ironic that he was going so far to develop his pictures when he could have driven only a few miles to the offices of the Akron *Beacon Journal*. 'I couldn't think kindly of that paper,' Filo explains. 'Six months earlier I had sent them a set of first-rate shots and they'd used them. Then they told me they were sorry but they'd lost the negatives. I said, "That happens. I'm sure you didn't mean it." So I had no negatives, no recognition, and no desire to lug these new negatives into Akron.'

When he reached the offices of the *Valley Daily News* he had a prudent idea. He handed over to the darkroom the roll that he felt had the least on it, as a precaution in case they didn't know their job. The technicians ran it through 'and everybody gasped, the pictures were so perfect. So I handed them the roll that I suspected had the good stuff, and when Chuck Carroll, the man in charge, saw the first staggering shots of the dead, the chaos, the Guardsmen looking like men from Mars, and that picture of the girl kneeling in the blood, he ran to the Associated Press transmitting wire and rang the bell vigorously to attract the attention of the retransmittal center in Philadelphia. But the wires were already loaded with interesting photographs coming from Kent and they wanted no interruptions. His bell was ignored.

'What pained me,' Filo says, 'was that the transmissions were coming from the Akron *Beacon Journal*, and I supposed they were scooping me. I was sure of it when Philadelphia broke in to scold us: "Akron is sending important pictures. Stand by." But Chuck interrupted and said, "I think we may have something here." Philadelphia asked, "So who in hell is the *Valley Daily News?*" And while we had the wire, Chuck put on the first of the good pictures, and for about an hour

Philadelphia kept everyone else off. You might say,' Filo says quietly, 'that we blew Akron right off the wire.'

His powerful portraits appeared in all the leading newspapers of the world: *New York Times, Asahi Shimbun* of Tokyo, three different dailies in Rome. Filo had asked no payment for his pictures, but editors everywhere recognized them as social documents, and when the excitement had subsided, the Associated Press volunteered to pay him at their top rates.

The county prosecutor

No one followed events at Kent with closer attention than a husky, quick-witted lawyer in Ravenna. Ron Kane, thirty-five years old, had had a colorful career and had acquired a vocabulary to match. When accused of being overly ambitious, he snorts, 'Why would I want to be a congressman? Wasn't it Mark Twain who said, "You can teach a flea anything you can teach a congressman"?'

Round of face, rapid in speech, enthusiastic in everything he does, he had been merely another small-town lawyer with a night-school degree when his shrewd older brother, Herb Kane, behind-the-scenes power in the local Republican party, had the bright idea of running him for county prosecutor. Ron, who had been a basketball player and who handled himself well, proved popular in large gatherings and won easily. He was good-looking, energetic and sharp; clearly he was on his way. Of the many persons mentioned in this book, Ron Kane is the one to remember, for he is bound to be heard from politically in the future.

There is some question as to whether Ron 'has it in for the university.' He attended a pre-law course there at one time, not too successfully, but in citing his own biography he avoids mention of this. He swears, 'Me? Mad at the university? Ridiculous! All I want is for it to behave like it's a part of Portage County . . . subject to our laws. I want its students to behave on our streets and its professors to shape up.' Friends who know Ron say, 'He's determined to make the university behave . . . his way.'

Kane knows that in the drug problem at Kent State he has a permanent issue which infuriates the people of Portage County. They want the drug traffic at the university eliminated and applaud whenever Kane goes into action. Technically, he could arrest 80 percent of the student body any time he wanted to, for under Ohio law, as we have seen, that proportion is probably guilty of at least one narcotics offense, but to make mass arrests would be self-defeating, so what Kane does is use a selective method of picking up the worst offenders or those whose arrest would serve some other purpose. He then announces that once more he is keeping check on the staggering narcotics ring operating out of the university.

His other public fight concerns traffic tickets, and here he seems to be on impeccable ground. 'Look at it our way,' he says, his close-cropped head bobbing enthusiastically. 'The damned university was using our public courts to enforce traffic violations on campus, but was pocketing the fines. Our boys did the work. Their boys got the gravy. What kind of game is that? So I instituted suit to recover $50,000 a year in fines, and you could hear them scream all the way to Columbus. I got the $50,000, too.' With this decision, his popularity increased, and it seems likely that he can be re-elected to his present position for as long as he cares to hold it. But observers are certain that older brother Herb has more exalted plans. 'Ron'll be governor one of these days, sure as hell,' Ravenna politicians say. 'Unless he prefers to be United States senator.'

Kane is a most amiable man, and dining with him and his charming wife in their historical house in the center of Ravenna is an enjoyable experience. He gathers about him the community leaders, fascinates them with yarns about the law, and quite captivates anyone who comes in contact with him. He has the gift of being able to tell jokes about himself. Of the Kent affair he says, 'Hell, I was the last man in the county to know. I'd played bridge Saturday night, and had informed my people that I wanted to be alerted the minute there was any follow-up on the Friday night rioting. So far as I knew nothing happened, so I came home and went to bed, but about 3:45 Sunday morning I got this phone call. Lot of excitement about a rape case in Aurora and a sodomy case down county. I got things straightened out and went back to sleep. Few more minutes and another phone call. Same rape, same sodomy. I explained matters again and went back to sleep. About 5:30, same goddamned phone. Rape and sodomy. So I blew my stack. When I finished exploding, the caller added weakly, "We've been under pressure tonight.

That fire at the university." "What fire?" I shouted. "The kids burned down the ROTC building." '

As dawn was breaking, Ron Kane thundered west on Route 59 and pulled up at the smoldering ruins. He was bitterly angry. He had for some time been convinced that sooner or later he was going to have to close down this university. Intuitively he felt, 'I ought to shut this place down right now.' Had he done so, the succeeding tragedy would have been averted. He recalled the morning he had stalked into a meeting at the university—some minor riot or something—with his sleek German shepherd at heel. 'Down, Shadow,' he had commanded, and the dog had quietly taken a position against the wall. 'Hell,' Kane had exploded, 'my dog is more obedient than your students.'

There is contradiction as to what happened next, but regardless of which version is correct, it proves that Kane was on the ball. Some people claim that one of the three phone calls had alerted Ron to the fact that something had gone wrong at the Portage County airport. Others insist that as he stood among the embers of the ROTC building he recalled that some weeks earlier he had received an anonymous phone call which had threatened that if the Liquid Crystals Institute continued to use the airport, the latter would be sabotaged. Of this incident, Kane says, 'Hell, I just had this gut-feeling, "They're bound to hit the airport." '

At any rate, on the spur of the moment Kane left the university, hurried eastward to the Portage County airport, and found that during the night someone had stolen a three-quarter-ton truck from the Umbaugh Pole Building Company, sneaked it onto the airstrip, and rammed six private airplanes, chopping them up pretty badly. The saboteurs had then set fire to a mobile home that was being used as the airport office and totally burned it. Money was stolen; records were destroyed; and a trainer which had cost $7,500 was wrecked. The total loss was about $40,000. This incident must be remembered when trying to assess the spreading spirit of fear that Sunday morning. Students had wrecked Water Street; they had burned down a university building and had threatened to burn more; and an airport some distance from the campus had been attacked and put out of business. Apprehension was justified.

Were students responsible for the airport sabotage? Ron Kane is certain they were, but when the Umbaugh truck was found abandoned, some hours later, it contained a penciled warning: 'If air and water pollution continues in Portage County, all the airports in the county will be burned.' The saboteur could have been a crank unconnected to the university; he could have been some ecology nut from the campus; he could have been someone fighting Liquid Crystals because of what he believed they had done to Che Guevara. In any case, the results were inflammatory.

'So I was busy all morning,' Kane says. 'As I told you, I went to the meeting with Governor Rhodes at the Kent firehouse and tried to persuade him to close the university down, but he thought he knew more about the situation than I did. If he'd listened to me, four kids would be alive now and Ohio would have avoided a scandal.

'Instead, what happened? On Monday at 12:28 I hear over the radio that four students have been shot and nine others wounded. Mad as hell, I called the governor in Columbus . . . about three in the afternoon . . . but couldn't get him. I told his assistant, "Look, we got people dead over here and we got bomb threats up your ass. We hear they're going to hit the town again, and the airport, and a lot of buildings on campus. I'm going to close that place down."

' "What authority will you use for such a thing?"

' "I'll close it down, then look around for the authority."

' "We beg you to postpone your decision for one hour. Governor Rhodes will call you back."

'So I waited for one hour and never heard a word from Columbus. But I hadn't been wasting my time. As soon as the announcement of the killings occurred, I told my legal secretary, "Start typing a petition for an injunction to close that place down." When the governor failed to call back, I carried this petition to one of the greatest judges in Ohio, Albert Caris, eighty years old and he's never had a case reversed by a higher court. I told him, "Judge, Kent State is in turmoil and has got to be closed down." '

Judge Caris, who is listening to this recollection, nods his head. 'That's how it happened,' he affirms. He is a splendid old man, intellectually sharp and devoted to orderly processes.

In this peremptory way a young prosecuting attorney and an elderly judge closed down a great university; in the wake of their decision, 760 major American institutions of higher learning either shut down or came close to doing so. The perilous aspect of the situation is that those in Ravenna who know Ron Kane best are satisfied that if the slightest justification arises, he will not hesitate to close the university again:

'He'll have his secretary type up another petition, and bets are good that Judge Caris will sign it.'

'Ron will never be happy until that place is shut down,' observers say. 'Last time, when he proved that he was right and the governor wrong, his vote-getting potential tripled. He would be very popular in this county if he could get rid of the university once and for all.'

Ron himself denies such animus. 'All I insist upon, as chief legal officer of this county, is that the university behave itself. And that goes equally for the wild-eyed kids and the radical professors.'

No one doubts that the ax is ready to fall.

Closing down

If at the beginning of the incident the administration of the university looked pusillanimous, at the close it looked superb. As soon as Ron Kane's injunction shut the place down, and 21,000 students, most of them without access to transportation, were left stranded but under strict orders to evacuate within the hour, David Ambler, dean for student residence life, had the brilliant idea of wheeling out the thirty-six university buses, loading them with students, and starting them off to Cleveland or Columbus, from which spots frantic students could catch what airplanes were available.

And so the huge blue and gray buses pulled up to arbitrary loading points while weeping girls and young men, paralyzed with rage at what they had seen, piled in for one of the most mournful caravans ever to start from a university town. 'It seemed like a group of dinosaurs,' one coed remembers, 'spreading out across a war-torn landscape. It broke your heart.'

There were some fantastic experiences. For example, Bill Warren, on his way home to New York, found himself sitting next to a book editor on the plane out of Cleveland; by the time the trip had ended, Bill had a contract for a book, *The Middle of the Country*, rushed into print a few weeks later, the first full-length work on Kent State.

Adding to the chaos on campus, at the first sign of trouble the telephone system collapsed. Some students believed 'the FBI ordered all telephones on campus disconnected so they could control everything that happened.' Others said that the telephone company simply closed down from sheer panic.

There was no truth to either of these rumors. It was true that campus telephones were out of order so that no calls were possible, but the reason was much simpler. The telephone system was so overloaded that normal functioning became impossible. It collapsed of its own weight and needed no outside shove.

George Towner, manager of the Kent Bell Telephone, explains, 'Instead of the average Monday load of 118,000 calls, we received more than 352,000 within a brief period. We were swamped; fuses in the dormitories had to be pulled. We did this at 1:00 P.M., or they would have blown. And for the first time in this area . . . maybe the first time anywhere in America . . . we put in Line Load Control. Here's the order.

> Line load control is a method of controlling outgoing calls, in the event of disaster, to insure continuous service to customers who have emergency functions directly contributing to the alleviation of disaster.

> To avoid affecting the service of all customers, switching arrangements are provided in most central offices whereby anyone can receive calls but only those customers whose service is classified as Essential can make them.

> Lines will be divided on a 10-45-45 basis, 10 percent to military and national defense systems, with incoming and outgoing facility; 45 percent service with incoming only; 45 percent to businesses related to the emergency with incoming only; but outgoing may be rotated equally between the Essential lines.

'When you have 21,000 students, each trying to make a long-distance call home, you have to take unusual steps. We did not panic.' The fact is, however, that fuses were pulled on campus and nowhere else, so that the students could not even receive incoming calls.

Students brave enough to remain in Kent had a difficult time. For example, Tim Butz was still having trouble avoiding violence. After the shooting he stayed in his quarters, then decided that he must get out of town. Slipping down side streets, he managed to avoid the police, until he turned a corner and found four policemen handcuffing Craig Morgan and Mike Alewitz.

'Now this was really crazy,' Butz says. 'Two more different guys you couldn't find. Morgan—very tall, very square and reserved. A conservative. Alewitz, short, red-hot leader of the socialists. A real radical. I see them handcuffed and up against the wall, and I do one of those Hollywood turn-arounds. You know, I'm walking toward the police and next step I'm walking away from them. I want to get far away.

'But the cops see me and call to another cop, "Arrest that guy!" So next thing I know I'm up against the wall too. I hear a car drive up, and I look around and there's five guys inside a station wagon, none of them in uniform, but all of them with rifles and shotguns. One of them had an M-16, and that's illegal in the United States. I tried to see who the five men were, but the police jabbed me and said, "You three, don't you look at that!" We turned our faces.'

When the police clicked the handcuffs onto Butz, Mike Alewitz made a wisecrack. 'You getting ready to shoot us, too?'

'Son,' one of the policemen said, 'I hope you have a good dentist.'

'Why?'

'Because if you say one more word, you're not going to have any teeth.'

In jail, Alewitz moaned, 'Outside, the whole world is falling apart, and here I am locked up in the clink.' Then he started to laugh. 'My first time in jail and I'm handcuffed to the top legal eagle in the university.'

Craig Morgan was that. He kept shouting at the guards, 'I'm a pre-law member of the A.C.L.U. and I demand my rights.'

A policeman told him, 'Being a member of that outfit's reason enough to keep you locked up forever,' but finally the students won the right to make one phone call.

'It was a serious decision,' Butz says. 'We were in trouble and had only one dime. Who should we call? Not our parents, because we knew they'd say "Let 'em stay there." We finally decided on Carl Moore. The professor with the red beard. We knew we could trust him.'

They placed the call, and within a few minutes Craig Morgan was sprung. Butz was kept in jail all night, then released. And Mike Alewitz, known to be a troublemaker, was charged with breaking curfew and fined $12. 'Discrimination at its worst,' Butz says.

The experience of Marshall Freeman, president of Wright Hall in Tri-Towers, symbolizes the reaction of those who were determined to hang around: 'Why should we allow them to throw us off our own campus? We'd paid our money and we had a legal right. They succeeded in throwing me out of the dorm, but I cut out across campus to a house where, as I suspected, a lot of my buddies were, and we sat around unable to believe what had happened. So we did the ouija-board bit and talked with the dead kids. I really loved Allison and Barry. They were a noble pair and it broke me up to think that we'd never see her again.

'We tried the astrology bit, seeing what might be in store for the dead ones, and then we ran through the Tarot cards. We were so deep into it, I was almost convinced that Allison was going to come through the door, tall, self-confident, repeating the last words she said to me Sunday night when she was crying after the riot at Tri-Towers. "No matter what happens, Marshall, try to keep your head non-violent." Then she put her arms about me and said, "Remember, you're president of a dorm. You can do things. Infiltrate the system and make things better for all of us." '

Freeman falls silent, and a deep intensity glows in his eyes: 'It was gloomy, man, it was gloomy. So we tried to conjure up the devil, and sometime after midnight he put in an appearance but he didn't have much to offer. It wasn't what you'd call a real grabber, so we went back to the ouija board. And then, about 3:00 A.M., we heard this terrifying thing. Two gunshots. Now nobody will admit that there were two gunshots that night, after all we'd been through, but I swear to you . . . and I wasn't hung up on the devil bit or the Tarot . . . I swear to you I heard two gunshots on campus.'

He was right. In spite of all that had happened, in spite of the Guardsmen everywhere, at some time after 2:00 A.M. determined revolutionaries had crept out to the edge of campus where Allerton and Rhodes Road intersect and had set fire to a sturdy barn in which the university stored athletic gear, snow fences and caretaking equipment. A highly skillful job of arson was done; from eight or nine flash points great flames leaped into the air, silhouetting two men as they escaped across the field. A Guardsman, stationed there to protect the building, got off two hasty shots in their direction, but missed.

The barn was a total loss. If a defiant gesture was needed to prove that Kent State harbored a hard core of revolutionaries ready for any adventure, this arrogant barn-burning provided it.

Students now scattered to all parts of America. The campus was rigidly closed down and not even President White was allowed to visit his office. The library was unavailable and laboratories containing the results of student investigations were padlocked. Rarely in American history has an educational institution been so totally quarantined and so totally empty. Only a handful of campus police roamed the vast, echoing buildings.

It was now that the administration and faculty showed their dedication. President White says, 'I cannot imagine how a body of men and women could have responded to a challenge more brilliantly than they. Aware that their students had to have final grades if they wanted to proceed with education next year—how would they get into law school or medical school?—our professors set up a hundred different variations for completing their classes and registering grades.'

It wasn't easy. The injunction forbade any meetings of any kind in Kent, so ingenious plans were devised whereby churches in Akron were used, and boy scout headquarters in other towns. Airmail seminars were instituted for students who found it impossible to convene. Professor Glenn Frank jumped in his car, drove a wide circuit through Pennsylvania, New Jersey and New York, holding area sessions wherever he went. Other professors hired mimeograph machines, lectured students by telephone, and typed lesson assignments through the night.

One cannot praise sufficiently the faculty of Kent State for its performance in these last days of spring. They saved many academic careers and won the respect of all.

There was one blemish on the faculty's performance, although when it took place it must have seemed quite the opposite. On Monday the four deaths followed by the total shut-down of the university left the faculty stunned; like other residents of Kent they huddled inside their homes as night fell, adjusting to the fact that they were living in a state of military siege.

By Tuesday their energies revived and they began casting about for some legal manner in which to express their reaction. Two courses seemed logical: either hold a general faculty meeting or convene the smaller and more powerful faculty senate. Younger members inclined toward the former alternative, for then they would be included; older professors preferred the latter, for then the more sober voices would prevail.

But each proposal proved impossible, as the faculty quickly learned, because Satrom's restrictions also applied to them. One astonished faculty member told his wife, 'I wasn't even allowed on the campus. I can't feed the animals in the experimental labs. I can't get my term papers, and I understand that President White isn't permitted to enter his own offices. This is really a blackout.'

Any general faculty meeting either on campus or anywhere within the city of Kent was impossible. Guardsmen prevented the former; the city curfew outlawed the latter. What to do?

On Tuesday morning a Unitarian church in Akron, eleven miles away, hearing of the embargo on faculty meetings within the Kent area, offered its auditorium to the professors, so a strung-out cavalcade of cars and station wagons was improvised, and the faculty convened at the church that afternoon. Of 1,170 eligible members, 550 attended, which is a high proportion for a university, but things were not to be so simple, because a large contingent of teaching fellows and graduate assistants forced their way into the meeting and demanded an equal voice in deliberations which involved them at least as deeply as the tenured professors who sometimes had little direct contact with students. It was these Young Turks who set the tone of the meeting and who were responsible for its excesses. Thus a problem which should have been grappled with long since—how best to incorporate the unaffiliated junior teachers into the full life and responsibility of the faculty—erupted at a time of crisis and further endangered the university. By force of their strong personalities and by virtue of the fact that they were the university personnel closest to the students who had been under gunfire, these young teachers constituted themselves ipso facto members of the faculty. Their resolution, hastily composed and adopted, contained much that was laudable and spelled out certain basic facts about advanced education, but these truths were so encompassed in rhetoric, questionable taste and lack of appreciation of the political situation in which the university then found itself, as to constitute civic irresponsibility. It was an unscholarly document released at an unfortunate time. It could only exacerbate emotions and not reduce them.

Many of the ideas expressed in the major resolution adopted that afternoon were in the great tradition of liberal education, and had they come a week later, when fears and tempers had cooled, they might have done much to bring discussion down to a reasonable level; that they burst upon the scene as the first university response to the weekend, showing no spark of comprehension of how the citizens of the area felt, was regrettable. Moreover, there were other statements which were not a part of the tradition and which were purely inflammable; we shall see later the aggravated response they drew from the community, doing the university great and perhaps permanent damage.

We the faculty of Kent State University, hereby affirming our belief that the faculty and students of a university constitute an indivisible community dedicated to the same ideals, and therefore regarding the deprivation of the life and liberty of any member of that community as our common deprivation, do strongly condemn the fatal shooting of four KSU students and the wounding of ten others by National Guardsmen on May 4, 1970.

We hold the Guardsmen, acting under the orders and under severe psychological pressures, less responsible than are Governor Rhodes and Adjutant General Del Corso, whose inflammatory indoctrination produced those pressures. We deplore the prolonged and unduly provocative military presence on the campus not only because we regard the use of massive military force against unarmed students as inappropriate in itself, but because it symbolizes the rule of force in our society and international life.

We regard student protest against this rule of force as their moral prerogative. We profoundly regret the failure of the Governor and other civil officers to understand the complexity and variety of the issues motivating our students, to comprehend the diversity of the students involved, and to adjust flexibly and humanely to their morally based unrest.

In this moment of grief, we pledge that in the future we shall not teach in circumstances which are likely to lead to the death and wounding of our students. We cannot keep the civil authorities from assuming control of our campus. But we can—and do —refuse to teach in a climate that is inimical to the safety of our students and to the principles of academic freedom. We pledge ourselves to a thorough consideration of the relationship between the university and the military establishment.

Finally, we protest the abridgment of our academic and civil liberties. While in no manner sanctioning violence to person and property by protestants, we find the massive peacetime imposition of martial law unconscionable. Not only were four members of our community deprived of life without due process, but all persons in our academic as well as local community have been subjected to abridgment of their rights to assemble and to move about.

We urge all our fellow citizens to consider the condition and the direction of our country: Why is there such hatred of dissident students? Why is there such intolerance of non-conformity? We respectfully but emphatically remind all that, especially under times of strain, Constitutional guarantees must be preserved and abided by and all universities must not only be allowed but be encouraged to perform their historic task of presenting and examining all points of view.

The community regarded this resolution as a challenge by the faculty, one which avoided and glossed over the question of student responsibility for the troubles. The phrases which were judged to be particularly galling were: 'student protest is a moral prerogative,' 'unarmed students,' 'we can and do refuse to teach,' and 'we protest the abridgment of our academic and civil liberties.'

The faculty did pass a second resolution deploring the use of violence 'by any member of the university community,' pointing out that 'student freedom carries with it student responsibility for mature action,' but the weight of this comment was lost for two reasons. Attention was given only to the first provocative resolution, so that the more sober second one was lost; and younger members of the staff insisted upon adding to the second a paragraph blaming everything that happened at Kent on the war in Vietnam, and this in a part of Ohio where the general citizen applauded the war and looked upon anyone who opposed it as subversive:

The faculty is convinced that we cannot view this tragic violence as a phenomenon separate from the violence in which the American government is involved in Southeast Asia. Our government's participation in the unpopular and apparently interminable war in Vietnam is chiefly responsible for the frustration and anger which is increasingly apparent among university students.

When these two resolutions hit the front pages, where they were given considerable prominence, citizens throughout the area formed an opinion which they would state with frequency and ferocity in the weeks ahead: 'Hell, the damned professors are no better than the kids.'

Several days after the university had closed, Ron Kane directed six detectives in a search of every room in Kent's thirty-one dormitories in an effort to show the people of Kent just how many guns the students had collected for the shootout. Obviously, if guns and ammunition were located, it would prove that the disturbance on campus had been much more serious than the general public appreciated. It would also prove that the National Guard had been justified in taking military action when it did.

Search continued for six days, after which Prosecutor Kane was ready to share the results with the press. On the tables in the gymnasium, the loot was lined up.

In bulk it was impressive, a scatter of so-called weapons spread over a large area. Television cameras scanned the tables. Still photographers flashed their bulbs. And reporters eyed the findings keenly, but with a growing sense of incredulity.

'Where are the guns?' they asked. 'Where's the hoard of ammunition?'

Upon inspection the weapons turned out to be the ordinary kind of junk one would expect to find in a college dormitory . . . or in the upstairs rooms of a family with two sons. There was a .22-caliber squirrel-hunting rifle, not recently used, a shotgun, some big-handle revolvers that had not been fired in the past decade. There were baseball bats which could prove quite lethal if used for cracking skulls. And a weird collection of sixty knives, some sharpened to razor's edge. There were bows and arrows, the latter equipped with steel tips; they could kill a person at fifty yards. There were three slingshots and several BB guns. There were also two hypodermic needles, 'used,' explained the people supervising the haul, 'for injection of heroin.'

The knives, it turned out, were ones which students had acquired when they were boy scouts. The baseball bats belonged to members of the Kent State nine. The bows and arrows were the property either of girls who were on the archery team or boys who had hunting licenses. And the two hypodermics belonged to diabetics who had left them behind when fleeing the campus under court order. The detectives did, however, find two hashish pipes and six marijuana plants growing in flower pots.

The search, the exhibition and the explanations were embarrassing to anyone who participated, but talk of 'the arsenal found in the dormitory rooms' flashed across the community and fell upon receptive ears. Many Kent residents sincerely believed that the students had been amassing arms in a planned attempt to take over the town.

On Sunday, May 17, Father Ernest Laperfido was saying in his Sunday sermon at St. Patrick's Cathedral on DePuyster Street, 'Events of two weeks ago were not the fault of the National Guard. They were not the fault of the students. We can have only scorn for what was found in those dormitory rooms. You could search any private house around here and find as much.' From the middle of the congregation an angry man rose, shook his fist at the cleric and cried, 'We don't want to hear your propaganda!' He strode from the church. Unabashed, Father Laperfido continued with his sermon of conciliation.

Next of kin

The death of four students by gunfire on campus shocked America. On the evening news that day, a disbelieving public watched in horror as the first tentative reports of the confrontation at Kent filtered across the screen. 'Two Guardsmen, two students killed,' the first broadcast had announced, but this was quickly set aright. Four were dead, but none in uniform: all were students. Two were nineteen years old; two were twenty—'the Kent Four,' as they came to be called.

That the news media were almost universally sympathetic to the dead students cannot be denied. Across the United States college students could identify with the innocent faces and the brief character sketches the newspapers provided. In virtually every magazine and newspaper around the country they read of Allison Krause, the girl who had placed a flower in a Guardsman's rifle, the heroine of the peace-and-love movement; Bill Schroeder, the 'all-American boy,' in his second year of ROTC training; Sandy Scheuer, the bubblingly happy Jewish girl, whose main joy was in making others happy; and Jeff Miller, the perplexed young man caught up in the troubles of his time, but not an activist.

'My God, that could have been me!' was the standard feeling of anyone between the ages of eighteen and twenty-five; to them, the news meant that their brothers and sisters had been killed. And not only did most of the American press embrace this sentiment, but similar reactions were expressed around the world. In Moscow, Soviet poet Yevgeny Yevtushenko rushed into print with a poem far below his usual average, but with a high propaganda content.

Allison Krause, you were killed because you loved flowers
. . . Ah, how fragrant are the lilacs,
But you feel nothing.
As the president said of you,
    you are a bum.
Each victim is a bum, but it is not his fault.

But what evoked sympathy in Russia and in the universities aroused choleric anger in many parts of conservative Middle America. Special resentment was expressed against newspapers which had published pictures of the four dead taken some years ago for their high school annuals. (The news agencies could be forgiven for this tactic, since no other portraits were available.) In the *New York Times,* John Kifner reported the comments of a grandmotherly-looking woman who had been a fraternity housemother at Kent for twenty years: 'The newspapers printed their high school pictures so people would think they were nice kids, but they weren't. They were dirty and had long hair.' In every city many people complained, 'The newspapers did a snow job on those kids. If they were out on that hill, they must have been hippies. There's probably a lot about those kids that'll never come out.'

In a sense, these criticisms were valid, for Allison Krause had changed in appearance from the sweet young girl with the gracious smile and string of white pearls around her neck, and the long-haired Jeff Miller of May 4 bore little resemblance to the youngster his high school picture depicts. Yet in the immediate aftermath of the event, the media were hampered in the gathering of data concerning the fatalities: the university had been closed, and friends and classmates of the students, who knew them best in their college milieu, were not available for comment. Thus reporters fell back on the partial knowledge provided by hometown friends and on testimonies to the dead made at the respective funerals; from these came hauntingly beautiful statements. In speaking of Allison, Professor Mike Lunine, who had known her well, said:

Allison was radical—if being young and bright and warm is radical.

Allison was radical—if having a great sense of justice and a sense of humor is radical.

Allison was radical—if being full of love and full of life is radical.

Then, my God, may we all be so radical.

And in Plainview, New York, mourners heard a long-time friend of Jeff Miller's say, 'It is ironic that Jeff gave his life for something he'll never find out if he truly believed in. College, radicalism—they were all games he played trying to get a perspective on life.'

For the immediate families, the shock of the death notification was profound. Ironically, each of the four students had been in contact with his family at some time over the weekend, assuring his parents that everything was all right. Jeff and Allison had spoken to their families as late as Monday morning, with Jeff saying to his mother two and one half hours before his death, 'Don't worry, Mom, I'm not going to get hurt. You know me, I won't get that involved.'

At 1:00 that afternoon, Mrs. Elaine Miller called her son's house to assure herself that he was still safe.

'Is Jeff there?' she asked.

The roommate to whom she spoke was so grief-stricken that all he could do was blurt out, 'He's dead.'

For Mr. and Mrs. Martin Scheuer, who were that day celebrating their twenty-seventh wedding anniversary, the news came in an equally brutal way. As Mrs. Miller had done, Mrs. Scheuer called Sandy's house, and the phone was answered by one of Sandy's roommates.

'You'd better come here right away, Mrs. Scheuer. Sandy's in the hospital, but that's all we know right now,' said Jan Reinstein. Less than two hours later the Scheuers had identified the body of their daughter at the Ravenna Memorial Hospital.

What the Krauses had to go through was indefensible. Mrs. Barbara Agte, Allison's closest friend on the faculty, says, 'No one in Kent felt responsibility for informing the parents of the dead students. Mr. Krause's brother lived in Cleveland and he heard a radio flash that there had been a disturbance at Kent State. Premonition warned him that his niece might have been hurt, so he called her family in Pittsburgh.

'The Krauses were also apprehensive and tried to telephone

Kent, but as you know, all lines were out. But somebody thought of the police band radio. They put in a call to the campus police, who assured the Krauses, "Everything is okay. Nobody was hurt."

'But the Krauses were still concerned, and on the 6:30 television news they saw the sketchy and somewhat garbled report that their daughter was dead. More frantic telephoning finally enabled the Krauses to reach the Ravenna hospital, where someone informed them coldly, "She was DOA."

'When they started to ask around, they found that not even this was true, because her constant friend, Barry Levine, who rode to the hospital in the ambulance with her, swears that she was still alive then, even though she had been left lying on the ground for twenty to thirty minutes before the ambulance came. Barry told me, "She was lying beside me, gasping for air. I asked the driver if there was any oxygen, and he just looked at me coldly and didn't even give me an answer." At the hospital, to which Allison was delivered still alive, no one would allow Barry in to identify her or even tell him whether she had lived or died. Finally a policeman appeared, seemed offended by my long hair, and said, "Go home."

'The university did not get around to sending the Krauses news of the death until late Tuesday afternoon.'

For five hours after the shooting many students were perplexed by the reports of one 'William Snyder, New York, not a student—dead.' In a house on Franklin Street four young men experienced growing panic when their roommate Bill did not show up as the 5:00 curfew approached.

'I think we started to face up to facts at curfew time,' a roommate says. 'We got that sick feeling that William Snyder was William Schroeder. It just wasn't like him to stay out after a legal curfew. Then about 5:15 Gene Pekarik called and told us that he'd seen Bill shot, he was only wounded. From then on, it was all downhill. About an hour later I was taken to the county morgue to identify him. I will never forget that feeling of seeing him lying there.'

'The people it was hardest on was the Schroeders,' he continues. 'Bill and his mother were extraordinarily close, and Mr. and Mrs. Schroeder didn't even find out about Bill until a Cleveland reporter called and asked them, "Is your son dead?" They contacted the Ravenna hospital at the suggestion of the Lorain police. Can you imagine that?'

One of the students wounded in the incident was deeply concerned as to how his parents would find out about his condition. Robert Stamps, twenty, who was shot in the buttocks, recounts his experience at the Ravenna hospital: 'I asked the nurses if they had notified my parents, and they said no. They said they couldn't get a line, but not to worry because they had notified the press that I had been shot, and that my parents would probably find out one way or the other. "Oh, wow!" I screamed. I asked them for a telephone so I could call myself, but they wouldn't bring one. They said I'd have to wait till morning.'

The first official statement from the university to the parents of the slain students came not on May 4, but on the following day, when President White sent a personal telegram to the parents: 'The thoughts of Mrs. White and I are with you in your terrible loss. As parents we are filled with horror and shock. We pray for support to you in this hour.'

And from President Nixon came personal notes of condolence on light-green White House stationery. 'Certainly nothing can lessen the extent of your tragic loss,' he wrote to the Schroeders, 'but I hope that the heartfelt sympathy of so many across the nation can in some measure ease its pain.' To the Scheuers, he wrote: 'As parents of two daughters, Mrs. Nixon and I feel especially keen the loss of one so young, so happy, so much a source of joy to her friends, and so full of the promise of life ahead.'

The parents acted with the dignity of the bereaved, but the anguish of one father was too great for him to keep silent, so, on May 5, Arthur Krause was broadcast on national television speaking of his daughter: '. . . She resented being called a bum because she disagreed with someone else's opinion. She felt that our crossing into Cambodia was wrong. Is this dissent a crime? Is this a reason for killing her? Have we come to such a state in this country that a young girl has to be shot because she disagrees deeply with the actions of her government?' Within five weeks after his daughter's death, Krause was to file a $6-million wrongful-death suit against Ohio officials, including Governor Rhodes and Guardsmen Del Corso and Canterbury. By mid-September similar suits had been filed by the parents of Jeff Miller and Sandy Scheuer, but the first suit to come to trial was speedily thrown out on the grounds that a sovereign state cannot be sued unless it agrees to it. As the presiding judge said, 'It is an historic precedent that "the Queen can do no wrong." '

In midsummer Bill Warren's *The Middle of the Country* was published. It was an angry and bitter statement compiled by eleven students and faculty members of Kent, written within a few days after the incident, conveying their gut-reaction to the horror they had seen on their campus. As such, there is little emphasis on presenting an objective or balanced account of what occurred, but for depth of emotion and fervor, it is highly representative of student thought.

But herein lies a danger which is coming increasingly to the fore in articles concerning Kent, or Jackson State, or Kansas State: there are blatant appeals only to the emotions, none to the mind. There is no better example of this than a magazine article by Erich Segal, in which the author purports to present a true picture of Allison Krause; in no way can his saccharine rhapsody be reconciled with facts which even the most casual research would have revealed. Statements such as 'none of the victims was in *any* way involved with the disturbances' and 'Allison Krause was killed because she happened to be in the line of fire when the National Guard began to shoot' preclude any critical evaluation of fact; this sort of glossing-over the truth should not be perpetuated if we are to arrive at any understanding of the continuing problem that faces us.

Letters to the editor

When Harold Walker left the field of the dead, he suspected that on his many rolls of film he might have captured some compelling shots, but like John Filo, he could not be sure until he saw them developed. So he did what he had been taught in journalism: 'If you think you have a scoop, get in touch with the newspaper you know best.' In his case it was *The Gazette and Daily*, of York, Pennsylvania, one of America's real odd-ball journals. Operating in the heart of the conservative Pennsylvania–German country and surrounded by people who vote Republican, it is liberal and outspoken. It is also interesting in that it is edited on a devil-may-care basis, with the editor saying pretty much what he likes. Among the American newspapers from cities its size, it has no peer. That many of its subscribers consider it communistic is a cross it has to bear.

Its reaction to the Walker photographs was typical. Calling Walker on the phone as he worked at Kent State, the editor said excitedly, 'These photos are too good to waste on a small-town paper like this. I've alerted the *Washington Post* and they want you to fly to their offices immediately.'

With some excitement young Walker caught a plane at Akron, and entered the *Post* editorial offices to find the entire staff gazing in bewilderment at the shots which he himself had·not yet seen. 'How did you get such photos?' some of the older men asked in admiration, but before Walker could explain, one of the senior editors delivered the crushing decision: 'We're not going to use any of them.'

Staff members of the *Washington Post* subsequently denied having said that the photographs were faked. They explained that some of the crucial photographs had been left behind in York, and that since they were unable to see the entire sequence they deemed it unwise to run what could only have been a portion of the total. They gave Walker some money for dinner and put him up at a hotel. Then he packed up his pictures and went back to York, where they appeared in the *York Gazette and Daily*.

The York editor came up with the logical idea of having Walker accompany his photographs with a verbal account of what had happened, and the young newsman ended his essay in the way most sensitive men his age would have done: 'I think that when people look at the situation—students shot without warning; the dead and the wounded—there will be sympathy across the nation, no matter what the political beliefs. As for the city of Kent, the whole town seems to be in sympathy with the students.' He concluded: 'I believe the incident may bring the student and the adult communities together. It may bring about mutual understanding.'

Never in his future career as newspaperman will Harold C. Walker, Kent State 1970, be more completely wrong, for even as the paper in York was printing these hopeful and constructive words, the newspaper in Kent was being forced to find space for what will be remembered as one of the most virulent outpourings of community hatred in recent decades. It seemed as if everybody in the Kent area suddenly wanted to unburden himself of resentments against young people, colleges and education which had been festering for years. The paper had to reserve a full page, day after day for several weeks, for this violent outburst, and anyone who wishes to explore the Kent phenomenon more deeply than this book allows, is directed to those terrifying broadsides, printed solid in compact type. They give a portrait of Middle America at the beginning of the 1970's that is frightening. The first group requires no comment.

Authority, law and order are the backbone of our society, for its protection. Would you want authorities to stand by if your home were threatened? Well, Kent State is my home by virtue of taxes spent funding it. What's more, it's their home by virtue of tuition paid. Playful children destroying a disenchanting toy.

How dare they! I stand behind the action of the National Guard! I want my property defended. And if dissenters refuse to obey the final warning before the punishment, hurling taunts, rocks (stones, they say), sticks, brandishing clubs with razor blades imbedded, then the first slap is a mighty sting.

Live ammunition! Well, really, what did they expect, spitballs? How much warning is needed indeed.

Hooray! I shout for God and Country, recourse to justice under law, fifes, drums, martial music, parades, ice cream cones—America, support it or leave it.

Ravenna housewife

When radical students are allowed to go through a town smashing windows, terrifying the citizens, and are allowed to burn buildings belonging to the taxpayers to the ground, I think it is high time that the Guard be brought in to stop them—and stop them in any way they can.

The sooner the students of this country learn that they are not running this country, that they are going to college to learn, *not teach*, the better.

If those students don't like this country or our colleges, why don't they go to the country from which they are being indoctrinated?

Concerned citizen

A surprising number of the writers referred to property rights and taxes. If there had been any doubt as to what values many citizens in this part of Ohio placed in paramount position, these letters settled that question.

We are paying a large percentage of our hard-earned money to support and educate these young people. For what? To let them burn and destroy property that more of our tax money has paid for? Who paid for the hose that was cut while our firemen were trying to stop a fire, set deliberately, all the while being pelted with rocks. Some innocent person's home could very well have burned while our firemen were busy fighting a fire on campus.

Concerned resident

I, and thousands of other old-timers, have been paying taxes for many years—even before some of the present troublemakers were born. These taxes were used, and are being used, to erect and equip modern campus buildings and to pay the salaries of professors (even those who support and condone the actions of the troublemakers) who have such a vital role in the educational process. How many buildings were erected and equipped from taxes paid by campus vandals? How many professors and other university personnel received salaries from taxes paid by campus vandals? This property does not belong to them. It belongs to me and thousands like me who have paid taxes for twenty, thirty and even forty years to provide the money for these facilities. We are lending them OUR facilities and we expect them to take care of OUR property. We do not expect these temporary occupants to burn, damage or destroy that which they have borrowed. We will gladly pay for these buildings, but we see red when OUR property has to be repaired or replaced because of the actions of a few irresponsible misfits who only want to damage or destroy.

A concerned old-timer

Only a small percentage of the letters printed in that period can be reproduced here, but each one chosen represents a score or more. On no subject was the comment more unanimous than on the right of the National Guard to do whatever was required to enforce discipline.

Some have questioned the need of the National Guard on campus and throughout our city. However, I shudder to think of the condition of our city today had they had not been present to protect and preserve what so many have labored endlessly to build.

Kent citizen

Are we the citizens of this fine town going to sit back and allow certain officials to persecute the National Guard for doing their duty? Are we going to accept the theory that these ones involved in this rioting and burning were JUST children?

Since when is rioting, looting, burning, assaulting a town called academic freedom? Is it freedom of expression? Why do they allow these so-called educated punks, who apparently know only how to spell four-lettered words, to run loose on our campuses tearing down and destroying that which good men spent years building up?

I plead with the citizens of Kent to take a stand, don't allow these tragic deaths to go for naught. Make your voice heard. Do not let the National Guard be blamed for something they did not create.

> Signed by one who was taught that 'to educate a man in mind and not in morals is to educate a menace to society'

Congratulations to the Guardsmen for their performance of duty on the Kent University Campus. I hope their actions serve as an example for the entire nation. The governors of our states cannot waste the taxpayers' money playing games. These men were alerted as a last resort to control mob action.

I extend appreciation and whole-hearted support of the Guard of every state for their fine efforts in protecting citizens like me and our property.

Mother of Guardsman

Not included in this sampling are the numerous letters, submitted by committees, with hundreds and even thousands of names, approving the behavior of the Guard. One of the most interesting themes was the recrudescence of an idea that had been born many years ago and which had enjoyed frequent revival through the decades. In April, 1933, at the depth of the depression, Representative William R. Foss, of the Ohio legislature, proposed that in view of the current oversupply of teachers, more than four thousand of whom were unable to obtain work, it would be a good idea to convert one of the four large colleges—Ohio State University was excluded—into a mental asylum. 'We intend to investigate this proposition thoroughly,' Foss warned, 'and to determine which college can most readily be converted. We're not bluffing.'

After a visit to Kent on May 4 of that year, Foss reported: 'Kent State has the finest, most modern buildings and, therefore, is most adaptable to welfare work. There would be no fire hazard in connection with the structures, and this is an important feature.' Later, referring obliquely to Kent, he said that 'one of the institutions visited was so adapted to welfare needs that it would be difficult to distinguish it from those built for that specific purpose.' The proposal came to naught and Kent State was spared.

However, two years later the idea of converting the college into an asylum surfaced again, and once more, serious consideration was giving to closing down the college, but an improvement in the economy saved it. Now, after the riots of 1970, the project was reopened.

> I have one possible solution to the problem. Build a fence completely around KSU, put President White and his 550 faculty members inside along with all the agitators that they understand so well and let them do their thing. We could also change the name from KSU to 'Idiot Hill.' Then Dr. White and his faculty and students could assemble and throw rocks at each other and play with matches and burn things down, because they understand each other's reasoning and don't want to be bothered. So be it! I have more ideas, but what's the use. In fact, who needs KSU? Not me.
>
> Kent taxpayer

Letters abusing student behavior were numerous. Their endless and bitter barrage startled the students and saddened the professors, who felt that a whole society was turning against the youth who would soon be constituting that society. One of the reasonable complaints against students follows:

> Last night on TV were several shots of protesting students and

a leader of these talked for some time about continuing the protest into the summer. The TV program showed pictures and named the student leader.

This student leader was not a student during 1968 and to October, 1969. Girls, wild parties, filthy living conditions and failure to pay bills featured this man; an acme of unreliability. Another man, said to be a leader of Kent SDS, lived with him for a time. His fine parents came to pay the bills he owed us when he disappeared. Word is that other creditors in the area were not so fortunate. Yet, this man is shown as depicting an important trend in our times.

Ravenna citizen

A surprising number of the letter-writers, and among them the most vehement, referred to themselves as members of the silent majority. Two examples follow:

When is the long-silent, long-suffering majority going to rise up in force to show the militant minority on the KSU campus exactly how they feel about them? It's hard to believe that the surly, foul-mouthed, know-nothing punks that have raised so much hell in this town the past few days are speaking for all of us, or half of us, or even one tenth of us. Yet, like any mob, they've got you outnumbered, and any sort of ideology is completely lost in the sadistic pleasure of sheer destruction. In other words, the would-be heroes are behaving exactly like the criminals they are.

As a person young enough to be more a member of their generation than that of their parents, I reject these creeps.

Anti-violent

Kent has tolerated these so-called misunderstood students long enough. The city of Kent should be off-limits to students. Keep them on the university grounds, and when they have completely destroyed it, they can go home and we will be rid of them.

If the National Guard is forced to face these situations without loaded guns, the silent majority has lost everything. The National Guard made only one mistake—they should have fired sooner and longer.

As for the parents of the dead students, I can appreciate their suffering, they probably don't know the truth. A dissident certainly isn't going to write home about his demonstration activities. Parents are learning the hard way and others should take heed. The high school photos that appeared in the paper were all very nice, but how do you explain the mother who refused to identify her own son at the hospital because of his appearance. This same boy had refused to go home on holidays.

I only hope the National Guard will be here the next time we need them. I am fully prepared to protect what is mine—property, home and life—at any cost against these mobs of dissidents in the event our law enforcement is prohibited to do what is necessary.

Ravenna citizen

Numerous letters spoke of the need for instituting some kind of vigilante movement to combat the students. Sometimes this was intimated; often it was spelled out.

There has been no other issue in recent years that has raised my wrath as much as student demonstration, including SDS leadership, against the Vietnam war and against anything else that occurs to the demonstrators.

So, it was refreshing to see a group of hard-hatted construction workers in lower New York do something about it. They went through those demonstrators like Sherman went through Atlanta, leaving sixty or seventy injured. That's exactly what we need . . . a harder line with demonstrators, not the easy, 'pat on the wrist' punishment for their crime.

I'm for raising a counterforce to neutralize the efforts of sometimes silly, and sometimes dangerous, and always unthinking students who want to go to a school without abiding by its rules.

Aurora citizen

My first reaction, and again I have been thinking of this for some time, was to arm both my home and my office. But during moments of more rational thought, I realize that probably all I would accomplish is to shoot myself in the foot. I abhor violence and I have no desire to traipse all over the country protecting other people's property. However, I feel an immediate and compelling responsibility to protect my own locality. I am thinking in the direction of a kind of citizens committee, under appropriate professional direction, who would bear arms against these people to protect our families and property. Further, I will support taxation to raise the funds to provide a capable effective force to deal with this problem.

Kent citizen

Many persons in the Kent area felt that students who dressed oddly or who wore their hair long ought to be disciplined. In fact, the bitterness which such appearance created was one of the recurrent themes in discussing the shooting. Several intimated that the penalty for non-conformity should be death.

It is too bad that a small minority of students feel that these damnable demonstrations must take place. If the slouchily dressed female students and the freakishly dressed, long-haired male students would properly dress and otherwise properly demean themselves as not to make show-offs of themselves, such trouble could be and would be avoided. It is difficult to understand why female students must get out and make such fools of themselves as they do, but it is understandable that male students do so largely to get their screwball mugs on television and in the press.

If the troublemaking students have no better sense than to conduct themselves as they do on our university and college campuses, such as throwing missiles, bottles and bullets at legally constituted police authority and the National Guard, they justly deserve the consequences that they bring upon themselves, even if this does unfortunately result in death.

Attorney-at-law

There were, of course, several letters which challenged the headlong rush to law and order. These writers endeavored to explain that the phrase required careful definition.

Where are the voices of 'law and order' when construction workers in New York City attack a peaceful, non-violent demonstration of anti-war protesters? I would suspect that the lawless action of the construction workers is condoned by the 'silent majority' because they aren't members of the 'effete corps of impudent snobs,' or they aren't 'bums.'

You see, the voices of the silent majority chose to remain silent on those issues. It would appear to me, then, that a double standard exists when people call for law and order—it's a good phrase when applied to young, long-haired dissidents and radicals, but it's a meaningless phrase when applied to the silent majority. I would submit that just as students are not above the law, neither are members of the 'silent majority.'

Ravenna citizen

And from time to time isolated writers would remind the public that four young people were dead, that something had gone fearfully wrong. They sounded like lost voices, except for the eloquence they sometimes introduced into their letters.

I am a KSU student. I am not a radical, but to quote Albert Camus, 'I should like to be able to love my country and to love justice, also.'

The letters I've been reading about the Kent deaths, and the people I've heard saying that the demonstrators deserved to be shot, frighten me. Many justify the slayings because of the property damage that had been done. But the crowd Monday was attacking no buildings. Did they shoot to avenge the burning of the ROTC building?

Revolutionaries and SDSers don't frighten me, nor do squads of police or National Guards. I am afraid of the people who say 'kill the demonstrators, because they destroyed our property.' I am afraid of these people who value property over human life. I am not afraid for my life, but for my soul, and for the sensitivity and humanity that is slowly being erased from our society.

Jesus said that no one can truly love God if he cannot love his fellow man. You people with the 'mow 'em down' philosophy, can you love God without loving Jeffrey, Bill, Sandy and Allison?

Ravenna student

On Monday, May 4, I witnessed the KSU killings. As horrible and frightening as the memories of those experiences are, they are not nearly so terrifying as the hostility that has been revealed in their aftermath. I am not a radical. I do not believe that arson and violence should go unpunished, but I know of no state in which arson carries a death sentence, and there are certainly none in which 'illegal' assembly is punishable by execution.

I have recently heard a multitude of comments such as, 'They should have mowed them all down' or 'I'll bet they think twice next time' or 'They got what they deserved.' It is in the people who make these statements that the real violence is to be found. They seem to be permeated with an intense desire to see destroyed or shackled anything they do not understand or anyone who does not concisely conform to their glorious social ideals about what is 'American.'

They are to be feared far more than are the campus dissidents, for they would destroy something far more precious than property, or even life—they would destroy freedom! And is not freedom supposed to be what America is all about?

Kent State student

It would be fruitless to reproduce all the savage attacks that were visited upon the faculty. The unfortunate resolution adopted in the Akron Church on Tuesday afternoon was referred to in a score of letters, with citizens rebuking them in harsh terms for their one-sided interpretation of what had happened on the campus. Only three letters need be cited here, a typical one of rebuke, and two reflections by university members on the tragedy that had overtaken a notable institution. They represent the kind of reevaluation that was being undertaken across the nation.

I do not understand why the teacher who was convicted of first-degree riot is permitted to teach at the university during the week and serve her time on weekends. She shouldn't even be allowed on the campus, much less be permitted to teach.

Ravenna resident

The meeting of the faculty of Kent State University held on Tuesday [in the Akron church] was deeply disturbing to me. The tone of the meeting seemed to me emotional and rhetorical—in short a mob. And I am sick of emotionalism, mobs and violence.

What is truly academic must be personal and humble. As I recall hearing it read, one of the items in the resolution stated that we will not teach under military coercion. Similarly, I don't see how we can teach under the social pressure of our own desire to reach unanimous decisions.

I want my students back, but I do not want to unite them behind any social issue or against any issue, such as the war in Indochina, even though I abhor that war. I want my students to wander a free campus, and I only want those who are 'academically inclined' to contemplate with humility and with intricacy. I am frightened of the mob—the mob in me.

Kent professor of English

The statement issued [by the faculty] from an Akron church Tuesday correctly expresses the angry mood of the majority of the faculty, but it is not enough. If academic democracy is to work, it must be self-enforcing. We must demonstrate clearly that we understand and are able to assume the responsibility for conduct of our university.

It is imperative that we defend academic freedom, which includes the right to dissent, as we have undertaken to do, but we must insure that the freedom we defend is clearly differentiated from license to destroy by violence. Our campus must remain open to those who would express unpopular ideas, but it must not be a sanctuary for those who commit felonious acts, no matter what purpose they avow.

I am not making just another appeal to 'law and order.' My position is that unless we insist upon the maintenance of orderly processes, the tragic circumstances of last Monday are the eventual and inevitable result.

All who have contributed to the blurring of the connection between the rights and responsibilities of free people must share in the guilt for the deaths of our students: those who have engaged in civil disobedience and have refused to accept the consequences, those who have cried for amnesty for those who have criminally violated the rights of others in pursuit of a worthy cause, those who have failed to understand that destroying a building is not a legitimate exercise of freedom of expression, and those who have stood silently by while this tide of passion has engulfed us in its tragic whorl.

Kent professor of journalism

The most deplorable aspect of these letters was not the explosive outpouring of hatred (which could be forgiven as an autonomic response to phenomena not understood) nor the obvious obsession with property values as opposed to human life (which is often observed in American life) but rather the willingness to condemn all students, perceiving them as a mass to be castigated. Nothing can excuse this error. We must constantly remember that only a small percentage of the Kent student body was involved. The following table has been revised continuously from the day this study started; it was refined whenever new police reports were made available or new photographs came to light. As it now stands, it incorporates the best guesses of many experts but reflects the personal conclusions of none. It is a composite.

Percentage of Student Body of 21,186
Participating in Disturbances

Incident	Total Persons Involved	Non-university Persons	University Persons	% age of Total Student Body Participating
Friday night downtown	1,000	600	400	01.9
Saturday night ROTC fire				
Passive spectators	1,500	250	1,250	05.9
Active participants	500	250	250	01.2
Sunday night sitdown	700	150	550	02.6
Monday noon rally				
Distant spectators	2,500	400	2,100	09.9
Passive on Blanket Hill	650	150	500	02.3
Active on Blanket Hill	450	50	400	01.9

Talk on the street

While the letter-writers were unburdening themselves in the local press, people on the street in Kent and Ravenna were being equally outspoken. The tone was set early by an esteemed Kent lawyer, who said in an interview with the Akron newspaper:

> We feel that the Guard did exactly what they are sent in to do: To keep law and order. Frankly, if I'd been faced with the same situation and had a submachine gun, there would not have been fourteen shot, there probably would have been 140 of them dead, and that's what they need.

Citizens less educated than this lawyer adopted the device

of flashing their right hands in the air, thumb folded down and four fingers extended. When a student asked what the sign meant, he was told, 'This time we got four of you bastards. Next time we'll get more.' Jim Banks was appalled by an incident which befell him: 'I was passing this out-of-town policeman imported for the trouble and he looked exactly like Rod Steiger in *Heat of the Night,* and as I drew equal to him he raised four fingers and whispered, "The score is four." ' Later this was elaborated into a jingle which ran:

> The score is four,
> And next time more.

Many hideous things were said in these first weeks. It became almost common for people to say, 'They should have shot most of the professors, too.'

Faculty members compiled a savage collection of letters from all parts of Ohio expressing regret that the professors had escaped. Dr. Harris Dante, a soft-spoken conservative in the education department, was told by one taxpayer, 'The only mistake they made was not to shoot all the students and then start in on the faculty.' In these letters, too, appeared the theme that if a person paid taxes he had the right to designate who should be shot. And considerable support built up for either closing the university permanently or converting it into the long-awaited asylum.

Obviously, more sober citizens like Bill Nash, LeRoy Satrom and the leaders of Kent avoided such excesses. Instead they began reconstructing, slowly and securely, a basis for cooperation between the city and the university. The old had been destroyed and everyone knew it.

When the flood of mail and speech had subsided, various persons began trying to decipher what the outburst had signified. These conclusions were suggested:

. . . The general population of Middle America was infuriated by what it saw happening to its universities and alienated by the presidents who administered them and the professors who taught in them. The average man downtown had little comprehension of what role a university ought to play in time of crisis or of its obligation to maintain discussion of all points of view; he was inclined to lash out at anyone who sought to change the university from what it had been when he was young. At Kent State some of the most vituperative comment came from alumni who rejected what their school had become.

   . . . These people were outraged that the university had allowed young radicals like Jerry Rubin, Mark Rudd and Bernardine Dohrn to speak on its campus. They were infuriated that students used profanity to college officials and campus policemen. And they were deeply disturbed that young men who in all past generations had marched off obediently to war should be questioning the authority of the President of the United States to send them to their war. This theme, expressed in various ways, echoed throughout the letters.

   . . . There was an honest longing for an old-fashioned college with old-fashioned problems. One citizen of Kent told a researcher, 'Why can't the kids come to college in the autumn the way they used to and worry about the things college kids always worried about. What fraternity to join? Where is the football rally going to be? Which of the coeds should I marry? Can I cut Professor Jackson's class one more time without his catching on? That's the way it used to be. What's all this moratorium stuff and the war in Vietnam? They can't do a damned thing about it.' This is a longing which is attacking all elements in our society; any change which offends it runs the risk of savage opposition.

   . . . No one could talk with a cross section of the local population without discovering that they were truly frightened by the more disreputable young people they saw on the streets of their town. When the facts were isolated, it became evident that the troublemakers were not university students but casual and unattached hippies who had clustered around Kent as the place where the action was. One woman summarized the town's feeling: 'My husband expects me to keep our house clean and myself neat. I take pride in it, just as I take pride in his advancement in his work. It's what we got married for. Then I go downtown and see these hippies, barefooted, filthy, boasting about the ragged clothes they wear, elbowing me off my own streets, and using language I've never heard my husband speak. What am I to think? Have they taken over the world? Have we got to surrender Kent to them?' The visual appearance of the young was terrifying to many people, and no amount of reassurance could relax their fears. The notorious Manson trial in California had something to do with this, because on any afternoon in Kent you could spot two dozen characters who, judging by appearances, would have fitted right into the dramatis personae of that trial.

. . . There seemed to be no possibility of reconciliation between the life styles of the young and the old. There was a wide gap, with unbridgeable differences in dress, cleanliness, hair fashions, attitudes toward work, politics, music, religion, patriotism and sex. One woman who had children at Kent said, 'There is no single thing on which we can agree any longer . . . except maybe food. They still like my cooking.' There seems little inclination on the part of the young to modify their present styles to accommodate their elders. Seemingly endless conversations were held on this, with the young people stubbornly reiterating, 'No one is going to make me change. I'd give up any job in the world if it meant surrendering the way I want to live. I will never cop out.'

. . . Sex plays a much larger role in this than was once apparent. Older townspeople both despise and envy the sexual freedom enjoyed by the young, and this theme recurs in constant non-sequiturs. A businessman will be saying, 'The thing I can't stand is the way they dress,' but he will add, 'And it's disgusting the way the girls sleep around.' Or a Kent housewife will explain, 'I could tolerate them if they had any manners,' but she will conclude in a lower voice, 'And the way they sleep together in those dormitories!' At the time of the shooting, six or seven communes operated in Kent—not on campus—apparently without any great promiscuity but with an ebb and flow of partners, and rumors of these infuriated the townspeople who heard of them. Two reactions were customary: 'The university should expel them all' and 'They ought to be horsewhipped.' Sexual jealousy appears to be a very strong determinant of the manner in which a citizen will react to the younger generation which he sees enjoying itself in a manner forbidden to him when he was young.

. . . There was a strong tendency toward vigilantism running through the community after the shootings. One heard, from the more aggressive townspeople, much talk of 'shooting the hippies on sight,' and from the students, of 'shooting back at them next time.' On each side, there was open discussion of weaponry and covert movement of it. To an uninitiated outsider, this constant reference to violence was appalling, but very real. In the weeks immediately following the May killings, Kent was close to violence and persons of all categories appeared prepared for it. One heard from literally scores of young people that they would 'be afraid of coming through this town in long hair and on a motorcycle.' There were stories of citizens taking pot-shots at passing long-hairs and much discussion of 'the *Easy Rider* syndrome.' A young person would say, 'I'm not hung up on the *Easy Rider* syndrome, but I wouldn't be surprised to be greeted by a blast from a shotgun any day.' A leading businessman confided, 'I was aghast when I saw who had been appointed special deputies . . . with permission to carry rifles and shotguns at all times. Three fellows in their early twenties who two years ago were members of the town's worst motorcycle gang.' This tendency toward vigilantism had started when blacks began to run wild, particularly after the vendetta shooting of policemen in Cleveland, and was born out of real fear of the public pronouncement of black leaders as to how they were going to shoot up the community. That it should have received its major subsequent impetus from the deaths of four students was a dreadful irony; one had to remind people constantly as they talked about the coming show-down that it was the students who had died; they had not done the killing. One recurring verbalism haunted the mind that long summer: 'I suppose there's bound to be a shoot-out.'

. . . The attitude toward blacks was ambivalent. At least one letter-writer and many speakers referred to the exemplary restraint of black students during the uprising, and when attempts to blame them for the rioting did surface, they were quickly squelched. 'You've got to say this for the blacks,' began a frequent comment, 'they kept their noses clean this time.' But accompanying this, especially on the part of the students, came the ominous suggestion, 'They're biding their time.' It became an accepted part of the legend that the blacks were furious about the shooting, not because four whites were killed, but because they had planned to take over the Administration Building that day and felt co-opted by the precipitate white action. The shootings did nothing to add to the bad feeling already existing between the races, but it did nothing to alleviate it either.

. . . Some townspeople were plain fed up with students. Larry Smith, a serious graduate student, suffered painful proof: 'I had just bought this new windbreaker. Looked like leather but was really one of the new vinyls. I wore it downtown a couple of days after the shooting. Debi Moreland was along and needed some cigarettes, so I stopped in this little store where three scruffy-looking townies were lounging and one of them asked me, "You one of them smart college kids?" I nodded, bought the cigarettes and walked out. When we'd gone half a block Debi said, "I smell something burning," and I looked around but didn't see anything, so we walked on. Then she cried, "Larry! You're on fire!" I told her to stop kidding, but she started slapping at my new windbreaker, and I saw that my entire back was ablaze. One of the guys in the shop had lit it with a match.'

. . . Finally, one of the strongest impressions coming from both the letters and the speeches, and one that none of the people associated with this book could have anticipated, was the virulence of the attitudes expressed by women. Notice has been taken of the violent speech of the coeds and of the fact that they were often the ones who took the more extreme positions, and this appears to be a phenomenon across the United States. But the response from conservative women was even more emphatic. An undue proportion of the demands for more killing came from women; the most intransigent opposition to students came from them, and the harshest dismissal of the young. Some thought that this resulted from a real sense of fear. There were numerous cases in which mothers on downtown shopping trips would clutch their children defensively if hippies wandered by. There was also the shattering experience of suddenly turning a corner and finding oneself face to face with seven or eight totally disheveled members of a commune, the men dressed like Daniel Boone, the women barefoot and in long tattered dresses. Even strong men were taken aback by such unanticipated confrontations; women were terrified. There were other factors, too. It could not have been coincidence that so many women referred with a sense of hatred to the young girls who were appearing in town without bras; this became a fixation with many, and was apparently an intuitive reaction to a symbol: 'If I've had to wear a bra all my life, why can't she?' This overreaction of women might be considered humorous, except that, as we shall see in the next section, it produced a terrible consequence when it occurred not in women generically, but in specific mothers.

What the students heard

While the faculty members who remained in Kent were getting their daily dose of shock from the page of letters to the editor—many felt that the things they had taught and believed in all their lives were being destroyed—their students were undergoing an even more shattering experience.

It began, symbolically, at three o'clock Monday afternoon when Daniel Gardner, a stocky, well-behaved, short-haired young junior with good manners and a deferential manner of speaking, went to his car under police protection, and in obedience to orders, left the campus with some other students from New England and started the long drive back home. He had been in no way involved in either the shooting or the activities that had led up to them. If one had wanted to find a 'normal' Kent State student who had come there for an education, Gardner would have been a likely choice, but the killings had made him think that perhaps the students had had a raw deal, and he expected non-campus society to agree with him. 'After all, 30.06 bullets against a gang of unarmed kids . . . too much, man, too much.'

He began to learn the facts when he left the Ohio Turnpike to enter the Pennsylvania. When the ticket-taker saw the Kent State sticker on Gardner's car, he snarled, 'Those Guards should of shot all of you.' When Gardner stopped at a bar on the outskirts of Buffalo, the men inside refused to allow the young people entrance. 'We don't want commies in here.' And after Gardner had dropped off his passengers at various points en route and arrived at his home on Cape Cod, his neighbors told him, 'Anybody who defied the Guard, they ought to be shot.'

When Bob Hillegas reported to work at his part-time job with General Tire, in Akron, he found that the dominant opinion among his co-workers was that 'those kids got what was coming to them.' Men in the shop were circulating a petition condoning the use of any weapons deemed necessary in future campus outbreaks and exonerating the Guard in advance if deaths resulted. 'I refused to sign such an un-American document,' Hillegas says, 'and now I'm regarded as a total outsider. I tried arguing with them, but they said, "If they were on the hill they were guilty and they deserved to be shot. Next time if they don't do what the Guard says, they'll all get shot."'

Karen Bowes, the unusually beautiful wife of a graduate student in business administration and an unaggressive, soft-spoken girl with a good education, works in the office of a manufacturing plant at Aurora, twelve miles to the north. She was still shaken by the deaths when she reported to work on Tuesday morning, but became more so when she heard the reaction of her associates: 'At my job in the factory everyone, and I mean every person I came in touch with, said they wished the students had all been shot. I must have shown my shock because they went on to elaborate. "Any student who was on campus that day should have been shot down." When I tried to explain that my husband, for example, had not only a right but an obligation to be there as a student, they said, 'He should have been shot. Students get away with too much and they should be shot." '

In various college towns throughout Ohio memorial services were held for the four dead students, but rarely without pickets. At the service in Toledo, women marched with signs reading:

> The Kent State four
> Should have studied more.

But one of the worst jolts came to the conservative fraternity men of the Sigma Chi house on East Main Street in the heart of town. On the front lawn the Sigma Chi's had some years ago erected a handsome Maltese Cross, representing one of the arcane teachings of the secret society. Across its face someone had printed in spray paint a huge, ominous black 4. It would remain there throughout the summer, all attempts at erasing it proving futile. Who had done it, and for what reason, remained unknown.

It was difficult to find any student who escaped a harsh confrontation with public opinion, but those who were subjected to even greater blows were the ones whose own parents said, 'Everyone on the hill should have been shot,' and when reminded that their son or daughter was there too, added defiantly, 'Well, if you were there when the Guard warned you to stay away, you should have been shot, too.'

Of the four hundred students whom the researchers of this book interviewed in depth, a depressing number had been told by their own parents that it might have been a good thing if they had been shot. If one requires documentation of a generation gap, this statistic is so frightening that it requires both substantiation and explanation.

The working wife of one student reports: 'My mother lives back East, and when I told her of the tragedy, she said, "I read about it in the papers. It would have been a good thing if everyone on that hill had been shot." When I reminded her that her own son-in-law had been there, she said, "That doesn't change my mind." '

An ex-army student, with a good record in Vietnam, got the treatment: 'When I reported home my mother said, "It would have been a good thing if all those students had been shot." I cried, "Hey, Mom! That's me you're talking about," and she said, "It would have been better for the country if you had all been mowed down." '

But no case of parental rejection equals that of a family living in a small town near the Kentucky border with three good-looking, well-behaved, moderate sons at the university. Without any record of participation in protest, the boys found themselves inadvertently involved at the vortex: the middle son ended up standing beside one of the students who was shot (at a great distance from the firing); the youngest was arrested for trespass and his picture appeared in the home-town paper, to the embarrassment of his family. When the family spoke to one of our researchers, the conversation was so startling that more than usual care was taken to get it exactly as delivered.

MOTHER: Anyone who appears on the streets of a city like Kent with long hair, dirty clothes or barefooted deserves to be shot.

RESEARCHER: Have I your permission to quote that?

MOTHER: You sure do. It would have been better if the Guard had shot the whole lot of them that morning.

RESEARCHER: But you had three sons there.

MOTHER: If they didn't do what the Guards told them, they should have been mowed down.

PROFESSOR OF PSYCHOLOGY (listening in): Is long hair a justification for shooting someone?

MOTHER: Yes. We have got to clean up this nation. And we'll start with the long-hairs.

PROFESSOR: Would you permit one of your sons to be shot simply because he went barefooted?

MOTHER: Yes.

PROFESSOR: Where do you get such ideas?

MOTHER: I teach at the local high school.

PROFESSOR: You mean you are teaching your students such things?

MOTHER: Yes. I teach them the truth. That the lazy, the dirty, the ones you see walking the streets and doing nothing ought all to be shot.

Why would mothers say such things? First, as women they are honestly frightened by the radical changes that are modifying society and which they feel powerless to oppose. Second, they so completely reject the new life style that they are willing to approve death as a reasonable penalty for it. Third, the fact that the four were killed by a law enforcement agency proves that the victims merited punishment. Fourth, all these fears and emotions are intensified by the fact that the young against whom they react are their own children. Finally, it is only charitable to point out that many of the women spoke in temporary anger, expressing themselves more harshly than they intended.

Of course, as the summer progressed, many of the parents retreated from their first harsh judgments and backed down from their initial wish that 'many more students ought to have been shot.' Communication with children was reopened and in many cases an understanding was achieved.

But in hundreds of other cases young students caught a terrifying glimpse of what their parents really thought. For a moment the veil that properly exists between young and old was sundered and the former were shocked by what they saw. Reactions varied.

'I doubt that I'll ever bother to go home again,' several students reported.

'I'm going on to Canada,' three of the young people said. 'I've had it.'

'I don't suppose I'll ever be able to talk with my parents again,' was a frequent reaction.

More frightening was the repeated admission that this sequence of events had alienated the students not only from their parents but from all society as they had known it. It is tempting here to use names, for some of the very finest young people appearing in these pages told compelling tales of their alienation; and to follow their psychological development would be fascinating for the reader, but since it is likely that some of them may subsequently reconsider and find an acceptable place in our society, it would not be fair to have on record a judgment made in anger of a moment, even though they were willing that their names be used. Each of the following statements was made by one of the characters of this book.

A conservative biology major: 'I was considered a square. But when my parents talked the way they did I found that my entire sympathy lay with the students, so I guess you'd say I've been radicalized. If I am, they forced it on me.'

A coed now living in a commune: 'When I left home to return to school this fall, after spending only three weeks with my family, I was crying so hard, my parents couldn't understand it. What they didn't know was that I realized it was the last time I would ever be with them again. Everything I'd said, they looked down on, and I just don't have it in me to fight them on it. So I've left for good . . . left forever the kind of life they represent.'

History major with a 3.4 average: 'During the years of the sit-ins and peace rallies, my parents and I disagreed, but we respected each other's opinions. But after Kent, when I saw how so many people, including my parents, truly feared and hated students, I realized there was no middle ground. Now I'm working against everything my family has worked for, and I will fight them as long as necessary.'

Delightful, wisecracking apolitical junior: 'I was raised in what you might call a military-oriented family. My father had been in the army, and when I was young, my brother and I always played "war games." Now he's in the army, too, and is really gung-ho Vietnam, and I'm on the other side, working against his silly war. So the few times I do go home, the only way we can keep the peace is not to talk about anything the least bit political. What kind of situation is that, when you can't talk to your own family about the things that really bug you? If people don't start talking and listening soon, this whole thing is going to blow up.'

After hearing a score of such confessions, one remembers that a major responsibility of all societies at all times is the reconciliation of young people with their elders. Today the problem has added urgency. The extravagant positions of each—'Mow 'em all down.' 'Death to the pigs.'—have got to be abandoned. There is nothing wrong in maintaining pressure for change, and this seems unlikely to diminish, but nothing is gained when in addition to legitimate pressure on sensitive subjects like the draft and war in Vietnam, grossly offensive behavior is paraded with an open challenge to the older society to combat it.

Kent proved that society has the power and the will to combat the young, extravagantly. It behooves all Americans to de-escalate passions, to restore some kind of dialogue. It may well be that some members of this generation of students, having been told by their parents that they should have been shot, cannot be won back. But it would be national suicide to engender in future cycles of students a similar rejection.

Universities, high schools, TV, newspapers, churches and all social agencies must strive to prevent this. The tragedy at Kent State did not produce the understanding that a hopeful young newspaperman like Harold Walker trusted it would; indeed, it produced just the opposite. But now that we know what the facts are, it is our job to respond intelligently, and understanding between the generations is the foundation upon which we must build.

Specifically, the young should be willing to make these concessions:

Act within the law. The correction of legitimate political grievances must be achieved in legitimate ways. The slow building of our democratic process required moral commitment and patience, but in the end it produced a notable society. People devoted to our nation and the vision of what it might become are understandably frightened by thoughtless assaults upon it.

Respect the other person's moral convictions. Young people are not obligated to pay allegiance to any church but they ought not ridicule those who do, for this is one of the easiest ways to generate antagonisms.

Tolerate those over thirty. There is probably some truth in the popular saying of those in their teens and twenties, 'You can't trust anyone over thirty,' but mutual respect is essential, and aggressive rejection is not the way to attain it.

Make some concessions on personal appearance. Young people are correct in thinking that the violent attitude of so many people toward long hair, beards and odd costumes is totally out of proportion. A young man should be allowed to wear his hair the way he wishes and a girl her skirt at the height which fits her best, but neatness and cleanliness do help society to function. They are the individual's personal ecology.

Sex is a private matter. Many older people covertly approve of the new sex mores but do not care to have them blatantly promenaded in public. It seems likely that recent excesses will create a demand for more restrictive rules covering books, plays, motion pictures and general public deportment.

Language should not be used as a weapon. The new freedom in language cannot easily be reversed, for it has opened up valuable new modes of expression, but its abuse infuriates the general public and makes communication difficult, if not impossible. A recent speaker at Kent State was greeted, at the end of his rather liberal lecture, by this question from the gallery: 'How does the university dare to bring onto this campus a motherfucking fascist like this to spread his bullshit?' Try as one might, it is impossible to see how such a question fits into any normal pattern of academic dialogue.

The older generation should be willing to make these concessions:

Acknowledge that the young are serious and rational in their protests. When the young first began to speak out against the Vietnam war they were branded as irresponsibles; perhaps they were the true patriots, and had we listened to them when they first spoke we might have saved our nation much embarrassment. What they espoused then has now become acceptable to senators, newspapers and churches. The same is true of the ecological concerns of the young, their dedication to a classless society, and their determination to find meaningful occupations. These are serious concerns which merit serious attention.

Stop being so irrationally opposed to hair styles. To the young, this seems one of the most extraordinary manifestations of middle-aged intransigence; they cannot comprehend why so many people object so strenuously to hair styles that were popular across the nation only sixty years ago. One young man with a copious beard took the trouble to search out photographs of his four great-grandfathers, and they were hairier than he. If one takes a hundred leading figures of American history, the bulk of them will look more like the hirsute youth of today than like the peeled and skinned fathers in their forties; and those historical figures who are not wearing beards will be wearing graceful and effeminate wigs.

Work out some rational system of drug control. The present system, sponsored by the older generation, is working havoc among the young, for it is irrational, arbitrary, and destructive of sensible decision. The earlier citation of the penalties to which the student body at Kent State is subject typifies the legal absurdity, and it is the responsibility of the older citizens to untangle this mess. The aim should be the elimination of all traffic in heroin, with life sentences if necessary, the logical control of lesser drugs, and some kind of sensible, agreed-upon way of handling marijuana.

Stop trying to defeat the reasonable aspects of the new life style. Dress, music, idiom, and new dating practices are matters of style, which change from generation to generation; older people should not allow themselves to become irritated by such trivial things. Use of drugs, bad sex habits, debasement of language, and a predisposition toward violence in settling arguments go much deeper than style and ought to be opposed where they are known to be destructive of either the person engaging in them or the society which he is attacking. The sagacious older person ought to be able to distinguish between the two.

Above all, maintain contact with the young. It would appear that the dialogue between generations is most often broken by the older group. (One acknowledges that in all periods of history some young people have been so withdrawn and secretive, so distrustful of parents, that they made dialogue impossible, but in the majority of cases this was not so.) Young people need older ones to argue with, to test their ideas on. The continuity of life is a most precious thing and must not be ruptured carelessly. If the dialogue has been broken, it must be restored, even though this may require humility on the part of those least accustomed to practice it. No wealth in this world is more valuable than the burgeoning talent of a new generation, and no expense is too great to spend on its cultivation. In even the most flagrant cases of parents' rejecting their children, there is always a chance for reconciliation; of this we are convinced. If this is to be achieved, children and parents alike must retract hasty statements, but—we repeat—the major responsibility lies with the parents.

One way for an older person to open his mind to what happened at Kent is for him to analyze the easy statement which so many elders indulged in after the shooting: 'It's a shame that four students had to be killed, but they shouldn't have been there in the first place.' It may help to follow the activities of only one of the many who walked the campus that day. No better case history could be provided than that of a girl we shall call Betsey.

She could be the representative senior in almost any coed college in America. Five-feet-four, blond, unusually attractive, with saucy eyes and a creamy complexion, she was so well thought of by her contemporaries and her faculty that she was chosen one of the resident student assistants at Prentice Hall, which happens to be the dormitory closest to where the killings took place. Late Sunday night she gave proof of her attitudes by organizing the bucket brigade which tried to put out the incendiary fire in the archery shed.

When asked why she had done so at some danger to herself, she said, 'I don't like to see things destroyed.'

On Monday, Betsey, probably as fine a student as Kent State produced that year, had a class in Van Deusen Hall, and as she walked back to Prentice Hall she followed a course which placed her in direct line of fire when the rifles went off. She was not killed, but she might have been. And at her death no one could conceivably have said, 'She had no right to be there.' As a top-notch scholar and an official of the dormitory to which she was returning, she had not only the right but also the obligation to be exactly where she was. What she did not have, and what none of the other students had, was the right to continue a rally after the riot act had been read, nor the right to abuse the National Guard in pursuit of their duties—but these things she did not do.

That night when she returned to her home in a small town in western Ohio, her nerves wracked by the tragedy she had seen, her parents said, 'It would have been better for America if every student on that hill had been shot.'

'Mother!' she cried in profound protest, 'I was there. Only a miracle of some kind saved me. What about that?'

'You would have deserved it.'

This story so startled the researchers that they set up the hypothetical question: 'If Betsey had been killed, what is the worst that could have been said about her?' They ran a thorough check on her, just as they did on the victims, and the worst thing they could uncover was that on October 15, 1969, she had attended a demonstration against the war in Vietnam. They uncovered one other fact. During four years she had maintained an average of 3.8 out of a possible 4.0. Has not this kind of student a right to be safe on a university campus?

Many readers may deride our contention that life style played an important role at Kent. Comparison should be made of two events which occurred in Ohio during a space of six months, one a riot at Kent State on a Friday night in

May, the other a riot at Ohio State on a Saturday night in the following November.

At Kent 1,000 people were involved; at Ohio State, 40,000. At Kent the riot lasted about two hours; at Ohio State, twelve hours. At Kent some dozen business establishments were damaged, without looting; at Ohio State, about sixty, with some looting. At Kent no one suffered bodily harm; at Ohio State many did, including a student who was shot. At Kent about $10,000 worth of damage was done; at Ohio State, about $30,000. By any index you choose, the Saturday night riot at Ohio State was three or four times more serious than the Friday night riot at Kent.

How, therefore, can one explain that Ohio went into a frenzy over the Kent riot and took the Ohio State disturbance in stride, without a strong reaction of any kind? At Kent the governor felt obliged to fly in and charge the participants with being worse than Brown Shirts; curfew was clamped down; vigilante groups were openly discussed; the National Guard was summoned with loaded rifles; four students were killed, nine others were wounded; and the university was closed down to general approval. At Ohio State none of these things happened.

For there was this significant difference. The Kent riot involved persons addicted to the new life style; it seemed to involve politics; and it was sensed as alien to our way of life. The Ohio State riot was conducted by persons who adhered to the older life style; it celebrated a football victory over Michigan, and it was recognized as a traditional part of our heritage. We knew how to handle it, how to jolly it along. Police were understanding in not attempting to break it up, and newspapers were jovial in cataloguing it as merely one more example of normal high jinks. This dual reaction of our establishment society—accept a football riot, punish a political one—is perhaps understandable and perhaps inevitable, but it highlights the necessity for explaining the nature of the new life style and those elements in it which lead to over-reaction.

The ghouls

One ghoulish aspect of the killings must be mentioned. The corpses were barely cold before citizens began circulating horrendous stories about them. Where these folk tales originated is not known for sure; some of the worst seem to have come from a woman attendant at the Ravenna hospital. It will be most effective merely to list them.

'It's all very well to feel sympathy for Jeff Miller, whose head was blown off, but I suppose you know he was so filthy that in the ambulance they had to keep the doors propped open so they could breathe.'

'You've heard about the mother who came to the hospital in Ravenna, took one look at the body, and cried, "This filthy thing is no son of mine." ' A version of this appeared in print in one of the letters quoted.

'The two dead girls were so covered with lice that the hospital attendants nearly threw up.'

'You know, of course, that neither of the girls wore underwear.'

For some peculiar reason, perhaps because she had been presented by newspapers outside of Kent as a charming girl who loved her cat Yossarian and placed flowers in the barrel of a soldier's rifle, particular vengeance was directed against Allison Krause.

'She was on drugs.'

'It was a mercy she was shot, because she was pregnant.'

'There's no reason to grieve over her death, because she was so ridden with syphilis that she would have been dead in two weeks.'

One coed living in Ravenna heard from her mother an explanation of why the housewives of that city were so volubly opposed to Allison. 'I suppose you know that she never allowed her parents to see her except in a bathrobe. That's a fact. The person who undressed her at the hospital told me. The poor girl had been tattooed from head to toe.'

This awful litany went on, and still does, as if by making the students repulsive, their deaths would be more acceptable. Repeatedly, those who knew the dead students would stop the calumniators and ask them, 'Suppose one of the girls did need a bath, would that be a just reason for shooting her?' Usually the answer was, 'In her case, yes.'

Many students whose parents recited these accusations against the dead asked, 'But suppose my clothes were dirty. Would that justify someone in shooting me?' Often the answer was, 'If you didn't obey the soldiers, yes.'

One must understand the psychological necessity and the historical precedent which generated these strong feelings. If the four had been criminals with known evil records, when they were safely dead, legends would have begun to weave about them, so that a century from now they would emerge as juvenile heroes. But if four non-criminal young people are killed by society, it is obligatory that they bear the onus for their own death: precisely because they were largely guiltless of any crime against society, they must be denigrated and torn down, because otherwise that society would have to declare itself guilty.

Rarely have four dead people been so vilified. What are the facts?

We have photographs of Jeff Miller taken at fairly close range on the commons. He is wearing his hair long, but not excessively so. He has on a cowboy shirt, untorn trousers and shoes—he does wear an Indian-type headband. We also have the numerous photographs taken of his corpse as it lies in the pool of blood, and these offer no evidence of a filthy man. In life and death Miller gives the impression of the young college student of his day.

We have an extraordinary photograph of Bill Schroeder climbing the hill at 12:02, that is, twenty-two minutes before firing began at the pagoda. He can be seen wearing army-type shoes, pants that could stand pressing, a striped T-shirt and what looks like an army jacket. His short hair is neatly combed and he is carrying an armful of books. He is right behind an active youth in headband who is waving a Vietcong flag, but Bill seems no part of the agitation. He is clean-shaven, as befits an ROTC member, and if he is in any way filthy, the camera at a distance of about six feet has failed to detect it.

What do the students who were with Jeff and Bill that day report? 'When Jeff and I first got to the rally,' says Dane Griffin, 'there was a close-knit feeling to the group—kind of like some of the rock festivals at Fred Fuller Park. But as the Guard started shooting gas, Jeff and I both got mad as hell. Maybe he threw back some tear-gas canisters—what else can you do when they land at your feet? When the Guard started moving back up to Taylor Hall after being down on the practice field, we were really excited. We thought we'd won. Jeff started jumping around like he always did when he was excited about something. Jeff was just Jeff, like any of hundreds of people you see around here, and not any kind of a hard-core radical.'

Gene Pekarik, who was with Schroeder up to ten minutes before he was shot, is very definite about Bill's reasons for being at the rally: 'He was peaceful. He wasn't a revolutionary or a radical. He went merely because he was curious. He was a psych major, and he had a big thing about making up his own mind about everything. He was there so he could understand for himself what was going on.' Lou Cusella, a long-time friend from Lorain, says, 'Look at that picture of him climbing the hill. A warm, wonderful guy detached from the whole operation . . . a beautiful spirit apart.'

As to the girls, there appears to be no photograph taken that day of Sandy Scheuer, for the very good reason that she did not participate in any of the action. There is, however, a fleeting shot of Allison Krause as she disappears over the hill at the pagoda, the last in a line of students who had been actively defying the Guard. That she was deeply involved in the incident, there can be no doubt. That photograph permits no deductions as to her dress, appearance or personal cleanliness, but there is another of her in a crowd, and in this she appears to be neatly dressed, and certainly her hair is combed.

There is a good deal of verbal testimony from students who were with the two girls that day. Sharon Swanson, Sandy's friend, says, 'I think I know how the rumor got started that the kids were on drugs. Someone at the hospital saw the needle mark in Sandy Scheuer's arm. From giving blood on Friday. Of everyone I know, Sandy would be the last person in the world to do dope. She didn't drink much, didn't smoke, and her moral standards were very high. I saw her about a minute before she was shot, and she was the same Sandy as always, just laughing and talking to some guy. When I saw her I called, "You heading for Speech Clinic?" She called back. "Yep." I told her, "Wait, and I'll go with you." Almost as soon as I said this, the shooting started. I ducked behind a sports car and a bullet went right through it, four inches above my head. Then I saw Sandy lying there . . . shot right through the eye. Alive? Who knows?'

Kent Miller has a chilling recollection of helping Allison: 'After the shooting stopped, I heard screams and turned and saw a guy kneeling, holding a girl's head in his hands. I ran to them, and was the first to reach them. The guy with her was getting hysterical, crying, yelling, shouting, "Those fucking pigs, they shot you."

'First I got him to lay her head on a coat and had to yell at him several times to get him to control himself. I treated her for shock and I immediately applied direct pressure to her wound with my handkerchief. She was shot just below the left armpit and her shirt was ripped apart and soaked with blood.

'She began to salivate. She seemed to be trying to swallow her tongue. I gave her mouth-to-mouth, but only for an instant. The bleeding slowed down, and I thought she would be all right. We got her into an ambulance, and it was only later that I found out her name was Allison Krause.'

But even with all this evidence from the colleagues of the dead students, and from their professors, the rumors which attempt to assassinate their characters persist.

'They were all communists.'

'When they got Allison Krause to the hospital they found she was carrying hand grenades.'

'She was the campus whore.'

'She was living in a commune.'

'They were all hopheads.'

The autopsies, performed almost immediately, told a much different story.

'We did complete autopsies on the students,' says Dr. Robert Sybert, Portage County coroner. 'Checked for morphine, barbiturates, amphetamines—nothing. No trace of it in any of the four, and no needle marks in the arm for drugs. There was no visible sign of venereal disease and no body filth. These were four clean, nice kids, and I see no basis for the rumors which I have heard going around.'

One reputable commission came to similar conclusions concerning drug usage: 'No evidence was found to establish that any of the casualties were under the influence of drugs at the time of the confrontation. A marijuana cigarette was found in a pocket of the jacket used to cover one of the wounded students, John Cleary, after he was injured. Cleary's father said, however, that the jacket did not belong to Cleary.'

After protracted investigation, and after learning as much about these four students as outsiders will probably ever be permitted to know, we feel obligated to offer our conclusions as to their characters and our guess as to their degree of political involvement.

Sandy Scheuer was an apolitical young woman of twenty who was traversing the parking lot as a casual observer on her way to class. Her only connection with campus agitation was that she knew Jeff Miller, the most modest kind of activist, and several other boys like him. Her death was pure accident, inexplicable and unjustified. Had she lived, Sandy would unquestionably have continued as she had in the past, uninvolved, charitable, loved by all her friends, and on the alert for some nice Jewish boy.

Bill Schroeder was a nineteen-year-old ROTC member who had never come close to political activity. A quiet young man, he was devoted to getting a good education, was interested in athletics, and spent his spare time working at odd jobs to make spending money. He had lived in Kent for only eight months, but in that time, had built an enviable reputation. We have talked with scores of his friends and have discovered not the vaguest adverse rumor. His death, too, was a cruel accident. Had he lived, he could not conceivably have become a radical.

Jeff Miller, aged twenty, emerges as a fairly complex young man, indifferent in his studies and insecure in his political beliefs. That he was in the forefront of the confrontation on Monday, there can be no question, for the photographs are definitive. He was active on the commons and on the hill, abusing the Guard verbally with obscene gestures; in one photograph, he is pictured giving the Guard the finger with each hand, in another he is seen throwing a tear-gas canister back at the Guard while they were on the football practice field. His position when shot was consonant with his previous behavior. Guardsman Carl Caldwell spotted him as one of the persistent troublemakers: 'I saw this guy running at one of our Guards, taunting him, giving him a really bad time. How did I know it was Jeff Miller? By the unusual cowboy shirt he was wearing.' One student, who could not have compared notes with Caldwell, is of the opinion that 'Jeff Miller had been giving one special Guard the finger all day and had been very abusive. I believe that when the Guards reached the top of the hill, this Guardsman whipped around and let Jeff have it. That's what started the shooting.' The fact that Miller was standing 224 feet from the firing line, and nineteen feet lower than the level line of sight, would discredit this theory.

At the time of his death he was not a radical. However, a letter exists indicating that he might have been on his way to becoming one. Written to a Kent friend days before the shooting, it shows Jeff to have been a prototype of the confused, idealistic young man and nothing more, but the person who received the letter and his circle of friends are convinced that had Jeff lived he would have inclined increasingly toward the radical position. Steve Drucker, who lived with Jeff, thinks not: 'He would never have gotten into politics. He would have become excited by ecology and he would have talked with wild enthusiasm—but politics? He never mentioned the subject.' Neil Phillips, who may have been closer to Jeff's thinking than anyone else, runs his fingers through his long hair and cries in real anguish, 'How in hell can anyone predict with certainty how this laughing, wonderful, drum-playing kid would have developed? I am sure of only one thing. When we lost Jeff Miller we lost a damned good right-fielder.'

Allison Krause, aged nineteen, appears to have been an activist who was in the thick of the disturbance on Monday. One investigatory team uncovered substantial evidence that she had been carrying small fragments of concrete and cinder block in the pockets of her jacket. She is reported to have given the Guard a bad time verbally, but this is contrary to her behavior on Sunday afternoon, when we know without question that she was amiable and conciliatory. However, many students have testified that they underwent a change of opinion Sunday night and it seems probable that she did so, too.

There is substantial evidence indicating that if Allison had lived she would have moved steadily, inconspicuously and probably non-violently toward the left. The young man who knew her best, Barry Levine, says, 'If she had transferred with me to Buffalo, she would be where I am now. Where's that? Alienated. Wondering whether to drop out. Looking for a better way of life.'

Rudy Gardner, a twenty-year-old from Columbus who often talked with Allison, says, 'If she had survived May 4 she would have become completely radicalized. Even more so than she was. The whole set of her experience was in that direction. But she would never have become a revolutionary.'

Regarding the ugly rumors which have collected around this dead girl, an expert witness is Mike Lunine, the nononsense dean of the Honors College of which Allison was a member. He has degrees from Iowa, Illinois and the University of Delhi in India. He speaks with a low and resonant voice and becomes quite tense when recalling his former student.

'She stood in the top 10 percent of all high school seniors in the United States, and she drew down grades that kept her in the top 25 percent of her honors class in college. One of the things I liked about her was that she volunteered her own time to work with mentally retarded children. I knew her well, and I categorically deny the rumors that have been circulating. Without qualification I reject charges that she was a revolutionary . . . or that she was personally filthy . . . or that she was anything but a lively-minded young girl trying to understand her society.

"Syphilis? How in God's name would I know?" Here Lunine jumps to his feet, tears in his eyes. After a moment's struggle to control himself, he asks, 'Just suppose she had? Has that become a cause for execution?'

On this point the coroner's report was specific and final: 'Miss Krause had no venereal disease.'

The verdict on this mercurial and sometimes contradictory girl will never be unanimous, but one of the most telling documents will be the essay she wrote at age seventeen when applying for entrance to the Honors College. It is in the possession of Mike Lunine, as part of Allison's file, and portrays her keen interest in self-education: 'I attend a progressive public high school. I have had a great deal of freedom in choosing what I want to learn and I have enjoyed this responsibility.' She speaks of her volunteer work at a camp for retarded children and says that she enjoys helping other people. She wants to be a psychologist and concludes with the confession that she finds it difficult to apply herself to either a subject or a personal relationship in which she has no immediate interest: 'I am inclined to work in spurts.' The essay bespeaks the mature intelligence of a woman in her mid-twenties.

When all the evidence appeared to be in, one of the researchers consulted with a high official of the secret grand jury that had issued indictments covering the four days of disturbance, and asked this hypothetical question: 'If Jeff Miller and Allison Krause had lived, and if you had had at your disposal the photographs and the testimony that you now have, would your jury have indicted them for their behavior on Monday?' Without hesitation the official replied, 'Unquestionably. We would have indicted them and on the evidence we had before us, they would have gone to jail.'

The disoriented

To the average American not involved in campus confrontations, as either parent or student, it is impossible to comprehend the psychological contradictions that can develop. Consider the case of Ed Truscott. Again this is a pseudonym.

He came from a small community, of which he says, 'Our attitudes were clear-cut. I heard fellows say, "If those civil-righters come out here to break any of my windows and loot my stuff, I'm gonna reach for my gun and blow their brains out." And then someone would always add, "Most of all, you got to watch those Jews. They're behind it all." ' College life was a revelation: 'I saw that the kids who had been big shots in high school were nobodies at Kent. They played no role at all. Because their ideas were used up. Dead. Busted. Cheer leader, big deal! But the fellows who had been quiet at high school became big shots at Kent. Why? Because they did have ideas. They had the gift of leadership. I discovered that I wanted to be like them. I wanted to participate. And you could participate only if you sat down and thought things out. Because it was ideas that counted.'

Ed had a difficult time determining his basic beliefs: 'Boy, the discussions we had at Moulton Hall. That was the first time I'd ever spoken to Catholics. Those characters knew what they believed, and in debate they argued you right down. But the more I talked the more I realized that I was a conscientious objector, so one of the Catholic boys took me to the Newman Center, where a priest told me how hard a row I had picked for myself. At the end of the first quarter I'd done so much arguing and so little studying that I busted right out of college. But I knew what I believed.

'I wanted to quit. I was ashamed of myself and started to drift, but as I talked with other fellows, I found that I had better ideas than they did. I was more sure of myself, and I came back to the next term with real dedication. That's the condition I was in Friday morning when the trouble started.

'At my 7:45 class that morning someone handed me a leaflet which showed President Nixon with an ax chopping down not a cherry tree but the Constitution. "Father of lies," the leaflet said. It explained how the Constitution was to be buried at noon because Nixon had killed it. So I looked up the leader of the affair, a tall graduate student named Sharoff, and told him, "I believe in what you're doing. I hear a Vietnam veteran with a lot of medals is going to burn his discharge papers." He nodded, and I said, "I'll volunteer to burn my draft card," and he said, "Get the hell out of here. They arrest you for burning draft cards, and the one thing we don't want is trouble." I told him I no longer cared if I sat in jail because I was against the war, but he told me to scram.

'So Friday night, after the accident at the traffic light, some of us marched around the campus—it must have been about 2:00 in the morning—chanting, "Watch the ROTC building go up in flames." But we did nothing about it.'

On Saturday evening a profound change came over Truscott, for when the time came to ignite the ROTC building he suddenly realized that the people who were sponsoring the fire were ones he had never seen before. 'I saw this one fellow with a long knife strapped to his left leg. "Let's go over to Tri-Towers," he kept shouting at us, but when the crowd left, he stayed behind. Then one of the professors handed me some leaflets which said: *Don't break anything.* And I knew then that I didn't want to see ROTC burn after all. In fact, I volunteered for the job of passing out the leaflets.'

His change of attitude led him to do something which would be remembered by many when they recalled the events of that wild night. 'When I saw that crowd rushing down over the hill, thousands of them, I knew they were a mob, uncontrolled. One of them broke out an American flag and started burning it. I shouted, "Stop that!" A photographer took a picture, and leaders in the mob screamed, "Get that film!" A very large man with a beard, someone I had never seen before on campus, lunged at the photographer and roughed him up. They broke open his camera, got the film and destroyed it.

'By this time the ROTC building was ablaze and firemen arrived to put it out. I lost my cool when I saw students hacking at the hoses with machetes, and I remember running into the center of the crowd and shouting as loud as I could, "Students! You have no right to do this!" A real brawl broke out and some guy tried to take a swing at me, but I kept shouting, "You have no right to destroy government property. It's your property."

'Several people shouted back, "President Nixon had no right to go into Cambodia," and I screamed, "He's your President too. You've got to respect him." I was ready to fight the whole mob to save that building.'

At this point, as we know from previous accounts, Professor Glenn Frank, assisted by other faculty members and student marshals, moved into the mob and hauled Truscott away. 'A couple of them grabbed me, pinned my arms, and tried to keep me from shouting, but I kept yelling at the barn-burners that they'd get into real trouble if they burned that building. Finally the faculty members dragged me into the

Student Union, making me do what they wanted by twisting my arm up behind my back. Professor Frank bought me a Coke, and after a while someone asked, "Now, Ed, have you settled down?" I said it was wrong to burn government property, and they said, "Sure, sure—but can you control yourself if we let you go back to the commons?" I said I could, and they let me go.

'When I got back to ROTC it was completely burned out. I couldn't believe it. I saw a fellow from my dorm who belonged to ROTC and he stood there with his girl, looking at the ashes, and he was crying. He and some of the rest of us hurried back to Moulton Hall, where we formed a committee to defend our dorm . . . I don't know against who. But we issued baseball bats, clubs and iron spikes. "If they try to burn this hall," I announced, "we'll knock their brains out," and we wove a protecting network of sheets and ropes between the pillars so no one could break his way in. As I looked out from behind our fortress I saw two black students acting as marshals, insisting that all blacks get off campus. "Stay out of sight," was the order and I thought how smart those cats were. They knew there was going to be trouble.'

On Sunday Truscott did something that still bewilders him. If you ask him about it now, he flushes, looks at his hands and says, 'All I know is that I did it.' It started when a large number of students began to gather on the commons in the late afternoon. Ed climbed atop the bell housing and yelled at them, 'Students, I warn you. Get off the campus. You'll never get the pigs out of here if you continue to gather in groups.' Nobody listened.

'Then I heard the rumor that at sunset they were going to burn the air force ROTC building too, and I did my best to keep away from it, but when they threatened to draw closer I ran down the hill to where the National Guard was, shouting as loud as I could, "They're going to burn the building. Don't let them. Kill them if you have to. Fire at them. Fire at them. This can't go on." Two of the Guardsmen said, "Don't worry, kid. We'll save it." I was gratified to hear this, but I was still afraid of what might happen, so I continued to run from one group of Guards to another, shouting, "If they come for the building, kill them. Kill them."

'Professor Frank ran up to me and shouted, "You want to get clobbered? You keep shouting things like that and somebody's going to get hurt." He ordered a couple of marshals to take me away from the Guard, but I kept free and told the

Guard again that before the night was out they'd have to shoot.'

'And then a very strange thing happened. I was trying to escape Professor Frank and at the same time begging the Guards to shoot if they had to, and it suddenly occurred to me that if anyone from my draft board happened to hear me they'd think I wasn't a conscientious objector at all. So I said nothing more that night, not publicly, that is. I walked among the Guard and told them, "I feel a great identity with you fellows, because you're draft dodgers, too." They understood what I meant and we had a long conversation. They told me they'd been at Ohio State University and Akron, on the road for a week. And now this dump with a bunch of screaming students, half of them girls. They'd been sleeping on cold football fields for a week, and one big fellow told me, "I'm getting damned ticked off. My mortgage is due tomorrow and here I am, earning $11.50 a day." It was a long night.'

On Monday, Ed had a 7:45 class in geology, and the professor said, 'I cannot teach on such a day,' but before the students could be dismissed, Ed leaped to his feet in protest. 'I came to Kent State for an education, and you professors have got to teach us.' A discussion was organized, but in spite of Ed's efforts, it strayed from geology and kept coming back to the burning of ROTC. 'What did you accomplish by burning it?' Ed demanded. 'It'll be rebuilt in concrete, and what will you do then? Use dynamite? Don't you see where this escalation has got to lead?'

His 12:05 class was no better. Professor Wilson was supposed to be teaching History 151, but when the helicopters kept dropping low over the building, he gave up. 'I can't teach in this war-time atmosphere,' he said, but before dismissing his class he cautioned, 'I warn you of one thing. If you go out on the commons instead of going back to your dorms, stay low, or somebody is bound to get hurt.'

In total confusion, Ed Truscott left his history class and wandered into the direct line of fire. He remembers thinking as he approached the Guard, 'I feel an identity with these Guards, because last night I found they were fellows just like me. But I also feel an identity with the students, because they're the best kids I've ever met. It's stupid that such people should be lined up against each other.' Then the shots rang out.

Back at Moulton Hall, Truscott sat in shock, not knowing what to think. Then a fellow from his hall appeared with a handkerchief darkly stained with human blood. It had been used in a vain effort to stanch the wounds of Allison Krause. The student's voice was low and ashen: 'In memory of her we're going to fly this symbol from our flagpole.'

'For Christ's sake!' a boy in the corner cried. 'Put that damned thing away. Can't you see it's making the girls sick?' And it was thrown into a drawer.

'At that moment,' Truscott remembers, 'my mind was made up. I could almost feel the decision cranking itself out. I knew that if ever again our campus faced bad trouble, I would have to be with the students. If rocks had to be thrown against the troops, I'd be throwing them.'

Many students experienced a change in values as a result of the shootings. Jamie Haines, the sorority pledge captain, says, 'I'm still a Young Republican, but now I'm a liberal Young Republican. It began when I heard ammunition exploding at the ROTC fire. I found myself asking, "Why would anyone have ammunition on campus? What are we teaching in this university that requires live ammo?" It continued when my mother came down the next day to drive me back home to Massachusetts. She's a wonderful mother and I felt very close to her as we sat in a Howard Johnson restaurant near New York. Then two mean-looking men sat down beside us and I think they changed her attitudes too, because one of them asked, "It that your car with the Kent sticker?" and when I said yes, he asked my mother, "You certainly aren't going to allow your daughter to go back to that communist outfit? It would have been better if they'd shot the whole lot of them." I started to protest, and they said, "Look, sister. From now on we're going to carry shotguns, and any damned kid we see with long hair, we're going to gun him down." Put it this way. Today when I see a traffic helicopter over Boston, I automatically choke up.'

For a young man seeking non-violence, Tim Butz was still having trouble. On the afternoon of June 1, sick of the questionings, the rumors, the counter-charges with which he was being bombarded, he went on a picnic and decided to go for a swim; when he dove into the water, a submerged stake scraped across his forehead, digging a gash so deep that it required ten stitches. Now the youthful veteran looks like Scarface or some ultra-tough saloon brawler. 'If you're non-violent,' he warns, 'stay away from picnics.'

Jeff Schoenfeld of Cleveland tells a moving story of how the May events affected one couple. 'I rented the Haunted House when Rick and Candy Erickson had to give it up. They went to jail, you know. But when they got out of jail they came back, late at night, to revisit the scenes that had meant so much to them.' Schoenfeld, a tall, bearded young man who had known the SDS group, continues, 'They obviously loved the place, but each reacted in his own way. Rick strode about the apartments, remembering events which had passed into history. "This was the war room," he told me. "This is where we had the tape recorder that night we fought with the radio station. And here is where we had the big meetings . . . the great ideas." He became quite excited. But Candy—have you ever seen her? Do you know what a beautiful woman she was? "The wallpaper's holding up. I'm glad to see the carpeting in the bathroom hasn't rotted. But they still haven't fixed the sink. There were some good people here in these rooms." '

Then Schoenfeld explains, 'You understand, they came separately. They've broken up. Candy's living in a commune somewhere in California. Rick's in one in Colorado.'

Disorientation was not confined to students. Professor Jordan Hodgkin, chairman of the geography department, left his office in McGilvrey Hall late Monday night to be stopped by a very young and nervous Guardsman, who cried bravely, 'Halt! You are not allowed to cross the campus, sir.' Hodgkin stopped, studied the young sentry and saw that he was in distress. 'Son,' he asked in fatherly tones, 'have you just wet your pants?' In acute embarrassment, the young soldier confessed that he done just that. 'Are you sick?' Hodgkin asked, and the boy replied, 'Yes, sir. I'm awful sick.'

The most effective response of the student body came, as it should have, in the form of poetry. Numerous laments were composed on subjects relating to the tragedy, and some were of high merit. Other students, driven by painful nostalgia to old year-books, came upon a poem written in 1929 by May H. Prentice, much-loved director of elementary education. She had been the first teacher at Kent Normal when it opened its doors.

She had left her mark on the university. The main gate, where Charles Madonio had talked with Specialist 4 Jim

Pierce on Sunday afternoon and where the student with the bullhorn had inflamed the action Sunday night, had been named in her honor, as had Prentice Hall. Her poem was a simple one, heavy with the sentiment of its day, and in its opening stanzas not very good:

Kent State College is set on a hill—
To win her door you must climb with a will,
And Kent State hill is weariful long—
But we trudge on together, a glad-hearted throng,
Climbing the hill at Kent.

What caused students to catch their breath was the third stanza, which could be interpreted as premonitory of what had happened:

For, the hills of the earth or the hills of the soul,
It is all the same, for they take their toll,
One of the body and one of the mind,
And the summit is hard to gain, we find,
Climbing the hill at Kent.

Among the contemporary poems, written in more modern idiom, the one that best summarized the reaction of the students was composed by Peter DeGroot, for it had the proper balance of grief and defiance.

Deride the eagle in us still.
Your words fall shattered,
Distilled but never still.
Who would know the anger force instills
The flower of our youth—
The innocent of that hill.
There is an eagle in us still.

Deride the death of four at Kent,
Those human lives unspent.
But still remember those are ours.
Forget the bayonet . . .
Not one of us is innocent.

And many students recalled that whereas in April they had heard Jerry Rubin cry, 'The first part of the Yippie program is to kill your parents,' in May they heard their parents say, 'You too should have been shot.' A bitter few concluded that Rubin had been right, but the prudent majority decided that something very wrong was happening in America, a malaise to which they themselves might have contributed, and they set out to make corrections. The stability which marked the fall and winter quarters, and on which older people congratulated themselves, should be attributed in large part to this central body of students who perceived the chaos toward which they might be lurching and called a halt.

The ecologist

Of the five students we have been following, only one survived the shooting, and for him the events of May 4 had a profound effect. Doug Wrentmore points to a line of mushrooms which have formed a fairy ring in a wooded area near the Kent reservoir, and says, in a soft, hesitant voice, 'The first part of the summer was hell. My brother was hitchhiking across country and I was cooped up at home with my right leg in a cast and not knowing whether my knee would ever work again. What bugged me especially was the constant flood of researchers who came to our house to interrogate me, as if I had done the shooting. FBI, highway patrol, Scranton Commission . . . they all rode herd on me, and I got tired of seeing anyone enter the room. A fit of deep depression set in, but then as my knee began to heal, my mind healed also.

'Facing death and being forced to decide what I honestly believed in produced exciting results. I began to see that one man has only a brief life and that in it he'd better concentrate on those things which bring him inner happiness. The rest can be ignored. My family has a little cottage behind our house. It's set in woods, and in my boy scout days I had learned to love nature, so I spent my time out there . . . just looking. I did a great deal of reading. Have you ever read *Summerhill*, by A.S. Neill? It helped me put everything together.'

Wrentmore was the sixth student who had volunteered the comment, '*Summerhill*'s the best book I read at the university.' An account of an experimental school in England, it asks probing questions as to what the true function of education is and shows how a young person can acquire such an education, even though he must attend traditional schools and colleges. 'It taught me priorities,' Wrentmore says. He has an advanced vocabulary and uses words well, which is understandable, for his family was interested in learning and discussed it with him. 'I was driven to identify what I truly believed, and the more I thought the more I saw that I was committed to non-violence. I had become acquainted with some Quakers and found their teaching instructive. I read many of their works and came to the conclusion that even though my draft board has given me a conscientious-objector status, so that I was excused from military service, I could not in conscience cooperate with the draft in any degree. I concluded that I would have to turn in my draft card.

'I discussed this with expert advisers, and they pointed out that if I did turn in my draft card, signifying my intention of rejecting the whole system, I would be subject to one to five years in jail, and that if I refused to serve when called, I would be subject to an additional one to five. My adviser asked me, "Do you really want to spend two to ten years in jail when you can escape the whole problem by keeping your mouth shut and holding on to your conscientious-objector status?" I thought about this carefully. I walked in the woods, with my mending knee, and decided that I never again wanted to be associated with violence in any form, and that if my government was going to use violence as an act of national policy, I could not conform. So I went to the post office and mailed my card.'

Wrentmore speaks with such quiet assurance that one intuitively feels he has thought out his position and will adhere to it. 'People ask me if I wasn't scared to send my card in, or was I driven to it by some kind of moral crisis. I tell them it wasn't anything as deep as that. It seemed the natural thing . . . the only thing to do, and I haven't regretted it for a minute. Since I performed this act I've been more spiritually content than ever before in my life.'

He has also dropped out of serious competition for a university degree. 'I take three hours a work . . . the least you can get away with. But I read constantly, in all sorts of exciting fields. For the first time in my life I consider myself a real student, and I propose to continue this way. If I ever settle down, I will work for some good cause, maybe ecology or saving natural wooded areas like this one. I want to save, not destroy.'

Wrentmore's next decision proves how profoundly his experience has cut. 'I can no longer take ordinary patterns of life seriously. If there's a chance that you may be shot dead tomorrow while walking to class, why bother with nonessentials? I found a girl who thought the same way I did and we announced that we were setting up a commune for a group of congenial people. Seven of us, five fellows and two girls will be in on it; it will be a kind of roving commune. We're buying a van and we're going to set out for each of the various regions of the United States . . . Maine, the deserts, the parks, even Canada. We're going to live in woods and open spaces and work as we have to. We are mutually determined to find a life that can be meaningful and relevant.'

A friend asks, 'But what will you be doing when you're fifty?' and Wrentmore replies, 'From what I read, many scientists believe we won't be here when I'm fifty, so that's not my problem. Water, air and earth will be used up, so I'm for living right now.'

The two flags

The haunting figure of Allison Krause continued to move across the pages of magazines and newspapers long after the other students had been forgotten. And the contradictions surrounding her increased rather than diminished. No incident was more difficult to assess than the one which occurred at her former school, the John F. Kennedy High School in Silver Spring, Maryland.

It started Monday night, after the shooting. Robert Barber, teacher of English, telephoned John Dorn, principal, and said, 'You remember Allison Krause? That fine girl we had last year? Well, she's dead.'

On Tuesday morning Principal Dorn had an early dental appointment and went to it directly before reporting to his school, but as he left the doctor's office he wondered, 'What ought we do about the school flag? Should we lower it or not?' The problem had been taken out of his hands, for when he reached the school he found a scene of considerable agitation.

'A group of students, deeply moved by the deaths at Kent State, had got their hands on a PA system . . . a young man in our audio-visual department had given it to them. They were making speeches and trying to drum up support for a demonstration over Allison's death. A large number of students listened to them.

'Well, the affair developed into an argument over whether the school flag should be lowered out of respect for Allison. There was active support for the suggestion, but also a good deal of opposition.'

One sophomore boy argued vehemently, 'I ain't got no feeling for this. People talking about this chick who was killed at Kent. Everybody's out mourning her death and wanting us to lower the flag. Two GIs from this school have been killed in Vietnam. Why didn't we lower the flag for them? They're in there fighting to keep the flag up.' Other students remembered that they had never liked her that much anyway.

Principal Dorn says, 'Finally we reached a compromise. As you can see, we have two flagpoles out front, so we found another American flag, raised one to the top of its pole and flew the other at half-mast. I judged that this would please everybody.'

Not so. In the afternoon smoke was smelled throughout the school, and when teachers went out to investigate, they found that students opposed to a Krause memorial had hauled down her flag and burned it in an upstairs trashcan. The school had been about evenly divided between those who felt that Allison had been a representative student whose death was worthy of commemoration and those who had felt that she was too radical to have the flag lowered on her behalf.

The teacher best qualified to judge where Allison stood in political matters was Robert Barber. He says, 'She was not a radical. She was a very thoughtful person, inclined to ask questions. She was the kind of girl . . . I mean, if I had girl children I wish they'd be like her.' Obviously, he remembers her with affection. 'She was a stunning girl. Tall, composed. She was a woman. She wasn't any skinny teenager. Allison Krause was no run-of-the-mill kid.'

It was not of Mr. Barber that Allison was speaking when she confided to her Kent State roommate, Carol Buchholz, 'I got along fairly well with most of my high-school teachers, but one of my English teachers really bugged me and would ride me about talking in class. So one day I got fed up, stood up, said in a clear voice, "Fuck you!" and walked out of class. I wasn't allowed back for two days, but I never regretted saying it.'

Principal Dorn says, 'I've been able to turn up nothing about the incident Allison boasted about to her roommate—swearing at an English teacher and being thrown out of class. If it did happen, it was probably less dramatic than she reported to her Kent State friends.'

Allison's other Kent State roommate, Gail Travaglianti,

may throw some light on this: 'Allison had developed a way to handle teachers and could really snow them. They all loved her, but they didn't know her like we did . . . living with her. You got a really different picture then.'

At any rate, when she graduated from John F. Kennedy, her teachers signed the following assessment:

Allison is a very mature and stable young woman with a diligent, persevering, and intellectually curious approach to education. She possesses a very positive attitude in her total approach to life and her personal endeavors. Allison entered John F. Kennedy high school in the tenth grade and displayed her flexibility and adjustive powers by acclimating herself quickly and positively to an innovative school with philosophies quite different than she had previously been exposed to.

She is a personable and attractive young woman with an admirable degree of sophistication. Her poise and perception of people contribute to her ability of making and keeping friends from both her peer group and adults.

Someone who studied Allison's record at various schools summarized her this way: 'If there is a key to Allison's character, it will be found, I feel sure, in a study of her relationship with her father, who loved, cherished and understood her much better in death than in life.'

However, such micrometer judgments are unnecessary when weighed beside the testimony of two students we have met before. Lou Urbano, who had wanted to put out the ROTC fire with his coat, and Nick Haskakis, who had been beat up when he photographed the burning of the American flag, were on duty at Johnson Hall on Sunday night at about 8:00. Urbano says, 'That night there was a lot of action around here. Students rushing in, rumors flying out as to ugly things that were going to happen. I was working at the desk when Pat Dolney, a student counselor in whom I had a lot of confidence, hurried up and whispered, "That chick coming in the door has two Pepsi bottles under her arms."

'I didn't know the girl by name but recognized her as Barry Levine's friend. Since Barry lived in Johnson, we often saw her around the dorm and considered her another loudmouth.'

Haskakis knew her name. 'Only a few days before, she had borrowed twenty-five cents from me. I knew Barry pretty well. We called him Jingles because of his beads and bracelets. But his girl was too much.'

Urbano says, 'She stormed past us and headed for the girls' bathroom, and all I could think was, "Molotov cocktails. She's going to burn this building." So I called to Pat Dolney, and he said, "Hey, wait a minute with those bottles!" And with this she stopped and cursed us out like you never heard before.'

Pat Dolney confirms this: 'She was like a cat trapped in a corner, prepared to claw back. She really bad-mouthed us, then banged her way into the bathroom.'

After a few moments she came out, and Dolney said, 'You have to give us those bottles,' but, as he explains, 'she gave us the language bit again, winding up with the threat, "I'm not giving you anything. Get away from me." She was so violent that the only thing that would have stopped her would have been a hard slap, and I wasn't prepared to hit a girl.'

Dolney continues, 'Barry appeared on the stairs and Allison ran to him, accusing us of having abused her. Barry said a strange thing: "You can call her a bitch if you want to, but don't you ever touch her." She led the way to the sundeck which overlooks the commons, where the action was. When they were gone, we inspected the bathroom, but the bottles were gone.'

Urbano explains, 'We didn't know what to do with this wild chick, so we called Bill Fitzgerald, resident director of our dorm, and he went onto the sundeck.'

Fitzgerald takes up the story. 'The men at the desk had been uptight that weekend and I didn't place much emphasis on what they'd said about the girl and the bottles and the bathroom. My job was to get the kids off the sundeck because we'd heard rumors about sniper fire and I didn't want anyone doing anything from our roof. I was well acquainted with Allison Krause and liked her. I saw her standing by the wall, and she had one bottle. I said, "All right, everybody off the roof," and she gave me no trouble. I did not frisk her, so I can't say what was in the bottle." '

Urbano, Haskakis and Dolney were sure that her plan was to throw the bottles at policemen—a trick that had been used during the Chicago riots at the Democratic convention.

This ought not to have been our last glimpse of Allison Krause, nor was it. That came late on a Saturday afternoon in October when Barry Levine returned to Kent State, wandering about the campus like a frail grandee in a play by Molière, his mustache and goatee glistening in the cold autumn sun. He said many things in a quiet voice which at times seemed near breaking. He was a young man who had borne an enormous loss, and from his fragmentary sentences one gleaned this impression: 'Allison was strong-minded . . . interested in everything . . . a girl of overwhelming compassion . . . she could get angry when she had to . . . she never spoke of owning things, only of the good she could accomplish . . . she often thought of the future . . . she was convinced it would be better than the present . . . sometimes her face would light up like a candle, slowly, flickering, until her whole face was glowing . . . she was gentle . . . she had a temper but she was gentle . . .'

His words faltered into silence. And in that quiet, one suddenly was overwhelmed by a deep sense of loss—of so many young people who could have contributed to our nation's future, slain not only in war but on our college campuses: Orangeburg, Kent State, Jackson State, University of Kansas. They leave an emptiness, and a grief that will never be assuaged.

VII

SIGNIFICANCE

The threat to education

If events like those which overtook Kent State were to continue to occur either at Kent or elsewhere, American advanced education would be in the gravest peril. Society would react with revulsion and would rebel against giving any further moral or financial support to education beyond the high school level, and the whole grand superstructure of advanced learning as we have known it would come crashing down. It is impossible to believe that this would benefit the United States or that it would be anything but a tragedy of enormous dimension, but there are many in our society who want to see it happen.

We must understand how it could happen, and anyone who was present at Kent during the summer and autumn of 1970 saw only too clearly how this could have been accomplished. Here are three scenarios that observers feared.

Scenario one. At the opening of school in early October a cadre of committed revolutionaries, nameless successors to the more peaceful radicals who had once dominated the Haunted House and the place on Ash Street, would declare war on society by either dynamiting a building or shooting a policeman. It was not necessary to look to university students for such action, because a message from the underground, purporting to have come from Bernardine Dohrn, had publicly threatened that the national revolutionary movement would soon dynamite Kent.

Regardless of who committed the act, the reaction would be the same. The student body, almost unanimously, would condemn this violent action, but to no avail, for the Ohio legislature in Columbus would demand immediate and ex-

439

cessive reaction, and the local authorities in Portage County would feel free to close the university down again, this time perhaps for a couple of years. Also, with the first intimation of trouble on campus, vigilante groups from the surrounding countryside would arm themselves and begin a private cleaning-up of anyone with long hair or habits offensive to them. There would be open gunfire, which would be responded to by those students who had managed to smuggle weapons onto campus. The students would lose. Because of Kent's symbolic significance across America, there would be anguished responses from other student groups in other universities, and one by one our great educational institutions would close . . . the list would grow each day. And some would stay closed for a year or more.

Scenario two. It was quite possible, in October, 1970, that violent disruptions in any college or university could have served as the spark for general student unrest. If the educational community at Wisconsin kept an eye on Kent, fearful of what might happen there, it was equally true that people in Kent were watching Wisconsin, and Colorado, and Michigan, and a dozen other schools. Any spectacular student rioting in any of those institutions would have ignited the entire student population of this country to the flash point. Suppose that some insane incident at Wisconsin, following in the wake of the August bombing there, had inflamed both the townspeople and the student body, with resulting confrontations and bloodshed. Surely the consequences would have reverberated around this nation, and students in Kent might well have reacted. From that point on, the counter-reactions of society would be the same as before, with similar results.

Scenario three. This is the most mournful, because it is the most likely, and it is likely because it grows not from some one insane act committed by some addle-pated idiot, but from the daily life and desperations of thoughtful students. It is this possibility that must be carefully considered.

The degree of radicalization that occurred at Kent State on May 4 when the guns went off is almost impossible to describe. Jocks who saw girls gunned down began to talk like revolutionaries. Greeks whose houses were invaded needlessly by police and who were gassed while sitting on their front porches sounded like YSA members of two years before. Students who had thought of themselves as straight suddenly found themselves discussing what they called 'the repressive nature of the police state.' And thousands of white students who had never paid much attention to black student demands began to say to one another, 'Maybe they have legitimate complaints.'

Colin Neiburger was standing on a train platform in Cleveland shortly after the shooting when a sorority girl from Kent rushed up to him, embraced him fervently, and cried, 'Colin! I should have listened to you last year.' One of the researchers had the opportunity of meeting with sixty fraternity men at Kent, the straightest group on campus, and came away in a state of near-shock. 'They talked like flaming radicals!' he reported. 'They despise Vietnam. They discuss openly whether they should flee to Canada to avoid the draft. They believe we're destroying our natural resources. And they claim that neither the university nor the national administration will listen to them. If parents in middle America believe that it's only the long hairs who are demanding action, they ought to listen to their conservative children.'

Now suppose that this large body of sensible students, already partially radicalized by events of the past two years, become convinced that there is no hope of modifying society through normal channels. Suppose they come to believe that their best professors are being intimidated by the FBI, or spied upon by the army. Suppose they grow increasingly resentful at the rumored presence of informers in the classroom. Suppose they feel, correctly or not, that they have no recourse at the administration level. Suppose our national leaders continue to belabor them publicly while diminishing economic support. And then suppose that the Vietnam war drags on interminably, with sporadic escalations and no diminution in the killing or no escape from the draft.

Is it not possible that students might interpret some otherwise trivial thing as the final indignity and overrespond to it? There would be mass protest of some kind, harsh reaction from the police, an irresponsible act by some student, and the quick mobilization of vigilantes. From there on, the descent is clearly marked out.

The end result of the three scenarios is the same. A substantial number of centers of higher education throughout the

United States would be immediately closed down. This must not be taken as a remote possibility. State legislatures and local governing bodies are itching for a chance to do this, 'to teach those snot-nosed kids and smart-aleck professors a lesson.' The important thing is not the temporary disciplining of the universities, for they could absorb that, but what might happen next.

As soon as the universities were closed, legislatures would take steps to emasculate the state-supported schools. The right of professors to criticize society would be abolished. Many departments would be eliminated permanently. Student enrollments would be cut 40 percent. Graduate schools would be dropped from many universities, and emphasis would be placed upon vocational education. Courses like The New Family, Karl Marx and Nineteenth Century Thought, The New York School of Action Painting, and The Protest Novel would vanish, and any professor brave enough to teach sociology, English or philosophy would be supervised by constantly running tape recorders whose contents would be reviewed not by university personnel but by civil authorities not connected with the university. The result would be the passing of stern laws prohibiting the enrollment of students from out of state; these would be popular with voters for two reasons. They see no reason why as citizens of State A they should pay for the education of students from State B; and they are convinced that it is outsiders, especially Jewish students from New York, who cause local disruptions, in spite of the fact that most of the known agitation has moved from west to east and involved only as many Jewish students as the percentage of Jews in the general population would have provided.

It is entirely possible that in each state certain state-supported institutions, especially those which had caused irritation in the past, might be closed permanently and their vast investment of campus and building diverted to other uses. Thus Kent State in Ohio and Temple University in Philadelphia, to take only two schools who have battled long and well for certain principles, might be shut down forever. Had a plebiscite been taken in Portage County in the summer of 1970, it is likely that the voters would have elected to get rid of Kent State once and for all. As late as October, when school had peacefully resumed, researchers for this book attended a series of informal dinner parties at which well over 80 percent of those present, responsible citizens all, were in favor of abolishing the university and turning its physical plant over to some other social use.

Nor would private institutions be exempt from such discipline. Boards would be pressured both from within and without to terminate all aspects of university life which cause trouble. Alumni, battered emotionally by what they had been witnessing over the past three or four years, would withhold contributions until such time as corrective measures were taken, and in the long run the private university might be in a more perilous position than the public, in that a legislature might be quicker to respond to public demand for reinstitution of some form of public education than a private board might be.

It would be very tempting to close major educational institutions, but for a democracy to do so would be insanity. This complex industrial democracy could not function if even one generation of its trained personnel were lacking. Who would plan the sewer systems? Who would design the new Pontiac cars? Who would invent the better plastic or print the better books? High school graduates cannot provide the medical and dental services required nor the leadership in law and engineering—and to believe that they can is preposterous.

More important, the constant study and evaluation of society which is required if a nation is to remain healthy can be carried on only in the university. Trained minds are essential for the understanding of where we are and where we are heading. Universities are needed more today than ever before, if only because the need for response to new problems is accelerated.

Two examples illustrate this condition. One of the subjects which most infuriate the outside observer is sociology. Of a hundred professors whom the laymen of this country would like to silence, a vast majority would be from this field, yet in no area of exploration is professional guidance more needed. The American system of courtship and marriage is undergoing the most violent change. Young people have struck out in bold new directions, and the trial marriage, which so infuriated Americans when Judge Ben Lindsey and philosopher Bertrand Russell first proposed it, is now commonplace, and in the very families of those whose parents objected most strenuously when the idea was first suggested. Communal living, new plans for rearing children and new attitudes toward the care of elderly people must all be studied, dissected and judged. The professor who directs his microscope to such subjects is not popular with the general public, but his work is essential and he must be protected while he carries it out.

The second example comes from a less inflammatory field. The great Penn Central railroad combine, one of the largest corporations in America and one of the important symbols of our business history, has for the past fifteen years been going quietly broke. Vast changes were under way in American life, and these produced sharp repercussions in the transportation industry, but the managers of the Penn Central seemed not to be aware of this. Because of the vital significance of railroading to this nation, there ought to have been in universities like Penn, Columbia and Chicago, to name only those in the major cities affected by the collapse of this particular railroad, college professors who were philosophically analyzing the nature of railroads in our democracy and issuing warnings that if the Penn Central continued the way it was going, it would soon be broke. Had there been such professors, and had they issued their warnings a decade ago, it is obvious that business leaders would have castigated them as meddlers and warned them to return to the campus and not interfere with real life. It is the job of the university to put all of real life under the microscope of reason and investigation. To consign the university to a lesser role would be stupid, for to do so would be to insure the collapse of this society.

The question, then, in this twilight age when great institutions may be closed for shorter or longer periods, is this: How can we have a disciplined university whose behavior conforms to generally accepted standards and at the same time preserve the freedom of investigation and discussion? If the universities cannot insure the former, the society will not provide the latter. And if free investigation vanishes, then this democracy will also vanish.

If we did close our schools, we could continue for a while without apparent loss, but soon we would no longer be able to maintain a creative society here at home, and we would fail in our competition with Russia and China abroad. Our industries would find themselves lagging behind those of Germany and Sweden. Our music and theater and magazines would begin to wither, and what imagination we had in television would vanish. Public services would begin to falter and there would be no inventions to keep factories alive. Worst of all, the yeast of ideas which makes life palatable would no longer operate and a terrible drabness would overtake us all, for the intellectual leadership which a modern society requires would be lacking.

We need education. We need intelligence. We need the inspiration and the fire of the young. And if we believe, even in moments of frustration and despair, that we can get along without them, we are trying to do what no other creative civilization in history has been able to do: function without trained minds. It is our job to restudy the role of education in a free society so that the historic functions of the university can continue after its weaknesses have been corrected.

The concept of sanctuary

One of the cherished concepts of humanity has been the sanctuary, a physical location to which a man in trouble could flee for protection from king, sheriff or police. Originally, the sanctuary was a land area in which fugitives could hide; today in Tahiti a central valley, girt by mountains, is still uninhabited because for centuries it was maintained as a sanctuary in which threatened islanders lived unmolested for years. In the Middle Ages any sanctified church served as a sanctuary, and thousands of men and women notable in history availed themselves of it. In the Renaissance, universities appropriated to themselves the right of sanctuary, but this was so abused by students and criminals that it had to be abandoned.

In 1918 students at the university of Córdoba in Argentina held their rector captive, without food or water, for several days, forcing the university to accept numerous demands, including abolition of examinations, open admission, student representation on the university council, and a revival of the old concept of the university as a sanctuary. Henceforth, police would not be permitted on campus.

The nation was not only inclined to grant this demand; it was eager to do so. Between 1900 and 1918 strong-arm politicians had tried to destroy university freedom and had instituted many repressive measures. Intellectual freedom was so abused that even conservative citizens cried, 'Our universities must again be free.' It would be wise, sensible men said, to remove the university from the reach of selfish politicians and arrogant police. Precisely the opposite result was obtained when sanctuary was granted. The campus did not become free; it became embroiled in political power struggles, street revolution and downright thuggery.

Students began to rob banks and flee back to the university, where they were secure from arrest or even police investigation. Student gangs became bolder and made frequent forays into the community, scrambling back to safety on the campus. Fidel Castro, as a pistolero at the University of Havana, is supposed to have murdered Manolo Castro (no relation) when the latter opposed him in a student election.

One of the most vicious results of this sanctuary was the creation of a class of overage students who enrolled for no courses but who hung around the campus year after year. The fossils, they were called, and in their forties they exerted a powerful influence on younger minds. José Revueltas, a student leader in the strike at Mexico's National University in 1968, was fifty-four years old. Numerous gangster-students past the age of thirty-five sought sanctuary after shoot-outs or bus-burnings in the various Latin American countries.

The classic illustration of what sanctuary means is the Central University of Caracas, Venezuela, where the theory was carried to its extreme. Central was made the headquarters for the Castro-backed Revolutionary Armed Forces, whose street fighters operated directly from the campus, retreating to it whenever they ran into danger. The university hospital was converted into a military field hospital for the treatment of their wounded, and two of the dormitories which they controlled were nicknamed Leningrad and Stalingrad. It became the custom for the movement to collect funds by robbing banks, and men who had gunned down bank guards or patrons found it convenient to scurry back to the university for sanctuary. Businessmen were kidnapped by gangs operating out of classrooms, and several assassinations were conducted by forty-year-old students.

The final outrage took place on December 13, 1966. Gunmen who had been hiding out in the university swept through the downtown section of Caracas in a stolen car, blazed away with submachine guns and murdered government officials. That day the cabinet declared a state of siege, and in predawn hours, steel-helmeted troops stealthily surrounded the university campus and moved in. A sharp fight ensued with the resident guerrillas, but the government prevailed. When the firing ended, more than one hundred so-called students had been arrested, along with an arsenal of guns, bombs and a revolutionary motor pool of fifty-one stolen automobiles. The police had known for some time that the cars were hidden on campus, but had been powerless to go in and get them.

Subsequent investigation disclosed many facts about the manner in which university sanctuary had functioned in Venezuela. The university press had been taken over for the publication of communist leaflets; student organizations were forced to give up their treasuries for revolutionary purposes; faculty appointments were controlled by Castro-led factions; scholarships were allocated at the discretion of communist cells and were awarded only to communists; university money was siphoned off to pay travel costs for students who wished to attend communist conferences in Europe, such as the meeting of International Federation of Students in Prague. It was proved conclusively that student gangsters, with only the most tenuous relationship to the university, had converted $22 million of the university budget to their personal purposes.

One member of the research team working on this book had a personal brush with the concept of sanctuary. While serving as a cultural ambassador to Venezuela, he had the most pleasant association with students and professors from the Central University and was eight times invited by them to speak at an assembly. Each time the meeting had to be canceled because minority cells on campus threatened to close the university down if an American imperialist was allowed to set foot on the campus. Clandestine meetings were arranged, but even these were called off because general student rioting was in progress. A professor explained, 'Of the 365 days in a year, the campus is closed about 200 because of one kind of riot or another.' Walking through the university was like touring a battlefield, and one wondered how education could possibly take place in such a climate.

It doesn't. Professor Lambros Comitas, currently teaching at Columbia University in New York, says of education generally in Latin America, 'When the universities were politicized, because of sanctuary and special privilege, the result was that no matter what you studied—law, medicine, science—you got not a teacher of law or science, but a politician. So we began to graduate M.D.'s who couldn't cure the sick and LL.B.'s who couldn't defend a man in court. They were politicians and not doctors or lawyers. The result has been that several nations became so starved for competent manpower that they quietly began to create something called institutes. Actually, they're universities on the American plan. Now, an institute has little prestige, but they do produce doctors who can practice medicine and lawyers who can quote you the law.'

The cultural ambassador, having been outlawed by the Caracas revolutionaries, was invited by the students and faculty of the University of Maracaibo in the western part of Venezuela to speak there. His lecture was scheduled for the library at 11:00 in the morning, but as his plane landed he saw plumes of fire rising from the campus. At 9:00 rebellious students claiming sanctuary had burned down the library. Ensuing riots sent students rampaging through the streets; battles with the police occurred and several people were killed. At dusk he was spirited aboard a high-speed motorboat and evacuated across Lake Maracaibo. Subsequent investigations convinced him that the theory of sanctuary has been a major factor in the near-destruction of education in many Latin American universities and would insure the demise of free education in the United States if the concept were allowed to take root here.

It is possible to argue that the decline which overtook Latin American universities when they adopted the concept of sanctuary has no significance for the United States, in that the standards of the Latin universities were not high, their instruction not first grade, and their students not serious. Young men in those countries who sought a real education went to France, Spain or the United States. No Latin American university stood in the category of Yale or Michigan, so that what happened to them could be dismissed as irrelevant to our problem.

But when one sees the fate that overtook the universities of Japan, he must acknowledge that institutions like Tokyo University are on a par with the best we have to offer and that what happened to them is relevant to what might happen to us. Trouble started with Japan's surrender in 1945. The whole society, morally outraged by the behavior of Japan's secret police in 1930–45, when they terrorized universities and exercised a most venal system of thought control, approved a plan whereby universities were granted sanctuary: it was forbidden for police to step on a university campus for any reason whatever. At the same time the nation swung away from the militarism which had brought it degradation; students, deluded in the belief that communism was the antithesis of militarism, formed a powerful student movement called Zengakuren, an abbreviation for Federation of All Japan Student Councils. Openly communist, this federation quickly dominated Japanese advanced education. Thus, from the finest motives—intellectual freedom and peace—a series of wrong choices was made and the stage was set for the emasculation of Japanese education.

The program of Zengakuren sounds familiar to anyone interested in recent American developments: 'We shall free millions of people from isolated lives they are now leading within our ailing society.' Japanese students were the first to speak of alienation, the first to make Che Guevara their hero. Everything that has happened in American universities first happened in Japan.

Zengakuren became so large that it broke into two divisions, one allying itself openly with the Communist party, the other finding organized communism too tame and too reluctant to sponsor rebellion in the streets. An unbridgeable gap developed and warfare between the two groups became common. In 1969, when one young man was suspected of contemplating a switch from the non-communist terrorists to the communist faction, his friends beat him to death to save him from that error.

The Zengakuren movement completely dominated Japanese higher education. It terrorized professors, controlled entire universities, conducted open warfare with the police, invaded the Diet and trained its members in the art of rioting.

A Zengakuren riot became a weapon of public policy. Two thousand screaming students, dressed in steel helmets, their faces covered with towels to fend off tear gas and prevent photographic identification, and armed with clubs and bags of rocks, descend upon a university hall or a foreign embassy, and within moments a massive brawl ensues. The target is twofold, to infuriate civilians and to battle the riot police. Says a Zengakuren publication:

> To the student, ours is a hostile society, and it is the riot police who represent the hostility. It is therefore the duty of the student to initiate major reform, and our front-line batch of enemies—the riot police—must be sternly dealt with.

After four or five years of practice in the streets of Tokyo and other large cities, Zengakuren students learned how to take over whole sections of a community, fight successfully for five or six hours, hold off the riot police and throw society into turmoil.

On one famous occasion a trainload of students left Tokyo after having been searched for weapons by the police. They were headed for a peaceful university a hundred miles inland.

On the long trip they sang student songs and had a jovial time, so that the secret service men watching them wondered, 'What are these kids up to?' About ten miles from their destination, their leader jerked the cord on the train, brought it to a halt, and supervised his troops as they rushed out to a cluster of haystacks, uncovered a cache of weapons which had been deposited there a week before, ran back to the train, and stormed into the unsuspecting city fully armed. Their take-over was complete.

What reasons have the Japanese students given for their rebellions? First bloodshed with the police occurred in 1960 when Zengakuren opposed ratification of the Japan–United States Security Treaty. Adult political forces supported the students, for members of only one party, the ruling Liberal–Democratic, attended the Diet session; the others were outside demonstrating with the students.

In 1964 students staged violent rallies outside the United States naval base at Sasebo to protest the visit of the first nuclear-powered submarine. Later, when B-52's started to bomb Vietnam from Okinawa, renewed protests swept Japan.

In 1965, when South Korea and Japan negotiated a sensible plan for resuming intergovernmental relations, students rioted for many days, demanding abandonment of the proposal on grounds that since Japan had occupied Korea for more than sixty years, any Korean–Japanese relations could only end in further Japanese exploitation.

In 1967, when Prime Minister Eisaku Sato sought to fly out of Haneda Airport for talks in Washington with President Johnson, more than 3,000 students converged on the airstrip, trying to prevent Sato's plane from taking off. A total of 662 students and 564 police were severely injured that day during violent demonstrations which lasted more than four hours.

In 1968 Zengakuren was successful in launching nation-wide riots against the United States' presence in Okinawa, once more throwing civil government into turmoil.

But the most devastating effect has been upon the universities themselves. Here terrorism has become a fine art, and learning has been suspended. Not long ago, nearly 100 universities were totally shut down and the remaining 700 suffered almost daily interruption. Students dug themselves into classroom buildings, which they occupied for over a year and from which they conducted brazen military operations against the police. At one university they beat a plainclothesman nearly to death because he had trespassed upon their campus while chasing a pickpocket. Fearing police retaliation, students everywhere began stockpiling rocks, clubs and Molotov cocktails; they became adept at making wooden shields and steel helmets. Open warfare was declared. For eighteen months the students succeeded in holding off the police and halting orderly education. The universities had ceased to function.

The students had overreached themselves. In January, 1969, a tough, resolute army of 8,500 riot police, armed only with bamboo sticks and tear gas, set out to clear the gangs out of Tokyo University and return it to the business of teaching. They succeeded in cleaning up the open spaces but found themselves unable to dislodge some 800 last-ditch students who had barricaded themselves in buildings which they had transformed into fortresses.

'Move in!' came the order. The resultant clashes, televised live on a national hook-up, gave the nation its first comprehensive view of what student rebellion meant. Molotov cocktails, rocks, pails of water rained down upon the police as they tried vainly to break into the student bastions. Night fell, with the students victorious and many policemen being hauled off to improvised hospitals.

On the second day of the siege the police came back with reinforcements. That turned the tide, and by nightfall the students had surrendered: 600 students arrested, 200 wounded, some of them requiring hospitalization, eight gravely injured. Tokyo University, one of the finest in the world, had to be kept closed. No examinations were given that year, and what was appalling to the young people of Japan, where entrance to Tokyo is more important than entrance to heaven, no freshman class was admitted. More than anything else, this brought home the fact that government could no longer tolerate student revolution.

Daniel Okimoto, a California Nisei with degrees from Princeton and Harvard, was studying for his doctorate at Tokyo University at the time and has recorded his reaction:

Alienated now from the administration and fellow students alike, hard-core radicals braced themselves to go down fighting, their ranks fortified by activists from other universities and youth organizations. Riot police, whose presence had helped ignite the strike, now came in to subdue the last remnants of opposition. Lifting barricade after barricade, the police laid siege to the final student stronghold, Yasuda Hall. In a fierce battle, involving helicopters, water hoses, tear gas, staves, rocks and Molotov cocktails, riot squads stormed into the building and cleared out the last radical resistance.

Cleaning up the rubble and repairing the destroyed property took armies of workers several weeks. Despite the return of normalcy to the campus, entrance exams had to be canceled, classes continued for months to be disrupted, graduation ceremonies were suspended, and many other functions were postponed for fear of rekindling the disturbance. During the long struggle, a year of study was lost, a year of faculty research squandered, hundreds of thousands of dollars wasted, and physical and emotional anguish was sustained by all parties involved.*

Reforms have been instituted. Professors are not so dictatorial as in the past, and the feudalism which lingered in the universities is diminishing. But the concept of the university as a sanctuary, not responsible to civil authority, has been dealt a deathblow. Police are not welcomed on campus, and during 364 days a year they stay off; but if either criminality or rioting occurs, they do come on campus, as they should.

What happened in Japan gives the best insight as to how the entire system of higher education could collapse if the relationship between the university and the rest of our society continues to degenerate.

What must be done

Society is going to demand some kind of stringent restructuring of advanced education. This 'shaking down,' as it has cynically been termed, will not be all bad, for any social institution requires constant review and alteration.

The state of Michigan has set the pattern in the legislative field with a set of six new rules governing its thirteen public colleges and universities.

1. Any student who damages campus property must be immediately expelled.

2. Any student found guilty of damaging property or committing violence against a person will lose any scholarship he may be holding.

3. Any institution which fails to enforce the above rules

*Daniel Okimoto, *American in Disguise*. Tokyo: Walker-Weatherhill, 1971.

(against faculty members, too, if they are involved) will lose all state funds.

4. No state funds can be used for salary or scholarship for anyone found with firearms on campus.

5. Faculty members cannot get paid unless they certify each week that they have been face-to-face with students in a classroom situation for at least ten, twelve or fifteen hours that week, depending upon the category of the institution.

6. Wayne State University will have its annual budget cut by $93,000, the amount it has been giving to a student newspaper which published 'obscene, seditious and anti-Semitic' material.

Oregon followed with an even more stringent code. Faculty, regardless of tenure, can be dismissed if convicted of either a felony or a crime involving moral turpitude, or if guilty of habitual neglect of duty. Students and faculty alike can be disciplined for nine additional reasons, including possession of firearms, obstruction of vehicular movement, unauthorized use of campus facilities, possession of illegal drugs, and inciting others to engage in any proscribed conduct. Whitney Bates, history professor at Portland State University, characterized the code as a 'shopping list for persons seeking means to discharge faculty members.' But the Board of Higher Education explained, 'Society has for long recognized the necessity for protecting colleges and universities against undue interference in order that an environment of freedom, which is indispensable to their efficient service to society, might be insured. In recent times it has become apparent that they must be protected also from coercion from within.' The board warned professors against 'the habitual or persistent introduction into a course of controversial matter that has no relation to the course content. The board does not wish any of its institutions to speak out with a corporate voice on public issues.'

The Ohio legislature responded quickly to the disruptions which had racked its major institutions, passing House Bill 1219, which alters considerably the rules under which state universities would henceforth function. Twenty specific crimes are listed, and the moment any student or faculty member is arrested for any one of them, he is automatically suspended, his rights and privileges are removed, and any salary or scholarship payments are stopped.

The twenty crimes cover such obvious felonies as intentional shooting or stabbing, assault and battery upon law enforcement officers, arson, and manufacture of fire bombs. But several less obvious crimes are listed, such as assault with an intent to rape, destruction of public utility fixtures, malicious injury to property, and campus disruption, which covers the actions of anyone who 'willfully or knowingly, with force or violence, disrupts the orderly conduct of the lawful activities of a college or university.' Punishment is swift and inescapable; a referee suspends the arrested person and he is remanded to trial. If found guilty, he is dismissed from the university. There are constitutional safeguards. The suspended person may appeal and the convicted person may apply for readmission after one year, which can be granted 'only upon terms of strict disciplinary probation.' Under House Bill 1219, all the disturbances which plagued Kent between 1968–70 could have been handled by the administration with the arresting assistance of the Ohio State Highway Patrol. Whether the terms of the new bill are too vague or too loosely drawn, the courts will have to decide, but enough will stand to give the university new powers to defend itself.

More important, in the long run, is a powerful document drawn up by a hard-nosed Select Committee of the Ohio Legislature to Investigate Campus Disturbances, for it spells out the future. In thirty-four closely reasoned pages, which are surprisingly non-hysterical if one considers the emotional climate in which they were written, the committee warns the universities what the latter must do to clean house so that the legislature will not have to step in and do the job:

It is appropriate, therefore, that the academic communities themselves solve these problems for which the remedies are within their power to administer. Failure will mean total loss of public confidence in the ability of administrators to govern the universities, of faculty members to fulfill their obligations as educators, and of students to pursue their studies with diligence, mature judgment and self-restraint. In that melancholy event, direct legislative involvement would be inevitable.

Recommendations of the committee are far-ranging, and are accompanied with a warning that the committee will be visiting each campus six months hence to check on what the universities have done to police themselves. Students are to be expelled or suspended for 'misconduct involving moral turpitude, drug abuse or persistent misconduct, whatever its gravity.' Faculty members are warned that the committee has heard of instances in which 'faculty members had condoned or actively encouraged disruptive activities by students and had even participated in such activities, had failed to teach the scheduled course content, had failed without excuse to meet scheduled classes, had made unwarranted and repeated use of obscene language in open class, and before other students had ridiculed and degraded students holding political and social opinions opposed to their own.' Appended to this list was the recommendation: 'The code of faculty conduct and discipline should provide that whether an offender is tenured or not is irrelevant to the imposition of appropriate sanctions for misconduct.' Administrators are chided for having surrendered so many of their prerogatives to faculty and student committees and are urged to take them back: 'In part, such committees represent administrative surrender to increasingly clamorous demands by faculty and students for control of university affairs. It was pointed out that such committees frequently deal with matters beyond the experience or competence of some or all their members, and require weeks and even months to reach decisions which a competent administrator might make in a matter of hours or days.'

From these samples it can be seen that many changes are going to be forced upon public education, some of them draconian; after a brief experience the most repressive will be ignored by both the legislature and the university. Others will persist and some of them will be salutary. Let us see what the necessary changes might be, remembering that they apply only to public universities; private colleges have their own special problems.

Regents and trustees. Both the public and the legislature will demand a higher level of performance from appointed boards, who will have to exercise more control than in the past. The senseless proliferation and duplication of fields of specialization ought to end. In a state like Ohio, or a region like the Rocky Mountains, where population is not concentrated, institutions should reach an agreement that each would do what it can do best. Libraries, staffs and students should be concentrated at the effective point and other institutions in the area should not try to compete in the same field.

Boards must insist that the universities get back to the problem of teaching and stop trying to be all things to all people. Specifically, research on military matters should not be conducted on university campuses nor subsidized by the military or industry. The many institutes of questionable teaching value—although of unquestioned investigative importance—should be removed from the university and located elsewhere. Balance between teaching and research must be achieved, and freshman and sophomore students should have at least some contact with full professors, for they are in their most formative years and would profit most from such teaching.

The question of open admission to the university must be reconsidered. Kent State is cluttered with students who have no vocation to be on campus. The young man whose previous education has not prepared him to read, write, figure or grapple with abstract ideas and who lacks the capacity to acquire those skills has no place in a university. He is destined, from the moment he sets foot on campus, to a life of frustration; too often he will become radicalized, and with bad luck, could become a revolutionary, for he knows that the university cannot fulfill his needs. For the poorly prepared student who does have a capacity to learn, the state should provide some kind of pre-university experience which would enable him to catch up; after two years or more of such educational therapy, the successful learner should enter the sophomore year with the probability that he will succeed.

Serious consideration should be given to a plan whereby a large system like Ohio's is broken down into three different kinds of universities. The first would specialize in technical training, with emphasis upon skills; every effort would be made to make this type of education respectable, and faculty and salaries should be no lower than in the next two types. The second would specialize in granting the bachelor degree in all fields, the master's in some, and the doctorate in a highly selected few. Emphasis would be upon teaching, with the faculty required to keep abreast of research being done throughout the nation. The third would be the traditional, full-fledged university competing with great schools like Harvard and Chicago. It would offer a complete roster of research and would contain law and medical faculties. Once a decision was made as to the kind of institution a given university was to be, regents and trustees should be watchful in protecting it against encroachments which would divert it from its responsibility; it should not be allowed to slip unobstrusively back into the sloppy tradition whereby each university, regardless of its capacity, tried to be everything to everybody. Obviously, a university of the third type ought not to permit open admission, because its curriculum and teaching would be so advanced that only the more literate high school graduate could profit. But there should be a fairly free interchange of students after the sophomore year, for by then students would have gained a clearer understanding of their interests and capabilities.

When such a proposal was discussed in Ohio, one knowing resident cautioned, 'It would never work. Ohio State University wouldn't enroll enough football players to retain its pre-eminence. And that the legislature would not allow.'

Administration. In the next decade American advanced education is going to make a grave mistake, but there seems no way to prevent it. Regents and legislatures will call for appointment of administrators from outside fields like business or the military in the mistaken idea that they will know how to run a university. Fortified by automatic laws like House Bill 1219 and the proposed Oregon statutes, these men will be able to keep the lid on for a while, but the outcome can only be second-rate education and a constant deterioration of that. University administrators are best when they come up through the ranks and have an intellectual competence, for they deal not only with buildings and budgets but also with young minds and the future of this nation. There is no 'administrative type'; there is only the trained educator who has a gift for administering complex organizations. If he is difficult to find in the local universities, Ohio must look elsewhere, and then start quickly to develop its own crop, for one such man, properly placed, can inspire the young people of an entire state.

During all but the last crisis, the administrators of Kent State performed well and no blanket condemnation can be justified by the facts. However, the legislative committee is correct when it recommends that every administration in Ohio recover to itself the basic functions of administration. Too many boards and committees have been allowed to grow up and to siphon off the responsibilities of the administrator. Faculty and students are entitled to representation on such boards as are decided upon, but a complex of such boards must not be allowed to stultify action.

It is regrettable that a university today must have a crisis plan, but if this is an age of crisis, not to be prepared is preposterous. The distinction in military circles between line and staff—those who are responsible for command and those whose job it is to see that command has the materials to do the job—is an admirable one. On every campus it should be clearly understood where the line of command runs and upon whom it devolves when swift decision is required.

Universities probably make a mistake when they place too much emphasis and hope on campus police. In Ohio, the pendulum has swung much too far in the direction of an armed guard poised to sweep down on evildoers; it is frightening to realize that under the new laws any one of these quasi-policemen has the power to arrest either a student or a faculty member and thus cause his instant suspension for a year or his loss of enrollment or job for life. This is much too close to the old Japanese and German systems which caused such vigorous and ill-advised countermeasures after the last war. The university would be better served by calling in outside police and reserving for its campus force various caretaking and supervisory jobs.

Faculty. Tenure for professors should be abolished. It is abused by men of little dedication, protects mainly the incompetent, does not protect the young who are on the firing line, and has no parallel in the adult life of a democracy except in the lesser jobs in civil service, where its principle produces even greater evil. It is an affront to those who best support education in that they enjoy no tenure. Its place should be taken by a guaranteed-employment contract renewable after review at ten-year intervals (or seven) with tenure till retirement after thirty years of satisfactory service.

Although it is preposterous to think of a university not founded on a basis of scholarship, and although major faculty emphasis must continue to be the search for truth and new understandings of it, there ought to be an equal opportunity for professional advancement for those members of the faculty who bear the major teaching load. Indulgent smiles used to greet those who proposed dividing the faculty into two categories, 'the scholars and the teachers,' for it seemed obvious that one became a scholar in order to teach and that no one had a right to teach unless he was a scholar, but many critics of the university are now satisfied that advanced research has become so highly specialized that the old belief is no longer viable. There is a place for the man who specializes in instruction, and no interview was more gloomy than the one in which a young graduate assistant confessed, 'When I reported to Kent for my job, the head of the department told me, "You have two responsibilities, teaching and research, and you must not get your priorities confused. It will take you at least two years to get your degree, but unless you maintain a 3.5 average your first year, you won't be invited back. Therefore, apply yourself to the courses you are taking and learn to get by in the courses you are teaching." '

The more that restrictive legislation hampers the traditional role of the professor, the more dedicated he must become. His impartial wisdom is needed now more than ever. As changes are forced upon the university, his experience and precaution are essential. And as our nation faces new problems, it requires the counsel of the best brains available. In recent years there have been harsh attacks on professors; to them there is only one reply: 'Could this intricate nation exist for one year without the help of trained intelligence?' Professors are more valuable now than ever before, more essential to the national well-being. They must continue as bastions of freedom, for this may be their finest contribution to America.

We spent many hours listening to a debate which confronts all large universities: Should teaching fellows and graduate assistants be made a formal part of the faculty? We have heard every reason why they should not, for example: 'They are too immature to have the best interest of the university at heart.' But not one counterbalances the overwhelming fact that much of the instruction first- and second-year students receive comes from these unattached young scholars. If they are not absorbed into the general faculty, they ought at least to be handled differently from the way they now are. To do otherwise is to lay the university open to the charge of employing sweated labor.

Students. Society is going to demand that students comport themselves more responsibly; if they don't, they are going to be thrown out of the university. Insofar as behavior is concerned, the new rules impose no added hardship on the young person who wants an education. For the most part they enforce laws already on the books, laws which the majority of society accepts but which in recent years have been overlooked where students were concerned. Arson is arson, and persons guilty of it should go to jail. Inciting to riot has been a felony for many years. And the enticing theory of sanctuary was never acknowledged in law.

While students should volunteer to respect accepted modes of behavior, they must not allow themselves to be muzzled in speech nor put in blinders intellectually. The university is a place for investigation, and the years from eighteen through twenty-five are a time for broad questioning. Political activity on the campus ought to continue as vigorously as in the past, for our democracy depends upon a constant inflow of young people committed to politics. All aspects of our political, social, economic and moral life ought to be subjected to scrutiny. Indeed, there is a greater need for the questing student now than there was ten years ago, for the rate of change has accelerated. But the excesses of recent years, when intellectual investigation led to physical violence, must be halted, and every sensible student acknowledges that.

In a time when the stress is on what students must not do, it may be helpful to remember what they should do. They attend a university to gain an education, and this presupposes intellectual, social and political participation. Our nation has prospered in part because so many of our young people have learned at university the full range of their capabilities, and any effort now to diminish the breadth of that experience would be folly, for it would impoverish our nation twenty years from now. Specifically, in addition to studying, students ought to (1) participate in the governance of the university; (2) help set rules of behavior; (3) help determine what is to be taught; (4) help evaluate their teachers; (5) help establish university priorities; (6) help in the political organization of the student body along democratic lines; (7) assume some responsibility for good relations with the surrounding community of which they will be a significant part for four years.

In the 1970's it is especially difficult to be a responsible student, because as the university relinquishes its role of *in loco parentis* and accords the student freedoms no previous students have known, he is obligated to use that freedom intelligently and with some restraint; behavior and speech patterns which accomplish only the alienation of the general community are counterproductive. Society is not yet wise enough to solve the marijuana problem, but when infraction of present rules can bring down upon a student three non-concurrent jail terms of twenty to forty years, prudent behavior is necessary until society does clarify its thinking. It is impossible to condone the decision of those students who believe that the only escape from American pressures is to emigrate either to Canada or Sweden; if the existing alternatives are judged to be morally unacceptable, a jail term in the United States would seem preferable. Finally, the breadth of the gap between parents and children seems greater now than in previous generations, and young people are obligated to do what they can to diminish this distance. If student life is more complicated now, it also seems more exciting and potentially rewarding. It is hard to muster sympathy for the recurring statement, 'Who cares? We may all be dead tomorrow.' That is not a legitimate student posture.

Finally, the student must identify his major goals and must not expect the university to fulfill those which it is not competent to handle. The student whose life goal is 'the complete restructuring of society' or 'the immediate abolishment of capitalism' or 'the end of racism in America' cannot reasonably demand that the university solve those problems. Kent enrolled many students in the years 1968–70 who sought from it not an education but a social revolution; they were frequently brilliant young people and often the most likable, but the university was not where they should have been fighting their battles; it would have been justified in asking them to leave. The overage student whose education has been interrupted by either military service or work from which he saved the money to attend college has an honorable place on campus, but not the overage revolutionary whose job is to inflame entering freshmen and divert their energies to rebellion.

If we had one major criticism of the Kent State student body, it would be that its most promising scholars had been so diverted by politics that they were ignoring those basic studies which have been the very foundation of political action. One did not find the young man whose mind was ablaze with the ideas of Immanuel Kant or the social theories of J. J. C. L. Blanc; he did not meet young women enraptured during their fall quarter with Palestrina and about to transfer their affections in winter quarter to the soaring work of Le Corbusier. There seemed to be a lack of dedication to knowledge, as if societies or lives could be held together without it. We were especially disturbed by the lack of formal knowledge on the part of the young radicals; they seemed not to know that men like Marx and Lenin studied endlessly before they developed their ideas and that Americans like Thomas Jefferson and Sam Adams were patient scholars before they became revolutionary leaders. They were irritated when we pressed for specific answers as to what they would do if their revolution succeeded; Abbie Hoffman's famous reply can be considered amusing: 'Abolish pay toilets, man, that's the goal of our revolution. Eternal life and free toilets.' Such a wisecrack has a place in any movement, for it jollies up the debate, but to accept it as a substitute for the hard, bitter analysis that men and movements require is to accept rubbish. The university is a gold mine from which the student can dig whatever ore he requires, but he must do the digging.

Parents. The relationship of the parent to the university has become clouded. As he has relinquished responsibility for disciplining his children, he looks increasingly to outside agencies to do the job, placing an unrealistic burden upon the university. When parents send their children away for an education, they should explain in precise detail what obligations are involved, what results are hoped for, and the degree to which the family will back up either the university or the police if major trouble ensues.

Parents pay, through taxes, for the creation of the university, and through registration fees, for its upkeep. They have not only a vested interest in it but a right to check upon what is being done in their institution. They should express their support of the regents and share with them their judgments. They should endeavor to understand what the administration is trying to do and should communicate with it. (After the May incident, President White received more than a thousand letters from parents throughout Ohio, most of them bitterly condemnatory, few showing any realization of the fact that four dead students were human beings representative of America's future; this imbalance bespoke a lack of understanding both of the university and of young people in general.) Parents ought to offer more than harsh criticism; if they ally themselves with the forces trying to hold this nation and its institutions together, they can accomplish much.

Finally, the whole burden of this book is that parents and children must try to understand each other. The 'generation gap' is no longer just an amusing truism. In an age of great social change, for these two groups to deprive themselves of association with each other is a tragedy that must not be perpetuated a day longer. We have said consistently that young people must offer conciliation; older people, who can be presumed to have more experience, are doubly obligated to do so.

Five arbitrary problems remain. These cut across all groups, from the legislature and the regents to the student and his parents.

Should the university attempt to outlaw the new life style? Many adults think it should. When dress and behavior codes are proposed, the targets are long hair, communal living, freedom of expression, and the tendency toward criticism. Parents, legislatures and editorial writers would enjoy seeing the university force its students back to a life style that was current two or three decades ago. This is a futile wish. The university is powerless to reverse trends established by society, condoned by it, and enthusiastically adopted by the young. The university cannot revoke history, and it cannot discipline students more severely than society would permit. It must accept students as society delivers them to its door, and by persuasion and precept lead them to broader perspectives. It must demonstrate the alternatives open to the intelligent man. Consequently, it need not sponsor the new life style, but it is powerless to veto it.

Should the universities resume parietal responsibility? No current concept is more appealing than the one which says, 'The university has got to teach our children the meaning of discipline.' It is amusing to hear parents who cannot discipline their sixteen-year-old son in his use of the family car, calling for the university to regiment the boy when he has reached the age of twenty and is operating in areas ten times more complex than automobiles. The only condition in which the university would dare to re-establish the parietal rules which prevailed in the 1940's would be if society at large undergoes a sharp revision of its attitudes and behaves in conformity to them. Legislatures would have to pass laws supporting the older attitudes, and courts would have to interpret those laws in favor of the university. Then Boards of Regents could risk dictating behavior patterns and could set up the machinery for enforcing them. This seems unlikely. What the university in the 1970's must do is accept young people in the condition to which their parents have brought them at age eighteen and educate them to be something better. One way to do this is to agree upon sensible rules which the entire campus will respect.

Should regulations governing girl students be tightened?

We have been constantly bewildered as to how we ought to report interviews like the two which follow. The first was conducted by one of the male researchers:

> RESEARCHER: Where was Chuck when this happened?
> GIRL: In bed with Olive.
> RESEARCHER: In your room? In the girls' dormitory?
> GIRL: Where else?
> RESEARCHER: Where were you?
> GIRL: In bed with Dave.
> RESEARCHER: Same room?
> GIRL: Of course. Fellows stayed all night whenever they felt they had to.
> RESEARCHER: You can see I'm writing this down. Am I free to quote you?
> GIRL: Why not?
> RESEARCHER: I was worrying about your parents.
> GIRL: What could they do about it?

The second was conducted by a young woman who talked with a coed and a boy, each of whom had known Jeff Miller.

> GIRL: I live in a four-person room in Beall Hall, but I can hardly ever get into it. Boyfriends of two of the girls have moved in with us on a permanent basis, so there's always a minimum of six in the room.
> BOY: Six isn't too bad. Lots of rooms have six.
> GIRL: But often one or two extra boys drop in for a couple of nights a week. There's simply no way I can study.
> BOY: You could study at my place. And if you like it, you can stay. We have plenty of room.
> GIRL: Thanks. I may give that a whirl. I'll drop by tomorrow.
> BOY: That's a deal. By the way, what's your name?

Out of a delicate regard for parents, such testimony has been filed without names, but its impact has been considerable and one does not need to be prudish to question whether recent relaxation of rules has been for the good. No moment in the preparation of this book was more poignant than the one in which a young man of eighteen confided, 'Verity and I lived together for more than a year and we decided that we'd probably not bother with marriage, either of us. It seemed like a drag.' One wondered if a boy of seventeen, his age when the liaison started, was capable of evaluating the meaning of marriage. One wondered if the normal occupation of a boy that age ought not to be study and speculation and occasional exploration with girls and the slow building of a set of values against which life could be judged in later years. One is not at all convinced that the blithe and easy manner in which young people slip into communal living is in the end fruitful. On the other hand, one suspects that the whole movement of society is in this direction and that the university is powerless to stop it. Certainly, the recent popularity of the women's liberation movement, and its substantial support on campus, would make one think that the liberation of coeds could not be reversed.

Should admission of out-of-state students be restricted? Throughout the Midwest there is popular support for the movement to raise out-of-state tuition so as to exclude students from states like New York, New Jersey and Pennsylvania. (Kent's tuition for Ohio residents is $240 per quarter; for outsiders, $540.) Justification is twofold: 'It prevents Ohio taxpayers from paying for the education of outsiders, and it keeps radical ideas from the East from contaminating our kids.' There is some reason for the former complaint, for the three eastern states mentioned have been notoriously delinquent in providing educational opportunities for their students; New Jersey is known educationally as 'the cuckoo state' because of its penchant for bearing children and sending them out of the state to be educated in other nests. A large university like Kent exists in part because neighboring states have not been facing up to their responsibilities; however, a Kent resident adds another reason: 'High tuition for outsiders is a good thing because it keeps out Jewish students, and they're the ones who cause the trouble.' A visitor is not long in Kent before someone informs him secretly, 'You've noticed, of course, that of the four students who were killed, three were Jewish. That was no accident.' For the Midwest, or any other section of the country, to impose restrictions against the free interchange of educational opportunities would be an error which could produce much damage. Perhaps Ohio prospers because some of the young people from New York and New Jersey stay there after completing their schooling; certainly the eastern states need students from Ohio. The same is true of faculty members; educational isolationism would be a dreadful step backward.

What should be done about outside agitators? If they behave legally, nothing. If they are revolutionaries inciting to violence, they should be arrested. Pains have been taken in this book to detail the considerable travel in and out of Kent by radicals, so that the reader could see for himself the pressure Kent State was under, but the point needs to be made now that all such travel was legal. When Mark Rudd and the other regional travelers came to Kent, they did so openly and were in violation of no laws. It was only when they began to preach and practice violence that they went underground; we have no secure knowledge of any visits after they became illegal travelers. Furthermore, we could have offered checklists of ultra-conservatives who came to Kent legally and who conducted meetings there. Traveling secretaries of fraternities and sororities visited, and famous professors, and editors, and popular entertainers, some of whom had acquired unsavory reputations. In other words, to a university of 21,000 comes an unceasing parade of visitors; the university would be delinquent in its duty if things were otherwise. The vast majority of these visitors represent the establishment and defend it; it is a basic principle of both democracy and education that critics also be heard. To halt the free flow of ideas to the campus would be preposterous, for then the campus could produce only second-rate minds trained to grapple with safe and second-rate problems. The campus should constantly be visited by outside agitators in the tradition of Socrates, Tom Paine, Alexis de Tocqueville and Hans Morgenthau, for they bring the ideas which produce fruitful lives. They should be of all political coloring, all economic persuasions, all academic pursuits, and any attempt to inhibit them is futile, because if their ideas are potent, they will penetrate any walls established to quarantine them. If they advocate violence or sedition or any overt assault upon law and order they should be arrested.

When these and other knotty problems have been tackled, there must be on the part of all a rededication to the great purpose of a university, to that sense of shared community in which each man is responsible for the whole, each group aware of its interrelationship with all others. Benson R. Snyder, in his study of what happened at Massachusetts Institute of Technology, *The Hidden Curriculum,* quotes a classic example of how purposes can be lost:

> One professor at a leading eastern university explained: 'When I first came down here, there were four of us, all sharp down from Harvard. We thought we'd really have a say in running the department. And we *were* allowed a voice in departmental matters. We each sought out bright students who were interested in the same things as we were and took them on as graduate students. We taught whatever courses we wanted in whatever way we chose. For us it was a grand life. The only trouble was that the university apparently went down the drain under our noses, and we never even knew it.'

Speculations

Among all types of students at Kent, there is vigorous disgust with two temporary aspects of American life—the war in Vietnam and the draft. This could be interpreted as 'cowardice on the part of young men who don't want to go overseas to fight,' except that the opposition of girls is equally strong.

It is therefore tempting to conclude that if only the war in Vietnam were terminated, which would also wipe out the draft, some kind of peace would return to America's campuses. For this hopeful belief, there is no justification. If Vietnam ended tomorrow, students would remain as agitated and confused as they are today. This does not mean that the war is justified; it merely means that the source of agitation lies elsewhere and that ending the war would not end discontent. Proof of this can be found by looking at Japan, France and Venezuela.

In Japan there is no foreign war and there is no draft; furthermore, there is exactly the national commitment to peace and anti-militarism that American students demand; the Japanese constitution outlaws war and forbids Japan ever again to participate in one. The military-industrial complex does not exist. Anyone listening to American protests would be justified in concluding, 'Japan has found the perfect solution to these problems. Students in Japan should be content.' Quite the contrary. The students of Japan are the most fierce of all young radicals, their assaults on society the most determined. In place of Vietnam and the draft, they have devised their own list of grievances, and these bear almost no resemblance to those promulgated by their American counterparts.

The surging disturbances in France, which came close to causing the downfall of de Gaulle, and the near-collapse of the nation's economy came after de Gaulle had courageously liquidated the Algerian war in accordance with the demands of intellectuals and students. In many ways this war had cut more deeply into France's moral life than the Vietnam war has into American life, so that its solution should have been more appreciated by the French students, but this was not the case. Nor did French students face the confused kind of draft Americans do. And whereas Japanese students could be excused for their agitation against American occupation of Okinawa and American air bases in Japan, there was no such occupation of French territory. In other words, the French students had none of the American causes to protest against and none of the Japanese, yet identical types of protests occurred.

In Venezuela, students had none of the American causes, none of the Japanese and none of the French, yet their protests were perhaps the most violent of all. With no war to fight against, no draft, no occupation and no dictatorship, the Venezuelans constructed their own body of causes: Pro-Castro sympathies, resentment of American investments, the need for a new system of government, and a plan for economic revolution. Not one plank in the Venezuelan program coincided with any in the United States, Japan or France, but the behavior of the students was identical, except that the pusillanimity of the Venezuelan government—for reasons which will be explained later—allowed those students to proceed further with their revolution than students were able to do elsewhere.

If one studied a dozen other countries, he would find this pattern repeated a dozen times: the causes for student unrest vary from nation to nation, but the end results are always the same.* This means that when we speak of *causes,* we are looking at surface causation and missing the underlying, basic reasons.

What fundamental reasons have caused this worldwide revolt? It is Marxist-based—Mao Tse-tung, Ho Chi Minh,

*For a philosophical extension of this thesis, see George Z. F. Bereday, 'Student Unrest on Four Continents,' in *Comparative Education Review,* Vol. 10, June 1966, pages 188–204, in which the author analyzes ethnic causes (Montreal, Canada), racial cleavages (Ibadan, Nigeria) social cleavages (Warsaw, Poland), and educational problems (Rangoon, Burma).

Che Guevara—and has led young people to reject the life styles of their parents and to commit themselves to the new life style which has been developing over the past two decades, and if one fails to see that the revolts in Japan, France, Venezuela and the United States are identical in every aspect that matters, he misses the whole point of what is happening in the world. And it behooves everyone—young and old— to insure that the radical divergence between life styles does not crystallize into permanent alienation. This does not mean that the older members of society have to surrender values which they have inherited and which they cherish; it does mean that there has got to be some understanding of what the young are trying to accomplish, and it is obligatory that older people not reject them automatically.

How many young people are involved in this challenge? Dan Petruchik, a conservative student at Kent State and the right-wing orator of Sigma Alpha Epsilon, makes a good point: 'Suppose that only 10 percent of the Kent State student body is ultra-liberal. When the total student body is around 20,000, this means that 2,000 students are available for any mass meeting that comes along, and on television or in the newspaper a crowd of that size is simply enormous. I believe that only 5 percent is radical, but that can produce a crowd of 1,000. If the truth were known, we probably have only 2 percent who are true radicals, but that makes 400, and that's a tremendous crowd, especially if others follow. Also, the real leadership of the 400 rests in the hands of about fifteen students, which is less than one-tenth of one percent.'

Petruchik continues, 'You must also remember that our university students are more radical to begin with than an equal number of young people who don't attend university. So that we are not talking about huge numbers of young people. We're talking about the conspicuous leaders . . . the ones who set the style. The vast majority of Kent State students are solid, responsible people. It's criminal that they should have been subjected to abuse because of the actions of such a pitifully small percentage of the whole.'

It is instructive to visualize this small minority as the Populists of the 1960's. In the latter years of the last century in America the Populist party cut a dramatic swath through our political life, pointing out in noisy confrontation scores of things that they deemed wrong with our system. Restricted amounts of money in circulation, suffrage, control of large corporations, abuses of interstate commerce, lack of freedom for labor and many other nuances of government became the subject of their agitation; because they were poorly led and too radical for their time, the Populists exerted little influence at the polls and won no great victories. But twenty years after their disappearance, most of the reforms they had preached were quietly adopted by the two major parties to become the American way of life. The Populists accomplished little for themselves, much for America.

At Kent State the agitation of the liberals started sedately in 1965 with a protest against war in Vietnam. Thirteen students participated, and one of them says, 'The campus looked at us as if we were freaks. People threw things at us, reviled us, threatened us with bodily harm. Professors ridiculed us and the newspapers had a holiday. Today many senators, most of the great newspapers, professors across the nation, everybody wants us to do exactly what we proposed six years ago—get out of Vietnam. Even President Nixon subscribes to our point of view.'

Of the four points in the original SDS program, all have become respectable. Leading commissions now recommend that universities do not undertake research on their campuses for the Department of Defense, and one great institution after another has determined within its own board of governance that it will no longer do so. Many universities have concluded that it makes more sense to conduct ROTC affairs off campus in some spot that is less conspicuous than an old Gothic armory which dominates the campus and becomes a focus for radical agitation; many private institutions have abolished ROTC altogether, although others have decided to retain it in modified form so as to permit those students who wish a military career to prepare for it. And a realization that campus police ought not to prowl a university armed with guns is growing. Several large universities are putting their campus force into distinctive blazers and arming them only with riot sticks; this may not be the wise thing to do in an age of escalating violence, but it does advertise to the general student body that these men are not armed but are their friends and assistants in a common cause.

Thus SDS, for all its fearful behavior, served in the 1960's as society's cutting edge and was the Populist movement of that period. By the 1980's most of its demands will have been generally adopted in educational institutions across the country. But immediately this has been said, two doleful warnings must be added.

First, the tactics of SDS were divisive, destructive, revolutionary and often illegal. Even though the aims were in some instances laudable, the means to those aims were unacceptable. There was inherent in SDS from the moment of its inception a germ of self-destruction; the course laid out at Berkeley and Columbia had to lead inevitably to the Days of Rage in Chicago and to the formation of the Weathermen with their program of nihilism, dynamiting and suicide.

Second, it is evident from what has just been said about Japan, France and Venezuela that even if all the SDS demands had been accepted at the moment of issuance, others would have been quickly forthcoming. Neither society nor Kent State could have purchased peace by concession. There was in these young people a determination to bring about radical change, and victory in one area would merely have led to increased demands in another.

Indeed, if one looks at four representative incidents which erupted while this book was being written, he sees through each of the four a common strand—a thread of terror—indicating that one element of society had declared war on another and that the quest for stable peace within our own society is our major obligation. The four incidents, in chronological order, were these.

1. The dynamiting of Mathematics Research Institute at the University of Wisconsin and the subsequent dynamiting of various buildings across the United States in response to a declaration of war issued by Bernardine Dohrn of the Weatherman underground. This is the ultimate response, the inescapable downward drift of the SDS idealists who had started their agitation with such high-flown sentiments as the rejuvenation of society and the restructuring of the university. These were acts of rage and of nihilism, the final rejection of society and the rules it has set up for its own revision. Worse, these explosions announced that henceforth the group responsible for them would operate underground for the purpose of 'bringing down society by any means available.' It is appropriate that such people be listed as public enemies.

2. The hijacking and dynamiting of international airliners by the Popular Front for the Liberation of Palestine in order to bring to the attention of the world its political aims. Precisely the same kind of mentality required for blowing up the buildings in the United States was required for this insolent and dramatic gesture. The perpetrators said, in effect,

'We are tired of ordinary negotiation, for it gets us nowhere. Now we shall attack international society as a whole.'

3. The kidnapping of two public officials in eastern Canada and the murder of one. This violent exhibition, so shattering to the peace of a nation which was doing its best to reconcile the sharp differences that existed between the two halves— one French, one English; one eighteenth-century rural, one twentieth-century urban; one Catholic, one Protestant; one separatist, one hopefully union—was an exact parallel to the Palestinian hijackings. Members of a political party, having in their opinion exhausted normal channels of communication, adopted the most violent means of confrontation: they declared themselves outcasts from society.

4. The slaying of Victor Ohta, California ophthalmologist, his wife, two of his children and his secretary, and the dumping of their bound and gagged bodies into a swimming pool. An example of this kind of irrational assault upon society should be cited to complete the picture of what happens when individuals or movements declare war on their own terms. This type of arbitrary group murder, the second example of its kind within the area, is what we must expect if large numbers of young people place themselves outside the normal controls of society. If such persons cluster together and convince themselves day after day that society has rejected them, or they society, then outbursts of irrational behavior will become commonplace and no one will be safe from them.

Running through these four hideous incidents is a cynical realization on the part of the perpetrators that a modern, interrelated, sophisticated society is vulnerable to the amoral individual who plots to bring it down. In the last century a determined gunman could hold up a stagecoach and rob it, but he could hardly hijack it a thousand miles across international boundaries, and if the passengers decided to fight it out with him, they could do so without the certainty of self-destruction. But one man with a toy gun jabbed into the back of a stewardess can accomplish ugly wonders. Water supplies, electrical systems, communication networks, and even mass emotional stability are all vulnerable to the individual who is determined to make a concerted attack upon them. The more intricate our social organism becomes, the more easily is it put out of commission. This is true of countries like Canada, or universities like Wisconsin, or private homes like Dr. Ohta's. Therefore, if we are all vulnerable, it is obligatory that we unite to protect ourselves against the forces that threaten to destroy us.

Our age can best be understood if we compare it to the year 1848 in European history. Then great revolutionary movements swept the continent, with crucial disturbances in France, Germany and Hungary and massive protest elsewhere. The old order established by Metternich and the Congress of Vienna was crumbling, and everyone knew it, but it still retained the power of self-defense, so one after another of the revolutions was crushed, leaving in cellars and other hiding places persistent ideas which did much to fertilize the rest of the century. The barricades in the streets were captured by the soldiers of the old regime; the barricades of the mind were possessed by the revolutionists.

An interesting sidelight to 1848 was that the United States profited spectacularly, because to our shores came thousands of the finest minds of Europe, seeking sanctuary from the subsequent repression. Men like Carl Schurz brought with them ideas which germinated in America and helped make us strong. Today, many able young Americans are fleeing the United States to seek a comparable sanctuary in places like Canada and Sweden. It was constantly astonishing at Kent State, which had no important heritage of international exchange, to find so many students who were seriously contemplating a permanent life abroad; case histories were compiled on at least twelve former students who had taken the big gamble and accepted permanent exile from their homeland. One hopes that they may become the new Carl Schurzes of their adopted homes but regrets that they felt they had to leave America.

The revolution of our times affects everyone. When Fireman Dave Helmling says, with almost tearful nostalgia, 'I do wish that Kent could become the peaceful old place it was and that the university would go away and leave us alone,' he is speaking for millions of Americans, most of whom live nowhere near a university. It is not Kent State which has altered the lovely old town so radically; it is the sheer number of people who must now be accommodated, and even if Kent had failed in 1910 to win this institution from competing towns, Kent itself would today be engulfed by practically every problem that Dave Helmling resents. The old, peaceful ways are lost. The habit of leaving one's doors unlocked has ended in a lot of towns other than Kent.

Young people with long hair are creating problems in lots of bars across this nation which do not face on Water Street.

It is naïve for the citizens of Kent to deplore the university or for the voters in Portage County to declare war on students. It is themselves they are fighting; it is their own children they are rejecting, and of a hundred problems which face them, ninety-nine would continue even if the university were abolished. Do communities with a General Motors plant instead of a university have it any easier?

The problem is one of conciliation. Where the problem is international, as with Israel and the Arabs, the good will of the entire world is required to help work out a solution. Where the difficulties are national, as in Canada and Ireland, they must be analyzed with intelligence and confronted with a mutual determination to achieve justice. Where they pertain to a community, like Kent, students and older citizens alike must be prepared to make concessions. And where they are restricted to individual families, as in many of the examples cited in this book, they can be solved only by love.

If the problem of generation-confrontation comes to open warfare, as leaders like Bernardine Dohrn recommend, the victors will be the older generation, for they have the police, the army and the power. It is therefore doubly obligatory that the young make concessions, and if they are reasonably intelligent they will do so; but one is convinced from hundreds of discussions at Kent that there is a limit to the concessions they will make.

Steve Sharoff indicated this limit: 'If you demand that I give up the life style I have evolved . . . I mean the music and the hair and modern dress and the new freedom . . . and if you try to enforce this by repressive laws and severe police action . . .' His voice trailed off. He wrapped his long legs in a knot, ran his fingers through his sideburns and concluded, 'If you try that, you and I are at declared war, and the only way you can preserve your way of life . . . keep the good things you've promoted for yourself . . . well, you have to do one of two things with me. Either lock me up for life or shoot me dead in the street.'

'But if you force a confrontation,' Steve was asked, 'don't you realize that the army and the police have the guns? They're bound to win.'

'They'll win, but it won't be a victory that you can live with.'

The hearings

Obviously, the people working on this book paid close attention to the various committees that investigated the tragedy at Kent. The most impressive was the President's Commission on Campus Unrest, which visited Kent in late August. Led by William Scranton, one of America's notable private citizens, and with a sterling cast of members, including three blacks, this committee handled itself commendably and brought in a solid report.

Scranton was at his best when chairing the three-day session held in one of Kent's science amphitheaters. With courtly aplomb he fended off persons who sought to make the hearings a sounding board for special pleading; he smiled courteously when one Kent woman explained that she could tell by looking at a student whether he could be trusted or not. It was a matter of hair. If it didn't reach down to his collar, he was all right, but if it touched his collar, watch out!

Scranton had the right of subpoena and used it constructively, bringing out evidence that had not been aired before, but he found himself powerless to bring the National Guard onto the witness stand, and this damaged the effectiveness of his report. He did prevail upon Generals Canterbury and Del Corso to testify, and they did an excellent job of defending the actions of their troops. Canterbury was especially effective, giving the appearance of a blunt soldier who had often faced civilian disturbances and whose men had behaved properly. Not even the tip of a wedge was driven into the solid front the Guard was presenting to the public, and it was apparent that the committee would find nothing substantial to say against it.

Many of the characters appearing in this book testified before the committee. Steve Sharoff told them, 'The students are embarked on a moral crusade to right the wrongs they perceive, and will not be deflected from their goals. They are vitally concerned with the older generation's preoccupation with property rights at the expense of human rights . . . and with a militarism which feeds a huge standing army and diverts the nation's economic strength from the goals it should be striving for. Students are acutely aware of the National Guard's capacity to use lethal weapons in a showdown but are not intimidated by them. Students will no longer allow themselves to be shot without shooting back.'

Mike Alewitz said, 'The National Guard travel from campus to campus in Ohio, small groups of armed men causing violence wherever they go. The student movement at Kent has been defeated because four persons were shot and many injured, but the movement goes on every day in this country. Students are fed up. Shutting the university only throws gasoline on the fire.'

Dr. Jerry Lewis testified, 'On Monday I couldn't figure out why the National Guard was guarding the burned-down ROTC building. It seemed very strange. If you were going to protect buildings, you would have stationed people around the Student Union, around the other buildings. But there was clearly a symbolic significance of some kind in the fact that the Guard protected only the burned-out ROTC building.'

Bob Pickett told the committee, 'This country is on its deathbed, man, and there ain't no doctor around. What doctors there are, like General Del Corso, are killing it, and as they do it, they're killing themselves. They're asking for a war and they're going to get it. Repression breeds violent reaction, and the mood of many students is such that it could propel them to the barricades.'

And Professor Frank said, 'The faculty marshals on Saturday night were not, and should never be, a police force. Our job was to talk with students to find out what the problem was and to see if something could be done to alleviate it. There were three things we were not there to do. We were not there to stop a demonstration. We were not there to stop peaceful protest. We were not there to stop anyone from being on campus. I have never in my seventeen years of teaching seen a group of students as threatening or as arrogant or as bent on destruction as the ones I saw and talked to that Saturday night.'

At the end of their hearings, the commission issued a report in two parts, one a general summary regarding the problem of student unrest as a philosophical matter, and a special volume dealing only with Kent State. (There was, of course, another special volume dealing with Jackson State in Mississippi.) The general essay was excellent, for it spelled out the causes of dissent and suggested ways to alleviate them. The commission prepared its own summary of its findings:

The report said campus unrest is not a single thing, but the sum of hundreds and thousands of individual beliefs and discontents, based broadly on:

—the war and the conditions of minority groups
—changing status and attitudes of youth in America
—the changing American university
—the escalating reaction to student protest and
the growing spiral of violence; and
—changes in western society.

The commission admonished universities 'to pull themselves together,' and face up to their responsibility to prepare for possible
campus disruptions. University officials who believe 'It can't
happen here'—and who, therefore, face disruptions without adequate plans, warning or sanctions—are 'worse than naïve,' the
report said, 'they are derelict in their responsibilities.'

The commission drew sharp distinctions in its report between
peaceful and disorderly protest, noting that peaceful protest was
not only safeguarded by the Constitution but 'was a healthy
sign of freedom and protection against stagnation.' To take a
'hard line' against peaceful protesters is not only wrong, but
could create greater alienation. On the other hand, the commission said, disruptive, violent or terrorist conduct is 'the antithesis
of democratic processes' and should not be tolerated either on
the nation's campuses or anywhere else.

What the commission called a 'new' culture is emerging among
students. Idealistic, fearful, and often scornful of the traditional
values held by their elders, its peculiarly dressed members
believe America has lost its sense of human purpose, the report
said. Impatient with the 'slow procedures of liberal democracy,'
these young people often are as scornful of the past experience
of others, as others are intolerant of the new culture's dress or
hair styles. The commission admonished against concluding that
a student who has a beard is a student who would burn a building. Almost no college student today, it stressed, is unaffected
by the new youth culture in some way.

The part of the report which provoked major reaction was
a section entitled 'For the President,' in which this passage
appeared:

We urge that the President exercise his reconciling moral leadership as the first step to prevent violence and create understanding. It is imperative that the President bring us together before
more lives are lost and more property destroyed and more universities disrupted.

We recommend that the President seek to convince public officials and protesters alike that divisive and insulting rhetoric is dangerous. In the current political campaign and throughout the years ahead, the President should insist that no one play irresponsible politics with the issue of 'campus unrest.'

We recommend that the President take the lead in explaining to the American people the underlying causes of campus unrest and the urgency of our present situation. We recommend that he articulate and emphasize those values all Americans hold in common. At the same time we urge him to point out the importance of diversity and co-existence to the nation's health.

To this end, nothing is more important than an end to the war in Indochina. Disaffected students see the war as a symbol of moral crisis in the nation which, in their eyes, deprives even law of its legitimacy. Their dramatic reaction to the Cambodian invasion was a measure of the intensity of their moral recoil.

The special volume on Kent State was not so impressive. It was conceived in haste, inadequately researched, written under heavy duress so far as time and lack of staff were concerned, and barely finished before the expiring date of the commission. But even though it had to contend with these limitations, it made few glaring errors, and its conclusions that students and Guards shared the blame for the four deaths appeared to be a logical deduction:

The conduct of many students and non-student protesters at Kent State was plainly intolerable. Violence by students on or off campus can never be justified by any grievance, philosophy or political idea.

For students deeply opposed to the Vietnam war, the Guard was a living symbol of the military system they distrusted.

Many students were legitimately in the area as they went to and from class. The rally was peaceful, and there was no apparent or impending violence. Only when the Guard attempted to disperse the rally did some students react violently.

The Guard's decision to march through the crowd for hundreds of yards up and down a hill was highly questionable.

The actions of some students were violent and criminal and those of some others were dangerous, reckless and irresponsible. The indiscriminate firing of rifles into a crowd of students and the deaths that followed were unnecessary, unwarranted and inexcusable. Even if the Guardsmen faced danger, it was not a danger which called for lethal force.

The Scranton report was rejected in both Washington and Ohio. The Nixon administration apparently felt that it was unreasonable of Scranton to call upon the President to exert moral leadership, while certain political leaders felt that a Republican former governor ought to have provided his party with a document more helpful in the impending election. Stories were leaked to the effect that the report would be ignored and that highly placed members of the administration would attempt to shoot it down. This Vice-President Agnew proceeded to do, castigating it as 'pablum for permissiveness.'

Meanwhile, in Portage County some fancy footwork was under way. Almost immediately after the shootings, County Prosecutor Ron Kane took a series of adroit steps to insure that all legal inquiries which might ensue remained under his control. On this point the law was clear; he was the official responsible for investigating and prosecuting the case. Unfortunately, he commanded insufficient funds to pay for a grand jury of the scope required, so he procrastinated, trusting that he could force the state to provide him with additional money without taking the investigation away from him. This was a grave miscalculation which he would later regret, for while he wasted June and July waiting for money from Columbus, state officials were devising a way by which they might snatch this publicity plum from him and establish a jury of their own choosing which might be inclined to hand down a set of indictments which would exonerate the governor, the National Guard and the state of Ohio while throwing all the blame on the students and faculty. If this could be achieved, it would be a neat trick.

Accordingly, on Thursday, July 30, Governor Rhodes' office wrote to Kane, informing him that 'early next week the necessary meeting can be held so that a final decision can be made as to how to finance grand jury inquiry into the Kent events.' Acting on the hunch that the money would be forthcoming, Kane decided on Friday to go ahead full steam, and on Saturday morning delivered to his friend Judge Albert L. Caris of the Ravenna bench a letter which set forth his intentions:

Please be advised that I am herewith making a formal request to reconvene the Portage County grand jury beginning August

17, 1970, for the purpose of a probe of the situation which occurred at Kent State University during the month of May, 1970.

Someone informed Columbus of Kane's plan, so early on Monday morning Judge Caris received notification that the state of Ohio was convening its own grand jury which would supersede anything Ron Kane might have in mind. The letter from Governor Rhodes to the state's attorney general empowering him to go ahead contained the hopeful sentence, 'Only a grand jury . . . can diminish the half-informed and mis-informed commentary on events at Kent State that is still heard.' Apparently Governor Rhodes believed that the report of his special grand jury would allay doubts and questions about the tragedy and give the public a final explanation which would forestall further discussion. He could not have been more wrong.

In accordance with instruction, Attorney-General Paul W. Brown convened his special grand jury and took its leadership away from Kane, handing it over to a lawyer from a different part of the state, Robert L. Balyeat, former prosecuting attorney from distant Allen County. He was assisted by a Ravenna lawyer whom we have met before, Seabury Ford, chairman of the Republican party in Portage County and the man who loaned Mayor Satrom the dime to make the phone call during the poker game at Aurora on Law Day.

Ford would be a major driving force of the grand jury; his attitudes, phrases and convictions would dominate the final report and the manner in which indictments were voted. He was a tall, lanky country lawyer who could have played the role of James Stewart's down-to-earth older partner in a Hollywood courtroom drama. Friends described him as 'a canny, cantankerous curmudgeon,' and always invited him to their informal meetings, for he had a fund of ribald stories. One of his favorites dealt with a brawl in the black section of town: 'Dinah was shot in the fracas and the bullet is in her yet.' When he finished this statement his long, narrow face would break into a grimace; he would hesitate, then add professionally, 'Ain't many women survive with a bullet in their yet.'

At sixty-eight, Seabury Ford led the Republicans capably and was much respected by his Democratic opponents. He had recently been proposed for a judgeship, but said, 'I can't afford to take it. Sure I'd like to be a judge, what lawyer wouldn't? But I'd have to give up my law practice and under that damned-fool law which the reformers put through, I wouldn't be able to stand for reelection when I was seventy, so I'd be a judge for only two years, and who wants that?'

Ford was strongly against reformers. 'Worst thing ever happened to this nation was Franklin D. Roosevelt. He really ruined us. But it all started when they took the election of senators away from the state legislature and turned it over to the people. The income tax was a backward step, too. You know what? They ought to pass a law which says that all taxes in this nation are paid in to the local county administration. What they have left over, they pass along to the state capitol, and what they have left over, they turn in to Washington. That's the only way to fight big government.'

Ford was probably the leading citizen of Portage County; his great-grandfather had been the last Whig governor of Ohio, and Ford's friends said, 'Seabury's the last living Whig in America.' He was known as an incorruptible, a man dedicated to the law. It was not surprising, therefore, when the state of Ohio chose him to help present evidence to the secret grand jury. What pleased Ford almost as much was the fact that he had recently received another signal honor.

Under House Bill 1219, which laid down stringent new laws for the control of student disturbances on Ohio campuses, any student or faculty member arrested for disrupting campus life, no matter how trivial the offense, must go immediately before a referee who, even prior to the trial or the accumulation of determinative evidence, would have the right to suspend the student or professor that day, halt any scholarship or salary payments, and not only keep him suspended for a year but deny him the right of entering any other Ohio state institution of learning. (If the court subsequently found the accused not guilty, the suspension would be lifted.) Each county housing a state university would have some eminent lawyer appointed referee and he would decide which students should be suspended. For Portage County, and therefore Kent State, the referee would be Seabury Ford.

The grand jury met in extreme secrecy in mid-September. Judge Edwin W. Jones, under whose jurisdiction it had been convened, handed down a series of commendable ground rules which required everyone serving on the jury or testifying before it to refrain from telling anything to anybody until the jury was finally dismissed. This meant that if John Smith were summoned before the jury to testify to an event in which he may have been involved, he was commanded to keep silent outside the jury room; but this restriction also applied to Henry Brown, who may have testified only to the fact that he saw John Smith doing something actionable. Newspapers and television crews were specifically forbidden to pry into the jury secrets or to publish whatever they discovered if they did pry.

The reason for these severe rules was twofold. In Cleveland, some years before, an Ohio court had allowed an infamous circus to develop around the trial of the osteopath Sam Sheppard, on trial for the murder of his wife. The indecorous exhibition, totally unrelated to justice, was caused partly by pressure from a Cleveland newspaper, partly by the inadequacies of the trial judge. The United States Supreme Court found it necessary to rebuke the Ohio court in harsh terms; Ohio judges and lawyers knew that the castigation was merited and did not want to see it repeated; there was a firm determination to keep the Kent Case free of sensationalism, and Judge Jones was commended for his unequivocal rules.

The second reason was equally persuasive. If word of impending indictments slipped out, the students and professors about to be arrested might flee the jurisdiction of the court in case of misdemeanor (where extradition is not pursued) or the country itself in case of a felony (where extradition from one state to another is customary).

No one believed that any National Guardsmen would be indicted; before the jury had even convened, Attorney-General Brown had told the press that he supposed none of the Guard would be touched.* Within the first few hours of the jury's convening, it was decided that under Ohio law the Guardsmen had to be held blameless in the killings, and it was further decided that no verbal strictures would be uttered against the Guard, either. The grand jury was meeting solely to arrest students and professors who had caused the trouble.

For the next four weeks word flashed around Kent that this person or that had appeared before the jury, and at late-night sessions extremely shrewd deductions were being made in dormitories and bars as to what was happening. Some clever student researched the law and found that a mere photograph of a person throwing a gas canister back at the

---

*Brown said, 'On the evidence we have available—and we have as much as anyone—I don't see any evidence upon which a grand jury would indict any guardsmen.' It was to be a hanging jury whose job would be to indict professors and students.

National Guard was not enough, for it is well known that photographs can be faked to show anything; what was essential was the confirming evidence of another human being who would say, 'Yes, that's John Smith and I saw him throwing that canister.' So one student after another went before the jury, studied the photographs, asked for better light to inspect the faces, and said, 'Never saw him. He must be an outsider.'

How many students and professors would the grand jury be justified in indicting? Taking the estimates which appear in the *Conclusions* to each of the days, it is obvious that the persons responsible for this book believe there was justification, if not conclusive evidence, for making the following arrests:

Day	Mis-demeanors	Minor Felonies	Major Felonies	Arrests Made on Scene
Friday	100	20	9	14
Saturday	80	80	18	31
Sunday	100	20	0	66
Monday	120	30	10	51
Totals	400	150	37	162

There were thus something like 587 possible arrests of which 162 had already been made. (This latter figure varies in different reports according to the time-span covered; the above figures are taken from records of the Kent police.) This means that the grand jury could logically indict about 425 young people, not all of them students; this figure does not take into account duplications from day to day, of which there would not be many. Irate citizens encouraged the jury to indict the lot. 'Let's teach those smart brats a lesson,' seemed to be the ruling sentiment. People spoke of '200 or 300 indictments and they'll all go to jail.' Special vengeance was voiced against the Kent professors, and many observers hoped that as many as ten might be put behind bars.

At this point the essential sanity of the community manifested itself. Credit goes to certain hard-headed bankers, a group of businessmen, a newspaper publisher. One says, 'We decided that our community could not absorb unlimited indictments being handed down one day in October. If no Guard were to be indicted, and if eight or ten of the most popular professors were to go to jail, and a couple of hundred students were nabbed, we could anticipate serious protest on our campus and across the nation. In fact, it would be logical for it to happen.'

So every effort was made to convey to those responsible for the jury the fact that restraint was essential. One Kent resident who participated in this effort said, 'We believed that the community could absorb as many as thirty indictments, some professors, some students. We felt that even the most excitable students would admit that real crimes had been committed on Friday, Saturday and Sunday and that punishment was in order. We had another fear. If mass indictments were handed down, they would constitute an invitation to a mass publicity trial, with someone like William Kunstler leading the parade. We also thought that if blanket indictments were issued, many of them would prove faulty, with attendant disorder in our courts. And finally, we didn't think we had the lawyers or the money or the time to try a massive number of cases. Everything pointed to restraint.'

There is pretty good evidence that the grand jury at one time wanted to indict about 125 persons; instead, they indicted only twenty-five.

A sigh of enormous relief swept over Portage County on Friday, October 16, when the grand jury made its report. Twenty-five defendants had been handed thirty-one indictments covering forty-three offenses. That it had not been vindictive was a tribute to our legal system. That it had been so meticulous in trying to bring in only just indictments whose reasonableness would be acknowledged by all was an assurance that justice was trying to be sensible and even-handed. Balyeat and Ford deserved credit for their judicious handling of this difficult problem, and there were thousands of people throughout the area who applauded them. Even those vindictive ones who had wanted '200 or 300 brats sent away for twenty years' accepted the judgment of the jury. It was one of the few good accomplishments in this whole sorry story.

There were, however, four unfortunate sidelights to the report, for in addition to bringing in the twenty-five indictments, the jury—more likely Balyeat and Ford, with emphasis on the latter—felt constrained to add a presentment expressing its reflections on what had happened at Kent State:

We find that those members of the National Guard who were

present on the hill on May 4, 1970, fired their weapons in the honest and sincere belief that they would suffer serious bodily injury had they not done so. They are not, therefore, subject to criminal prosecution under the laws of this state for any death or injury resulting therefrom.

We find that the major responsibility for the incidents occurring on the campus on May 2nd, 3rd and 4th, rests clearly with those persons who are charged with the administration of the university. The administration has fostered an attitude of laxity, overindulgence and permissiveness with its students and faculty to the extent that it can no longer regulate the activities of either and it is particularly vulnerable to any pressure applied from radical elements within the student body or faculty.

Among other persons sharing responsibility for the tragic conse-quences must be included the 'twenty-three concerned faculty of Kent State University' who composed, and made available for distribution, an unusual document [which deplored the presence of the Guard on campus]. If the purpose of the authors was simply to express their resentment to the presence of the Na-tional Guard on campus, their timing could not have been worse. If their purpose was to further inflame an already tense situation, then it surely must have enjoyed some measure of success.

The most discouraging aspect of the university's role is that the administrative leadership has totally failed to benefit from past events. On Wednesday, October 7, 1970, the YIPPIES were granted permission to use the auditorium. On Sunday night, October 11, 1970, two appearances were scheduled for a rock music group known as the Jefferson Airplane. During the second performance color slides were projected onto a screen behind the group consisting of psychedelic colors, scenes of the Ohio Na-tional Guard on Kent State campus, and scenes of the shooting on May 4th, complete with views of the bodies of the victims. On October 12th the YIPPIES scheduled a second meeting which was supposed in some manner to relate to the activities of this grand jury. What disturbs us is that any such group of intellectual and social misfits should be afforded the opportunity to disrupt the affairs of a major university to the detriment of the vast majority of the students enrolled there.

By willfully, and in a sense vengefully, offering these *obiter dicta* the grand jury exceeded its commission, thus nullifying the good work it had accomplished in holding the number of indictments down. The gratuitous essay had these grave faults: (1) most of what was said was erroneous in that conclusions were reached contrary to the evidence; (2) it intruded upon the problems of governing a university when the members of the jury knew little about the matter and appeared to rely upon the prejudices of their community; (3) the National Guard was exonerated on the basis of certain evidence when there was a mass of other evidence pointing to the fact that it shared responsibility; (4) and by prejudging the defendants in the essay, the jury seemed to be serving as both indictor and judge, thus denying the defendants their right to a fair trial.

The sharpest criticism came from those who found the grand jury report to be a counterbalance to the more moderate conclusions of the Scranton Commission. One studious critic said, not unjustly, 'It's a rural, conservative, know-nothing answer to the Scranton report, which was urban, liberal and carefully studied.' Another man, a Republican, said, 'It's a damned good Republican campaign document for the elections in November.' It was generally believed that at least 90 percent of the citizens of Portage County approved the report, especially the three sharp sentences at the end of the section on the Guard:

> The grand jury takes note of some who have advocated that the Guard be committed to action without live ammunition. With this we cannot agree. Guardsmen should be furnished with weapons that will afford them the necessary protection under the existing conditions.

An extraordinary situation now developed. In its *obiter dicta,* and not in conjunction with the indictments, the grand jury had bitterly castigated President White, yet because he had testified before the jury, he was forbidden to reply. In the absence of any defense, the general public assumed that the jury had been correct, that the fault was White's and that his position was so feeble, it could not be defended. This enforced silence was probably unprecedented in recent American law, and numerous protests were voiced; White kept his mouth shut; the condemnation stood; the tensions gradually relaxed.

On the whole, the acts of the grand jury met with general approval. The restrained number of indictments proved popular with liberals who wanted to avoid further campus disruption. The total exoneration of the Guard was popular with the general public. The castigation of the university administration and its faculty was popular with everyone except the university community. And the rejection of the Yippies was popular everywhere. Arrests were made in due course and things settled down to normal.* It was hoped that most of those indicted would plead guilty and that the judges would deal with their cases quietly and leniently.

'Not for quotation'

And then the roof blew right off the courthouse. Seabury Ford, who keeps a Confederate flag in his law office and a Colt .45 under a brown paper bag on his desk on grounds that 'You never know when some damned fool may be mad at you,' gave an interview to a canny reporter from the Knight newspaper in nearby Akron. There is some confusion as to whether the man posed as from Detroit, which also has a Knight newspaper, or whether he declared himself as an Akron man. At any rate, crusty old Seabury unlimbered. What he said made headlines across the nation:

> One of the three special prosecutors of the Kent State grand jury said Friday that National Guardsmen on campus last May 'should have shot all' troublemakers.

> 'There is no question that those boys [the Guardsmen] would have been killed up there—if they hadn't turned around and fired.

> 'I think the whole damn country is not going to quiet down until the police are ordered to shoot to kill.'

*Of the persons who appear in this book, the following were indicted: Professor Tom Lough, sociology and anthropology, with his doctorate from Michigan; he was the man who angered some people because he had discussed in a classroom a front cover of *The New York Review of Books* which showed how to make a Molotov cocktail. Craig Morgan, president of the student body, whose indictment was interpreted by students as an attempt to discipline them by indicting a leading campus figure; it was widely believed that Morgan had done no more than what a score of less conspicuous students had done. In late January, Ruth Gibson, attractive in large wire-rimmed glasses and camping outfit complete with knapsack, reported voluntarily to the Portage County courthouse to answer to the indictment against her. She had been out of the state and unable to report earlier. 'I came back at this time,' she explained, 'because today is the forty-ninth anniversary of the assassination of Rosa Luxemburg. Right on! Rosa Luxemburg was a real heavy sister.' She said that she had come back from San Francisco, where she had gone 'to earn some bread and get my head together.' In a prepared statement she added, 'The grand jury's exoneration of the Ohio National Guard does not wash the blood from their hands, but serves only to further demonstrate the injustice of the American political and judicial systems.'
*Since the Guard was on campus May 2, 3 and 4 and since figures cited earlier showed a total of 458 troublemakers on those days, Ford seems to have been calling for a total of 458 shootings, which is even more than the figure proposed by those who growled, 'They shouldn't have shot four, but 400.'

He said he agreed with what he called the 'average' opinion of most people in the Kent–Ravenna area: 'Why didn't the Guard shoot more of them?'

Referring specifically to the volley of National Guard bullets that killed four students and wounded nine others, Ford said: 'The point is, it stopped the riot—you can't argue with that. It just stopped it flat.'

Publication of this interview caused a hurricane of excitement throughout the Kent area, and when the turmoil subsided, three things emerged. Seabury Ford would, in the normal course of events, help prosecute those indicted by the secret jury of which he had been a part, so that the question arose as to whether it would be proper for him to do so if he harbored such vindictive attitudes. Also, since he was still part of the jury process and since he was still under court order not to speak of its operations, he was apparently in contempt of court. And, since he was special referee under House Bill 1219, responsible for dispensing an even-handed justice when arrested students and faculty were brought before him, what kind of justice could students and professors expect from a man with such opinions?

Official reaction was swift. The Akron *Beacon Journal* said in a long editorial:

Now comes Mr. Ford, who was privy to all that went on in the jury room and who may have written part or all of the report, with remarks that are not only outrageously prejudicial but highly inflammatory.

The jury had indicted twenty-plus members of the crowd on charges of inciting to riot, second-degree riot and first-degree riot, the maximum penalty for which is three years in prison.

But Mr. Ford, sworn to uphold the Constitution and the laws under it, seems to believe it was right and proper to inflict capital punishment as a penalty for the crime of rioting. Moreover, he seems willing to countenance punishment without trial —shooting the guilty and the innocent alike!

There was great danger of a new outbreak on the campus on the part of students who had suspected all along that the grand jury was rigged and who had rejected its *obiter dicta* as biased. Twelve Kent clergymen, Catholic and Protestant alike, combined to petition Washington for the convening of a federal grand jury, and in doing so, expressed resentment at the grand jury's willingness to condemn only the students and administration, which it termed "unfair and false.'

> It is our conviction that long prior to May 1 the social fabric of our nation was rent by violent forces to which all of us have contributed; which forces were expressed anew in the events of May 1.

Once more prudent counsel was needed to keep things on an even keel, and it was forthcoming. Leaders with a determination to keep things quiet moved among the students, counseling prudence and suspended judgment. Proper legal moves were made to lift the imposition of silence on President White, for most observers believed it illegal for a judge to impose silence on a man who had suffered no indictment but who had been abused in extraneous matter.* And things seemed to be moving toward a peaceful settlement which would probably include the resignation of Seabury Ford from his role as arbiter of student conduct.

Then something happened which nobody could have foreseen and which precipitated a crisis which could no longer be swept under the rug. It came from an unexpected quarter.

Professor Glenn Frank studied the Seabury Ford statement, the gag rule on President White, the exoneration of the Guard, and the general condemnation of a university he loved and a student body he respected. It was more than he could take. Seeking out a reporter, he delivered some lines which will be long remembered in Kent State history:

> Someone on this campus must sacrifice himself. I speak now in contempt of court, in contempt of the naïve and stupid conclusions of the grand jury, specifically as to their reasons for the May 4 disturbances, in contempt of Judge Edwin Jones for the gag rules placed on President White, and personal contempt for Lawyer Ford for his lack of understanding after sixty-eight years of what I believe is a wasted life.

---

*Through this difficult period President White conducted himself well. When forbidden by the Ravenna court to speak, he did not indulge in self-pity; when released from this silence by the Cleveland federal court, he did not engage in recrimination. He spoke boldly and often in defense of intellectual freedom. Notable was the fact that Robert Dix, president of the Board of Trustees, stood with him and resisted efforts to force his resignation or dismissal; if the Two Bobs had worked together to build the university, they now cooperated in its salvage. On February 18, 1971, White formally requested permission to resign and resume his old job of teaching in the School of Education, which he had left in 1963 to become president.

Since Frank had testified before the grand jury, he was technically in contempt of court at the moment he opened his mouth, and of this he was fully aware. Lest he be misunderstood, he added:

Ford is a troublemaker. It is my feeling that the Republican party must smash this student uprising in order to stay in power. Ford has made his statement in order to convince people who do not know the facts that he is a law-and-order man who will crack down on anyone who disagrees with the system he represents. However, that should not allow a prosecutor to make what I consider to be a farce out of justice for his own gain or to gain favor with voters.

Freedom of speech is greater than Judge Jones. I defy Judge Jones to arrest me for contempt of court because I cannot see a system I believe in and respect subverted by man. I cannot live with a conscience that permits people to say 'they should have shot all' the troublemakers.

Ford's outburst had occurred on Saturday; Frank's riposte, on Sunday. On Monday the two men were haled into court, and charged with contempt, on recommendation of the Portage County Bar Association, and both pleaded guilty, which was about the only thing they could do under the circumstances. Ford said he was misquoted; Frank said that he had spoken out only after Ford had broken the court order with his alleged statements.

That afternoon the Kent State faculty senate went on record as supporting Professor Frank, with the statement: 'We share his indignation over the grand jury's findings and over the gag rule imposed on participants in the grand jury proceedings.' Ford obviously embarrassed by the brouhaha he had caused, retained his salty composure. 'I was misquoted,' he claimed. 'I never said I wanted anybody shot . . . certainly not for publication.'*

---

*On January 28, 1971, in a federal court sitting in Cleveland, U.S. District Judge William K. Thomas ordered the report of the Portage County Special Grand Jury to be destroyed on grounds that its publication of the notorious *obiter dicta* violated the command to secrecy. He did, however, allow the twenty-five indictments to stand because 'they were separate and self-sufficient.' He added, 'The vice of the violation of secrecy is that the grand jury finds commission of criminal offenses and ascribes guilt to participants. If allowed to stand, these findings and conclusions will irreparably injure their right to a fair trial.'

The FBI 'report'

Constantly adding to the confusion was the existence of a secret FBI report—which certain people had seen but were not allowed to quote from, and which others had not seen but were free to guess about. Immediately after the shootings, a huge squad of FBI men moved into Kent, took over one of the gymnasiums and set up an establishment of some 300 people to sift the facts. They interviewed with assiduity and perception and sent out urgent calls for on-the-spot interrogations in places as distant as Florida and California. A great number of students suddenly found themselves being questioned by the FBI. Two cases are typical.

A boy with long hair sat in a bar in Cleveland giving his rather colorful interpretations of what had happened on May 4. When he was finished, a man from a nearby table came over, identified himself as an FBI agent, and the boy became the subject of an intensive investigation covering four weeks and involving three different officers who visited him at various times and for differing purposes. Actually, the young man knew nothing and could contribute nothing intelligible to the information already on hand.

A lovely, uninvolved coed, whose name appears elsewhere in this book in connection with another incident, happened to be sitting in the Student Union during Kent's summer session when a television crew came along, seeking local color, and asked her opinion of May 4. Inspired by the idea of appearing on television, the young lady became rather expansive, and two days after the show was aired, an FBI agent visited her home, started checking on every aspect of her life. She says, 'After they had been to see me about four times, one of them tried to catch me off base by suddenly saying, "Wouldn't General Henderson be ashamed to think that his son had been dating a girl who thought the way you did about Vietnam?" I hadn't dated the general's son for two years, but they knew about it. I may have jolted them when I said, "As a matter of fact, the general's boy is also against the war." ' In this instance, too, the girl had nothing substantial to add, for she had not witnessed any of the crucial incidents, but the FBI with amazing thoroughness tracked down even the most trivial leads.

The researchers have stumbled upon about a dozen instances in which students with no apparent connection with the weekend troubles were caught in the FBI web and subjected to lengthy and probing interrogations, and apart from the panic caused in middle-class households when the dreadful phrase 'Our son is wanted by the FBI' flashed through the village, no fault could be found with the FBI operation. They were careful and they were thorough but they did not abuse their prerogatives, except, perhaps, in their interrogations of students in an attempt to ascertain what certain professors had been saying in their classrooms.

The result was a report covering 7,500 typewritten pages, which were kept under lock in Washington. Hundreds of adroit reporters tried to penetrate the veil of secrecy, but with no success. Official commissions, of course, were granted permission to study the findings, so that the Scranton Commission had access to them, as did the secret grand jury. But ordinary citizens did not.

However, news of what the findings contained did begin to leak out, and it was generally believed that the FBI data proved two things: that the riots were not communist-led and that the Guard was so culpable of unprofessional behavior that court action might be warranted. The latter finding, if true, would be disturbing in a state which had whole-heartedly supported the Guard.

Then, on July 23, someone associated with the Akron *Beacon Journal* got hold of a fourteen-page analysis of the massive total report; it had been prepared not by the FBI itself but by the Justice Department as a guide to any governmental agency which might be contemplating legal action regarding the incident. It was thus merely one person's opinion founded on facts, and it must be remembered that if a different person had reviewed the same facts, he might come up with a different opinion. In any case, the disclosures were sensational.

The shootings were not necessary and not in order.

No Guardsmen were hurt by flying rocks or projectiles and none was in danger of his life at the time of the shooting. There was no hail of rocks beforehand.

One Guardsman fired at a student who was making an obscene gesture; another fired at a student preparing to throw a rock.

Altogether, thirteen students were hit with bullets, all but four in the back or side.

The report lists names, ranks, outfits and home addresses of six Guardsmen who could be charged.

Release of this information, which was published as FBI findings, provoked bitter debate, with J. Edgar Hoover reminding the press that the FBI never drew conclusions from its investigations and that what was purported to be FBI thinking was merely a summary drawn by some Justice Department individual who had seen the material.

But then Senator Stephen Young, of Ohio, got into the act; one would have to conclude from his comment that he had in some manner found access to the Justice summary, for he castigated the Guard on the basis of what appeared to be inside information. He made a series of grave accusations, including the two specific charges that they had fabricated the story that their lives were in danger and that they had gathered after the event and agreed upon a common explanation to which all would adhere.

And there the matter rested until October 31, 1970, when the field team responsible for the studies reported in this book were preparing to leave Kent. As they were departing the city, the *New York Times* arrived bearing the summary of a more complete text of FBI findings prepared by the Department of Justice, which had apparently been so outraged by the findings of the Portage County grand jury and so irritated by Senator Young's partial but accurate charges that it leaked the full story. The conclusions were unequivocal:

Most of the guardsmen who did fire do not specifically claim that they fired because their lives were in danger. Rather, they generally simply state that they fired after they heard others fire or because after the shooting began, they assumed an order to fire in the air had been given. As a general rule, most guards add the claim that their lives were or were not in danger to the end of their statements almost as an afterthought.

Six guardsmen, including two sergeants and Captain Srp of Troop G stated pointedly that the lives of the members of the Guard were not in danger and that it was not a shooting situation. The FBI interviews of the guardsmen are in many instances quite remarkable for what is not said, rather than what is said. Many guardsmen do not mention the students or that the crowd or any part of it was 'advancing' or 'charging.' Many do not mention where the crowd was or what it was doing.

We have some reason to believe that the claim by the Guard that their lives were endangered by the students was fabricated subsequent to the event. The apparent volunteering by some guardsmen of the fact that their lives were not in danger gives rise to some suspicions. One usually does not mention what did not occur. . . .*

A chaplain of Troop G spoke with many members of the Guard and stated that they were unable to explain to him why they fired their weapons.

The guardsmen were not surrounded. Photographs and television film show that only a very few students were located between the Guard and the commons. They could easily have continued in the direction in which they had been going. No guardsman claims he was hit with rocks immediately prior to the firing, although one guardsman stated that he had to move out of the way of a three-inch log just prior to the time that he heard shots. Two guardsmen allege that they were hit with rocks after the firing began.

Although many claim they were hit with rocks at some time during the confrontation, only one guardsman, Lawrence Shafer, was injured seriously enough to require any kind of medical treatment. He admits his injury was received some ten to fifteen minutes before the fatal volley was fired. His arm, which was badly bruised, was put in a sling and he was given medication for pain.

There was no sniper. The Guard clearly did not believe that they were being fired upon. No Guardsman claims he fell to the ground or took any other evasive action and all available photographs show the Guard at the critical moments in standing position and not seeking cover. In addition, no guardsman claims he fired at a sniper or even that he fired in the direction from which he believed the sniper shot.

Seven members of Troop G admit firing their weapons, but also claim they did not fire at the students. Five persons interviewed in Troop G, the group of guardsmen closest to Taylor Hall,

---

*In his book *The Killings at Kent State: How Murder Went Unpunished*, A New York Review Book, 1971, I. F. Stone accepts the charge that Guardsmen did conspire to fabricate evidence and asks what America's reaction would have been had it been students who had done the fabricating. 'In a country so passionate about law and order, it should not be necessary to remark that falsification of evidence is a crime, and agreement to do so in concert with others is conspiracy to obstruct justice. Were students to shoot down National Guardsmen or other law officers, and were the FBI then to turn up evidence that those who did the shooting agreed among themselves to tell the investigators a fabricated story, it is hard to believe the news would be relegated to the back pages and met with indifference.'

admit firing a total of eight shots into the crowd or at a specific student.

Specialist 4 James McGee claimed that it looked to him like the demonstrators were overrunning the 107th. He then saw one soldier from Company A fire four or five rounds from a .45 and saw a sergeant from Troop G also fire a .45 into the crowd. He claims he then fired his M-1 twice over the heads of the crowd and later fired once at the knee of a demonstrator when he realized the shots were having no effect.

Specialist 4 Ralph Zoller claims he heard a muffled shot which he alleges came from a sniper. Thereafter, he heard the Guard shoot and he fired one shot in the air. He then kneeled, aimed and fired at the knee of a student who he claims looked as if he was throwing an object at Zoller.

Specialist 4, James Pierce, a Kent State student, claims that the crowd was within ten feet of the guardsmen. He then heard a shot from the Guard. He then fired four shots—one into the air; one at a male ten feet away with his arm drawn back and a rock in his hand (this male fell and appeared to get hit again); he then turned to his right and fired into the crowd; he turned back to his left and fired at a large Negro male about to throw a rock at him.

S. Sgt. Barry Morris claims the crowd advanced to within thirty feet, and was throwing rocks. He heard a shot which he believes came from a sniper. He then saw a 2nd lieutenant step forward and fire his weapon a number of times. Morris then fired two shots from his .45 'into the crowd.'

Sgt. Lawrence Shafer heard three or four shots come from his 'right' side. He then saw a man on his right fire one shot. He then dropped to one knee and fired once in the air. He then saw a male with bushy, sandy hair, in a blue shirt (Lewis) advancing on him and making an obscene gesture. This man had nothing in his hands. When this man was 25–35 feet away, Shafer shot him. He then fired three more shots in the air.

We did not have access to any summary of FBI reports and, until the *New York Times* release, did not have any clear idea of what they contained, but by the time we were well into the mass of rumor, fact and contradiction, we became convinced that our conclusions would have to parallel those of the FBI. We could not believe that two different groups of individuals studying the material we were uncovering could reach divergent conclusions. When we saw the summary, we were gratified that our findings confirmed theirs. This does not, of course, imply that had the FBI taken the time to investigate the background to May 4, they would have interpreted those events as we did; they would have uncovered much more material than we did, and their dossiers on participants would have been fuller, but their conclusions could not be radically different.

In one area the FBI investigation had to be immeasurably more complete. Because of injunctions restraining us from talking to the Guards, because of the policy of strict secrecy on the part of the Ohio National Guard, and because we had no power of subpoena, we were not able to interrogate specific Guardsmen who fired the rifles. It should be obvious to the reader, however, that we talked quietly, and often late at night, to quite a few Guardsmen who were on that hill, and perhaps, unknowingly, to some who fired, but the kinds of interviews the FBI got we could not get. In spite of this, we know almost exactly what happened, save the crucial matter of whether there was, at the practice field, any kind of order or agreement which triggered the firing a few moments later.

It is inconceivable that the seventy-six men who were penned in on the field that day will be able to maintain their wall of silence indefinitely. In the years that lie ahead, someone will talk, and a flood of testimony will be released. We think that the ultimate truth will not be vastly different from what has been suggested in these pages.

The girl with the Delacroix face

Many who have studied the incidents at Kent State in detail have commented on the youth of the participants. Evidence is overwhelming that at least half the young people involved in the trashing of Water Street were younger than university age, and there is responsible proof that of those who burned ROTC, several of the ringleaders were below college age. Also, at Monday's large assembly on the commons, it seemed to many observers that a vast majority, perhaps as high as 80 percent, of the participants were freshmen and sophomores. 'There were few upperclassmen there that day' was a constant comment of witnesses.

This raises two questions: Is rioting the occupation of the young? Does disenchantment begin at a much lower age than we used to think?

As to the first, the answer seems to be that rioting is especially alluring to the young, but becomes effective only when launched, supervised and directed by older people with specific goals of disruption in mind. Therefore, the young require protection from the cynical old who would use them.

As to the second question, every school in America, almost from kindergarten on, ought to start right now to analyze what is happening to its students. The radicalization of the young is proceeding at a terrifying pace and should be halted. Jerry Rubin said at Kent, 'From here on I am going to work mainly in high schools.' One of Kent's leading revolutionaries told a researcher, 'I'm getting a job in high school. That's where you can really convert people.' Jerry Persky, one of Kent's rising new breed of activists, says excitedly, 'Man, hearing Rubin tell us to concentrate on the kids really fired me up. That very weekend I went home to Cleveland and gathered all the kids in the neighborhood and taught them "Ho, ho, ho! Ho Chi Minh." They loved it.' Seasoned observers at Kent said repeatedly, 'It's the incoming freshmen who are the wild-eyed ones. They've been indoctrinated before they get here and our radicals have a hard time keeping up with them.' The large majority of committed radicals in the university who consented to be interviewed for this book stated that they had been radicalized before they reached Kent. For a chilling view of what this means, one should read *The High School Revolutionaries* by Marc Libarle and Tom Seligson, in which high school boys and girls explain how they have been radicalized.

Kent offered dramatic illustration of the youthful revolt when the television and newspapers flashed across the country John Filo's famous photograph of the tall coed with the Delacroix face, kneeling over the dead body of Jeff Miller, her arms raised in the air. This photograph was the epitome of grief, the perfect symbol of university youth in turmoil. Soon the nation would learn that the supposed coed was a fourteen-year-old runaway from a Florida junior high school.

Her story is needed to complete any explanation of present-day university life. It begins at the fairy-tale town of Opa-locka, which was launched in 1923 by a man with a crazy vision. Glenn Curtis, the aviator, returning from a junket through the Middle East, selected some undeveloped land on the outskirts of Miami, and announced, 'Here I will build my dream village.' It became a sprawling development which tried to reproduce the whimsy and mystery of Arabia. Its building laws decreed that every structure erected in Opa-locka had to have a Middle East motif. The result was a hodgepodge of 'mosques, minarets and minor marvels' pink and peeling in the hot sun, seeking shade under a cobweb of high-tension wires. In recent years blocks of three-room bungalows have appeared along the streets called Alibaba, Sesame, Aladdin . . . and Silah.

If Opa-locka is Baghdad, then Silah is the Casbah, a kind of cul-de-sac of scrawny, postage-stamp lawns, barking dogs and cycling children, all dirty. The Vecchios—Frank, his wife, fourteen-year-old Mary and her sister Sharon, age three —live at 1091 Silah.

There is little doubt that Mary has put the Vecchio family on the map. They hope this will produce financial rewards. 'Forty percent,' says Mrs. Vecchio to no one in particular, 'that's what our lawyer says we get.' She is speaking about a legal hassle the Vecchios are now embroiled in with a group on the Berkeley campus. It seems the Californians are re-producing posters and T-shirts bearing Mary's picture as she crouched over the body of Jeff Miller at Kent State. 'This would be all right,' Mrs. Vecchio points out, 'but they aren't paying us our cut. So our lawyer, Philip Vitello—he's the son of Frank Sinatra's lawyer—he sent a disguised investigator to go out to California.

'The trouble is,' Mrs. Vecchio goes on, 'Mr. Vecchio is making his own T-shirts, and the California outfit was cutting into our business.' The Vecchio version is white with the blue figure of Mary in the middle, bending over Jeff Miller. Below her picture there are the words: *Now Will You Listen,* accompanied by her autograph signed in a childish hand. 'We sell them at $2.50 each. You can buy them at The Great Train Robbery and some of the other good stores.'

Where is Mary? She won't be back till afternoon. She is attending North Dade Junior High School, morning sessions, and she also has a job at the Royal Castle, a ham-and-eggery three miles down the road. 'She had it tough in school,' says Mrs. Vecchio, 'but only because the principal didn't understand her. He didn't get along with any of the kids. So he suspended her and she ran away.' She pauses to recall something else. 'Oh, and they started busing in Negro kids last fall. She didn't like that at all.'

Now Mrs. Vecchio grows angry. 'The police arrested our girl after she came back. Picked her up at four in the morning. And released her name to the papers. They're not supposed to do that. Mary is a minor.' So the Vecchios are suing the city of Miami for $1,000,000.

'You ought to see the letters we get since Mary became famous,' Mrs. Vecchio says. 'They come from all over, wanting autographs. Most of them are real nice, but one fellow said he wanted to do us the way they did those Tates in California.'

Now Mary herself appears, and one's first reaction is, 'What a large child.' She is no less than immense at five-feetten and a hefty 190 pounds, most of it in her legs. Her hair is long and she wears blue jeans and a red sweatshirt. She frequently gazes off into space, at nothing in particular, and ignores the words around her. Finally, she mumbles a one-syllable answer, vague, cryptic. She apologizes, says she is out of sorts because she had just been fired from her job as a waitress at the Royal Castle. 'They did it without warning and I'm upset because they're deducting an apron from my final check.'

Why had she left home? 'I was suspended from school and they were going to lock me up. Besides, my parents had confined me to the house for two weeks.' Had she run away before? 'Many times. I liked to go to the beach at Sunny Isles. It's not far away. I'd sleep there alone in the sand. I was thirteen when I ran away for the first time. They suspended me from school. That time I stayed at an apartment with two girls. They were about seventeen, I think, but I came home four days later.'

Looking toward the television, she says, 'It was a Sunday, February 4, I think, that I decided to run away . . . for keeps. I wanted to see California.' But there was a more pressing reason. 'They had suspended me again and I was afraid the fuzz would lock me up.

'First off, I went to Grenoylds Park. A lot of kids hang around there . . . just doing nothing. Some of them come from California or from someplace else and I thought maybe I could catch a ride to somewhere. I met this French girl. She asked me for a cigarette and right away I told her I was looking for a place to stay.' Mary does not know how old the girl was, and of course they did not exchange last names. 'But she was French and was called Sue, and she had some friends in a place called Chamblee, Georgia.' Over the course of the afternoon, they decided to make their way west together, at least as far as Chamblee, where Mary would break off on her own for California. That afternoon they started hitchhiking and got as far as Fort Lauderdale.

The girls spent two weeks at Fort Lauderdale, sharing an apartment with two boys who sold dune buggies. During the daylight hours Mary would panhandle along the streets. 'I always got a little money because I had no shoes. I'd left home with only the clothes I was wearing and nothing else.'

In Opa-locka, her parents had notified Police Chief H. L. Chastain that Mary had run away. A bulletin was circulated statewide, but it accomplished nothing, because hundreds of girls were running away that year.

At the end of two weeks the dune-buggy salesmen decided to leave for California, and this was just what Mary had wanted, but Sue talked her into stopping off first in Chamblee, so the opportunity passed.

It took three days for the girls to reach Chamblee, hitchhiking along the superhighways, passing through small and sleepy towns. 'No one gave us any trouble,' Mary recalls, 'not even the cops.' They spent two nights in sleeping bags in the high grass at the side of the road, and one night, when it was very cold, in the back of a station wagon that had broken down and was parked on the shoulder of the highway. 'I don't know where the owner was,' Mary says, 'I guess he'd gone for a tow truck and decided to spend the night somewhere.'

Chamblee was not what Mary expected. Sue's friends were elderly and married. And it was cold. There was snow on the ground and Mary was still barefoot, so she went in to Atlanta to panhandle for some shoes. While she was standing in the snow in Piedmont Park in downtown Atlanta, 'A nice man gave me $5. I spent half of it on a pair of cheap tennis shoes.' Couldn't she have bought the tennis shoes in Chamblee? 'Well, it wasn't only the shoes I was thinking of. There was this rock concert scheduled in Piedmont Park that weekend. When you write, don't call them festivals. They're really concerts.'

With her new shoes, Mary wandered into a Community Center run by the city for youth who were homeless, and a woman there had a list of couples who had agreed to take runaways into their homes, and it was to one of these that Mary was assigned. 'There was me and another girl, and two boys. They fed us and I took a hot shower and spent the night.'

The couple who sheltered them made an impression on Mary. 'They were about fifty and were very nice. The house was clean, and the food, well, it was great. Like I'd never done anything or seen anything like that before, you know.' It was a vast improvement on the bungalow on Silah Street.

At the concert, Mary vaguely expected to meet up again with the French girl, Sue, but they failed to make contact and Mary never saw her again. When asked about this, she does not recall being concerned. 'Sue was sort of nice,' she says.

She remained in Atlanta during February and March. At first she panhandled; later she met a group of runaways who peddled an underground paper for grubstakes. 'They called it *Great Speckled Bird* and some of them made as much as twenty dollars a day selling it. They'd never make less than twelve.'

And so Mary became a newsgirl, hawking the *Speckled Bird* through Atlanta's hippie community. She would, each week, buy the papers for eight cents a copy, sell them for fifteen. 'It was all about what was happening. It told you about what concerts were coming up and what rides were available to where, who was doing what.' At night she shared a crash pad with the other peddlers, newsboys and their girls. An apartment had been rented by the publisher of the paper, a young man of nineteen, who collected a modest rental from the girls.

California still obsessed her. 'But I'd think about going over those mountains, and I'd get scared. I mean, hitchhiking out there in the winter.' Why had she not taken a ride? Many free ones were advertised in the paper she sold. Her face goes blank. 'I don't know,' she says.

She is also vague about why she quit her job as newsgirl. 'I don't remember. I just quit, that's all.' The listener suspects that she may be trying to hide something. Maybe the newsboys told her to leave, for some reason. Possibly she did not pay her rent. On the other hand, perhaps she was bored. 'I don't remember.'

So it was back to panhandling, back to the Community Center for free lodging. But even this was temporary, because several days after she left the *Speckled Bird* commune she met two couples while begging. 'They were going to Youngstown, Ohio. The two boys lived there and wanted to go home. They had this old Plymouth, a sedan, that didn't look as if it could get us there.' The two couples had altogether $5, but Mary chipped in $10 from her panhandling, and kept another $7 stashed away. They decided that with this much capital they could make it to Youngstown, and for the moment California was forgotten.

And so, at the end of March, Mary Vecchio moved north, and when the gang ran out of money they all took to panhandling, and while engaged in this occupation Mary learned who her companions' were. 'The boys had driven down to Florida to hear a concert in West Palm Beach. They had just gone down there like a lot of kids come from the North to get away from the cold and the snow up there. One of the girls was from Miami, like me, and her name was Barbara. The other was called Linda and I don't know where she was from, but both of them had run away from home. Like me.'

When the old Plymouth chugged into Youngstown, the snow was knee-deep and Mary's tennis shoes had worn through, so she threw them away and went barefoot. 'It was crazy. There I was without shoes in all that snow and I never got sick or caught a cold. In Florida, where it was warm, I used to catch colds all the time.'

For one and a half months Mary kicked around Youngstown. 'I must have stayed in thirty places. Welfare homes, friends, crash pads, sometimes the streets. It was warm in the all-night hamburger stands, but I got real hungry sometimes. Have you ever been real hungry?'

It was about the end of April when she met Noel, a boy from Campbell, Ohio. 'He was French. Well, not French, really, but he said he was born there. I liked him. Every weekend he'd drive up to Kent State for the action. He told me there was a place there called J.B.'s where they had live music and there was a dance all the time.'

On Friday, May 1, Mary went to the Red Barn, a gathering place for Youngstown youth. It was in the morning, and she met six other youngsters with a car who said they were going to Kent State that night. They told her, 'Noel is already there.' Why hadn't she gone with him? She can't remember. It isn't certain that Noel ever existed; but perhaps he was someone attractive that she had met briefly at the Red Barn. 'I don't remember much about how I got to Kent but I do know the boys were from Atlanta. And the girls—there were two twins and then two other girls from Youngstown. I forget how I met them.'

The group of seven arrived at Kent at 8:00 P.M. that night and promptly dumped Mary at J.B.'s. 'I don't know where they went,' Mary recalls. 'They were there and then they were gone. I didn't have any money. No place to stay. So I went around and panhandled a little. On the sidewalk and in J.B.'s. Then I met a girl who was splitting for California and she had a dog, a kind of half-collie and half-German shepherd. She said she couldn't take it with her and so she gave it to me. He was just a puppy.' So now there were two of them together, the dog and Mary, and he, perhaps, was something she could count on.

Mary left J.B.'s at midnight, she remembers, still clutching her dog, and she saw trouble on the street. 'Cambodia,' she says. 'Cambodia did it. They built a fire out there and were circling around, chanting. There were quite a few of them. Oh, I don't know, maybe a couple of hundred.' Mary joined them, dancing about the trash fire in the street. It was what was happening and she wanted in. It was at the fire that she first saw Ann, no last name, only Ann, who seemed to be a leader. 'Ann was yelling the loudest,' Mary remembers. Then the crowd got nasty and began to throw rocks, charging down the street and shattering windows. And Mary tagged along, a big lumbering girl, throwing rocks like the rest. 'But then I saw three cops come,' she says, 'and I ran. I didn't want to be arrested and sent home. I knew the police might be looking for me, and if they caught me they'd lock me up. You know, I was already on probation and there was Silver Oaks waiting.'

In the confusion Mary met some college kids who had been on Water Street. 'I told them I needed a place to stay real bad and that the people who I had come up with had just left me. I didn't know where to go.' The college kids put her up for the night. 'They had an apartment off Main Street. It was real nice. They had a swimming pool in the back, but I don't remember who they were.'

Saturday night she decided to go to the campus. 'I saw flames in the sky and I wanted to get a close look. So I collected my dog, and headed for the ROTC building. I'd never seen a National Guard up close. They had on their helmets and I was scared. I couldn't get near the building, so I walked over to Tri-Towers and went inside and sat down, figuring I could sleep there because it was part of a college.' Then she recognized the girl she had met on Friday. 'It was Ann, who had been leading at the fire. I asked her if she could put me up for the night, and she said, "Why not?" '

Mary was taken to the house on Ash Street, where she met about ten students. Shortly after she and Ann arrived, seven other girls came in. 'There was a whole bunch of kids, all talking about the demonstrations and what ought to be done next.' When the police questioned her three months later, Mary Vecchio would learn that Ann was one of the SDS leaders at Kent State. 'God, I didn't even know what SDS was. Ann was just a nice girl.' (Confirmed by Paul Probius: 'On Saturday, after the burning of ROTC, I was drifting around with nothing to do and happened to stop by the house on Ash Street, and there was this big coed I hadn't seen before. There was discussion under way and she joined it, just like everyone else, and later on she trailed off to bed. I assumed she was a new recruit to the movement, but I never saw her again until her photo was in the papers. I couldn't believe she was only fourteen.')

'Sunday was for nothing,' Mary says. 'I left the house and walked over to the campus. A lot of people were around taking pictures of the building that had been burnt down, but it was very quiet.' She was alone with her dog now, and she wandered down the street toward J.B.'s, but it was closed, so she panhandled enough money for a meal for herself and scraps for the puppy. At the restaurant, Mary met a Canadian girl about seventeen and not a student. As usual, Mary can't recall her name, but the two girls had no trouble finding some students with whom to crash. 'They thought there would be trouble Monday and it would be smart not to go to classes,' Mary recalls. 'But I took a shower and went right to sleep.' (Confirmed by Randy Gardner, freshman basketball player from Columbus: 'I was just jaywalking around the campus on Sunday afternoon when I saw this big girl in a red sweatshirt carrying a dog. She moved with the crowd and gave no one any trouble. She seemed like a good kid along for the fun.')

On Monday, Mary and the Canadian girl rose at 11:00, picked up the dog, and wandered off to the campus. 'There was a big crowd down by Taylor Hall, sitting on the grass. There was about 200 of them more or less and I sat down with them and started to ask around what was happening. Just about then the police and the Guard started to throw tear gas at us. Some of the kids got up and were throwing rocks. I figured the dog would get hurt, so I took him inside of Taylor Hall and put him in a room, a room with a lot of typewriters. I guess it was an office. Then I went back outside.' (Confirmed by a coed named Becky Adams, from Maumee: 'I was in the Student Union about 10:00 that Monday morning, sitting in a booth with a friend. Two nice-looking Guardsmen took the booth next to us and had breakfast. We offered them a few friendly words, but one of the soldiers looked up and cried, 'Wow! Look at that!' We all turned to see a very big girl with a rather handsome face. She was wearing a red sweatshirt, with no bra. She carried a dog, and stopped to smile when she saw the Guards staring at her. I told the men, "She's a coed," but all they could say was, "Wow!" ')

Outside, it was happening. 'The kids were throwing gas canisters, anything they could find. I picked up some rocks and started to throw them at the Guard.' Mary was losing her fear now. She was doing what everyone was doing and that made it all right. 'The Guard went over the hill and down into the middle of a field.' What field? 'Just a field.' And what happened? 'There was a parking lot there with some cars, a lot of cars, and the soldiers were raising their rifles, pointing them at us. I was near some kind of building about forty or fifty yards away from them. They put down their rifles and started to go back up the hill, a little hill, and we were walking after them. I was kind of on the fringe of the crowd. I was walking slowly with a guy and I turned and asked him what was happening. I can't remember just what I said, I did ask him his name though, and he said, "Jeff." ' What happened then? 'They started shooting and everybody fell down. I was laying down on the ground with my arms over my head, and I said, "This is silly because they're shooting blanks," but everyone else was down, so I lay down too.' How long? 'Until the shooting stopped and it was quiet again. Then I turned my head and I saw him. There was blood coming out of his nose and mouth and it looked like he had two apples in one cheek. "My God," I thought. "He's dead." ' Was she close to him? 'Like I could reach out and touch you.'

Mary said she was stunned . . . did not realize what had happened. Then she got to her feet. 'I wanted to help him. I just got down next to him and started to cry. Then I got up and walked away. I saw a girl on the ground and someone was trying to hold her head off the grass. So I went back to Jeff and there was a big crowd around him and there was a whole lot of blood now. Some guy jumped up and down in it, yelling and screaming, and the blood was spattering all over us. I got some on my shirt and on my pants. I never saw this guy before. He just came out of nowhere, I guess.'

At this point Mary followed the crowd back to Tri-Towers, where later she would board an evacuation bus which happened to be headed for Columbus. 'But just as I got on the bus, I remembered my dog, but I didn't go back to find him. I just wanted to get out of Kent as fast as I could.' (Confirmed by Rita Rubin, a senior from New York: 'After the horror of the shooting I sat in Tri-Towers trying to calm myself, and saw this big coed wearing beat-up clothes and sandals come in. She sat beside me and was quite vacant. I asked her where she was heading, now that school was closed, and she said in an absent-minded sort of way, "I may go to Colorado. I hear there's good action at Boulder. But what I'd really like to do is split for California." She was completely out of focus—spacey, you might say. I remembered her distinctly, and a couple of days later, saw her picture and found out that she was the runaway girl from Florida.')

She arrived in Columbus about 4:00 Monday afternoon, and with a homing-pigeon instinct, went straight up North High Street to the campus of Ohio State University and made contact with students, who found her a pad just off 13th and High, where not many nights before, the pitched battle had occurred between Ohio State students and police.

On Tuesday she roamed the campus and decided, 'I just didn't want to be around colleges any more. Same soldiers standing around the same buildings with the same tear gas. I just wanted to get out. I'd had enough of that, so I met this girl who thought she might like to hitchhike to Indianapolis. We joined forces and what money we had and I left Ohio.'

She says that Indianapolis was all right. 'I just walked around the city, panhandled a little, stayed with a girl I met. I didn't know what I ought to do. But it was getting warmer and I started thinking of California again.'

By Friday night Mary had heard the radio report that she had been identified, and suddenly—in the low-life hang-outs of Indianapolis—she was a heroine. She was pumped for information about Kent State; everyone wanted her to go to a party; people invited her to stay with them, free meals and all. 'I was a celebrity. That night a girl came up to me on the street and said, "I know you're the runaway, but I won't tell the police." She asked me if I would speak to a friend of hers about what had happened at Kent, and I said, "Well, why not?" Who do you think her friend was? A reporter from the *Indianapolis Star,* but he promised me there would be no cops around. So we went to this girl's place and I gave him the story. And you know what? Ten minutes after he left, the cops arrived.'

And so Mary Vecchio came home to Silah Street. Nothing much had changed, she found, except that people said hello to her, which was something they had not done before. One reporter asked her if she was going to run away again, and she said, 'Why should I? I have friends now. I'm a celebrity.' She says that one of these days she may want to go to college. For the present there are the T-shirts and the open road, and the rock concerts, and the vision of California beyond the mountains.

The living room is dark, with only the flicker of the color TV. On the floor, the dogs twitching in their sleep. 'Hey,' Mary cries with real enthusiasm, 'are you really going back to Kent State? Would you do something important for me? Would you find that room with the typewriters and ask the people if they know what happened to my dog? I worry about him all the time.'

AFTERWORD

Shortly after the tragedy of May 4, Andrew Jones, Princeton 1944, a senior editor of the *Reader's Digest*, was sent to Kent to see whether a team of writers might be able to collect enough information to throw light upon that chaotic event. He was accompanied by John Hubbell, University of Minnesota 1950, who helped with the initial digging and interviewed persons involved in the various incidents. They worked for some weeks, and concluded that with a trained team, a good book might result. They reported this fact to their home office.

Later, Jones returned to Kent for a more extended stay, delving more thoroughly into aspects of the story and generating the enthusiasm that would mark his long association with the project.

In mid-August he returned for yet a third time to conduct specific interviews and to start his negotiations with the Ohio National Guard which led to the remarkable reconstructions offered here.

In mid-September he returned for a fourth time to complete the solid spadework. People in many walks of life in Kent now recognized him as a thoroughly grounded expert, and because he was an ex-marine, he was able to acquire military and political data which another could not have done.

Leslie Laird, Vanderbilt 1970, went to New York upon graduation, determined to find a job. She landed one with the *Reader's Digest* as a researcher, one of the band of experts who make the publication of any magazine possible, but before she could even find her way around the office, she was dispatched to Kent to study the story from the students' point of view, and it was not uncommon to see her returning from interviews perched on the rear seat of a motorcycle. She met with literally hundreds of these students, and the reconstruction of the lives of the five students was possible only because of her careful researches.

Nathan Adams, Colby 1958, assumed responsibility for visiting the other Ohio institutions which had experienced campus disorders in the spring of 1970, and his detailed reports on Ohio State University, University of Ohio and Miami University (of Ohio) would be worth publishing as separate documents. He also lived for some time in a little-known Ohio commune and contributed interpretations on contemporary changes in life style. It was he who made the trip to Opa-locka.

Eugene Methvin, Georgia 1955, came to Kent to work on the problem of student rebellion, a subject in which he is an international expert and on which he had just written a long book. He was able to provide guidance in relating the Kent experience to what was happening in other centers across the country.

Mari Yoriko Sabusawa, Antioch 1944, stayed in Kent for several weeks, meeting with students and faculty, and relating this experience to her knowledge of Ohio education as gleaned at one of its best and more adventuresome private colleges.

Six Kent students attached to the School of Journalism were employed on a part-time basis to provide guidance and to assist in interviewing students. Their help proved invaluable. Linda Peterson, Kent 1971, had worked in the women's department of the Cleveland *Plain Dealer*. Ben Post, Kent 1971, had already landed a good job with the local *Record-Courier* and was on the way to becoming an ace reporter. Jeff Sallot, Kent 1970, had a similar job with the Akron *Beacon Journal* and was their specialist in university affairs. Larry Rose, Kent 1971, was just back from duty in Vietnam, while Scott Mueller, Kent 1971, had spent his summer vacation working for United Press International in Cleveland. John P. Hayes, who was involved in much of the action, served as stringer for two papers. These six were already skilled newspaper people and many of the leads which uncovered fruitful information came from them.

Howard Ruffner, Kent 1971, and John Filo, Kent 1971, provided the basic photographic work for the book and also some of the best stories. That they were heroic young men their photographs show; that they were thoughtful and informed should be evident in what is said about them in these pages. If two young men ever started at the top of their profession, it is these two.

That leaves me, Swarthmore 1929, and perpetually concerned about what young people are doing. I entered the picture late, after Jones and Hubbell had surveyed the field. I arrived by car in early August, slipped into a motel, spent a week walking around the city and reading back copies of the *Record-Courier* and *The Daily Kent Stater,* the university paper. I spent my nights in the bars on North Water Street, sitting in a corner and listening. It was eight days before anyone knew who I was; by then I had a feel for Kent and had made a series of friendships which would continue throughout my stay.

How did I work? Guided by what Jones and Laird were uncovering in their long discussions, I let it be known that I was eager to listen to anyone in Kent who had strong ideas about what had happened during the first four days of May. I sat in the window of a motel where any student could get my attention by tapping on it. I took a jog each day through the back streets near the campus and stopped off whenever a fraternity or sorority group flagged me down to heckle me with questions. I spent a good many nights at Orville's drinking ripple wine and listening to the gossip. And I passed many precious hours with faculty members who wanted to talk about their institution and its grave confrontations.

When a practiced writer does this, quietly and with enough time so that he is not hurried, he finds an amazing sequence of visitors coming to his door. Some of the most extraordinary came after midnight, hoping that the police would not spot them. Some called and arranged meetings at strange places. Others refused to give their names. And one lovely girl of twenty, with a remarkable story to tell, swore us to secrecy with the best reason I ever heard for anonymity: 'It would break my mother's heart if she learned I had been in jail.'

Because there has had to be some masking of names—always acknowledged in the text—I must here certify that I believe everything in this book to be true; every person referred to is a real person; every bit of dialogue as accurate as memory and sometimes sketchy notes will permit. In a few cases, where testimony of two different observers conflicts, we have allowed the contradiction to stand. Crucial data were taken down on a tape recorder by either Jones or Laird, so that errors can be attributable only to me. In the four conspicuous cases where pseudonyms are used—one of the Guardsmen, the involved radical, the disoriented student, the house on Ash Street—modifications have had to be introduced to obscure identities. Because of legal restrictions placed upon us, we were not able to interview everyone we wished, but we missed only a few. Also, when, as happened in several instances, our team uncovered evidence which might have been used to prosecute informants who had committed minor offenses without having been identified by the police, we deemed it prudent not to use names.

This is as true a picture of one small aspect of a great state university as we could construct.

James A. Michener

Kent, Ohio
July–December, 1970